Students, Professors, and
the State in Tsarist Russia

Studies on the History of Society and Culture
Victoria E. Bonnell and Lynn Hunt, Editors

Students,
Professors,
and the State
in Tsarist Russia

Samuel D. Kassow

UNIVERSITY OF CALIFORNIA PRESS
Berkeley · *Los Angeles* · *London*

University of California Press
Berkeley and Los Angeles, California

University of California Press, Ltd.
London, England

© 1989 by
The Regents of the University of California

Library of Congress Cataloging-in-Publication Data
Kassow, Samuel D.
    Students, professors, and the state in Tsarist Russia / Samuel D.
Kassow.
        p.   cm. — (Studies on the history of society and culture)
    Bibliography: p.
    Includes index.
    ISBN 0–520–05760–0
        1. Student movements—Soviet Union—History—20th century.
2. College teachers—Soviet Union—History—20th century. 3. Higher
education and state—Soviet Union—History—20th century. 4. Soviet
Union—Politics and government—1894–1917. I. Title. II. Series.
LA838.7.K37   1989
378′.198′1—dc19   88–040237
                                                                CIP

Printed in the United States of America
1 2 3 4 5 6 7 8 9

*Dedicated to the memory of my father,
Jacob Kassow, 1912—1987*

Contents

List of Tables   ix

Acknowledgments   xi

Introduction   1

1. Higher Education in Russia   13
2. Students in Search of Identity   48
3. The Student Movement Erupts, 1899–1901   88
4. Rethinking the Student Movement   141
5. The Professoriate at the Crossroads   198
6. 1905   237
7. New Possibilities, 1906–1910   286
8. Confrontation   343

Conclusion   387

Appendix A: Russian University Students   407

Appendix B: Russian University Professoriate   413

Bibliography   417

Index   429

Illustrations follow p. 140

List of Tables

1. Distribution of Population Aged 20–24, 1859–1914   16
2. Enrollment of Women in Russian Higher Education, 1900–1916   22
3. Distribution of Students in Russian Universities, by Field   25
4. Occupations of Fathers of Moscow University Students, 1905   65
5. Students Aided at Moscow University, 1901   68
6. Moscow University Student Vote to Resume the 1899 Strike, by Faculty   111

Appendix A: Russian University Students

A-1. Regional Origins of Moscow University Students, 1891, 1904, 1913   407
A-2. Social Origins of Students, 1880   408
A-3. Social Origins of Students, 1900 (excluding Kiev)   409
A-4. Social Origins of Students, 1912   410
A-5. Social Origins of Students by Field of Study, 1894, Moscow University   411
A-6. Social Origins of Students by Field of Study, 1904, Moscow University   411

Appendix B: Russian University Professoriate

B-1.   Listed Property of Professoriate   413
B-2.   The Russian Professoriate by Social Background and
          Specialty, 1913   414
B-3.   Russian Professors Who Prepared at Either Moscow
          University or Saint Petersburg University   415

Acknowledgments

I am very grateful to the many people who helped me in the preparation of this book. Professor Cyril Black, Professor Arno Mayer, Professor V. P. Iakovlev, and Professor Jerome Blum all made excellent suggestions that greatly facilitated the writing of the original doctoral dissertation.

Many colleagues and friends read all or part of the manuscript. Special thanks go to John Gillis, Judy Coffin, William Fuller, Carol Heim, Noreen Channels, Miriam Silverberg, and James Flynn. My colleagues in the Trinity College History Department—especially James West, Kim Steele, and Michael Lestz—gave freely of their time and advice. Joseph Fasano helped me with photographic reproduction, and my colleagues Olga Hasty and Natasha Roklina steered me through some especially difficult translations. I owe a special debt of gratitude to J. Ronald Spencer, who carefully read a draft of the manuscript and gave me invaluable comments, as well as to Jane-Ellen Long for her superb copyediting and Mary Renaud for supervising the project. Of course, responsibility for any shortcomings and mistakes that remain is mine alone.

I would also like to thank the Danforth Foundation, the International Research and Exchange Board, the American Council of Learned Societies, and Trinity College for fellowships and grants that facilitated my research. Deans Borden Painter and Andrew De Rocco were always ready to finance incidental—and not so incidental—expenses. For vital assistance in locating materials, I am very grateful to the staffs of the Hoover Institution Library, the Slavonic Division of the New York Public Library (especially Mr. Edward Kasinec), the Trinity College Library, the Central State Historical Archive in Leningrad, the Central State Archive of the October Revolution, and the manuscript division of the Lenin Library. Mary Santomeno, Francine Bretton, Pat Kennedy, and Gigi St. Peter provided major help in typing the manuscript.

Finally, I would like to thank Sheila Levine of the University of California Press for her patience and encouragement.

Introduction

This book is about government, professors, and students in Russia from 1899 until the Revolution of 1917. Most of the story will center on the student movement and its crucial role in defining the position of the universities in tsarist Russia. On a more fundamental level, the book is about a part of a now extinct Russia—the Russia of the universities, zemstvos, voluntary societies—and about the constant conflict and tension that marked the history of Russia's institutions of higher education. The Russian universities were cast squarely in the middle of a conflict that lasted until the very end of the Romanov dynasty, a conflict between two contrasting views of how Russia should be governed. Would Russia remain a centralized and bureaucratized country, completely controlled by the state, or would there be room for local initiative, collaboration between the bureaucracy and the educated classes, respect for entreprencurship, individual freedom—in short, would there be room for a nation alongside the autocratic state?

Between 1899 and 1911 recurrent waves of student strikes and demonstrations disrupted Russia's institutions of higher education. Tensions reached a peak during the Russian Revolution of 1905 when most institutions of higher education (*VUZy*)[1] closed for almost two academic years while government officials, senior faculty, junior faculty, and stu-

---

1. *VUZ* is an abbreviation for *Vysshee Uchebnoe Zavedenie* and refers to any institution of higher education, universities as well as technical institutes. Strictly speaking, this is a Soviet term, but it is a convenient abbreviation and will be used throughout this work.

1

dents confronted one another with varying degrees of intensity and mutual suspicion.

Although the universities played an important symbolic role, they were not merely, to use N. I. Pirogov's phrase, the "barometers" of society, nor did they simply reflect tensions outside the academic world. They had their own histories and were political actors in their own right. More often than not, the universities were out of step with the pace of extramural political life and marched to their own peculiar tempo. Six major student strikes erupted between 1899 and 1911, but only the 1905 strike coincided with mass movements outside the universities.

This study assumes that the Russian student movement, the government's policy toward the universities, and the attitude and politics of the professoriate are issues that can be understood only in relationship to one another. To write about the Russian student movement without dealing with the other aspects of the "university question" would create a distorted impression. Furthermore, these relationships must be studied not only statistically or structurally but also within the context of an evolving chronological pattern where outside political developments influenced but did not always determine the stance of groups within the academic community.

The relationship of the universities to the surrounding society was a complicated matter that does not easily lend itself to clear conceptualization and neat categorical questions. Like universities in any other country, the Russian universities were highly complex entities answering to several constituencies and expected to perform a variety of different and often conflicting functions. Government bureaucrats wanted them to train obedient and loyal civil servants and professionals. Professors resented the government's emphasis on the teaching function of the universities, arguing instead that the primary purpose of the universities was to serve the nation by promoting independent research, because only a research university could train a self-reliant professional class and an enlightened civil service. Revolutionary intellectuals saw the universities as convenient recruiting grounds and reservoirs of political discontent. Furthermore, Russian universities were the incubators of a student subculture, a meeting place where thousands of provincial youth, often poor but having little in common with the popular masses and even less with the ruling elite, joined a proud new social group, the *studenchestvo,* and then left to become teachers, doctors, lawyers, civil servants, or, in a few cases, embittered revolutionaries. Had these students accepted the professors' view of the university, had they been content to sit quietly for five years and then leave with diploma in hand, there would have been no student movement.

Forced to meet so many varied demands, Russia's universities depended for their continued existence on attaining some semblance of a consensus about their underlying role and purposes, a consensus about what they could and could not do. But in the last years of the Romanov dynasty, such a consensus proved to be an elusive goal. In a time of persistent political uncertainty and underlying cultural conflict, the universities, in exposed positions in Russia's urban centers, became painfully vulnerable to the slightest disruption, easy prey to attacks from all directions. To the right, they symbolized an alien force undermining Russian tradition, an engaged ally of the Jews, liberals, and revolutionary parties. To the left, they were a convenient base for revolutionary recruitment and for holding meetings. As the leading educational institutions in a country undergoing so many upheavals, they became lightning rods of discontent, worshipped by some, detested and feared by others, but never able to achieve internal peace or outside acknowledgment that they should avoid direct participation in the nation's political battles.

The very ideology of the autocracy, with its heavy emphasis on the outward maintenance of public order, gave the *VUZy* a political importance far out of proportion to the tiny percentage of the Russian population who studied in them. The *VUZy* were located in the major urban centers, where a small but highly visible student population posed the constant threat of public demonstrations and, worse yet, confronted government officials with the specter of a militant union of the student and labor movements. As this book shows, the autocracy seriously misjudged the student movement. But in our effort to better understand the relationships between state and society in prerevolutionary Russia, it is instructive to examine the reasons for official perceptions of social movements, however erroneous. After all, in trying to forge a policy concerning the universities and other institutions of higher education, the autocracy confronted in miniature the crux of one of its most bothersome problems: how to reconcile the imperatives of economic development and social stability. It is all too simple to label tsarist educational policy willfully reactionary, and this book will not do so. While searching for ways to suppress student unrest, a problem which loomed much too large in their perception of the university issue, most government officials did recognize the importance of higher education to the nation's development. They also knew that limiting access to higher education to the richest and presumably the most politically reliable threatened to deprive Russia of much-needed trained labor. The autocracy's university policy was one test of its skill in solving difficult internal problems and of its ability to find common ground with the educated public.

Apart from the students, the group most directly affected by the twists and turns of state policy was the Russian professoriate. This study will proceed from the assumption, developed by Walter Metzger, that professors had a dual professional identity. Not only were they chemists or historians, but they also had a cross-disciplinary identity stemming from their common relationship to the university. Throughout this study, discussion of the professoriate will emphasize this cross-disciplinary identity and the common interest of the profession in securing the abrogation of the 1884 University Statute.

Important issues divided most of the professoriate from the government. One of the most sensitive of these issues concerned the very purpose of the university. The government tended to take a utilitarian view of higher education. It saw the universities essentially as state teaching institutions whose primary purpose was to train civil servants, teachers, and professionals. This view of course justified state regulation of the most trivial aspects of university life and fostered a policy of favoring specialized technical education over a more humanistic approach to scholarship. But the professoriate held a totally different view of the role of the university, one that borrowed from the German model its emphasis on pure research and academic freedom but added a vision of university governance where appointment decisions stemmed from the faculty at large rather than from individual departments. This model was a happy combination of ideology and self-interest: the professor was a scholar, not just a teacher, and therefore needed academic freedom, secure power within the academic structure, and a free hand in enforcing internal university discipline. Furthermore, prominent professors argued, the universities were the linchpin of Russia's system of higher education, since they stood above class interest and promoted pure knowledge. Knowledge, or *nauka*, not only developed character, thus guaranteeing a competent civil service and dedicated professional class, but also was a vital component of Russian national power. In short, the professors claimed that they deserved the state's trust, not its suspicion. Like other professionals, the professoriate enjoyed a highly ambivalent relationship with a state that both set up preconditions for professional progress and pursued policies that threatened professional prerogatives. Unlike other professionals, however, Russian professors had little possibility of reducing their dependence on the state by entering some form of private practice. With few means at their disposal for exerting pressure on the government, Russian professors could only hope for a relationship based on cooperation rather than confrontation. For the most part, this did not happen. Relations between the government and the professoriate remained tense and even worsened.

One reason for the strained relationship was the student movement. Another was the often-overlooked point that the ideology of *nauka,* knowledge in the nation's service, could cut both ways, supporting conservative arguments against university autonomy as well as liberal arguments as to why such autonomy was vital. In short, the experience of the professoriate in fighting for professional goals illustrated a point that held for other professions as well: the obstacles that stood in the way of effective professional unity were created not only by the state but also by basic tensions within the professions themselves.

The professoriate saw the student movement as a major obstacle in the fight for academic freedom and university autonomy. Student unrest and protest led to government interference, with the professors usually caught in the middle—especially during the turbulent autumn of 1905. When conflict arose between the government and the students, the faculty councils raised the banner of a fragile "neutral university," whose survival was too important to Russia to risk its being destroyed in the cross fire between the right and the left. But at the same time the professors used the student movement as convenient ammunition in making their case that the government's university policies had failed and that to increase academic freedom and grant more authority to the professoriate were the only answers to the problem of student unrest. In turn the professors dodged charges from both sides. Government ministers and the tsar himself accused them of being negligent dupes, too feckless to maintain order, while student groups condemned their "spinelessness" and "cowardice."

Perhaps an analysis of the problems and dilemmas of the Russian professoriate will offer additional insight into a much-discussed but inadequately understood subject, Russian liberalism. Along with the zemstvos, the universities were critical institutional laboratories for liberals, who saw them as vital arenas of autonomous social initiative in which to fight to discredit the tradition of omnipresent but incompetent bureaucratic rule. It may be argued that the tension between the student movement and Russian liberalism represented, on a deeper level, a conflict between the assumptions and tactics of an important wing of Russian liberalism and its skeptical but vital future constituency. If liberalism could not win the allegiance of those in the student movement—Russia's future professional classes—if it could not control university politics, then did this failure have any implications for its wider political prospects?

Russian professors could hope for academic freedom, but they could not forget that they were state employees. They could try to persuade the government to enact academic reforms, but they had very little political power and genuinely feared that revolution from below would lead to anarchy and the destruction of higher learning in the country. Afraid of the masses and lacking a strong political base, Russian professors, like many liberals outside the universities, could only rely on the good intentions of the government, on its willingness to grant reform from above and engage in fruitful collaboration with the educated middle classes. But what if the government chose reaction and a return to police rule? The few options open were those faced by the Kadet party after 1906. Just as some Kadet leaders flirted with the extreme left, so too a few professors, especially after 1905, called for closer collaboration with the student movement and the restive junior faculty. But most professors preferred to hope for eventual government moderation. After all, the professoriate feared not only disorder in the streets but also upheaval within the universities, in particular the demands of the junior faculty and student demands for shared power.

This book attempts to show how, during a period of intense political upheaval, the professoriate tried to maneuver between the government and the student movement while struggling to reach internal consensus about its corporate position. How could the professors ignore the widespread demands in 1905 that the universities as such declare their support of the liberation movement or that the academic profession join other professional groups in the Union of Unions? For a short time it seemed that the professors would drop their aversion to corporate political involvement. They formed the Academic Union, passed political resolutions, and signed the well-known "Declaration of the 342" linking academic reforms to political changes. But the flirtation was short-lived, and this book tries to show why.

Objections may be raised to the characterization of the professoriate as "liberal." But insofar as professors undertook explicit political actions, the Russian press characterized them as liberal. The professoriate as a group after 1906 elected its own representatives to the State Council, and these deputies mostly aligned themselves with the center or the

left wing of the council. In addition, the elected representatives of the
professoriate had all signed the manifesto of the Academic Union. Furthermore, the faculty council resolutions, especially important in 1904
and 1905, serve as reliable indicators of corporate consensus. To be
sure, many professors saw themselves as conservatives or even sympathized with the extreme right. After 1905 in some universities, such as
Kiev and Odessa, this group even constituted the majority. Three of the
ministers of education most detested by the majority of the Russian professoriate—N. P. Bogolepov, A. N. Schwartz, and L. A. Kasso—were
former academics. But critics of the professoriate, ranging from Prime
Minister Peter Stolypin to Vladimir Lenin, agreed that, as a group, the
senior faculty was most at home with the Kadet party. It must be added,
however, that even when it took a clear political stance, the professoriate as a group was clearly opposed to direct confrontation and to
collaboration with the revolutionary left. In 1905, for example, the Academic Union was the most moderate of the professional associations.

Given its view of the purposes of the universities, it is hardly surprising that the professoriate had little sympathy with or patience for the
widespread mystique of the Russian intelligentsia. During the period
covered in this study, several prominent professors criticized the intelligentsia for laziness, lack of patriotism, absence of respect for law, low
level of culture, political immaturity, and personal immorality. It is
highly revealing that these well-known academics—Maxim Kovalevskii, Bogdan Kistiakovskii, Evgenii Trubetskoi, Pavel Vinogradov—un-
questioningly accepted the term *intelligentsia,* with its peculiar social
and psychological properties. Reading between the lines, we can see that
behind their condemnation of the intelligentsia, these professors offered
a revealing glance of their own ideology and their vision of the place of
the universities in Russian society. Russia needed individuals who were
disciplined, competent, and efficient, people who knew their job and did
it well. This picture of a disciplined and efficient professional class con-
trasts sharply with the professors' view of the intelligentsia as lazy and
incapable of seeing the importance of "small deeds," that is, of helping
the people through steady and often unglamorous work at one's chosen
profession. Such a professional class would have a healthy sense of Russian patriotism, and the brains to see that opposition to the policies of
the tsarist government did not preclude support of Russian national interests. The universities would train citizens who understood the importance of a civic culture where single-minded dedication to revolutionary politics did not destroy respect for education, literature, or other

people's opinions. Furthermore, the universities themselves had an important political role to play, not as direct participants but as training grounds for alert citizens who would understand that procedure was often as important as dogma and who would recognize the incremental nature of progress.

The authority that the professoriate claimed and thought it deserved was under constant challenge from the student movement—a term that itself raises some difficult methodological problems. Students were a transitory group, recruited from various social classes and usually staying at the *VUZy* no more than five or six years. How, then, can one speak of a "student movement" over a fifteen- or twenty-year period? And just what does *student movement* mean? Does it include students who joined revolutionary political parties or those who engaged in political activities outside the universities? What constitutes the activities of a student movement? Strikes? Street demonstrations? Does it include the prosaic but important work of organizing student cooperative societies and self-help organizations, and of publishing newspapers? No one will dispute the fact that there was a constant series of strikes, demonstrations, and intensive organizational work in the universities. But unless these had purpose and direction, a sense of student tradition, can this unrest in Russia's *VUZy* be termed a student movement?

This book argues that there was a student movement, at least insofar as a significant proportion of Russia's students saw themselves as constituting a unique and distinct subgroup in Russian society, the *studenchestvo*, with its own history, traditions, institutions, code of ethics, and responsibilities. This sense of tradition, the consciousness of being part of a unique social group, was at the bottom of most student protest and justifies the term *student movement*. As this book attempts to show, the student movement had an independent identity, quite distinct from the revolutionary left. When the major revolutionary parties tried to use the student movement as a convenient tool for their own purposes, they usually failed. Student unrest was more likely to break out because of corporate grievances or to protest police repression of fellow students than as a reaction to events outside the universities. Only one major student strike out of six coincided with social ferment outside the universities.

Although most of their demands were of a corporate or a liberal character, the students gave their rhetorical allegiance to the radical left. For example, the Social Democrats crushed the liberal Kadets in student-body elections in 1906 and 1907. What was behind this rejection of political liberalism? And if the students voted for revolutionary platforms and radical slogans, why was it that the student movement kept its distance from the revolutionary left?

To complicate matters, the student movement faced major problems concerning tactics, ideology, and ultimate goals. Were students a force in their own right or, as Marxists argued, were they a temporary group who had to ally with the proletariat in order to achieve anything at all? If the latter, did that mean students had to subordinate their own concerns to those of the working class or the local Marxist groups? The most politically committed students argued that to protest university conditions or even police repression of fellow students not only was a waste of time, but was selfish and narrow-minded. The main concern was to save energy for the decisive showdown with the government, a showdown where the students would at best play the role of auxiliaries to the worker and peasant armies. But time and time again, the student masses, although they voiced Marxist slogans, confounded the leftists by striking or demonstrating in response to corporate concerns while ignoring pleas to strike in support of outside party causes. What could student protest actually achieve, however, and what tactics should the students use? Student strikes were a handy weapon, but such strikes hurt the students themselves and, obviously, caused the state less harm than strikes in factories did. The major alternative was the street demonstration, but most of these were quickly broken up by the police, and participants were more likely to be arrested and expelled from the university. If neither tactic was effective, then why did student demonstrations and strikes constantly recur, despite the danger of expulsion from the universities, the lack of outside support, and growing criticism from within the student ranks of the notion that the students were a special group, representing a significant political and social force?

This book tries to answer these questions by looking behind the formal slogans and resolutions and analyzing the students' self-image. The concept of the *studenchestvo*, the studentry or student estate, is especially important here, as is a consideration of the prospects the students thought they faced after graduation from the university. In short, the student movement must be related to the place of the university in Russian life as well as to the various problems that hindered the development of strong professions and a middle-class identity which could forge—or reflect—coalitions between hitherto disparate social groups.

Far from home and frequently living on the edge of poverty, Russian students relied heavily on their peer group. The feeling that they had become a part of a special estate with its own rich traditions was a powerful antidote to the pressures of student life. Joining the *studenchestvo* meant accepting certain obligations to fellow students, submitting to the judgments of student courts of honor, admitting certain undefined but important obligations to those not fortunate enough to receive a higher education. Belonging to the *studenchestvo* involved accepting a code of behavior that emphasized upholding the ideals of previous student generations and that stressed student solidarity in the face of government repression. This code of behavior was heavily influenced by the perception that, in the second half of the nineteenth century, West European, especially German, students had betrayed their ideals and had chosen self-interest over social commitment.

As Russia's student population grew and as the political role of the students began to shrink relative to that of other social groups, especially after the Revolution of 1905, there was a growing feeling that the old, close-knit *studenchestvo* was dying. Numerous articles warned that Russia's students were following in the footsteps of their bourgeois German counterparts. The so-called crisis of the *studenchestvo* is central to any analysis of the Russian student movement. That students worried about such a crisis is as important as whether there actually was one; that they thought they were betraying their past and their traditions is as significant as whether that past was indeed as heroic as they dreamed it had been. It also reflected a larger process: the ongoing tension between traditional forms of social perception and new forms of self-definition generated by rapid social and economic change. There was also, it should be remembered, a "crisis of the *kupechestvo*" (which P. P. Riabushinskii wanted to replace with a self-assertive bourgeoisie) and a "crisis of the intelligentsia."

Quite clearly a basic tension existed between the mystique of the student tradition and the opportunities for material and social advancement the Russian universities and technical institutes offered their graduates. The line between "selling out" and ruining one's life by getting expelled for protesting was not always easy to define. On the one hand, group solidarity was a basic tenet of the student code. On the other, few students wanted to sacrifice their university careers. Most Russian students found it very hard to take the step from a rhetorical allegiance to the revolutionary left to a positive but dangerous personal commitment to the revolutionary cause.

It will be argued here that the Russian student movement must be analyzed within the context of this psychological dilemma. The student movement, the mystique of the *studenchestvo*, was a way of protesting without making an extreme and dangerous commitment to the revolutionary movement. Furthermore, the student movement reflected the anxiety many students felt about following in their fathers' footsteps as ineffectual "Chekhovian heroes," acquiescent civil servants or frustrated professionals vaguely unhappy with the autocratic system but too timid to do anything but accommodate themselves to it. In a sense, to borrow Michael Miles's point about the American student movement of the 1960s, the Russian student movement was a preparatory protest directed against what students saw themselves becoming but what few had the determination to avoid. The student movement involved the politically dissatisfied but uncommitted majority of students. As a rule, the radicalized, politically committed minority was outside their ranks. Indeed, this small minority did its best to discredit the value of student protest and student politics. Nevertheless, the student movement shared with the revolutionary movement a hostility to liberalism. The student movement kept reminding the professoriate that under the circumstances that prevailed in Russia, even liberal goals often required radical tactics.

CHAPTER I

Higher Education in Russia

Writing from exile in 1929, Professor A. A. Kizevetter recalled the annual celebrations marking Tat'ianin Den' (12 January), the traditional founding day of Moscow University. Long before the tedious official ceremony started, officials, students, professors, and alumni from all over Russia filled the main auditorium. After sitting through the obligatory prayers, the long scholarly paper, and the rector's remarks, the throng would rise, sing the national anthem, and then depart for a day of festive partying in Moscow's restaurants. This was one day in the year when the police would look the other way as crowds of students in their distinctive uniforms sauntered down the Tver and Strastnoi boulevards to the Romanovka and other favorite hang-outs. Meanwhile, the alumni—professors, doctors, lawyers, civil servants, even a few industrialists and businessmen—would leave for smaller, more intimate gatherings all over Moscow. In the late afternoon, they would start making their way toward the large hall of the Bolshoi Moskovskii Traktir in the center of town. After more speechmaking and drinking, troiki began taking the alumni to the Iar'. On this day, the famous restaurant served only revelers from the university. All the rooms were packed. New guests would arrive to cheers from the crowded rooms inside. V. O. Kliuchevskii, the great historian, would recite humorous couplets, while the famous lawyer F. N. Plevako improvised speeches on topics shouted from the audience.

> This was a joyous holiday. It was very pleasant for everyone to feel, even once a year, that they belonged to a larger group of cultured individuals

bound by common memories and sharing the same mood. All the barriers
that separated people—age, politics, occupation—were swept away. . . .
What was this, this one-day Moscow carnival? Was it just revelry and
merrymaking? No, this was a celebration of the conscious unity of cultured
Russia. That cultured Russia was divided by many disputes . . . but on
Tat'ianin Den' the feeling of belonging to the same alma mater outweighed
all the divisions.[1]

Not everyone shared Kizevetter's lyrical view of the "one-day carnival." In some years, ugly brawls broke out between the carousing students and the tough butcher-boys from the nearby Okhotnyi Riad market. Student organizations crusaded against the public drunkenness of
Tat'iana and issued appeals for the students to uphold the traditions
and honor of the *studenchestvo*—preferably by attendance at speeches
discussing the terrible plight of the dark masses who stood totally outside the university world. For many, Kizevetter's family of "cultured individuals," the alumni of Moscow University, bore a closer resemblance
to a panoply of characters from Chekhov's plays: bored and ineffectual
doctors and civil servants, for whom university days seemed like a faded
dream.

Thus even Tat'iana symbolized the ambiguities of the universities'
position in tsarist Russia. The clashes between privileged students and
their poorer contemporaries, the uneasy conscience which led many students to reject merrymaking in order to express concern about the
underprivileged masses, the uncertainty as to whether the university
produced a class united by common culture or only a pale imitation of a
civil society that would disintegrate under the pressures of Russian
life—all underscored the paradoxes of Russian higher education.

The root paradox was that institutions such as Moscow University
were the creatures of a Russian state that had a profound mistrust of
that very "conscious unity of cultured Russia" which Tat'iana was cele-
brating. Until almost the very end of the autocracy, there was no alternative agent—no churches, individuals, or cities—that could develop
and support institutions of higher education without state participation.
And, ironically, this Russian state, in many respects so reactionary, was
a powerful source of revolutionary change, as its policy on higher education proved. Putatively dedicated to preserving the principle of estates,
the inviolability of Russian orthodoxy, and the prerogatives of the aristocracy, the autocracy founded universities and institutes that undercut

---

1. A. A. Kizevetter, *Na rubezhe dvukh stoletii* (Prague, 1929), pp. 315–318.

the principle of privilege and status determined by birth. Open to young people from all estates, the institutions of higher education, especially the universities, posed yet another long-term threat to the state. Their dedication to *nauka*, the principle of education based on pursuit of scientific truth, implied an openness to inquiry and a connection to a cosmopolitan academic culture that would defy any attempt at strict regimentation and control and would clash with an ideology based on the personal authority of the tsar and official orthodoxy.

RUSSIAN HIGHER EDUCATION

In the last half-century of Romanov rule, imperial Russia developed a system of higher education marked by diversity and, especially in the 1905–1917 period, by rapid growth. Between 1897 and 1914, the proportion of the student-aged cohort attending some form of institution of higher education increased markedly (see Table 1). Furthermore, the ratio of higher-education enrollments to enrollments in primary and secondary education remained at its historically high level.[2] One historian of Russian higher education has gone so far as to argue that such an imbalance, caused by the "emphasis of the state on extensive education for a few rather than modest schooling for the many," helped to sharpen "social differences and antagonisms even more rapidly than liberal or radical rhetoric was able to bridge or ameliorate them."[3]

To what degree the state, especially after 1890, consciously emphasized and pursued a policy aimed at "extensive education for a few" is open to question. By the end of the nineteenth century, education bud-

2. Michael Kaser has calculated that for every 1,000 primary pupils in 1914 there were 72 secondary and 15 higher-education enrollments. Corresponding figures for secondary and higher-education enrollments in earlier years were 106 and 14 in 1835, 93 and 9 in 1875, and 67 and 10 in 1905 ("Education in Tsarist and Soviet Development," in Chimen Abramsky, ed., *Essays in Honor of E. H. Carr* [London, 1974], p. 235).

3. James C. McClelland, "Diversification in Russian-Soviet Education," in Konrad Jarausch, ed., *The Transformation of Higher Learning, 1860–1930* (Chicago, 1983), pp. 182–183. Certain objections can be raised to the points made in this provocative and stimulating essay. First, the apparent weakness of primary as opposed to secondary and higher education is accentuated by extremely low levels of reported schooling in non-Russian areas. In zemstvo provinces, with their Great-Russian peasant population, a surprisingly high percentage of the children were receiving some form of education. (A. G. Rashin writes that, by 1915, 78.2 percent of the 8–11-year-olds in Tula *guberniia* were receiving primary schooling: see A. G. Rashin, "Gramotnost' i narodnoe obrazovanie v Rossii v 19om i nachale 20ovo vekakh," *Istoricheskie Zapiski*, no. 37 [1951]: 68.) Second, as Michael Kaser ("Education," p. 245) points out, many acquired literacy outside the formal school system. Kaser cites a district in Moscow *guberniia* in 1883–1884 where only 38 percent of literate factory workers had studied in formal schools.

TABLE I   DISTRIBUTION OF POPULATION AGED
20−24, 1859−1914

	1859	1880	1897	1914
Total aged 20−24	61,648,000	97,705,000	125,640,000	166,347,000
University students	5,000	8,045	15,000	69,000
Institute students	3,750	7,110	15,000	58,000
Total	8,750	15,155	30,000	127,000
Students per 10,000 total population	1.4	1.5	2.4	7.6
Students as percentage of those aged 20−24	0.014%	0.016%	0.024%	0.076%

SOURCE: Based on table compiled by Patrick Alston in "The Dynamics of Educational Expansion in Russia," in Konrad Jarausch, ed., *The Transformation of Higher Learning, 1860–1930* (Chicago, 1983), p. 107. These figures include women.

gets clearly favored primary and secondary over higher education. In the university sector, the trend was toward less state involvement and greater reliance on student fees and local, rather than state, money to start new institutions, although the state still provided 60 percent of total university budgets in 1914. The tremendous spurt in higher-education enrollments was the result of a complex interplay of factors. On many occasions state policymakers talked of trying to slow the growth of the higher-education sector, to encourage more practical schooling on the primary and secondary levels, and to increase the inducements for young people to consider alternatives to a higher-education diploma.[4] But the incentives for a young urban Russian to acquire higher education were overwhelming. Furthermore, the state, the zemstvos, and the private sector needed skills—especially medical,

4. Tsar Nicholas expressed this wish on a number of occasions. See his remarks to a 6 April 1901 interministerial conference on higher educational policy (Tsentral'nyi Gosudarstvennyi Istoricheskii Arkhiv [hereafter referred to as TsGIA], f. 721, op. 2, ed. kh. 295). Examples of ministerial concern are the December 1909 and January 1910 meetings of the Council of Ministers to consider a new university statute (TsGIA, f. 733, op. 154, d. 471, ll. 182–198).

teaching, and technical skills—taught by the institutions of higher education. Pressure for new institutions of higher education, both universities and institutes, came from various sources: ministries anxious for skilled personnel in their particular area of competence;[5] towns pledging large sums of money to train a local elite and keep their young people close to home after graduation;[6] and high government officials convinced that universities and institutes in the non-Russian areas of the empire would spread Russian culture and initiate a benign and politically healthy process of cultural assimilation.[7]

Besides opening the doors to the civil service, medicine, law, high-school teaching, and specialized technical professions, a higher-education degree became increasingly important for private employment and for zemstvo positions.[8] Moreover, it was widely recognized that a sec-

---

5. Examples, to be discussed below, are the role the Ministry of Finance played in setting up the polytechnics and the initiative the Ministry of Trade and Industry took in changing the status of the commercial institutes.

6. An example of this local initiative can be seen in the records of the 10 April 1907 Council of Ministers meeting, which considered the question of starting a new university in the country. The Minsk city administration pledged 500,000 rubles and 16 desiatines of land if the government would approve a university there. Vitebsk promised 600,000 rubles, with "more pledged from the local merchants." Voronezh promised 950,000 rubles over a four-year period. Nizhni-Novgorod promised 650,000 rubles and a city building valued at 150,000 rubles. Saratov promised 1,000,000 rubles, and the local zemstvo pledged another 150,000 rubles. Astrakhan and Penza sent briefs supporting Saratov's position. State financial involvement was essential, as no offer exceeded 50 percent of the cost of setting up a new university. For financial reasons, the council decided on Saratov, which opened with one medical faculty in 1909. See Sovet Ministrov, *Osobyi Zhurnal ob Osnovanii Novovo v Rossii Universiteta*, 10 and 13 April 1907.

7. See, for example, the arguments made by Viceroy Vorontsov-Dashkov in May 1912 in favor of founding a new polytechnic in Tiflis, or the 1904 memorandum of Minister of Education V. G. Glazov to Tsar Nicholas advocating increased government support of Iur'ev and Warsaw universities. Both minimized the dangers of founding institutions of higher education in non-Russian areas and emphasized the success of Strasbourg University, which was allegedly strengthening the ties of the Alsatians to the German empire (Sovet Ministrov, *Osobyi Zhurnal ob Uchrezhdenii na Kavkaze Vysshevo Uchebnovo Zavedeniia [24 May 1912]*; TsGIA, f. 922, op. 1, d. 143).

8. See the comments of Professor E. N. Trubetskoi to the 1902 commission on university reform: Komissiia po preobrazovaniiu vysshikh uchebnykh zavedenii, *Trudy* (Saint Petersburg, 1903), vol. 1, p. 34. State service, as Charles Timberlake points out, offered significant material advantages over many branches of private service. For example, many state jobs offered housing allowances and generous pension plans, as well as the right to wear an "Anna on the Neck." In order to help certain institutions created by the Great Reforms (zemstvos, city Dumas, judicial institutions) compete for personnel, the tsarist government extended some civil-service benefits to certain of their employees. "As a result the distinction between the 'private' and the 'public' sector in Russian society was blurred" (see Timberlake, "Higher Learning, the State and the Professions in Russia," in Jarausch, *The Transformation of Higher Learning*, p. 337). Some professors criticized what they perceived as a hypocritical tendency on the part of students to engage in protest while they were at the university and then to prefer state to private employment after graduation. See, for example, I. Kh. Ozerov, *Na temy dnia* (Moscow, 1912), p. 179.

ondary school diploma by itself (either from a classical gymnasium or from a *realuchilishche*) offered relatively few opportunities unless the student continued on to higher education.[9] A higher-education degree allowed young people from the so-called subject estates (the peasantry and the *meshchanstvo*) to acquire "honorary citizenship," to improve their legal position, and to enter the Table of Ranks.[10] Students received a deferment from military service and served for a shorter time. For Jews a degree was a ticket out of the Pale of Settlement. A mere diploma from a classical gymnasium or a *realuchilishche* gave few privileges unless the student had won a gold or silver medal. As Minister of Education I. I. Tolstoi pointed out in 1906:

> To a very large extent this explains why many graduates of gymnasia, pro-gymnasia, and *realuchilishcha* strive so relentlessly for a diploma from an institution of higher education, despite all the material obstacles that stand in their way. For the son of a peasant or a *meshchanin*, a non-Russian [*inorodets*], or even the son of a merchant not having enough money to set himself up in trade . . . higher education constitutes the only means of entering government service and securing personal status [*lichnye prava*].[11]

There were several types of institutions of higher education (*VUZy*): closed schools, military academies, specialized institutes, women's institutes, polytechnic institutes, commercial institutes, private universities and institutes such as Moscow's Shaniavskii University, and state universities. The universities and several institutes were under the control of the Ministry of Education. Control over the rest of the higher-education establishment was distributed among several ministries.

---

9. Professor M. M. Novikov recalled that his father, who was sure the family would not be able to afford to give his son a higher education, decided to send him to a commercial high school, since gymnasia and *realuchilishcha* only "prepared for higher education" (Novikov, *Ot Moskvy do N'iu-Iorka* [New York, 1952], p. 26). In a Ministry of Education survey of the 4,378 students who earned their high school diploma (*attestat zrelosti*) from a gymnasium in 1900, more than 98 percent stated their intention of entering either a university or a special technical institute (79.7 percent wanted to go to university, 18.5 percent to specialized institutes). Of the 7,491 high school graduates in 1910, 76.2 percent wanted to go on to university, and 14.9 percent to specialized institutes (*Otchët* of Ministry of Education for 1900 and 1910). Of 4,376 graduates of *realuchilishcha* in 1912, 75 percent wanted to go on to higher education—14.7 percent to universities and 60.4 percent to specialized institutes. Of the remainder, 12.3 percent wanted to start military service and 9.5 percent were undecided. Only 3.0 percent wanted to enter either private employment or state service immediately after high school graduation (*Otchët* of Ministry of Education for 1912).

10. First-class-degree graduates of universities and most technical institutes entered the civil service at rank X, second-class-degree graduates at rank XII. Holders of doctorates entered at rank VIII; those with a master's degree entered at rank IX.

11. TsGIA, f. 733, op. 153, d. 174, l. 55.

The closed schools, to train the government elite, included the Pazhe-skii Korpus, the Alexandrovskii Lycee, and the Institute of Law (Uchi-lishche Pravovedeniia).[12] Enrollments were small and selective. On the eve of World War I, just 290 students attended the Alexandrovskii Lycee, while 350 studied in the Institute of Law. One reason was cost: about 800 rubles a year for tuition, room, and board in the older classes— double the cost of attending a university. The closed schools were unique in the higher-education system in that they were open only to the sons of hereditary nobles. Honors graduates of the Pazheskii Korpus, the Insti-tute of Law, or the Alexandrovskii Lycee started with the ninth rank in the civil service, whereas the rest entered state service at the tenth rank. (By comparison, only university graduates with a master's degree en-tered the civil service at the ninth rank, and only honors graduates of the universities entered at the tenth rank.)[13]

The specialized institutes prepared trained specialists—engineers, sur-veyors, agronomists—not only for state service but also for private en-terprise and zemstvo employment. Admission to these institutes, by ex-amination only, was highly competitive and prompted the oft-repeated charge that a high proportion of university students were rejects from these institutes.[14]

From 1860 on, the government's higher-education policy favored the specialized institutes.[15] A 1916 Ministry of Education memorandum noted that between 1866 and 1916 the government founded fourteen new specialized institutes but only two universities, and those only par-

12. V. R. Leikina-Svirskaia, *Intelligentsiia v Rossii vo vtoroi polovine 19ovo veka* (Moscow, 1971), p. 75.

13. Alumni of these schools did well. The 1897 edition of the *Almanakh sovremennykh russkikh gosudarstvennykh deiatelei* listed eighty-four officials who were members of the State Council, ministers, or department chiefs (*glavnoupravliaiushchie*). Of this group, only twenty-three were university graduates, including twenty-one alumni of Moscow University or Saint Petersburg University. Thirty-seven graduated from the closed schools, and fifteen received a military education. (The rest either had a secondary education or graduated from a specialized institute, or their education was not indicated.)

14. See the comments of the Ministry of Finance at the March 1909 interministerial conference to discuss government financing of the universities (TsGIA, f. 733, op. 154, d. 471, l. 114). In 1891 there were 213 applications for 21 vacancies at the Institute of Communications and 250 applications for 40 places in the Institute of Civil Engineers. See "Vnutrenee obozrenie," *Russkaia Mysl'*, no. 9 (1891). For 665 places in six specialized institutes in Saint Petersburg during the 1899–1900 academic year, there were 3,261 applicants.

15. James C. McClelland has argued that the state's higher-education policy in fact lavished too many resources on the universities (*Autocrats and Academics: Education, Culture, and Society in Tsarist Russia* [Chicago, 1979]). As will be argued below, state expenditures on nonmedical university education tended to stabilize after 1885.

tially staffed.[16] Many of the institutes were not under Ministry of Education control. For example, the Ministry of the Interior directed the Electrotechnical Institute in Moscow, the Ministry of Trade and Industry supervised the Saint Petersburg Mining Institute, and the War Ministry oversaw the Military-Medical Academy. *VUZy* attached to ministries other than the Ministry of Education traditionally allowed their students a great deal more freedom than students in the universities enjoyed. For example, students in the Saint Petersburg Mining Institute maintained, with official permission, a library and a dining hall, as well as having the right to hold meetings (*skhodki*).[17]

One difference between the student bodies of the institutes and those of the universities was that the former were more likely to come from estates other than the nobility and civil service and also tended, as time went on, to be better off financially.[18] Some contemporary observers noted that not only the merchants (*kuptsy*) but also the peasants wealthy enough to give their sons a higher education preferred the prospects

16. TsGIA, f. 733, op. 226, d. 206, l. 14. The memorandum argued in favor of more universities, citing regional needs and the shortage of physicians and high school teachers. The more important specialized institutes in St. Petersburg (excluding polytechnics and commercial institutes) with date of founding and number of students in 1912 were the Mining Institute (1773), 640; the Military-Medical Academy (1799), 900; the Forestry Institute (1803), 560; the Institute of Communications (1810), 1,384; the Technological Institute (1828), 2,525; the Institute of Civil Engineers (1842), 810; and the Electrotechnical Institute (1886), 750. In Moscow the most important institutes were the Lazarev Institute of Eastern Languages (1815), 141; the Higher Technical School (1830), 3,000; the Petrovskii Agricultural Academy (1865), 1,000; and the School of Engineering (1896), 580. Important provincial institutes included the Riga Polytechnic (founded in 1862; not to be confused with the polytechnics started by Witte in 1898), 1,753; the Kharkov Technological Institute (1885), 1,400; the Ekaterinoslav Mining Institute (1899), 480; the Tomsk Technological Institute (1900), 1,171; and the Don Polytechnic (1907), 704. See Nicholas Hans, *A History of Russian Educational Policy, 1701–1917* (London, 1931), pp. 239–240.

17. A good description of the special privileges and traditions of the students at the Mining Institute can be found in *Konovalovskii konflikt* (Saint Petersburg, 1905); cf. *Na puti k pobede* (Leningrad, 1925). On the spirit of the Military-Medical Academy, see Daniel Brower, *Training the Nihilists: Education and Radicalism in Tsarist Russia* (Ithaca, 1975), p. 131.

18. In 1914, of 9,704 students at six technological institutes of the Ministry of Education, 26.5 percent came from noble and civil-service families, 2 percent from the clergy, 14 percent from the merchants and the honorary citizenry, 31.5 percent from the *meshchanstvo* and artisans, and 22 percent from the peasantry. In the same year, of 35,695 students enrolled in the universities, 35.9 percent came from noble and civil-service families, 10.3 percent from the clergy, 10.9 percent from the merchants and the honorary citizenry, 24.4 percent from the *meshchanstvo* and artisans, and 13.3 percent from the peasantry. See V. R. Leikina-Svirskaia, *Russkaia intelligentsiia v 1900–1917 godakh* (Moscow, 1981), pp. 15, 24.

offered by the specialized institutes.[19] But fragmentary evidence suggests that in at least some of these institutes, students shared with their counterparts in the universities a deep ambivalence about their studies and their future careers.[20] Prospective students would sit exams at several institutes and would go to whichever one accepted them. Often the match was less than perfect.[21]

A major milestone in the history of Russian higher education was the decision of the Ministry of Finance, with some important financial support from leading merchants and industrialists, to build a network of polytechnic institutes in Saint Petersburg, Warsaw, and Kiev between 1898 and 1902.[22] The ministry, dissatisfied with the performance of university graduates, wanted to develop managerial as well as technical skills. For example, the Saint Petersburg Polytechnic added an economic-legal section to the existing departments of metallurgy, electromechanics, and shipbuilding.[23] By 1913, the Saint Petersburg Polytechnic, with an enrollment of 5,215, was the "second-largest technical institute in the world."[24]

Another important area of prewar Russian higher education was higher commercial education, concentrated in the Moscow and Kiev commercial institutes. In 1912 the Moscow Commercial Institute had 4,261 students, and 3,800 studied in the Kiev Institute during the 1913–1914 academic year. The Ministry of Trade and Industry fought hard to

19. G. Gordon, "K voprosu o material'nom polozhenii nashevo studenchestva," *Vestnik Vospitaniia*, no. 7 (1914): 175. A 1901 Tomsk census reported in this article found that 79.2 percent of the university students, but only 59.5 percent of the technology students, lived on less than 25 rubles a month.

20. See the discussion, in Chapter 7 below, of the 1909 census at the Saint Petersburg Technological Institute.

21. One complication was the fact that some towns had only a classical gymnasium and no *realuchilishche*, or vice versa. A graduate of a *realuchilishche* could enter a university only after passing examinations in Latin and Greek (later only one classical language was required), while a graduate of a gymnasium who wanted to enter a specialized institute was often at a disadvantage when taking the competitive examinations.

22. A polytechnic opened in Novocherkassk in 1908. On the founding of the Kiev Polytechnic Institute, see Alfred J. Rieber, *Merchants and Entrepreneurs in Imperial Russia* (Chapel Hill, 1982), p. 107. The best source on the Saint Petersburg Polytechnic Institute is Gregory Guroff, "The Legacy of Pre-Revolutionary Economic Education: Saint Petersburg Polytechnic Institute," *Russian Review*, no. 3 (1972).

23. See Gosudarstvennyi Sovet, *Otchët za 1902 god* (Saint Petersburg, 1903), pp. 266–280. When the State Council objected that this was the purview of the universities, Witte pointed out their defects. True, he argued, the universities taught law, but their graduates received insufficient practical preparation in economics and took too long, as civil-service experience showed, to acquire practical skills.

24. McClelland, "Diversification in Russian-Soviet Education," p. 185.

TABLE 2   ENROLLMENT OF WOMEN IN RUSSIAN HIGHER EDUCATION, 1900–1916

	Women's *VUZy* by Type			Coed *VUZy*		Total
	University	Agricultural	Technical	Commercial	Other	
1900–1901	2,588	—	—	—	1	2,589
1906–1907	8,533	97	224	289	1,350	10,493
1910–1911	24,588	531	485	1,084	2,730	29,418
1913–1914	31,786	1,401	520	1,400	3,000	38,107
1915–1916	36,164	1,753	1,200	1,500	3,400	44,017

SOURCE: These figures are based on a table in Ruth Dudgeon, "The Forgotten Minority: Women Students in Imperial Russia, 1872–1917," *Russian History*, no. 9 (1982):9.

upgrade their status. In 1912, graduates of these institutes became eligible for the civil service and estate privileges granted to other officially recognized institutions of higher education.

Of all the sectors of Russian higher education in the last years of the autocracy, institutions for women showed the fastest rate of growth (see Table 2). This occurred despite an almost total lack of financial support from the state.[25] In the deliberations preceding the promulgation of the 1863 University Statute, the state had considered making the universities coeducational, but most faculty councils opposed the idea, and the student demonstrations of 1861–1862 convinced the government that coeducation would lead to further unrest. By 1873, however, a special commission had concluded that the pressing need for female doctors and teachers justified the establishment of some form of higher education for women. In 1876 Tsar Alexander II permitted permanent women's courses in Moscow, Saint Petersburg, Kiev, and Kazan, as well as women's medical courses in Saint Petersburg. By 1910 the two largest institutions of higher education for women were the Bestuzhev-Riumin courses in Saint Petersburg, with an enrollment of 5,897 students, and the Moscow women's courses, with 6,477 students. At the Women's Medical Institute in Saint Petersburg 1,525 women were studying medicine, while 2,450 were enrolled in the Kiev women's courses.

The extraordinary growth of enrollment of women, despite the fact that for women a diploma brought few of the legal and civil privileges enjoyed by male graduates, and despite the heavy expenses involved, offers impressive evidence of the value and regard that growing numbers of young women attached to higher education.[26] It also induced a change

25. For example, 90 percent of the total 1912 budget of the Moscow Higher Courses for Women came from tuition fees. As Ruth Dudgeon points out, of the 7.5 million rubles spent by the Ministry of Education in 1911–1912, only 230,000 rubles (3 percent) went for women's education, and of that amount all but 12,000 rubles went to the Saint Petersburg Women's Medical Institute ("The Forgotten Minority: Women Students in Imperial Russia, 1872–1917," *Russian History*, no. 9 [1982]: 4). See also TsGIA, f. 1276, op. 2, d. 515, l. 8. This document summarizes the 4 September 1908 meeting of the Council of Ministers, at which Minister of Education A. N. Schwartz submitted a memorandum outlining the state's policy toward the higher education of women.

26. One commentator on Russian student life wrote in 1914 that "it was only yesterday that the average provincial citizen [*obyvatel'*] reacted with disgust to his daughter's dream of getting a higher education. Only yesterday such an admission meant a bitter argument with parents and a break with home. [Parents] feared the distance from home, the prospect of their daughter living in a strange city, the effects that higher education would have on the girl! Going to the 'courses' meant a break with the past and future at the same time. And then came 1905 and the provinces, the very citadel of these humdrum types [*tsitadel' etovo obyvatelia*], themselves became the source of the [mania for higher

in the government's policy of withholding rights. The law of 19 December 1911 gave women graduating from a few state-recognized institutions all the legal privileges enjoyed by male graduates except the right to enter the state service and the Table of Ranks.[27]

Most women students came from a professional, civil service, or mercantile background.[28] Upon graduation, most became teachers or doctors.[29] By 1914, however, they had won the right to begin the long process that led to admission to the bar.

THE UNIVERSITIES

For men not wishing to proceed to a specialized technical career, the basic institution of higher education remained the university. On the eve of World War I, there were ten universities in imperial Russia. Six—those in Moscow, Kharkov, Kazan, Kiev, Odessa, and Warsaw—consisted of four departments: law, medicine, history and philology, and natural sciences and mathematics. Saint Petersburg University had a department of Eastern languages but did not train doctors. Tomsk University had departments of law and medicine, and Saratov University had only a department of medicine. Iur'ev University, in Dorpat, had, in ad-

education] which until now had come from the capitals" (L. Kleinbort, "Russkaia kursistka," *Sovremennyi Mir*, no. 9 [1914]: 22).

27. Dudgeon, "The Forgotten Minority," p. 4; K. Shokhol, "K voprosu o razvitii vysshevo zhenskovo obrazovaniia v Rossii," *Zhurnal Ministerstva Narodnovo Prosveshcheniia*, no. 7 (1913): 7. From 1901 on, the state began to widen opportunities for women to enjoy a teaching career. In September 1901, women graduates won the right to teach in women's gymnasia. In August 1906, they were allowed to teach in the lower six classes of male gymnasia. The December 1911 law gave women equal status with men in secondary teaching.

28. According to a census of students in the Bestuzhev courses in Saint Petersburg, 24.4 percent of the women's fathers were "free professionals"; 13.5 percent were in state service; 9.9 percent were on pension; 13.9 percent owned industrial or commercial enterprises; 8.3 percent were landowners; 7.5 percent lived on rents from a house or invested capital; 5.6 percent were clergy; 4.8 percent were employees in industrial or commercial establishments; 2.2 percent were employees in the transport sector; 1.7 percent were workers or artisans; and 1.7 percent were peasant cultivators. See A. Kaufman, "Russkaia kursistka v tsifrakh: Perepis' v Bestuzhevskikh Kursakh," *Russkaia Mysl'*, no. 6 (1912): 65–66. The census also corroborates the obsolescence of traditional estate rubrics. While the fathers of only 1.7 percent of the students were "peasant cultivators," 11.5 percent of the students indicated that they came from the peasant estate.

29. Of the employed alumnae of the Bestuzhev courses, 67 percent were in teaching. As Ruth Dudgeon points out, this career was not necessarily the first choice of women students: "Seventy percent of the respondents in the humanities and natural sciences expected to become teachers although only 7 percent of the science students and 37 percent of those in the humanities indicated a preference for teaching" (Dudgeon, "The Forgotten Minority," p. 11).

TABLE 3   DISTRIBUTION OF STUDENTS IN RUSSIAN
UNIVERSITIES, BY FIELD

	1880	1885	1899[a]	1912
Eastern languages	0.4%	0.8%	1.1%	0.8%[b]
History and philology	11.3	9.8	3.9	8.5
Law	22.3	30.2	43.1	38.3
Medicine	46.0	38.0	28.1	27.5
Natural sciences and mathematics	20.0	21.2	22.9	24.9

SOURCE: Figures for 1880, 1885, and 1899 are from Paul Miliukov, "Universitety v Rossii," in E. A. Brokhaus and I. A. Efron, eds., *Entsiklopedicheskii slovar'* (Saint Petersburg, 1897–1903), vol. 58, p. 799. Figures for 1912 are from Ministerstvo Narodnovo Prosveshcheniia, *Otchët za 1912 god* (Saint Petersburg, 1913).
[a] Figures for 1899 do not total 100 percent in the original data.
[b] Eastern languages in Saint Petersburg, and theology in Iur'ev.

dition to the four basic departments, a department of theology. Enrollment patterns in the universities, as can be seen from Table 3, showed that most students studied law and medicine.

Few professors would have argued with L. I. Petrazhitskii, a noted Saint Petersburg jurist, when he tried to defend the central role of the universities in Russia's higher-education system:

> For state posts and public functions in general, where one seeks an idealistic, principled, and humane approach rather than entrepreneurial deftness and economic or utilitarian practicality—for example, judges, gymnasium teachers, doctors, posts in general internal administration, or supervisory responsibilities in the Ministry of Education—the university type of education is most desirable.[30]

Petrazhitskii did not believe that the technical schools had attained a level of "psychic and ethical culture that would permit one to expect a spirit of disinterested honesty."

Elsewhere, Petrazhitskii's colleagues amplified these arguments by pointing out the fundamental relationship between strong universities and national power. For Moscow's N. V. Speranskii, the source of archrival Germany's vitality was obvious:

30. Quotes from Petrazhitskii are taken from Leikina-Svirskaia, *Russkaia intelligentsiia*, p. 11. See also the review of L. Petrazhitskii's *Universitet i Nauka* in *Sovremennyi Mir*, no. 7–8 (1907).

To whom does Germany, which was once so abased and poor, owe its present power and fame? Above all, to the universities. Who preserved the feeling
of national unity when Germany was fragmented? The universities! Who
maintained the German spirit? . . . Who created the basis of Germany's economic power? . . . Who smashed the barriers to national unification?—the
universities.[31]

In a suggestive and cautionary comparison, Speranskii then turned to
France. Quoting Louis Pasteur, Speranskii argued that the French had
lost the Franco-Prussian War because, in its obsession with industry,
trade, and agriculture, France forgot that "there is no such thing as applied science, only the application of science."

At about the same time, the famed geologist V. I. Vernadskii voiced
the concern, shared by many of his colleagues, that the state's higher-
education policy, concentrating as it did on specialized technical education rather than universities, was shortsighted. Universities, Vernadskii
argued, were "a weapon in the universal struggle for survival, a weapon
stronger than dreadnoughts."[32]

Founded by the state in the eighteenth century to train civil servants,
from their very inception the universities embodied a variety of distinct
and potentially contradictory features. A basic problem was the tension
between the identity of the universities as state institutions and their
various other roles: their dedication to the principle of the pursuit of
"pure knowledge," their service to the emerging Russian public, and
their teaching functions. As the Kharkov University Faculty Council argued in a 1901 memorandum, the university as an institution was "sui
generis" and therefore needed a large degree of autonomy. Writing in
the middle of the nineteenth century, Nikolai Pirogov, the liberal curator of the Kiev educational district, argued that it was easier to define
the Russian universities in terms of what they were not than in terms of
what they were:

If it is difficult to define the West European universities, it is even more difficult to define ours. . . . The Russian university is not an institution of applied
learning, but it is also not a scientific research institution [*svobodno-nauchnoe
uchrezhdenie*]. It does not impart general education, but neither is its main
purpose moral education. In character it is not based on the estate principle,
nor is it a church institution, a private-philanthropic institution, a purely bureaucratic institution, or an institution modeled on the lines of a medieval

31. N. V. Speranskii, *Krizis russkoi shkoly* (Moscow, 1914), p. 38.
32. V. I. Vernadskii, "Vysshaia shkola v Rossii," *Ezhegodnik Gazety Rech' za 1914
god* (Petrograd, 1915), p. 317.

corporation. And yet, in varying degrees, each of the above principles is incorporated into our university structure.[33]

Pirogov then made the case for granting faculty councils a large degree of autonomy in internal university governance.

The first real debate over the function of the Russian universities and their relationship to the state took place during the era of the Great Reforms, in the early 1860s. Shaken by the student unrest of 1861–1862, some conservatives wanted to turn the universities into closed institutions modeled on the elite Alexandrovskii Lycee. Others held up the model of mid-nineteenth-century Oxford and Cambridge, where the main goal of the university experience supposedly was "moral education" (*vospitanie*). Unlike the German model, tutorials rather than lectures, and "Christian values" rather than *Wissenschaft,* were to be the centerpiece of higher education. Some liberals, such as N. I. Kostomarov, looked to the French model of the Collège de France. Kostomarov advocated turning the universities into completely open institutions where anyone could attend lectures. Other noted scholars, such as Moscow University's B. N. Chicherin, argued against all these views, claiming that the German model of the university, with its emphasis on the lecture system, the pursuit of pure knowledge, faculty prerogatives in internal university governance, and student guidance based on an examination system, offered the best direction for Russia's higher-education system. The best source of moral education was, they argued, scientific research, not tutorials. Furthermore, strong universities were essential to the future welfare of the nation, and only universities, not specialized institutes, could develop scientific knowledge.[34]

The 1863 University Statute represented a victory for the arguments of Chicherin and Pirogov. Student rights were severely circumscribed, and the professors were given extensive powers. They were authorized to elect rectors and other professors and were granted jurisdiction over student discipline. In a significant departure from the German model, faculty councils rather than individual departments voted on new faculty appointments—a procedure meant to symbolize the principle of the unity of science as well as the unity of the university.

33. Quoted in A. Filippov, "Moskovskoe studenchestvo," *Russkoe Obozrenie,* no. 5 (1897): 457.

34. These debates are summarized in G. A. Dzhanshiev, *Epokha velikikh reform* (Moscow, 1900), pp. 265–270; and Alexander Vucinich, *Science in Russian Culture* (Stanford, 1970), vol. 2, p. 38.

The 1863 Statute, however, was short-lived. Student unrest led to calls for more government control over university governance and teaching. In 1879 the government relieved faculty councils of all responsibility for student discipline and instead appointed outside "inspectors." Meanwhile, influential conservatives such as Mikhail Katkov, the editor of *Moskovskie Vedomosti,* dreamed of using an outside examination system to guarantee government control over the content of university teaching. The assassination of Tsar Alexander II in 1881 and the ensuing appointments of I. D. Delianov as minister of education and Dmitry Tolstoi as minister of the interior increased the pressure on the universities.

At the end of 1882, Tolstoi submitted a project for a new university statute to the State Council.[35] The project, which was approved and became the 1884 University Statute, represented a drastic shift in power in university governance, from the faculty councils to the minister of education and his appointed curator. It provided that the curator would convene meetings of the faculty council and individual departments. Faculty councils and rectors lost the right to communicate directly with the minister of education; they now would have to address all requests to the curator. The rector, who had previously been elected by the faculty council, now became an appointee of the minister of education. Deacons of departments, who had hitherto been elected by the faculty councils, were now to be named by the curator. The minister of education would assume control of faculty appointments. Article 100 of the statute gave him the choice of either filling a vacancy himself or asking the faculty council to select a candidate, who would then be subject to his approval. The faculty council lost all power over the disbursement of university funds and now found itself limited to functions of a purely formal nature: deciding student prizes, conferring degrees, and approving doctoral dissertations. The council would have to secure ministerial approval for such decisions as electing honorary members of the university or founding learned societies. Authority over student discipline would be vested in an inspector appointed by the curator. One of the inspector's more important powers would be that of determining which students would receive scholarships. The draft statute also incorporated

35. On the deliberations leading to the 1884 Statute, see P. A. Zaionchkovskii, *Rossiiskoe samoderzhavie v kontse 19ovo stoletiia* (Moscow, 1970), pp. 320–322; Allen Sinel, *The Classroom and the Chancellery* (Cambridge, Mass., 1973), pp. 122–125; G. I. Shchetinina, *Universitety v Rossii i ustav 1884ovo goda* (Moscow, 1976), pp. 127–154; Gosudarstvennyi Sovet, *Otchët za 1884 god,* pp. 231–392.

Katkov's idea that all university graduates would have to pass state examinations administered by outside examiners.

The statute encountered strong opposition in the State Council. Baron A. P. Nikolai pointed out that the statute betrayed "an insulting lack of trust in the professoriate." Even K. P. Pobedonostsev, the procurator of the Holy Synod, voiced doubts about such aspects of the statute as the state examination system. Although the majority of the State Council voted against the statute, Tsar Alexander III ratified it on 23 August 1884.

IMPLEMENTATION OF THE NEW STATUTE

In his valuable survey of Kharkov University, which appeared in 1905, Professor V. Buzeskul divided the history of the implementation of the 1884 Statute into three periods. During the first period, 1884 to 1888, the Ministry of Education tried to follow the new statute to the letter. From 1888 to 1899 it was forced to modify many of its basic principles significantly. The outbreak of massive student disorders in 1899 brought about the third period, marked by "the total collapse" (polnoe krushenie) of the statute.[36]

Yet the 1884 Statute would remain in force until 1917; its history shows just how difficult it was for the autocracy to realize its intention of asserting state control over university teaching, university governance, and student discipline. It soon became clear that in dealing with the universities, laws by themselves offered little guarantee that the government would have its way. By 1905 the statute was, as Buzeskul pointed out, in shreds. What is truly extraordinary is that although the government recognized the need to replace the statute as early as 1901, it lasted until the fall of the autocracy.

Ministerial interference in faculty appointments was most pronounced in the years immediately following the introduction of the 1884 Statute. While the Ministry of Education practiced relative restraint in appointing university rectors, replacing only a few of the previously elected incumbents, it did undertake a minor purge of the professoriate.[37] Even before the statute went into effect, professors I. I.

---

36. V. Buzeskul, *Istoriia Khar'kovskovo Universiteta pri deistvii ustava 1884ovo goda* (Kharkov, 1905), p. 1.

37. Only one elected rector, Professor Tsekhanovetskii of Kharkov University, was replaced immediately. In 1887 Delianov installed Professor M. I. Vladislavlev as rector of Saint Petersburg University, a move that led to some student unrest.

Mechnikov, A. S. Posnikov, and V. V. Preobrazhenskii had been forced out of Odessa University. Delianov also fired, in 1887, two popular professors of the Moscow University juridical faculty, M. M. Kovalevskii and S. A. Muromtsev. Professor F. G. Mishchenko was forced to leave Kiev University for "Ukrainophile leanings." The new minister dismissed *privat-dozent* V. I. Semevskii from Saint Petersburg University because he did not like what he heard about Semevskii's lectures on the 1861 emancipation of the serfs. Professor I. I. Ditiatin had to resign the chair of Russian law at Kharkov University. In 1890 the famous chemist D. I. Mendeleev resigned from Saint Petersburg University after receiving a reprimand from Delianov for passing on a student petition.[38] The brunt of the ministry's attacks on the professoriate occurred in the 1880s. During the following decade, the Ministry of Education began to pay more attention to the opinions of the professoriate in filling vacancies—although it always had the legal right to overrule faculty recommendations.[39]

When it introduced the 1884 Statute, the Ministry of Education told the professoriate that "university teaching . . . must serve the interests of the state; it must be patriotic."[40] To this end, new examination rules went into effect in 1885.[41] University teaching was now divided into "primary" courses, for which students would be responsible when taking the state examinations, and "secondary" courses, on which they would not be examined. The new rules were designed to have their greatest impact on the two most politically sensitive departments: history and philology, and law. The curricular emphasis in the former was shifted toward a heavy concentration on the classics; subjects such as Russian literature and philosophy now became "secondary."[42] As for the juridical faculty,

38. A good source on these dismissals is S. G. Svatikov, "Opal'naia professura 80-kh godov," *Golos Minuvshevo*, no. 2 (1917). In justifying his decision to fire Kovalevskii, Delianov wrote to the curator of the Moscow educational district that "it is better to have a professor of mediocre capabilities than to have an especially gifted professor who has a deleterious effect on the minds of the students."

39. See Buzeskul, *Istoriia Khar'kovskovo Universiteta*, pp. 17–27; Th. Zelinskii, "Universitetskii vopros v 1906 godu," *Zhurnal Ministerstva Narodnovo Prosveshcheniia*, no. 8 (1906). Zelinskii does point out that this restraint lacked any legal underpinning. Bogolepov's unceremonious dismissal, after the 1899 student disturbances, of Nikolai Kareev and Ivan Grevs from the Saint Petersburg University faculty reminded the professors of their vulnerability under the law.

40. Buzeskul, *Istoriia Khar'kovskovo Universiteta*, p. 5.

41. The full text of the examination rules for all departments is reprinted in Ministerstvo Narodnovo Prosveshcheniia, *Alfavitnyi spisok zakonopolozhenii i rasporiazhenii po Sankt Peterburgskomu Uchebnomu Okrugu* (Saint Petersburg, 1893), pp. 1260–1279.

42. A. I. Georgievskii, one of the architects of the statute, pointed out that Russian literature was an undesirable subject because Russian writers "have followed only one

the new statute abolished the teaching of foreign constitutional law and turned such politically sensitive fields as state law into secondary subjects. Attention now focused on Roman, civil, criminal, and church law.[43] The new examination rules instructed professors to glorify the Russian autocracy and stop comparing it to other governments. Furthermore, they were to emphasize concrete facts rather than spend too much time on "abstract legal theories."[44]

The new rules, however, soon disappointed those who had seen them as an effective vehicle to ensure state control over university teaching. As the State Council majority had in fact predicted, the scarcity of qualified personnel soon led to a situation where state examination commissions had to be composed of the very professors whose teaching they were supposedly regulating. The examinations themselves soon became so standardized that students could pass them by taking two-week cram courses.

Dissatisfaction also mounted with the curricular changes mandated by the new statute. On the history and philology faculty, the unpopularity of the forced concentration on classics and the mass flight of students to other faculties forced the ministry to beat a hasty retreat. In 1889 Delianov announced the restoration of the pre-1884 division of the faculty into classics, history, and Slavic departments.[45]

Criticism of the juridical curriculum also mounted; even other government departments implied that the 1884 Statute had failed to raise the level of legal graduates. The Ministry of Justice complained that the

---

goal: to point out . . . the defects . . . of the contemporary state and of the social order. Given the sociopolitical bias of Russian literature, the lectures of the professors . . . are full of harmful nonsense." See G. I. Shchetinina, "Universitety i obshchestvennoe dvizhenie v poreformennyi period.," *Istoricheskie Zapiski*, no. 84 (1969): 196. These changes were not popular with students. Enrollment in this faculty fell from 11.3 percent of all students in 1880 to 3.9 percent by 1900.

43. In his memoirs A. N. Naumov describes the basic course prescribed by the 1884 Statute for law students. In the first year the courses, all required, included the history of Russian law, the history of Roman law, political economy, and the encyclopedia of law. During the second year students took Roman law, Russian state law, financial law, church law, and the history of legal thought. The basic subjects in the third and fourth years included criminal law, civil law, international law, police law, and commercial law, as well as electives in such fields as forensic medicine and penology (*Iz utselevshikh vospominanii, 1868–1917,* [New York, 1954], vol. 1, p. 82).

44. Ministerstvo Narodnovo Prosveshcheniia, *Ekzamenatsionnye trebovaniia, pravila i programmy ispytaniia v komissii iuridicheskoi* (Saint Petersburg, 1885), p. 2.

45. A critical view of the history and philology curriculum at the turn of the century can be found in S. P. Mel'gunov, *Vospominaniia i dnevniki* (Paris, 1964), pp. 79–81. Mel'gunov complained about his educational experience in Moscow University, where the professors supposedly discouraged research in contemporary topics. A more positive view can be found in Kizevetter, *Na rubezhe dvukh stoletii,* pp. 50–92.

excessive number of courses students had to take precluded the development of critical legal skills. To press his case for economic-administrative education in the polytechnics, Finance Minister Witte cited the deficiencies of the university juridical faculties. A 1902 review commission appointed by the Ministry of Education recommended the reintroduction of the teaching of foreign constitutional law. Other critics complained that the statute barred students on the juridical faculty from taking courses such as logic or psychology, which were taught only on the history and philology faculty.[46]

While the medical and natural science faculties did not come under the same political scrutiny as did the departments of history and law, they too suffered from another stricture of the statute: inflexible staffing guidelines which failed to keep pace with scientific developments and the demand for new faculty positions. The 1902 commission on university reform pointed out that the 1884 Statute left the natural science departments severely understaffed, while medical teaching demanded new chairs in obstetrics, bacteriology, pediatrics, medical physics, and psychiatry.[47]

In order to improve the quality of teaching and encourage professors to compete in tailoring their courses to the requirements of the new examination system, the statute introduced the German institution of the *privat-dozent* as well as the honorarium. *Privat-dozenty* received the right to compete with senior professors by offering the same courses, while all students had to pay their teachers an honorarium of one ruble per course-hour. Thus high enrollments would bring financial reward and would presumably encourage professors to concentrate on preparing students for the state examinations.

Here, too, reality fell far short of the expectations of the government. *Privat-dozenty,* whose prospects for an academic career depended on the favor of their senior faculty mentor, would rarely risk alienating the senior faculty by giving parallel courses. Another reason real competition did not develop was the chronic shortage of qualified teaching personnel. Making German *Lehrfreiheit* and *Lernfreiheit* work in Russia presupposed a supply of qualified university professors that the country simply did not possess. Because there was a shortage rather than a sur-

46. Komissiia po preobrazovaniiu, *Trudy,* vol. 1, pp. 123–125; O. F. Shershenovich, "O zhelatel'noi postanovke iuridicheskovo obrazovaniia," *Pravo,* no. 4 (1900); Sergei Zhivovo, "Chevo nedostaët v universitete nashim budushchim iuristam?" *Russkaia Mysl',* no. 10 (1902).
47. Komissiia po preobrazovaniiu, *Trudy,* vol. 1, pp. 104–105, 133.

plus of university teachers meeting the requirements of the 1884 Statute, the honorarium led to gross inequities; it benefited those lucky enough to be teaching required courses in departments with large enrollments but did little to encourage healthy competition to raise the quality of teaching.[48]

One major reason for the teaching shortage was the numerous obstacles that the statute put in the way of aspiring professors. Jews and women were automatically barred from the professoriate. The 1884 Statute provided for two faculty ranks—associate (extraordinary) and full (ordinary) professors. But in order to meet the statutory requirement for an associate professorship, a young man had to earn two research degrees, a master's and a doctor's degree, each requiring a long dissertation. In practice, this meant that many university teaching posts were filled by individuals who did not meet the statutory requirements. In 1908, for example, out of a total of 474 statutory professorships and associate professorships in Russian universities, 115 were "vacant," that is, they were staffed by professors who were teaching beyond the normal retirement age or who did not have the required doctor's or, in some cases, even the master's degree.[49] Those who opposed calls for more universities argued that the "vacancy rate" proved that Russia did not have enough teaching personnel even to staff the existing institutions and therefore should not start building new ones. This was met by the counterargument that the fault was the government's: it allocated too little to graduate fellowships and clung to an unrealistic and outmoded two-dissertation requirement.[50]

48. In 1899 the historian P. G. Vinogradov argued that one motive of the Ministry of Education for introducing the honorarium was to divide and demoralize the academic profession. It did lead to wide disparities in compensation. In 1906, law professors at Saint Petersburg University received an honorarium 1,250 percent higher than the honorarium of history professors, and at Kiev University they received 830 percent more. In 1897, of sixty-seven professors in Saint Petersburg University, thirty-four received less than 500 rubles a year in honorarium, whereas five earned more than 4,000 rubles. By 1909, a professor on the juridical faculty of Saint Petersburg University averaged 9,229 rubles in honorarium a year, while a colleague teaching Oriental languages averaged 76 rubles. In 1902 a law allowed faculty earning less than 1,000 rubles in honorarium to collect a 20 percent raise in their basic salary. (See P. G. Vinogradov, "Uchebnoe delo v nashikh universitetakh," *Vestnik Evropy,* no. 10 [1901]; D. I. Bagalei, "Ekonomicheskoe polozhenie russkikh universitetov," *Vestnik Evropy,* no. 1 [1914].)

49. Ministerstvo Narodnovo Prosveshcheniia, *Otchët za 1908 god.* Of these vacancies 38 were filled by professors who had passed the mandatory retirement limit, 47 were taught by *privat-dozenty,* and 30 were not taught at all.

50. There is an extensive literature on this subject. See Komissiia po preobrazovaniiu, *Trudy,* vol. 4, pp. 132–164; A. M. Mironov, "Pravovoe i material'noe polozhenie privat-dozentov v russkikh universitetakh," *Vestnik Vospitaniia,* no. 1 (1906). For a defense of the two-degree requirement see Novikov, *Ot Moskvy do N'iu-Iorka,* pp. 71–72. Novikov

One risk of formalizing relations between government and universities in an all-inclusive statute was that it became more difficult to respond quickly to changing economic needs and circumstances. The professoriate wanted higher salaries and increased state expenditures on higher education. Although the Ministry of Education was sympathetic, little changed between the introduction of the statute and the onset of World War I, in part because of opposition from the Ministry of Finance, in part because of the government's failure to modify or replace the 1884 Statute. Full professors earned 3,000 rubles in addition to honorarium; associate professors, 2,000 rubles in addition to honorarium. These salaries had not changed since 1863 and were much lower, faculty councils contended, than those of other civil servants in the same grade.[51]

Unlike members of some other elites (such as the State Council) few professors had a nonuniversity education. A significant percentage had a degree from either Moscow University or Saint Petersburg University. The social profile of the university professoriate showed marked differences from that of the student body it was teaching. (Estate categories, however, have limits as scholarly tools.) On the eve of World War I only 20.3 percent of the professoriate came from the *meshchanstvo,* the merchant estate (*kupechestvo*), and the peasantry and honored citizenry (*pochetnoe grazhdanstvo*), whereas 45.7 percent of the student body claimed these estates as their origin. The percentage of nobles ranged

---

contended that the shortage of qualified professors in the country guaranteed academic jobs for those who managed to win the support of a powerful member of the senior faculty. Therefore the goad of two degrees and a public defense was needed to encourage research. Few of Novikov's colleagues shared his opinion; the 1906 Tolstoi Conference (see Chapter 7, below) recommended abolishing the two-degree requirement.

51. In a response to a 1901 Ministry of Education questionnaire, the Moscow University Faculty Council made the case for higher academic salaries. It took the average *privatdozent* lucky enough to secure an academic post 10.8 years to attain an associate professorship and 14 years to attain a full professorship. In short, he had to wait a long time before he could earn even the 2,000 rubles given an associate professor. When he became a full professor, he would attain the fifth rank in the civil service and realize that other ministries awarded much higher fifth-rank salaries (e.g., 67 percent of the civil servants in the Department of Transport received between 6,000 and 8,000 rubles a year). The faculty council reminded the Ministry of Education that even in 1863, 5,000 rubles had been recommended as the optimum salary for a full professor. Eight years later, arguing that professors had too easy a life (considering their vacations and extramural earnings), the Ministry of Finance opposed higher salaries and expressed skepticism about the efficiency of the universities in the nation's higher-education system. Professor Bagalei pointed out that by 1914, many gymnasium teachers could earn more than an associate professor. See Imperatorskii Moskovskii Universitet, *Suzhdeniia Soveta Imperatorskovo Moskovskovo Universiteta* (Moscow, 1901), pp. 64–68; TsGIA, f. 733, op. 154, d. 471, l. 114.

from 46.2 percent for historians and 48.1 percent for mathematicians down to 29.3 percent for medical faculty. It was not a rich profession, nor did it appear to have close links with the landed nobility. Of the professoriate, 83.5 percent owned neither landed property nor a house. The profession was becoming more homogeneous in religion: 75.7 percent over the age of 65 were Russian Orthodox, and the proportion increased to 86 percent of those between the ages of 35 and 54.[52]

Between 1884 and 1917 the state made only limited increases in its financial support of higher education, and these small additional sums were allotted mainly to medical education. By 1914 the state was allocating about 5.5 million rubles a year to the universities, 60 percent of their total budget. Six years earlier a professorial conference called by the Ministry of Education had recommended raising annual outlays to 13 million yearly. As of 1914 the Russian universities had 7.8 million rubles outstanding in requests for urgently needed construction.[53]

The universities coped with these financial limitations by relying more heavily on student fees and junior faculty. Student fees made up an ever-expanding part of the university budget as enrollments increased, and since the statute made it difficult to establish new professorial chairs, the universities made growing use of junior faculty to teach new courses and keep pace with rising enrollments and the expansion of subdisciplines.[54] Still, the ratio of teachers to students tended to deteriorate, especially after 1900. For example, at Moscow University between 1900 and 1914, teaching staff increased by 21.7 percent, while enrollments increased 161.8 percent.[55]

As the junior faculty members assumed an ever larger role in university teaching, they became increasingly dissatisfied with their failure to win the role in university governance and the improvement in financial status to which they felt they were entitled.[56] The road to an associate professorship was long and grueling. An aspiring academic had to be

---

52. This paragraph is based on the 1913 service lists of the Ministry of Education. See Appendix Table B-2 in this volume.

53. Bagalei, "Ekonomicheskoe polozhenie."

54. In 1912 there were 649 *privat-dozenty,* 350 of whom taught in either Moscow University or Saint Petersburg University. Subjects neglected by the 1884 Statute, such as bacteriology and mathematical physics, were often taught by *privat-dozenty.* See N. Kol'tsov, *K universitetskomu voprosu* (Moscow, 1909), p. 4.

55. *Istoriia Moskovskovo Universiteta,* ed. M. N. Tikhomirov (Moscow, 1955), vol. 2, p. 372.

56. On the position of the junior faculty, written from a junior-faculty point of view, see Kol'tsov, *K universitetskomu voprosu;* Mironov, "Pravovoe i material'noe polozhenie privat-dozentov."

recommended by his university, undergo a risky and feudal relationship
with an academic advisor, write and publicly defend two dissertations,
secure the approval of the curator of the educational district, and then
put in long years as an underpaid *privat-dozent* until a position became
available.

Senior faculty kept the well-remunerated courses for themselves. Of
the ninety-five *privat-dozenty* teaching in Saint Petersburg University in
1895, only eleven received an honorarium of more than 600 rubles,
while sixty earned less than 300 rubles a year, and eighteen earned
nothing at all. Fixed salaries were laughable. In 1908 a *privat-dozent*
reading two lectures a week could count on 80 rubles for the academic year.[57]

But in order to become a *privat-dozent,* a student had to earn an advanced degree. Stipends for graduate study were quite small. Of eighty-
five aspirants in Moscow University in 1908, ten received scholarships
from the Ministry of Education, twenty-four obtained scholarships
from other sources, and the remaining fifty-one had to support themselves. Ministry of Education scholarships awarded the recipient 600
rubles yearly—about half the starting salary of a teacher in a classical
gymnasium. Thus *privat-dozenty* and graduate students had to undertake outside work.

A major complaint of the junior faculty members was their almost
total lack of professional rights. They were excluded from faculty council meetings and could not even attend a meeting of their own department except by invitation. They were at the mercy of their dissertation
supervisors and also of the curator, who could discharge them at any
time. Thus resentments built up not only against the Ministry of Education but also against the senior faculty. These resentments were to surface in 1905, when the junior faculty would demand that the senior
faculty share some of its newly won powers, and the senior faculty
would refuse.[58]

THE STATUTE UNDER FIRE

The outbreak of large-scale student unrest in 1899 forced the government to confront the question of revising the 1884 Statute. The inves-

57. Kol'tsov, *K universitetskomu voprosu,* p. 5.
58. See, for example, the report of the January 1906 commission created by the
Moscow University Faculty Council to study the junior faculty's demand for the right to
elect delegates to attend faculty council meetings (Tsentral'nyi Gosudarstvennyi Istoricheskii Arkhiv Moskvy [hereafter referred to as TsGIAM], f. 418, op. 249, ed. kh. 97).

tigatory commission headed by General P. S. Vannovskii concluded that
a major reason for the chronic student unrest was the unsatisfactory
state of the universities and the failure of the 1884 Statute to achieve
its objectives.

Acting on Vannovskii's report, Minister of Education N. P. Bogolepov
convened a conference that recommended key changes in some of the
basic assumptions of university policy. A fundamental feature of the
1884 Statute had been the clause that contact between students and
professors be limited to the classroom and laboratory. Another assumption was that students were "individual visitors" of the university, with
no corporate identity (see Chapter 2, below). The conference now admitted the unfeasibility of these assumptions and accepted the alleged
connection between student unrest and the deficiencies of government
university policy. The conference recommended that the government
take steps to improve the conditions of student life, to encourage more
interaction between students and professors, and to ensure that the students spend more time on their academic work. It proposed that the
government start building dormitories, that the Ministry of Education
encourage previously banned, extracurricular "scientific circles" under faculty direction, and that professors modify the lecture system
by teaching more seminars and giving students more frequent work
assignments.

P. S. Vannovskii, who became minister of education in 1901, gave the
professoriate an opportunity it had long been denied under the 1884
Statute: to arrive at and express a professional consensus about the entire university structure. On 29 April 1901, Vannovskii sent to the faculty councils a list of eighteen questions on possible directions for university reform. Analysis of the replies of the faculty councils to these
questions permits the conclusion that despite individual differences of
opinion among the professors, the academic profession as a whole
seized the opportunity presented by Vannovskii and began to speak
with one voice.

THE PROFESSORIATE CALLS FOR CHANGE

The 1884 University Statute confronted Russian professors with a
basic tension between their identity as independent scholars, loyal to
specific disciplines, and their relationship to that complex and highly
fragile institution, the university, for which they felt primary responsibility but over which they had insufficient control. This tension emerged
in the subtle but crucial difference between two major professional

goals: academic freedom and scientific freedom. As Walter Metzger points out:

> Academic freedom is the ideology of a profession-across-the-disciplines, the profession created out of the common circumstance of an academic appointment in a college or university and of the common duties and anxieties that this entails; scientific freedom is the ideology of the diverse professions-within-the-discipline, the professions based on regularized advance of knowledge in distinctive fields.[59]

The contrast between growing scientific self-confidence and humiliating state tutelage, epitomized by the 1884 University Statute, became increasingly sharp with the passage of time. The steady growth in membership and activity of learned societies signified increasing confidence in the ability of Russian scholarship to reach the highest professional standards.[60] In addition, the learned societies brought professors together with other members of educated urban society—bureaucrats, lawyers, doctors—and provided the academic profession with a significant opportunity to exert cultural influence and leadership.[61] Indeed, when one remembers the *lex Arons* in Germany and the gross violations of academic freedom in the United States at the time, and when one considers that professors fired from state universities could teach at other ministries' *VUZy*, one may well argue that the conditions of Russian life were not completely inimical to scholarship, even when compared to those in more "advanced" countries. (Nikolai Stepanovich, the hero of Chekhov's "A Boring Story," certainly seemed content with his achievements.) It was not in scholarship but in defining their relationship to the state and the nature of their professional identity that the Russian professors faced their most serious challenge.

The issue of state tutelage was complicated by the absence of an eco-

59. Walter P. Metzger, "Academic Freedom and Scientific Freedom," *Daedalus* 107, no. 2 (1978): 107.

60. On learned societies see Vucinich, *Science in Russian Culture*, vol. 2, pp. 204–209; Leikina-Svirskaia, *Russkaia Intelligentsiia*, pp. 91–92; A. D. Stepanskii, "Liberal'naia intelligentsiia v obshchestvennom dvizhenii," *Istoricheskie Zapiski*, no. 109 (1983): 64–94. An excellent exposition of the dichotomy between state interference and the growing self-confidence of the professoriate can be found in V. I. Vernadskii's "1911 god v istorii russkoi umstvennoi kul'tury," *Ezhegodnik Gazety Rech' za 1911 god* (Saint Petersburg, 1912). It should be noted that relations between the government and some of the learned societies were delicate. For example, in 1899 the Ministry of Education ordered the Moscow Juridical Society closed, after a "seditious" speech by its president, S. A. Muromtsev.

61. On the role and influence of the Moscow Juridical Society, see Kizevetter, *Na rubezhe dvukh stoletii*, pp. 25–27.

nomic base capable of providing a real alternative to state-financed university education. This confronted the professoriate with two interrelated problems. The first was that of deciding whether the professor was a civil servant or an independent professional. The second was the issue of how to defend professional rights in case of state attack. As Kendall Bailes has pointed out, one dilemma of Russian professionals was "to free themselves from the tutelage of the state, while still using the state for their own ends."[62] This was a dilemma the Russian professor could not escape.

Except for the short-lived Academic Union of 1905 (discussed in Chapter 5, below), the Russian professoriate never created a nation-wide professional organization. The focal point of professors' scholarly identities was the laboratory or the learned society, while their cross-disciplinary identities centered on the faculty council. Yet even here there was a strong conservative minority which argued for the primacy of individual departments in university governance, especially with respect to the election of new professors.[63] The attitude toward faculty council powers, so sharply curtailed by the 1884 Statute, was a basic litmus test of "liberalism" and "conservatism" within the academic profession. Liberals argued that a strong faculty council signified not only belief in the "unity of science" but also the professoriate's dedication to the principle that the university was more than the sum of its parts, that there was in fact a profession-across-the-disciplines with common interests centered on the universities.[64]

Indeed, one reason that the 1884 Statute was so disturbing to the majority of the professoriate was that it showed how professional arguments could cut both ways. Most professors would agree that from their point of view, the worst ministers of education turned out to be their ex-colleagues, Bogolepov, Schwartz, and Kasso. These ministers, representing a significant minority of the professoriate, believed that it was

---

62. This paper represents the conclusion to the as yet unpublished "Professions in Czarist Russia," edited by Harley Balzer and Kendall Bailes. This book is based on various papers, including one by this author on the university professoriate, delivered at an NEH–AAASS–sponsored Conference on Professions and Professionalization in Tsarist Russia, held at the University of Illinois in June 1982.

63. See, for example, V. Sergeevich, "Germanskie universitety i nashi," *Vestnik Evropy*, no. 3 (1905). The case for departmental as opposed to faculty council powers rested on the assertion that when the latter decided academic appointments, political considerations tended to outweigh scholarly issues.

64. See, for example, the record of the meeting between the rectors of Saint Petersburg and Moscow universities with Minister of Education Schwartz in October 1908 to discuss his draft statute (TsGIA, f. 733, op. 154, d. 269, l. 3).

not the government that was violating professional norms, but, rather, the majority of their colleagues, who engaged in "political intrigue," "pandering to students," "diluting standards," and so forth. Such professors saw the state as an essential protector against the tyranny of their colleagues, just as the statute was regarded as a professionally honest document that tried to protect educational excellence from extraneous considerations. In short, the complexity of the university and the tension between scholarship, teaching, and institutional responsibility combined to provide a coherent alternative to the dominant professional ideology.

The experience of the Russian university professoriate under the 1884 Statute was to show that defining the obstacles to academic freedom was much easier than deciding just what academic freedom actually meant; that the professoriate's "professional ideology" assumed a consensus among academics, government, and students on what the university should be; that this consensus, because of the complex nature of the Russian universities, did not exist; and, finally, that the almost hopeless tactical situation of the professoriate severely hampered its prospects of attaining its professional goals. By the eve of World War I, relations between the Russian government and the professoriate were worse than at any time since the reign of Nicholas I. Tsarist Russia developed great scholars and scientists but failed to develop a stable university system or a satisfied academic profession.

Major reasons why most of the professoriate disliked the 1884 Statute were its emphasis on the utilitarian functions of the universities and its failure to recognize the essential interrelationship of scholarship, research, and teaching. Professors who taught and trained future civil servants found it difficult to explain why the government should not treat them as employees and regulate the universities. But professors who devoted their lives to pure research, which in turn was the only guarantee of effective teaching, could make a much stronger argument for academic freedom and university autonomy.

There was yet another reason why expecting the universities to train students or impart practical skills threatened the professional interests of the university professoriate. The tremendous explosion of knowledge, the creation of new subdisciplines, and the demands of various ministries for civil servants with better training and more specialized skills threatened to make the university obsolete and to undercut claims that the state should recognize its primacy over the specialized institutes.

Therefore defenders of the university had to stress the primacy of method over content as the basis of university teaching.[65]

University teaching would, proponents argued, prepare students for future careers, but only indirectly. Strictly avoiding all "practical" or "applied" courses, the universities would instill a respect for free research and an understanding of scientific methodology that would provide the nation with independent, critical thinkers who would be dedicated civil servants and professionals.[66]

If Harold Perkin's thesis of two conflicting ideals in the formation of middle-class identity—the entrepreneurial, and the professional—is valid, then it is certainly the latter that the professoriate propagated.[67] The professionals' claims to status rested on the mastery of scientific and conceptual rather than on merely applied knowledge; on their claim that the practice, application, and development of this knowledge demanded autonomy, especially from the state; on their self-proclaimed aloofness from the naked battle for economic self-interest. Professionals, to be sure, demanded their fees, but only as deserved compensation for the vital services they performed for society as a whole. In theory, at least, the academics constituted an elite among professionals. They not only communicated knowledge but also created it. Their power to grant university degrees, as Joseph Ben-David has pointed out, controlled a basic standard for entry into other professions.[68]

Only through such universities, professors argued, could Russia develop effective free professions or an honest and capable civil service. It

65. Among many articles on this issue, one example is that of E. D. Grimm, "Organizatsiia universitetskovo prepodavaniia po proektu novovo ustava," *Russkaia Mysl'*, no. 4 (1916). After complaining about the government's preference for specialized technical education, Grimm pleads with the government and the Russian public not to demand more from the universities than they can or ought to give—that is, a good grounding in scientific (*nauchnyi*) thinking. "An individual," Grimm points out, "who has had a serious scientific education can easily and quickly absorb the 'practical knowledge' the government and the public [*obshchestvo*] demand. He will not find himself lost, either when he pursues his own intellectual interests or when he is confronted by various problems encountered in the hard school of life" (p. 117).

66. A typical defense of the key role of the universities in educating competent professionals and honest civil servants can be found in Vinogradov, "Uchebnoe delo v nashikh universitetakh."

67. Harold Perkin, *The Origins of Modern English Society, 1780–1880* (London, 1969), pp. 218–339. I owe much to conversations with other participants in the June 1982 conference on professions in tsarist Russia, and especially to the comments of Kendall Bailes.

68. Joseph Ben-David and Randall Collins, "A Comparative Study of Academic Freedom and Student Politics," in S. M. Lipset, ed., *Student Politics* (New York, 1970), pp. 149–150.

followed from this that the university, rather than the specialized institute, should be the linchpin of the nation's system of higher education. Universities based on science would become, the liberal professoriate hoped, a driving force behind government policies serving the interests of the nation as a whole rather than those of separate social groups; moreover, they would pave the way for the gradual democratization of Russia while avoiding the pitfalls of revolution from below. Also important was a belief held by many liberal professors that the university was an essentially "democratic" institution—not because the senior faculty regarded junior faculty and students as equals, but because the universities were scientific institutions based on the principle of meritocratic achievement.[69]

Most professors would have agreed with George Young's statement that the function of the nineteenth century had been to "disengage the disinterested intelligence, to release it from the entanglements of party and sect . . . and to set it operating over the whole range of human life and circumstance."[70] Businessmen, entrepreneurs, and merchants, albeit important as creators of wealth, could not be trusted to develop a sense of the common good.[71]

Ironically, the easiest way to achieve the common good in tsarist Russia was to work with, rather than against, the state—if the state would only cooperate. Moscow University's Professor I. I. Ianzhul, more politically conservative than many of his colleagues, did not find much disagreement when he argued the case for strong state intervention to temper many of the evils of capitalism and ensure balanced economic development. Naturally, the state would be well advised, Ianzhul argued, to call on professors and other experts to ensure that the government was "maintaining the proper equilibrium" among classes and

69. See, for example, E. N. Trubetskoi, "K nachalu uchebnovo goda," *Moskovskii Ezhenedel'nik,* no. 34 (1907).

70. In Perkin, *The Origins of Modern English Society,* p. 260.

71. In the *Iuridicheskii Vestnik,* the organ of the Moscow Juridical Society, can be found numerous references to the alleged backwardness of the *kupechestvo* and the industrial entrepreneurs. In a typical reference, the *Vestnik* bemoans their "lack of consideration for the worker, their lack of concern for the common good" ("Raznye zametki," *Iuridicheskii Vestnik,* no. 10–12 [1880]: 70). In turn, as Albert Rieber and James West have pointed out, many merchants and/or industrialists resented these attitudes on the part of the professional intelligentsia (A. J. Rieber, *Merchants and Entrepreneurs in Imperial Russia* [Chapel Hill, 1982], pp. 319–323; James West, "The Riabushinskii Circle: Russian Industrialists in Search of a Bourgeoisie, 1909–1914," in *Jahrbücher für Geschichte Osteuropas,* no. 3 [1984]). Of course, not all professors shared this hostility; a prominent exception was I. Kh. Ozerov of Moscow University.

groups.[72] And while relations between the government and the professoriate were far from smooth, the state did in fact make extensive use of academic consultants.[73] Yet while the government collaborated with professors as individuals, it distrusted the profession as a corporate entity.

A major obstacle to recognition of the professoriate's professional demands was the student problem, specifically, the differences that constantly surfaced between students and professors over how to respond to perceived government attacks on the universities. The professoriate, which almost always counseled students to "take the long view" and show restraint, represented a perfect target for the *studenchestvo*. In the eyes of many students, the professoriate embodied the hypocrisy of Russian liberalism in its pursuit of self-serving ends disguised by the rhetoric of lofty ideals. That many students glimpsed their own future position embodied in the professors' behavior only added to their bitterness. Heavy criticism of the alleged cowardice of the professoriate and its unwillingness to match the courage of the *studenchestvo* in defending the universities was to figure prominently in the student movement.

The professoriate's very definition of the university and of its own professional role left it open to criticism. There was a large gap between the professional ideology and the reality of university life. In theory, students went to a Humboldtian university where they eagerly listened to the lectures of eminent scholars and honed their characters by learning the methodology of, and respect for, pure academic research.[74] Many students indeed met these expectations.[75] But, as was the case in many other countries as well, most students entered the university with little idea of exactly what they wanted to do and therefore had only vague and contradictory expectations of what their university education should give them. Furthermore, the professors, with their own professional in-

72. I. I. Ianzhul, "Bismark i gosudarstvennyi sotsializm," *Vestnik Evropy*, no. 8 (1890): 729–730.
73. There are many examples of "scholarship in the nation's service." S. A. Muromtsev did valuable work in legal codification; V. O. Kliuchevskii tutored the royal family and submitted memoranda in 1905 on institutional reform; A. I. Chuprov undertook important studies that affected railway policy; I. I. Ianzhul worked as a factory inspector; I. Kh. Ozerov served as a consultant on tax policy and cooperated in Zubatov's attempts to create police unions; and V. V. Dokuchaev, V. I. Vernadskii, and D. I. Mendeleev undertook vital surveys of the nation's natural resources.
74. A good exposition of this theory is offered by Ivan Grevs, in "Zabytaia nauka i unizhennoe zvanie," *Nashi Dni*, 20 December 1904.
75. Such students formed organizations such as the Scientific-Literary Society in Saint Petersburg University in the 1880s and the Historical-Philosophical Society of Moscow University, founded in 1902 and directed by Professor Sergei Trubetskoi.

terests at stake, gave the students a nonvocational "elite" rather than an "expert" education.[76]

It was not clear, however, that the kind of elite the universities were preparing—a professional elite—would in fact be running the country. In addition, most of the roles for which the universities were preparing the students, especially those of physician, lawyer, high school teacher, and zemstvo employee, involved entry into professions and occupations that were either fighting the state over issues of professional autonomy or whose professional activities were often stymied by perceived government obstructionism. Furthermore, even professionals who worked for employers other than the state—zemstvo physicians, for example—often encountered the hostility of such entrenched elites as the landed aristocracy, who often showed little sympathy for the professional ideal.[77]

Adding to the tension between professors and students was the steady worsening of the faculty-student ratio between 1880 and 1914. Excellent teaching was the exception rather than the rule.[78] The examination system encouraged rote memorization rather than creative learning, especially in departments, such as law, with large enrollments. But many professors suspected that calls for better teaching and more direct supervision of students' work masked an attempt to turn them into "high school teachers," and they fought back by making extravagant claims for the intellectual and the moral superiority of the lecture system, even if the lectures were poorly delivered and boring.[79] Frustrated by the stu-

76. I have borrowed the terms *elite* and *expert* universities from Ben-David and Collins's highly suggestive article "A Comparative Study of Academic Freedom and Student Politics." *Elite* universities did not try to give their graduates practical training; *expert* universities did. The authors also distinguish between *model* and *non-model* systems. In the former, the universities train graduates for positions and responsibilities that have clear models in the wider society; in the latter, universities are "created by a traditional, or at any rate uneducated, elite for the purpose of eventually reforming themselves or increasing their efficiency through training new and better qualified people of a kind that do not yet exist in the country" (p. 162).

77. Nancy Mandelker Frieden, *Russian Physicians in an Era of Reform and Revolution, 1856–1905* (Princeton, 1981); John F. Hutchison, "Society, Corporation or Union? Russian Physicians in the Struggle for Professional Unity, 1890–1913," paper delivered at the June 1982 Conference on Professions in Tsarist Russia, held at the University of Illinois, Urbana.

78. Mark Vishniak, *Dan' proshlomu* (New York, 1954), p. 47; N. I. Astrov, *Vospominaniia* (Paris, 1941), p. 191; Mel'gunov, *Vospominaniia i dnevniki*, pp. 79–81.

79. This was especially true after 1899, when the Ministry of Education decided that better teaching and more seminars would be a useful antidote to student unrest. See N. Kazanskii, "Eshche o prepodavanii na iuridicheskikh fakul'tetakh," *Zhurnal Ministerstva Narodnovo Prosveshcheniia*, no. 1 (1901). For a defense of the centrality of the lecture system, see the review of L. Petrazhitskii's *Universitet i Nauka* in *Sovremennyi Mir*.

dent problem, the professoriate tended to blame unrest in the universities on the government's treatment of the academic profession and pointed to Germany as an example of how government respect for professors led to good relations between professors and students.[80]

The collective frustration of the university professoriate finally found a legally sanctioned outlet when the faculty councils were asked to reply to the 1901 Ministry of Education questionnaire. The dominant tone of the replies was reflected in the Moscow University Faculty Council's statement that it made little sense for the government to entrust the educational development of the students to professors who were not allowed to elect their own colleagues, appoint rectors, determine lecture schedules, or oversee student discipline.[81] All the councils asked for the right to elect their own rectors as well as for control over student discipline, higher salaries, abolition of the honorarium, and more faculty power—vested in the faculty council, rather than in the department—in making new appointments. The professors also favored retention of the rights and privileges associated with the university degree, as well as the replacement of the moribund examination system. The Saint Petersburg Faculty Council argued that it would be unfair for the universities to lose these privileges while they were retained by graduates of the specialized technical institutes or the closed schools. The Kiev and Kharkov faculty councils pointed out the importance of these inducements in ensuring a capable civil service. Removing them would open the way to favoritism and patronage.

Yet the professors left no doubt that they preferred to work with rather than against the state. In their replies to the Vannovskii questionnaire, the faculty councils stressed the fundamental compatibility of university autonomy, which they preferred to call self-rule (*samoupravlenie*), with the autocratic system. The Kharkov University Faculty Council argued that ideas needed freedom but conceded that as soon as an idea "entered the realm of word or deed, then it fell under the jurisdiction of the . . . laws ensuring public order and peace." If such a distinction held in Germany, which combined *Lehrfreiheit* and university autonomy with a stern commitment to defend the existing social order, then why

---

80. In his Tat'ianin Day speech of January 1904, Professor Sergei Trubetskoi appealed to the Russian educated public to look to the example of Germany, "where no possible political or social upheaval could upset the consensus that the universities were inviolable and independent" (*Russkie Vedomosti*, 12 January 1904).

81. The replies of the faculty councils to Vannovskii's questionnaire are found in TsGIA, f. 733, op. 226, d. 95.

could not such a distinction, the Kharkov professors asked, gradually be introduced into Russia? The Moscow Faculty Council bluntly rejected the assumption of the 1884 Statute that the universities needed strong government control. Why, the faculty council asked, did the government distrust an academic profession that was totally loyal?[82]

The government responded with some apparent concessions. In 1902 the Ministry of Education named a commission composed of professorial appointees to consider the replacement of the 1884 University Statute. The recommendations of the commission, whose deliberations ran to five volumes of closely printed text, largely agreed with the faculty council replies of the previous year. Some recommendations were immediately implemented—for example, the conclusion that graduates of *realuchilishcha* and seminaries be allowed to enter universities upon passing examinations in Latin and Greek.[83]

At the same time, the ministry granted a major demand of the professoriate by allowing the faculty councils to elect disciplinary courts to deal with student disciplinary infractions. Each court was to consist of five professors, approved by the local curator, who would hear cases referred to it by the rector. Cases falling under the jurisdiction of the courts included conflicts between students and professors, student infractions of university rules, and student violations of the "rules of morality and honor." The court was empowered to issue punishments ranging from a reprimand to expulsion.[84] Unfortunately, the rules establishing the disciplinary courts did not clearly delineate where the authority of the professors ended and where that of the curator began. Nor would the curators approve what they considered to be the lamentable practice of over-lenient sentences. It would not be long before the two key issues of jurisdiction and punishment would transform the courts into a major area of conflict between the professoriate and the government.

In the end, little was to come of these government initiatives. The 1902 commission report was consigned to the archives. By 1903 the government was attacking the disciplinary courts for the leniency of

---

82. "We suggest that the main danger facing Russia is not the development of phantasmagoric republics rejecting the authority of the government . . . but, rather, the overabundance of chancelleries which interfere everywhere . . . and deprive citizens on the local level of the possibility and desire to accomplish something" (ibid.).

83. Seminarists already had the right to enter the universities of Tomsk, Warsaw, and Iur'ev.

84. *Russkie Vedomosti*, 29 August 1902. During the 1902–1903 academic year the courts heard forty-four cases, involving 1,985 students. Of these, 1,453 students received "light" sentences—reprimands, censure, fines—and 376 were acquitted. See TsGIA, f. 733, op. 151, d. 299.

their sentences. Both Vannovskii and his successor, Professor G. E. Sanger, were forced to resign. After the assassination of D. S. Sipiagin in November 1902, V. K. Plehve, the new minister of the interior, orchestrated a tougher policy not only against the universities but against the specialized *VUZy* as well.

On the eve of the Revolution of 1905, therefore, the 1884 Statute was in tatters. Yet it remained on the books, a constant reminder that the status of the Russian academic profession rested on a precarious legal foundation. The professoriate was beginning to realize more clearly than ever that the major priority of the government's university policy was to curb the student movement, not to enlist the cooperation of the faculty in undertaking a general reform of the universities.

CHAPTER 2

Students in Search of Identity

Sometime in February 1901 a student at Saint Petersburg University, E. K. Proskuriatov, wrote a poem protesting his classmates' passivity before the government's decision to draft 183 Kiev University students into the army. He had expected Russia's *studenchestvo* to react with demonstrations and strikes. Instead the students milled around indecisively, torn between the instinct for solidarity and the obvious fear that they too would be drafted.

> Ia pomniu dni: sem'ëiu druzhnoi
> My smelo vyshli na bor'bu.
> Togda nikto nemalodushno
> Ne triassia za svoiu sud'bu.
> Nikto iz nas pokoi svoi sytyi
> V tsel' zhizni vsei ne vozvodil
> I molcha, kak teper', obidy
> I oskorbleniia ne snosil.[1]

I remember the days when as one close-knit family we entered the fray, when no one cowered for his own skin, when no one made his own personal interests the highest purpose of his life, when no one, unlike now, passively accepted insults and outrage.

Proskuriatov assumed that he and his colleagues spoke a common language and understood one another. The themes were clear: the sense of

---

1. Handwritten copy in Tsentral'nyi Gosudarstvennyi Arkhiv Oktiabrskoi Revoliutsii (hereafter referred to as TsGAOR), f. DO, 3ch. 125t. 1/1898, l. 93a.

a student family; the dichotomy between self-interest and the self-sacrificing ideals of the collective; students' obligation to uphold a common code of behavior, especially when their "family," the *studenchestvo*, was insulted and oppressed; finally, the implication that they were somehow inferior to previous student generations, who would have acted more courageously.

> Tovarishchi! Muzhaites' dukhom!
> Pust' tuchi chërnye krugom,
> My smelo, brat'ia, drug za drugom
> V bor'bu neravnuiu poidem.
>
> No pozabyv, chto my studenty,
> Ne stanem my v sem'e svoei
> V nadezhde poluchit' protsenty
> Chitat' Suvorinskikh rechei.
>
> Ne stanem—net—my slishkom chestny
> I gordy
> I eti tseli neizvestny
> Sredi studencheskoi sredy!

Comrades! Heads up! The black clouds may gather around, but together we will still enter the unequal struggle. We will not forget that we are students, we will not start reading conservative trash and dream of living off comfortable savings. No, we won't do that, we're too proud and too honorable, and such things are unknown to the student world.

Even if the forces were unequal and defeat was all but certain, the students still had to uphold their honor by fighting. Above all, they had to resist the temptation of looking ahead to the possibility of a secure life and comfortable job. As a 1903 Riga student proclamation put it, "The *studenchestvo* is the social group that is most able to forget its own egotistical interests and continue the struggle."[2]

Some years later, in 1910, one student newspaper told its readers that despite the great changes the universities were undergoing, what held the students together was more significant than the forces driving them apart:

The *studenchestvo* is a separate corner of Russian life. It lives in its own separate world, shaped by special chacteristics formed out of a long history of suffering. The *studenchestvo* is not a random, mechanically assembled mass of separate individuals. No, it is like a miniature people [*narodets*], its firm

---

2. "Brozhenie v vysshikh uchebnykh zavedeniiakh," *Osvobozhdenie*, no. 15–16 (1904).

sense of solidarity coming from the basic aspects of its collective existence. Notwithstanding the heterogeneity of its class structure . . . the Russian *studenchestvo* has many vital unifying elements, which bring together its different groups and blur party and social differences.[3]

But many students began—in growing numbers after 1905, but some even earlier—to deny the very existence of a *studenchestvo*, arguing that Russia's students were indeed little more than a random mass of individuals from different backgrounds and fated to go their separate ways, which mostly led upward. Still other articles conceded that a sense of corporate solidarity and identity may once have existed, but claimed that the vast increases in higher-education enrollments, as well as the political and social changes that were transforming Russia, were eroding the sense of community that was at the core of the notion of *studenchestvo*.

Thus *studenchestvo* had acquired a normative as well as a descriptive significance. It implied standards of ethics, solidarity, and idealism that were hard to meet and that led many students to assume that their predecessors were somehow better than they. The 1901 student-poet who compared the cowardice of his comrades with the heroism of previous student generations might have been surprised to learn that in the 1870s a writer in the revolutionary journal *Vperëd* had made the same invidious comparisons between his comrades and the students of the 1860s.[4] And in 1896, the United Council of Moscow University lamented the wide gulf in moral standards between the students of the 1890s and those of the 1860s and 1870s: "Then the description of the [*studenchestvo*] as the 'hope of Russian society' or the 'flower of the nation' . . . was richly deserved. . . . But how ironic that sounds when it is applied to us!"[5] Two points, however, remain clear: the sense of a student past, and the need of successive generations of Russian students to define their identity and their place in Russian society.

All along, of course, there had been other voices, some quite cynical, that dismissed the notion of *studenchestvo* as an exercise in self-delusion, a last chance to play with idealism and courage before the students became judges, civil servants, and comfortable lawyers. In February 1899, when the attention of educated Russia was focused on an unprecedented nationwide student strike, Anton Chekhov wrote to a friend:

3. *Studencheskii Mir,* no. 1 (1910).
4. R. V., "Studenchestvo i Obshchestvo," in S. G. Svatikov, ed., *Put' studenchestva* (Petrograd, 1916), p. 34.
5. S. P. Mel'gunov, "Studencheskie organizatsii 80–90kh godov v Moskovskom Universitete," *Vestnik Vospitaniia,* no. 4 (1907): 172.

As long as they are still students and *kursistki* [women students], then they are an upright, good community; indeed, they are the future of Russia. But as soon as these students and *kursistki* take their own road in life and become adults, then the hope and the future of Russia go up in smoke . . . and we see rentier-doctors, voracious civil servants, dishonest engineers.[6]

Clearly Chekhov, in referring to the students as the "future of Russia," was parodying what not only the students but also educated Russians tended to think of the *studenchestvo* (and of the intelligentsia). If the concept of *studenchestvo* gave a moral purpose to Russian student life, it also enabled university graduates to enjoy a vicarious identification with its ideals, to the point of using the memory of student experience as a convenient surrogate for political involvement and professional success. As P. Ivanov described them:

The average Russian *intelligent* puts too heavy a burden on the *studenchestvo*. . . . He hides behind the student whenever he has to confront the issue of idealism. . . . He hopes that the *studenchestvo* will stand up for itself—and for him—whenever it is necessary to fight.

"When I was a student . . ." is the slogan of most average Russian *intelligenty*. . . .

"Why are you so inert? . . . Why do you so easily swim with the tide? Why do you not fight against social evil?"

"When I was a student, . . ." the weak, whining voice replies. . . .

"We know, we know! But what about now?"

"Now?" A heavy sigh. "Now there is family, children, work, the dreariness of provincial life [*provintsial'naia tina*]. I am surrounded everywhere by boring people. . . ."

"But remember, you used to go to student *skhodki*. . . ."

"Shh! . . . The director is coming!"[7]

Russia needed hard-working doctors, efficient civil servants, productive landowners, diligent engineers, enterprising merchants, and imaginative industrialists. But for writers like Chekhov, as such scholars as Edith Clowes have perceptively observed, this in itself was not enough. These groups had to form alliances, develop cultural, social, and political ties. They had to overcome the mutual estrangement so brilliantly portrayed in *The Cherry Orchard* and begin working together.[8] In short,

6. A. N. Dubovnikova, "Pis'ma k Chekhovu o studencheskom dvizhenii 1899–1902," *Literaturnoe Nasledstvo* (Moscow, 1960), vol. 68, pp. 449–476.

7. P. Ivanov, *Studenty v Moskve: Byt, nravy, typy* (Moscow, 1918), p. 283. This is a reprint of a 1903 edition.

8. Edith W. Clowes, "The Moscow Art Theater, 1898–1905: The Commercial-Industrial Sector and the Rise of New Literary Institutions," paper presented at the National Meeting of the American Association for the Advancement of Slavic Studies, New York, November 1984.

they had to become a "middle class." In order to do this, they had to go beyond traditional categories of self-definition—*intelligent, kupets, dvorianin*—and find new symbols that could mobilize hitherto isolated groups into effective common action. The traditional labels dated from a time when the state formed society and defined social groups. To transcend these traditional categories demanded the mobilization of new forces—the theater, the universities, professional associations—that could provide a basis for "middle-class" identity.

Studenchestvo can be seen as one such traditional label. It implied negation of a hypothetical opposite: *meshchanstvo,* self-satisfied philistinism, and, by implication, *bourgeoisie.* One of the most common themes of Russian student pamphlets and articles in the Russian student press was rejection of the alleged path taken by German students after 1848: the path from *studenchestvo* to *bourgeoisie.* In a basic sense, the Russian student movement derived much of its actuality from a deep collective ambivalence about the nature of the "middle-class" identity that the universities gave their graduates a chance to achieve. And much of this ambivalence derived from the very real political and social obstacles facing those who wished to forge coalitions among commercial, professional, and landowning groups and to endow them with a sense of collective possibility and identity.

The Russian student experience was, for many, a complex combination of privilege and deprivation; of exalted status and humiliating treatment; of high intellectual expectations and disappointment in the actual educational experience; of intense commitment and self-sacrifice and equally intense frivolity and dissipation.

The notion of a *studenchestvo,* a student estate with its own code of behavior, organizations, traditions, and sense of mutual obligation, dates from the sudden changes that transformed the Russian universities, as well as the rest of Russian society, following the death of Tsar Nicholas I in 1855. Before then the students were on the whole prepared to follow the advice proffered by one curator in 1847: play cards, get drunk, chase women, but stay away from politics.[9]

Determined to ensure the reliability of the universities, Nicholas I had enforced a strict code of military discipline. Inspectors posted to watch the students meted out harsh punishments for improperly worn

9. S. Ashevskii, "Russkoe studenchestvo v epokhu 60-kh godov," *Sovremennyi Mir,* no. 6 (1907): 14.

uniforms or long hair. One student in Kiev University who appeared at a compulsory religious service in an incomplete uniform found himself shoved out of the church by an inspector and expelled from the university the next day.[10] The writer P. A. Boborykin, recalling his freshman year in Kazan University in the early 1850s, emphasized the students' political apathy. Not only did they show little inclination to start their own organizations, but they took hardly any interest in the outbreak of the Crimean War.[11] The only groups of students distinguished by their network of organizations and corporate feeling were the Germans of Dorpat University and the Poles. But neither Germans nor Poles showed much interest in fraternizing with their Russian classmates.[12]

Soon after Nicholas I died, the government began to undo the harsh regime he had imposed in the universities. The abolition of the 1850 rules limiting the size of the student body led to a dramatic rise in enrollment. In 1855 there were 476 students in Saint Petersburg University; three years later the number had more than doubled, to 1,026.[13] The government reinstituted the practice of sending young men abroad to prepare for university professorships and restored the teaching of philosophy and constitutional law. In 1859 the Ministry of Education relaxed the strict censorship rules governing the acquisition of foreign books by university libraries.

At the same time, the ministry abolished the requirements that students wear uniforms and engage in drill. In Kiev, Polish students began to march the streets in Polish national dress, while in Moscow and Saint Petersburg some students took to wearing peasant costumes. In Kazan students celebrated the new era by marching through the streets in animal skins. The new students coming into the universities were clearly different from their predecessors.[14] As Dmitry Pisarev recalled, they did not have the same reverential attitude toward authority and quickly "became masters of the university."[15]

10. I. Solov'ëv, *Russkie universitety v ikh ustavakh i vospominaniiakh sovremennikov* (Saint Petersburg, 1914), p. 19.

11. P. A. Boborykin, *Za polveka: Moi vospominaniia* (Moscow, 1929), p. 69.

12. An interesting discussion of the relations between Russian and Polish students in Saint Petersburg University around 1860 can be found in L. F. Panteleev, *Vospominaniia* (Moscow, 1958), pp. 168–184; see also the Kiev University memoirs of A. V. Romanovich-Slavatinskii in Solov'ëv, *Russkie universitety*, p. 190.

13. Daniel Brower, *Training the Nihilists: Education and Radicalism in Tsarist Russia* (Ithaca, 1975), p. 121.

14. Ashevskii, "Russkoe studenchestvo v epokhu 60-kh godov," *Sovremennyi Mir*, no. 7–8 (1907): 2.

15. In Brower, *Training the Nihilists*, p. 121.

This new era in the universities coincided with the intense public discussion of the impending abolition of serfdom. Frequent appearances of well-known writers and public figures at university gatherings gave the students a growing sense of their own importance. To paraphrase Franco Venturi, the universities became one of the "battlegrounds" where liberalism and populism fought for influence.[16] And if populism did not score an outright victory, it at least succeeded in setting the stage for what was to become one of the persistent themes of the student movement: the tension between the student corporation and the liberal to moderate elements of the professoriate. In the student movement that would soon erupt, the students would for the first time openly confront not only the government but also their liberal teachers, who would argue that despite periodic provocations, the university as such should not become involved in confrontational politics.

At the same time the students began to develop a clear sense of corporate identity. By 1861 the students, who only a short time before had been known mainly for their rowdiness and political passivity, engaged in nationwide demonstrations in defense of their rights. Over time, a wide network of institutions and organizations—*zemliachestva*, the *skhodka* (student meeting), discussion groups, newspapers, representative organs—would nurture this emerging sense of corporate identity.

Within a few years after the accession of Tsar Alexander II, students began showing a new determination to defend their rights. In Kazan University, the student body demanded that incompetent professors be dismissed. Students also defended popular professors (e.g., N. I. Kostomarov) against official harassment. In September 1857, a policeman broke into an apartment where a group of Moscow University students (mostly Poles) were drinking and demanded the surrender of a thief the students were allegedly hiding. When those inside asked him to leave, he returned with a group of police and firemen, who beat the students. The student body of Moscow University reacted with rowdy meetings demanding an official investigation and punishment of the police officers, not only on behalf of their injured comrades but also to satisfy their offended sense of corporate honor.[17] A report of the university faculty council observed that the incident "caused the students to think of their unity. Until then there had been no common goals, and therefore no *skhodki*. . . . The students had not thought of themselves as a corpora-

16. Franco Venturi, *Roots of Revolution* (New York, 1966), p. 223.
17. Svatikov, *Put' studenchestva*, p. 10.

tion. . . . The violence against some of their comrades was seen as an attack against all." [18] The students elected course representatives to push their demand for an investigation. The young tsar shared the students' outrage, but his sympathy would soon give way to anger and frustration as the *studenchestvo* began to show a new aggressiveness.

Another sign of a new era in the universities was the emergence of new student organizations. Under the benevolent curatorship of N. I. Pirogov in Kiev, students at Kiev University established a court of honor, a library, and a credit society—institutions which they themselves ran. [19] In Saint Petersburg University, students began publication of a literary journal in 1856. Its editorial board soon started a self-help society (*kassa*) to help the large numbers of needy students who entered the university after 1855. To raise money, the editorial board began organizing concerts. By 1859 the *kassa* had actually disbursed more money (9,000 rubles) than did the administration of the university. [20] When the students suspected the treasurer of the *kassa*, Butchik, of embezzlement, they turned to their law professors for help in organizing a court of honor. [21] Such courts were to become a student tradition.

Episodes such as the Butchik affair raised the question of how students would meet to discuss their needs and reach joint decisions. Thus arose the tradition of the *skhodka*, an assembly of the student body to discuss issues of common concern. An individual or a group would call for a *skhodka* to assemble, usually in the university courtyard or in a large auditorium. At first, students had little experience in running such meetings: there was neither a clear agenda nor a presiding officer. Soon the practice of the *skhodka* became more refined. Students met and elected a president of the *skhodka*. The latter then recognized speakers and called for a vote on a given issue.

As Daniel Brower has noted, the forming Russian student community was

> completely unlike the German model of student organization. The Russian manner of organization, especially in the assemblies, resembled the egalitarianism of the peasant communes, whose meetings also had the name of

18. V. I. Orlov, *Studencheskoe dvizhenie Moskovskovo Universiteta v 19om stoletii* (Moscow, 1934), p. 159.

19. Ashevskii, "Russkoe studenchestvo," no. 7–8 (1907): 34. A good overall source on the development of student corporate identity at this time is Brower, *Training the Nihilists,* pp. 116–134.

20. Ashevskii, "Russkoe studenchestvo," no. 7–8 (1907): 32.

21. S. Ashevskii, "Russkoe studenchestvo v epokhu 60-kh godov," *Sovremennyi Mir,* no. 10 (1907): 36.

skhodka. This fact led Dimitry Kavelin, the Saint Petersburg University history professor, to conclude that the student community forming around him had somehow found inspiration in Russian cultural traditions. He argued that "educational institutions, especially universities, assume a form like their contemporary social institutions." Western medieval universities developed as guild-like corporations, resembling urban society of the time. The German student fraternities preserved some of these traditions, but Russia had not followed this social path, and its universities could not reproduce the same social patterns. Its students, whose concern for social prestige faded as their interest in learning increased, expressed egalitarian sentiments as did the peasantry. The two communities had nothing in common except a disdain for any authority but that emanating from the group. The students, privileged by official educational policy, denied any privilege among themselves. In an authoritarian society their style of life was anarchistic.[22]

The appearance of the *skhodka* really marked the advent of a student corporate identity. The *skhodka* was eventually to become the source of legitimacy for all collective student action, the basis of an unwritten student constitution. It implied the supremacy of direct democracy, the notion that the *studenchestvo* possessed a general will capable of instant response when the need arose.

Alarmed by the growing independence of the *studenchestvo,* in 1861 the government tried to tighten its control of the universities. It raised tuition fees, banned *skhodki,* and tried to force all students to sign a handbook, the *matrikul,* spelling out the new regulations.

The students reacted with defiance. *Skhodki* resolved not to sign the *matrikuly* and voted to ostracize any student who did so.[23] In Saint Petersburg a crowd of students marched down the Nevskii Prospekt:

> A sight like it had never been seen. It was a wonderful September day. . . . In the streets the girls who were just beginning to go to university joined in together with a number of young men of differing origins and professions who knew us or merely agreed with us. . . . When we appeared on the Nevsky Prospekt, the French barbers came out of their shops and their faces lit up and they waved their arms cheerfully, shouting "Revolution! Revolution!"[24]

A strike at Saint Petersburg University forced the government to keep that institution closed for the greater part of the next two years. The disturbances spread to the provinces. In Moscow and the provincial

22. Brower, *Training the Nihilists,* p. 124.
23. One student song of the time praised the defiance of the *studenchestvo:* "Honor and glory to those students who did not sign the *matrikul,* who did not fear the casemates, and who did not lose heart."
24. Venturi, *Roots of Revolution,* p. 227.

universities, the police urged shopkeepers and butchers from the nearby Okhotnyi Riad (Hunters' Row) to attack students marching toward the house of the local governor.[25]

By 1863 relative calm had returned to the universities, and the government approved a university statute that gave the professors a good deal of power in the universities while allowing the *studenchestvo* far fewer rights than the students would have liked. Routine disciplinary authority was now vested in a faculty court, which was much more lenient than the old inspectorate, but students were still forbidden to hold *skhodki* or maintain organizations. After the abortive attempt on the tsar's life in 1866, government surveillance of the students grew more stringent, but this did not quell student disorders, which broke out in 1869, 1874, 1878–1879, 1880–1881, and 1882, over such diverse issues as the right to maintain student organizations, conflicts with professors, and demands that the universities become more accessible.[26]

This last complaint reflected growing anger with the government's policy of limiting eligibility for university admission to male graduates of classical gymnasia. In addition to barring graduates of seminaries, *realuchilishcha,* and women, in 1887 the government imposed limits on the enrollment of Jewish students in the universities. Furthermore, the 1884 Statute imposed higher tuition fees (raised to 100 rubles in 1887) and limited the number of students receiving tuition waivers to 15 percent of the class.

On the whole the Ministry of Education had only mixed success in regulating the social composition of the student body, notwithstanding the higher fees imposed in 1887, the celebrated "Cook's Circular" of that same year calling for limitations on the admission of children from the "lower orders" into the classical gymnasia, and the *numerus clausus* restricting the entry of Jewish students.[27] The ministry was most successful in limiting the admission of Jews.[28] However, the policy of restricting

25. Ibid., p. 230. A number of sources provide information on the student disorders of the early 1860s. See Brower, *Training the Nihilists,* pp. 127–130; Alain Besançon, *Education et société en Russie dans le second tiers du 19ᵐᵉ siècle* (Paris, 1974), pp. 135–164; William Mathes, "The Origins of Confrontation Politics in Russian Universities," *Canadian Slavic Studies,* no. 2 (1968).

26. S. G. Svatikov, "Russkoe studenchestvo prezhde i teper,'" in his *Put' studenchestva,* p. 13.

27. For a well-reasoned interpretation of the "Cook's Circular," see Patrick Alston, *Education and the State in Tsarist Russia* (Stanford, 1969), pp. 107–139.

28. For a detailed discussion of the deliberations leading to the *numerus clausus,* see TsGIA, f. 733, op. 153, d. 175, l. 55. As A. N. Schwartz argued in a lengthy 1908 memorandum surveying the history of the *numerus clausus,* numerous exceptions and exemptions had led to significant discrepancies between the number of Jewish students actually

seminary students' access to universities conflicted with the ministry's desire to direct more Russian students to Iur'ev and Warsaw universities as well as the need to lure students to the newly opened (1888) and un-inviting university of Tomsk. All three universities dropped restrictions on the enrollment of seminary graduates. Restrictions on graduates of *realuchilishcha* also came under increasing scrutiny, in part because of the government's own admission that it had to reform the secondary school system as well as because of the growing conviction, reflected in the deliberations of the 1902 commission on higher-education reform, that graduates of schools other than classical gymnasia should have a chance to enter a university if they chose, albeit with the proviso that they take additional examinations mandated by the faculty councils.[29] Male graduates of classical gymnasia faced restrictions in gaining ad-mission to a university only if they wished to enter some medical fac-ulties (which required competitive examinations because of shortages in classroom space) or, between 1899 and 1906, if they wished to go to a university not designated to admit graduates from their particular edu-cational district.

Total enrollment in the universities increased from 8,120 in 1880 to 13,548 in 1900. On the eve of the Revolution of 1905 it stood at 21,506. The impact of the revolution—almost two years of interrupted classes as well as a temporary but drastic liberalization of admissions restric-tions in 1906—led to a sharp increase in enrollment, to 31,433 in 1906 and 38,440 in 1909. After that year, restrictions newly imposed by the Ministry of Education resulted in a gradual decline of enrollment, to 34,110 in 1912. The share of the two central universities in total univer-sity enrollment increased from 43 percent in 1880 to 56 percent in 1900. After that year, various residence rules, especially with regard to medical admissions, led to a moderate decline in their share, to 48 per-cent of total enrollment in 1912 (see Appendix Tables A-3 and A-4). The most significant change in enrollment patterns between 1880 and 1912 was the displacement of the medical faculty by the juridical fac-ulty as the department with the most students. Enrollment in the natural sciences and mathematics faculty gradually increased, and the history

in the universities and the stipulated legal limit (Schwartz, "O priëme evreev v vysshie i srednie uchebnye zavedeniia Ministerstva Narodnovo Prosveshcheniia," unpublished memorandum of 15 May 1908, located in the library of the Harvard University Law School).

29. Komissiia po preobrazovaniiu vysshikh uchebnykh zavedenii, *Trudy* (Saint Peters-burg, 1903), vol. 2, p. 173.

and philology faculty, too, which had suffered a sharp decline in popularity as a result of the 1884 Statute, began attracting a higher proportion of students after 1900 (see Table 3 in Chapter 1).

The popularity of the juridical faculty was in part a result of the fact that it answered the needs of students who wanted to earn a university degree but were unsure about their future choice of career.[30] It also attracted students who started studies in the natural sciences and found themselves unable or unwilling to keep up with the work.[31] One alumnus of Moscow University, N. I. Astrov, recalled that

> young people who received their leaving certificate from the gymnasium flocked to the juridical faculty. It should be stressed that few did so because they were devoted to the prospect of a legal career or because they were enthralled . . . by the law. Many chose this faculty because it was the easiest, it did not commit one to strict specialization, and it seemed to give a general education.[32]

To be sure, Astrov added, some students had specific reasons for wanting to study law: the hope of making a great deal of money, for example, or the dream of becoming a "defender of the oppressed." Some radical students liked this faculty because it afforded the only opportunity in the university to study political economy.

> But for the majority the question of whether or not to enter the juridical faculty was solved by a process of elimination. They became sick of philology in the gymnasium, did not like mathematics, had practically no preparation in the gymnasium for the natural sciences. So the juridical faculty was the only choice left. "I'll enter it," they said, "and then I'll see what happens."[33]

A major choice facing a graduating student in the juridical faculty was whether to enter state service or to pursue a career at the bar, in the zemstvos, or in some type of private employment. By 1913, over ten thousand civil servants, judges, prosecutors, and other experts with legal training staffed the Ministry of Justice and the court system.[34] A

---

30. The juridical faculties, at least in Moscow University, tended to attract more sons of nobles and civil servants than did other departments, while enrolling fewer students from the peasantry and the *meshchanstvo*. See Appendix Tables A-5 and A-6.

31. A survey of 1,900 male gymnasium graduates showed that more of those who wanted to enter universities intended to study natural sciences (32.4 percent) than any other subject. Law was a close second (31.6 percent). Yet enrollments on the juridical faculty stayed at the 40 percent mark, while natural science enrollments remained in the 22–24 percent range. See Ministerstvo Narodnovo Prosveshcheniia, *Otchët za 1900 god*.

32. N. I. Astrov, *Vospominaniia* (Paris, 1941), p. 191.

33. Ibid.

34. V. R. Leikina-Svirskaia, *Russkaia intelligentsiia v 1900–1917 godakh* (Moscow, 1981), p. 36.

like number were practicing attorneys.[35] The Ministries of Finance and the Interior also demanded legally trained personnel and put pressure on the universities to provide a more rigorous legal education.[36] State service was secure and well paid. But to a much greater extent than was the case for technically or medically educated students, state service for graduates of the legal faculties implied acceptance of the existing system and readiness to defend its policies. It also carried the stigma of "careerism."[37] Although private legal practice proved financially rewarding for many lawyers, various government restrictions led to a growing polarization between the legal profession and the state.[38]

The medical faculties of the universities trained a substantial number of the 20,659 physicians practicing medicine in Russia in 1903. Of these, 33 percent were in private practice, 13 percent worked for the zemstvos, 16.3 percent worked in hospitals and clinics, while another 34.4 percent were in government employment. (The remaining 3.3 percent either were employed elsewhere or did not indicate where they worked.)[39] Although Russia desperately needed trained physicians, graduates of the medical faculties did not have an easy time finding a job. The very class that most required medical care, the peasantry, lacked the means to pay for it. As Nancy Frieden points out, "a bitter irony of medical work in Tsarist Russia was that underemployment and even unemployment coexisted with a desperate need for medical services."[40]

35. Leikina-Svirskaia cites a figure of 11,800 attorneys (*prisiazhnye poverennye*) and assistant attorneys (*pomoshchniki prisiazhnye poverennye*) in 1916; ibid., p. 78.

36. In a case cited by Roberta Manning, a recent graduate of the Moscow University juridical faculty, Vladimir Maibordov, started his service with the Bessarabia Provincial Board of Peasant Affairs in 1904 but discovered that he was expected to "know the law very well" and quickly resigned; see *The Crisis of the Old Order in Russia* (Princeton, 1982), p. 410. On Interior Minister Plehve's concern for the educational training of officials entering the Ministry of the Interior, see I. I. Ianzhul, *Vospominaniia* (Saint Petersburg, 1910), p. 55.

37. Brian Levin-Stankevitch, "Toward a Study of Professionalization in the Russian Legal Occupations, 1864–1917," unpublished paper; cf. Iu. Martov, *Zapiski sotsialdemokrata* (Berlin, 1922), p. 61. Martov complained that "all the future careerists and civil servants" headed for the juridical faculty. He chose the natural sciences faculty, in part because it had the reputation of being the "most democratic."

38. See Levin-Stankevich, "Toward a Study of Professionalization"; Leikina-Svirskaia, *Russkaia intelligentsiia*, pp. 82–84. Stankevich concludes that "the more highly developed the legal professional's dedication to his profession and to the goal of service to society, the more alienated he became from that society. The government's policies tended over time to polarize what had begun as a united profession. The state legal professions were increasingly dominated by careerists, with the exception of the 'old guard' which had entered service shortly after the court reform. The bar became increasingly 'missionary' as the government prosecuted its members for performing their lawful functions."

39. Nancy Mandelker Frieden, *Russian Physicians in an Era of Reform and Revolution, 1856–1905* (Princeton, 1981), p. 210.

40. Ibid.

Competition for state posts, which offered more security, became more intense after 1890. Only a few prospered in private practice, while zemstvo physicians often endured an uneasy relationship with their superiors. Physicians not only suffered from unemployment and underemployment but also had to battle for social prestige and government recognition of professional rights. Compared to other occupations requiring the same degree of education but much less exertion, physicians' salaries were low.[41]

Study in the history and philology or the natural sciences and mathematics faculty most often led to a career in high school teaching or, for some science and mathematics students, further study in a technical institute. High school teaching certainly offered a modicum of financial security: beginning teachers in the gymnasia of the Ministry of Education earned 900 rubles a year, a salary which could rise to 2,500 rubles after twenty years of service. Pensions paid 1,800 rubles a year.[42] Since there was a growing shortage of high school teachers, the only serious obstacle—but it was a real one—to receiving a post was securing the approval of the curator of the educational district.[43] But there were drawbacks to this profession as well. Not all students had fond memories of their own experience in the gymnasium where, to judge from memoirs, many of their teachers resembled the Mr. Belikov in Chekhov's "Man in a Case."[44] And while there were always jobs available, most entailed living in some small provincial town.

Thus a common feature of the professions that university-trained graduates (and technical graduates as well) would enter was their ambivalent relationship to the state. High school teachers, physicians, lawyers, and even civil servants both needed the state and resented in varying degrees its tutelage and interference. Only a certain number of students would be able to find posts in the capitals; most would go to the provinces, where they would be exposed to the vagaries of local authorities enjoying wide powers under the 1881 Emergency Decrees, unpredictable zemstvo boards, or educational curators who could sum-

41. Ibid., p. 213. The average physician's earnings were about 1,200 rubles.
42. Leikina-Svirskaia, *Russkaia intelligentsiia*, p. 62.
43. In 1912 there were about 1,900 "vacant" teaching positions in male gymnasia and progymnasia of the Ministry of Education. See Ministerstvo Narodnovo Prosveshcheniia, *Otchët za 1912 god.*
44. "The real world irritated and frightened him and kept him in a constant state of nerves. Perhaps by forever praising the past and what never really happened, he was trying to justify this timidity and horror of reality. The ancient languages he taught were essentially those galoshes and umbrella in another guise, a refuge from everyday existence." (Translation by Ronald Kiss.)

marily dismiss a high school teacher for political unreliability. Some level of financial security was indeed guaranteed to most university graduates; even the most poorly paid university graduate would earn much more than a factory worker. But in return the graduate was usually expected to grant obedience. Professional status, autonomy, and independence were much harder to achieve. In 1905 a student wrote to *Russkie Vedomosti* that the reasons for student unrest were not hard to find: he and his comrades could only look forward to a future lived as "Chekhovian heroes." Strikes and demonstrations were his only way of fighting back.[45] This was to be a frequent theme, as will be seen, in student protest literature.

Available data make it difficult to ascertain with any precision the social origins of the *studenchestvo*. Estate categories, the most readily available statistic, provide little insight into relative wealth or into the occupational backgrounds of the students' families. Nonetheless, if used with caution, they furnish some useful information, especially when supplemented by student censuses and enrollment lists that specify such points as the civil service rank of the student's father.[46] Available information from estate categories shows that the trend between 1880 and 1914 was for a sharp increase in enrollment of students from the *meshchanstvo* and the *krestianstvo* and a moderate decline in students from civil service and noble families.[47]

Some generalizations, however, can be made. Most university students came from the middle ranks of Russian society—mid-level civil servants, minor landowners, merchants, priests, and relatively well-off artisans. Very few came from the working class or the peasantry. Most students, as of 1905, represented the first generation of their family receiving a higher education. On the whole, technical institutes tended to recruit a smaller proportion of their students from noble or civil service families than did the universities, and fragmentary evidence seems to suggest that students in the specialized institutes came from families with slightly higher incomes. Most students came from small provincial towns and thus had to leave home to study at the university.[48] For many,

45. *Russkie Vedomosti*, 24 February 1905.
46. It is possible to assume, for example, that a "peasant" listing, though not necessarily signifying that the father actually tilled land, would preclude his inclusion in the higher ranks of the civil service. A Jew would not be a hereditary noble, while an "honorary citizen" would be more likely to have received a higher education than would a member of other categories.
47. See Appendix A.
48. In Kharkov University, for example, 90 percent of the students came from out of town. In Moscow this figure was about 75 percent.

therefore, it was their first experience of independence. Russian students tended to be somewhat older than their counterparts in some other countries.[49] Nor were the very wealthy a significant percentage of the student body.

In 1900 an article in *Sankt Peterburgskie Vedomosti* stated that

> educating a son or daughter in a gymnasium or university, if you include an apartment, costs at least 300 rubles a year. Clearly, then, teachers, *feldshers*, and other such poor people cannot send their children [to the university] . . . even if they have only one son or daughter. All other inhabitants of the countryside—zemstvo employees, doctors, middle landowners—cannot educate more than one or two children.[50]

The following year, the Kharkov University Faculty Council, responding to a Ministry of Education questionnaire, stated that

> the very rich have no trouble [financing their university educations] while the very poor can [at least] get certificates which free them from having to pay fees. . . . But those in the middle have a hard time. The civil servant or the landowner receiving 2,000 rubles a year income from a salary or an estate, the artisan or *meshchanin* owning a home in a provincial backwater and earning several hundred rubles a year in income, . . . these have a hard time sending their children to the university. *And most students at the university come from these kinds of families.* It is hard for them to give their children enough money for expenses.[51]

To a certain extent, various student censuses supplement available statistics on the social backgrounds of the student body. For example, at the beginning of 1905, Doctor M. A. Chlenov conducted a census of the sexual habits of Moscow University students. About half the student body (2,150 students) responded to Chlenov's questionnaire, which included questions about their social background. Twenty-six percent of the fathers had a higher education, 32.3 percent had a secondary education, 22 percent a primary education, 15.2 percent were educated at home, and 4.5 percent had no formal education. Of the students' mothers, 5.6 percent had a higher education and 37.3 percent had finished secondary school. The families of 56.5 percent of the students came from central Russia, 7.2 percent from northern Russia, 11.1 percent from the

---

49. An age chart of Moscow University students in 1902 shows that 5 percent were more than 28 years old; 21 percent were between 25 and 27; 30 percent were 23 or 24; 34 percent were 21 or 22, and only 10 percent were under 21.

50. Quoted in A. E. Ivanov, "Universitetskaia politika samoderzhaviia nakanune pervoi russkoi revoliutsii," Kandidat dissertation, Moscow State University, 1975, p. 38.

51. TsGIA, f. 733, op. 226, ed. kh. 96 (emphasis added).

south, 5.6 percent from the Urals and Siberia, 12.2 percent from the western provinces, 5.8 percent from the Caucasus, 0.5 percent from central Asia, and 0.9 percent from Europe. Most students' families lived in cities: 80.7 percent, according to the census; only 19.3 percent defined their place of residence as being in a village. Of the 1,698 students who said they came from cities, only 38.4 percent said they lived in large cities.[52] These figures are congruent with detailed information about geographical background available from student lists.

Chlenov's census indicated that 9.2 percent of the fathers were landowners, 3.1 percent were factory owners, and 12.1 percent were merchants. One in four (24.8 percent) was a member of the civil service or the military, while 11 percent were salaried employees or officials in zemstvos or municipal government. Physicians, lawyers, and high school teachers made up 15.5 percent; priests, 5.8 percent; petty traders and clerks, 6 percent; and college professors, 0.3 percent. Only 3.4 percent of the respondents said that their fathers were agricultural cultivators (*khlebopashets*), workers, or artisans; and only 1.2 percent said that their fathers worked as primary school teachers. The fathers of the remaining students represented a wide scattering of occupations or there was no indication of what they did (see Table 4).

The same sample, broken down by estate (*soslovie*), showed that 42.3 percent of the students' fathers were nobility or civil servants, 11.2 percent merchants, 9.3 percent honorary citizens, 16.8 percent *meshchanstvo*, 5.9 percent peasants and Cossacks, and 11.2 percent priests; 3.3 percent were unclassified. Of the students' mothers, 79 percent did not work, 6.3 percent were teachers, 2.4 percent were in medicine, 0.7 percent were writers, 0.4 percent were artists, 6.6 percent were landowners (*pomeshchitsa*), and 3.9 percent were in trade.

This survey, with all its shortcomings, tends to confirm the impressionistic evidence of student social origin gleaned from other sources: the *studenchestvo* came from the middle ranks of the civil service and the urban strata of Russian society, with a large proportion coming from the smaller provincial cities. Sons of peasants and workers made up only a minuscule percentage of the student body.

When asked to define the economic status of their families, 66 percent of the students answered that they fell into the "intermediate" cate-

52. M. A. Chlenov, *Polovaia perepis' Moskovskovo studenchestva i eë obshchestvennoe znachenie* (Moscow, 1909), pp. 24–29. Chlenov did not specify these geographical areas further.

TABLE 4 OCCUPATIONS OF FATHERS OF
MOSCOW UNIVERSITY STUDENTS, 1905

Occupation	Percentage of Fathers Engaged in Occupation
Landowner	9.2
Agricultural cultivator (*khlebopashets*)	1.4
Zemstvo employee	2.0
Factory owner	3.1
Employee in industrial concern	4.3
Worker	0.3
Artisan	1.7
Merchant	12.1
Petty trader	3.1
Employee in trade	2.4
Building manager	0.8
Servant	0.1
Civil servant	22.3
Military	2.5
Priest	5.8
Clerk	2.9
Professor	0.3
Zemstvo functionary (*delatel'*)	1.2
Municipal functionary	1.1
Physician	5.9
Lawyer	3.9
Artist, actor	0.7
High school teacher	5.7
Primary school teacher	1.2
Other	3.5
No occupation	2.5

SOURCE: M. A. Chlenov, *Polovaia perepis' Moskovskovo studenchestva i eë obshchestvennoe znachenie* (Moscow, 1909), p. 5.

gory, 13.5 percent saw themselves as being "higher than average," and about 20 percent regarded themselves as coming from "lower than average" families.[53]

A computer analysis of the 1902 Moscow University student body reveals some important additional details about those students whose fathers were civil servants. Less than one percent of the student body came from the top three ranks of the Table of Ranks (*kantsler, deistvitel'nyi tainyi sovetnik, tainyi sovetnik*). The next five ranks (*deistvitel'nyi statskii sovetnik, statskii sovetnik, kollezhskii sovetnik, nadvornyi sovetnik,* and *kollezhskii assessor*) provided 24.5 percent, and 8 percent came from the lowest ranks.[54] By 1913 the percentage of students with fathers in the civil service category had dropped to 19 percent, of whom 14 percent were in the middle five ranks and 5 percent in the lowest ranks.

The student censuses conducted in various universities and technical institutes between 1872 and 1914, though methodologically far from perfect, provide valuable information about the economic status of the *studenchestvo*. Response rates were often low, as those responsible readily admitted, and only a few of these censuses elicited information about the occupational, as opposed to the estate, background of the students' families. Yet if read carefully, the censuses yield some interesting insights.[55]

Professor N. Bunge conducted the first such census, at Kiev University in 1872.[56] Approximately half the student body (355) returned the census forms. Bunge calculated that a normal student budget should have been 375 rubles a year, computed as follows: 80 rubles for a room, 120 rubles for food, tuition and fees of 40 rubles, 66 rubles for clothes, 24 rubles for lighting and laundry, and 45 rubles for books and incidentals. One observer, *dozent* V. V. Sviatlovskii of Saint Petersburg University, considered Bunge's budget to be too low. Out of 328 students living on their own, however, only 36 spent more than 300 rubles a year. Sixty-five spent less than 150 rubles a year, 104 spent between 151 and 200 rubles, and 123 spent between 200 and 300 rubles. (Twenty-seven students lived with relatives or parents.) A major source of student income was derived from tutoring high school students, but the average

53. Ibid., p. 29.

54. These figures are based on an analysis of Imperatorskii Moskovskii Universitet, *Alfavitnyi spisok studentov*. I used every fifth name.

55. For an important general discussion of these censuses, see V. V. Sviatlovskii, "Studencheskie perepisi v Rossii," in his *Studenchestvo v tsifrakh* (Saint Petersburg, 1909).

56. In ibid., pp. 13–15.

pay was only about 25 kopecks an hour, and 121 out of the 171 students reporting tutoring jobs made less than 15 rubles a month. Of the students responding to the questionnaire, little more than a third got some form of scholarship aid.

After allowing for a generous margin of error, Bunge figured the total amount of student need at approximately 170,000 rubles. Of this amount, 14,000 rubles were covered by tuition waivers, 25,000 rubles by scholarships, and 30,000 to 40,000 rubles by income derived from tutoring. This left 90,000 to 100,000 rubles not covered. Bunge asks, "How can students exist in the face of such deprivation? Some are students in name only but really cannot study, because they spend so much time tutoring. Others leave the university, sometimes for a year at a time, to earn money to enable them to finish."[57]

The census conducted in Tomsk University and the Tomsk Technological Institute in 1901 was distinguished by its extremely high response rate: 73.2 percent for the university students and 74.4 percent for the students of the Technological Institute. The census provided some statistical backing for what many observers had been saying: that the most financially secure students tended to come from the *kupechestvo* and the *meshchanstvo* rather than from the nobility, and that students receiving a higher technical education were somewhat better-off than those going to the universities.[58] The budgets of 79.2 percent of the university students and 59.5 percent of the students at the Technological Institute were below 25 rubles a month. Only 19.5 percent of the former but 37.1 percent of the latter lived on 25 to 50 rubles monthly. Of course, Tomsk University did contain an exceptionally high percentage of impecunious seminarists, but a 1914 article in *Vestnik Vospitaniia* argued that the census reflected a situation characteristic of Russian higher education as a whole.[59]

By 1914, inflation had pushed the level of an "adequate" student

57. Ibid., p. 12.
58. The census also provides another example of all-too-rare statistics on the actual occupations of students' fathers. Of the fathers of students at Tomsk University, 60.4 percent were priests; 15 percent were members of the civil service and free professions; 8.1 percent worked in trade and industry; 7.3 percent were in private or railroad employment; 4.2 percent were in agriculture; 4.2 percent were rentiers; and 0.8 percent worked as artisans. Figures for the adjoining Tomsk Technological Institute show a strikingly different profile. Only 5.9 percent of the fathers of students were priests; 38.8 percent were members of the civil service and free professions; 20.4 percent were in trade and industry; 20.4 worked in private or railroad employment; 5.9 percent were in agriculture; 5.9 percent were rentiers; and 2.7 percent were artisans (including one worker).
59. G. Gordon, "K voprosu o material'nom polozhenii nashevo studenchestva," *Vestnik Vospitaniia*, no. 7 (1914).

TABLE 5   STUDENTS AIDED AT MOSCOW
UNIVERSITY, 1901

Faculty	Total Number of Students	Number of Needy Students	Number of Students Aided
History and philology	273	170	160
Law	1,523	734	654
Mathematics	468	235	225
Medicine	1,149	697	638
Natural sciences	604	300	280
Total	4,017	2,136	1,957

SOURCE: Imperatorskii Moskovskii Universitet, *Doklad komissii izbrannoi sovetom Imperatorskovo Moskovskovo Universiteta 28ovo fevralia, 1901ovo goda dlia vyiasneniia prichin studencheskikh volnenii i mer k uporiadocheniiu universitetskoi zhizni* (Moscow, n.d.). Note that the Moscow University Faculty Council lists the mathematics and the natural sciences faculties separately.

budget to 450 rubles yearly in Saint Petersburg and 400 rubles in the provinces. These figures included tuition fees of 100 rubles. At this time unskilled laborers earned 200 rubles a year, office workers about 500 rubles a year, and minor clerks 700 rubles a year.[60]

An important source of information on the economic situation of Russian students is the February 1901 report of the commission elected by the Moscow University Faculty Council to examine the causes of recent student disorders. In identifying "needy" students, the commission used data provided by the university inspectorate, which tended to understate the degree of need. Table 5 presents a breakdown of needy and aided students by faculty. Of the 1,957 students receiving some form of financial aid, 1,499 were awarded full tuition waivers. Of these, 874 received some form of scholarship aid in addition to the full waiver. The rest received either partial waivers or grants.

Obviously Russian students depended very heavily on financial aid—and, compared to those of other countries, the universities in Russia tried hard to oblige. The four basic sources of aid were university scholarships, discretionary grants, tuition waivers, and grants from chari-

60. Ibid., p. 178. D. Margolin, however, in his *Spravochnik po vysshemu obrazovaniiu* (Petrograd, 1915), maintained that a student in Saint Petersburg could live adequately on 350 to 400 rubles a year (including tuition).

table organizations, especially from the Society for the Aid of Needy Students in Moscow and similar organizations in other cities.[61]

Despite the constant efforts of the Ministry of Education to force students to go to the university designated for their high school district, large numbers of students from all corners of the country flocked to the two central universities. Some, like A. A. Kizevetter, dreamed of coming to Moscow University to study with the great man V. O. Kliuchevskii. Others, like the young V. B. El'iashevich in far-off Irkutsk, decided that going anywhere but Moscow University was out of the question. In any case, Tat'iana was a celebration shared by all university graduates in Irkutsk, whether or not they had graduated from Moscow University.[62] A major reason for the preference for the central universities was the hope that Moscow and Saint Petersburg might offer more part-time work and scholarship money.[63] As a result, both Moscow and Saint Petersburg universities enjoyed strong growth in student enrollment, which in turn increased pressure on available financial resources.[64]

> If not three-quarters, then at least three-fifths of our students rely on outside earnings for their existence, and here we find ourselves in a sort of vicious circle: the cost of living in Saint Petersburg and Moscow is incredibly high and it would seem to be easier to stay in the provinces, but on the other hand there are no positions [for student jobs in the provinces].[65]

61. During the 1899–1900 academic year at Moscow University, students received a total of 150,000 rubles in scholarships, 125,000 rubles in tuition waivers, 41,695 rubles in discretionary grants from the university, and 36,300 rubles from the Society for the Aid of Needy Students. The society also disbursed free meals, valued at 58,879 rubles. A valuable description of the work of the society is contained in A. A. Kizevetter, *Na rubezhe dvukh stoletii* (Prague, 1929), pp. 309–315.

62. V. B. El'iashevitch, "Iz vospominanii starovo Moskovskovo studenta," in G. B. Sliozberg, ed., *Pamiati russkovo studenchestva* (Paris, 1934), p. 106.

63. Rafael Vydrin, *Osnovnye momenty studencheskovo dvizheniia v Rossii* (Moscow, 1908), p. 67. See also A. L., "Naselenie universitetov," *Vestnik Evropy*, no. 9 (1896). The *Otchët* of the Ministry of Education for 1902 shows that Moscow University awarded 195,124 rubles in discretionary aid and scholarships and Saint Petersburg awarded 113,085 rubles, whereas Kazan University awarded only 69,000 rubles and Kiev University awarded 42,445 rubles.

64. Because so many students went to the two central universities (about half of the total), their scholarship funds did not translate into a significantly larger amount of aid per capita. According to the 1909 *Otchët* of the Ministry of Education, of 35,329 students in the nine Russian universities on 1 January 1909, 4,784 received tuition waivers, 942 received both tuition waivers and scholarships, and 752 received scholarships alone, for a total of 18.3 percent of the student body receiving some form of financial aid. A total of 693,744 rubles was available for scholarship aid, in addition to tuition waivers, which were worth 100 rubles a year apiece. Resources per capita varied wildly: 11.5 rubles yearly at Saint Petersburg University; 25.17 at Moscow; 18.82 at Kharkov; 25.67 at Kazan; 14.37 at Kiev; 17.37 in Odessa; 10.98 in Iur'ev; 57.80 at Tomsk; and 36.10 in Warsaw.

65. Vydrin, *Osnovnye momenty*, p. 67.

Financial aid did not keep pace with the growing student population. In 1880 an average of 62 rubles in scholarship aid per student was available. This figure declined to 23 rubles in 1891, and to just under 16 rubles by 1912.[66] In 1880 19.6 percent of all university students received tuition waivers. This number fell to 16.5 percent in 1891 and to just over 12 percent by 1912. The government made little effort to match the rise in student enrollment with a corresponding expansion of its financial aid budget. This increased the importance of tuition waivers, the efforts of private aid societies, the cheap student dining halls, and the activities of the *zemliachestva* as time went on. Another result of the effective decrease in student aid was that large numbers of students were forced to leave the university because they could not pay fees. In the first semester of the 1899–1900 academic year, for example, 480 students, or 12 percent of the student body, were suspended by Moscow University for nonpayment of fees.[67] During the 1901—1902 academic year, 3,793 out of 17,453 university students dropped out, at least temporarily, because of economic reasons.

Even those awarded aid had worries. Few scholarships paid more than 25 rubles a month, a sum that assured only bare subsistence. Most financial aid came in the form of tuition waivers, leaving students with the problems of finding accommodations and feeding themselves during the academic year. Few students could count on their parents to finance their university educations completely. A survey of Moscow University students conducted in 1893 showed that only 20 percent of the respondents received more than 35 rubles a month from their parents; 25.4 percent received less than 25 rubles a month; and 25 percent received nothing from home.[68]

For many students, then, staying in the university depended on their finding work. As the student population steadily rose, especially in Moscow and Saint Petersburg, competition for jobs grew more intense and hourly earnings fell. Meanwhile, prices steadily inflated, especially in rents. Tutoring remained the major source of student employment: unlike their American counterparts, Russian students shunned "putting themselves through college" by engaging in common physical labor.[69] To

66. Paul Miliukov, "Universitety v Rossii," in E. A. Brokhaus and I. A. Efron, eds., *Entsiklopedicheskii slovar'* (Saint Petersburg, 1897–1903), vol. 58, p. 799. These figures, however, do not include tuition waivers, or scholarships from private sources.

67. P. Ivanov, *Studenty v Moskve*, p. 59. This book is an invaluable source of information about student life in Moscow at the turn of the century.

68. Sviatlovskii, "Studencheskie perepisi v Rossii," p. 20.

69. P. Ivanov, *Studenty v Moskve*, pp. 72–87; for comments on Russian students' aversion to taking manual jobs, see *Studencheskoe Delo*, no. 7 (1912).

earn 30 rubles a month, however, a student would have to tutor twenty-five hours a week. In 1900, average monthly tutoring earnings for Moscow University students were 18 rubles a month. But tutoring jobs were not easy to obtain, especially after 1902 when the government began to de-emphasize classical languages in the high schools. Once again, it was the first-year student who had the hardest time obtaining work.

Finding a place to live was also a major problem. Many landlords refused to rent to students at all, on the grounds that they always left during vacations. Students everywhere tried to live near the university and, over time, well-defined student neighborhoods took shape: Vasilevskii Island in Saint Petersburg; the Nikitskii-Tver Boulevard area of Moscow—70 percent of Moscow University students lived here or in the Presnia-Iamskaia section of the city. Since a decent room in a good location was hard to obtain for under 25 rubles a month, many students had to share a room or live in substandard accommodations.[70] About one-fourth of Moscow University students lived in buildings without indoor plumbing. A 1907 housing census conducted by N. A. Kablukov concluded that more than half the students of Moscow University and two-thirds of the students at the nearby commercial institute lived in quarters that gave them less space per person than the hygienic minimum calculated by Professor F. F. Erisman.[71]

After the 1899 student disorders, the government began building some dormitories, but they could accommodate only a small fraction of the student population. Moscow's Nicholas II dormitory offered library and medical facilities, cheap meals, and well-lighted and spacious rooms. Room and board for a single room cost only 260 rubles for an academic year—but the dormitory had room for only 150 students.

Cheap dining halls played an important role in student life, providing not only food but also a meeting place where students could trade news and make new contacts. The Saint Petersburg University dining hall, financed by a local philanthropic organization but run by students, had four large rooms with electric lighting and a choice of more than thirty newspapers and magazines to read. The executive board included two student representatives. Students could buy cutlets for 6 kopecks apiece, a plate of borscht for 3 kopecks, and a potato for 1.5 kopecks. In Moscow the Society for the Aid of Needy Students ran dining halls

---

70. A particularly notorious example of substandard student housing was the Hirsh apartment block near Moscow University, where an enterprising landlord jammed 360 students into 123 rooms.

71. N. A. Kablukov, *Studencheskii kvartirnyi vopros v Moskve* (Moscow, 1908). Kablukov cites Erisman on p. 44.

which served an average of 100,000 free meals a year between 1892 and 1902 to students able to show proof of financial need.

The government was not entirely happy with these dining halls. After the February 1899 clash between students and police in Saint Petersburg's Rumiantsev Square (discussed below), excited students assembled in the dining hall to discuss possible responses. During student disorders and strikes, the dining halls became vital centers of protest activity. On 6 April 1899, Minister of the Interior Goremykin wrote to Minister of Education Bogolepov that "the state of affairs in the Saint Petersburg University dining hall cannot be allowed to continue."[72] After the student disorders of 1902, the government closed the dining hall, allowing it to reopen only after all students had been removed from the governing board.

How did a student qualify for financial aid? What criteria were used? From the students' point of view, perhaps the most objectionable feature of the financial aid system was the role played by the hated inspectorate, which was responsible for drawing up lists of needy students. Students who found themselves in any sort of trouble with the inspectorate had difficulty qualifying for aid. Most scholarships were reserved for upperclassmen and were awarded on the basis of not only financial need but also a student's academic performance. First-year students had particular difficulty getting aid, and this began a vicious circle. A poor freshman, in order to survive his first year in university, had to live in substandard accommodations and spend many hours looking for work. This often affected his performance on the yearly exams and thus diminished his chances of qualifying for financial aid the next year.

The inspectors, who were all expected to possess university degrees, cooperated with the police in keeping track of students outside the universities and drew up lists of those eligible for financial aid. They also had to enforce the official rules on student behavior. For example, students were required always to appear in uniform, even outside the university. They could not marry, or even go to lectures in other departments, without permission. If they came from "subject estates"—the peasantry or the *meshchanstvo*—they had to present a certificate freeing them from tax obligations. In order to secure admission to the university, they had to present a certificate from the local police attesting to their good behavior (*svidetel'stvo o blagonadezhnosti*). The rules for-

72. TsGIA, f. 733, op. 151, d. 49.

bade all student-run organizations: "reading rooms, dining halls, snack bars, theaters, concerts, balls, any meetings not having an academic character." In the same vein, students could not form *zemliachestva* (clubs uniting students from the same region) even if the latter "pursued no harmful goals." If students wanted to join organizations off the university premises, they were subject to the general laws governing associations or organizations, and even here, they needed to secure the approval of the inspectorate. Since students were regarded as "individual visitors" in the university, they had no corporate rights, not even the right to submit collective petitions or to meet to discuss grievances. Nor were they allowed to show any "signs of approval or disapproval at lectures." [73]

Punishments could be levied by the inspectors, the rector, or the university administration. These included admonitions, confinement in the *kartser* (the university jail) for terms ranging up to four weeks, suspension, and expulsion. Suspended students could, under certain circumstances, enter other universities. If sentenced to the *kartser,* a student could leave to attend classes.

In its February 1901 report on the reasons for student unrest, the Moscow University Faculty Council laid much of the blame on the inspectorate:

> The students are unanimous in their [negative attitude] toward this institution. . . . If a student, imbued with the old but dying tradition, enters the university with a feeling of reverence . . . then he quickly becomes disillusioned. . . . There are the subinspectors, who stand at the entrance of the lecture hall in order to check, and who patrol the corridors between classes, marking down those students whose uniforms are not in order. At every step the beginning student hears their remarks, comments, and warnings. . . . At first all this surprises the beginning student; later this lack of trust . . . turns into a fiery anger when the student sees that he is always being followed, that the [inspectors] . . . are always trying to see whether or not he is "reliable." When the student is in the university he feels he must always be careful. [74]

In time, the report continued, most students adjusted to this regime, but turned sullen and came to despise not only the inspectorate but also the entire university administration and even the faculty. The latter, stripped

73. TsGIA, f. 733, op. 151, d. 629.
74. Imperatorskii Moskovskii Universitet, *Doklad komissii, izbrannoi sovetom Imperatorskovo Moskovskovo Universiteta 28ovo fevralia, 1901ovo goda dlia vyiasneniia prichin studencheskikh volnenii i mer k uporiadocheniiu universitetskoi zhizni* (Moscow, n.d.), p. 11.

by the government of all power in the university, became an object of contempt. The faculty council complained that the students saw their teachers not as "friends and senior guides in the pursuit of knowledge but, rather, as employees of the administration."

In his memoirs of student days at Moscow University in the late 1880s, A. N. Naumov—hardly a revolutionary—recalled that inspector Bryzgalov barged into his room at 10:30 one night and asked him to name those of his friends who belonged to the Simbirsk *zemliachestvo*. When he refused, Bryzgalov threatened him with immediate expulsion from the university.[75] Professor E. V. Anichkov recalled that the members of the inspectorate would spend hours in the university buffet trying to eavesdrop on conversations. When they tired of this, they would pass the time studying photographs of individual students.[76]

Right after the big 1899 student strike, the Ministry of Education reminded the inspectors that in addition to maintaining order in the universities, they had to show "genuine and positive concern" (*blagozhelatel'noe popechenie*) about their charges. They were told to help them with their lessons and to assist them in finding work and suitable living quarters. At the same time the ministry ordered a large increase in the staff of the inspectorate. These measures, however, did little to improve relations between the inspectorate and the students.

Outside the university, the students suffered from the attentions of the police, who had no trouble following the uniformed students, and of the house janitors, who reported on their conduct, especially when any suspicion of illegal student meetings was involved. Of course students who lived with their parents had fewer problems with the inspectorate, but they were a distinct minority everywhere. A student had to register with the police as soon as he arrived back at school, and if he had to leave the university for any reason, such as academic failure or inability to pay, he had to endure good-natured but humiliating taunts at the police station when he came to pick up his passport for the trip home.[77]

Since most students could afford only the cheapest accommodations, they lived in close quarters with certain urban elements who resented

---

75. A. N. Naumov, *Iz utselevshikh vospominanii, 1868–1917* (New York, 1954), vol. 1, p. 75.

76. E. V. Anichkov, "Ustav 1884 goda i studenchestvo na pereput'e: Iz utselevshkih vospominanii," in Sliozberg, ed., *Pamiati russkovo studenchestva*, p. 42. The inspectors, it should be noted, complained that the steady increase in the student population made their job—which required that they know students by name—more and more difficult. Hence the time spent studying student photographs.

77. P. Ivanov, *Studenty v. Moskve*, p. 156.

their privileged status. In Moscow, for example, brawls between students and the butchers and delivery boys of the Okhotnyi Riad were common occurrences. When such fights erupted, students suspected police complicity. Relations between students and police also suffered from the 8 February 1895 incident in which a group of police and janitors beat up some drunken students leaving Saint Petersburg's Palkin restaurant. It had long been a custom for students to celebrate the university holidays—such as 12 January in Moscow University and 8 February in Saint Petersburg—with a variety of activities ranging from lectures and banquets to alcoholic binges. Students expected the police to look the other way, and they usually did, especially in Moscow. But because students expected privileged treatment, they were all the more likely to be shocked and surprised when on occasion they were treated like anyone else. This was to be a major cause of the unexpected 1899 nationwide student strike, which erupted from just such a holiday confrontation between police and students in Saint Petersburg.

Yet, for all these difficulties, few entering students would forget their first days in the university, their first lecture, when professors called them "gentlemen" (*milostivye gosudari*) and often dropped broad hints about the better days that science and knowledge would bring to Russia.[78]

> *Studenchestvo!* This meant that the chains were gone as well as all the tortures we had had to go through before we got our certificates from the gymnasium. The very word opened many doors and promised much in the way of new knowledge and interests. Now I felt that my ego would be liberated.[79]

For many it was the first time in a large city. Theaters and museums gave students cut-rate tickets.[80] And although the uniform made them more conspicuous, the distinctive visored cap, blue tunic, and green trousers also marked them, for all to see, as members of a special group.[81]

---

78. See, for example, Victor M. Chernov's description of his first lecture, in *Zapiski sotsialista-revoliutsionera* (Berlin, 1922), p. 108; also Astrov, *Vospominaniia*, p. 192; Martov, *Zapiski sotsial-demokrata*, p. 61.

79. Anichkov, "Ustav 1884 goda," p. 36.

80. On the importance of the theater to students, see Kizevetter, *Na rubezhe dvukh stoletii*, pp. 175–180; S. I. Mitskevich, *Revoliutsionnaia Moskva, 1888–1905* (Moscow, 1940), pp. 57–58. In Moscow the students' favorite theater was the Malyi. They would "fill the upper galleries and their reaction would determine the success or failure of a play."

81. One former student activist, V. I. Orlov, even developed his own "theory of the green trousers." Putting them on, he said, gave an *intelligent* a revolutionary orientation. But once he took them off, he became a "Chekhovian hero or a stupid civil servant." See Arkhiv Instituta Istorii Akademii Nauk (henceforth referred to as AIISSSR), f. 5

For many, the high hopes of the first days came true. They certainly did for the young A. A. Kizevetter, who came to the university knowing that he wanted to be a historian and study under the superb guidance of P. G. Vinogradov and V. O. Kliuchevskii; and for Genrikh Sliozberg, a Jewish youth from the Pale of Settlement who came to Saint Petersburg University to study law with N. S. Tagantsev.[82] Praise was almost unanimous for such professors as K. A. Timiriazev, M. A. Menzbir, and A. I. Chuprov. A lecture by Maxim Kovalevskii or V. O. Kliuchevskii would fill even the largest hall.[83] This is how one former student recalled a typical Kliuchevskii lecture:

> All eyes turned to the sound of tumultuous applause coming from the direction of the doors. In walked a stooped figure, looking like a scribe, wearing a black coat and glasses. . . . Raising himself slowly on the lectern and brushing back his unruly hair, Kliuchevskii cast a glance at the auditorium, turned sideways, and then began. It was really not a lecture, not an analysis of what happened in the past, but an actual reproduction of the past, in an artfully woven verbal texture, in the deliberate intonation of actual historical figures. Of course one lecture could not give knowledge. But it called forth no less significant aesthetic emotions. And just as the lecture hall met Kliuchevskii with applause, so too did wild applause usher him out.[84]

But not all professors had Kliuchevskii's skills; as is the case in universities everywhere, the general teaching level was quite uneven.[85] Many professors read the same lectures year after year, and students quickly learned that they could easily pass the end-of-the-year exams (especially on the juridical faculty) without attending lectures. Exams were not overly difficult provided that students crammed at the last minute. Professors admitted that there were too many students and too much material to be covered for them to conduct examinations in a proper manner.[86] (Of course, because of the nature of the subjects, study

---

(M. N. Pokrovskii), op. 5, ed. kh. 58, l. 35. These are Orlov's unpublished memoirs of the 1901–1902 student movement.

82. G. B. Sliozberg, *Dela minuvshikh dnei* (Paris, 1934), vol. 1.

83. The rule that students could not attend lectures in other departments was not always strictly enforced; see Mark Vishniak, *Dan' proshlomu* (New York, 1954), p. 52.

84. Ibid., p. 52.

85. According to G. B. Sliozberg, only a tiny minority of Russian professors knew how to teach; see "Dorevoliutsionnoe russkoe studenchestvo," in his *Pamiati russkovo studenchestva*, p. 89.

86. On the professoriate's unhappiness with the examination system, see the replies of the various faculty councils to the 1901 Ministry of Education questionnaire in TsGIA, f. 733, op. 226, d. 95. A good description of the examination system from the students' point of view can be found in Alexander Saltykov, "Moskovskii Universitet v 1890–95

on the medical or natural sciences faculty demanded more dedication and certainly afforded more supervision.) [87]

For many students, therefore, the initial enthusiasm quickly wore off; comradeship took the place of academic dedication. This was hardly surprising, since most students were far from home and lonely. Faculty-student contact was in any case quite limited. Describing his first weeks at Kiev University, Vladimir Medem, the future leader of the Jewish Labor Bund, wrote that "everything was strange and different . . . even the air smelled different than it did at home . . . all of a sudden I really felt it: I was away from home." [88] Like so many others, the young Medem joined a *zemliachestvo* composed of fellow students from his home district.

There were *zemliachestva* at virtually all Russian institutions of higher education, and students joined them despite their being formally banned. Some were limited to a particular *VUZ*, others were citywide, uniting all students who came from a specific area. Non-Russian students, such as Poles, Armenians, and Georgians, had their own national *zemliachestva,* and these were on a much more secure financial footing than their Russian counterparts. [89]

The *zemliachestva,* which dated from the late 1850s, were highly diverse. Most of them pursued the goals of mutual economic aid and

---

godakh," in Sliozberg, ed., *Pamiati russkovo studenchestva,* pp. 100–101. Professors on the examination boards often did not know their students by name, and this led to frequent cheating. Some students would find substitutes to take their exams. Mark Vishniak recalled that "only an idiot" would fail the final exams on the Moscow University juridical faculty. P. Ivanov, in *Studenty v Moskve,* p. 236, emphasized that although the exams did not require much original thought, they did force students to do a good deal of cramming.

87. Some valuable memoirs of students in these fields include Andrei Belyi, *Na rubezhe dvukh stoletii* (Letchworth, 1966), pp. 397–464; S. Abramov, "Meditsinskii fakul'tet Moskovskovo Universiteta 90-kh godov," in V. B. El'iashevich, A. A. Kizevetter, and M. M. Novikov, eds., *Moskovskii Universitet 1755–1930: iubileinyi sbornik* (Paris, 1930), pp. 365–404; A. Krapavin, "Teni proshlovo," in Sliozberg, ed., *Pamiati russkovo studenchestva,* pp. 115–123.

88. Vladimir Medem, *Fun mayn lebn* (New York, 1923), vol. 1, p. 142.

89. A. Filippov, "Moskovskoe studenchestvo," *Russkoe Obozrenie,* no. 3 (1897): 382. It is not within the scope of this work to discuss extensively the non-Russian students. It should be mentioned, however, that although students from the Caucasus identified with the Russian student movement, the Polish students were divided, with the National Democratic party counseling Polish students at Russian universities to stand aside from Russian student disputes. Sometimes, as during the 1899 strike, Polish students would demand from their Russian comrades, as a price for their joining the strike, support of Polish national demands. As will be seen in Chapter 6, Jewish student groups were disenchanted with the failure of the *studenchestvo* to protest the Kishinev pogrom as well as by the students' refusal to treat the issue of Jewish rights as a separate and specific problem. At Iur'ev (Dorpat) University, the German element totally ignored the Russian students and their demonstrations.

"moral education." Funds came from membership dues, alumni contributions, and the proceeds of parties and concerts given in the members' home towns. According to Nikolai Iordanskii, a future editor of *Sovremennyi Mir,* there were about fifty *zemliachestva* in Saint Petersburg University when he was a student there in the late 1890s. While some counted more than a hundred members, the average was thirty.[90] In 1894 in Moscow University, seventeen hundred students were organized in forty-three *zemliachestva.* Although some commentators speak of their having suffered a decline in popularity in the decade before the Revolution of 1905, there is general agreement that they enjoyed a strong revival between 1906 and 1914.[91]

While some *zemliachestva* were well organized and were able to raise enough funds to help their poorer members, many barely scraped by. Since most students had little money to spare for membership dues, the major purpose of the *zemliachestva* turned out to be companionship rather than material help. By joining a *zemliachestvo,* an organization forbidden by statute, the student was committing an illegal act. Nevertheless, most *zemliachestva* vigorously avoided any hint of political involvement.

In a proclamation issued on 14 December 1896, the United Council of *zemliachestva* of Moscow University explained to the public why university students joined these organizations and why they should be made legal:

> We have constant troubles with the police and can't even leave Moscow without their permission. Instead of being regarded as the intellectual cadres of the future, the government insists on regarding us as "separate visitors" in the university [with no right to any corporate life]. Spies follow our every step. Instead of comradely ties with our professors, we have an official relationship of client and civil servant. Instead of a university administration interested in helping us meet our material and spiritual needs, we have a group of police agents whose aim is to keep order. We have no right to express our collective opinions. Most of us have no families in Moscow, and we spend most of our time just trying to exist.[92]

90. Nikolai Iordanskii, "Missiia P. S. Vannovskovo," *Byloe,* no. 9 (1907): 86.

91. *Trudy soveshchaniia predstavitelei studencheskikh ekonomicheskikh organizatsii o nuzhdakh studenchestva* (Saint Petersburg, 1908), pp. 3–8. An enlightening article on the strength of the *zemliachestva* on the eve of World War I can be found in *Russkie Vedomosti,* 5 January 1914.

92. Hoover Institution, Boris Nikolaevskii Collection, file 109, box 6, packet 60, no. 140.

In an earlier proclamation the United Council explained the crucial role played by *zemliachestva* in helping younger students adjust to the university:

> The membership of a *zemliachestvo* consists of students of varying degrees of knowledge and experience, students of differing ages and levels of intellectual development. . . . This helps the younger members develop that sense of inquisitiveness and curiosity which the gymnasium tried to stifle. It also fosters an ability to work independently. . . . The libraries of the *zemliachestva* play a very important role in this regard.[93]

Of course, not all the *zemliachestva* conformed to these lofty descriptions. Not infrequently, *zemliachvestva* disbanded because of bickering among the members. A. Filippov recalled how at the founding meeting of his *zemliachestvo,* the students were full of high hopes for an organization which was to supply their native province with idealistic doctors, lawyers, and zemstvo workers. By the third meeting, arguments about dues and organizational differences threatened to split the organization.[94] Nikolai Iordanskii asserted that the *zemliachestva* reminded him of the Zaparozhe "Sech'," an old Cossack band that "anyone who believed in God and drank vodka could join."[95] V. A. Posse, however, who joined the Nizhegorod *zemliachestvo* in Saint Petersburg University in the 1880s, recalled the great mutual respect and tolerance that characterized the relations between the "tiny layer" of students who were sympathetic to the ideals of the revolutionary movement and those students who believed in the philosophy of "small deeds." In his *zemliachestvo,* according to Posse's perhaps idealized account, students spent most of their time studying and discussing various books and articles.[96]

One of the more important functions of the *zemliachestva* was indeed, as Posse indicated, to provide a way students of differing political and social views could meet and learn from each other. In the 1880s the philosophy of "small deeds," that is, liberal reformism, was especially strong in the universities, as the memoirs of Kizevetter and V. A. Maklakov and the example of Saint Petersburg University's Priutino brotherhood attest.[97] Respect for the reforms of the 1860s and the achieve-

93. Hoover Institution, Paris Okhrana Archive (hereafter referred to as POA), XVIb(7), 14C.
94. Filippov, "Moskovskoe studenchestvo," p. 372.
95. Iordanskii, "Missiia P. S. Vannovskovo," p. 87.
96. V. A. Posse, *Moi zhiznennyi put'* (Moscow, 1929), p. 35.
97. Kizevetter, *Na rubezhe dvukh stoletii,* pp. 38, 168–169; V. A. Maklakov, *Vlast' i obshchestvennost' na zakate staroi Rossii* (Paris, 1936), pp. 79–81; "Vospominaniia

ments of the zemstvos, as well as a genuine aversion to the terrorism of
the Narodnaia Volia (People's Will, the organization that assassinated
Alexander II in 1881), led many students to believe that diligent and
competent work in one's chosen profession, not revolutionary violence,
was the best way to serve the nation. This hostility to direct action was
reflected in the *zemliachestva,* which for the most part rejected overt
political commitment.

The disparities between the various *zemliachestva,* as well as some of
their common problems and characteristics, can be gauged by comparing some of their annual reports.[98] In its report for 1891, the Siberian
zemliachestvo of Moscow University complained that the alumni were
indifferent and the library was in terrible condition. In order to inject
some life into the organization, the students founded four different discussion groups and began expelling comrades who showed little interest
or whose behavior reflected badly on the good name of the *zemliachestvo.*[99] Another *zemliachestvo,* with fifty members, raised 600 rubles
a year in annual income, which enabled it to maintain a library of 184
books and give some financial help to twenty-two students. To facilitate
intellectual interchange, the *zemliachestvo* followed common practice
by dividing into five discussion groups, which would come together during the organization's general meeting. Yet many felt that the *zemliachestva* should be doing more. One student, who was to be arrested
for going to an illegal All-Russian student congress in 1901, disgust-
edly wrote:

> [The *zemliachestva*] unite the students mainly on the basis of financial aid
> and protest against the university structure. . . . In our *zemliachestvo* there is
> a group studying political economy, a group that worries about student af-
> fairs, a group that is thinking about doing propaganda, a group that is orga-
> nizing a statistical survey of the *studenchestvo.* There's a group that bothers
> everybody else and, finally, there's a group that does absolutely nothing.[100]

The Caucasus *zemliachestvo* in Moscow seemed much better placed.
After its founding in 1884, it grew slowly, for students were afraid of

---

peterburzhtsa o vtoroi polovine 80-kh godov," *Golos Minuvshevo,* nos. 10, 11 (1908);
Terence Emmons, *The Formation of Political Parties and the First National Elections in
Russia* (London, 1983), pp. 65–67.

98. Fragmentary copies of Moscow University *zemliachestva* reports are on file in the
Arkhiv Biblioteki Moskovskovo Gosudarstvennovo Universiteta imeni M. V. Lomonosova
(hereafter referred to as BMGU), f. V. I. Orlova.

99. BMGU, f. V. I. Orlova, 5dt., no. 309.

100. TsGAOR, f. DO/1898 3ch. 1L, B–1, l. 44 (purloined letter of Alexander Tarasov,
22 March 1900).

seeming to be members of a revolutionary-political organization. But after 1890 an influx of more energetic students brought the *zemliachestvo* to active life. Successful lotteries brought in money for scholarships, but the students agreed that the main purpose of the organization was "spiritual" rather than "utilitarian" union. Unlike other *zemliachestva*, the Caucasus students forbade subgroups, since they "defeated the main purpose" of the organization. Instead, all students participated in a "self-development circle." Unlike other groups, a report proudly noted, this group banned discussion based on reading of outside texts. Each student instead had to prepare an original report on a topic of common interest; often the *zemliachestvo* appointed an "official opponent" to keep the debate going.[101]

During the 1880s and 1890s, most *zemliachestva* in various university towns tended to form coordinating councils, partly in response to the nationwide outbreaks of student unrest in 1887 and 1890 to protest the 1884 Statute, the inspectorate, and other aspects of the university system. Many *zemliachestvo* members wanted to prevent such sporadic outbreaks on the grounds that they were counterproductive. In the early 1890s several Moscow University *zemliachestva* revived a United Council. By 1894 the council included forty-three *zemliachestva* representing seventeen hundred members.[102] The council declared that its main goals were "to raise the intellectual and moral level of the *studenchestvo*," "to prepare its members for public activity," and to improve the material conditions of student life. The United Council was composed of one delegate from each participating *zemliachestvo*.

The council administered a number of commissions as well as a student court. The commissions undertook such functions as monitoring the financial claims of students asking for aid, gathering statistical data on the *studenchestvo*, and overseeing relations between *zemliachestva*.[103] The student court handled appeals from the individual *zemliachestvo* courts, as well as any disputes between the latter and the United Council. During the 1893–1894 academic year the court heard forty-three cases. Five involved student complaints against professors (who, not surprisingly, ignored the court and did not appear), and the remaining thirty-eight cases involved students. Of the latter, five cases dealt with students accused of spying for the police or the university adminis-

101. BMGU, f. V. I. Orlova, 5dt., no. 266.
102. Hoover Institution, POA, XVIb(7), 14C (Proclamation of the United Council, 28 December 1894); also Mel'gunov, "Studencheskie organizatsii," p. 150.
103. Mel'gunov, "Studencheskie organizatsii," p. 147.

tration, four cases involved students who were accused of compromising the honor of the *studenchestvo* by their public behavior, six involved accusations of receiving financial aid under false pretenses, another six concerned accusations of unruly behavior (*buistvo*), and two dealt with students accused of "crimes against the honor of women." The court also tried students for such offenses as using counterfeit coins or cutting articles out of publications at the university library. Students found guilty were either fined, ordered to perform certain chores, or sentenced to ostracism from the student community.[104] In its report for the 1894–1895 academic year, the court declared that its chief obligation was to ensure that the *studenchestvo* protected its honor.[105] Similar courts existed in other universities. Vladimir Medem recalls attending a trial, at Kiev University, of a student accused of making an anti-Semitic remark and thus "violating the traditions of the *studenchestvo*."[106]

The United Council made other attempts to raise the tone of student behavior. It campaigned against the customary alcoholic binges associated with Tat'ianin Den'. It also encouraged such initiatives as that of the Viatka *zemliachestvo,* which suggested that students act as museum guides for peasants and workers.

During the 1890s the tone of student life underwent a subtle change. The famine of 1891, the accession of Tsar Nicholas II, and the growing ideological battle between populism and Marxism led to new attempts to define the place of the *studenchestvo* in Russian life. In the mid-1890s major student demonstrations broke out, especially in Moscow and Saint Petersburg universities.[107] Many members of the Moscow University United Council began a process of intellectual self-definition that tended to isolate them from the politically inchoate *zemliachestva* they represented.[108] Ironically, it was the very absence of political self-

104. Ibid., p. 156.
105. BMGU, f. V. I. Orlova, 5dt., no. 285 ("Otchët sudebnoi komissii za 1893–94 god"). The court complained that too much work remained to be done in making the students take pride in their corporate honor. Public drunkenness, petty theft, dishonesty among scholarship claimants, and pilfering of coats and boots from university cloakrooms were common. Furthermore, many students disputed the authority of the student court over public behavior outside the university. The students who entered the university after 1890, however, had a much better attitude, according to the court.
106. Medem, *Fun mayn lebn,* vol. 1, p. 145.
107. In Moscow, student protest was directed against various professors: Ianzhul for refusing a United Council request not to lecture on the anniversary of the emancipation of the serfs, Kliuchevskii for eulogizing the deceased Alexander III, and Zakharin for allegedly unethical behavior in his private medical practice. These demonstrations were not sanctioned by the United Council, which tried to act as a moderating influence.
108. Future Marxists on the United Council included N. A. Semashko and V. G. Groman. At the same time the United Council included Victor Chernov, a future leader of the Social Revolutionary party.

definition by most *zemliachestva* members that made them more, rather than less, likely to participate in student disorders at this time and led to tensions between the United Council and its constituent organizations. For those students leaning toward Marxism, the arguments against student unrest were convincing. Victor Chernov recalled that Marxist sympathizers on the United Council were willing to concede that in the 1860s and 1870s, the *studenchestvo* was a clearly defined group capable of independent action, but that was before the rise of the proletariat and the social and economic shifts that were destroying the cohesion of the *studenchestvo*. The *studenchestvo* was increasingly being replaced with a heterogeneous student body that merely reflected the interests of the various groups who sent their sons to the universities. Student disorders were now futile and only resulted in needless expulsion from the universities. Moreover, after the rise of the proletariat the students could no longer flatter themselves with the romantic illusion that they were the nation's political barometer. If students wanted to protest, they should seek general political change rather than pursue narrow corporate goals. Better yet, they should become Marxists and try to establish contact with the workers.[109]

Like the Marxists, the populist students on the United Council in the mid-1890s opposed spontaneous outbreaks of student unrest over local, corporate issues. But unlike the Marxists, they did not believe that the political role of the intelligentsia in general, and that of the students in particular, was finished. Chernov recalled that some of the students on the United Council organized an inter-*zemliachestvo* committee to consider the role of students in history, the part played by European students in 1848, and the future place of the Russian *studenchestvo*.[110] One of the papers presented to the committee argued that the political role of students and student movements varied from country to country. In Russia, because of the peculiarities of its economic and social development, the students were still an important force:

> The development of capitalism in different countries is . . . uneven. . . . The cultural achievements of the bourgeoisie vary widely. . . . In some countries they are high. Such countries see the flowering of bourgeois progressivism

109. Chernov, *Zapiski sotsialista-revoliutsionera*, p. 118.
110. Ibid. A copy of the agenda of this committee can be found in the BMGU, f. V. I. Orlova, 5dt., no. 270. Some specific questions on the agenda were: "(1) Is the *studenchestvo* . . . a progressive social group with an active relationship to surrounding events, or are the students an inert group, occupied only with their own specific interests? and (2) Shouldn't the aim of student groups be to establish a network of student organizations that could influence the surrounding society?" If uneducated German workers could do it, a preconference memorandum asked, then why not the educated Russian *studenchestvo*?

and bourgeois liberalism; there the intelligentsia subordinates itself to the bourgeoisie and its spirit more easily. In other countries, the bourgeoisie is weaker and crawls at the feet of the older and more privileged classes. . . . In such countries . . . [the intelligentsia is more independent] and becomes the political and moral vanguard of the nation. . . . But the intelligentsia has nowhere to turn except to the people. . . . Thus, the student movement and student organizations are a significant political factor and have a real role to play in Russia.[111]

This populist view of the student movement was reflected in the proceedings of a national student congress that the Moscow University United Council organized in 1894. P. S. Shirskii, a future Denikin adjutant in the Civil War, was sent out to establish contact with various universities, and delegates came to the congress from Saint Petersburg, Kazan, Odessa, Kiev, and Kharkov. Victor Chernov represented the United Council. The conference resolved that the *studenchestvo* "was an integral part of the revolutionary intelligentsia and a natural vanguard of the popular movement. . . . It should not confine itself to narrow academic interests. . . . The academic structure was just a part of the general system." [112] But the conference also resolved that "the *studenchestvo* should not lose its own organizational unity. The *studenchestvo* as such should stand ready for united action in a spirit of harmonious solidarity; it should be prepared to struggle against the academic regime which is itself but a part of the general regime." [113] The conference warned, however, against spontaneous student disorders over concerns that would not engage the sympathies of the wider public. Aware of the traditional hostility that such urban groups as the butchers and the porters felt toward the students, the conference wanted to ensure that in the future, student unrest would not be viewed as the "carousing of well-fed rich brats." To that end, it recommended that henceforth students mark such anniversaries as the emancipation of the serfs.

The conference clearly demonstrated a strong consciousness of *studenchestvo,* which differed markedly from the Marxist line. In its final protocol the conference called on the present student generation to emulate the example of its predecessors in the 1860s and 1870s. Chernov, who drafted the protocol, ended the document with stanzas from Minskii's "Pesni o rodine," a poem that glorified the political role of youth.[114]

111. Chernov, *Zapiski sotsialista-revoliutsionera,* pp. 118–119.
112. Ibid., p. 121.
113. Ibid., p. 122.
114. Ibid. "In the whole world there is nowhere where youth, spurning all the good things of life, so honestly and purely dedicates itself to the service of strict justice as here [in Russia]."

In 1895 and 1896, the United Council tried to focus student protest and to give it a more general appeal. A call for major student demonstrations at the Vagan'kov cemetery to mark the second anniversary of the Khodynka catastrophe led the Okhrana, in November 1896, to arrest the entire council membership. Relations between the latter and the *zemliachestva* had already become strained, under accusations that the United Council was acting too independently.[115] A second United Council replaced the first but had a hard time establishing its authority. Thus, on the eve of the 1899 strike, the student movement in Moscow struck some observers as lacking leadership and organization.[116] At the same time, however, most *zemliachestva* members were unhappy with the conditions of university life and supported the concept of student protest as a means of fighting for such goals as the repeal of the 1884 Statute. In December 1896, the second United Council took a poll of *zemliachestva* members: 51 percent favored "well-organized student protest," 34 percent were opposed, and the rest abstained.[117]

In Saint Petersburg University, in addition to the *zemliachestva*, there was another important student organization, the Kassa Vzaimopomoshchi Studentov Sankt Peterburgskovo Universiteta (Saint Petersburg University Mutual Aid Society). The *kassa* was composed of delegates elected by student *kruzhki* (circles), which had been formed on an ad-hoc basis by students who knew each other and had interests in common. These circles typically encompassed between five and twenty students each. According to M. N. Mogilianskii, about one-quarter of the student body belonged to circles represented in the *kassa*.[118] Each circle sent one representative to the assembly (*predstavitel'noe sobranie*), the legislative organ of the *kassa*. The executive body was composed of the president, the treasurer, and, after 1898, a board consisting of five students. The *kassa* never had enough money to become a real credit union, but in time, it assumed de facto control of the university dining hall, thus acquiring a steady source of funds.

Mogilianskii, who became a president of the *kassa* at the end of the 1890s, recalled that when he entered the university in 1893, he shared with most of his fellow members of the *kassa* an exalted view of the *studenchestvo*, its traditions, and the political importance of student

115. TsGIA, f. 733, op. 151, d. 72, l. 116.

116. Ibid. These are the notes of Nikolai Rudnev, a member of the United Council, on the Moscow student movement in the late 1890s. They were confiscated when Rudnev was arrested at an abortive national student conference in Odessa in 1900.

117. Hoover Institution, Boris Nikolaevskii Collection, file 109, box 6, packet 60, no. 140.

118. M. N. Mogilianskii, "V devianostye gody," *Byloe*, no. 23 (1924): 141.

disorders. But his disillusionment with his *zemliachestvo* (composed of Ukrainian students) quickly led him to reconsider his earlier views. In the *kassa* Mogilianskii discovered that many students shared his impatience with *skhodki, zemliachestva,* and student protest. The basic demand was always the same—abrogation of the 1884 University Statute. The outcome, too, seemed always to be the same. The university administration would patiently explain that students had no right to make collective petitions, nor could they, of course, tell the government what to do. The students would mill around, complain, and then disperse.

By the middle of the 1890s the *kassa* began waging a propaganda campaign in the university against student disorders and *skhodki*. To a certain extent this reflected the growing influence of Marxism on the *kassa* leadership. The workers' strikes of 1895 and 1896, as well as the scientific rigor of Marxist analysis, made a deep impression.[119] At any rate, the *kassa* began using the same arguments against the student movement that Victor Chernov had heard on the Moscow University United Council.

But many *zemliachestvo* members resented the *kassa*'s claim that the *studenchestvo* was disappearing and that student unrest was pointless. The *zemliachestva* maintained that the students remained a distinct group and had to defend their rights and dignity against the policies of the government. Through the student movement, many students would come to develop a sense of personal dignity and political responsibility.[120]

Meanwhile, the 1890s saw a number of student protests. Unrest broke out in 1894 after the student body petitioned the new tsar to repeal the 1884 Statute. The beating of students by police and janitors outside the Palkin restaurant in February 1895 caused deep resentment and protest *skhodki*. In November 1896 the Moscow University United Council sent a delegate to Saint Petersburg to ask *kassa* support of the demonstration the Muscovites were planning to commemorate the victims of the Khodynka catastrophe. The *kassa* refused, advancing the familiar Marxist arguments against student demonstrations. But when news reached Saint Petersburg of the arrests following the Moscow demonstration, students ignored the *kassa* and held a number of stormy *skhodki,* thus underscoring the strong feelings of comradeship and mutual responsibility which linked students and which still outweighed arguments that *studenchestvo* solidarity was an anachronism.

119. Ibid.
120. Iordanskii, "Missiia P. S. Vannovskovo," p. 90.

The strong hold of *studenchestvo* solidarity became dramatically apparent in March 1897, after the self-immolation of M. F. Vetrova, a student at the Bestuzhev women's courses who had been arrested at the end of 1896 and sent to the Peter-Paul fortress. Rumors quickly spread through the Saint Petersburg student population that Vetrova had killed herself after having been attacked by Kichin, an assistant prosecutor. Vetrova's fellow students in the Bestuzhev courses then called the *studenchestvo* of the capital to come to a large memorial demonstration in front of Kazan Cathedral on 4 March 1897. Between two thousand and four thousand students milled about on the Nevskii Prospekt in front of the Cathedral and began singing, "Vy zhertvoiu pali v bor'be rokovoi" ("You fell, a victim in the fateful struggle"). Police quickly broke up the demonstration, but it showed once again how sensitive Russian students were to police mistreatment of fellow students. By contrast, when, just a few weeks later, a nonstudent committed suicide in prison, attempts to rally students for a demonstration proved unsuccessful.[121] The Vetrova demonstration also highlighted many of the unresolved tensions affecting the student movement. The *kassa* wanted to turn it into an overt political protest, whereas the *zemliachestva* preferred to emphasize that the Kazan Square episode was a "non-political" memorial to a dead comrade.

Thus, by the end of the 1890s the student movement was beginning to reflect the interaction of traditional attitudes and emerging ideologies. A tension was developing between the notion of student solidarity, reflected in the concept of *studenchestvo,* and changes in the nation at large that were fostering alternative ways of defining the place of students in Russian society. Meanwhile, each year a few thousand young students, fresh from the provinces and untouched by these emerging ideological debates, entered the universities and replenished the ranks of the *studenchestvo.* The constant influx of new students kept alive the idea of student solidarity. In 1899 the students were to surprise everyone, including themselves, by organizing an All-Russia strike and undercutting the skeptics who had declared that student protest and student solidarity were obsolete holdovers from a long-gone era.

121. V. Levitskii, *Za chetvert' veka* (Moscow, 1926), pp. 68–69.

CHAPTER 3

The Student Movement Erupts, 1899–1901

The most important period in the history of the Russian student movement spanned the six years between the outbreak of the nationwide student strike of 1899 and the Revolution of 1905. During these years the student movement reached the high point of its political importance and internal intensity. Between 1899 and 1902 the students were the principal mass protest movement on the Russian scene. Many contemporary observers argued that the student movement acted as a major catalyst in the intensification of the revolutionary and liberal opposition movements before the outbreak of the Russo-Japanese War.

During this period, three major questions stood out. What did the students want? How did their self-image change? What impact did they make on the rest of Russian society? The obvious chronological guideposts—the 1899 student strike; the government decision to draft protesting students; the street demonstrations in February and March 1901; the students' rejection of government concessions in late 1901; the protest strike in February 1902; the theoretical debate on the student movement which followed the apparent failure of the 1902 strike—all help the historian impose some kind of structure on a complex chain of events taking place in several different university towns. But there is the danger that such an orderly framework may fail to convey the very complicated process of self-definition the student movement was undergoing, a process which was hardly unilinear, logical, or predictable. Like Dostoevskii's Underground Man, the students often seemed to spend much of their time refusing to admit that two plus two equalled

four. Much to the consternation of their self-appointed leaders, they resisted direction or ideological definition. Some historians paint a neat
picture tracing the evolution of the student movement at this time from
"corporate" to "political" protest, from apolitical strikes to more radical street demonstrations to close collaboration with the revolutionary
parties, all leading to the grand finale of 1905 when the students turned
the universities over to the workers and then stopped being a major political force.[1] Such a scheme may be compelling, but it fails to explain
what really happened.

The 1899–1905 wave of student protest confronted its participants
with many more questions than answers and sparked an intense but ultimately unsuccessful search for an ideology of student activism. This
search gained urgency from the fact that the student movement was
making an impact, both on the urban public and on the revolutionary
movement. It was, then, all the more natural for the students to ask
what exactly it was that they were doing and how effective their actions
really were.

Several issues, some not entirely new, faced the students during this
period. The first and most important was whether their goal was "political" or "academic" protest. Should the students eschew demands for
general legal and political reforms and confine their aims to the attainment of academic and corporate rights? This issue led to another:
whether the attainment of corporate rights was at all possible within the
framework of the traditional autocratic structure. Yet another major
problem concerned the importance of the student movement. Had the
students become a major political force, strong enough to wrest concessions from the government and politicize other social groups, or were
they still a transient mass of little importance, unable to agree on goals
or to mount a sustained protest? And if indeed the latter were the case,
should the students abandon the student movement altogether?

There was also the question of tactics. In 1899 the students "discovered" a new weapon, the strike. The student strike made it easy to mobilize large numbers and publicize student demands. But critics quickly
pointed out that apart from causing the government some embarrassment, student strikes harmed only the students themselves. Furthermore, these critics argued, the strike reinforced the students' isolation
from the rest of urban society, especially the working class. By 1901,

---

1. See, e.g., P. S. Gusiatnikov, *Revoliutsionnoe studencheskoe dvizhenie v Rossii*
(Moscow, 1971); G. Kiss, *Die gesellschaftspolitische Rolle der Studentenbewegung im
vorrevolutionaeren Russland* (Munich, 1963).

radical students were advancing arguments in favor of street demonstrations: they frightened the government and made more of an impact on the general population. But the government dealt much more harshly with demonstrators than with strikers, and since few students were prepared to run such risks, it quickly became apparent that the more openly radical the student movement became, the fewer the number of students who were willing to participate. This tactical conundrum was closely related to the question of whether students should try to coordinate their protests with those of other social groups, especially workers. That issue in turn led to the controversy over student organizations. Should the students abandon their traditional all-student councils and *zemliachestva* in favor of new organizational forms based on political preference? Opponents of traditional student organizations argued that the unity of the *studenchestvo* was a myth, that the students should recognize the fact that they came from different social groups reflecting widely divergent goals. In turn, supporters of these organizations asserted that the *studenchestvo* was still alive, still able to mount effective protests in defense of its own interests.

THE 1899 STRIKE

Russia's first nationwide student strike broke out over a seemingly unimportant incident in Saint Petersburg University. A few days before the traditional 8 February celebration of the founding of the university, rector V. I. Sergeevich warned the students that alcoholic binges or raucous processions down the Nevskii Prospekt would lead to severe punishment under the general provisions of the law concerning public hooliganism.

For some time the police had tolerated student rowdiness on 8 February, but recent incidents had strained the relationship between the authorities and the *studenchestvo*. In 1895 a public brawl had broken out between students and janitors in front of the Palkin restaurant, and the students had afterward accused the police of calling in the janitors to provoke them. In 1897 a crowd of five hundred students broke through police lines and marched on the Winter Palace, where they planned to conduct a public serenade. The *gradonachal'nik* (chief of police) persuaded them to disperse peacefully. In 1898, students had repeated their impromptu concert, refusing to disperse and clashing with the police.

Now the government was determined to maintain public order. In posting his notice, rector Sergeevich was merely conveying a warning he had received from the Ministry of Education. But the rector's warning angered the Saint Petersburg students, who resented the implication that the whole *studenchestvo*, and not just a small number of troublemakers, was guilty of alcoholism and misconduct. What made things worse was the fact that the students, on their own, had already decided to act in a more decorous manner this year. The tone of the rector's notice offended their sense of corporate pride. Resentments flared when the warning appeared in the city's newspapers, a move that many students saw as a public humiliation.[2]

On 8 February the traditional anniversary ceremonies began in the usual setting: the main university auditorium packed with government dignitaries, professors, and thousands of students, all prepared to sit through the usual speeches in honor of the university and *nauka*. But when Sergeevich took the floor, a storm of howls and catcalls interrupted his speech. When the flustered rector sat down, the students quickly stopped their protest. All rose in respectful silence for the playing of the national anthem, and many students even demanded an encore.[3]

The real trouble began as the students left the crowded auditorium. Stung by the rector's insinuations that they did not know how to behave, the students had posted monitors outside all exits to ensure that all would leave the hall in small groups and then immediately disperse. But as the students tried to cross the Dvortsovyi Bridge connecting Vasilevskii Island to the central city, they found the way blocked by police, who had also closed off the river, by breaking the ice in the far channel.[4] A large crowd of uniformed students milled around the Dvortsovyi Bridge and then turned west, toward the Nikolaevskii Bridge. When the students reached Rumiantsev Square, two mounted policemen rode into the crowd. The crowd thought that they were on their way to block the Nikolaevskii Bridge and thus cut the students off from the central city. As the two riders found themselves surrounded by the crowd, a detachment of mounted police suddenly descended on the students from the direction of the Academy of Sciences. When the high-spirited students

---

2. TsGIA, f. 733, op. 151, d. 244 (hereafter referred to as Doklad komissii Vannovskovo); G. M Libanov, *Studencheskoe dvizhenie 1899 goda* (London, 1901), pp. 8–12.

3. B. G., "V. I. Sergeevich i studencheskie bezporiadki v 1899 godu," *Istoricheskii Vestnik*, no. 113 (1911): 232.

4. Libanov, *Studencheskoe dvizhenie 1899 goda*, pp. 11–12.

responded with a volley of snowballs, the police unsheathed their *nagaiki* (whips) and began to beat students over the head. Several students and passersby suffered minor wounds.

The police had been issued the *nagaiki* the night before and apparently relished the prospect of settling scores with the students, who, they felt, "caused them too much trouble and extra work." One officer testified to the Vannovskii Commission that on the previous evening he had reminded one of his colleagues that "students are not workers." The colleague had replied that "the orders were to beat." [5]

The news of the beatings on Rumiantsev Square shocked students and general public alike. The strike about to break out proved an elementary but fundamental point: students in the imperial Russian capital at the beginning of the twentieth century agreed that the police had neither the moral nor the legal right to beat them in the streets. The strike was to be not a radical demonstration, but, rather, a mass movement aimed at reminding the government to respect basic rights the students assumed they already enjoyed as Russian subjects. The students did not want to be treated like peasants.

As excited students crowded into the dining hall on the Tenth Line to demand a protest *skhodka* for the next day, their more politically committed comrades shrugged off the whole episode. That night, as the more radical students gathered at the usual 8 February Marxist and populist evenings, to hear speakers and discuss politics, few expected anything to come out of the next day's *skhodka*.[6] Mogilianskii, for example, thought that the "green" students would pass a few resolutions, let off some steam, and then return to class. As radicals, the members of the *kassa* considered the beatings a logical outcome of the system, a reminder to the students that basic rights were incompatible with the autocracy. They certainly did not see them as an unexpected and heinous violation of guaranteed civil procedures.

Nikolai Iordanskii was still in his room the next day, 9 February, when a friend rushed in to tell him that three thousand students had broken into the main auditorium and that the *skhodka* was still going on. Iordanskii rushed to the university, which looked as if a "storm had

5. The quotes come from Doklad komissii Vannovskovo, pp. 12, 14; see also Libanov, *Studencheskoe dvizhenie 1899 goda*, p. 12.
6. M. N. Mogilianskii, "V devianostye gody," *Byloe*, no. 24 (1924): 95. As the Vannovskii report makes clear, these meetings took place with the permission of the police.

just hit it."[7] Without prior direction or organization the *skhodka* (which had recessed and then reconvened the following day) elected an Organization Committee and surprised the leftists by calling for a strike. The *skhodka* wanted to end the weary pattern of previous student protest— petition and deadlock—and voted a forcible closing of the university until its demands were met. The demands included publication of all circulars and rules governing police procedures for handling crowds, an official investigation of the 8 February beating, and confirmation that the principle of inviolability of person was a basic feature of Russian law.[8]

The Organization Committee elected on 10 February to direct the strike consisted mainly of *kassa* members with vague Marxist or populist sympathies. According to Mogilianskii, however, none had made any definite commitment to a political group and the 1899 strike was their first important political experience.[9] This first Organization Committee was made up of Pavel Shchegolev, Vladimir Danilov, Ivan Ladyzhevskii, Sergei Saltykov, Vladimir Elpatevskii, Nikolai Perovskii, Nikolai Iordanskii, Sergei Volkenshtein, Gregorii Nosar, Alexander Korshunov, and Arkadii Velikopol'skii. Six were twenty-four years old or older, and only one had attended a Saint Petersburg gymnasium. Seven were nobles, one was the son of a civil servant, two were from the peasant estate, and one was from the merchant estate. Nine had been members of the *kassa*.[10] Nosar was to become president of the Saint Petersburg Soviet in 1905; Saltykov later served as a Menshevik Duma deputy; Iordanskii went on to a career as editor of the leftist journal *Sovremennyi Mir*.[11]

Although many members of the Organization Committee were also in the *kassa*, serious friction immediately clouded relations between the two groups. On 9 Feburary the *kassa*'s assembly met in emergency session to discuss the strike, and several speakers urged adherence to the basic Marxist line condemning the student movement as useless and self-destructive.[12] But the members of the Organization Committee told the *kassa* not to "ruin the students' mood" by trying to squelch a spontaneous mass protest against police brutality. After some debate the

---

7. N. Iordanskii, "Missiia P. S. Vannovskovo," *Byloe*, no. 9 (1907): 98.
8. Libanov, *Studencheskoe dvizhenie 1899 goda*, p. 15.
9. Mogilianskii, "V devianostye gody," p. 124.
10. The details on the membership of the Organization Committee come from a police list found in POA, index no. 1, folder 16, vols. 22–23.
11. Mogilianskii, "V devianostye gody," p. 124.
12. Ibid.

kassa decided to "sanction" the strike and the Organization Committee. Committed Marxists on the *kassa* rationalized this decision by arguing that the strike might radicalize students and attract potential recruits to the revolutionary movement.

According to Iordanskii, the Organization Committee members of the *kassa* had to fight the influence of the *Rabochaia Mysl'*, whose "economist" ideology argued that the working class would become a revolutionary force only after a long period of preparatory struggle based on economic issues. The "economists" therefore rejected the notions of establishing political coalitions between the workers and other social groups, allowing nonworkers to lead the labor movement, and, of course, attempting to forge an alliance between students and workers.[13] The upsurge of the student movement between 1899 and 1902 played a major role in the decline of "economism" and the concomitant rise of such new groups as *Iskra* and the Social Revolutionary party, groups that recognized the importance of political struggle against the autocracy based on coalitions of various social groups: the bourgeoisie, students, and workers.

Although the *kassa* hoped that the strike would quickly acquire political overtones, the majority of the student body wanted to steer clear of any hint of political protest. Despite their private views, the members of the Organization Committee respected their mandate from the students and especially their hostility to political demands.[14] When Mogilianskii told a *skhodka* in the university auditorium that their demands could not be attained without fundamental political changes, the students howled him down. And when a member of the Organization Committee made a joking reference to the tsar's portrait, the *skhodka* "raged like a wounded animal."[15]

It was clear that during the first stage of the strike most students saw neither contradiction nor incompatibility between the ideal of a *Rechtsstaat* and the Russian autocracy. As one student summed up the prevailing consensus, "we are fighting for the law, not against it."[16] While the Organization Committee was not as sanguine about the student view that the fight was for the recognition of legal guarantees that al-

13. One economist tract urging workers to keep their distance from the student movement was reprinted in *Nakanune*, no. 7 (1899).
14. Iordanskii, "Missiia P. S. Vannovskovo," p. 103.
15. Ibid.
16. Ibid., p. 102.

ready existed, it carefully avoided raising political questions, which would not only have isolated the committee from the mass of students but would have also made it liable for prosecution under the articles of the criminal code spelling out the penalties for belonging to "revolutionary organizations." [17]

Meanwhile the Organization Committee redoubled its efforts to enlist public support and even government sympathy for the students' cause. A few days after the strike began, the committee published a detailed explanation of what the students wanted. Under existing Russian law, the committee explained, citizens found it difficult to file complaints against police abuses, especially since the Department of Police had to approve all such requests for investigation of police behavior. The committee emphasized that the students wanted *all* citizens to have the right to file complaints against the police in the courts without having to secure prior approval from the Department of Police. The committee also set forth its demands concerning time limits on investigations of police misconduct and the publication of all rules governing police behavior toward citizens.[18]

By focusing their demands on the issue of police brutality, the Saint Petersburg University students quickly secured the support of the city's other *VUZy,* including the higher technical institutes and the women's schools. All backed the university's basic demands.[19] Even the students at the elite Institute of Communications, who had never engaged in any form of protest, joined the strike, though only after dispatching a humble telegram to the tsar asking him to protect the students against police brutality.[20]

The strike soon spread across the country as Organization Committee envoys reached the provincial towns and worked to secure their students' support. The Organization Committee sent Sergei Saltykov to Moscow University. The response to his account of the Rumiantsev Square incident belied the fears expressed to him by a few student veterans that the Moscow students were too disorganized to join the strike. On 15 February the students of both Moscow University and the Moscow Technological Institute voted to halt classes. The university elected

17. Ibid.
18. *Nakanune,* no. 6 (1899).
19. On the spread of the strike to other Saint Petersburg *VUZy,* see Libanov, *Studencheskoe dvizhenie 1899 goda,* p. 27.
20. *Nakanune,* no. 3 (1899).

an Executive Committee to direct the strike and maintain contact with other institutions of higher education.[21]

Vladimir Medem, a future leader of the Jewish Labor Bund, recalled years later how he and his fellow Kiev University students first heard the news from Saint Petersburg. Although the students did not like the police, they had assumed that, unlike peasants, students enjoyed a certain deference, an immunity against being beaten on the streets. When Saltykov arrived to address the Kiev students, the lecture hall was packed. "He spoke calmly and distinctly," Medem wrote, "and the hall began to seethe with indignation."[22] Kiev's student leaders were a little disappointed that the Organization Committee had failed to couch its demands in more radical terms (Iordanskii deprecated the well-known "verbal radicalism" of the Kiev students), but the students overwhelmingly voted to join the strike.[23]

Within two weeks, as the provincial universities and technical institutes joined the protest, the strike had become an impressive demonstration of nationwide student solidarity. Perhaps nothing better captures the mood of the 1899 strike than its anthem, "Nagaechka," written by an anonymous Saint Petersburg student shortly after the 8 February incident. The song became the symbol of the student movement and retained its popularity until the Revolution of 1917. In its clever puns comparing the pharaohs of ancient Egypt with Piramidov, the Okhrana chief whom the students blamed for the beating, the song captured that mixture of playfulness and seriousness that was so characteristic of the student movement:

> Nad shirokoi rekoi
>   molchalivoi chetoi
> Para sfinksov sidit,
>   ukhmyliaetsia.
>
> . . . .
>
> Nagaechka, nagaechka, vos'movo fevralia,
> Nagaechka, nagaechka, proslavim my tebia.

21. For a police summary of the Moscow student movement in 1899, see TsGAOR, f. 124, op. 8, ed. kh. 194–1899, l. 110.

22. Vladimir Medem, *Fun mayn lebn* (New York, 1923), vol. 1, p. 160. For police reports on the 1899 student movement in Kiev, see TsGAOR, f. 124, op. 8, ed. kh. 199/1899.

23. Iordanskii, "Missiia P. S. Vannovskovo," pp. 100–101; TsGAOR, f. 124, op. 8, ed. kh. 199/1899, l. 307.

Faraony krugom
    vsekh kolotiat knutom,
Piramidov-prokhvost
    otlichaetsia.

. . . .

A na tekh, kto potom
    ne dovolen knutom,
Desiat' kaznei zaraz
    nasypaetsia

. . . .

Ves' narod pred bozhkom
    vozlegaet nichkom
I reka kazhdyi god
    razlivaetsia.

A odin krokodil nam
    nedavno tverdil
Chto zakonom strana
    upravliaetsia.

Over the broad wide river, like a silent couple a pair of sphinxes sit and smirk.

Little whip, little whip of February eighth, we will glorify you and make you famous.

The pharaohs all around beat everyone with a knout; the scoundrel Piramidov excels.

And those who are not content with the knout are heaped with punishment in one fell swoop.

All the people fall face down before the idol, and the river overflows its banks every year.

And one crocodile recently maintained to us that the country is ruled by law.[24]

As the 1899 strike spread into the provinces, the students there added their own grievances to the basic Saint Petersburg demands. Kharkov University adopted a resolution insisting that students receive "adult" treatment and corporate rights:

Our education is too narrow, too specialized; on the whole it is disappointing. There is a constant undercurrent of dissatisfaction in the *studenchestvo*

---

24. This text is based on handwritten copy found in TsGAOR, f. 102, 3 ch. B–1898, l. 206. *Pharaoh* is a slang term for "police." I am grateful to my colleague Professor Olga Peters Hasty for her help with this translation.

and even one incident could set off serious disturbances. . . . Financial aid
should be decided by students, not by the inspectorate . . . only lackeys
and grovellers get scholarships. . . . Recently police repression has become
more frequent.[25]

Demands for a change in the inspectorate and reform of the system for
determining financial aid became common features of the resolutions
adopted by students joining the strike.[26]

Few defied the strike, for roving bands of students disrupted those
few lectures that managed to meet. In Saint Petersburg University some
professors tried to continue lecturing but gave up after police squads
stationed themselves in the classrooms. By 15 February the police had
arrested sixty-eight Saint Petersburg University students, including many
members of the first Organization Committee. The committee, however,
immediately replaced arrested members with substitutes selected in advance. More serious was the wave of arrests that decimated the provincial *studenchestvo*.[27] Yet the students held firm, showing no signs of
ending the strike.

On 16 February the Saint Petersburg University Faculty Council,
meeting in emergency session, asked for a temporary closing of the university, the release of all students arrested by the police, and the removal
of the police from the university.[28] But the council gave no sign of supporting the students' wider demands. While many professors privately
expressed sympathy with the students' cause, the professoriate as a
whole failed to give collective support to the student movement, although several professors signed various petitions couched in the mild
tone of the Saint Petersburg Faculty Council resolution. Years later, in
the middle of the Revolution of 1905, Professor N. A. Gredeskul would
confess in the authoritative liberal journal *Pravo* that in 1899 the professoriate should have done more to support the students, who had
shown more insight into the true character of the autocracy than their
teachers had.

Even in 1899, a few scholars managed to render the students some
marginally effective help. On 17 February, Professors N. N. Beketov and

25. TsGIA, f. 733, op. 151, d. 48, l. 21.
26. TsGIA, f. 733, op. 151, d. 48, contains numerous student proclamations justifying support for the strike.
27. Libanov, *Studencheskoe dvizhenie 1899 goda*, p. 32; POA, index 1, folder 16,
vols. 22–23; TsGIA, f. 733, op. 151, d. 51.
28. Libanov, *Studencheskoe dvizhenie 1899 goda*, p. 34.

A. S. Famintsyn, both members of the prestigious Academy of Sciences, secured an audience with Tsar Nicholas to explain the student movement. Beketov, as he later smilingly explained to the amazed members of the Organization Committee, told the tsar that the students would have been "unworthy of bearing the name of Russian" had they meekly accepted the police beatings! While neither professor condoned the strike, they both urged the tsar to show leniency and understanding.[29]

Meanwhile the government bureaucracy was sharply divided. Seizing the opportunity to embarrass his arch-rival I. L. Goremykin, who headed the Ministry of the Interior, Finance Minister S. Iu. Witte despatched a memorandum to the tsar calling for an investigation of the Rumiantsev Square incident. Unlike previous student protests, Witte explained, the strike had no political overtones. Like young people everywhere, students were "touchy," especially when beaten; an investigation would probably end the whole matter.[30] Joining Goremykin in opposing Witte's idea were Minister of Education N. P. Bogolepov and Minister of War A. N. Kuropatkin. Outside the Committee of Ministers, in high court and bureaucratic circles, there was a general feeling that the police had gone too far.[31]

On 20 February the tsar took Witte's advice, appointing an investigatory commission, headed by General P. S. Vannovskii, to report on the 8 February affair. For some, like Grand Duke Sergei Alexandrovich, the announcement was a "terrible mistake . . . a dangerous concession to public opinion which would lead to further concessions . . . and an eventual plunge into the abyss."[32] As for the student leaders, the announcement of the commission left them in a quandary. While nobody on the Organization Committee knew Vannovskii, his reputation as the reactionary general whom Alexander III had appointed to stamp out liberalism in the army inspired grave apprehensions about how he would conduct the investigation.

The real question facing the Organization Committee was whether to end the strike. To be sure, the government had met one of the students' basic demands, the appointment of an investigatory commission. But the police had already arrested hundreds of students all over the em-

---

29. Iordanskii, "Missiia P. S. Vannovskovo," p. 105.

30. A copy of Witte's memorandum can be found in the Hoover Institution, Boris Nikolaevskii Collection, file 109, box 6, packet 60, no. 7.

31. Iu. B. Solov'ëv, *Samoderzhavie i dvorianstvo v kontse 19 veka* (Leningrad, 1973), p. 140.

32. Ibid., p. 141.

pire. Ending the strike meant breaking that bond of comradely solidarity so important to the *studenchestvo*. Yet fighting on was dangerous. Now that the government had announced the commission, it was
difficult to justify the strike on the grounds that the students were fighting "for, not against, the law." To continue the strike could well be interpreted as a blatant challenge to the authority of the government.

What ensured the Organization Committee's decision to recommend
continuing the strike was the failure of the government to promise quick
release and readmission of arrested students.[33] Most students, however,
were ready to give the Vannovskii Commission the benefit of the doubt.
Pro-strike sentiment began to waver; on 23 February many of the Saint
Petersburg higher technical institutes voted to end the strike. In Saint
Petersburg University, the Organization Committee called a 1 March
skhodka to decide whether to follow suit.

The week leading up to the 1 March *skhodka* saw an intense pamphlet campaign waged between pro- and anti-strike students.[34] Supported by the professors, anti-strike students argued that the Vannovskii
Commission would correct the worst abuses in the government-student
relationship and would finally tame the excesses of the police. Pro-strike
pamphlets emphasized the students' moral obligation not to give up the
struggle until the authorities released the hundreds of students expelled
and arrested during the previous few weeks, especially in Moscow and
Kiev.[35] Both groups freely used poetry as well as prose. One pro-strike
broadsheet mocked the students' readiness to give up:

> My zh dadim urok prekrasnyi
>   pokoleniiam drugim,
> Kak vesti protest otvazhnyi
>   i chto znachit smelym byt'.
> Eto znachit postoianno
>   otstupat' ot slov svoikh
> I, konechno, ne narochno,
>   tseli dela pozabyt'.
> Eto znachit kliatvy vernosti
>   prinimat' lish' na slovakh,

33. Iordanskii, "Missiia P. S. Vannovskovo," p. 104.
34. Many of these pamphlets can be found in TsGAOR, f. 102, 3 ch. 1LB/1899,
no. 4; Libanov, *Studencheskoe dvizhenie 1899 goda*, p. 59.
35. An example is the proclamation of the "Group of the 147," TsGAOR, f. 102, 3ch.
1LB/1899, no. 4, l. 18.

A v delakh velikoi krainosti
im bez strakha izmeniat'.[36]

We will give a wonderful lesson to other generations on how to make a daring protest and what it means to be courageous. It means always to retreat from your word and to forget (not intentionally, of course) the goals of the cause. It means to take the oath of loyalty and shamelessly betray it as soon as things get tough.

Meanwhile the Organization Committee, which was trying to mobilize pro-strike sentiment, tried going outside the university in order to convert nebulous public sympathy into more solid support. The committee decided to despatch Nikolai Iordanskii and S. N. Saltykov to a meeting of well-known writers and professors that consisted of L. F. Panteleev, Th. D. Batiushkov, V. G. Korolenko, V. A. Miakotin, and M. I. Sveshnikov. By this time the Okhrana was conducting an energetic dragnet for members of the Organization Committee. In order to move freely, Iordanskii rid himself of his beard and student uniform, donning dark glasses in the pious hope that this would render him inconspicuous.[37]

The meeting proved a bitter disappointment. The young emissaries realized that the student movement, for all its "moderation" and "naive" belief that the autocracy could be persuaded to act like a *Rechtsstaat*, was still far ahead of the rest of the Russian educated public in its willingness to undertake collective open protest against government policies. When Iordanskii asked the assembled writers what they advised the students to do, Korolenko replied that the answer to that question depended on what the students wanted to accomplish. If their major goal was protest, then they should continue the strike. But if they wanted to achieve specific, practical results, then they should return to classes. The delegates then asked whether the students could count on any degree of support, since the *studenchestvo* by itself was too weak to force significant concessions from the government. The answer was clear and disappointing: sympathy, yes; overt support, no.[38]

Much to the disgust of the Organization Committee, the 1 March *skhodka* voted to stop the strike. Indeed, a few days later Vannovskii managed to secure the return of those students arrested in Saint Petersburg, although he made no promises about the fate of students from the

36. TsGAOR, f. 102, 3ch. 1899, no. 4, l. 88.
37. Iordanskii, "Missiia P. S. Vannovskovo," p. 122.
38. Ibid.

provincial universities. In Moscow University on 5 March, the students disregarded a pro-strike appeal from Kiev University and voted to return to classes, after securing a promise from rector Tikhomirov that he would petition the police to return arrested students.[39]

Believing that the strike was finally over, the Saint Petersburg *kassa*, which until then had remained aloof, decided to issue a public statement on the political and theoretical significance of the student movement. The *kassa* had smugly expected the students to greet the Vannovskii Commission by ending their strike; nonetheless, the scope and intensity of the previous month's student protest had surprised many leftists who realized that the movement might be more important than they had thought. Perhaps the student action was a sign of impending changes in the relationship between the autocracy and the educated public.[40] A major reason for the *kassa* statement was the perception that a correct analysis of the student movement would have important implications for the debate just beginning within Russian Social Democracy as to whether workers' organizations and Social Democratic groups should participate in or aid nonproletarian political and social movements.[41]

Was the bourgeoisie ready to move? Based on his observations of the student movement, at least one of the *kassa* leaders, Mogilianskii, concluded that the answer was yes. If so, then the students were the best-organized group in the bourgeois camp. Furthermore, Mogilianskii argued, bourgeois political activism could have an important effect on the labor movement, leading the workers to strike for political and not just economic reasons.[42]

Immediately after the 1 March *skhodka*, Mogilianskii raised to the executive board of the *kassa* the question of issuing such a proclamation. The populist students rejected any attempt to issue a Marxist interpretation of the recent strike, and Iordanskii and other Organization Committee members warned that trying to attach political labels to the student movement was a mistake. It was still possible that the student masses would become disillusioned with the Vannovskii Commission—burning bridges was bad policy.[43] Mogilianskii, however, waved these

---

39. P. S. Tkachenko, *Moskovskoe studenchestvo v obshchestvenno-politicheskoi zhizni Rossii vtoroi poloviny 19ovo veka* (Moscow, 1958), p. 235.

40. For example, see bulletin 19 of the Saint Petersburg *kassa*, in TsGAOR, f. 102, 3ch. 1LB/1899, no. 4, l. 25.

41. Mogilianskii, "V devianostye gody," pp. 122–123.

42. Ibid.

43. Ibid., p. 124.

objections aside and issued his proclamation on 5 March, a few days after the students voted to end the strike.

The *kassa* proclamation represented an important departure from previous Marxist appraisals of the student movement. For the first time, a Marxist group emphasized its political significance, albeit as a bourgeois protest movement. By labeling the student movement *bourgeois,* Mogilianskii took dead aim at those comrades who preferred to think of the *studenchestvo* in traditional terms as the idealistic vanguard of the Russian intelligentsia. At the same time, Mogilianskii indirectly attacked the accepted Marxist line on the student movement; it was more than a temper tantrum staged by "insulted kids." It was, in fact, an important signal, the first sign of an imminent political struggle that would soon mobilize the entire Russian bourgeoisie against the autocracy. Of all the groups constituting the bourgeoisie, the students "were the most idealistic segment . . . and the most dedicated defenders of their class. For this reason, and with a fateful inevitability, they are in chronic, not sporadic, opposition to the arbitrariness [of the autocracy] and its attacks on the principle of human rights." Furthermore, the recent student strike showed that the students were ready to seize the initiative. Unlike their fathers, they were willing to take risks to defend the principles of their class. Thus the student movement was not only "political" but also "combative" (*nastupatel'no boevoe*), one of "several budding social movements which will despatch Russian absolutism to its grave." Mogilianskii continued his analysis of the student movement:

> The basic cause of the student movement is the bourgeois struggle for human dignity, dignity that was violated [by the recent policies of the police]. The ideals of the bourgeoisie always relate to the individual; they are permeated through and through with the concepts of *freedom* and *property.* Therefore the positive role of the bourgeoisie is its introduction into public life of the principles of personal inviolability, freedom of speech, and conscience, as well as other variants of the "natural rights of Man." [44]

There was another side to bourgeois political behavior: "liberal opportunism." The students had revealed this trait, the proclamation complained, when they decided to end the strike. The cause of the final paralysis of the student movement was quite clear: the students were not

---

44. A complete text of the *kassa* proclamation can be found in the Hoover Institution, Boris Nikolaevskii Collection, file 109, box 6, packet 60.

revolutionaries. "A revolutionary mood," the *kassa* warned, "cannot be created just by words and proclamations." Now that the student movement was over (or so Mogilianskii thought), the *kassa* could invite the *studenchestvo* to consider its mistakes and ponder its future course. As far as the *kassa* was concerned, that course was clear: all individuals, regardless of social class, should join in a common struggle aimed at the overthrow of the autocracy.

The *kassa* proclamation was hardly an instant success: Saint Petersburg University students reacted with fury. In the university dining hall on the Tenth Line, infuriated students tore up and trampled copies of the proclamation. One of the most fervent protesters was Ivan Kaliaev, who later joined the Social Revolutionary Battle Organization and was hanged for the assassination of the Grand Duke Sergei Alexandrovich in 1905. By this time Kaliaev, along with future terrrorist Boris Savinkov, had joined the Organization Committee.[45]

Kaliaev mirrored the mood of a sizable minority who rejected both the "cowardice" that ended the strike and the Marxist "sectarianism" of Mogilianskii's tract. While continuing to steer clear of party politics, students were developing a new attitude that stressed a fundamental incompatibility between the autocracy and the students' demand for a system based on the rule of law.

POLITICAL FALL-OUT

In short, after the 1 March *skhodka,* three major trends developed in Saint Petersburg University. The first, reflected in the 1 March vote to end the strike, was marked by a refusal to see the student movement as a protest against the autocratic system, and by a readiness to trust in the Vannovskii Commission. The second, represented by the *kassa* group around Mogilianskii, emphasized the political importance of the student movement but regarded it as representing a larger class, the Russian bourgeoisie. Only revolution, not reform, would change the system, but in the meantime the student movement could play a useful role, since the students were the best-organized segment of the bourgeoisie. The third trend argued that the *studenchestvo* should admit that the strike was not just an isolated incident, but was really aimed at a law-

---

45. Ironically, Mogilianskii evolved in the opposite political direction and later joined the Kadet party.

lessness and arbitrariness endemic in the political system. But unlike the Marxists, these students rejected the assertion that the *studenchestvo* was just a subgroup of the bourgeoisie. For many, the 1899 strike was indeed a radicalizing experience. In time, some would join the revolutionary parties, but few had embraced, during the period of the strike, either Marxism or populism. Yet within this group there was a growing tendency to equate liberalism with cowardice.

The major representative of this trend was the Organization Committee, which issued a manifesto shortly after the 1 March *skhodka*.[46] Not knowing whether the strike would ever resume, the Organization Committee resolved to make public its own interpretation of the student movement. The manifesto was a hard-hitting document which admitted that, regardless of what many students thought they were doing, the Organization Committee had from the beginning seen the strike as a protest against the entire system. If the committee had refrained from openly stating that fact before, that was only because its goal had been to sustain the widest possible degree of support from the student masses, many of whom had not yet broken with certain illusions about the true nature of the autocracy. "We were not just protesting against the 8 February beating. The latter was just a particular manifestation of the present Russian system, a system based on arbitrariness, secrecy and the total . . . absence of the most necessary . . . sacred rights essential for the development of the human personality." The manifesto reported that during the first period of the student strike, the Organization Committee had managed to keep the students united by carefully avoiding demands or programs "linked to narrow party platforms." Unfortunately, the unanimity of purpose which had at first united the student movement vanished after the naming of the Vannovskii Commission:

> The student masses trusted in the Vannovskii Commission and forgot the initial and more fundamental significance of their protest. They also forgot about their initial demands. The students have chosen the slippery path of submitting petitions and asking for favors. . . . If the student masses had really been serious and conscientious about the movement . . . they would have realized that the movement was really aimed at an order of things where rights and law mean nothing, where only petitions and appeals count. Educated and emasculated under the dead regime of the eighties and nineties, the student masses . . . did not rise to the occasion.

46. A complete text of the Organization Committee's manifesto can be found in BMGU, f. V. I. Orlova, Otdel Rukopisei (no number).

The manifesto excoriated not only the students but also the apathy and cowardice of the Russian public, and especially the fecklessness of the "liberal 'well-wishers' who tore the control of the movement from our hands after the announcement of the Vannovskii Commission. They tell us that our strength lies in public sympathy for our cause. Yes, we counted on it but we were mistaken. The liberal hogwash we heard at the beginning of the strike clouded our vision, and we lost sight of the star which should have guided us forward. Sure, the public sympathizes . . . but doesn't dare express its sympathy openly."

Nonetheless, the initial impulse of the Organization Committee had been sound. The student movement was not yet over. Many students were soon disappointed in the Vannovskii Commission. Reports from interrogated students reinforced the impression that the aim of the commission was not to investigate the Rumiantsev Square incident but to prove that the student movement was the product of outside manipulation. The general himself, however, impressed the students as an honest if simple soldier, especially after he began to give credence to their denials of a hidden political hand behind the strike. Indeed, as Vannovskii began to believe that the students were defending, however wrongheadedly, the "honor of their uniform" or their "comrades" sitting in provincial jails, he began to show the students a certain sympathy.[47] Kleigels, the police chief, felt Vannovskii's hostility so keenly that he protested in a personal letter to Tsar Nicholas that the commission was biased against the police.[48] Yet most students shared Iordanskii's impression that while Vannovskii meant well he lacked the power to put the Department of Police in its place. The fact that Iordanskii had to elude a police dragnet in order to meet an appointment with the general did not help create an impression that Vannovskii could really do very much to change things.[49]

Even more disquieting to most students in Saint Petersburg was the continuing police repression in the provinces, especially in Warsaw and Kiev. While in Moscow and Saint Petersburg arrested students could re-

47. Iordanskii, "Missiia P. S. Vannovskovo," pp. 115–116.

48. A copy of Kleigels' letter to the tsar (no date) can be found in TsGAOR, f. DO, 3ch. t1/1898, l. 289. Kleigels' anger focused on two points. First, the students attacked the police on 8 February yet managed to win the sympathy of "many people in high places and even some ministers." Second, Vannovskii and his commission interrogated Kleigels in a particularly insulting way: "They questioned me just as if I had been a student." Kleigels cautioned the tsar not to underestimate the political potential of the student movement and reminded him that Kleigels had been warning of large-scale disturbances since 1896.

49. Iordanskii, "Missiia P. S. Vannovskovo," pp. 115–116.

turn to their *VUZy*, mass arrests continued in those provincial cities. The Kiev students taunted their Saint Petersburg comrades for leaving them in the lurch, "firing the first shot and then deserting the battle-field." The Kiev United Council, which directed the strike there, also criticized the Saint Petersburg *kassa* proclamation as reckless and stupid, because it jeopardized provincial students who now were bearing the full brunt of the police repression:

> Your decision to declare that the student movement was "political," once you decided that the strike was over, was a tactical blunder. While the movement may be over in Saint Petersburg, it is still going on in the provinces. . . . We'll do our best to keep your proclamation from getting wide circulation. . . . By basing the student movement on the general principle of the defense of human rights [instead of sectarian political doctrines] we were able to unite students of differing political views. Also, espousing such a principle saves us from even worse repression.[50]

The news from the provinces led to heated discussions in Moscow and Saint Petersburg; as usual, the student dining halls were the centers of debate and pamphleteering, places where students who wanted to resume the strike could meet in a relatively secure atmosphere.

The Saint Petersburg Organization Committee finally responded to Kiev's appeals, calling a *skhodka* on 16 March at the university to consider the question of resuming the strike.[51] After the usual ritual of breaking down locked doors, approximately a thousand students stormed the university auditorium and voted to resume the strike. But anti-strike forces argued that the vote did not reflect the real mood of the student body and demanded a second *skhodka,* which met the following day. The university became the scene of intense activity, as students crowded around bulletin boards to read exhortatory poems hung by the Organization Committee and to argue about resuming the strike. On 17 March Sergei Volkenshtein, the president of the *skhodka* and a member of the first Organization Committee, opened the meeting by asking the students to reaffirm their vote of the previous day.

There was a clear difference in mood between these *skhodki* of mid-March and the tumultuous meetings that followed the beating in Rumiantsev Square. If they resumed the strike, the students knew, they would be coming closer to political protest, openly challenging the gov-

---

50. TsGIA, f. 733, op. 151, d. 48, l. 275; TsGAOR, f. 102, 3ch. 1LB/1899, no. 4, l. 121.
51. TsGIA, f. 733, op. 151, d. 48, l. 241; Iordanskii, "Missiia P. S. Vannovskovo," pp. 125–127.

ernment by an implicit declaration of "no confidence" in the Vannovskii Commission and taking the student movement in a new, uncharted direction. Volkenstein reminded the students not to harbor illusions about the seriousness of their position or about the implications of a vote to resume the strike.[52] The students could no longer contend, as they had in February, that they were protesting the Saint Petersburg police department rather than a general political system that made such outrages possible. A second strike carried little guarantee of success and certainly offered much less prospect of outside sympathy.

The clear differences between the February and the March *skhodki* in Saint Petersburg University hinted at important and complex changes taking place in the student movement. In February the outrage stood out more clearly; more students came to the *skhodki* and the near-unanimous dislike of the police, along with the expectation of public support, led to a jubilant, festive attitude. The students had then felt that there was little danger in striking, especially for a just cause that even important circles in the government could support.

Now, in March, the situation was different. Fewer students attended the *skhodki,* but those who did seemed more receptive to political speeches, although they still opposed any attempt to inject specific ideological or party platforms. The *skhodka* even applauded when one speaker read letters from Berlin and Lausanne hailing the political importance of the student movement and openly attacking the autocratic system.[53] According to Iordanskii, who attended the March *skhodki,* the political temper of the crowd came as a complete surprise to the Organization Committee, who remembered the cautious mood of the previous month. But he quickly discerned a crucial nuance, an ambivalence that would become a crucial and constant feature of the Russian student movement right up to the Revolution of 1917: the tension between verbal, formal radicalism and the reluctance to make any specific activist commitment on behalf of actual political parties or ideologies.[54] The same crowd that applauded the Lausanne student letter containing the slogan "Down with the Autocracy" avidly protested the reading of Mogilianskii's manifesto, partly because of its Marxism, and partly, as we have seen, because the students preferred to see themselves as *intelligenty* rather than as the "vanguard of the Russian bourgeoisie."

52. Iordanskii, "Missiia P. S. Vannovskovo," pp. 125–126.
53. Ibid.
54. Ibid.

The students were actually acting in a revolutionary way [*delali revoliutsiiu*] but were afraid to tell themselves that they were doing so, in part because they did not want to lose the advantage of "legality," their supposed "legal" right to protest the police action. But it seems to me that the students were not so much afraid of embarking on a revolutionary course as they were mistrustful of old-style conspiratorial revolutionary organizations. In the effort to create a "political" rather than a "revolutionary" movement, the students were not only reflecting the influence of "liberal-oppositional" ideology but also attempting to find a new form of revolutionary struggle that would permit the possibility of a mass movement.[55]

In a few years the students would lose their fear of passing revolutionary resolutions, but their ambivalent relationship to the organized revolutionary left would remain a constant feature of student unrest in late imperial Russia. The student movement, by its nature a mass movement, would find itself in an ambiguous and tense relationship to the leftist political parties pushing to impose ideological and organizational coherence on mass protest. Nevertheless, as Iordanskii himself noted, the student movement would drift slowly leftward; the political and legal realities of the Russian empire undercut the February 1899 position that student protest could be "legal" or "nonoppositional." This was to be a slow process, with many reversals along the way, but, in the end, exhibiting striking continuities. As an oppositional protest movement, essentially dependent on the readiness of the student masses to take part, the student movement would soon face important ideological and tactical problems. Could an oppositional mass movement resist party domination or function without a preconceived ideological and/ or tactical doctrine? Could the students devise an ideology that could exert a broad enough appeal to unite a critical mass yet at the same time retain enough coherence to provide a theoretical underpinning for student protest? These issues, which moved to the center of attention in 1901 and 1902, first began to surface in 1899, as the student movement underwent an inchoate, subtle, yet important change in mood.

THE STRIKE RESUMES

After long arguments between the pro-strike and anti-strike forces, the 17 March *skhodka* reaffirmed the decision to resume the strike, by a vote of 825 to 601.[56] The next day the administration closed the univer-

---

55. Ibid.
56. Libanov, *Studencheskoe dvizhenie 1899 goda*, p. 67.

sity and suspended the student body. Students had five days to petition for readmission; the price was a promise not to participate in *skhodki* or "illegal" student groups. On 20 and 21 March, the Okhrana—without consulting Vannovskii, who felt that he had given his word to Saint Petersburg student leaders that they were safe from arrest—apprehended all suspected members of the Organization Committee and expelled them from Saint Petersburg.[57]

Meanwhile, the Ministry of Education decided to break the strike, which by this time had resumed in the provincial universities, by forcing all students to take their regular oral examinations during the last week of March. In Saint Petersburg, pro-strike students responded by disrupting the examinations; university authorities then called in police to keep order. Tension escalated as clashes broke out between pro-strike and anti-strike students. The government tried to minimize the impact of the disorders by forbidding the press to publish anything on the student movement and by issuing a 2 April communiqué in *Pravitel'stvennyi Vestnik* asserting that secret revolutionary organizations were behind the academic turmoil.[58] This move further undercut Vannovskii's credibility, although the general had had nothing to do with the report. A few days earlier, pro-strike students in Saint Petersburg University called a street demonstration in front of the main university buildings to protest the presence of police at lectures and exams. On 31 March the police encircled the crowd of students and arrested 540 of them. By the first week of April about one-third of the student body of Saint Petersburg University had been arrested. The police quickly released all these students to the custody of their parents, which meant that all those who were not natives of Saint Petersburg had to leave the capital. By means of these repressive measures, the government had managed by mid-April to impose a rough kind of "order" on the city's *VUZy*. Similar scenes characterized the course of student protest in the provinces.[59]

In Moscow University the students also decided to resume the strike. There were two principal reasons. On 8 March rector Tikhomirov angered the student body by posting an announcement forbidding student meetings without his permission. The second reason was, of course, the students' anger over the persistent failure of the police to release students in Kiev and Warsaw.[60]

57. For an account of Vannovskii's acute embarrassment, see Iordanskii, "Missiia P. S. Vannovskovo," pp. 128–129.
58. Libanov, *Studencheskoe dvizhenie 1899 goda*, p. 71.
59. Ibid., pp. 70–73.
60. TsGIA, f. 733, op. 151, d. 48, l. 76.

TABLE 6   MOSCOW UNIVERSITY STUDENT VOTE TO
RESUME THE 1899 STRIKE, BY FACULTY

	Year	For Resuming the Strike	Against Resuming the Strike
History and philology	1	26	1
	2	23	6
	3	1	14
	4	17	7
Law	1	239	8
	2	90	21
	3	16	31
	4	—a	—
Mathematics	1	74	14
	2	62	8
	3	39	4
	4	18	9
Medicine	1	181	26
	2	176	25
	3	104	28
	4	16	92
	5	0	177
Natural sciences	1	116	14
	2	65	50
	3	26	74
	4	38	15

SOURCE: TsGIA, f. 733, op. 151, d. 48, l. 201.
a The figures for final-year law students are not indicated.

The results of the strike vote conducted by the Moscow University
Student Executive Committee provide some interesting insights into the
mood of the Moscow students. The overall vote in the university was
2 to 1 for resuming the strike. Students voted as indicated in Table 6.
About half of the enrolled students voted. These figures show that
younger students tended to be more combative; older students tended to
be either less willing to resume the fight, or, as in the case of last-year
medical students, downright determined not to let the strike disrupt the
beginning of their professional careers.[61]

61. Certain anomalies, such as the overwhelming anti-strike sentiment among third-
year science students in an otherwise pro-strike department, might be explained by these
students' concern over the fate of the ongoing individual research projects that were required at that level. This is only an educated guess. Other anomalies, such as the vote of
the third-year history and philology students, defy easy explanation.

As in Saint Petersburg and other university towns, in Moscow University the authorities met this second strike with mass arrests and expulsions. The administration forced all students in the university to petition for readmission and then refused to readmit 778 of them. Counting previous arrests and expulsions, a total of 840 students were expelled by the university administration and an additional 199 were sent out of Moscow by police order.[62] A list of these students has been preserved in the archives of the Ministry of Education.[63]

An analysis of this list affords some insight into the types of students who participated in the 1899 disorders. Of the 888 students on the summary list, 269 were from the medical faculty, 285 from the juridical faculty, 207 from natural sciences, 95 from mathematics, and 32 from the history and philology faculty. Almost 21 percent of the medical students, 16.4 percent of the law students, 25 percent of the natural sciences and mathematics students, and 14 percent of the history students were listed as participants. Thirty-two percent of the listed students were freshmen and 31 percent were second-year students, while first-year students comprised 30.5 percent and second-year students 25.6 percent of overall enrollment. About 23 percent of the entire student body had attended Moscow secondary schools, but only about 11 percent of the listed students appear to have done so.[64] The list included 20 percent of all sons of civil servants enrolled at the university, 23 percent of nobles' sons, 18 percent of those of merchants and honorary citizens, 20 percent of the sons of *meshchane,* 20 percent of the peasants' sons, 23 percent of those of the clerical estate, and 26 percent of officers' sons.[65] Nineteen percent of the students had a record of previous involvement in student disorders. Although 50 percent of the entire student body received some form of financial aid, only 28 percent of the listed students were scholarship recipients.[66] Ten percent of the listed students were Roman Catholic and 5 percent Jewish, compared to a general Roman Catholic percentage of 5.8 and a Jewish representation of 3.5 percent. Assuming that most of the Catholic students were Poles, the high degree of involvement of these students indicates that feelings of student solidarity led them to ignore nationalist calls to avoid the

62. TsGIA, f. 733, op. 151, d. 48, l. 269.
63. This list can be found in TsGIA, f. 733, op. 151, d. 51.
64. I made these calculations on the basis of the summary list, the *Otchët za 1899 god* (Moscow, 1900) of Moscow University, and the student roster for the 1898–1899 academic year, *Alfavitnyi spisok studentov za 1899 god* (Moscow, 1900).
65. Ibid.
66. TsGIA, f. 733, op. 151, d. 51.

strike on the grounds that a Russian student movement had nothing to do with them.[67]

Although the social composition of the active students did not differ significantly from that of the general student population, the above analysis suggests certain differences between the profile of the activists in 1899 and that of the general student body. The activists tended to be first- or second-year students, although their overrepresentation was not overwhelming—64 percent of the activists as opposed to 55 percent of the general student population. Students on the natural sciences faculty, Roman Catholics, and nonscholarship recipients were overrepresented among the activists, and students who had attended Moscow high schools were underrepresented. Since Moscow students probably lived with their parents instead of with fellow students, their striking under-representation in the activist group suggests a clear relationship between student activism and living arrangements that helped create a student subculture. Younger students from the provinces relied more on their comrades for emotional support and were more likely to respond to a call for student solidarity. It is possible to surmise as well that many students not receiving scholarships may have harbored grudges against the university inspectorate, which made such decisions, and thus were more likely to protest.

By April the 1899 student strike was clearly on the wane. The mass arrests and expulsions were having an obvious effect. In an effort to chart a general strategy for the student movement, the Moscow University Executive Council called an All-Russian student conference to meet at the end of April. But before it could convene, the Okhrana arrested all the students present, including delegates from Moscow, Tomsk, Kazan, Warsaw, Odessa, Kharkov, Kiev, Iur'ev, and Saint Petersburg. These arrests completed the process of ending the student strike.[68]

The 1899 student strike forced the government to reexamine its higher-education policy. In its final report the Vannovskii Commission

67. The Polish National Democratic movement issued a proclamation condemning the participation of Polish students in the Russian student movement and reminding Polish students of how little support their Russian comrades had given them when they tried to defend Polish national interests, such as demanding a chair of Polish history in Warsaw University. See TsGIA, op. 151, ed. kh. 48/1899, l. 283. See also Jerzy Braun, "Położenie i ruch organizacyjny młodzieży akademickiej na uniwersytecie warszawskim w latach 1890–1904," *Roczniki Uniwersytetu Warszawskiego*, vol. 5 (1963): 92.

68. The interrogation reports on the arrested students are an extremely valuable source for assessing the 1899 student movement. They certainly show that anger against the police and feelings of comradely solidarity were as important in the provinces as they were in Saint Petersburg. See TsGAOR, f. 124, op. 8, ed. kh. 194/1899.

contradicted the official government communiqué by emphasizing that the student movement was not the work of a handful of conspirators or outside agitators, but was, rather, the result of the students' deep dissatisfaction with their living conditions and with the academic system.[69] The report also lambasted the police for negligence in their handling of the Rumiantsev Square incident. The commission made a number of specific recommendations. The *VUZy* should admit no more students than they could properly educate. Professors should assign more work to their students and supervise their studies more closely. The commission recommended abolishing the honorarium on the grounds that it encouraged professors to court popularity by espousing liberal ideas in the lecture hall. It also urged an increase in the university inspectorate and the repeal of those articles in the 1884 Statute that denied the students a corporate identity and the right to form student organizations. The commission concluded that the universities should emulate the specialized technical institutes and permit the students to have libraries and *zemliachestva* and to elect course representatives.

In June the Ministry of Education responded by issuing circulars expanding the professoriate, announcing plans to build more dormitories and, in a move that would arouse much resentment, forcing students to attend the university closest to the educational district of their secondary school.[70] The ministry also announced plans to raise the educational level of the inspectorate and urged the inspectors to establish close relationships with their student charges.

At the same time the government went beyond the Vannovskii Commission recommendations by issuing the 29 July 1899 Temporary Rules, which empowered special boards to conscript students involved in disorders, for varying periods of military service. The idea for the rules was Witte's. Witte carefully counterbalanced his earlier liberalism by urging a move that even the arch-reactionary K. P. Pobedonostsev had opposed a few years earlier.[71] The Temporary Rules ran up against the solid opposition of Minister of War Kuropatkin, who told the tsar that the army resented any implication that the barracks were a reform school. None-

---

69. TsGIA, f. 733, op. 151, d. 244.
70. TsGIA, f. 733, op. 226, d. 111.
71. The case for Witte's role rests on two sources. The first is the 1 March 1901 entry in A. A. Polovtsev's diary, where he records Kuropatkin's complaint as well as the war minister's assertion that the idea came from Witte ("Dnevnik A. A. Polovtseva," *Krasnyi Arkhiv* 3 (1923): 87). The second is a letter from Witte to Interior Minister Plehve, written in the summer of 1902, defending the rules as a measure that furthered the students' "moral education" (*vospitanie*). See TsGAOR, f. DP 00, 3ch. 78/1898, l. 215.

theless, the tsar approved the rules, not anticipating the trouble they would later cause the government.[72]

The Temporary Rules, Bogolepov's circulars, and the Vannovskii report all showed that government circles were sharply divided in their perceptions of the student movement and how to deal with it. While Vannovskii denied that the student movement had any political overtones, the Ministry of Education issued a secret circular in April 1900 warning all curators that the major purpose of the student movement was to foment anti-government political agitation.[73]

The Moscow Okhrana meanwhile argued that it should no longer investigate student disorders, on the grounds that the student movement was academic rather than political. Furthermore, the Okhrana contended, the 29 July Temporary Rules covered all student protesters and thus superseded previous procedures whereby some student demonstrators had been prosecuted under Article 1035 of the Criminal Code or Article 318 of the Statute of Punishments. After all, the Temporary Rules implied that the government now regarded student protests as a separate category of disturbance. S. V. Zubatov listed another reason why the Okhrana should no longer investigate student protests. By its very nature, the student movement differed from the revolutionary movement, in that student protests were of a mass character. They were spontaneous outbursts, with many participants, unlike the revolutionary movement, and student matters overloaded the strained resources of the Political Police.[74]

At the same time Minister of the Interior D. S. Sipiagin issued a directive to the local police on how to deal with the students. He warned them to avoid a repetition of the 1899 Rumiantsev Square incident by exercising a "lenient" attitude toward ordinary rowdiness during the 1900 student holidays. But he told the police to suppress any large street demonstrations and to hand over students apprehended in such disturbances to the special boards established by the Temporary Rules.[75]

In short, the 1899 strike produced a potentially disruptive countermeasure—the draft—but no fundamental consensus within the government about basic policy toward the student movement. Overall the reaction to the strike was surprisingly mild. Most students arrested in 1899

---

72. Solov'ëv, *Samoderzhavie i dvorianstvo*, p. 143.
73. TsGIA, f. 733, op. 151, d. 199.
74. TsGAOR, f. DP OO, 3ch. 78/1898, l. 215 (letter of Zubatov to L. A. Rataev, 18 September 1899).
75. TsGAOR, f. DP OO, 3ch. 78/1898, l. 73.

were allowed to return to their studies. The tsar, disregarding the advice of his uncle, accepted the spirit of the Vannovskii report, that the strike reflected police stupidity and structural problems within the universities rather than outside revolutionary agitation. Such an appraisal of the student movement strengthened the case against the 1884 Statute and especially against those provisions that denied the corporate identity of the student body.

There was, however, another side to the strike. Unlike previous student disturbances, the 1899 strike focused on fighting for a presumption of right stemming not only from status as a student but also from status as a Russian subject. For the first time students engaged in nationwide and sustained collective protest over an issue—inviolability of person—that transcended narrow corporate concerns. It was ironic, but from the point of view of the government potentially disquieting, that the furious reaction to the Rumiantsev Square incident broke out not because of, but, rather, in opposition to revolutionary political sentiments. (It will be recalled that the first reaction of politically committed students was to ignore the episode; because they did not expect a *Rechtsstaat,* evidence of police arbitrariness enraged them less.) The strike was a mass movement, not the work of an ardent minority. What this showed was that a relatively large group, concentrated in the major cities of the empire, had developed certain expectations and was prepared to fight for them. If the government chose to ignore these expectations, the student movement could well take a more radical turn.

Although the 1899–1900 academic year passed quietly, without major student disorders, the 1899 strike made a clear impression on the *studenchestvo.* For some students, including many former members of the Saint Petersburg Organization Committee, the experience of the strike steered them toward a personal commitment to the revolutionary movement. Iordanskii emphasized the role played by veterans of the strike in preparing the way for the demise of economism in Saint Petersburg Social Democratic circles.[76] The student strike showed even the vast majority who shunned politics that their protest could make a public impression and force the government to listen to their demands. As a Riga student pamphlet proclaimed:

> 1899 showed us that (1) the Russian *studenchestvo* can successfully and intelligently function as a clearly defined and separate group, (2) that active protest from this group can arouse strong concern and confusion in government

76. Iordanskii, "Missiia P. S. Vannovskovo," p. 130.

circles, and (3) that the Russian government correctly perceives in the student movement symptoms of discontent which it must suppress at all costs. For the government the *studenchestvo* is an especially dangerous enemy.[77]

The 1899 strike left another legacy. Those who had consigned the glories of the *studenchestvo* to history now had to admit that the students had shown unexpected vitality. Such songs as "Nagaechka" entered the student subculture as new symbols of comradeship and defiance. If not a victory, the 1899 strike at least came to be seen as a comforting reminder that the Russian *studenchestvo* was still unready to follow the bourgeois path of its West European counterparts.

The strike also renewed student efforts to develop an ideology of the student movement. In October 1899 the Kiev University United Council published an "Open Letter to the Kiev Studenchestvo" analyzing the significance of the 1899 strike and outlining possible directions for the student movement.[78] The council admitted that it was still difficult for students to understand the broader significance of what they had done but argued that the 1899 strike had proven two points. First, the breadth and intensity of the strike, as well as the ability of the *studenchestvo* to unite around a liberal-political rather than a narrow corporate platform, belied the Marxist assertion that student protest was unimportant or that students were too heterogeneous to count as a political force. Second, the student strike gave the Russian general public an example of how citizens could fight for their rights. The students had shown that the political task of the hour was to forge broad coalitions based on widely acceptable demands such as legal rights or administrative accountability—coalitions that, by ignoring potentially divisive issues, could unite wide sections of Russian society into a powerful political force. In this regard the *studenchestvo* could play *the* decisive role. To a certain extent, therefore, the Kiev students accepted Mogilianskii's tactical conclusions, outlined in his *kassa* manifesto, while rejecting his characterization of the *studenchestvo* as a bourgeois group.

The letter asked the students to ponder some basic questions. Was it possible to unite the student movement on a liberal-political or even on a corporate platform? Could either a central student bureau, a newspaper, or periodic national student conferences serve as a focal point for the student movement? (The council recommended a student journal

77. Tsentral'nyi Gosudarstvennyi Istoricheskii Arkhiv Moskvy (hereafter referred to as TsGIAM), f. 459, op. 7, d. 5291.
78. TsGAOR, f. 124, op. 8, ed. kh. 201/1899.

that would propagandize left-wing views but pay more attention to student life than journals such as *Rabochaia Mysl'* or *Vpered*.) Finally, how could the *zemliachestva* and other student organizations adapt themselves to the lessons of the 1899 strike?

"What now?" was also a question that bothered students at other universities. In Moscow the 1899–1900 academic year saw growing tension between the *zemliachestva,* who wanted to keep the student movement within corporate bounds, and leftists, who tried to create political organizations and forge links to Social Democratic and workers' groups outside the university. In early 1900, radicals grouped in the Chernigov and Voronezh *zemliachestva* elected an Executive Committee to organize a national student conference and lay the groundwork for a coordinated student movement, with a newspaper and central organization.[79] The new Executive Committee was headed by the twenty-five-year-old Nikolai Rudniev, a landowner's son from Voronezh who had already been arrested for participating in the 1896 and 1899 disturbances. Rudniev and his friends succeeded in convening a national student conference, which met in Odessa on 16 June 1900. Unfortunately for the twenty-nine delegates, however, the police knew all about their plans and arrested the entire group on the first day of the conference. The documents confiscated by the police showed that two major issues preoccupied the conference: what, if any, relationship should there be between the workers' and student movements; and how should left-wing students react to the unwillingness of the majority to go beyond corporate or broadly liberal concerns?[80]

One memorandum, written by twenty-one-year-old Archid Dzaparidze, a reservoir manager's son from Tiflis, questioned the hostility of his fellow Moscow University delegates to student corporatism. The determination with which students fought for issues they cared strongly about promised more long-term results than doctrinaire attempts to deny the legitimacy of student protests on the grounds that the workers were allegedly more important. After all, Dzaparidze argued, there was nothing wrong with any group fighting for its own concerns. If other social groups emulated the students and defended their own rights, then in time the autocracy would face a serious situation. The student movement had its own particular character and purpose, one created by the

---

79. TsGIA, f. 733, op. 151, d. 72, l. 116. This is the Okhrana report on the 1900 student conference. The report includes letters and other written materials taken from the arrested students.

80. Ibid.; also TsGAOR, f. 102, 1 ed. kh. 90, 3ch. 2LE/1898, ll. 111–116.

overall position of the universities in Russian society: "[The task of student organizations] is to maintain a spirit of protest . . . against the efforts of the government to turn us into civil servants devoid of any sense of public responsibility, who carry out orders from on high without even daring to criticize them. . . . The task of . . . the student movement is to protect those ideals . . . against [government attempts to destroy them] by promises of careers and material rewards."[81] The memorandum also cautioned student organizations against trying to link student protest with the labor movement. While Dzaparidze praised "those few" students who were trying to make contact with the workers, he would have reminded the conference that a vast gap separated the world of the student from that of the worker and that the two strands of social protest were fundamentally different.

FROM STRIKE TO STREET:
THE 1901 DEMONSTRATIONS

For obvious reasons, the 1900 conference was stillborn. Although no clear answers emerged to the questions raised by the Kiev United Council and the delegates to the 1900 conference, student protest continued to take its own unpredictable course. On 23 November 1900, a group of Saint Petersburg students disrupted *Sons of Israel,* an anti-Semitic play being staged at the Malyi Theater.[82] The management knew that it faced trouble and refused to sell tickets to anyone in a student uniform. But enough students made their way into the theater to cause a scene, which led to the suspension of thirty demonstrators by the university administration. *Skhodki* met in the university to discuss possible student reactions, but the majority of participants rejected a sympathy strike on the grounds that the Malyi Theater demonstration, albeit for a good cause, took place outside the university and did not affect the direct corporate interests of the students.[83] But these November *skhodki* had an important consequence: the students elected an Organization Committee to direct any future protests by the student body.

In Kiev University, the fall term had seen a number of lively *skhodki,* none of which appeared to have the sanction of the university's United Council. Politically radical students complained about the "narrow cor-

81. TsGIA, f. 733, op. 151, d. 72, l. 116.
82. Hoover Institution, Boris Nikolaevskii Collection, file 109, box 6, packet 60, no. 146.
83. Ibid.

porate character" of these *skhodki*.[84] For example, on 13 November 1900, the Kiev students met to discuss two comrades who had allegedly beaten up a cab driver after refusing to pay him. Some students complained that the two had "violated the honor of the student uniform," and the *skhodka* demanded their expulsion from the university. Other *skhodki* met to protest the poor lectures of Professor O. O. Eikhelman on the juridical faculty, and the actions of two students who had allegedly stolen a gold ring from a singer at a local restaurant.[85]

The university inspectorate took down the names of several students at the 13 and 15 November *skhodki*. A university court then sentenced four students to confinement in the *kartser,* the university jail. Much to the consternation of the district curator, who complained that Russian students lacked the good sportsmanship of their German counterparts (who accepted the *kartser* as a hallowed part of university life), two students, Tseretelli and Pokotilov, refused to enter the *kartser*. The authorities then expelled them.[86]

The expulsion touched off an immediate reaction from the Kiev students: a well-attended *skhodka* took over the main university auditorium on 7 December to demand the return of Pokotilov and Tseretelli and the abolition of the *kartser*. After the students refused orders to disperse, the Kiev governor-general asked the university rector if he could handle the situation on his own. When he replied that he could not, the governor-general sent an infantry battalion and a Cossack mounted detachment to the university. The students finally left the building after presenting their demands to the rector. The university authorities noted the names of 406 students attending the *skhodka*. Of these, a special disciplinary board sentenced 183 to immediate military service on the basis of the July 1899 Temporary Rules. Two hundred and seventeen students received less severe punishments.[87]

By applying the July 1899 Temporary Rules for the first time, the government showed the *studenchestvo* that its new strategy for quelling student disorders was no empty threat. Minister of the Interior Sipiagin clearly expected a lot of trouble when the *studenchestvo* heard the news from Kiev and seemed to welcome the opportunity to hurl down the

84. Ibid.
85. TsGIA, f. 733, op. 151, d. 199 (this file contains the reports of the curator of the Kiev Educational District to the minister of education).
86. Ibid.
87. Gusiatnikov, *Revoliutsionnoe studencheskoe*, p. 45.

gauntlet. In a secret circular issued immediately after the Kiev affair, he warned the local authorities in university towns to quell any street demonstrations as quickly as possible, employing all means up to and including military force.[88]

When the students returned from their Christmas holidays to take stock of the situation, they found themselves caught between their sense of duty to their Kiev comrades and their fear of military induction. Adding to the general feeling of helplessness was the widespread belief that the Russian public would do no more to help the students than it had in 1899. The Kharkov University United Council told the students there that "we can rely only on ourselves," a sentiment echoed practically everywhere else.[89] But alongside the confessions of weakness, two themes emerged in the dozens of hastily prepared proclamations issued in January 1901: moral duty, and comradely solidarity. The Odessa Organization Committee urged the students not to recognize the Temporary Rules, which "deprive us of the right to discuss our corporate concerns and which subject us to demeaning punishment for the expression of comradely and corporate solidarity."[90] A group of Moscow University medical students warned:

> If we don't do anything, then both the government and the public will see that all that is needed to extinguish the student movement are the Temporary Rules. Then the government will manage to convince the public that if the Temporary Rules suffice to cow the students, they can't be really serious [about their various demands]. As a result the public will come to think that the whole student movement was nothing more than the work of a few troublemakers. The students would then lose public sympathy, their only hope for eventual success. . . . We must act now.[91]

Another pamphlet, signed by "267 women students," foreshadowed the important role women would play in the student demonstrations that would soon be mounted against the Temporary Rules. The pamphlet echoed once again the common theme that "if in the best years of our lives we think about 'caution and moderation,' then what will we be like later on?" Only the students, not the oppressed masses, could fight against arbitrariness (*proizvol*). Moreover, the pamphlet declared, Mos-

88. TsGAOR, f. DP 00, 3ch. 78/1898, l. 98 (Sipiagin circular of 4 December 1900). Also l. 107, circular of 27 February 1901.

89. TsGIA, f. 733, op. 151, d. 64, l. 45.

90. TsGIA, f. 733, op. 151, d. 64, l. 42.

91. TsGIA, f. 733, op. 151, d. 241, l. 115.

cow's students faced the moral obligation of "restoring to the *studenchestvo* the general respect it used to enjoy."[92]

The pamphlets reveal many conflicting emotions: anxiety about the students' public image, loneliness, fear, despair that the public would once again leave the students to fight alone. The students were afraid of fighting but knew that somehow the tradition of the *studenchestvo* demanded that they must do so. At bottom was the nagging question: if we do not fight now, what will we be like as adults?

About this time a long poem began circulating around Saint Petersburg. Entitled "Togda i Teper'," the poem (quoted at the beginning of Chapter 2) appealed to the students to live up to their traditions.[93] Such appeals had no immediate effect. Most Moscow University students seemed cowed by the Temporary Rules. In the third week of January, *skhodki* at Kharkov, Kiev, and Moscow universities called for protest strikes, but most students ignored the resolutions and continued to attend classes.[94]

In Saint Petersburg University the Organization Committee elected after the November Malyi Theater incident tried to organize a protest strike. But it ran into the opposition of the *kassa*, whose current leadership had reverted to the pre-1899 view that student disorders were futile; the Kiev affair proved that they were dangerous as well.[95] When the Organization Committee issued an appeal to the Saint Petersburg public to support the students, the *kassa* published a counterappeal rejecting the Organization Committee's flirtation with the liberals and its efforts to organize a student protest against the Temporary Rules:

> Students! Two hundred of our comrades have been sent into the army. We should protest. But how? We're told to start disorders [*bezporiadki*]. But in fact disorders lead to passivity [*molchalinstvo*]. The majority participates unwillingly because they are afraid of being called cowards. But they hope to squirm away at the first opportune moment, leaving the most talented and dedicated comrades to bear the brunt of the danger. For most students disorders provide an education in TREACHERY. It is not true that disorders strengthen the oppositional spirit. The latter is the cause, not the result, of disorders and is created by the general conditions of life. The student dis-

92. TsGAOR, f. 124, op. 10, ed. kh. 441, 1901, l. 55.
93. Handwritten copy in TsGAOR, f. DO, 3ch. 125t. 1/1898, l. 93a.
94. Curators' reports and student pamphlets in TsGAOR, f. 124, op. 10, ed. kh. 441, 1901; TsGIA, f. 733, op. 151, d. 64.
95. For a comment on the mood of Saint Petersburg students and their fear of the Temporary Rules, see POA, XVIb(7), folder 6 (letter of Nikolai Rudevich). See also G. Engel' and V. Gorokhov, *Iz istorii studencheskovo dvizheniia 1899–1906* (Moscow, 1908), p. 20.

orders are valves . . . through which the accumulated energy of the students drains away. The proof of this is that even successful disorders, like the Vetrova demonstration and the first 1899 strike, are followed by a period of passivity. . . . The political development of the *studenchestvo* proceeds not BECAUSE OF BUT DESPITE DISORDERS.[96]

The *kassa* tried to convince the Saint Petersburg students that the only real beneficiary of the student disorders was the police, who were able to score an impressive series of cheap victories at the expense of the students. It was time to realize that students had to transcend their own corporate concerns and start struggling against the system as a whole.

> We should protest not with impotent flickers of rage but with STRUGGLE—struggle against the political system in Russia. . . . Comrades! Is it really true that we can protest only when they beat us or send us into the army? Is it true that we can protect only our own corporate interests and remain indifferent to the sufferings of those who don't wear a student uniform? . . . Is it true that the student with all his bourgeois narrowness can turn a deaf ear to the voice of the times and remain satisfied with the miserable demand that the rule of law should apply only to students? Is it true that the Russian student will not join the general battle for freedom, equality and brotherhood?[97]

The *kassa* ended its proclamation by reminding students that joining the revolutionary movement was not only most useful but also safest. The chances of being caught by the police and getting sent into the army were much higher for those participating in *skhodki* or strikes. If students wanted to change their tactics, the *kassa* suggested, they could make a useful beginning by giving 5 percent of their monthly income to the revolutionary parties.

Although the *kassa* proclamation was an interesting restatement of the conventional Marxist position on the student movement, its practical effect was small, since most Saint Petersburg students were already too frightened by the Temporary Rules to protest the fate of the Kiev comrades. They had good reason to be afraid. When the Organization Committee called a protest *skhodka* for 25 January, the administration sentenced twenty-eight ringleaders to varying terms in the army. One of these students, E. K. Proskuriatov, soon committed suicide.[98]

96. Engel' and Gorokhov, *Iz istorii*, p. 21.
97 Ibid.
98. For a list of the names and social origins of those involved, see TsGIA, f. 733, op. 151, d. 241, l. 110. Of the twenty-eight, nine were sons of civil servants, three sons of priests, two each were sons of doctors, engineers, officers, and teachers, and one each was the son of a lawyer, a mining official, a railroad official, and a *feldsher*. The social origins

What was left of the Organization Committee issued a frantic appeal on 6 February, entreating the Saint Petersburg University student body to remember the glorious student generation of the 1860s and uphold the traditions of the *studenchestvo:* "Comrades, we are living through a critical moment! It is now a question of 'to be or not to be' for the Russian *studenchestvo* which for so many years has been the only vibrant force amid . . . the ugliness of Russian life." [99] But this appeal was no more successful than that of the 25 January *skhodka* in convincing the student body to strike.

By the beginning of February, some students were writing home that "the time had come to bury the student movement." [100] The Temporary Rules had made their point, and the promising new tactic of 1899, the strike, had failed to mobilize student support for the 210 already drafted into the army. It was at this point that the student movement took another major turn. Since the calls for a strike met with little success, various students trying to organize a protest movement began thinking about street demonstrations against the Temporary Rules. Even if most students stayed away, enough might come to ensure an impressive turnout, especially in large centers such as Saint Petersburg. Furthermore, demonstrations offered the prospect of encouraging other social groups to express solidarity with the students.

As was the case with the 1899 strike, the idea to organize the February and March 1901 demonstrations cannot be traced to any specific individual or group. What is clear is that by the beginning of February the Saint Petersburg University Organization Committee had been able to establish an informal network of student representatives from several men's and women's *VUZy* in the city.[101] A figure who would play an important part in the organization of the demonstrations was the young Vladimir Levitskii, then beginning his career in the revolutionary movement. Another important participant was Pokotilov, one of the two Kiev students whose refusal to enter the *kartser* had sparked the crisis.

By Levitskii's account, Pokotilov at this time was a rather neurotic character, an alcoholic whose face was heavily scarred with eczema. Like many others who came to take an active role in the student move-

---

of the remaining four students were not indicated. For an illuminating account of what happened to the students during their brief stint in the army, see L. A. Sobolev, "Vospominaniia studenta-soldata," *Byloe,* no. 5 (1906).

99. TsGIA, f. 733, op. 151, d. 242, l. 43.
100. TsGAOR, f. 102, op. 226, ed. kh. 3ch. 125t. 1–A/1898, l. 48.
101. TsGAOR, f. 102, op. 226, ed. kh. 3ch. 125t. 1–A/1898, l. 10.

ment, Pokotilov had no clearly formed political views except an obsession with "comradeship."[102] By the beginning of February, Pokotilov had arrived in Saint Petersburg, where he began intense agitation to get the Saint Petersburg students to support their Kiev comrades. At one gathering he took violent exception to those who said that the student movement was finished—leaping onto a chair, he screeched, "We need a demonstration!" and then fell off the chair in hysterics.[103]

In contrast, the hostile stance of the economist Soiuz Bor'by dlia Osvobozhdeniia Rabochevo Klassa, still the largest Social Democratic group in Saint Petersburg, complicated preparations for the demonstration.[104] The Soiuz Bor'by maintained its suspicious attitude toward the student movement and told its members not to cooperate with students who came asking for help in organizing a public demonstration.

Unlike the situation in 1899, however, there was now a new trend in Russian Social Democracy, expressed in the journal *Iskra*. *Iskra* welcomed the student movement and urged Social Democrats and workers to ignore the Soiuz Bor'by and give the students active support. The student movement became a focal point in the argument between the Soiuz Bor'by and *Iskra*. In an important *Iskra* article entitled "Conscription of the 183 Students," Vladimir Lenin urged Social Democrats and workers to support the student movement:

> The working class has already begun the struggle for its liberation. But it should understand that this important struggle carries with it important obligations. The worker cannot free himself without having at the same time liberated all the people from despotism. Above all he must respond to and support every political protest. The best members of our educated classes have proven with the blood of thousands of revolutionaries their willingness to shake off the dust of bourgeois society and join the socialist ranks. That worker who can look on with equanimity as the government uses the army against the students is not worthy of bearing the name *socialist*. The student has [in the past] gone to the aid of the worker—the worker must go to the aid of the student.[105]

In conclusion, Lenin urged workers to participate in street demonstrations.

---

102. V. Levitskii, *Za chetvert' veka* (Moscow, 1926), pp. 94–96.
103. Ibid., p. 148.
104. Ibid., p. 144. See also N. V. Iukhneva, "Studencheskoe dvizhenie v Peterburgskom universitete i pervye demonstratsii 1901 goda," *Ocherki po istorii Leningradskovo universiteta* (Leningrad, 1962).
105. "Otdacha v soldaty 183-kh studentov," *Iskra*, no. 2 (1901).

In January and February 1901 there was as yet no *Iskra* group in Saint Petersburg. In March two smaller socialist groups, the Rabochee Znamia and Sotsialist, would proclaim their allegiance to the *Iskra* line, but until then, they too opposed the idea of actively helping the student movement and collaborating in a public demonstration.[106]

Meanwhile, events began to move at a more rapid pace. On 14 February Peter Karpovich, a disgruntled ex-student, showed up for an appointment with Minister of Education Bogolepov, calmly pulled out a revolver, and shot him fatally in the chest. News of the assassination exacerbated the tension in the atmosphere. At the same time certain student members of the Soiuz Bor'by rejected the economists' negative attitude toward the student movement and began agitating for street demonstrations. One such student, A. N. Karasik, founded an organization entitled the Soiuz Spravedlivykh. It consisted of himself and a hectograph machine, but he succeeded in fooling the Okhrana and many students into thinking that there was a formidable organization ready to take the student movement on a new tactical course.[107] Leadership was coming from other sources as well. Vladimir Fridolin, one of the few members of the Saint Petersburg University Organization Committee who had escaped the arrests of late January, started making the rounds of the city's *VUZy* and recruited a Delegate Conference to discuss tactical options available to the students. Like Pokotilov (who was now working on his own, because other students found him too hysterical to include in their plans), Fridolin had no specific political views. Levitskii described him as "an idealist, a little unworldly, trusting and impractical, burning with the desire to 'suffer' and share the fate of his comrades."[108]

After a few inconclusive meetings, the Delegate Conference met on 16 February to decide whether to call a student demonstration at the Kazan Cathedral for 19 February, the anniversary of the emancipation of the serfs. To reach the apartment where the meeting took place, the sixteen delegates had to pass several cages housing the inmates of a mental institution located on the first floor. To the accompaniment of a strange assortment of sounds, the argument about the demonstration began. V. V. Filatov, the delegate from the Mining Institute, attacked the idea, arguing that the demonstration would fail and demoralize the *stu-*

---

106. Iukhneva, "Studencheskoe dvizhenie"; Levitskii, *Za chetvert' veka,* p. 144.

107. Levitskii, *Za chetvert' veka,* p. 130. One of Karasik's pamphlets can be found in TsGAOR, f. 102, op. 226, ed. kh. 3ch. 125t. 1–A/1898, l. 30.

108. Levitskii, *Za chetvert' veka,* p. 130. For a police report on Fridolin, see TsGAOR, f. 102, op. 226, ed. kh. 3ch. 125t. 1–A/1898, l. 30.

denchestvo even further. He counseled abandoning purely student-based protests in favor of working with revolutionary groups. Opposing Filatov was Vasilii Adamov, an army officer and a friend of Fridolin's, who argued that a student street demonstration would have a major impact on the public and would undermine the government's political position.[109]

After long and inconclusive debate, the delegates decided to make a rough count of the students they thought would be ready to take to the streets, two thousand being the agreed-upon minimum necessary to ensure the success of a demonstration. The count came up five hundred short. At that point, the police broke in and led the whole group to jail, past the cages of the screaming inmates.

Much to the surprise of the police, the arrests disrupted but did not cripple the plans for a student demonstration. One student, a certain Baumstein, escaped arrest and distributed flysheets calling for students to assemble at Kazan Square at noon on the nineteenth. Rumors that the demonstrations had been called off kept the turnout low, but about four hundred students, mostly women, assembled at the appointed time. The police ringed the small group (some accounts speak of beatings) and arrested 244 students and onlookers, who were released after the police recorded their names. Of the 244, 128 were female students, 71 were male students, and 45 were nonstudents.[110]

Although the turnout for the 19 February demonstration was relatively small, those student leaders who had managed to escape arrest were encouraged by the public sympathy the demonstration attracted, especially since the demonstration had not been widely publicized and many students erroneously believed it had been postponed at the last minute. After the arrest of the Delegate Conference, the Saint Petersburg University Organization Committee issued an appeal to "all classes of society" to join in a public demonstration in front of Kazan Cathedral on 4 March, a Sunday. The Organization Committee called the demonstration to defend "basic human rights" and invited the public to join forces with the students. One veteran of the student movement noted two distinct tendencies among the proponents of the Sunday demonstration. Whereas the Organization Committee appealed to the middle-class educated public, other students, Marxists who did not agree with the negativism of the Soiuz Bor'by, attempted to win workers' support for the

109. Levitskii, *Za chetvert' veka*, pp. 154–155.
110. TsGAOR, f. 102, op. 226, ed. kh. 3ch. 125t. 1–A/1898, l. 21.

demonstrations.[111] Although these efforts were generally unsuccessful, the students did succeed in publicizing the planned demonstration.

Contemporary police reports, as well as some leading historians, ascribed the major role in the preparation and organization of the 4 March demonstration to the revolutionary movement.[112] But available evidence fails to support this contention. The impetus for the demonstration came from the students. And *Iskra* itself attacked Social Democratic organizations for not participating in planning the demonstrations—not only in Saint Petersburg, but in Kharkov and Kiev as well.[113]

The 4 March Kazan Square protest, one of the largest street demonstrations the Russian capital had ever seen, made a profound impact on the Russian public and showed once again the ability of the Russian student movement to embarrass the government and raise the political temperature of the nation.

All morning, crowds of students streamed toward Kazan Cathedral. One eyewitness, the writer R. V. Ivanov-Razumnik, who was then a student at Saint Petersburg University, responded to the call of the University Organization Committee to protest the Temporary Rules and made his way to the square:

> Time of action—midday on the fourth of March 1901; scene of action—Kazan Cathedral Square in Saint Petersburg. A vast crowd overflows the square: students of every branch of learning, the majority regular members of the university but also including a large number of post-graduates—technologists, mining and railway engineers. There are young girls from the higher courses for women. There are also many ordinary members of the public, not a few of whom are middle-aged. In the crowd I catch sight of the grey-bearded figure of the well-known journalist and writer, N. F. Annensky, with his usual expression of gaiety and enthusiasm. Standing near me are two rising stars of the Marxist firmament, P. B. Struve and Professor M. I. Tugan-Baranovskii of our university. . . . But youth is predominant, thronging the whole huge square in a closely packed mass. Other spectators jostle on the pavements of the Nevskii Prospekt, some simply out of curiosity, some out of secret sympathy. All are aware that exactly at noon, when the cannon fires from the Petropavlovsky fortress, the students are due to march down the Nevskii Prospekt in a demonstration.[114]

111. Engel' and Gorokhov, *Iz istorii,* p. 33; Levitskii, *Za chetvert' veka,* p. 162. According to Levitskii, the Soiuz Bor'by changed its mind at the last minute and decided to support the 4 March demonstration.

112. For example, see Allan Wildman, *The Making of a Workers' Revolution* (Chicago, 1967), p. 211; Gusiatnikov, *Revoliutsionnoe studencheskoe,* p. 56; TsGAOR, f. DP 00, 3ch. 78/1898, l. 160 (Sipiagin circular of 5 December 1901).

113. *Iskra,* no. 3 (1901).

114. R. V. Ivanov-Razumnik, *Tiur'my i ssylki* (New York, 1953), p. 19.

Another participant in the 4 March demonstration, Ariadna Tyr-kova-Williams, recalled nearly fifty years later the deep impression made by the students:

> For the first time in my life I saw a large street demonstration. When politics hits the streets, it can produce noisy flashes of human freedom or it can peter out in silence. . . . The beginning of that Sunday was quiet. But as soon as we reached the Nevskii, we could see right away that something had deeply disturbed the life of Saint Petersburg. The gates of all the buildings . . . were shut tight, as if it were the middle of the night. The trams didn't run. From time to time a cab-driver appeared . . . but quickly turned onto a side street. . . . Everybody was heading toward Kazan Cathedral. They went in small groups, composed mainly of students. Their young faces shone with a proud sign: WE ARE GOING TO PROTEST.[115]

Accompanied by the noted economist Mikhail Tugan-Baranovskii, Tyrkova-Williams disregarded the friendly advice of a mounted Cossack to go home. She edged her way through the crowd toward the steps of the cathedral, where students raised a large sign: "Down with the Temporary Rules." The sea of student caps and sheepskin hats, the "unofficial uniform" of the *kursistki,* left no doubt that the overwhelming majority of the demonstrators were students. Buoyed by the large turnout and rumors of successful student street demonstrations in Moscow and Kharkov, the crowd was in high spirits.[116]

Riding into the crowd without warning, the Cossacks pushed hundreds of people against the steps of the cathedral, blocking all avenues of escape. Then the beatings began. The government communiqué later said that the students started the violence by throwing rocks at the Cossacks' horses, but most onlookers believed that the attack on the crowd was unnecessary and unprovoked.

> A girl was hanging on to the bridle of a Cossack horse . . . the rider knocked her hat off with his *nagaika*. Her hair streamed out around her face, blood flowed down her cheek. Not far away two students were fending off the *nagaiki,* covering their faces with bloody arms. Two policemen were dragging off a screaming girl.[117]

115. A. Tyrkova-Williams, *Na putiakh k svobode* (New York, 1953), pp. 67ff.
116. Ibid.
117. Ibid., p. 69. Numerous accounts of the demonstration can be found, including a long pamphlet from the Saint Petersburg University Organization Committee describing the events of 4 March (TsGAOR, f. DO, 3ch. 125t. 1, 1/1898, l. 162). The official government communiqué was issued on 7 March. Long accounts, exaggerating the casualties, can also be found in *Iskra* and *Revoliutsionnaia Rossiia.*

As Tyrkova-Williams and her companion watched the chaotic scene, wanting to help but not knowing what to do, Peter Struve, the well-known writer and political thinker, bumped into them. He was waving his arms and yelling frantically:

> "The devil take them! How dare they? How dare they hit me on the legs with a *nagaika?* You understand?—me!" He pounded his coat to show where the *nagaika* had left its dirty marks. We were . . . horrified by what was going on around us. But life loves to mix tragedy with comedy. As I looked at his dishevelled red hair and red beard . . . and kept hearing his repetitive, disjointed, ridiculous cry, "me! me!" it was all I could do to keep from laughing.[118]

Soon it was over. By the bloodier standards of a later era, the demonstration of 4 March was a tame affair. Although there were wild rumors to the contrary, no one died or even suffered serious wounds. Under police escort, 775 people marched through a cold drizzle to jail. Most of the detainees were students, the numbers almost equally divided between men and women; the Russian *kursistka* was carrying a disproportionate share of the fight against the Temporary Rules.[119]

Their treatment in prison reflects the curious mixture of deference, paternalism, and repression that marked the old regime's attitude toward the *studenchestvo*. Ivanov-Razumnik recalls a not unpleasant experience: the jailers allowed the students to organize a theater, give lectures attended by the prison governor, hold chess championships, and receive ample parcels. One student's father, the well-known tobacco manufacturer Shapsal, sent in several shipments of ten thousand cigarettes each. "From the very first days of our stay we took so many liberties with the regulations that our prison life was converted into a kind of student picnic. Every cell resounded with shouts, laughter, songs, and choruses."[120] The prison also allowed the students liberal visiting rights:

> Men-students who had no relations in the city were visited by fictitious "fiancées," girl-students had their "fiancés." One of our company was visited by three "fiancées" at one and the same time, whereupon the Chief of Prison sent for the fortunate young man and begged him to state which of his "fiancées" was the real one. But that was the whole difficulty—none of them was. So after that the girls decided they would take turns to visit him. Noise and hilarity prevailed throughout these unusual prison visits.[121]

118. Tyrkova-Williams, *Na putiakh k svobode*, p. 70.
119. A police summary of the arrest list is in TsGAOR, f. 102, op. 226, ed. kh. 3ch. t1LB/1898. Of the arrestees, 349 were male students, 323 were female students, 24 were female teachers, and 79 (50 men and 29 women) were *raznochintsy* [*sic*].
120. Ivanov-Razumnik, *Tiur'my i ssylki*, p. 23.
121. Ibid.; translated and annotated by P. S. Squire as *The Memoirs of Ivanov-Razumnik* (London, 1965).

But the authorities drew the line when Ivanov-Razumnik asked for an evening's furlough to attend a subscription performance of the Moscow Art Theater. He told the Chief of the Prison that he promised "on his word of honor as a student" to return by midnight.

> The Chief of the Prison—a man of some irony—explained with great politeness and every appearance of gravity that he had all possible confidence in Mr. student's word of honor, but did not Mr. student think that out of some hundreds of men and women students there might be dozens whose pockets also contained identical tickets? He would readily release Mr. student on his word of honor, but in that case he would also have to release a whole crowd of people on the same basis. Did not Mr. student think that in many respects this would be inconvenient and for him, the Chief of Prison, even impossible? [122]

After a week all the arrestees appeared for cursory interrogations at which they were asked whether they belonged to revolutionary organizations and why they had participated in the 4 March demonstration. Almost all the students were expelled from their *VUZy* and forbidden residence in university towns for periods from one to three years.[123] The government was, however, clearly having second thoughts about applying the Temporary Rules. Furthermore, the apparent harshness of the penalties suffered by the Kazan Square demonstrators was mitigated by their speedy annulment. That summer the government allowed most conscripted and expelled students to reenter the *VUZy* for the fall term.[124]

If the students had wanted to stage a successful demonstration, win public sympathy, and exert pressure on the government to abrogate the Temporary Rules, then they had certainly succeeded. The demonstration proved that even a small minority of students could make an impact on the general public and the government:

> Exaggerated rumors flew across the city about a vicious attack by the Cossacks and police on the demonstrators. Saint Petersburg seethed with indignation. Saint Petersburg supported us. This was the first outburst of the liberation movement [*obshchestvennovo dvizheniia*]. Especially affected were the central quarters of the city, where the wealthier classes and the intelligentsia lived. We were later told that the workers were also angry. Maybe. I saw no workers either on the square or among the arrestees . . . the demonstration was a student affair, far from the concerns of the workers, but it deeply touched the educated public. Public opinion supported the students so unanimously that the government became confused. It realized that a certain turn-

---

122. Ibid., p. 27; trans., Squires, p. 6.
123. TsGAOR, f. 102, op. 226, ed. kh. 3ch. 125t. 1LB/1898, l. 99.
124. Ivanov-Razumnik, *Tiur'my i ssylki*, p. 27; Engel' and Gorokhov, *Iz istorii*, p. 40.

ing point had been reached on Kazan Square, that the opposition movement had received a new impetus.[125]

The news of the police brutality in Kazan Square, widely disseminated in a series of somewhat exaggerated bulletins put out by the Saint Petersburg University Organization Committee, finally touched off an academic strike in the capital's *VUZy*.[126] At the same time 150 writers, lawyers, and professional people sent a petition to the Ministry of Justice charging premeditated police brutality and asking for the punishment of those responsible.[127]

The Kazan Square demonstration also intensified conflicts within Russian Social Democracy. *Iskra* seized on the absence of workers at the demonstration to step up its attacks on economism and press its claims for hegemony in the Russian Social Democratic movement:

> There is no doubt that instead of a simple beating of the people by the authorities, the demonstration would have been the scene of a real battle between the people and the government if only the socialist groups . . . had appealed to the workers [to join the demonstration] and organized separate demonstrations on the outskirts of the city. . . . Some workers finally did come but they arrived too late.[128]

Events in other university towns—Moscow, Kharkov, Kiev, Tomsk— followed roughly the same pattern as the development of the student movement in Saint Petersburg. When the majority of students balked at striking to protest the Temporary Rules, a more committed minority embraced the idea of street demonstrations as a way out of a tactical dilemma.[129] Repression of the demonstrations or news of police brutality in other cities then induced the other students to strike. In all these cases there seemed to be no coordination between university towns, no prior plan, and certainly little or no collaboration with revolutionary groups or workers' organizations. Once again the student movement was following its own distinct rhythm.

In Kharkov, for example, the United Council made several unsuccessful appeals in January for a strike to support the drafted Kiev students. After these appeals failed, some radical students planned a street

125. Tyrkova-Williams, *Na putiakh k svobode*, p. 73.
126. Police reports describing the strike are found in TsGAOR, f. DO, 3ch. 125t. 1/1898, l. 161.
127. TsGAOR, f. DO, 3ch. 125t., 1/1898, l. 198.
128. *Iskra*, no. 3 (1901).
129. Engel' and Gorokhov, *Iz istorii*, p. 26.

demonstration on 19 February and secured the support of local Social Democratic groups that were more sympathetic to the *Iskra* line than were their counterparts in Saint Petersburg.[130] But, as if to underscore the independence of the student movement, the students disregarded the advice of the Social Democrats to hold the demonstration in the evening so that more workers could participate. When a small group of students assembled in front of the main cathedral at noon on the nineteenth, the anniversary of the emancipation of the serfs, they distributed pamphlets couched in remarkably moderate tones: besides demanding the repeal of the Temporary Rules, they praised the "Tsar Liberator" Alexander II. When the small crowd of students started marching to the university, mounted Cossacks encircled and beat them. Pro-strike forces in the university and the Technological Institute began to gain the upper hand, and a strike finally broke out after news of the Kazan Square demonstration reached Kharkov.[131]

In Moscow University an Executive Committee formed at the end of January to direct the student protest against the Temporary Rules. Although this committee included several students who would in later life join the revolutionary movement, it at first proceeded quite cautiously, waiting until events elsewhere made the Moscow students more willing to fight.[132] When news came of the 19 February demonstrations in Saint Petersburg and Kharkov, the Executive Committee distributed a questionnaire asking how many students would appear at a *skhodka* on 23 February. Nine hundred and seventeen said they would, although far fewer actually came.

As soon as the *skhodka* began, a large crowd of students and their relatives and friends gathered in front of the university and watched the students inside hang out a large banner proclaiming "Down with the Temporary Rules!" A crowd of gendarmes then stormed into the auditorium and began to escort out the three hundred students who refused to disperse to the Manezh, a large exhibition hall and cavalry barracks across the square from the university. (The authorities hastily cleared out the bird show then running in the hall.) A long chain of police separated the arrested students from the enthusiastic crowd of well-wishers.

130. On the Kharkov student demonstrations, see the report of the acting minister of education, N. A. Zver'ev, to Tsar Nicholas II, 22 February 1901, in TsGIA, f. 733, op. 151, d. 64, l. 24. See also *Iskra*, no. 2 (1901).

131. TsGIA, f. 733, op. 151, d. 64 (report of Kharkov curator to acting minister of education, 13 March 1901).

132. On the activities of the Moscow University Executive Committee during this period, see the unpublished memoirs of V. I. Orlov in AIISSSR, f. 5, op. 5, ed. kh. 58.

A member of the Executive Committee, N. V. Korshun (a future member of the Social Revolutionary party), climbed a street lamp and called on the students in the crowd to join the group being led to the Manezh. About two hundred students then broke through the police lines and joined their arrested comrades.[133] After a boisterous and rowdy night in the Manezh, where a crowd of sympathizers stayed all night and entertained those inside with choruses of "Nagaechka," "Dubinushka," and other student songs, the police transferred the male students to the Butyrka prison and released the women.

Of the 358 Moscow University students on the arrest list, 32.5 percent were juridical students, 8.6 percent came from the history and philology faculty, 8.6 percent were mathematics students, 24.3 percent were students of the natural sciences, and 26 percent were medical students. (In other terms, 9.8 percent of the students from the history faculty, 6.7 percent of those from mathematics, 13.9 percent from the natural sciences, 6.9 percent of the juridical students, and 8.1 percent of the medical students went to the Manezh.) Of the students' fathers, 15.2 percent were nobles, 22 percent were middle-level civil servants, and 11.3 percent were either lower-level civil servants or civil servants of unspecified rank; 17.2 percent of the arrested students came from the *meshchanstvo*, 9 percent from the *kupechestvo*, 7 percent from the priestly estate, 7 percent from the honorary citizenry, and 5 percent from the peasantry.[134] Eighty-six percent had graduated from high schools outside Moscow. Once again the natural sciences faculty was significantly overrepresented, as were students from provincial backgrounds. More than 60 percent were either first-course or second-course students, but this reflected the general proportion of these students in the university population. As was the case in 1899, students from all estates were involved in the movement. The students on the arrest list this time were, however, a smaller proportion of the general student body than in 1899, representing that minority which was clearly ready to defy the express orders of the police and go to jail. Police interrogation reports show that the major reason for these students' decision to protest was comradely solidarity and anger at the Temporary Rules.[135]

133. Ibid.
134. These figures are compiled on the basis of the arrest list in TsGAOR, f. 124, op. 10, ed. kh. 441, 1901.
135. G. A. Vesëlaia, "Massovye obshchestvennye vystupleniia Moskovskovo studenchestva, v kontse 19ovo–nachale 20ovo veka," Kandidat dissertation, Moscow State University, 1974, p. 117.

The events at the Manezh stirred up the city and led to an unexpected but sizable street demonstration the following Sunday, 25 February. Crowds of students gathering in front of the governor-general's house on the Tverskoi Bul'var were soon joined by several hundred onlookers, including a few workers. The crowd marched up and down the central streets of the city, singing songs and ignoring the repeated demands of the police that they disperse.[136] The Executive Committee was heartened by the public support, especially the alleged turnout of "many workers," but obviously felt that the crowds came to support the students' specific grievances rather than to make a general political protest against the regime.[137] The next day the committee asked the students to refrain from further demonstrations, since the public had already shown its sympathy and more street outbursts would only result in needless arrests. This position provoked a sharp retort from *Iskra:*

> These partisans of a "purely student movement" naively assume that the crowd demonstrated, sacrificed itself, and took risks only to . . . influence the government to accept the students' demands and that it will stop its agitation as soon as the students get what they want. . . . The Executive Committee is afraid that the student movement might turn into a political movement.[138]

Why did the nonstudents in fact come? Specific motives are, of course, hard to establish, but the truth lies somewhere between the *Iskra* position that they came to demonstrate against the government and the Executive Committee view that their main motive was to support the students. As was the case with the Kazan Square demonstration, some of the participants were probably onlookers who got carried away by the excitement of the crowd. It should be remembered that demonstrations on this scale were, to put it mildly, a novelty, especially in the central districts of Russia's major cities. Both the 4 March Kazan Square and the 25 February Moscow demonstrations took place on Sundays on main thoroughfares, the Nevskii Prospekt and the Tverskoi Bul'var. Although these streets were close to the universities and the student districts, they were far removed from the working-class areas. Therefore

---

136. TsGAOR, f. 124, op. 10, ed. kh. 441, 1901, l. 105.

137. For the text of the Moscow Executive Committee bulletin, see TsGIA, f. 733, op. 151, d. 64, l. 236. In his memoirs, S. I. Mitskevich states that "many workers" indeed came to these demonstrations, but he added that these demonstrations were "spontaneous" and that the Moscow Social Democratic Committee had no role in them (*Revoliutsionnaia Moskva, 1888–1905* [Moscow, 1940], p. 283).

138. *Iskra,* no. 3 (1901).

workers who did come to demonstrate probably had a specific political purpose in doing so. The nonstudents arrested at the Kazan Square demonstration were professionals and intelligentsia, but the profile of the nonstudent arrestees in Moscow is somewhat different. More workers came to the Moscow demonstrations, and even more "employees"— shop clerks and such—nonetheless, to quote one eyewitness, "most workers were untouched by the student demonstrations."[139]

It should be reiterated that, as was the case in Kharkov and Saint Petersburg, the Moscow students were divided into several groups. Most sympathized with the Kiev students drafted into the army but, out of fear, refrained from striking or demonstrating. A smaller number of student activists, quite conscious of the traditions of the student movement, wanted to organize some sort of student protest in reaction to the Kiev incident. At first this group favored the strike, which had enjoyed such success in 1899. But these students soon despaired of convincing their comrades and began to espouse the idea of street demonstrations. When the demonstrations finally began in Moscow, however, they were an unplanned reaction to the arrest of the 23 February *skhodka*. And although these student activists wanted to attract public support for their demonstrations, they balked at advancing political demands that went beyond the 1899 platform. There was also a smaller group of radical activists who wanted to establish close links between the students and the labor movement. This group was itself split into two factions. One faction recognized the political potential of the student movement, whereas the other faction agreed with the economists that the student movement was useless.[140]

An academic strike broke out in most *VUZy* by the beginning of March, but this did not happen in Moscow University, mainly because of the intervention of the university's faculty council. The faculty council made a direct appeal to the students to avoid strikes or demonstrations: student disorders were self-defeating. The 1899 strike had produced nothing but the Temporary Rules; by demonstrating against them now, the *studenchestvo* was backing the government into a corner, forcing the authorities to defend their prestige by retaining the draft. Nor was it appropriate for the students to strike. After all, the faculty council argued, the universities were not factories.[141]

139. AIISSSR, f. 5, op. 5, ed. kh. 58, l. 13 (V. I. Orlov memoirs).
140. Ibid.
141. This appeal can be found in TsGIA, f. 733, op. 151, d. 241, l. 17.

In a sharp reply, the students' Executive Council accused the professors of cowardice; they worried only about keeping their jobs and did little to defend either student or academic interests. "What did you do for us in 1899? Which of you followed the example of Kovalevskii, Menzbir, and Miliukov? . . . How can we see you as 'pillars of science' when your lectures get filtered through ten layers of censorship? How can we believe that you professors are even in a position to help us when your very appeal to us is illegal according to the University Statute?"[142]

What most distinguished Moscow from other universities was the decision of P. A. Nekrasov, the curator of the Moscow educational district, to head off a student strike by allowing the faculty council to appoint a commission to investigate and report on the causes of student unrest. The commission's deliberations mollified most Moscow students, averted a strike, and confirmed that most students would still respond well to any hint of reforms from above.[143]

Tsar Nicholas seemed to be reaching the same conclusions: a change in educational policy might succeed where the Temporary Rules had failed, in ending the student movement. On 16 March the tsar convened an interministerial conference on higher-education policy.[144] Four days later, on 20 March, he wrote a telling letter to his uncle, Grand Duke Sergei Alexandrovich, the Moscow governor-general, sharply disagreeing with the latter's gloomy assessment of the situation created by the student movement. Sergei Alexandrovich, discouraged by the February and March demonstrations, had told Nicholas that he wanted to resign. The tsar was more sanguine. Perhaps the root cause of student unrest was bad educational policy. If so, then the time had come to correct it. "I think a real government is strong when, openly admitting its mistakes, it immediately corrects them without worrying about what others will think or say." Yes, the student movement was troublesome, but the

142. TsGIA, f. 733, op. 151, d. 242, l. 97.
143. TsGIA, f. 733, op. 151, d. 242, l. 81.
144. The tsar asked the assembled ministers whether the time had come to put all *VUZy* under unified control. Although N. A. Zver'ev, the acting minister of education, liked the idea, Witte argued that the real problem lay in the inability of the Ministry of Education to control the universities, whose students, he asserted, usually took the lead in fomenting student disorders. K. P. Pobedonostsev, the ober-procurator of the Holy Synod, agreed and argued that "the universities were based on Western models . . . which were totally unsuited to Russia's character." The conference also heard suggestions from D. S. Sipiagin, the minister of the interior, on how to relieve the alleged overcrowding of the *VUZy*. The government, Sipiagin argued, had to reform secondary education so that a high school graduate would not have to go on to higher education in order to obtain social and employment opportunities. See TsGIA, f. 721, op. 2, ed. kh. 295.

vast majority of the population was loyal. "Don't think I am minimizing the importance of these disorders but I sharply distinguish disorders within the universities themselves from street demonstrations. The time has come, though, to reform our entire academic structure . . . things can't get worse." The tsar ended his letter by disclosing that he intended to give the job of reforming Russian education to a "military man": General P. S. Vannovskii.[145]

News of Vannovskii's appointment seemed to restore the faith of most students that the government would abrogate the Temporary Rules and overhaul the whole system of higher education. Indeed, the rescript that accompanied Vannovskii's appointment promised such reforms and a softer line toward the students. The rescript asked teachers and administrators to "enter into close association with the students and . . . further the moral education of youth on the basis of heartfelt concern [*serdechnoe popechenie*] for their well-being." [146]

At the beginning of April, Vannovskii announced a thorough review of the University Statute of 1884 as well as a reconsideration of the 29 July Temporary Rules. In fact the government did not apply the rules to the hundreds of students arrested during the spring demonstrations; that August the authorities released the Kiev and Saint Petersburg students who had already been conscripted.

In April it was clear that the spring wave of student protests had run its course. An April *skhodka* resolution at Saint Petersburg University expressed the general attitude: a 1,675 to 271 vote passed the resolution that "the *studenchestvo* trusts the good intentions of the government" but asked Vannovskii to put off the spring exams until the fall so that students arrested that spring would not suffer. After some initial reluctance Vannovskii agreed.[147]

As the students went home for summer vacations many pondered the lessons of this latest episode in the student movement. Most agreed on one point: they had won. The Temporary Rules were gone, and Vannovskii promised further reforms. Moreover, it all came as something of a surprise. They had begun the semester frightened of the Temporary Rules, unable to repeat an 1899-style strike in support of their conscripted comrades. But, just as in 1899, an unforeseen tactical inno-

145. Letter of Tsar Nicholas II to Grand Duke Sergei Alexandrovich, 20 March 1901, TsGAOR, f. 646, ed. kh. 71, l. 55.
146. Text quoted from M. K. Korbut, *Kazanskii Gosudarstvennyi Universitet imeni V. I. Ul'ianova-Lenina za 125 let, 1804/5–1929/30* (Kazan, 1930), vol. 2, p. 146.
147. Engel' and Gorokhov, *Iz istorii,* p. 40. Both authors played an active role in the student movement at Saint Petersburg University. Their book is as much a memoir as it is a secondary source.

vation had confounded the pessimists and cynics who denigrated the importance of the student movement.

Compared to the 1899 strike, the 1901 street demonstrations certainly carried some tactical advantages. First, of course, a far lower level of student participation sufficed to convey an illusion of success. Fewer students actually participated in the demonstrations, but the sense of victory was greater. Second, street demonstrations forged links between the student movement and other social groups. The 1901 street disorders were mainly *student* demonstrations, but they nevertheless made a major impression on Russian urban society and gave students the feeling that the student movement counted after all.

As Allan Wildman has perceptively observed:

> The street demonstrations of March 1901 in the major cities of Russia marked the advent of yet another phase in the long conflict of radical society with the prevailing order. The heroism and initiative of the students in combatting the "provisional regulations" of 1899 gave the revolutionary intelligentsia and their liberal fringe a new focal point for their political hopes and helped free them from the spell of the working masses. With the defection of such leading theoreticians as Struve, Tugan-Baranovskii and Bulgakov, the intellectual pre-eminence of Marxism had rapidly dwindled. The once captive authors and scholars, the impressionable ex-Populists and liberals, the Worker-phile students, lawyers and zemstvo employees now responded to new strategies and theoretical justifications for their mounting aspirations for change. In exposing themselves to the blows of Cossack whips, to the dangers of arrest and the loss of social position, they developed a new sense of their own dignity and social import which Marxism had denied them.[148]

As they reflected on the import of the 1901 student demonstrations, many former participants in the student movement believed that the outbreak of student protest also influenced the shift in Russian Social Democracy away from economism. Once again Wildman, a leading historian of Social Democracy during this period, agrees:

> To be sure they still regarded the working class and their Social Democratic champions as important "allies" in the shaping struggle, but other social factors now entered their political computations. The overly simple view, so popular a few years before, that the momentum of the workers' movement would of itself burst the shackles of the autocracy, gave place to the feeling that "all live forces" should now join in the battle for political liberty. . . . In response to these events, which momentarily put the workers' movement in the shadow, Russian Social Democracy rapidly completed its shift from "economics" to "politics."[149]

148. Wildman, *The Making of a Workers' Revolution*, p. 214.
149. Ibid., p. 215.

In short, the 1901 spring demonstrations showed the *studenchestvo* that the student movement could be important. It could influence other social groups and even force the government to meet student demands.

The events of the spring also underscored the key role played by women students, the *kursistki,* especially in the capitals. Women's higher education was gaining increasing acceptance not only from the elite but also from more conservative merchant groups. In addition to the problems faced by their male counterparts, women students had to contend with special obstacles—their inferior legal status, nettlesome discrimination in employment, government harassment of women's institutions of higher education—which guaranteed a tense relationship with the state. During the 1890s the long battle for women's rights to higher education and the slow development of mutual aid groups and networks finally began to bear fruit. The 1897 Vetrova demonstration made a powerful impression on women students, and the 1899 strike showed that the Russian *kursistka* was now ready to join her male counterpart in the student movement.[150] In the battle against the Temporary Rules, feelings of comradely solidarity merged with the special nature of the issue. After all, if women were exempted from the draft, it is not illogical to assume that they felt an added responsibility to support their comrades who were not exempt.

Underneath this illusion of victory, the tactical and ideological questions facing the student movement still remained, to reemerge in full force in the following academic year. Tactically, the street demonstration, for all its advantages, had a major drawback. Once demonstrators had made their stand on the street, what could they then do except passively await arrest? And "ideologically" the apparent success of the 1901 demonstrations—Vannovskii's promises of corporate reforms and the de facto abrogation of the Temporary Rules—now raised a new problem for the student movement. Should students accept academic or corporate reforms in isolation, or should they link their own demands to more general political reforms of the autocracy? The relationship of academic to political reforms had surfaced in the 1899 strike. In the fall of 1901 it would become the major issue of the student movement.

150. A fine treatment of this issue is the Harvard 1986 B.A. thesis of Catherine Schmidt, "Pushed into Politics: The Radicalization of Women Students in Saint Petersburg from 1889 to 1901," esp. pp. 46–56.

The Kassa Vzaimopomoshchi of Saint Petersburg University, ca. 1900. (V. V. Mavrodin and V. A. Ezhov, eds., *Leningradskii Universitet v vospominaniiakh sovremennikov*, volume 2 [Leningrad, 1982])

A group of Saint Petersburg University students drafted into the army, 1901. (V. V. Mavrodin and V. A. Ezhov, eds., *Leningradskii Universitet v vospominaniiakh sovremennikov*, volume 2 [Leningrad, 1982])

G. I. Chulkov, in student uniform, awaiting transport to Siberia, 1902.
(G. I. Chulkov, *Gody stranstvii: Iz knigi vospominanii* [Moscow, 1930])

G. I. Chulkov and fellow students in the *taiga*, 1902. (G. I. Chulkov, *Gody stranstvii. Iz knigi vospominanii* [Moscow, 1930])

Transporting students by barge up the Ienisci, 1902. Note the red flag at the front. (G. I. Chulkov, *Gody stranstvii: Iz knigi vospominanii* [Moscow, 1930])

The Moscow Ispolkom and the Saint Petersburg Kassa Radikalov, Alexandrovsk Central Prison, 1902. (G. I. Chulkov, *Gody stranstvii: Iz knigi vospominanii* [Moscow, 1930])

The Alexandrovsk Central Prison, 1902. (G. I. Chulkov, *Gody stranstvii: Iz knigi vospominanii* [Moscow, 1930])

Moscow students in Butyrka Prison, 1902. (*Istoriia Moskovskovo Universiteta,*
M. N. Tikhomirov, ed., volume 1 [Moscow, 1955])

CHAPTER 4

Rethinking the Student Movement

In the autumn of 1901, Russia's students returned to the classroom amid widespread expectations that the government was ready to grant important concessions on such matters as university autonomy and student corporate rights. But hopes for a better relationship with the government quickly gave way to deep disillusionment and opened a new cycle of confrontation that culminated in the nationwide student strike following the January 1905 Bloody Sunday massacre.

If, in 1901, most students still believed that university reform was possible even without wider political reform, this was no longer the case a year later. The student movement, without losing its concern for corporate issues, took the direction of political confrontation with the government. If, in 1901, the overwhelming majority of the professoriate still trusted in the good intentions of the tsar and the Ministry of Education, by 1905 the academic profession had begun to take the first cautious steps toward rebellion.

Both the *studenchestvo* and the professoriate felt misled by the government's unwillingness to implement the implied promise of major reforms contained in the rescript appointing Vannovskii minister of education. For its part, the government was caught between its recognition that the University Statute was obsolete and its fear of losing control of the universities. What it finally granted satisfied no one.

Frustrated and disappointed by Vannovskii, the students began to accept the link between corporate demands and politics. In so doing they tried to give their protest wider significance. During the nationwide strike that followed the publication and rejection of Vannovskii's reform proposals, the students passed resolutions emphasizing the role of the student movement as a catalyst for wider social protest. Their example supposedly would encourage other social groups to fight for their rights.

The problem with this view of the student movement quickly became apparent. How exactly would the student movement act as a catalyst? What issues should the students raise? What tactics should they use? What should they do once other social groups actually did start protesting? For the *studenchestvo,* the transition to confrontation occurred during a time of growing political instability in the nation. The rise of the Social Democratic and Social Revolutionary parties, peasant riots, strikes, and the organization of the Union of Liberation all served to alter the context of student unrest. In 1899, 1901, and 1902, the students largely acted alone. A short time later this was no longer the case. In fact, just when the student movement quieted down after the 1901– 1902 academic year, unrest swept the country. Peasants rioted in the south, bitter strikes broke out in Rostov and Baku, a savage pogrom ravaged Kishinev in 1903—but the *studenchestvo* as such did not respond. Yet this seeming lack of concern for events outside the universities coincided with an intense effort to rethink the place and purpose of the student movement. And student protest went on as before—but in response to provocations occurring within the universities and directly affecting the students.

A major theme of this period is the search for a suitable ideology of student protest, as well as the student response to the process of political mobilization that culminated in the 1905 Revolution. Once students accepted the political dimensions of student unrest, they had to define what their relationship would be to emerging political parties and consider whether, in the light of changing political circumstances, the student movement had lost its raison d'être. Was there still any justification for an independent student movement, or should politically conscious students join the ranks of the revolutionary parties? If so, what should their attitude be toward recurrent outbreaks of student protest?

A second major theme is the constant tension between attempts to impart a specific direction to the student movement and the unwillingness of the student masses to listen to their would-be leaders. Even if congresses and conferences formulated new theses on the student movement, it still remained to be seen how effective their resolutions would be.

RADICALIZATION, 1901–1902

Most students started the new academic year ready to give the government and Vannovskii the benefit of the doubt; they expected at any moment the announcement that the government would abrogate those sections of the 1884 Statute forbidding students to organize, to meet, or to claim a corporate identity. Opposed to this majority, nicknamed academics, were the so-called politicals, who greeted the reformist expectations of the majority with cynical scorn and argued that the student movement should reach out to other social groups and link academic goals with general political reforms.[1] As will be seen below, the politicals themselves were a highly disparate group with widely differing views about the student movement. Their base in the fall of 1901 was their control of the organizations that had emerged the previous spring to direct the demonstrations and strikes, such as the Saint Petersburg University Organization Committee, the United Councils of Kiev and Kharkov universities, and the Moscow University Executive Committee.

In October these organizations, apparently acting separately, all called *skhodki* to inject a tone of militancy into the student movement. These "political" *skhodki* tried to mobilize the students against Vannovskii by demanding the readmission of *all* students expelled during the spring demonstrations, the abolition of all Jewish quotas, the admission of women to all-male *VUZy*, and the lifting of restrictions on the admission of seminary graduates.[2] But none of these *skhodki* attracted much student interest and the efforts of the politicals to renew the previous spring's academic strike ended in failure. This did not discourage them from redoubling their efforts to discredit the government and coax the rest of the student body to drop its "illusions" about Vannovskii. For example, the Moscow University Executive Committee told the students that they had *forced* the government into concessions and that only continued militancy would guarantee further success.[3] In October the committee issued a proclamation telling the students:

> Compare the student movement of 1899 with [last spring's]. . . . In 1899 the students demonstrated great solidarity and yet they got nothing but the 29 July Temporary Rules. . . . Compare that with the movement that broke out at the beginning of this year . . . only about one-eighth of the students really participated, but they managed to attract thousands of workers [*sic*] and members of the intelligentsia. . . . Compare the two movements and then decide yourselves which method of struggle is more productive. . . . If you want to achieve your academic demands, make wider demands as well

---

1. An excellent source on student moods in September and October 1901 is the collection of weekly police reports on the student movement contained in POA, index no. 16B, folder 14a. Also valuable are the memoirs of A. Anisimov, "Kniaz' S. N. Trubetskoi i Moskovskoe studenchestvo," *Voprosy Filosofii i Psikhologii*, no. 1 (1906).

2. POA, index no. 16B, folder 14A.

3. TsGAOR, f. 124, op. 10, ed. kh. 442, 1901, l. 33.

and you will get the support of the workers and the intelligentsia [even for your corporate goals].[4]

During the fall semester, such appeals had little direct effect. It was not until the majority of students became disillusioned with government promises that the politicals began to make headway. This disillusionment, however, was not long in coming.

In the middle of October, Vannovskii's "new course" faced its first crucial test in a controversy about the right of the *studenchestvo* to protest in a legally sanctioned manner a newspaper article that almost all students believed was sexist and insulting to their corporate honor. The article appeared in the 11 October issue of *Grazhdanin*, the organ of Prince Meshcherskii, an ultra-conservative editor who was personally close to Tsar Nicholas II. Meshcherskii accused the students of wanting coeducation in order to satisfy their sexual needs and made unflattering comparisons between Russian women students and their West European counterparts. Russian *kursistki*, Meshcherskii wrote, were physically and morally "sloppy."[5]

As a wave of anger and disgust swept through the *VUZy*—the article united the *studenchestvo* in a way no purely political issue ever could— the students debated how to respond. In past years such a provocation would immediately have led to illegal protest *skhodki*, but this time, not wanting to alienate Vannosvkii, students asked permission from academic authorities to meet and discuss how to respond to the insult. In turn Vannovskii allowed protest *skhodki*, as long as the students discussed only the Meshcherskii article.[6] Most students saw this as a sign that the Ministry of Education was about to make a fundamental change in its relationship with the *studenchestvo* and recognize their right to some form of corporate existence.

But allowing the students to let off steam about the Meshcherskii article was as far as Vannovskii was prepared to go. The disillusionment with the "new course" promised the previous April may best be traced by focusing on events in Saint Petersburg and Moscow universities. The Saint Petersburg students met, heard a legal opinion warning them that they would lose a slander suit against Meshcherskii, and then decided to insert an advertisement in the newspapers expressing the *studenche-*

4. Ibid.

5. A file on the incident, including the article in question, can be found in Gosudarstvennaia Publichnaia Biblioteka imeni V. I. Lenina, Otdel Rukopisei (hereafter referred to as GPB im. V. I. Lenina), f. 158, nos. 1–3.

6. The real motive here was to prevent unauthorized *skhodki*, which could get out of control. On Vannovskii's intentions, see TsGIA, f. 733, op. 151, d. 264, l. 175.

stvo's "disgust" with the Meshcherskii article. But the government then disappointed the students by refusing to allow the advertisement to appear in print.[7]

In Moscow University, the students also experienced bitter disillusionment with the outcome of the Meshcherskii protests. At first it seemed that the students would be allowed to organize a response to the Meshcherskii article. The Executive Committee, the political student organization, made little headway in its guerrilla campaign against Vannovskii. While the committee told the Moscow students that the only fitting way to protest was to convene a general *skhodka* and defy the university authorities, most students ignored these appeals and accepted a proposal from the faculty for a joint student-faculty commission to discuss ways of reacting to the Meshcherskii article.[8]

Encouraged by Nekrasov, the Moscow curator, the faculty saw such a commission as the best way of isolating the politicals from the majority of the student body and asserting faculty authority in the university. On 29 October the faculty council elected a commission of twelve professors under the chairmanship of historian P. G. Vinogradov to supervise student discussion of the article. In turn the students of each faculty course were to meet and elect three delegates each to the commission.[9]

The Vinogradov Commission was much more significant than its immediate role would suggest. Almost everyone in the universities saw it as an acid test of the "new course," a key indicator of the possibility of achieving some degree of academic autonomy within the framework of the autocratic system. If students and professors could elect a commission to discuss specific problems, then several of the key provisions and assumptions of the 1884 University Statute would fall to the ground: the students as "individual visitors" of the university, with no right to corporate identity or organization and the professoriate as a body not allowed to discuss internal disciplinary affairs. No wonder that the Executive Committee launched a fierce campaign against the commission, arguing that a general *skhodka* run by the students themselves was more dignified than course meetings supervised by professors. But while agitating for a general *skhodka*, the Executive Committee still ran its own candidate slate for the Vinogradov Commission elections.[10]

The high hopes riding on the Vinogradov Commission quickly evapo-

7. TsGAOR, f. 124, op. 10, ed. kh. 455, 1901, l. 6.

8. See the letter of Moscow curator P. A. Nekrasov to Vannovskii, 30 October 1901, in TsGIA, f. 733, op. 151, d. 264, l. 191.

9. For the records of these elections, see GPB im. V. I. Lenina, f. 158, no. 6.

10. POA, index no. 16B, folder 14A.

rated. On 4 November Vannovskii came to Moscow University and met with the students who had been elected delegates to the Vinogradov Commission. The students, who came to hear Vannovskii detail the forthcoming reforms planned by the Ministry of Education, were instead treated to a rambling discourse about the therapeutic qualities of military ties (they kept one from catching colds).[11] When asked a direct question about whether *all* students expelled the previous spring would be allowed readmission, Vannovskii replied in the negative. Furthermore, he told the students, the government had no plans to abolish the quota on Jewish enrollments, nor was the Ministry of Education willing to legalize student courts of honor.

After the conversation with the students, Vannovskii met with Vinogradov about the Meshcherskii matter and immediately threw cold water on the high expectations raised by the Vinogradov Commission. Vannovskii told the historian that although he sympathized with the students over the Meshcherskii article, the government had nonetheless resolved to forbid any collective student protests and, on the insistence of the Ministry of the Interior, to ban all newspaper advertisements by student groups to protest the article.[12] To add insult to injury, Vannovskii then told Vinogradov that in the future any such faculty-student bodies would have to meet in the presence of the inspector and the rector. When Vinogradov reported this conversation to the student members of the commission, they decided to resign. A few days later the faculty council decided that it could not accept faculty-student commissions if the ministry insisted that the rector or inspector monitor their meetings.[13]

The collapse of the Vinogradov Commission disillusioned many students and professors; Vinogradov himself decided to leave the country and take up a post at Oxford University. In a conversation with a student, A. Anisimov, shortly before his hasty departure for England, Vinogradov expressed deep despair about the future of the Russian universities. According to Anisimov, Vinogradov saw the Russian universities as "about to face a great crisis" and condemned the government for pursuing a "blind policy. Very soon there will be room for only two parties in the universities: the government and the revolutionaries. Anyone hoping for a legal solution to the university question will lack the support of both the right and the left and will become equally hateful to

11. TsGIA, f. 733, op. 151, d. 294, l. 429.
12. TsGIA, f. 733, op. 151, d. 294, l. 430.
13. TsGIA, f. 733, op. 151, d. 294, l. 432.

both sides." [14] Sergei Trubetskoi, the noted philosopher, almost left the university as well but finally decided to stay "until the very end." [15]

Zubatov, the director of the Moscow Okhrana, also saw the collapse of the Vinogradov Commission as a major mistake on the part of the government. Shortly after the fiasco he wrote a sharply critical memorandum attacking the government's university policy as a misguided program that would push the students toward the left:

> The revolutionaries are trying to exploit the student movement for their own purposes. Purely political appeals found little sympathy among the broad masses of students so the revolutionaries shifted their attention to the academic sphere and tried to connect very minor incidents in the university with the Russian political structure. . . . Both the liberals and the conservatives misunderstand the student movement. . . . The conservatives think that the student movement is the work of a small group of agitators. The liberals think that all students are the carriers of their beloved ideals. . . . In reality the students are divided into many groups: moderates, radicals, and the indifferent. . . . The most active students are the freshmen. . . . We must get the basic control of student life into the hands of the "moderate majority." [16]

The collapse of the Vinogradov Commission, according to Zubatov, was a textbook blunder by the Ministry of Education. When Vannovskii allowed the formation of the commission, it appeared that the ministry was finally learning the lessons of long years of student disorders and was strengthening the hand of the "moderate majority." It was hoped that this commission would be allowed to develop into a permanent organ, in which case it would have come to resemble some of the workers' associations that were safely under police control and that served as a useful counterpoint to the influence of the revolutionaries. "Unfortunately the minister of education did not seem to understand the significance of this highly original initiative and by his tactless and clumsy interference, he incited turmoil [*smuta*] among the professors and the students. The result was the strengthening of the Executive Committee and increased activity among the revolutionary groups." [17] Zubatov was right. The failure of the Vinogradov Commission, Anisimov recalled, quickly changed the atmosphere in the university, and the Executive Committee soon gained influence.

The unpublished memoirs of V. I. Orlov shed some light on the Mos-

---

14. Anisimov, "Kniaz' S. N. Trubetskoi," pp. 157–160.
15. Ibid.
16. TsGAOR, f. 124, op. 10, ed. kh. 442/1901, ll. 35–40.
17. Ibid.

cow University Executive Committee, which was to play a major role in the disturbances of 1901–1902.[18] Although outside observers thought the Executive Committee to be a tightly organized and thoroughly politicized organization, in fact it reflected the serious tensions and uncertainties dividing the entire student movement.

When Orlov entered Moscow University in the fall of 1901 he had no ideological views except a clear preference for the politicals over the academics. The first month gave him the opportunity to develop contacts with like-minded students. Since he was a native of Moscow, Orlov did not join a *zemliachestvo* but instead entered a *desiatka,* one of a number of loose discussion groups that argued various issues, especially the student movement, and co-opted new members. In October, Orlov went to a concert at the Romanovka restaurant, organized by the Executive Committee "to bring radical students together." During the intermission, Orlov was asked if he wanted to join the Executive Committee.

The next day the committee met in Orlov's room in the dank Hirsh building on Tverskoi Bul'var and the young freshman got his first look at this mysterious group that had been leading the fight against Vannovskii. He quickly got to know its leaders. There was V. V. Rudnev from the Voronezh *zemliachestvo,* a landowner's son and veteran of the 1899 student movement, one of the organizers of the aborted 1900 student conference. Orlov described him as "correct, restrained, mildmannered, a 'soft character.' . . . He called everyone *kamerad* and it sounded like the cooing of a dove." I. Ia. Tseilikman, from the Smolensk *zemliachestvo,* a twenty-one-year-old Jewish law student ("well-read and capable") was a leader of the "moderate" wing of the committee. Other members included the future writer and Bolshevik G. I. Chulkov, and A. A. Khovrin, a future Social Revolutionary, the son of a minor civil servant from Tambov province. Another important member was I. V. Baev, a twenty-six-year-old mathematics student who was a "puzzling cross between anarchist and law professor."[19] (All these men had been arrested numerous times for participation in the student movement; that they were still in the university serves as a needed reminder that most students expelled for participating in student disorders eventually won readmission.) Of all the Executive Committee members, none enjoyed more authority than Iracli Tseretelli, a future Menshevik leader.

18. These memoirs can be found in AIISSSR, f. 5, op. 5, ed. kh. 58.
19. These descriptions are taken from AIISSSR, f. 5, op. 5, ed. kh. 58, p. 64.

At first I am a little disappointed. There is nothing charismatic or theatrical about him. When he begins to speak the feeling of disappointment mounts. It's as if he's not talking but thinking aloud, in a quiet voice with a light Georgian accent . . . but half an hour later one becomes totally captivated. An incredible intelligence. An iron will. . . . Among the Moscow students there were better orators, there were students who knew more . . . but no one had more influence than Tseretelli.[20]

(Perhaps passages like these suggest why Orlov's memoirs remained unpublished.)

When Orlov joined the Executive Committee at the beginning of November, he was disappointed to see that the committee was deeply divided and seemed to have no clear plan of action apart from distributing pamphlets attacking Vannovskii. At the first meeting he argued for a sharp change of course, with the committee to issue anti-government slogans, downplay corporate issues, and try to organize street demonstrations that would link the students with other social groups—especially the workers. Most members of the Executive Committee opposed Orlov, on the grounds that the committee could not alienate itself from the mass of the students by taking too political a line or embracing causes that did not affect the students' direct interests. But there was another, highly significant reason for the reluctance to change course. Even on the Executive Committee, there was a strong undercurrent of loyalty to the "traditions of the *studenchestvo*." These student leaders had little patience for those who argued that the *studenchestvo* was dead.

THE OTHERS: We're students, after all. If we follow your plan the other students won't listen to us.

ORLOV: What's the *studenchestvo* anyway? It's not one group. It has no common interests. What in fact binds a radical student to someone who "buys learning cheap in order to sell it dear" later on?

THE OTHERS: Of course we have common interests. We're all in the university. Do you really have no regard for the honor of the student uniform?

ORLOV: I regard myself as a Russian citizen compelled for a certain length of time to wear a student uniform. . . . I would gladly exchange it for regular clothing.

What I said did not go down well with the others.[21]

20. AIISSSR, f. 5, op. 5, ed. kh. 58, p. 65.
21. AIISSSR, f. 5, op. 5, ed. kh. 58, p. 70.

These sharp exchanges steadily escalated during November, as Or-lov, Chulkov, and Tseretelli pressed the moderates to take a more active line. But beyond wanting to declare openly that the student movement was part of a general political mobilization to change the system, they too had no clear idea where to go or how to proceed. In effect, the mod-erates on the committee argued that it was possible to have one's cake and eat it too: to stick to student issues (thus avoiding the tough penal-ties meted out to revolutionaries), maybe even call street demonstra-tions (à la Kazan Square, in defense of student rights), and yet at the same time attract public support and make a general political impact. Could a purely student-supported movement have any real effect? It was an old question, but it began to split the Moscow University Execu-tive Committee. As will be shown below, the new Saint Petersburg Uni-versity Kassa Radikalov was simultaneously debating these same issues and developed a short-lived but coherent ideology of the student move-ment that seemed to provide the answers.

While the Moscow University Executive Committee debated these questions, the academics set up a rival organization in the university. This organization, which called itself the Partisans of Academic Free-dom (SAS), issued a general proclamation to the student body on 15 November in which it announced a program based on the conviction that there was no necessary connection between the academic and the political policies of the government. "An improvement of the conditions of academic life," the statement said, "is possible even if it seems to con-tradict the general direction of state policy." The purpose of the new organization was to be "the struggle for academic freedom . . . using academic means."[22]

This new organization, which included such future political figures as M. E. Adzhemov, a Kadet Duma deputy, and Mark Vishniak, hardly advocated passive surrender to the government. Despite the misgivings caused by the Vinogradov incident, the group reflected the feelings of many students that the Ministry of Education deserved a chance to fulfill the promise of the April rescript and announce permanent re-forms of the 1884 Statute. If the students did not get what they wanted, then as a last resort a strike could be considered. Even street demonstra-tions were permissible "when students were locked out of the university and chased into the street."[23] Actually, the differences between the Par-

22. Anisimov, "Kniaz' S. N. Trubetskoi," pp. 157–160. For the text of the 15 No-vember SAS proclamation, see TsGIA, f. 733, op. 151, d. 291, l. 50.
23. Mark Vishniak, Dan' proshlomu (New York, 1954), p. 57.

tisans of Academic Freedom and the moderate wing of the Executive Committee were not as great as many students imagined. What really divided the two groups was the question of whether academic reform was possible without more general political reform.

On the one hand, therefore, by the middle of 1901 most students at Moscow University still refused to make the student movement into a catalyst for wider political protest or pressure. But, on the other hand, the very existence of such organizations as the Executive Committee and the Partisans of Academic Freedom indicated a striking growth of student consciousness and a certain maturing of the student movement. Now, as opposed to their actions in 1899 or 1901, the students were not just reacting to provocations or specific repressions but instead were planning possible responses to government policies. If these policies proved disappointing, then the question of the connection between the student movement and wider political issues would immediately take first place on the student agenda, even for the vast majority who did not belong to the Executive Committee.

THE 1901 TEMPORARY RULES

Events at Saint Petersburg and other universities in the fall of 1901 followed the same general course as at Moscow University, albeit with certain local differences. October had seen the failure of the politicals to make much headway among the *studenchestvo*. And, like their counterparts in Moscow, the students showed that although they were ready to wait for the Ministry of Education to announce promised reforms, they had a self-confidence, inherited from the previous spring, that made them ready to fight such perceived provocations as the Meshcherskii article. At Saint Petersburg University, for example, the whole student population reacted with outrage to the news that a police agent had entered the Electrotechnical Institute to arrest a student.[24] The students believed that police had no right to enter the premises of an educational institution without the prior approval of the academic authorities. Tempers cooled after the students learned that the agent had been dismissed from the service.

As in Moscow, the Saint Petersburg professors got permission from the ministry to allow the students to form temporary elected organizations, pending the introduction of more permanent reforms. At Saint

24. POA, index no. 16B, folder 14A.

Petersburg University the chief organization of the politicals, the old Kassa Vzaimopomoshchi, split over the question of participating in these elections. Advocates of participation left to form a new group, the Kassa Radikalov, which would soon play an important role in the history of the student movement.[25] The Kassa Radikalov won a plurality in the mid-November elections, but this was more the result of better organization and the *kassa*'s readiness to work for the students' corporate interests than it was an indicator of any sudden politicization of the student body. Like their counterparts in Moscow, the Saint Petersburg students supported a moderate academic line. For example, a *skhodka* rejected holding a demonstration to commemorate the fortieth anniversary of the death of the literary critic Nikolai Dobroliubov. A *skhodka* on 20 November clearly showed the corporatism of the Saint Petersburg students, even while making demands of the government:

> 1.   The *skhodka,* by a vote of 499 to 109, resolves that the students of Saint Petersburg University form one autonomous corporation.
> 2.   The members of this corporation should be granted the rights of self-administration, freedom of person, and freedom of speech.

The resolution also demanded that for all academic offenses students be tried by a student court.[26]

This resolution did not sit well with the Moscow University Executive Committee. By the time news of it reached Moscow, the Executive Committee, under the influence of Tseretelli, Chulkov, and Orlov, had moved further to the left. As a result, the Executive Committee issued a stern counterproclamation warning that the time had come for the student movement to go beyond the fight for corporate interests:

> The Saint Petersburg students, quite unjustifiably, are demanding special exemption from the regime of arbitrary police rule that hangs over everybody [not just students]. These demands contradict the self-evident truth that academic freedom is impossible [where political tyranny reigns]. . . . The student movement should be a political movement.[27]

Meanwhile, two developments clarified the issues and helped radicalize the student movement. The first was the mass expulsion of the

25. G. Engel' and V. Gorokhov, *Iz istorii studencheskovo dvizheniia 1899–1906* (Moscow, 1908), p. 57.

26. TsGAOR, f. 124, op. 10, ed. kh. 455, 1901, l. 22.

27. TsGAOR, f. 124, op. 10, ed. kh. 442, 1901, l. 52.

entire freshman class of the Kharkov Veterinary Institute after the students called a strike against an incompetent professor. (The director suspected the connivance of a "secret revolutionary party.") Sympathy demonstrations by students from Kharkov University and Kharkov Technological Institute led to police repression, and the news from Kharkov angered students in other parts of the country.[28]

The second, and the major, catalyst to a renewal of intense student protest was the long-awaited announcement of the "Vannovskii reforms." During the fall semester several interministerial conferences had been considering the government's student policy, with the goal of drafting uniform rules on student organizations and disciplinary procedures and ending the wide disparities that marked the policies of the various ministries controlling institutions of higher education. The major issue facing the ministers was whether to allow students the right to hold general *skhodki*.[29] The ministers reached agreement on other fundamental points, such as allowing students to hold course meetings under faculty supervision. But Minister of the Interior Sipiagin insisted that it would be dangerous to allow general *skhodki*. Such *skhodki* were impervious to governmental controls and would pass political as well as academic resolutions. Pobedonostsev, chief procurator of the Holy Synod, agreed with Sipiagin. The government, he argued, had made a major error in 1884 when it failed to legalize the *zemliachestva*, thereby pushing the moderate students into the arms of the radicals. "But now it is too late," the old conservative warned. "We cannot permit general *skhodki*." Minister of Finance Witte disagreed. He told his fellow ministers that "the *skhodka* is a basic need of academic life. If you push it out the door, it will crawl in through the window. If we do not allow *skhodki* in the *VUZy*, they will take place somewhere else. . . . The government must get the *skhodki* under its control [*vziat' skhodku v svoi ruki*]."

Sipiagin would not budge. By November he had become convinced that the student movement had become a real danger to the autocracy, an integral part of a well-orchestrated campaign by the revolutionary left to embarrass the government and wreck public confidence in it.[30] Although the students did not know it, the next outbreak of student protest would lead to punishments of unprecedented severity.

28. TsGAOR, f. 124, op. 10, ed. kh. 442, 1901, l. 57.
29. The records of the interministerial conferences are contained in TsGIA, f. 733, op. 151, d. 286.
30. TsGAOR, f. DP 00, 3ch. 78/1898, l. 160 (Sipiagin circular, 3 December 1901).

Meanwhile the ministers drafted the "Temporary Rules on Student Organizations," which would apply to all *VUZy*, regardless of ministerial jurisdiction. The rules allowed students to organize libraries, dining halls, music clubs, credit unions, discussion groups, and drama clubs. There was one major catch: such groups could meet only under the direct supervision of a professor appointed by the rector. If any student organization strayed from its permitted agenda, the minister had a right to close it down. The supervising professor had to approve the agenda of all student groups, especially discussion groups. The rules forbade all books, meetings, newspapers, and proclamations in the student dining halls. The rector also had the right to ban specific books from student libraries.[31]

At first the ministers had decided to allow general *skhodki* under strict supervision—much like the *skhodki* allowed during the fall to discuss the Meshcherskii article—but Sipiagin insisted that such *skhodki* would be dangerous. In effect, the Temporary Rules thus abolished a concession the students thought they had already won. Students could meet only by faculty course and only in the presence of a professor, who had to approve the agenda in advance and close the meeting if there were digressions. Furthermore, the rector could veto any student leaders elected by the organizations provided for under the new rules. Each course could elect two representatives to deal with the university administration, but joint meetings of course representatives were forbidden— thus abrogating another concession the students assumed had already been granted.

At their 18 November meeting, the gloomy ministers had no illusions that the Temporary Rules would meet a warm reception in the *VUZy*. Both Witte and Vannovskii expected new disorders; Sipiagin agreed but argued that at least that would give him the chance to identify and arrest the leaders of the student movement.[32] On the one hand, the Temporary Rules were a de facto admission that a major concept of the 1884 Statute, the refusal to recognize the students as a corporate group, had been a total failure. But, on the other hand, in trying to draft a coherent policy to rectify this mistake the ministers once again showed the constraints and fears that hampered the autocracy's ability to deal with the grievances of various social groups, even when those grievances were

31. TsGIA, f. 733, op. 151, d. 294, ll. 285–313.
32. TsGIA, f. 733, op. 151, d. 286, l. 144.

seen to be justified. The ministers were caught between their recognition of student complaints and their fear of losing control of the *VUZy*. In the end they chose a paternalistic half-measure that made matters worse. The rules banned *skhodki* and tried to destroy the character of the students' major social centers, the dining halls, by banning meetings and printed material there. The rules replaced the 1884 ban on student organizations with what the *studenchestvo* regarded as an insulting paternalism. It is a telling comment on the government's decision-making process that even though the ministers believed the rules would not work, they decided to publish them.

Until the publication of the rules in November 1901, the government had a good chance of reaching a compromise with the students. A "student bill of rights" guaranteeing the right to *skhodki* and corporate organization would have assured, at least for the time being, the isolation of the politicals. But the Temporary Rules now undercut the argument that student corporate rights and academic needs could coexist with the autocracy.

One of the most galling provisions of the new rules was the ban on general *skhodki*, the quintessential symbol of the *studenchestvo*. On this point most students agreed with the politicals in arguing that students forbidden general meetings "resembled a body without a head." Take the *skhodka* away, many felt, and the *studenchestvo* would become a random collection of individuals bereft of corporate identity or a sense of shared traditions and moral attitudes.[33]

RENEWED PROTEST

As the students returned from their Christmas vacations, the academics united with the politicals in opposing the new rules. For example, on 15 January 1902 the Moscow University Partisans of Academic Struggle offered to join the Executive Committee in a united protest.[34] In an added blow to government hopes, important segments of the professoriate and even some curators considered the new rules to be a grave mistake. Both the Moscow and Saint Petersburg university faculty councils

---

33. Rafael Vydrin, *Osnovnye momenty studencheskovo dvizheniia v Rossii* (Moscow, 1908), p. 63.

34. TsGAOR, f. 124, op. 10, ed. kh. 442, 1901, l. 113.

warned that the new announcement destroyed any remaining hopes for pacifying the universities.[35]

A major question at the beginning of 1902 was whether the inevitable protests against the new rules might be harnessed to produce some fresh answers to the perennial problems of the student movement: ideology and tactics. One group that tried to develop a new doctrine of student protest was the Saint Petersburg University Kassa Radikalov. Two *kassa* veterans, G. A. Engel' and V. A. Gorokhov, in their account of its activities published in 1908, called the new doctrine "student Radicalism."[36] "Student Radicalism" was the most ambitious attempt yet in the history of the Russian student movement to provide a coherent doctrine of student protest. What the *kassa* developed was a synthesis of the political and academic views of the student movement. The core of the *kassa*'s argument was that student protest, even if it responded to the students' own corporate concerns, was of crucial political significance.[37] The student movement was a key catalyst in politicizing potentially significant social groups. The events of 1899 and 1901 had shown that student protest in the urban nerve centers discomfited the government and reminded the middle classes as well as the proletariat that it was possible to fight.

Unlike the politicals, who saw student protest as a waste of time, the Radicals argued that in a country whose government viewed any public protest as a threat, even seemingly juvenile protests about student rights carried disproportionate political weight. But although student leaders should recognize the legitimacy of corporate demands, the Radicals argued, they should also use every opportunity to make the student masses see that their movement was part of a larger fight against the autocracy. Because the Radicals viewed the student movement as a crucial catalyst, they favored the street demonstration as the best tactic of student protest, allowing the students to carry their struggle outside the university and thereby involve other social groups. Within the university, student leaders should strive for the broadest possible coalition and avoid needless party and doctrinal battles. Beyond the slogan "Down with the Autocracy," the Radicals offered no coherent political doctrine, although

35. TsGIA, f. 733, op. 151, d. 286, l. 387.
36. Engel' and Gorokhov, *Iz istorii*, pp. 57–62. In the discussion of "student Radicalism" developed below, all adherents of the specific doctrine of the Kassa Radikalov will be referred to as Radicals (upper-case).
37. Various proclamations by the *kassa* outlining this position can be found in TsGAOR, f. 124, op. 10, ed. kh. 455/1901.

Engel' and Gorokhov, the best sources on the Kassa Radikalov, say that many in fact sympathized with the Social Democrats. In a sense the Radicals foreshadowed the Liberation Movement of 1905. Even moderate liberals could interpret "Down with the Autocracy" in their own way; it was a slogan that could forge a wide coalition.

The Radical synthesis lasted no longer than a year; by the beginning of 1903, detractors began to argue that the only useful role students could play was as members of specific political parties. In their account of the Kassa Radikalov Engel' and Gorokhov point out that in the end student Radicalism would fail to provide a satisfactory answer to the key problem of tactics. Even though the *studenchestvo* was not a class in the same sense as the proletariat, the Kassa Radikalov argued, it could still radicalize "society," especially through street demonstrations. At the same time, the *kassa* believed that student protest would develop real strength only from student unity. Experience showed that students were not likely to react to issues or provocations that did not affect them directly. Furthermore, the only tactic that attracted mass student support was the academic strike, but the strike isolated the students from other social groups, failed to embarrass the government as effectively as street demonstrations did, and raised the touchy moral issue of using force against fellow students and faculty who ignored the calls to shut down the universities. The *kassa* also recognized the contradiction of using an academic tactic, the strike, to achieve political goals.

The other alternative, the street demonstration, left the students dangerously vulnerable to police repression. Why should the "best" and "most conscious" students march lemming-like to jail? Did not the government in fact welcome demonstrations as a convenient opportunity to demoralize and dismantle the student movement? Furthermore, there were problems with the idea of the student movement as a catalyst. If "society" was not ready to join the fight (as proved to be the case in 1902), then the students were putting their necks into a noose. But if "society" was already politicized enough to join the demonstrations, then why the need for an independent student movement?

Such were some of the inherent paradoxes and contradictions of student Radicalism. But at the beginning of 1902 these were overshadowed by the general hostility to the new rules and the widespread determination to protest. Disappointed in the government, most students could no longer deny a connection between corporate reforms and wider political issues. Therefore, even though Kassa Radikalov did not start a formal organizing campaign elsewhere, the student movement as a whole arrived at a general, if vague and temporary, acceptance of the fundamental tenets of student Radicalism.

Mass protests started immediately after the beginning of the new semester.[38] Shortly after news arrived from Kiev University that the students there had decided to strike against the new rules, the Kassa Radikalov began distributing pamphlets at Saint Petersburg University, explaining why it had broken off from the old Kassa Vzaimopomoshchi and outlining its new doctrine of the student movement. The old Kassa Vzaimopomoshchi had reverted to its "doctrinaire" attitudes and no longer believed in the potential of the student movement. The Kassa Radikalov, in contrast, told the students that they and their fight were important: for the government, they had long been the hardest nut to crack. "Comrades!" they wrote, "There have been many parties and oppositional groups in Russia—the Decembrists, the Kolokol, the Narodniki—but all were suppressed by the government. Only in the universities was the government beaten. Only there has it failed to introduce its police regime or eliminate the spirit of protest."[39] In another pamphlet, issued at the end of January, the Kassa Radikalov explained why the student movement was important in preparing the downfall of the autocracy and why the chief task at the moment was union of all groups, not party bickering:

> Everyone should struggle on their home ground and use the tactics that are most suited to their immediate possibilities. Professionals should make use of their congresses, students the universities, and workers the factories. But all should know that they are fighting a common political battle and share a common enemy. Everybody has the same goal: political freedom. Let us forget our party differences. The student movement will slowly and even imperceptibly corrode the foundations [of the autocracy], thus preparing the way for the heavier and decisive blows that will come from the proletariat.[40]

Other *kassa* pamphlets emphasized the revolutionary role of the European universities in 1848 and the unique position of Russia's universities as the Achilles' heel of the autocratic system, the fragile nodal point where the conflict between the government's fear of social autonomy and its need to foster economic development came to a head:

---

38. A weekly chronicle of these protests, compiled by the Department of Police, can be found in POA, index 16B, folder 14A.

39. TsGAOR, f. 124, op. 10, ed. kh. 455, 1901, l. 59.

40. TsGAOR, f. 124, op. 10, ed. kh. 455, 1901, l. 69.

It is perfectly natural that the government sees the universities as a Gordian knot. . . . On the one hand, the universities epitomize the development in Russia of European norms, culture, and progress, a development the government is trying to throttle. On the other hand, economic necessity forces the government to rely on the very groups that come out of this process of Europeanization. It is in the universities that the conflict between economic needs and the instinct of self-preservation confronts the autocracy most clearly. Hence the hesitation and indecision of the government's university policy.[41]

The immediate problem for the Kassa Radikalov was that although it preferred massive street demonstrations, the logic of its own doctrine, as well as the mood of the *studenchestvo*, dictated the academic strike as the only tactic that would unite rather than divide the students. On 5 February 1902 the *kassa* convened a large *skhodka* in Saint Petersburg University which voted 1,063 to 5 in favor of a protest strike against the new rules.[42] Students in the city's elite technical institutes, angered that the new rules would also be applied to them, voted to join the strike. After voting to strike, the February *skhodka* passed a resolution declaring that the current student movement was basically a political movement fighting for the fundamental freedoms of speech, the press, and assembly. To direct the strike the *skhodka* elected an Organization Committee, which issued the following statement: "We're beginning a new phase of the student movement. . . . While the student movement has always been objectively political, only now has this fact penetrated the consciousness of the student masses."[43] By the middle of February the strike had spread to most of Russia's *VUZy*, universities as well as institutes. As in 1899, the academic strike was accompanied by forcible disruption of classes. Toward the end of February the *kassa* called for a massive street demonstration to be held on Sunday, 3 March, on the Nevskii Prospekt.

Although by this time most of the *kassa*'s leadership had been arrested—ringleaders of the 5 February *skhodka* had been sentenced to Siberian exile—the 3 March demonstration attracted an impressive turnout, with estimates ranging from *Iskra*'s thirty thousand to the Saint Petersburg Okhrana's five thousand.[44] Although *Iskra* stressed the

41. TsGAOR, f. 124, op. 10, ed. kh. 455, 1901, l. 228.
42. TsGIA, f. 733, op. 151, d. 292, l. 217.
43. Engel' and Gorokhov, *Iz istorii*, p. 64.
44. A full list of the arrested Kassa Radikalov members is contained in TsGAOR, f. 124, op. 10, ed. kh. 455/1901, l. 70.

crowd's proletarian makeup, sixty-three of the day's ninety-two arrestees were students.[45] From that point on the student movement in
Saint Petersburg slowly began to lose momentum. A large demonstration had followed a massive academic strike, but most members of the
kassa were on their way to Siberia and the tsarist government was still in
place. Clearly the hopes entertained by the Kassa Radikalov that the student movement would inspire protest elsewhere had not been fulfilled.

THE MOSCOW EXECUTIVE COMMITTEE

Although there appeared to be no direct contact between the Kassa
Radikalov and the Moscow Ispolkom (Executive Committee), the latter
organization faced the same questions and, to a certain extent, took a
similar course. The real difference between the *kassa* and the committee
at this point (December 1901–February 1902) was that the *kassa* had
worked out a coherent ideology of student protest, however short-lived,
whereas the Executive Committee kept groping for a suitable rationale
for its actions and in the end made plans it knew had no chance of
succeeding.

Two important "student" issues, the Vannovskii rules and the mass
expulsion from the Kharkov Veterinary Institute in November, had
guaranteed second-semester protests. Shortly after the new semester began, the academic SAS at Moscow University had publicly offered to
join the Executive Committee in fighting the government's new academic line but continued to insist on a sharp distinction between corporate and political protest.

The Moscow committee found itself caught between its aversion to
pure student protest and its confusion about just what alternative it had
in mind. In the words of one committee member, the student organization was beginning to go around in circles: "We have to agitate in order
to develop an organization. We have to have an organization in order to
organize a demonstration. And we have to have a demonstration in
order to agitate. The only way out of this dead end is a good theory."[46]
But a "good theory" was exactly what they did not have. Unlike the
Kassa Radikalov, the Executive Committee was unsure about the theoretical context of the student movement and certainly failed to articulate

45. A list of those arrested in the 3 March demonstration can be found in TsGAOR, f.
124, op. 10, ed. kh. 455/1901, l. 193. For a police report on the demonstration, see "Studencheskoe dvizhenie 1901–1902 gg.," *Krasnyi Arkhiv* 89–90 (1938): 290–293.
46. AIISSSR, f. 5, ed. kh. 58, l. 90 (V I. Orlov memoirs).

a coherent link between student protest and the radicalization of wide sectors of Russian society. Its more assertive members were thinking about joint action with the workers, but there is no evidence that any were members of Social Democratic groups or that they were as yet well versed in Marxist theory.

On 27 January the Executive Committee gathered around a long table covered with hors d'oeuvres and wine bottles and argued about what to do next. The news had just arrived that the Kiev students had proclaimed a strike to protest the Vannovskii rules. Beating his spoon against a cup, Iracli Tseretelli opened the meeting by warning his comrades that they had to act now or become passive spectators of what promised to be another wave of student protest. Such a stance had done much to discredit Saint Petersburg's Kassa Vzaimopomoshchi in 1899. Did the committee want to emulate Kiev and call for a student strike, or did it want to organize a demonstration? If the members decided on a demonstration, then did they want to attract workers? If so, then the demonstration must take place on a Sunday. In a telling admission, Tseretelli warned the group not to count on the assurances of "contacts" that workers were ready to participate in a student-called demonstration. They could only be sure of a reliable nucleus of about eight hundred students.

Another member of the committee, A. S. Syromiatnikov, then supported the idea of a street demonstration. "The university," he warned, "is a trap. If we really want to turn the student movement into something bigger, then we have to [take to the streets]." [47] But at that point an air of gloom settled over the meeting. Just like the Kassa Radikalov, the Executive Committee members gathered around the table realized that the only way to mobilize mass student support was to base the protest in the university and stress academic as well as political issues. Getting eight hundred students to gather in the university would be far easier than calling them into the streets. Although the students had succeeded in organizing impressive demonstrations in the spring of 1901, especially in Saint Petersburg, the issue then in question—forced conscription—had been more conducive to arousing public indignation than the new rules on student organizations were.

Tseretelli then summed up the situation. The committee had to face facts: the only possible strategy was to call a *skhodka* in the university, time it for a Sunday, and then hope that the students would either march

47. AIISSSR, f. 5, ed. kh. 58, l. 102.

into the city or attract crowds of citizens (workers, it was hoped) to the university. But even as he was outlining the plan, Tseretelli was admitting probable defeat. The police would most likely enter the university, haul them off to jail, and then exile them from Moscow. "If the workers support the students," Tseretelli concluded, "well and good. And if not, then at least we'll go down with honor." [48]

The decision to call a *skhodka* produced an odd feeling of relief. Orlov recalled that "a load fell from our shoulders. It seemed as if the room had gotten brighter. We were doomed. But so what? At least we had made a decision. The main thing was that we were no longer plagued by indecison." [49]

There was certainly ample reason for their pessimism, especially where the workers were concerned. Early 1902 was a low point in the fortunes of Moscow Social Democracy and its influence over Moscow's workers, who in a few short weeks would show their loyalty to the autocracy by streaming to a huge Okhrana-orchestrated demonstration in the Kremlin. [50] Yet, faced with the choice of doing nothing, leading a corporate student protest, or starting a general political demonstration doomed in advance, the committee chose the third course.

As will be seen below, the 9 February *skhodka*, whose implications were misinterpreted by both Soviet and non-Soviet historians, would give rise to considerable bitterness and recrimination. But the Executive Committee meeting also revealed the importance of psychological momentum in the student movement. Having argued for so long that the students had to make theirs a political and not an academic movement, people like Tseretelli, or Orlov and Chulkov, could not instantly become *Realpolitiker* and admit that they should either do nothing or return to the tradition of corporate protest. In the end, the gesture became an end in itself. Without intending to do so, the Executive Committee arrived at the same conclusion as the Kassa Radikalov: student protest, even if based in the university, could perhaps serve as an important catalyst for wider protest movements.

Unfortunately for the committee, the Okhrana knew all about its plans and, on Sipiagin's orders, arrested the entire organization on 31 January. [51] The government greatly feared the possibility that student

---

48. AIISSSR, f. 5, ed. kh. 58, l. 104.

49. Ibid.

50. Jeremy Schneiderman, *Sergei Zubatov and Revolutionary Marxism* (Ithaca, 1976), p. 207.

51. TsGAOR, f. 124, op. 10, ed. kh. 442, 1901, l. 129. Overrepresented on the committee were sons of middle-level civil servants, students of the natural sciences, history

street demonstrations might radicalize the workers and now prepared to suppress the student movement with unprecedented harshness.

The 29 January arrests failed, however, to cripple the planned 9 February *skhodka*. The committee prepared for the possibility of arrest by designating a shadow group, which issued bulletins calling the students to the university. On 6 February the new group notified all students that Sunday's *skhodka* was of "extraordinary importance."[52] Russian society was seething with discontent and was waiting for the students to set an example; the government was very afraid of the student movement. The *skhodka* would send shock waves through the system and "lay the foundation stone for the future rule of law in Russia." Tensions rose further when the moderate SAS announced that the "tactics of moderation" had failed to secure any real gains for the students. "We can secure our right to legally recognized student organizations," the SAS concluded, "only by struggle and illegal organization."[53] Many students erroneously interpreted this to mean that the Executive Committee and the SAS had joined forces to turn the *skhodka* into a corporate protest against the new rules on student organization. Finally, in another development that strengthened pro-strike sentiment, word arrived at Moscow University that a 5 February *skhodka* at Saint Petersburg University had voted a protest strike.

On Saturday morning, hundreds of students streamed into the university. Onlookers could see the students hanging protest banners from the university windows. Police and troops occupied Manezh Square but allowed students to enter the university buildings. When some of the leaders of the SAS entered the university auditorium the crowd inside greeted them with loud applause, but sharp disagreements soon split the politicals from the academics.[54] After a few hours, about three hundred moderate students left the university but were immediately arrested and sent to the Butyrka prison.

Meanwhile, in a mood of optimistic solidarity, the *skhodka* adopted the most politically radical resolution yet. After calling for freedom of

---

students, and students from non-Moscow high schools; law students were underrepresented.

52. A copy of this bulletin can be found in BMGU, f. VI. Orlova, 5dt., no. 34.

53. TsGIAM, f. 459, op. 2, ed. kh. 8270, l. 22.

54. There are several descriptions of the 9 February *skhodka*. One valuable memoir, written from the point of view of an SAS participant, is Ivan Kheraskov's "Iz istorii studencheskovo dvizheniia v Moskovskom Universitete," in V. B. El'iashevich, A. A. Kizevetter, and M. M. Novikov, eds., *Moskovskii Universitet 1755–1930: iubileinyi sbornik* (Paris, 1930), pp. 442–444.

speech, the right to strike, the eight-hour day, and the removal of all restrictions on non-Russian nationalities, the resolution declared that since the autocracy could not make such concessions, the students demanded a constituent assembly. The resolution concluded by announcing that the students would immediately "take our protest into the streets where, together with the cadres of workers' organizations, we will back up our demands with force."[55]

Soviet historians of the student movement have made much of the resolution, which allegedly proved that the student movement had finally and irrevocably entered a new, Marxist phase.[56] This is an overstatement. It is clear that the students at the February *skhodka* were not fully aware of the implications of the resolution. The mood within the university was as festive as it was serious, and demands such as the eight-hour day and threats to use force were tacked on with wild abandon and with little serious discussion.[57] The SAS had left, most members of the Executive Committee were in jail, and the leaders of the new committee were even more inexperienced than their arrested comrades. Despite what the resolution said, they obviously had no contacts with workers' organizations (although the government was frightened enough to station troops in the workers' districts). To be sure, such a resolution was, as events soon proved, a risky step. It would have been unthinkable in 1899 or even in 1901. Disappointed in Vannovskii, the *studenchestvo* in early 1902 was in fact drifting toward a stance of political opposition, but the bombastic declarations concealed clear and important continuities with the traditions of student protest. Camaraderie, a sense of self-importance, and a feeling of historic mission created a mood tinged with a mixture of euphoria and apprehension. Spontaneity rather than calculation, fellowship rather than organization underlay the 9 February *skhodka*.[58]

55. The text of the resolution can be found in "Studencheskoe dvizhenie," pp. 278–279.

56. For example, P. S. Gusiatnikov, *Revoliutsionnoe studencheskoe dvizhenie v Rossii* (Moscow, 1971), p. 81.

57. An excellent unpublished memoir of the 1902 student movement discusses this point. See "1901–02: Iz zapisok svidetelia," which appeared in *Nashi Tovarishchi*. This is a hectographed collection of essays on the student movement which appeared in 1903. A copy can be found in the Lenin Library.

58. A good source on this *skhodka* and the second thoughts entertained by some of its participants is the collection of letters of the arrested students published in G. A. Veselaia, "Pis'ma studentov i kursistok iz Butyrskoi tiur'my," in V. G. Verzhbitskii, ed., *Materialy po istorii Rossii v period kapitalizma* (Moscow, 1976), esp. pp. 27–28. See also "1901–02"; and "Pis'mo kursistki," in P. A. Zaionchkovskii, ed., *Moskovskii universitet v vospominaniiakh sovremennikov* (Moscow, 1956), pp. 398–400.

THE GOVERNMENT REACTS

Even before the government heard about the latest student resolution in Moscow, the changed attitude toward the student movement portended an unprecedented crackdown. Sipiagin saw the latest round of student disorders as an integral part of a plan to destabilize the empire.[59] One reason he came out so strongly against allowing general *skhodki* during the discussions of the rules on student organizations was that he believed that provoking the students might provide a welcome opportunity to cripple the student movement before it got even more dangerous.[60] As for Witte, he now abandoned his 1899 belief that the student movement was basically harmless, arguing that the student movement had become very dangerous, especially because the students were trying to radicalize the workers.[61] (Even if he really did not believe in what he was saying, it may not be excessively cynical to assume that Witte found such an argument a convenient weapon in his ongoing battle against the Zubatov movement.) Grand Duke Sergei Alexandrovich, determined to crush the students and avert the possibility of a Sunday demonstration, ordered police and troops into the university on the night of 8–9 February.

Inside the university, the students made themselves at home. After the SAS supporters walked out, about 550 students remained, including 73 women.[62] A helpful *privat-dozent* allowed the students to use his nearby apartment for making tea and cooking. Groups of students used chairs and beams to barricade all entrances. Because a few students had daggers or pistols, there was some talk of resisting arrest, but in the end the students decided on a course of passive resistance. The evening passed in singing and storytelling; by midnight many students had fallen asleep. Plans for the next day were somewhat vague but called for students to leave the university and attempt a march into the center of the city.

Anxiously waiting outside the university gates, Grand Duke Sergei Alexandrovich expected the worst—a bloody pitched battle between the police and the students.[63] At two A.M. a student yelled, "They're

59. TsGAOR, f. DP 00, 3ch. 78/1898, l. 160.
60. TsGIA, f. 733, op. 151, d. 286, l. 144.
61. TsGIA, f. 733, op. 151, d. 293, l. 63.
62. See "1901–02."
63. Iu. B. Solov'ëv, *Samoderzhavie i dvorianstvo v kontse 19 veka* (Leningrad, 1973), p. 159.

coming!" The students inside looked out and saw an eerie spectacle: the glare of firemen's flashlights reflecting the fixed bayonets of the soldiers marching into the main university building.[64] Some laughed at the sight of such military force employed to clear out a few students; others were more frightened. An officer entered the auditorium with a drawn pistol and warned that if the troops met any armed resistance they would shoot. The soldiers quickly took 509 students to the Manezh, and from there marched them in small groups to the Butyrka prison. On the way the marching students tried to wake up the sleeping city with rousing choruses of the "Marseillaise" and "Dubinushka."[65] Back at the university, a relieved Sergei Alexandrovich, who had been clutching a cross all night, fell into the arms of D. F. Trepov, his police chief.[66]

Coming so soon after the Saint Petersburg *skhodka* and the Kiev street demonstration, the mass arrest in Moscow touched off a spreading student strike that quickly affected most of the country's *VUZy*.[67] Although the strike itself began to lose momentum after the Easter vacation, the events of February and March had thrown the government into confusion. Were the Temporary Rules on student organization still in force? Did the 1899 rules on conscripting student protesters still apply? Witte pointed out that the decision to exile the Moscow and Saint Petersburg students nullified the 1899 rules and thus left the government once again with no coherent policy regarding the student problem.[68] The Okhrana, in a 12 March memorandum, admitted that it was worried about student disorders—they were destabilizing and undermined "public safety and security"—but cautioned against any public admission of concern. Nevertheless, on 12 March a communiqué in the *Pravitel'stvennyi Vestnik* glumly noted that the student movement had taken a "political turn."[69]

The arrested Moscow and Saint Petersburg students immediately suffered the consequences of the government's growing worry about the political implications of the student movement. Grand Duke Sergei Alexandrovich successfully insisted on unprecedented severity, a view

---

64. "Pis'mo kursistki," pp. 399–400.
65. Report of Moscow procurator to Ministry of Justice in TsGAOR, f. 124, op. 10, ed. kh. 442, 1901, l. 160.
66. Solov'ëv, *Samoderzhavie i dvorianstvo*, p. 159.
67. POA, index no. 16B, folder 14A.
68. TsGAOR, f. DP OO, 3ch. 78/1898, l. 215.
69. The Okhrana memorandum is quoted from TsGAOR, f. 102, ed. kh. 2ch. 3LG, l. 14. The communiqué is taken from a copy of the article found in TsGAOR, f. DP OO, 3ch. 78/1898, l. 199.

enthusiastically supported by Tsar Nicholas II.[70] Despite some mis-givings within the government, a 20 February conference deciding the fate of the Executive Committee members and the Moscow University students arrested at the *skhodka* decided to sentence 95 to Siberian exile for terms ranging from two to four years, and 567 to jail for three to six months.[71] The Siberian penalty was applied only to students from Saint Petersburg and Moscow, but students elsewhere also received jail terms or banishment to their home towns.

Although the students in Butyrka and other prisons got the punish-ments usually reserved for real political prisoners, they neither looked like nor were treated like dedicated revolutionaries. One student in Butyrka recalled that his cell consisted of rather exotic cliques, each with a distinctive nickname—the "Dagomeitsi," Armenians and Geor-gians who kept everyone awake with their all-night singing and their demands for snacks; "yellow-bellies" who covered themselves with iodine out of solidarity with a sick comrade; "turtles" who prided them-selves on their ability to ignore everything else and sleep around the clock. The *zemliachestva* continued to meet. There were also the "revo-lutionaries" who stood apart, but they were a small minority.[72]

As before, student prisoners received privileged treatment. In Butyrka the students put out two jail newspapers and organized a choir and a debating society.[73] During their daily walks in the prison courtyard sev-eral students built a "tribune" of piled snow in the prison yard and yelled political speeches to the criminals in the upper stories. At first the prison authorities did not interfere. During the evenings, a wandering storyteller named Sladkopevtsev went from cell to cell entertaining the students with stories and anecdotes.

The Butyrka group, which by the end of February totaled 624, also conducted a census to gather information on the students' social back-ground and financial situation.[74] One of the more important findings of the census was that there was no relationship between financial depriva-

70. TsGAOR, f. 102, op. 10, ed. kh. 442/1901, l. 173. In fact, the Grand Duke wanted all the arrested students sent to Siberia. On 11 February 1902 the tsar called for "drastic measures." See G. Nikol'skaia, "Iz revoliutsii Nikolaia Romanova," *Krasnyi Arkhiv* 63 (1934): 130.

71. TsGAOR, f. 124, op. 10, ed. kh. 442/1901, l. 224; TsGAOR, f. DP 00, 3ch. 78/1898, l. 199.

72. Sergei E—v, "Iz istorii studencheskikh bezporiadkov," in G. B. Sliozberg, ed., *Pamiati russkovo studenchestva* (Paris, 1934), p. 75.

73. Ibid.

74. The results of this census can be found in "1901–02," p. 226.

tion and the decision to participate in the 1902 student movement. Even the members of the Executive Committee were at least as well off as the average student.[75] Of the entire student body, 14.2 percent found themselves in Butyrka: 15.2 percent of the medical students, 20.6 percent of the natural science students, 10.1 percent of the juridical students, 17.2 percent of the history and philology students, and 13 percent of the mathematics students. Ratios of participation ranged from nearly 25 percent of the freshman natural science students to only 6.5 percent of the senior juridical students. A most striking difference between the Butyrka students and the general student body was the fact that only 13.3 percent of the former but 26 percent of the latter had gone to a secondary school in Moscow. The arrested students also tended to be younger. Only 4.4 percent of the arrestees, as opposed to 7.8 percent of the general student body, were over twenty-seven years old; 19.3 percent of the arrestees, as opposed to 31.2 percent of the general student body, were between twenty-four and twenty-six years old, and 40.4 percent of the arrestees, as opposed to 25.7 percent of the general student population, were under twenty-one years old.[76]

After a few weeks, relations between the prison administration and the students began to deteriorate. Rumors that guards were insulting women students led to a hunger strike and snowball attacks on the guards.[77] During the week of 20 March, while most of the Butyrka students began their three- to six-month terms in various jails, the Saint Petersburg and Moscow "ringleaders"—members of the Kassa Radikalov and the Executive Committee—were put on a train for Siberia.

G. I. Chulkov, veteran of the Executive Committee, gave a vivid description of the convoy:

> No group of political prisoners sent to Siberia was as numerous and high-spirited as ours. Ours was the happiest group of exiles. . . . We sang songs the whole way and held onto our precious red flag; at every stop crowds welcomed us. . . . The authorities and guards—thrown into total confusion by this unusual group and its irrepressible high spirits—had no idea how to

75. Of thirty-four students on the Executive Committee who volunteered information on their means of support, twenty were supported by their parents. Sixteen lived on a monthly budget of less than 25 rubles a month, nine received between 25 and 35 rubles a month, and nine lived on more than 35 rubles a month; at that time, the average budget of a Moscow student was 25 rubles a month. A detailed survey of the arrested committee members, including their financial situations, can be found in BMGU, f. V. I. Orlova.

76. This is based on a comparison of the arrest list found in the police archives with a computer profile of the Moscow student body based on every fifth name found in Imperatorskii Moskovskii Universitet, *Alfavitnyi spisok studentov za 1902 god* (Moscow, 1903).

77. TsGAOR, f. 124, op. 10, ed. kh. 442/1901, l. 280.

subject us to regular discipline. The authorities were used to the dour and sullen resistance of underground veterans, to their asceticism and defiance. All of a sudden they confront our good-natured insolence, our youthful daring, our open insubordination.[78]

In Tula the train carrying the Saint Petersburg Kassa Radikalov joined the Moscow contingent, and the convoy rolled east. Relations between the two groups got off to a bad start when the Saint Petersburg students walked into the car where the women were staying and rejected the *kursistki*'s appeals to leave. They told the women students that sexual segregation was an outmoded bourgeois prejudice, but retreated after the Moscow male students intervened. A short time later some of the men held a meeting and decided to marry their female comrades in order to protect them from the wild animals and other rigors of their impending exile. When a student entered the women's car to inform them of this decision taken on their behalf, he was surprised to find himself seized by a hefty *kursistka* who hurled him out of the car amid shouts of indignant approval from her female colleagues.[79]

After a few weeks the students finally arrived at the Alexandrovsk Central Prison on the Angara River. From there they were to be dispersed among various settlements. But days went by, and the students began to demand that the authorities tell them exactly where each of them would be going.[80] When they failed to get a prompt answer they barricaded the prison yard, chased out the guards, and raised a red flag. The students received welcome support from other political detainees in the prison, including Felix Dzerzhinskii, future head of Lenin's secret police, who offered to guard the flag that waved above the wooded stockade. The prison authorities told the students where they would be going and the siege ended. Still wearing their uniforms, the students now boarded barges for the long upriver trips to their remote destinations. On the way they still expected and received special treatment. One group of students bound for Iakutiia, including Executive Committee members Khovrin and Chulkov, refused to part with the red flag and carried it with them up the Lena River. Finally, one official boarded the

---

78. G. I. Chulkov, *Gody stranstvii: Iz knigi vospominanii* (Moscow, 1930), p. 17. Chulkov later became a poet and literary critic.

79. See "Sibiriada," an extremely valuable hectographed memoir of the Siberian trip written by an unnamed but unmistakably pro-Marxist veteran of the trip. This can be found in BMGU, f. V. I. Orlova, no. 1237. Cf. Chulkov, *Gody stranstvii*, p. 19.

80. Chulkov, *Gody stranstvii*, p. 21; see also the 12 May 1902 report of the Irkutsk vice-governor in "Studencheskoe dvizhenie," pp. 298–300.

barge and ordered Khovrin to hand over the flag. Khovrin calmly replied that as far as he knew the color red was supposed to bother only oxen and bulls. He kept his flag.

The Siberian odyssey affected the students in different ways. Some, like Chulkov, enjoyed the scenery and used the opportunity to get to know the political exiles and make a deeper personal commitment to the revolutionary cause. Indeed, the experience caused many politically inclined students to take a new look at their comrades, and it strengthened their doubts about the student movement.[81] Had the student movement been worth the severe punishment? What had it achieved? Supposedly the exiled group included the cream of the Saint Petersburg and Moscow student movement, the leadership of the Kassa Radikalov and the Executive Committee. They had all organized *skhodki* and faced down the fear of arrest, exile, and expulsion. Had they expressed contrition, they might have gotten off with three- to six-month jail terms, but they had refused. Yet some students noticed a puzzling incongruity between the personal courage of their comrades and their frivolity.[82] Though unafraid of arrest, once in jail they seemed interested only in reading cheap novels, singing songs, playing cards, or flirting with women.

Iskra had reported the Siberian exile with the hopeful comment that the government had now begun the "mass production of revolutionaries."[83] But one anonymous veteran of the Siberian trip cynically remarked that *Iskra* just did not understand the student movement.[84] The Moscow *skhodka* had called for the overthrow of the autocracy, and it was true that a mysterious "student congress" issued a manifesto that the students must join the Social Democratic movement.[85] But all this,

81. BMGU, f. V. I. Orlova, no. 1237.
82. Grigorii Nestroev, who would later join the Social Revolutionary party, was arrested about this time for student disturbances at Kharkov University; he mentions, with great chagrin, the same incongruity marking the attitudes of the jailed Kharkov University student leaders. See Grigorii Nestroev, *Iz dnevnika maksimalista* (Paris, 1910), p. 10.
83. *Iskra*, no. 19 (1902).
84. BMGU, f. V. I. Orlova, no. 1237.
85. The full text of the manifesto can be found in POA, index no. 16B, folder 14A. It appeared in February 1902, after the arrest of the Kassa Radikalov and the Moscow University Executive Committee. In the absence of leadership from the central universities, it is hard to avoid the impression that Gusiatnikov errs in labeling this manifesto the work of an "All-Russian student congress" (*Revoliutsionnoe studencheskoe*, pp. 75–76). Grigorii Nestroev is closer to the mark when he emphasizes students' resentment of the manifesto and their feeling that it was issued by an unrepresentative and totally unknown group ("K istorii studencheskovo dvizheniia v Rossii," *Katorga i ssylka* 28–29 [1926]: 133). An educated guess is that the Marxist document was issued by an Armenian students' meeting called at the Riga Polytechnic Institute in February 1902. See "Studencheskie gody Stepana Shaumiana," *Proletarskaia Revoliutsiia* 9 (1923).

the memoirist concluded in his hectographed "Sibiriada," was long on rhetoric and short on political sense. The long trip east reinforced his suspicion that the student uniform, which they all wore, symbolized what seemed to be an unbridgeable gap between the intelligentsia and the masses. For the most part the guards were respectful and stood aside while the students regaled the curious crowds at the stations with revolutionary songs. But he suspected that most of the peasants they saw on the way regarded the students as "privileged characters" (*studentov ne tronut*).

Thus, the Siberian experience led some students back to the orthodox Marxist view that the student movement was a waste of time and that only a commitment to the revolutionary movement made sense. But other students in Siberia drew different conclusions from their exile. A sizable group reaffirmed their commitment to the Kassa Radikalov position that the student movement was vitally important both as a catalyst to mobilize other social groups and as a reminder of the autocracy's basic impotence. In *Osvobozhdenie*, the journal Peter Struve founded in 1902 to form a wide-ranging coalition against the autocracy, these students found a sympathetic forum. It was clear, from a long letter written by this group which appeared in *Osvobozhdenie*, that some students in Siberia saw their arrest and exile as a victory, not a defeat. They had discredited the government and proven that the student movement was growing in size and importance.[86] Sending the students to Siberia had made the government look weak and foolish. The government had no coherent policy for dealing with the student movement and went from one policy to another. Meanwhile all social groups in Russia, including the aristocracy and the bourgeoisie, were becoming more alienated from the state. The real conflict in Russia, the letter continued, was not between classes but between "Europeanization" and traditional autocratic forms. The universities were the focal point of this confrontation and the student movement was in the vanguard of the political struggle. Of course, the Marxist exiles rejected the *Osvobozhdenie* letter and sent their own article to *Iskra* that documented the ideological polarization within the exile group and affirmed the leading role of the proletariat in the coming political showdown.[87]

Soon another issue split the student exiles: the government's offer of

---

86. "Otkrytoe pis'mo ot soslannykh v vostochnuiu Sibir' v 1902 studentov i kursistok," *Osvobozhdenie*, no. 14 (1903). Commenting on this letter, Peter Struve noted that these students "showed a clarity of political understanding . . . which representatives of more radical political strands in Russia often lack."

87. "Eshche o studentakh v Sibiri," *Iskra*, no. 30 (1902).

partial amnesty and permission to return to Russia.[88] Once again the autocracy was wavering in its student policy. Almost as soon as the students arrived in Siberia the government had second thoughts about its new tough line. In August 1902, Prince Sviatopolk-Mirskii, then assistant minister of the interior, was sent to Siberia to meet with the exiles and discuss the possibility of amnesty in exchange for promises of good behavior.[89] Some students wanted to accept Sviatopolk-Mirskii's offer; others refused to meet him. The minister tried to be polite. He told the students who met him that their parents were very upset and asked them whether in fact they had been guilty of anti-government demonstrations the previous February.[90] In a comment on the Sviatopolk-Mirskii mission published in *Osvobozhdenie,* Struve pointed out that the Russian government, having fixed the punishment, now decided to ask the accused whether they had indeed committed any crime![91] Although many students persisted in their boycott, Sviatopolk-Mirskii recommended freeing all the exiles. The returning students were divided into three categories with varying conditions of police supervision and residence restrictions.[92] The abrupt about-face on the Siberian exile was seen by the students and the émigré press as a victory of the students over the government.

A NEW POLICY

Now that Siberian exile had gone the way of the July 1899 Temporary Rules on conscription and the November 1901 Temporary Rules on student organization, the government went back to the drawing boards for a new student policy. On 13 August 1902, an interministerial conference admitted the unworkability of the Temporary Rules of the previous fall. At the same time the conference emphasized that there could be no return to one of the fundamental principles of the 1884 Statute: the notion that students were "individual visitors" in the university with no corporate rights. What the ministers now recommended involved the abrogation of yet another key assumption of the statute,

---

88. A good account of these disagreements can be found in *Iskra,* no. 30 (1902), and also in BMGU, f. V. I. Orlova, no. 1237.

89. "Studencheskoe dvizhenie," pp. 303–304.

90. BMGU, f. V. I. Orlova, no. 1237.

91. "Missiia Sviatopolka-Mirskovo i eë rezultaty," *Osvobozhdenie,* no. 13 (1903).

92. The students who had been jailed the previous spring were also released; see TsGAOR, f. 124, op. 10, ed. kh. 442/1901, l. 469.

the idea that the professoriate should assume no responsibility for internal university discipline.[93]

In a major policy shift, the August 1902 conference recommended the institution of a professors' disciplinary court, as well as new rules on student organizations. As we have already seen, the guidelines establishing the disciplinary courts failed to define adequately some crucial issues: punishments, the type of offenses to be handled by the courts, and the clear delineation of authority between the new courts and the state-appointed rectors and curators.[94] The new rules on student organizations allowed meetings by courses but stubbornly upheld the ban on general *skhodki*. Course meetings, as well as meetings of student extracurricular groups now legalized by the new rules, had to secure the supervision of a professor. As before, collective student petitions were forbidden.[95]

Clearly, the constant cycle of student unrest was forcing the government to continue the piecemeal abrogation of the 1884 Statute. In time, the August 1902 rules were to go the way of previous attempts to solve the university question. The disciplinary courts would intensify the friction between the government and the professoriate, while most students persisted in their refusal to accept any rules that denied them their right to *skhodki* or collective petitions. Nonetheless, the August 1902 guidelines did make some important changes in academic life. For the first time since the mid-1880s, the government allowed organizations in the universities in which professors and students could meet in a relatively informal atmosphere to discuss academic issues of mutual concern. One of the most important of these new organizations was the Historical-Philosophical Society in Moscow University. Chaired by Professor Sergei Trubetskoi, the society sponsored a trip to Greece and encouraged students to read papers and compositions on philosophical and historical themes. The society became an object of bitter criticism by politically minded students who argued that such a forum merely propagandized the liberal dream of a "university above politics" and revived the discredited myth that a free university was able to function in an autocratic state.[96]

---

93. TsGAOR, f. DP 00, 3ch. 78/1898, l. 230.
94. A summary of the rules under which the disciplinary courts operated can be found in *Russkie Vedomosti*, 29 August 1902.
95. TsGAOR, f. DP 00, 3ch. 78/1898, l. 230.
96. Anisimov's "Kniaz' S. N. Trubetskoi" gives an excellent description of the society. The historian S. P. Mel'gunov, who had been a student member, takes a more ambivalent

THE MOVEMENT RESPONDS

At this time, politicals had to face some very difficult questions. In contrast to the previous two academic years, 1902–1903 passed quietly; the passivity of the students proved an embarrassing contrast to the quickening of the political pulse in the nation at large. In an open letter to the *studenchestvo*, the Saint Petersburg Committee of the RSDRP (All-Russian Social Democratic Workers party) demanded to know why the students, after years of struggle, now seemed indifferent to the Rostov strike, the peasant riots in the south, and the Kishinev pogrom: "The peasantry is protesting, the worker is protesting, the timid liberals are raising their heads, and the Russian *studenchestvo*, the 'barometer of Russian life,' is quiet."[97] This reproach underscored the problems of student Radicalism as well as the pitfalls of underestimating the autonomy of the student movement. Other groups were in action, but the students seemed untouched by these developments outside the universities. How, then, could one justify the traditional proud claim that the *studenchestvo* was the vanguard and the conscience of Russian society?

To be sure, there were student protests over local issues in various *VUZy*—Warsaw, Tomsk, Moscow, and Saint Petersburg universities, as well as in the Saint Petersburg Women's Medical Institute.[98] But, unlike the situation in 1901 and 1902, there was now no national issue to unite the student movement, no simultaneous wave of student strikes and protests. The Partizany Bor'by of Saint Petersburg University, a successor to the Kassa Radikalov, attributed the universities' passivity to ideological confusion. The student movement was in transition; it was searching for new answers in the elusive quest for an ideology of student protest.[99] Others saw a simpler explanation in the arrests at the beginning of the year, which "decapitated" the student movement.[100]

An important new element in the student movement was the emerging conflict between the adherents of Social Democracy and supporters of the Social Revolutionary party. A key issue was whether there should be

---

view. He compares the government's motives in encouraging the society to those of Zubatov in setting up his police unions (*Vospominaniia i dnevniki* [Paris, 1964], p. 73).

97. *Iskra*, no. 5 (1903).

98. Curators' reports to the Ministry of Education on these disturbances can be found in TsGIA, f. 733, op. 151, d. 597.

99. See the Partizany Bor'by pamphlet "Chto zhe nam delat'," *Osvobozhdenie*, no. 20–21 (1903).

100. This was the view expressed in "Nashe znamia," a hectographed pamphlet that can be found in BMGU, f. V. I. Orlova, no. 1238.

a united student movement or a student movement divided along clear party lines. As the Siberian debates showed, many students believed that the main lesson of the 1902 arrests was that the idea of a united student movement, the student Radicalism of the Kassa Radikalov, had outlived its time. To win maximum student support, politically committed students had to sacrifice too much doctrinal clarity and political direction and devote too much effort to academic concerns. The Kassa Radikalov had argued that this was the way to achieve a strong student movement, which in turn would spark protest from other social groups. Now this position seemed less plausible, for the rest of society was stirring, while the universities were quiet. One pamphlet that circulated in Saint Petersburg University, "K aktivnomu studenchestvu," asked whether a key assumption of student Radicalism, the importance of attracting large numbers of students to demonstrations and strikes, was really worth the price. The pamphlet conceded that students were more prone to protest than other social groups, but unlike the proletariat, they were unwilling to fight to the end. The reason was the constant tension between their dissatisfaction with university policy and the knowledge that a relatively comfortable life awaited them when they left.[101]

Iskra threw its support behind the 1902 manifesto of the anonymous group that called on students to ally with local Social Democratic organizations.[102] But this call for partisan self-definition met with a hostile response from several student organizations. The Kiev United Council of Zemliachestva and the Organization Committee of the Kiev Polytechnic Institute responded in an open letter asserting that the *studenchestvo* as such could not ally with either of the two revolutionary factions, although it could serve as a recruiting base for both.[103]

The Social Revolutionary party now entered the dispute with stinging attacks on *Iskra* and the Marxist view of the student movement.[104] The *studenchestvo*, it editorialized, was a transitional group and could not make party commitments. The Social Revolutionaries also accused the Marxists of systematically underestimating the importance of the student movement itself, citing the impact of the student protests of the past three years. The students, even while defending their own interests, had awakened Russian society and had embarrassed the government.

101. TsGAOR, f. 124, op. 10, ed. kh. 442/1901, l. 283.
102. "Opekaemoe studenchestvo," *Iskra*, no. 31 (1903). See also note 85, above.
103. In *Revoliutsionnaia Rossiia*, no. 13 (1902).
104. "Studenchestvo i revoliutsiia," *Revoliutsionnaia Rossiia*, no. 17 (1902); "K uchashcheisia molodëzhi," *Revoliutsionnaia Rossiia*, no. 19 (1903).

They had shown other groups, especially the workers, that it was possible to protest. Furthermore, it was pointless and counterproductive to force the *studenchestvo* and the intelligentsia into the procrustean bed of Marxist class theory. The Social Revolutionary newspaper told the students to avoid the "either-or" of the Marxists: strikes or demonstrations, united student movement or party organization, *zemliachestva* or political study groups. Everything was useful that helped mobilize support against the autocracy. Since the universities were part of the system, even academic struggle was useful and instructive. In effect, the Social Revolutionaries were supporting the Kassa Radikalov line of the previous year.

If student Radicalism seemed obsolete, Marxism posed some psychological problems of its own. Even student Social Democrats admitted a certain frustration at following a theory that assigned primacy to the working class and lowered the self-esteem of the *studenchestvo*. In 1899 and 1901 the student movement had caught the Marxists up short, but few really believed that such surprises were likely to happen again soon. So was the answer to be the abandonment of the student movement and the formation of Social Democratic organizations?

In 1903 a hectographed volume of essays on the student movement, "Nashi tovarishchi," appeared in Moscow. The authors were Siberian returnees, veterans of the 1901–1902 Moscow University student movement.[105] One essay, "K molodëzhi," described with uncanny insight the problems faced by the students as they watched the process of party formation in the wider society. The students, the essay asserted, were "stupid" as they ran back and forth between ideologies and tried and discarded tactics in rapid succession:

> Morally separated from the bourgeoisie and fundamentally distinct from the working class, the [*studenchestvo*] cannot adopt either the triumphant philistinism [*torzhestvuiushchei poshlosti*] of the former or the clear consciousness of the latter. . . . Unable to believe that it is an independent force in its own right, the *studenchestvo* vainly tries to assume foreign identities.

Liberalism, the essay argued, stood for cowardice and was thus fundamentally unattractive to the *studenchestvo*. Social Democracy, with its clear and logical ideology, its proud self-confidence that it ruled the future, was attracting many students. But there was a problem here,

---

105. Textual similarities with the unpublished V. I. Orlov memoirs suggest that Orlov wrote at least some of these essays.

too: "There are two strands in Social Democracy. One says that 'Social Democracy is the ideology of the working class.' The other says that 'Social Democracy will win because of the inevitable logic of economic development.' Fine, but what about us? We're not workers! And you can't love the inevitable, you can only bow to it." In Russia the intelligentsia stood alone. Unlike other classes in Russian society, the intelligentsia was defined by idealism, not economic self-interest. As the most organized part of the intelligentsia, the *studenchestvo* too had to make choices that were not self-seeking. At the present moment, the essay argued, the best choice for the *studenchestvo* was to collaborate with Social Democracy without adopting Marxist ideology. The Social Revolutionaries flattered the students' egos by telling them that their movement counted. But unfortunately the Social Revolutionaries did not have the political or the ideological consistency to bring down the autocracy. Their obsession with terror and "action" was appealing but ineffectual. Their advice to the students—constant protest—promised little but defeat: "Let us forget our [traditions] of . . . splendid isolation. . . . We think that the students should collaborate with the Social Democrats not because of ideological affinity but because of tactical expediency. Our demands for social and political freedom arise not from an analysis of the capitalist system but out of the belief that each individual has the moral right to work out his own fate." Ironically, this attitude suggested closer affinity to the subjectivist position of the Social Revolutionaries, or even to liberal individualism, than to the dialectical materialism of Marxism. But only Social Democracy, the essay argued, was "strong enough" to bring down the system.

In short, "K molodëzhi" argued that the days of an independent student movement were gone. The students should become "fellow travelers" of Russian Social Democracy without forgetting that socially and psychologically they were quite separate from the working class. And once the autocracy fell, individuals would be free to seek and realize their own ideals.

Clearly, therefore, in advising the students to support Social Democracy, the author of "K molodëzhi" did not endorse either a socialist Russia or the dictatorship of the proletariat. In fact, he was propagating the liberal ideal of individual freedom while rejecting political liberalism and the perceived revolutionary romanticism of the Social Revolutionary party as possible means of securing the essential precondition to its realization, the overthrow of the autocracy.

Many students found themselves unable to accept these calls to bury the student movement and affiliate with political parties. Unable, however, to defend student Radicalism or make any other case for an independent student movement, some student organizations openly threw up their hands. In December 1903, for example, the Kiev University United Council dissolved itself and issued a valedictory proclamation that emphasized the conflict between the old myth of the *studenchestvo* and the new changes taking place in the country. Old student traditions seemed outdated, the United Council stated, and student organizations did not know how to respond to new challenges. But the members of the United Council could not make the break, as they themselves admitted:

> We are experiencing a very difficult period. New challenges demand immediate solutions but we cannot free ourselves from the traditions of the past which bind us so tightly. The thankless job of resolving the contradictions of the student movement has fallen on our shoulders. Student organizations, which were the main foundation of the student movement, have begun to lose their vitality, but alternatives have yet to appear. A purely student-oriented movement, which in the past seemed the most suitable form for struggle and protest, now appears to be losing its rationale. . . . The present members of the United Council feel that they are at a crossroads between the old and the new [and are at the same time unable to break with the traditions of the past]. . . . We resign in full confidence that a new group not so closely bound to the legacy of the past will lead the *studenchestvo* on a new course which will be just as glorious as was the old one.[106]

One attempt to give the student movement a new sense of purpose came from Grigorii Nestroev, a former Kharkov University student who had been arrested in 1902 for participating in the student movement there. (Later on Nestroev would become a leading member of the Maximalist faction of the Social Revolutionary party.) Although the frivolousness of some of the Kharkov student leaders had annoyed Nestroev, he was at the same time unable to accept the Marxist condemnation of the student movement. He had seen the psychological impact of the student demonstrations in Kharkov and believed that the *studenchestvo* could remain an important force if only it resolved some of its ideological problems.

The solution Nestroev advocated was "nonparty socialism." Students would feel free to sympathize with any party but would, he hoped, collaborate within the universities. In 1903 Nestroev founded the jour-

106. TsGIA, f. 733, op. 151, d. 639, l. 212.

nal *Student* as an organizational and ideological focus for the student movement.[107]

In its first issue *Student* asked the students: "Should we admit that our movement is spontaneous, that it resists any attempt to give it direction, and that it cannot be bent to our will and our reason?" It was time for the students to recall what their European counterparts had accomplished in 1848 and turn the student movement into a coherent force. But first they had to abandon the conceit of "splendid isolation. . . . Only we students have not yet joined the general social movement, only we students still harbor the stupid and dangerous illusion that we can create a little state within a state."[108]

In November 1903, *Student* organized a national student conference in Odessa. Saint Petersburg University sent a delegate representing a student Social Revolutionary group, as well as G. A. Engel', a veteran of the Kassa Radikalov and now a member of a student Social Democratic group. There were also delegates representing the editorial board of *Student,* and delegates from Kharkov, Moscow, Odessa, Riga, and Kiev universities.[109]

From the first day of the conference, it became clear that Social Democratic sympathizers exerted the predominant influence. The conference elected Engel' as its president.[110] The deliberations lasted three days, during which the students drafted a manifesto deciding the future principles of the student movement. It was not an easy job—Nestroev recalls that during the last twenty-four hours of the conference, the students became so involved in debate that they forgot to adjourn for meals.

The report reflected the Social Democratic line. The *studenchestvo* as a self-contained group imbued with a sense of corporate traditions and separate identity was disappearing. The rise of the working class meant that the era of massive, politically important student movements on the

107. Nestroev, "K istorii," pp. 131–133; "Na vernyi put'," *Student,* no. 1 (1903). The first issue of the journal was dedicated to the memory of S. V. Balmashev, the student who had assassinated Minister of the Interior D. S. Sipiagin in 1902. Three issues of *Student* appeared in 1903, all in Switzerland.

108. "Na vernyi put'."

109. G. Engel', "1905g. i studencheskoe dvizhenie v Peterburge," *Krasnaia Letopis',* no. 2 (1925): 97–98; Nestroev, "K istorii," p. 145. Some preparatory materials for the conference—questionnaires, letters, etc.—can be found in BMGU, f. V. I. Orlova, 5dt., no. 50.

110. Engel' joined the Bolshevik party in 1904. After the October Revolution he became a professor of social sciences at Leningrad University.

scale of those of 1899, 1901, and 1902 was also passing into history. Political and social differentiation was destroying the *studenchestvo* and forcing the students to see the political party as the ideal form of student organization.[111]

To replace the old United Councils, Executive Committees, and Organization Committees, the conference report urged the formation of student coalition councils consisting of representatives of political groups—Social Democrats, Social Revolutionaries, and others. In a major departure from the traditions of the student movement the report recommended banning the *zemliachestva* from participation unless they represented a definite ideology. The major task of the new coalition councils was to harness the energies of the students to serve the political goals of the major revolutionary parties. Instead of reacting to corporate issues, as they had in the past, students would now show self-restraint and save their demonstrations for major political anniversaries such as 19 February or 1 May. Neither the student Social Democrats nor the student Social Revolutionaries would sacrifice any of their independence by their collaboration on the coalition councils. The primary role of the councils was to be tactical, not doctrinal. It was hoped that they would gradually turn the student masses away from illusions about the student movement and lead them in more useful directions, such as carefully orchestrated demonstrations to suit the convenience of the revolutionary parties.

The universities would not accept the decisions of the Odessa conference. Although the adherents of student Radicalism had lost a lot of their confidence, the students still showed a stubborn loyalty to the traditions of the *studenchestvo* and an independent student movement. The events of the 1903–1904 and 1904–1905 academic years showed that the goal of harnessing the energies of the students to the needs of the revolutionary parties proved much easier to talk about than to realize. The new coalition councils were to have a very hard time controlling the student movement.

Within a month of the Odessa conference, the formation of new United Councils in Moscow and Riga showed that many students rejected the call to replace the traditional forms of student organization, such as the *zemliachestva*, with coalition councils based on political groups. The new Moscow University and Riga Polytechnic United Coun-

111. A copy of the conference report can be found in TsGIA, f. 733, op. 151, d. 638, l. 226.

cils issued proclamations making unflattering comparisons between the constant bickering of the revolutionary parties and the traditional unity and sense of purpose of the *studenchestvo*. As the December 1903 Riga proclamation showed, loyalty to student traditions died hard: "Naturally the *studenchestvo* should energetically struggle against this system . . . of evil and despotism. Since it is composed of young people, the *studenchestvo* has a lot of energy. Other social groups are based on mutual rivalry; students are immune from this and are relatively insulated from the corrosive influence of self-interest."[112] The Riga United Council made it quite clear that the students needed no outside guidance.

There was yet another telling reminder that the Odessa conference may have been premature in proclaiming the end of an independent student movement. On 10 November 1903, a large *skhodka* met in Saint Petersburg University to discuss supporting a strike in the higher women's courses. The immediate cause of the women's strike was an obscure incident in which a policeman insulted a *kursistka*. What is significant about the *skhodka* is that it was a completely spontaneous expression of solidarity with fellow students— exactly the kind of demonstration that the Odessa conference had declared a waste of time. Student Social Democrats were hard put to explain why students ignored workers' strikes, yet rallied to support their own.[113]

When sixty-three students were summoned to appear before the professors' disciplinary court, the university Social Democratic organization found itself faced with an unattractive choice: either to ignore the incident or to join the Radical Partizany Bor'by in organizing a demonstration against the court. The Social Democrats chose to participate. Over a hundred students jammed the stairwell and tried to keep the court from convening. Unimpressed, the professors suspended seventeen students for one academic year.

The incident forced the Radicals and the Social Democrats into unwilling cooperation, but it also exacerbated the hostility that the Social Democratic students felt for the traditions of student Radicalism. Engel', the president of the Odessa conference and the leader of the student Social Democratic organization, resented the incident.[114] He felt that the more politically mature students had been dragged into a confrontation with the authorities at an inopportune time and because of a secondary

112. Quoted in "Brozhenie v vysshikh uchebnykh zavedeniiakh," *Osvobozhdenie*, nos. 15–16 (1904).

113. TsGIA, f. 733, op. 151, d. 639, l. 97.

114. Engel' and Gorokhov, *Iz istorii*, p. 95.

issue. The suspensions were yet another example of the futility of student Radicalism and the student movement. Engel' called for a greater effort in the propaganda campaign against student Radicalism.

The Partizany Bor'by drew different conclusions. While the Radicals admitted that the *skhodka* fell short of unqualified success, it nonetheless proved that the students were still very sensitive to issues directly affecting the interests of the *studenchestvo*. The *skhodka*

> shows how much revolutionary energy still lives in the bosom of the *studenchestvo*. At the same time we face the most painful and burning question, that of student organization. . . . Everywhere we see that the *studenchestvo* is completely confused about the tactics, goals, and ideological content of the student movement. . . . There is an intense search going on for new directions. . . . We need a collective effort in order to give the student movement a new theoretical basis and to find a place for it in the general structure of the Russian [public] movement.[115]

The Social Democrats had a coherent ideology but little control over events; the Partizany Bor'by and student Radicals elsewhere were more in touch with the mood of the students but were losing confidence in the workability of their ideology. Outside Saint Petersburg, student Social Democratic groups did not seem to have the same cohesion that they had achieved in the capital, but they felt the same sense of confusion and uncertainty concerning the student movement. In a very short time, however, the Russo-Japanese War and Bloody Sunday would force the students in new directions.

THE ONSET OF REVOLUTION

The onset of the Russo-Japanese War in January 1904 found the students deeply divided. Many participated in patriotic demonstrations, while others passed anti-war resolutions.[116] In Saint Petersburg University a 28 January *skhodka* adopted a patriotic statement and then broke up in a confused flurry of fistfights after the patriotic students ejected hecklers from the hall. A new right-wing student group, the Dennitsa, enjoyed a brief period of influence in the university.[117] That same day a

115. TsGIA, f. 733, op. 151, d. 639, l. 125.
116. A survey of how the outbreak of war affected the universities can be found in "Kazënnyi patriotizm i russkaia molodëzh'," *Osvobozhdenie*, no. 18 (1904); also A. E. Ivanov, "Rossiiskie universitety i russko-iaponskaia voina," in Akademiia Nauk SSSR, Institut Istorii, *Problemy otechestvennoi istorii* (Moscow, 1973), pp. 268–282.
117. Vladimir Voitinskii, *Gody pobed i porazhenii* (Berlin, 1923), p. 10; Engel' and Gorokhov, *Iz istorii*, p. 100.

few hundred students marched across the river to the Winter Palace, where they sang the national anthem and cheered N. V. Kleigels, the chief of police. But elsewhere in the city, the picture was different. At the Mining Institute a *skhodka* condemned the war, and the women at the higher courses rejected the patriotic message that their professors, along with every other faculty council in the country, sent to the tsar. The same lack of unanimity marked the students' reaction in other university towns. Probably most students were mildly patriotic at the very beginning of the war, but this mood soon gave way to growing antigovernment feeling.[118]

Apart from serious disruptions at the Saint Petersburg Mining Institute and the Kharkov Technological Institute (for reasons that, as will be shown below, had little to do with the war), the second semester passed relatively quietly. Spring came; the students took their exams and went home. Russia had been at war five months. What serious student unrest there was followed traditional patterns—protest against government assaults on student prerogatives. The war did lead to the formation of some coalition councils, modeled on the 1903 Odessa recommendations, but they were singularly unsuccessful in mobilizing the student movement.[119] For many observers this continued passivity of the *studenchestvo* only reinforced the growing suspicion that at long last the universities had ceased to be the "barometers of Russian society." The rapidly growing opposition movement in the country, however, once again began to focus the attention of various groups and parties on the political potential of the universities.

The summer of 1904 dashed hopes of a quick victory over the Japanese and began Russia's slide into political crisis. After Plehve's assassination on 15 July, the tsar signaled a more liberal policy by appointing Prince Sviatopolk-Mirskii as his successor. But it was a case of too little too late. On 30 September, representatives of various liberal and revolutionary organizations met in Paris to draft a common tactical program. The Paris meeting, which included Struve's Union of Liberation as well as the Social Revolutionaries, agreed to collaborate in fighting the tsarist regime. Liberals like Miliukov and Struve, who had by

---

118. Voitinskii, *Gody pobed i porazhenii,* p. 10.

119. Engel', "1905g. i studencheskoe dvizhenie," p. 99. Two pamphlets that discuss the state of the student movement after the outbreak of the Russo-Japanese War can be found in BMGU, f. V. I. Orlova. These are "Nashe znamia," no. 1238, and "Ob organizatsii," no. 883. The author of "Nashe znamia" reveals his Social Democratic sympathies but dismisses the November 1903 Odessa conference as "useless" in providing direction for the student movement.

now abandoned his earlier support of the war, were now prepared to look to the left for allies.

A good way of crafting an effective anti-government coalition, Struve claimed, was to abandon traditional liberal scruples about student unrest and recognize the political value of the student movement. In September *Osvobozhdenie* published a lead article on "The Student Movement and the Tasks of Opposition." Like it or not, *Osvobozhdenie* told Russian liberals, the student movement was a fact of life. "Even now, even with the growth of the revolutionary parties, the labor movement, peasant unrest, and the growing oppositional stance of wide segments of the educated public, the student movement is of great political significance." Contrary to a widely held belief, furthermore, the student movement was a phenomenon distinct from the revolutionary left. "It differs from the revolutionary movement," the article explained, "in that it is spontaneous [rather than directed] and because it embraces the wide masses of the student population."[120] The revolutionary parties were not prepared to lead the student movement and indeed failed to understand it. They wanted to recruit individual students, not encourage or lead a student movement that in their view deflected energies from more valuable goals. Instead of encouraging the "revolutionary minority" to lead the student movement on the basis of common concerns and aims that all students could share, the left-wing parties wanted to exploit it for their own purposes.

Nevertheless, the student movement would not go away, and the liberal opposition had to consider whether the leadership vacuum in the universities did not in fact offer tempting political opportunities:

> The students are a natural part of the liberation movement. One might shrink from accepting moral responsibility for their sacrifices. One might be shocked at the idea of collaborating with politically immature students. But there is an answer to this objection. . . . No matter what we think, the students will not refrain from political action. The value of their sacrifices and the maturity of their political outlook will depend on our own attitude toward the students.[121]

In an editorial comment that appeared alongside the article, Struve reiterated the demand that the liberal opposition organize both the students and the professoriate for political action.[122] (Time would show

120. "Studencheskoe dvizhenie i zadachi oppozitsii," *Osvobozhdenie*, no. 56 (1904).
121. Ibid.
122. P. B. Struve, "Chto zhe teper'?" *Osvobozhdenie*, no. 56 (1904).

that the professoriate would respond, albeit with deep reservations; the student movement would keep its distance from both the liberals and the revolutionary parties.)

The 1904–1905 academic year, which ended abruptly after Bloody Sunday, underscored Struve's assessment that the student movement was not really controlled by anyone. In the fall of 1904 there was a clear tension between those attempting to use the student movement to serve wider political ends and the students' tendency to protest on their own terms and over their own issues. During this period the Social Democrats saw that they needed the students to make the street demonstrations that were necessary to remind the Russian public that Social Democracy had not accepted liberal leadership of the opposition movement. Many students were indeed willing to demonstrate, but resented being told when and how.

The fall of 1904 also saw the final "surrender" of student Radicalism to the recommendations of the Odessa conference for coalition councils based on party groups. The dynamics of student protest still buttressed the Radicals' claim of an independent student movement, but the wider political context—a losing war and the radicalization of Russian society—made it hard for them to cling to the definition of the student movement as a political catalyst. The year 1904 was not 1902. But because the students in fact continued to act independently, and often spontaneously, a gap developed between the coalition councils and the actions of the student masses.

Student protest in various cities showed the same characteristics and moved in the same general direction, but there was little coordination or direction, no structurally unified student movement. In the summer of 1904, Engel' and the Saint Petersburg student Social Democrats tried to call another national student congress to "finish off the remnants of student Radicalism" and coordinate the student movement. But not enough prospective delegates promised to come, and Engel' called off the meeting.[123]

It would be a mistake, however, to assume that the failure to assemble a student congress indicated political apathy in the universities in 1904. Vladimir Voitinskii, a student at Saint Petersburg University and later a leading member of the Menshevik party, recalled that that fall most students in the university saw themselves as being politically opposed to the autocracy but nonetheless resisting affiliation with any par-

---

123. Engel' and Gorokhov, *Iz istorii*, p. 104.

ticular political party.[124] The average student, Voitinskii recalled, had little interest in overt demonstrations but welcomed Japanese victories because they embarrassed the government. Indifferent to the political student organizations, most students still showed great interest in left-wing literature. Meanwhile, conservative groups like the Dennitsa had quickly lost the temporary popularity they had gained in the first heady days of the war.

According to Voitinskii, the widespread interest in Marxism was academic rather than actively political. Students read Struve as much as they did Lenin, and such comparatively moderate teachers as E. V. Tarle, L. I. Petrazhitskii, and M. K. Pokrovskii were radical enough for the majority of students. To be sure, some student organizations and even *zemliachestva* had become politicized; V. V. Sviatlovskii's economic study group was especially popular among Marxist students. But on the whole, the political differentiation claimed by the Odessa conference did not seem far advanced in Saint Petersburg University, much less elsewhere.[125]

The major Radical organization in the university, the Partizany Bor'by, after concluding that the student movement had little future as a catalyst, decided to join the Social Democrats and Social Revolutionaries in a coalition council.[126] Within the council, the Partizany Bor'by accepted a certain division of labor. While the student Social Democrats would find out what the adult revolutionary organizations had in mind, the Partizany would form a Central University Organ to work with the majority of the student body, who were opposed to the regime but unwilling to join a specific political group.[127]

The major task of the Central University Organ was to persuade the Saint Petersburg students not to demonstrate or protest until the coalition council gave the signal. There had not yet been any large-scale labor or peasant unrest, especially in the capitals and the central Russian cities, and the council did not want the students to act alone or waste their energies on student issues.

The students, however, once again confounded the calculations of their political leaders by protesting against the "wrong" issue at the

124. Voitinskii, *Gody pobed i porazhenii*, pp. 10–30.
125. A good source on student life in Saint Petersburg University in 1904 is Sergei Kamenskii, *Vek minuvshii* (Paris, 1967), p. 34.
126. N. V. Doroshenko, "Vozniknovenie bol'shevistkoi organizatsii v Peterburgskom Universitete i pervye gody eë sushchestvovaniia," *Krasnaia Letopis'*, no. 2 (1931): 83–85. In 1905 Doroshenko, a leader of the coalition council, also became a member of the Petersburg Committee of the RSDRP. He soon left the party. After the revolution, he worked in Gosplan.
127. Engel' and Gorokhov, *Iz istorii*, p. 106.

"wrong" time. No sooner had the academic year begun than many students wanted to fight new restrictions on the operation of the student dining hall.[128] With much effort, the coalition council managed to head off a protest *skhodka* scheduled for 2 October. This move led to a great deal of bitterness against the council, which many students accused of trying to destroy student traditions.[129] On 11 October, the Central University Organ answered these critics in a pamphlet arguing that corporate protests were out of date: "We are asked, 'If you are against student disorders, what do you propose replacing them with?' We answer, 'Get rid of the idea that the essence of the student movement lies in disorders [*bezporiadki*]. Forget the old memories, get to work, study Russian reality.'"[130]

The tension between student traditions and the political agendas of the coalition council surfaced again after the 8 October suicide of Ivan Malyshev, a jailed student. In the past such incidents (for example, the 1897 Vetrova affair) had aroused strong feelings of student solidarity, and Malyshev's death proved no exception. On 14 October, more than seven hundred students gathered in front of the Kresty prison to escort his body and then planned a public memorial to take place in front of Kazan Cathedral three days later. The Malyshev incident embarrassed the coalition council. Although at first they agreed to the proposed 17 October public funeral, they quickly changed their minds after the city committee of the Social Democratic party suggested keeping the students off the streets until the "workers were ready" for a massive demonstration of their own.[131]

The coalition council's problem was to control student unrest, not to convince the students to oppose the government. In the fall of 1904 the general oppositional drift of Russian society was reflected in student resolutions. Student *skhodki* in October and November passed resolutions that staked out ground to the left of the liberal opposition. Various *VUZy* demanded a constituent assembly and an immediate end to the war.[132]

At the time these resolutions did not cause the government great con-

---

128. An excellent official account of all student disorders in Ministry of Education *VUZy* for the first semester of the 1904–1905 academic year is A. Georgievskii, "Bezporiadki v vysshikh uchebnykh zavedeniiakh v 1904–05gg.," in TsGIA, f. 733, op. 152, d. 196.

129. TsGIA, f. 733, op. 152, d. 176, l. 3.

130. TsGIA, f. 733, op. 152, d. 176, l. 16.

131. A detailed report on the impact of the Malyshev affair on the students is available in POA, index no. 13c(2), folder 6C.

132. Police reports on the *skhodki* and their resolutions can be found in POA, index no. 13c(2), folder 6C; and TsGIA, f. 733, op. 152, d. 176, l. 42.

cern, but they assume a certain significance when considered in the political context of the autumn of 1904 and especially in light of the relationship between the liberal and the revolutionary movements. The Union of Liberation had already adopted a policy of "no enemies on the left," and Struve had already angered some moderate liberals by questioning the idea that politics had no place in the universities.[133] The revolutionary left, however, was divided on the question of cooperating with the liberals, an issue that became even more pressing after the November zemstvo congress. Although the congress elected the moderate Dmitri Shipov as its president, it adopted a platform that brought the zemstvo movement closer to the views of liberal militants such as Struve and Miliukov. The platform included a popularly elected legislative organ as well as guaranteed freedom of the press, speech, religion, association, and assembly.

The growing militancy of the liberals confronted the Social Democrats with the possibility that the Union of Liberation would effectively contest the leadership they had hoped to exercise among the peasantry and the workers. The Bolsheviks and the Mensheviks faced a tactical dilemma. To cooperate with the radical liberals was to risk a loss of political initiative and independence, which was one reason why they refused to join the Social Revolutionaries in the Paris bloc. But noncooperation carried the risk of political isolation, especially after the zemstvo congress turned its back on the moderates' pleas to settle for a consultative rather than a legislative assembly.

Massive street demonstrations, especially in the major cities, were one way the Social Democrats could remind the liberals and the government of their independent presence.[134] In this context, the student movement assumed an immediate importance for the radical left—if the students would follow orders. The student Social Democrats in Saint Petersburg formed a United Social Democratic Organization of Saint Petersburg Students and reported to the city party committee that the October *skhodki* showed that enough students were in a fighting mood to make large demonstrations possible.[135] The problem, as has been seen, was to keep the students at the beck and call of a city Social Demo-

---

133. Many years later, in exile, V. A. Maklakov, a prominent member of the "moderate" wing of the Kadet party, bitterly denounced *Osvobozhdenie*'s line on the student movement (*Vlast' i obshchestvennost' na zakate staroi Rossii* [Paris, 1936], pp. 182–187).

134. I follow here the interpretation of John L. H. Keep, *The Rise of Social Democracy in Russia* (Oxford, 1963).

135. "Otchët ob"edinennoi sotsial-demokraticheskoi organizatsii studentov Sankta-Peterburga," *Tretii s"ezd RSDRP Aprel'-Mai 1905: Protokoly* (Moscow, 1959), p. 561.

cratic organization to which they felt no particular allegiance. But the latter, having made little impact upon the capital's working class, kept putting back the date of the proposed demonstrations.

By the middle of November the student Social Democrats, afraid that their constant appeals for restraint were wearing thin, called a demonstration on their own initiative. The demonstration was scheduled for 18 November, called off, then rescheduled. A key question was whether workers would attend. The student Social Democrats were divided on this issue. After all, it was precisely against the idea of purely student-based demonstrations and actions that the coalition council and the student Social Democrats had been lobbying since September. At any rate, the police had ample warning. By the day of the demonstration, furthermore, the continual changes in plan had left everyone thoroughly confused.[136]

No workers attended the 28 November demonstration, which ended in complete failure. At 12:30 P.M. about a hundred and fifty students unfurled a red flag in Kazan Square and began singing revolutionary songs. Almost immediately, mounted police rushed out of the adjoining city Duma building and began beating the students. The police quickly arrested most of the demonstrators and scattered the rest.[137]

The next day more than two thousand students gathered at a *skhodka* in the university to protest the beatings. But this spontaneous expression of collective anger only served as another reminder of the innate tension between the student movement and the attempts of the coalition council to harness its energy for particular ends. After all, the decision of the Radicals at the beginning of the academic year to join the coalition council meant that practical control of the student movement had passed into the hands of the student Social Democrats. But they too had little to show for their efforts and had certainly discovered how difficult it was to implement the decisions of the Odessa conference. Early in the fall they had barely succeeded in keeping the student body from engaging in independent protests against the government, and they soon found that they risked losing control of the student movement unless they agreed to some action. The student Social Democrats got little help from the city party organization, and the failure of the November dem-

---

136. Ibid. For a Menshevik view, see N. Cherevanin (pseud. of F. A. Lipkin), "Dvizhenie intelligentsii," in L. Martov, ed., *Obshchestvennoe dvizhenie v Rossii* (Saint Petersburg, 1910), vol. 2, part 2, p. 162. Cherevanin emphasizes the independence of the student movement in the autumn of 1904. See also "Na zare 1905ovo goda," *Krasnaia Letopis'*, no. 2 (1925).
137. Voitinskii, *Gody pobed i porazhenii*, pp. 28–30.

onstration led to the collapse of the United Social Democratic Student Organization in Saint Petersburg. As a result, the organization would play little part in the hectic development of the student movement that followed Bloody Sunday.[138]

As in Saint Petersburg, the political crisis in other parts of Russia confronted a student movement searching for answers to the dilemmas of student Radicalism. Student Radicals had found the Odessa conference recommendations unsatisfactory. But, as in Saint Petersburg, the fact that the *studenchestvo* no longer enjoyed its former near-monopoly on visible urban protest caused psychological and practical problems for the Radicals. Therefore, in most cases the student Radicals did not contest the rise of the coalition councils. The party groups had not found directing these councils to be an easy task. In any case, the majority of students maintained their attitude of mostly passive opposition to the regime without taking any steps toward explicit affiliation with a political party. As the Social Revolutionary student group at Odessa University noted in a pamphlet of November 1904:

> As a result of last year's [Odessa conference] a new organization, the coalition council composed of Social Democrats, Social Revolutionaries, and Radicals, replaced the old United Council which had been based on the *zemliachestva*. As a result the *zemliachestva* members who were not members of the political groups felt excluded [from the coalition council] and had little chance to influence student affairs. The lack of any organization for Radical students who were not members of the party groups left a strong imprint on last year's student movement in our university. The majority of students did not know what was happening . . . or what goal to strive for. The proclamations of the coalition committee did not satisfy the majority of Radical students. . . . They did not like the role of silent spectators; they demonstrated a perfectly justifiable wish to discuss what was going on. They wanted to direct matters themselves. But there was no satisfactory framework for the Radical students. At present this problem is especially acute. . . . [Nonparty students] have nowhere to turn. And all the while there is a pressing need for solidarity, for common action. . . . We feel paralyzed.[139]

138. The student Social Democrats, in their report to the third congress of the RSDRP, stated that "internal arguments made it impossible for the organizations to exercise a cohesive influence on the student movement of January and February [1905]. In each institution of higher education, the Social Democratic student group acted by itself" ("Otchët ob"edinennoi," p. 561). Gusiatnikov, however, maintains that the student Social Democrats directed and controlled the student response to Bloody Sunday, all the while following the orders of the city Social Democratic Committee (*Revoliutsionnoe studencheskoe,* pp. 140–141). This assertion seems erroneous.

139. TsGIA, f. 733, op. 152, d. 196, l. 296.

Some students, convinced that the student movement could never overcome its inherent limitations, decided to abandon it in favor of an exclusive commitment to the regular revolutionary parties. One of these students was Mark Vishniak, who began the 1904–1905 academic year as a course representative on Moscow University's United Council. A few months later he decided to leave the student movement. "My experience convinced me," he recalled, "that the student movement was going in the right direction, but it was too amorphous, too undefined. It included too many different elements. In order to wage an effective struggle against the autocracy a large degree of unity was needed, as well as more agreement on the tactics and goals of struggle. [As opposed to the student movement] the political parties offered this. Many [other] students reached the same conclusion."[140]

Of course, only a small minority followed Vishniak on the road to open revolutionary commitment. The very spontaneity and amorphousness of the student movement, which Vishniak labeled its major weakness, struck such observers as Struve as a source of its strength. Difficult to direct and control, the student movement was by the same token hard to destroy.

The pattern of student protest elsewhere in the fall of 1904 showed striking parallels to Saint Petersburg. In Moscow the first major outbreak of student unrest occurred on 15 October 1904, when students seeing off classmates to the front were suddenly assaulted at the Iaroslavl' station by railway porters and troops who seemed to associate student uniforms with lack of patriotism. The next day, after Professor Kliuchevskii finished his always popular history lectures, many students stayed in the hall and held a *skhodka* to discuss the incident. They soon left the university and marched up Nikitskaia Street singing the "Marseillaise" and yelling anti-war and anti-government slogans. Some students tried to march to nearby factories and rally workers to their cause, but they were headed off by police. After some beatings and a few arrests the demonstration broke up, but it made a marked impression on the Moscow student body. According to *Osvobozhdenie*, the "demonstration was completely unplanned yet was a total success despite its lack of organization."[141]

The student party groups, both the Social Democrats and the Social

140. Vishniak, *Dan' proshlomu*, p. 98.
141. "Studencheskaia manifestatsiia v Moskve," *Osvobozhdenie*, no. 59 (1904); see also TsGIA, f. 733, op. 152, d. 173, l. 8.

Revolutionaries, expressed their opposition to the unplanned demonstration and asked the Moscow students to refrain from further protests until they gave the signal.[142] At this time a United Council based on the *zemliachestva* was still the major student organization in Moscow University; as yet there was no coalition council. The United Council called a *skhodka* for 20 October to discuss the Iaroslavl' station incident, but the idea met with strong opposition from the Social Revolutionary and Social Democrat student groups.[143] Unwilling to contest with the political groups any longer for the leadership of the student movement, on 23 October the United Council called for the establishment of a coalition council and issued a proclamation challenging the party groups to prove that they could in fact give the student movement leadership and direction. The abdication of the student Radicals from the leadership of the student movement was occurring in Moscow, as it had elsewhere.

During November the new coalition council in Moscow University devoted its main efforts to making sure that student demonstrations would not take place without its prior approval. When the news reached Moscow of the brutal suppression of the 28 November demonstration in Saint Petersburg, the student Social Revolutionary group called a *skhodka* for 1 December and asked the Social Revolutionary town committee to give the students permission at last to organize a major street demonstration. The committee called for a demonstration on 5 December, and the student Social Democrats reluctantly went along.[144]

As in Saint Petersburg, the workers stayed away and it was mostly students who assembled on Tverskoi Bul'var and began to march toward the home of the Moscow governor-general. Vishniak recalled, "I didn't pay much attention to the proclamation. In fact I had no idea that a Social Revolutionary committee even existed. . . . But the call for a public expression of 'professional' solidarity with my fellow students in Saint Petersburg made me respond. I decided to go to the demonstration."[145] Before they could reach their destination, the demonstrators were surrounded by squads of police and Cossacks who pressed the trapped crowd against the locked doors of the large Filippov bakery. Ac-

142. TsGIA, f. 733, op. 152, d. 173, l. 35.
143. TsGIA, f. 733, op. 152, d. 173, l. 45. It is important to note that one reason why the resolutions of the Odessa conference were not popular in Moscow was the absence from the conference of any delegate from Moscow University. See "Nashe znamia," in BMGU, f. V. I. Orlova, no. 1238.
144. TsGIA, f. 733, op. 152, d. 173, l. 50; Gusiatnikov, *Revoliutsionnoe studencheskoe*, p. 135.
145. Vishniak, *Dan' proshlomu*, p. 92.

cording to one eyewitness, the bakers joined the police in attacking anyone in a student uniform.[146]

The Moscow *studenchestvo* reacted swiftly to a traditional issue—
police brutality against students. On 7 December a large *skhodka* at
Moscow University voted to strike until at least after the Christmas
vacation. The students asked the faculty to support them. In a major
break with the traditions of the Russian professoriate, the teaching staff
strongly protested the police action and tried to shield the participants
of the 7 December *skhodka* from police reprisals. (The faculty response
will be discussed in greater detail in Chapter 5.) The faculty council
elected a commission of sixteen professors who urged a faculty boycott
of the professors' disciplinary court. In accepting the committee's recommendations on how to handle the 7 December *skhodka,* the Moscow
Faculty Council took the unprecedented step of declaring that any reform of the universities depended on general political reforms in the
country.[147]

For the first time, the younger faculty emerged as an organized independent force in the university, a fact that impressed and frightened the
curator of the Moscow Educational District. On 11 December more
than a hundred junior faculty members signed a statement declaring
their conviction that "normal academic life is possible only if the whole
political structure is reconstructed on the basis of personal inviolability,
freedom of conscience, freedom of the press, and freedom of speech, all
guaranteed by the participation of popular representatives in the legislative process."[148] The emergence of the junior faculty occurred in provincial universities as well.

The December events in Moscow University serve as an important
reminder of the essential autonomy of the student movement in the fall
of 1904 and the persistence of traditional patterns of student response
despite the changing political situation in the country and recurrent attempts to integrate the student movement with party differentiation as a
new organizational factor in Russian society. The basic tension between
studenchestvo and party group reflected, perhaps, a more general tension in the wider society between traditional forms of social definition

146. An excellent eyewitness account of the demonstration is found in BMGU, f. V. I.
Orlova, 5 dt., no. 32. See also the report of Moscow curator P. A. Nekrasov to V. G.
Glazov in TsGIA, f. 733, op. 152, d. 173, l. 52.
147. TsGIA, f. 733, op. 152, d. 173, l. 88.
148. TsGIA, f. 733, op. 152, d. 173, l. 80; a very useful survey of senior and junior
faculty response in Ministry of Education *VUZy* can be found in the Georgievskii report
"Bezporiadki."

(estate, professional group) and the rise of newer forms of self-definition, epitomized by the political parties.

The 7 December *skhodka* was the biggest student action in the fall of 1904 and it showed that the *studenchestvo* responded better to traditional calls for solidarity than to party appeals. Only a small minority of students had demonstrated on the fifth, but the student body and faculty rallied to their cause after hearing of the police beatings.

Elsewhere—in Kiev, Kazan, Odessa, Tomsk—the students showed the same pattern of growing interest in politics, oppositional resolutions at *skhodki,* and a stubborn passivity in the face of the efforts of student party groups to organize the student movement. As was the case in the capitals, a significant development became apparent: the growing reluctance of the professoriate to cooperate with the Ministry of Education in disciplining recalcitrant students.

A NEW STRIKE

The students heard the terrible news of Bloody Sunday while they were still on Christmas vacation. Both government and faculty knew that there would be trouble when they returned. On 12 January Minister of Education Glazov told Sviatopolk-Mirskii, the chairman of the Council of Ministers, to keep the universities closed until the labor movement calmed down, but he soon changed his mind. For reasons of prestige, the universities, as state institutions, had to remain open.[149]

The government's determination to keep the universities open in the aftermath of Bloody Sunday put the professoriate in a difficult position. Long opposed on principle to student strikes, most faculty councils feared bloody confrontations between students and police if the *VUZy* were kept open. Besides, the professors' own political views were changing, and a student strike could serve their purposes.

What happened in the central universities after Bloody Sunday formed a pattern of response that occurred at all other institutions of higher education, with the notable exception of the closed schools.[150] Defying a ministry warning that they were violating the 1884 Statute, the Moscow University Faculty Council decided to poll the students at faculty-supervised meetings in order to ascertain student attitudes toward the

---

149. N. I. Pavlitskaia, "Peterburgskii Universitet v revoliutsii 1905–07gg.," *Vestnik Leningradskovo Universiteta,* no. 11 (1948): 141.
150. See Georgievskii, "Bezporiadki."

idea of returning to work in the second semester. Although a strong bloc of conservative professors opposed the poll, arguing that professors had a moral duty to teach regardless of political circumstances, neither at Moscow nor at other universities could they overcome the consensus of their moderate and liberal colleagues that the universities faced an unprecedented situation in which they could no longer conduct business as usual.

Professor Sergei Trubetskoi, who observed one of the Moscow student meetings, expected a strike vote but was astonished by the intensity and bitterness shown by almost the entire student body. On 8 February a *skhodka* of approximately three thousand students in Moscow University voted almost unanimously to strike until 1 September, at which point the decision would be reviewed in light of the political situation. Students also caucused separately, by class and course. Even relatively conservative constituencies such as fifth-year medical students and older juridical and history and philology students put aside graduation hopes and added their support to the strike vote. A harbinger of things to come was the *skhodka*'s demand not only for basic political reforms in the country but also for a reform of university governance to include students and junior faculty.[151]

Similar *skhodki* were held in every institution of higher education in the country when the students returned from vacation after Bloody Sunday. The only exceptions were closed schools such as the Pazheskii Korpus and the Alexandrovskii Lycee. By all accounts these meetings attracted an unprecedentedly large turnout. They all passed practically identical resolutions: an academic strike until 1 September, and a call for a constituent assembly.[152] But there is no evidence to suggest that either inter-university coordination or any outside party influence lay behind this remarkably uniform reaction to Bloody Sunday.

The years of student protest beginning with the 1899 strike had forced the government to continue its retreat from the 1884 Statute and

151. See the protocols of the Moscow University Faculty Council for January and February 1905, in TsGIAM, f. 418, op. 249, ed. kh. 95.

152. D. [A. Diakonov], *1905 i 1906gg. v. Peterburgskom Universitete* (Saint Petersburg, 1907), pp. 9–10; M. I. Matveev, *Studenty Sibiri v revoliutsionnom dvizhenii* (Tomsk, 1966), p. 128; TsGIA, f. 733, op. 152, d. 183 (Kiev University); *Khar'kovskii Gosudarstvennyi Universitet imeni A. M. Gor'kovo za 150 let* (Kharkov, 1955), p. 173; M. K. Korbut, *Kazanskii Gosudarstvennyi Universitet imeni V. I. Ul'ianova-Lenina za 125 let, 1804/5–1929/30* (Kazan, 1930), vol. 2, p. 211; A. E. Ivanov, "Demokraticheskoe studenchestvo v revoliutsii 1905–07gg.," *Istoricheskie Zapiski*, no. 107 (1982): 174–177.

seek help from the professoriate in finding the solution to the university problem. But the retreat was not steady; it alternated with periodic attempts to deal with the students by strengthening discipline and control. The appointment of the Vannovskii Commission, sporadic admissions that reforms were necessary, conciliatory gestures toward arrested students, and attempts to establish better ties with the professoriate alternated with forced conscription, attacks on the disciplinary courts, and a refusal to allow student *skhodki*.

Unlike the demonstrations of 1899, 1901, and 1902, the nationwide student strike that followed Bloody Sunday was closely linked to events outside the universities. By 1905, the student movement, for all its spontaneity, amorphousness, and resistance to direction and control, had clearly moved beyond the political ambivalence of the 1899 strike or even the 1901 protest against the Temporary Rules. In those days the students were ready to respond to gestures of goodwill from the government; the student movement had not yet linked protest against university conditions with wider political issues. By 1905, most student *skhodki* were calling for a constituent assembly.

Yet, ironically, by deciding to strike the *studenchestvo* in effect dissolved itself at a crucial time. Certainly the strike violated the spirit of the November 1903 Odessa conference, which hoped to turn the student movement into a useful adjunct of the revolutionary parties. In short, even the events of 1905 showed some strong continuities with the traditions of the student movement.

But the students were no closer in 1905 than they were in 1901 to arriving at a clear understanding of their role and their relation to other social groups. Nor did the students easily adapt to the attempts of some of their comrades to impose the directives of outside party doctrines. Traditional patterns of behavior—loyalty to arrested students, the continued sway of *studenchestvo*—clashed with calls for students to adopt political models of self-definition and recognize that the "student family" was disintegrating. Proponents of traditional student solidarity found themselves in the paradoxical position of having the facts on their side but lacking the coherent ideological underpinning needed to contest the bid of party-minded students for leadership of the movement. Perhaps the tension in the student movement between tradition and new forms of self-definition pointed to a problem that also affected groups outside the universities: the difficulty of creating coalitions that could unite disparate groups in Russian society for common action. The coincidence of student protest with ferment outside the universities still remained the exception rather than the rule.

As the events of 1905 unfolded, both the students and the professoriate faced unprecedented pressure to define more exactly their positions and the proper role of Russia's universities during a time of political crisis.

CHAPTER 5

The Professoriate
at the Crossroads

The revolution of 1904–1907 set off a complicated struggle for control of the Russian universities. Intense conflict among the student movement, the senior faculty, the junior faculty, and the government meant that between January 1905 and September 1906 Russia's institutions of higher education stayed open for a grand total of one month. This turmoil marked one of the most important periods in the history of Russian higher education, as the autocracy seemed to signal the end of the 1884 Statute. Many key restrictions on university admissions lapsed. University enrollments doubled between 1904 and 1907. The professoriate won a large degree of autonomy in the management of university affairs. These new opportunities presented the professoriate—especially its moderate liberal majority—with unforeseen problems. Just when the professoriate had begun to celebrate its newly gained primacy in university affairs, it had to defend its authority against challenges from all sides—government, the emergent junior faculty, and the students.

Even before 1899, the senior faculty had attacked student unrest as an irresponsible tactic which, in pursuit of a few praiseworthy goals, played into the hands of reactionaries and endangered Russian higher education, and thus hampered rather than enhanced the chances for political and intellectual progress. But the political turmoil that engulfed the country in 1904 forced the professoriate to consider the very questions the student movement had been raising for a number of years. Could academic freedom remain separate from the wider issue of far-reaching political reforms? If not, then what besides direct action and confrontation would force the autocracy to grant those reforms?

Many professors, even those who endorsed the aims of the liberation movement, feared making compromises involving the professoriate or the universities *as such* in the revolution. Yet would a society in the middle of a revolution grant the professors the luxury of upholding the universities' claim to be "above politics"? And could the professoriate support political democracy outside the university while insisting on German-style rule over students and junior faculty within? Although the senior faculty would have no trouble reconciling political liberalism with academic authoritarianism, other groups within the academic community—students and junior faculty—would refuse to surrender their demand for "institutional democracy."

By 1904 a few leading academics openly admitted that the academic profession had to reexamine its attitudes and priorities. Some even questioned whether the student movement had not been right all along in insisting that university autonomy had to be gained through struggle, not compromise. For example, Kharkov juridical professor N. A. Gredeskul admitted in the prestigious *Pravo:*

> The liberation movement in the universities began long ago, certainly much earlier than last year. But in all honesty, for a very long time its only adherents [in the universities] were the students. The student disorders of 1899 were imbued with the same liberating ideal that the whole of Russian society has now embraced. Its essence is that a real cultural life worthy of human dignity is incompatible with [the autocracy]. . . . This system [the autocracy] now blocks any forward movement. The students were saying this in 1899 and after . . . but we professors did not listen. . . . Even those of us who did not want to be only bureaucrats [*chinovniki*] . . . [told the students then] that first it was impossible to change the system [at least in the near future] and, second, that the system was flexible enough to allow real cultural progress, such as university autonomy [even without more general reforms].[1]

In raising the issue of whether the professor was a government bureaucrat or whether his first obligation was not to his employer—the state—but to Russian society at large, Gredeskul touched on one of the key questions the Russian professoriate was forced to confront in 1905. Many professors would argue that if the academic profession sat out the political confrontation between state and society, it would emerge the

---

1. N. A. Gredeskul, "Rol' universiteta v sovremennom dvizhenii," *Pravo*, no. 40 (1905).

loser. In times of national crisis, professors had to take a stand or risk forfeiting the public respect they considered to be a basic precondition for strong, flourishing universities. But too much political commitment risked a total rupture with the government, increasing polarization within the professoriate, and the establishment of a very dangerous precedent that could endanger all future appeals for a university "above politics."

Prodded by public pressure as well as their own consciences, Russia's professors tried to overcome their deep reluctance to making a professional commitment to the political battle against the autocracy. They formed an Academic Union, passed anti-government resolutions, and even tried to show more sympathy toward the student movement. This sympathy stopped short of outright endorsement of the student strike that closed the universities from February until September of 1905. But the development of the revolution quelled the professors' initial doubts and convinced them that in the end only they, of all the nation's professions and social groups, really cared about the survival of the universities. Russia's slide into confrontation politics left the professoriate back where it started—deeply uncertain about the limits of the universities' political obligations and very much hoping for a change in government policy that would enable reform from above to forestall revolution from below.

THE BEGINNING OF CONFRONTATION: THE DISCIPLINARY COURTS

Between 1899 and 1904 the government repeatedly raised the professors' hopes that they would regain the authority over university governance and student discipline denied them by the introduction of the 1884 Statute. Each time, however, the government backtracked, fearful of losing control over the universities. Vannovskii's 1901 questionnaire gave the faculty councils a chance to articulate their criticisms of the statute. After two decades of depriving the professoriate of jurisdiction over student life, the government, stung by the student disorders of 1899, now started talking about "closer relations between students and faculty" as a panacea for the student problem. But if the faculty was to cooperate in persuading the students to remain quiet it wanted a quid pro quo—a repeal of the 1884 Statute and more power within the university. Hopes for the repeal of the statute rose even higher when, in

1902, Vannovskii's replacement, G. E. Sanger, appointed a commission to study the matter and make recommendations. As we have seen, the commission report, which ran to five thick volumes of proceedings, finally came to rest in the archives.

Still, the pressure of the student movement forced the government into a continual retreat from the 1884 Statute. In August 1902 the establishment of the professors' disciplinary courts seemed to meet a long-standing faculty demand that enforcing student discipline was the job of the professoriate, not the government.

In December 1903, the Odessa University Disciplinary Court met to consider the cases of students involved in *skhodki* organized that fall to protest anti-Semitic incidents in the university. The court justified its lenient sentences by pointing out that the disturbances were local in scope and showed no evidence of being part of a planned pattern of student unrest. This led to a complaint from the Odessa district curator to the ministry in Saint Petersburg that the professors were neglecting their duties. The arch-conservative rector of the university, A. N. Derevitskii, secured a directive to take over the functions of the court himself or dissolve it and hold elections for a new one.[2]

The same mistrust of the professoriate surfaced in Warsaw University, when the court's leniency angered curator A. N. Schwartz. After the disciplinary court meted out light sentences to the students involved in disorders in November 1903, Schwartz warned the ministry that "as it is now constituted, the court is not a suitable means of quelling mass disorders."[3]

When disorders broke out in Kharkov University following the advent of the Russo-Japanese War in February 1904, M. M. Alekseenko, the curator in Kharkov, asked Lukianov, the acting minister of education, if he could bypass the court altogether in punishing the students involved. "The court," he complained, "acts too slowly." Upon getting Lukianov's permission, Kuplevskii, the university's rector, expelled twenty students and suspended thirty-two. As a result the entire court—Professors L. L. Girshman, D. N. Ovsianko-Kulikovskii, V. A. Steklov, N. A. Gredeskul, and M. P. Chubinskii—resigned. Along with the Moscow University Faculty Council's December 1903 declaration, this was one of the most important examples of academic protest since

2. TsGIA, f. 733, op. 151, d. 299, l. 26.
3. TsGIA, f. 733, op. 151, d. 299, l. 38.

Vinogradov's departure for England three years earlier. It signaled that the patience of the professoriate was finally beginning to wear thin.[4]

Clearly V. K. Plehve, the minister of the interior, was now setting the tone of the government's get-tough policy toward both the professoriate and the students. By the beginning of the war, the tsar had not yet named a replacement for Sanger, whom Plehve had fired in 1903 after deciding that he lacked the firmness required to deal with the student problem.[5] For Plehve, however, the attack on the disciplinary courts was just a first step in pacifying the *VUZy*. At the beginning of 1904 he launched a frontal attack on the specialized technical institutes, whose students had traditionally enjoyed much more autonomy than their counterparts in the universities. In March and April 1904, Plehve's new policy led to the temporary closing of the Saint Petersburg Mining Institute and the Kharkov Technological Institute. The minister of the interior was determined to force a unified government policy toward the *VUZy*, abolishing the wide disparities of treatment that had up to now characterized the status of *VUZy* subordinated to other ministries.[6]

Both the students and the faculty of the Saint Petersburg Mining Institute had been intensely proud of the traditions of their school.[7] Over the years the students and faculty had established a close rapport. The students had set up a library, dining hall, and other mutual aid organizations, which had been tolerated by the Ministry of Trade and Industry, to which the institute was formally subordinated. In the past the students had been comparatively moderate in their protests, except when it appeared that the government intended to encroach on their privileges. In 1901 the students had voted not to participate in the Kazan Square demonstration because they did not want to violate the long-standing tradition against carrying student protest outside the walls of the insti-

4. In December 1903 the Moscow University Faculty Council questioned the government's commitment to the new disciplinary courts, in view of its constant displeasure with the court's decisions. A copy of the protest declaration can be found in GPB im. V. I. Lenina, f. 131, V. O. Kliuchevskovo, folder 29, no. 20. On the incident with the Kharkov Disciplinary Court, see TsGIA, f. 733, op. 151, d. 638, l. 254; the Kharkov Disciplinary Court's letter of resignation appears in *Osvobozhdenie*, no. 56 (1904).

5. Plehve praised Sanger's replacement, acting minister of education Lukianov, for firmness in dealing with the Kharkov and Odessa incidents. See TsGIA, f. 922, op. 1, l. 9. This is the summary of the first interview between Tsar Nicholas II and General V. G. Glazov after Glazov's appointment as minister of education in 1904. The tsar emphasized that he relied heavily on Plehve's advice in formulating his policy toward students and professors.

6. TsGIA, f. 922, op. 1 (Glazov's notes on conversation with Plehve, April 1904).

7. An excellent collection of memoirs of student life in the Saint Petersburg Mining Institute is *Na puti k pobede* (Leningrad, 1925).

tute. (They did join the 1899 strike, however.) In February 1902 the students decided to fight Vannovskii's rules on student organizations, since they were meant to apply to all *VUZy* and thus to equalize the status of students regardless of the ministry to which the particular school reported. They called a strike that led to the expulsion of 332 students. (All won readmission the following fall.)[8]

As part of his drive to impose uniformity on higher-education policy, Plehve appointed Professor D. P. Konovalov from Saint Petersburg University to assume the directorship of the mining institute at the beginning of 1904. At the same time he appointed a new director of the Kharkov Technological Institute, Professor N. N. Shiller. (Unlike the mining institute, the Kharkov Technological Institute answered to the Ministry of Education.) Konovalov had the reputation of being an archconservative. Upon his appointment he told the professors of Plehve's determination to subject the students to stricter discipline. Trouble began on 3 March 1904, when Konovalov entered the student dining hall and ripped a picture of German Socialist leader August Bebel from the wall. He later tore up the protest resolution delivered to him by two student representatives. An escalating series of charges and countercharges concerning his behavior led to a large student *skhodka* on 15 March, which voted to strike. The following day the institute closed. On 19 March, six leading professors resigned from the faculty. Konovalov managed to complete the academic year with the support of a small group of anti-strike students and conservative faculty, but the episode polarized the mining institute and became a cause célèbre throughout the country.[9]

Repression at the Kharkov Technological Institute also began in March. The Ministry of Education had dismissed a *privat-dozent* from Kharkov University because of an allegedly unpatriotic speech he had made at the beginning of the Russo-Japanese War. The students of the technological institute called a *skhodka* to express their solidarity with the university students who were protesting the dismissal of the *dozent*. The *skhodka* drew only a small crowd but gave an excuse for Shiller, the new director, to begin fulfilling his new mandate. He closed the institute on 5 March and expelled 207 students without consulting the

8. G. Rokov, "Iz noveishei istorii studencheskikh volnenii," *Vestnik Vospitaniia*, no. 3 (1906). The best single source on the 1904 dispute in the mining institute is the voluminous *Konovalovskii konflikt* (Saint Petersburg, 1905). This is the stenograph of the informal court of honor that met at the beginning of 1905 to adjudicate the various charges being traded between the pro-strike and anti-strike factions of the previous year.
9. Rokov, "Iz noveishei istorii," gives a concise summary of the affair.

disciplinary court. He then reprimanded six faculty members who protested this action. After consulting with Plehve, Shiller escalated matters by asking the six professors to resign. When the rest of the faculty joined the protest, Shiller deprived several professors of their fellowships for foreign study. On 14 May the tsar affirmed Shiller's dismissal of the six professors from the institute.[10]

These two incidents have certain similarities. The government appointed reactionary directors who antagonized the faculty by arrogating to themselves disciplinary functions that had previously been under faculty control. Furthermore, Konovalov and Shiller used relatively minor student protests to provoke a confrontation with the faculty. In doing so, they clearly invoked Plehve's direct support. The attacks on these institutes certainly contributed to the growing alienation of the educated public from the government. At the same time, the mounting evidence of the increasing politicization of the government's higher-education policy, exemplified by the constant attacks on the disciplinary courts, began to push the professoriate toward a reappraisal of its relationship with the government.

A NEW MINISTER OF EDUCATION

Had the professors known what was on the tsar's mind, they would have had even less reason to feel encouraged. On 10 April 1904 the tsar appointed an ex-general, Vladimir Gavrilovich Glazov, to head the Ministry of Education. Brushing aside Glazov's protests that he was unqualified for the job, the tsar made it clear that now the top priority in the nation's educational policy was not reform but housecleaning and pacification.[11] During his interview with the minister, the tsar told Glazov that the root of the problem lay with the professoriate. "There [were] decent people in the professoriate," the tsar said, "but very few."[12]

Glazov made a conscientious effort to learn his new job and even recommended policies that could have established a good working relationship with the majority of the professoriate. After touring the universities, Glazov sent a memorandum to the tsar recommending sharply

10. "Razgrom Khar'kovskovo Tekhnologicheskovo instituta," *Osvobozhdenie*, no. 56 (1904).
11. TsGIA, f. 922, op. 1, l. 9; cf. "Dva razgovora: Iz dnevnikov V. G. Glazova," *Dela i Dni*, no. 1 (1920).
12. In turn Glazov ventured the remark that perhaps one reason for the poor quality of the professoriate was low pay.

increased funding levels and emphasizing the political advantages of a strong university system, especially in the non-Russian areas.[13] In addition, he supported more state funding for scholarships. It would not serve the national interest, he pointed out in a letter to the tsar, to turn the universities into closed schools for the very wealthy. (Besides, there were not enough wealthy students to fill them.) But Glazov's relationship with the faculty councils was bound to suffer from the fact that he relied heavily on the advice of assistant minister Lukianov and former Moscow University rector A. A. Tikhomirov for recommendations on university policy. Neither had a good relationship with the liberal or moderate elements of the professoriate. Shortly after his appointment, Glazov received a memorandum from Tikhomirov blaming his former colleagues, the senior faculty, for the terrible state of Russia's universities and concluding that because the main problem was the "de-Christianization" of Russia's educated classes, the malaise of Russian higher education was so deep-rooted that anything the ministry did in the way of decrees or legislation would have little effect.[14]

Of course Glazov knew that what the government (in other words, Plehve) expected of his ministry was placid universities, not innovative policy. But Plehve's crackdown on the professoriate in 1903–1904 could not be justified by any objective threat the universities posed to the security of the state. The student movement was in the throes of an identity crisis and lacked direction and central leadership. Student unrest in 1903 and even after the beginning of the war did not match the intensity of the 1899–1902 period. Why, then, did the government pursue a counterproductive course bound to lead to a confrontation with a professoriate that at heart much preferred order to revolution?

One answer was that the autocracy was the prisoner of its own "ideology of order," a fixation that robbed it of any flexibility in dealing with public expressions of discontent. Any expression of public protest, no matter how unimportant, was seen as a serious challenge. Bureaucrats who argued otherwise risked jeopardizing their careers. As a result there was an inherent tendency, despite occasional spates of tolerance, to overreact to disturbances in the universities, especially because they were conspicuously located in the nation's urban centers. One key option for the autocracy was to "depoliticize" institutions such as the uni-

---

13. TsGIA, f. 922, op. 1, d. 143.
14. TsGIA, f. 733, op. 226, d. 90. Nonetheless, Tikhomirov's pessimism did not prevent him from recommending a major increase in financial aid allocations for needy students.

versities so that their problems could be dealt with without involving the prestige of the government.

The problem of depoliticization was a major challenge posed by the Revolution of 1905 to the government in general and to the Ministry of Education in particular. With regard to the universities, major steps toward depoliticization could have included transferring disciplinary powers to the professors and granting them wider rights in choosing rectors and determining curriculum—in short, repeal of the 1884 Statute. In August 1905, the government would indeed follow this course, at least for a time. But in 1904, it was moving in the opposite direction.

Glazov, a military man, had no patience with the professors' disciplinary courts. On 25 September 1904 he asked the tsar to sanction further limitations on the professors' disciplinary powers. In cases of "mass disorders or political agitation" Glazov advocated telling the rector to consult with the curator and then to bypass the disciplinary court and judge the cases himself. He would also be able to expel or suspend students without having to consult the court. The tsar approved Glazov's recommendations, which were issued as Ministry Circular No. 38, on 3 October 1904.[15]

The 3 October circular guaranteed further deterioration in faculty-government relations. During the fall semester of the 1904–1905 academic year the faculty councils watched large-scale suspensions from Kiev, Odessa, Kazan, Iur'ev, and Moscow universities effected without consultation with the disciplinary courts.[16] As the country grew more restless, the senior faculty was beginning to lose patience with the government and started taking a new look at its conviction that the academic profession as such "had to stay out of politics."

The growing student unrest in the fall of 1904, especially the violence following the November and December street demonstrations in Moscow and Saint Petersburg, put even more pressure on the professors. In the case of Moscow University, the aftermath of the 5 December demonstration, as we have seen, led the faculty council to issue a report that verged on open defiance of the government. Another new factor was the emergence of the junior faculty as an assertive force.[17]

Even before Bloody Sunday, therefore, relations between the senior faculty and the government had reached the crisis stage. The massive

15. TsGIA, f. 922, op. 1, d. 162.
16. TsGIA, f. 1276, op. 1, d. 51.
17. A. Georgievskii, "Bezporiadki v vysshikh uchebnykh zavedeniiakh v 1904–05gg.," in TsGIA, f. 733, op. 152, d. 196.

student strike and the general public outcry following the Bloody Sunday massacre put more pressure on the professors to define their attitudes and responsibilities during an escalating revolutionary situation. For the professoriate the situation created by the student strike offered both dangers and opportunities. Professional tradition and pride made it hard to openly support the principle of a student strike, yet common sense argued that a resumption of classes might lead to bloody violence in the universities, especially if excitable students picked fights with the police.

Furthermore, the strike offered the professoriate a chance to win long-sought professional goals: repeal of the 1884 Statute, elected rectors, more academic freedom, and a restoration of the authority of the disciplinary courts.

CANVASSING THE PROFESSORIATE

In early February the government unwittingly gave the professoriate a legal opportunity to discuss professional demands and grievances when it decided to poll the faculty councils of all the nation's institutions of higher education on the question of resuming classes.[18] There was sentiment within the government for letting the strike run on—who needed thousands of angry students milling around the cities?—but closed universities raised questions of prestige and undercut claims that normal life was returning. Acting on the recommendations of a January interministerial conference, the government asked the professors for help in restoring normal academic life.[19]

The faculty responses showed a striking degree of agreement. Not one university agreed to resume teaching. All the faculty councils, university and nonuniversity, asserted that wider political reforms were an essential precondition for peace in the *VUZy*.[20] The professors were uncharacteristically defiant, especially because they all saw plainly the irony of the government's seeking their help after having told them in 1903 and 1904 that it had lost confidence in their ability to handle student discipline. The similarity of faculty council responses permits the assumption of a basic professional consensus in 1905. All *VUZy*, how-

18. TsGIA, f. 1276, op. 1, d. 51.
19. Ibid. In its report to the tsar the conference recommended immediate reconsideration of the 1884 Statute.
20. The replies of the various faculty councils are contained in TsGIA, f. 733, op. 152, d. 196.

ever, also had sizable conservative minorities that issued dissenting opinions and called for an immediate return to classes.[21] Later on, this conservative opposition would become more important, especially in the provincial universities.

A typical response was that submitted by the Moscow University Faculty Council.[22] While the council opposed the idea of a student strike, it could not agree to reopen the university under the present circumstances. The university had to stay closed "in order to protect the students from themselves." What about the long run? That, the council implied, depended on radical changes in the government's political and academic policies.

The Moscow professors placed the blame for the parlous state of Russia's universities squarely on the government's shortsightedness, especially with regard to the 1884 Statute, a document that undercut faculty morale and prestige and made it impossible for the professors to gain the students' respect. The government, of course, had heard exactly the same thing in the professors' responses to the 1901 Vannovskii questionnaire; in the ensuing four years little had happened except further deterioration of the state of the universities. Because the universities had no autonomy, and the professors no authority, the students cared about neither. They saw the universities as diploma mills, the professors as hapless state employees. It was hardly surprising, therefore, to see the students taking out all their frustrations—political and academic—on the most readily available target, especially since they had no notion of how vital the universities were to the nation's future.

Any meaningful reform of higher education, the Moscow University Faculty Council argued, had to begin with a fundamental redefinition of the purposes of the universities. The government had to accept the professors' contention that the main task of the universities was the propagation of scientific thinking, not the training of middle-level civil servants. "The basic purpose of university teaching," the faculty council pointed out, "is not merely the imparting or communication of knowledge to students. Even more important is the need to arouse interest in scientific work and the need to acquaint students with the methods of scientific inquiry."[23] If this were done, the nation would find itself with

21. In Odessa University, for example, the faculty council voted 32 to 25 against a return to classes.
22. TsGIA, f. 733, op. 152, d. 173, ll. 379–383 (Postanovleniia Soveta Imperatorskovo Moskovskovo Universiteta, priniatyia v zasedaniiakh 6ovo, 12ovo i 15ovo Marta, 1905ovo goda, po voprosu o merakh, sposobnykh obezpechit' pravil'noe techenie universitetskikh zaniatii).
23. Ibid.

better civil servants and professionals in the bargain. The professors called for the formal abolition of the already emasculated state examination system and a transition to an elective curriculum that would emphasize specialized and independent inquiry rather than rote learning. Making science rather than teaching the main function of the university provided the ideological underpinning for the faculty council's demand for major changes in academic governance that would give the senior faculty control over the election of rectors, the filling of vacant chairs, and supervision of student life. By clearly establishing the professoriate as scholars and as masters in their own house, such reforms would show students two important reasons for respecting and obeying the senior faculty. As a result the students would be more likely to heed the professors' pleas to put the integrity of the universities above the passing frustrations of the moment.

At this point, the faculty council statement ran into certain problems, a reflection of the delicate position of the professoriate as a whole. Along with their colleagues elsewhere, the Moscow professors considered general unspecified political reforms a sine qua non for the resumption of normal academic life. But too strong an insistence on political reforms seemed uncomfortably close to involving the professoriate in a political strike—which made the senior faculty uncomfortable. The Moscow University Faculty Council had indeed endorsed the 18 February Bulygin rescript, with its vague promise of a consultative Duma, as a measure that "opened the way for Russia to reorganize her life on a new foundation." But only the most naive professors believed that a consultative Duma would satisfy the students or even the Union of Liberation. Yes, the senior faculty was making political demands—but very moderate ones.

The Moscow professors called for *immediate* control over internal university administration. But a return to the classroom before the resolution of underlying political tensions risked, as the professors themselves admitted in the same statement, confrontation with the students, obstruction of classes, and police interference. The faculty council explicitly recognized the dilemma: "University autonomy will not bring peace to the university unless it is accompanied by general political reform. Although it realizes this, the faculty council sees no way out of the present difficult circumstances other than the immediate realization of full academic autonomy."[24] The council explained that the professors could not assume the role of passive bystanders awaiting the advent of a

24. Ibid.

more favorable political situation, and it warned that "Russia faced a stormy period that might last several years . . . during which there was every likelihood that some form of student disorders would continue."[25] In such a situation it was absurd to keep the universities closed until the end of the student movement. But given the likelihood that disorders would continue, the professors argued that they themselves were best qualified to deal with such problems—provided they first received university autonomy.

Quite clearly the Moscow University Faculty Council, like its counterparts elsewhere, did not want a major confrontation with the government. The professors were cautiously trying to reconcile the increasingly contradictory roles of scholars, civil servants, teachers, guardians of the universities, and, last but not least, proud members of Russia's educated elite who wanted to guard their status in the eyes of the public.

GOVERNMENT POLICY: CONFRONTATION OR COMPROMISE?

The government did not make the professors' position any easier. When he sifted through the various faculty council responses, Glazov saw only their impertinence and ignored their pleas for a new era of cooperation between the state and the academy. One clear example of the ministry's shortsightedness was the fate of a potentially important initiative undertaken by P. A. Nekrasov, the curator of the Moscow Educational District.

Nekrasov sensed that many professors were uncomfortable with the growing involvement of the senior faculty in the liberation movement and decided to organize a conference to explore possible solutions to the academic crisis. Without seeking Glazov's permission, he asked the faculty councils of all the VUZy in Moscow province, regardless of ministerial affiliation, to elect delegates. He knew, of course, that technically his action was illegal; the 1884 Statute made no provision for any such

25. Ibid. It should be noted that eighteen members of the faculty council signed a statement opposing the majority declaration. These conservative professors declared that they could not agree with the assumption that "the authority of the professoriate in the eyes of the students and the Russian public depends on the enjoyment of its 'corporate rights.' . . . For those students who understand their obligations, as well as for those citizens who have achieved a certain level of culture, the measure of the authority of the professor has been and will be solely that of talent, knowledge, and devotion to teaching" (TsGIA, f. 733, op. 152, d. 173, l. 288).

conferences, much less those that united professors across ministerial boundaries.[26]

The Nekrasov conference held several meetings in March and April. While ruling out the prospect of an early return to classes, the professors encouraged Nekrasov by reaffirming their loyalty to the principle of an organic link between the state and higher education, which in turn would determine the context of any definition of academic freedom. At the same time, they reminded Nekrasov that the collapse of the universities began *before* Bloody Sunday and that there was a separate university crisis, *in addition to* the general political crisis. However, by endorsing the concept of state-controlled higher education and the goal of academic freedom within the framework of that control, the professors strengthened Nekrasov's belief that the academic community could be detached from the widening anti-government coalition.[27]

Glazov reacted with shocked surprise when he learned of the conference and refused to meet with a delegation elected by the conference to talk to him about university reform. The old general then summoned Nekrasov to Saint Petersburg to explain why he had allowed the meeting.[28]

In mid-April, replying to the summons, Nekrasov told Glazov that the government had an opportunity to win the professoriate to its side and would be foolish to let baseless suspicions interfere. He urged Glazov to approve one of the main recommendations of the Moscow conference: a national conference, composed of elected representatives of the professoriate, to meet and draw up a replacement for the 1884 Statute. The Moscow professors, Nekrasov concluded, far from being a threat, were actually meeting under the "banner of true autocracy."[29]

Glazov, unimpressed, ordered Nekrasov to stop the conference, threatening him with immediate disciplinary action if he failed to comply. The tireless curator fired back another letter, pleading with the minister of education to stop viewing the professors as inevitable opponents of the regime. The ministry's insistence on holding professors' discussion to the narrow range of subjects allowed by the statute only served to prevent moderate elements from organizing to counter growing anti-government agitation. (Glazov was obviously unconvinced, since his

26. The protocols of the conference can be found in TsGIA, f. 1276, op. 1, d. 51, ll. 439–497.
27. TsGIA, f. 733, op. 152, d. 173, l. 318.
28. TsGIA, f. 733, op. 152, d. 173, l. 326.
29. TsGIA, f. 733, op. 152, d. 173, l. 318.

comments in the margin of Nekrasov's letter equated Nekrasov's suggestions with the disastrous decision to encourage Father Gapon in Saint Petersburg.) The curator emphasized again that the government should allow a nationwide professors' conference to draft a new statute. "The conference," Nekrasov predicted, "will demand academic autonomy. We have to expect that. But we must demand that this academic autonomy be consistent with loyalty to the tsar, that it be organically linked to the government." The curator reiterated his belief that the majority of the senior faculty shared this view.[30]

The government decided to give the professoriate a symbolic slap in the face. In a development that sharpened the tension between the state and the academic profession, the *Pravitel'stvennyi Vestnik* on 23 April published a warning that if the universities did not reopen in the fall, the entire teaching staff, as well as the student body, would be suspended. Professors from all over the country reacted with indignation and fury. A common response was that the warning made it more difficult than ever for the professoriate to pursue a moderate course, since the public would now suspect it of acting only out of self-interest.[31]

One sign of the growing anger and assertiveness of the professoriate was the defiant tone of the Moscow professors' conference, which continued to meet despite Glazov's orders. After the 23 April threat, the conference responded with its own warning, telling Glazov that the professoriate would not accept any new statute drawn up by bureaucrats. Only university reform charted by the elected delegates of the professoriate would have any legitimacy.[32]

While Glazov persisted in his hard line toward the professoriate, he also realized that the government needed more of a university policy than just the threat to expel students and fire professors if the *VUZy* stayed closed in the fall. At the beginning of June, Glazov sent a memorandum to the tsar that showed that although the general was a disciplinarian, he was far from being an arch-reactionary. Glazov admitted that the only sure way of solving the student problem was to change existing admissions policies and turn the universities and technical institutes into closed schools on the model of the Alexandrovskii Lycee. The minister warned that such a course was not only "impossible but also undesirable."[33]

30. TsGIA, f. 733, op. 152, d. 173, l. 335.
31. A 2 May protest letter signed by thirty-four professors can be found in TsGIA, f. 733, op. 152, d. 173, l. 363.
32. TsGIA, f. 733, op. 152, d. 173, l. 367.
33. TsGIA, f. 922, op. 1, d. 163, l. 1.

Like most responsible officials in the government, Glazov clearly did not want to turn higher education into the preserve of the wealthy nobility. Besides, could this group by itself staff the professions and the higher civil service? As the government learned when it tried to implement the 1884 Statute, there were simply not enough trained personnel or potentially trustworthy recruits to staff the various institutions of Russian society and government if the autocracy was indeed determined to follow a course of coherent counterreform.

There was the alternative, which Glazov now began to advocate, of depoliticization. One key proposal of Glazov's memorandum was that the government expand the disciplinary powers of the professoriate. Such a policy, Glazov wrote, "would shift to the shoulders of the faculty councils a burden which now seems so tempting and so desirable to the majority of professors." The government would benefit, for the onus of future student disorders would fall on the professors, not the state. At least that was his hope. "One has to believe," he concluded, "that it will turn out this way; if this new policy does not work one would have to conclude regretfully that the university as a form of higher education does not suit Russian circumstances and is inconsistent with the level of the civic development of Russian society."[34] Glazov thought that the government would still exercise a significant degree of control over higher education as long as the curators continued to act as watchdogs over the *VUZy*.

Ignoring the warnings of the professoriate, Glazov convened a conference on 10 June to draft a new university statute. In addition to himself and his two chief aides, Tikhomirov and Lukianov, the conference included three arch-conservative professors invited by Glazov.[35] In his opening remarks Glazov told the group that aside from wanting to abolish the privileges associated with a degree, the tsar had no specific guidelines for a new statute.

Two years earlier the government might have been able to impose a new statute without much opposition from the professoriate. But the situation had obviously changed, and the deliberations of the June conference proceeded in an atmosphere of unreality. Having rejected Nekrasov's advice that he put the relationship between the government and the professoriate on a new footing, Glazov continued to believe that a new university statute could be worked out in the secret chambers of the Ministry of Education and be implemented without consulting the

34. TsGIA, f. 922, op. 1, d. 163, l. 3.
35. Ibid.

professoriate as a whole. While clearly in keeping with the political traditions of the autocracy, such an attitude was totally out of date by the summer of 1905. The Russian professoriate was losing its patience with government tutelage.

THE PROFESSORIATE BEGINS
TO ORGANIZE

The deliberations of the various faculty councils between December and March were only one aspect of the searching reevaluation by the professoriate of its political and professional obligations and identity. As political tensions mounted, the academic community realized that it had to answer not only to the government but also to the liberation movement, whose influence was rapidly growing. Many professors, of course, were ready to enter the political fray as individuals. The major issue was whether the Russian professoriate as a professional group was ready to collaborate with the liberation movement.

Some leading academics—Professors V. I. Vernadskii, P. I. Novgorodtsev, S. A. Kotliarevskii, and I. M. Grevs—had participated in the July 1903 Schaffhausen conference convened by Peter Struve to establish the Union of Liberation.[36] The conference, Struve hoped, would unify the two divergent strands of Russian liberalism, the zemstvo moderates and the radical constitutionalists. The professors who made this early political commitment soon discovered that they were closest to the moderate wing of the Union of Liberation.

Two issues that exposed potential rifts between the liberal professoriate and the more radical elements of the liberation movement were the nature of political liberalism in Russia and attitudes toward the Russo-Japanese War. The first problem centered on priorities. Should liberals link demands for political reforms and libertarian guarantees with demands for social and economic justice? Should these goals be given equal priority? Replying to an essay by Struve arguing that Russian liberals had to link social with political demands, Professor S. N. Bulgakov of Kiev University spoke for many of his colleagues in warning that Russian liberalism "too easily sacrifices the interests of political liberalism and political freedom on the altar of the interests of a democratic social policy."[37] As will be seen below, another powerful argument in this vein

---

36. Shmuel Galai, *The Liberation Movement in Russia, 1900–1905* (Cambridge, England, 1973), p. 177.
37. Ibid., p. 181.

was to be developed by Professor Paul Vinogradov in his "Political Letters."

Nor did the professors share the widely held view that military defeat was preferable to victory. When hostilities broke out with Japan at the beginning of 1904, each faculty council sent a declaration of loyalty to the tsar.[38] A basic component of academic liberalism in Russia was its disdain for the lack of patriotism long held to be an integral part of the traditions of the intelligentsia. The academic community believed that the universities could play a major role in helping Russia compete with other European countries, that science and knowledge were powerful weapons which could be mobilized to serve the national interest. Indeed, a major reason why academic attitudes toward the government began to harden was the angry conviction that bureaucratic obstruction of higher education was playing a major role in Russia's defeat.

Shortly after the start of the war, the eminent geologist V. I. Vernadskii, soon to be a prominent figure in the organization of the Academic Union, wrote a gloomy letter to a Moscow colleague, the philosopher Sergei Trubetskoi.[39] Vernadskii bitterly assailed the defeatists who "misunderstood the role of Sevastopol" in Russian history. Vernadskii, like many of his colleagues, distinguished between the existing autocratic system (*samoderzhavie*) and the Russian state (*gosudarstvo*). The interests of the latter required a fundamental modification of the former. The lesson of Sevastopol was that no state could long survive unless it could put knowledge at the service of national power. Liberal professors supported the idea of a powerful state, but one that would employ their talents. Their opposition to the autocracy stemmed not only from their liberal instincts but also from their basic aversion to a system whose bureaucratic incompetence was subverting the national interest and Russia's ability to compete internationally. On hearing the news of the fall of Port Arthur, Trubetskoi wrote that he was filled with "sadness, pain, anguish, and a shame that cried for vengeance, a shame that was unforgiving."[40]

When the renowned jurist Boris Nikolaevich Chicherin died just after the war began, Trubetskoi wrote a eulogy whose major theme would echo in the writings of many of his colleagues. He declared:

38. A typical declaration, that of the Saint Petersburg University Faculty Council, can be found in Imperatorskii Sankt-Peterburgskii Universitet, *Zhurnaly zasedanii soveta za 1904g.* (Saint Petersburg, 1905), p. 13.

39. Ol'ga Trubetskaia, *Kniaz' S. N. Trubetskoi: Vospominaniia sestry* (New York, 1953), p. 74.

40. Ibid., p. 100.

> We are not breaking our ties with Russia's past. We do not renounce the
> foundations of its national greatness; we want to strengthen them and make
> them indestructible. . . . That same patriotism, that powerful state instinct
> which gathered Russia around the throne of the rulers of Moscow and made
> her the greatest and largest power in the world should now receive its histori-
> cal justification . . . the tsar should now realize his real historical mission—
> to give freedom to the Russian nation and thereby achieve a closer harmony
> between tsar and people.[41]

The assassination of Plehve in July 1904 and the string of Russian de-
feats in the Far East increased the fears of the moderate liberals that unless the government made concessions quickly, the country would slip
into revolutionary anarchy.

One important advocate of this position was Prince Evgenii Trubetskoi, a professor of philosophy at Kiev University, who would also
play an important role in the organization of the Academic Union. On
26 September, *Pravo* published his article entitled "The War and the Bureaucracy," which one historian has described as "a turning point in the
annals of the Russian press." Trubetskoi called on the autocracy to forestall revolution by initiating reforms from above. He blamed the "bureaucracy" (a euphemism for the autocracy) for strengthening the revolutionary parties. If the government would only change its policy, "then
we will not need to fear either the internal or the external enemy."[42] The
article prompted Struve in turn to publish an "Open Letter to Prince
E. N. Trubetskoi," which appeared in *Osvobozhdenie* on 14 October
1904. Struve warned that "as long as the stronghold of autocracy has
not been destroyed, anyone who is fighting against it represents not a
'grave danger' but a great blessing. . . . In Russia there is no internal
enemy apart from the autocracy. . . . Solidarity between all our oppositional forces constitutes the first commandment of a sensible political
struggle." The contrast between these two viewpoints—"no enemies
on the left" versus "better reform from above than revolution from
below"—underscored the choice facing the professoriate. After half-
hearted flirtations with the oppositional movement, the bitter experi-
encc of the revolution would rekindle their faith in the government at
the first sign that "reform from above" was actually possible.

But Evgenii Trubetskoi's moderate political views did not keep him
from urging his academic colleagues to reevaluate their stance of corpo-

41. Ibid., p. 77.
42. Galai, *Liberation Movement*, p. 219.

rate political noninvolvement. Up to now, Trubetskoi wrote, the professoriate had "loudly proclaimed that the university should serve science and then would sit back and hope for the best. But such a claim rings hollow when we ourselves cannot teach what we want."[43] He and his colleagues, Trubetskoi admitted, had been wrong to assume, as they had told the students in the past, that academic freedom was compatible with political autocracy. Even if the autocracy satisfied all the professors' demands and repealed the 1884 Statute, the student movement alone would suffice to wreck normal academic life. Logic dictated that the professoriate had a direct stake in the political showdown between state and society.

Shortly after the publication of Trubetskoi's article, Vernadskii made a public appeal to the professoriate to break with its past traditions and organize.[44] "Internal emigration," Vernadskii argued, was no longer an alternative for Russia's academics. Besides, the government demanded more of its employees than mere neutrality, and the professors had to face up to the fact that they were independent scholars and teachers, not hacks on the state payroll. They should no longer let themselves be treated as if they were "teaching on some godforsaken Philippine Island." They had to organize, join the fight for political reforms, and stand ready to fill the vacuum created in the universities by the slow collapse of the 1884 Statute.

A few days later the new and influential liberal newspaper *Nashi Dni* hurled a direct public challenge to the professoriate in a blunt editorial entitled "The Professor: Is He a Civil Servant or Not?"[45] The paper declared that "the universities must now choose on whose side they stand." Were they *chinovniki,* or would they join the political mobilization of Russian society? In a not very subtle hint, the newspaper warned that the independence of a scholar was incompatible with the status of a hired civil servant.

By the end of 1904, therefore, a full-scale press campaign was under way to pressure the academic profession to join the political lineup against the autocracy. The campaign gathered momentum when Ivan Grevs, a Saint Petersburg University historian, wrote a hard-hitting article in *Nashi Dni* questioning the basis of the professoriate's "professional ideology." Most professors believed that

43. "Universitetskii vopros," *Pravo,* no. 50 (1904).
44. "O professorskom s"ezde," *Nashi Dni,* 20 December 1904.
45. "Chto takoi professor: Chinovnik ili net?" *Nashi Dni,* 24 December 1904.

a teacher of science acting in good conscience should help his students become adults by fostering a serious atmosphere of dedication to knowledge.
In order to realize this educational purpose he should dissuade them from
premature political diversions. Therefore he refrains in his teaching from discussing politics. Instead he expounds a very wide and progressive theoretical
idealism.[46]

By adopting such an approach, the Russian professor hoped to "preserve his influence on the students . . . and gradually develop in them a
conscious and critical attitude toward the contemporary world." This
was well and good in "normal countries" and in "normal situations,"
but Grevs argued that under Russian circumstances, such a lofty view of
the academic calling was a "pipe dream." Students formed their views
not in the classroom but in the student movement, through the "thick
journals" and under the influence of the mystique of the intelligentsia.
All too often, Grevs complained, the professor was caught between the
student movement and the autocracy and was "forced into complicity
with the disciplinary actions of the administration." Grevs argued that
the professoriate had allowed the government to place it in a position
incompatible with its professional honor. Because they had allowed
themselves to become compromised, the professors enjoyed low status
in the eyes of the Russian public. It was time to change this image—by
courageous action and organization.

Many other academics took advantage of Moscow University's 150th
anniversary, which took place in January 1905, to issue statements supporting Vernadskii and Grevs and calling for a nationwide professors'
conference.[47] A common theme of these statements was that unless the
professors won the respect of the general public and the students there
would be little hope for the restoration of normal academic life.

Thus, by the end of 1904, the professors were under growing external and internal pressure to make a corporate commitment to the liberation movement. But here they faced a serious problem, one with grave
implications for the future. The Union of Liberation had adopted a policy of "no enemies on the left." But the professors were naturally wary
of any collaboration with the revolutionary parties or political up-

46. "Zabytaia nauka i unizhënnoe zvanie," *Nashi Dni,* 28 December 1904.
47. See, for example, S. Bulgakov's "Bez plana," *Voprosy Zhizni,* no. 1 (1905).
Bulgakov reminded his colleagues that as of January 1905 only the students had taken any
collective stand concerning Russia's social and political crisis. Although some individual
professors had written articles, the universities as such had "been silent and remain
silent."

heavals, which might threaten the vulnerable universities. Yet the academic community could no longer shield itself from the deepening political crisis. Individual faculty councils were already raising their voices in favor of political as well as academic reform. The government showed no signs of encouraging lone individuals within the educational bureaucracy who urged building trust and understanding between the senior faculty and the state. The professoriate now began to undertake a step that was clearly illegal: the organization of an Academic Union.

THE "DECLARATION OF THE 342"

The second congress of the Union of Liberation met in Saint Petersburg on 20 October 1904. During this meeting the union endorsed the decisions taken at the Paris conference with the revolutionary parties the month before, thereby ratifying the adopted policy of collaboration with the left. The union also adopted a four-point plan of action, and it called on members to participate in the upcoming zemstvo congress and to raise constitutional demands at zemstvo assemblies. Finally, it decided to organize a nationwide banquet campaign for 20 November and to begin a propaganda drive to form a Union of Unions consisting of newly organized unions representing the free professions. The plan envisioned the organization of the professoriate, as well as doctors, lawyers, engineers, and others.[48]

In December 1904 the Union of Liberation entrusted Professor L. I. Lutugin with the job of organizing an academic union.[49] Lutugin contacted Professor A. A. Brandt of the Saint Petersburg Electrotechnical Institute and asked him to gather signatures for a political statement that would form the basis for the new union. Brandt reluctantly accepted the charge. He would later write that not only he but

> many other professors felt that it was already too late for a constitution in Russia. It should have been bestowed, if not during the reign of Empress Ann, then immediately after the emancipation of the serfs. At that time Russian industry had not yet developed and there was no Russian proletariat. . . . The first Russian Dumas would have consisted almost exclusively of nobles. . . .

48. Galai, *Liberation Movement*, p. 223.
49. A. A. Brandt, *List'ia pozheltelye: Peredumannoe i perezhitoe* (Belgrade, 1930), p. 26. The other professional unions, such as the Union of Lawyers, began with demonstrative banquets. But Brandt noted that the idea of a collective political banquet made the professors somewhat uncomfortable.

But in 1904 a constitution would lead to serious consequences; it would produce not political but social revolution.[50]

Caught between their anger at the government and their fear of social revolution, professors now began a delicate and risky journey down the road of political organization.

During the first week of January 1905, Brandt's group drafted a statement of political and academic principles that could bring the majority of the academic community into a union. The group planned to publish the statement on 12 January 1905, the sesquicentennial of Moscow University. It was signed by 16 members of the Academy of Sciences, 125 professors and adjunct professors, and 201 junior faculty members.[51] This statement, the "Declaration of the 342," would attract more than 1,650 signatories by August, more than half of the professoriate and the junior faculty.[52]

The "Declaration of the 342" was a turning point in the history of Russian higher education. For the first time, the Russian academic profession was making a collective statement affirming the incompatibility of decent education with the political status quo.

> A stream of government decisions and regulations has reduced professors and other instructors at the institutions of higher education to the level of bureaucrats, blindly executing the orders of higher government authorities. The scientific and moral standards of the teaching profession have been lowered. The prestige of educators has dwindled so much that the very existence of the institutions of higher education is threatened. Our school administration is a social and governmental disgrace. It undermines the authority of science, hinders the growth of scientific thought and prevents our people from fully realizing their intellectual potentialities. . . . The tragic state of our educational system does not allow us to remain on the sidelines. It compels us to express our profound conviction that academic freedom is incompatible with the existing system of government in Russia. The present situation cannot be remedied by partial reforms but only by a fundamental transformation of the existing system. . . . Only a full guarantee of personal and social liberties will assure academic freedom—the essential condition for true education.[53]

50. Ibid.

51. A list of the signatories can be found in *Vsemirnyi Vestnik,* no. 4 (1905).

52. By August the Academic Union had 550 members in Saint Petersburg, 111 in Kiev, 112 in Kharkov, 72 in Odessa, 400 in Moscow, 57 in Kazan, 49 in Dorpat, 41 in Warsaw, 100 in Tomsk, 16 in Ekaterinoslav, 22 in Novo-Alexandria, 11 in Iaroslavl', and 3 in Nezhin (S. D. Kirpichnikov, *Soiuz soiuzov* [Saint Petersburg, 1906], p. 20).

53. This is Alexander Vucinich's translation as it appears in his *Science in Russian Culture* (Stanford, 1970), vol. 2, p. 483.

Since the "Declaration of the 342" coincided with the beginning of the nationwide student strike, the Academic Union feared the Russian public might assume that the professors endorsed the students' action. Therefore an early priority of the union was to make it clear that the idea of the organization had arisen before Bloody Sunday and that the professors were acting completely independently of the student movement. The Academic Union had to walk a delicate line. On the one hand, the union signified an explicit commitment by the academic profession to the political campaign against the autocracy. But, on the other hand, as events would later underscore, a major purpose of the Academic Union was to safeguard the integrity of the universities during a period of political and social ferment. This ruled out endorsement of an academic strike as a tactic of political struggle—although the "Declaration of the 342" implicitly endorsed what amounted to the same thing. In short, the professors, not quite sure of themselves in their new role, wanted both to keep their distance from the student movement and to retain the option of dissociating themselves, if the need arose, from the political decisions of the Union of Liberation.

In March 1905, two leading members of the Academic Union, Ivan Grevs and S. E. Savich, expressed the union's attitude toward the student movement. It was complicated by a grudging recognition that the students had not been totally wrong. Grevs, while expressing "disappointment" at the students' decision to strike, called on his colleagues to be realistic.[54] Opening the universities would lead to violence. Furthermore, an honest observer had to conclude that perhaps the students had no choice but to strike. All in all, Grevs wrote, the professors found themselves in a "tragic" situation, torn between the struggle for political reform and their loyalty to the principles of higher education.

Savich argued that the key to restoring the universities to good health was for the professors to prove to everyone, especially the students, that they had the courage of their convictions. Matters would not return to normal until the public and the students saw the professors "not as supine scholars who meekly bowed to all government demands . . . but as firm-willed public figures [*obshchestvennye deiateli*]."[55] Their past diffidence had been a major cause of the student movement. But what about the short run? How should the Academic Union treat the student

54. Ivan Grevs, "Vozroditsia u nas podorvannoe nauchnoe prosveshchenie?" *Pravo*, no. 9 (1905).
55. S. E. Savich, "Zabastovka v vysshikh uchebnykh zavedeniiakh," *Pravo*, no. 11 (1905).

strike? Savich regretted the strike: closed universities weakened Russian liberalism in its two-front struggle against the government and the extreme left. After all, Bloody Sunday did not keep doctors and lawyers from working, and Russia needed universities more than ever. Of course, Savich admitted, there was now a clear incompatibility between "detached devotion to knowledge" and "civic duty." What the Russian professoriate had to do was save the universities by making a corporate commitment to the liberation movement.

As these articles revealed, the professoriate had to balance two commitments: the first to the notion of some sort of corporate involvement in the liberation movement, the second to the idea that the basic position of the universities was "above politics." In addition, the professors had to keep their distance from the student movement without agreeing to resume classes before the government made concessions. While many professors questioned this attitude from the right, only a very few were prepared to criticize this emerging professional consensus from the other political direction. One exception was the biologist K. A. Timiriazev, who publicly objected to his colleagues' attempts to put some distance between themselves and the student movement.[56] The European ideal of the apolitical university did not fit Russian circumstances, nor did Russian reality justify the professoriate's patronizing attitude toward the students. Russian students were much more mature and sensitive than their European counterparts, Timiriazev argued. If the state forced them to fight, the students had a right to ask what they were fighting for. Timiriazev compared the academic strike to a hunger strike in a prison. Both were acts of moral desperation; both were the only vehicles of protest available to essentially powerless groups.

As events would show, few professors shared Timiriazev's views. Their immediate problem was to make sure that the Russian universities took advantage of the opportunities offered by the revolution while avoiding the many pitfalls.

THE ACADEMIC UNION

After several preparatory meetings in Saint Petersburg, the first congress of the All-Russian Academic Union met in the capital on

56. K. A. Timiriazev, "Akademicheskaia svoboda," *Russkie Vedomosti*, 27 November 1905.

25 March.[57] The congress passed a political resolution calling for "general and equal" suffrage and rejecting a consultative parliament. The resolution condemned "national, religious caste, and class privileges" and declared that the nation was "on the brink of an abyss"; speedy reforms were absolutely necessary.[58] Here the consensus ended, as the Academic Union was to prove itself among the most moderate of the professional unions. The doctors' and the lawyers' unions called for a constituent assembly, but the professors did not, a decision that stood in sharp contrast to the resolution passed by the third congress of the Union of Liberation, which was meeting at the same time.[59] The Academic Union could not agree on such matters as the general basis of the new electoral law, suffrage for women, and the principles of agrarian reform. The Union of Liberation, however, supported these goals. Nor could the professors even agree whether the Academic Union was mainly a professional union or also a political organization. One way around these difficulties was to allow local organizations wide autonomy in passing their own resolutions.[60]

The delegates had less trouble reaching consensus on an academic platform. They declared: "We regard teaching, lecturing, holding seminars, and examinations as being morally impermissible while repression and force pervade the universities. We have firmly decided not to teach."[61] The congress also demanded that any reforms of higher educa-

57. A complete listing of the seventy-one participants of the Saint Petersburg preparatory meetings is given in TsGAOR, f. DO, ed. kh. 999, 4/1905, l. 12. Fifteen of the participants (eight professors and seven *privat-dozenty*) came from Saint Petersburg University, twelve from the Saint Petersburg Polytechnic, eight from the women's medical courses, five each from the institute of communications and the technological institute, and the remainder from other *VUZy* in the city. Professors Brandt and Salazkin secured Governor-General Trepov's permission to hold these meetings, after assuring him that their sole purpose was to formulate a new university statute. Clearly Trepov was becoming increasingly critical of Ministry of Education policy; later he became the moving force behind the adoption of the 27 August 1905 Temporary Rules. As comments on the listed professors make clear, the Okhrana was far from happy with the widespread practice of letting a professor fired from one *VUZ* transfer to a *VUZ* of another ministry.

58. For the text of the resolutions passed by the first congress, see *Russkie Vedomosti,* 30 March 1905.

59. Galai, *Liberation Movement,* pp. 244–245.

60. On this, see the unpublished memoirs of N. I. Kareev, GPB im. V. I. Lenina, f. 119, ed. kh. 49, l. 317. According to Kareev, most of the delegates to the first congress saw the Academic Union as a professional organization whose main goal was to rally the Russian academic profession around the banner of academic freedom. For more on the differences between the Academic Union and the other professional unions being formed at this time, see N. Cherevanin (pseud. of F. A. Lipkin), "Dvizhenie intelligentsii," in L. Martov, ed., *Obshchestvennoe dvizhenie v Rossii* (Saint Petersburg, 1910), vol. 2, part 2.

61. *Russkie Vedomosti,* 30 March 1905.

tion be worked out by a representative assembly rather than by the government.

Commenting on this resolution, Professor N. A. Gredeskul of Kharkov University declared that the professoriate had "crossed the Rubicon."[62] The Academic Union, had, after all, endorsed a strike in deed if not in name. But there was one important ambiguity. Part of the resolution called on the government to grant "temporary powers" to the faculty councils. Thus the professors left open the possibility that they might return to the classroom even before they got all they wanted.

A short time later Vernadskii, addressing the Moscow professors' conference organized by curator Nekrasov, discussed the tasks of the Academic Union and its first congress.[63] Many of those present had attacked the "temporary powers" clause as constituting a possible escape hatch from the professors' new political and moral commitment not to teach until political freedom had been attained. Vernadskii's reply was significant, especially in light of the post-1905 relationship between the professoriate and the government. He distinguished between "temporary powers"—which he defined—and "academic freedom"—which he did not. The former bore a striking resemblance to what the government would actually grant in August—permission for faculty councils to elect rectors and assume responsibility for student discipline and internal affairs in the universities. This was different, Vernadskii pointed out, from "academic freedom," which was "incompatible with the present conditions of the Russian state and could not be realized until the country receives the popular representation promised by the imperial rescript of 18 February."

At that point there were more objections from the audience. Would the professoriate not be falling into a trap if it shouldered the responsibility for student discipline before it was certain that Russia had finally achieved political freedom and academic autonomy? Again Vernadskii's response reflected the sense of what made the professors unique and separated them from other professionals. "We professors are in a special position. When we discuss events we cannot do so solely in our role as Russian citizens. We must also act as the guardian of science and education. . . . Our first duty is not to let the *VUZy* suffer during this period of social upheaval."

This notion of a "special position" set the Russian professoriate apart

62. Gredeskul, "Rol' universiteta."
63. The text of Vernadskii's speech can be found in TsGIA, f. 733, op. 152, d. 173, l. 359.

during the Revolution of 1905. Articles published by leading professors in this period conveyed the distinct impression of a profession "fighting on all fronts." The political commentaries of Vinogradov, Kovalevskii, Trubetskoi, Vernadskii, and others developed themes that emerged as the major contours of professorial liberalism. One important theme was the assertion that the autocracy not only bore the blame for Russia's defeat but also misunderstood its role in the nation's history. Rather than being something "specifically Russian, tsarism was introduced to Russia from abroad . . . in stages, under the pressure of external necessity."[64] Pskov and Novgorod, Kovalevskii argued, showed that there was as much precedent for popular initiative in Russia's history as there was for stultifying bureaucracy.

Fear of mass revolution, however, led to the hope that the government would see reason and collaborate with the educated classes to forestall revolution from below. Vinogradov, for example, expressed a clear preference for "1848" over "1789."[65] But these academics did not ignore the shortcomings of liberalism in Western Europe. Vinogradov, arguing that Russian society was "basically democratic," opposed an electoral law based on property qualifications, or an upper house.[66] While liberalism in Europe had tied itself too closely to selfish class interests, Russian liberalism would speak for the nation as a whole. Evgenii Trubetskoi, for example, opposed the electoral law to the Bulygin Duma on the grounds that it was inconsistent "with the major task before the Russian government: the achievement of social harmony and the reconciliation of antagonistic groups."[67] Like Vinogradov, Trubetskoi called for reforms based on "democratic" principles.

Another theme was the clear line the professors drew between themselves and the intelligentsia. The enemy was as much on the left as on the right. Vinogradov wrote that he shuddered at the thought of a "disruption of all existing relations in society, a break with the national past, a risky gamble with unknown political forces."[68] Russia needed

64. M. M. Kovalevskii, *La Crise Russe* (Paris, 1906), p. 19.
65. P. G. Vinogradov, "Politicheskie pis'ma," *Russkie Vedomosti*, 5 August 1905.
66. Commenting on Vinogradov's letters, V. I. Lenin wrote that they underscored the fact that the "bourgeoisie does not want, and indeed because of its class character cannot want, a revolution. It only seeks a deal with the autocracy at the expense of the . . . people." At the same time Lenin discussed the special role the professoriate played within the bourgeoisie by virtue of its relative freedom from the profit motive or narrow class interests ("Chevo khotiat i chevo boiatsia nashi liberal'nye burzhuia," in his *Sochineniia*, 3d ed. [Moscow, 1936], vol. 8, pp. 189–193).
67. "Blizhaishaia zadacha gosudarstvennoi dumy," *Syn Otechestva*, 23 August 1905.
68. "Politicheskie pis'ma."

"thinking people" who were disciplined, competent, patriotic, and efficient, people who knew their job and did it well. The members of the intelligentsia were too lazy and intolerant to see the vital necessity of helping the nation by undertaking steady and often unglamorous work at one's chosen profession. They were also too narrow-minded, too given to simple answers.

These professors also made a clear distinction between the autocracy and the nation and, in so doing, defined a major task for the universities—to strengthen the nation by creating a professional class with a strong sense of Russian patriotism. They had no patience with the defeatism that marked the attitude of many educated Russians toward the Russo-Japanese War.[69] The universities would also train citizens who would understand the importance of a civic culture and shoulder the burden of overcoming caste and class differences. An essential choice was between taking a risky and reckless leap into the unknown or starting a steady march forward based on collaboration between an able administration and the nation's educated elite.[70] In short, the universities were essential to the rise of a Russia that was strong, unified and "democratic." Because they were so important, could they be jeopardized by direct involvement in politics?

The very logic of this definition of the place of the universities in the nation's life set the stage for what many unsympathetic observers called the beginning of a full-scale retreat of the senior faculty from the political idealism and courage that underlay the "Declaration of the 342." At any rate, as the spring wore on, the deepening of the nation's political crisis increased the pressure on the Academic Union to define the nature of its relationship to other political organizations such as the Union of Unions, an umbrella body of professional unions organized by the Union of Liberation. By its first congress, on 8 May, the Union of Unions included fourteen professional unions; the Academic Union found itself together with such radical groups as the engineers' and the railway workers' unions, whose leaders were already charting the strategy for a general strike to overthrow the autocracy and call a constituent assembly.[71] Professor P. I. Novgorodtsev told the delegates that the Academic Union empowered him to attend the congress as an observer

69. "We always speak of the Russian people and the Russian government as if they were opposites. We never refer to the Russian state [gosudarstvo], which includes both" (ibid.).
70. V. I. Vernadskii, "Tri zabastovki," Russkie Vedomosti, 5 July 1905.
71. Galai, Liberation Movement, p. 248.

rather than as an active participant, a clear sign that it was deeply divided about its identity as a political organization.[72] Although the congress elected a relative moderate, the historian Paul Miliukov, as the chairman of the Union of Unions, its center of gravity was beginning to shift rapidly to the left.[73]

A few days later a stunned nation learned of the crushing defeat at Tsushima, where Admiral Togo sent the hapless Russian fleet to the bottom of the Pacific. Quickly taking advantage of this blow to the government's prestige, the Union of Unions called an emergency congress on 24 May which issued a dramatic appeal to the nation to overthrow the government: "All means may now be legitimately used to fight the danger represented by the continued existence of the present government. . . . Bring about the immediate elimination of the bandit gang that has usurped power and replace it with a constituent assembly . . . so that it will as quickly as possible end the war and the present regime."[74] Both the Academic Union and the Union of Zemstvo Activists, which also included several faculty members, boycotted the emergency congress; the Union of Unions had become too radical. The liberation movement was showing clear signs of estrangement between radicals and moderates. While the emergency congress of the Union of Unions was taking place, the moderates were holding a coalition congress that attracted more than three hundred delegates. Its own response to the Tsushima disaster was to send a delegation to the tsar to urge immediate reforms in order to forestall revolution.[75] The delegation, headed by Moscow professor Prince Sergei Trubetskoi, met the tsar on 6 June. Trubetskoi made an eloquent personal appeal to the tsar to listen to the moderates:

> Your subjects must feel themselves to be Russian citizens, equal and without differences. . . . It is necessary that all your subjects, even though they be of a different faith or race from you, see in Russia their fatherland and in you their sovereign. Just as the Russian tsar is not the tsar of the nobility or of the peasantry or of the merchants or of classes, but the tsar of all the Russias, so the persons elected by the entire population should serve the interests of the entire polity and not of classes.[76]

The tsar listened politely, but Trubetskoi's appeal had no effect on government policy, especially on the important deliberations being con-

---

72. D. F. Sverchkov, "Soiuz soiuzov," *Krasnaia Letopis'*, no. 3 (1925).
73. Galai, *Liberation Movement*, p. 253.
74. Ibid.
75. Sidney Harcave, *The Russian Revolution of 1905* (London, 1964), p. 159.
76. Ibid.

ducted under the chairmanship of Bulygin. By early summer the public had learned the main outlines of the proposed reforms—and they fell short of what even moderate liberals had expected. The government was planning to offer a consultative assembly elected by a complicated ballot that would favor the nobility and the peasantry.

On 6 August the tsar announced the law establishing the so-called Bulygin Duma. Most non-Russians were excluded from the vote. Property qualifications were set so high that most wage earners and urban small-property holders were excluded as well. Nor was the proposed Duma to have much power. The law specified that the Duma was to "provide preliminary consideration and discussion of legislative proposals, to be transmitted through the State Council up to the supreme autocratic sovereign."[77]

TEMPORARY RULES OF 27 AUGUST 1905

In the summer of 1905 the Academic Union faced two major decisions. Would it join most of the other professional unions in the Union of Unions in boycotting the Bulygin Duma? Second, would it recommend a return to the classroom in the fall?

The Academic Union had to act against the backdrop of growing popular violence. Heavy fighting broke out in Poland, widespread May Day demonstrations pointed to growing restiveness among the working class, and in June the mutiny aboard the *Potemkin* led to violence that claimed two thousand lives. On 1 July the third congress of the Union of Unions met in Terioki and voted to boycott the elections to the proposed Duma.[78] This decision led to a split. Three unions, including the Academic Union, opposed the boycott. Paul Miliukov sided with the minority position and lost his chairmanship. He then proceeded to organize the moderate minority of the Union of Unions. Through professors Brandt, Trubetskoi, and Vernadskii, the Academic Union kept in close touch with Miliukov. On 7 August, the Okhrana raided Miliukov's summer home; among those arrested was Professor Brandt.[79] This arrest ended Miliukov's association with the Union of Unions, which now turned its attention to the organization of a general strike. Meanwhile

77. Ibid., p. 162.
78. Kirpichnikov, *Soiuz Soiuzov*, p. 14.
79. TsGAOR, f. 102, op. 5, ed. kh. 00, 3ch. 25/1905.

the fourth congress of the Union of Liberation, which met in Moscow on 23 and 24 August, voted to accept the Bulygin Duma and to participate in the elections, with the aim of "transforming the Duma into a legislative assembly" and changing the electoral laws in accordance with the formula of direct, equal, secret, and universal suffrage. At this point the Union of Liberation decided to dissolve and form the Constitutional Democratic party, which would participate in the coming elections.[80]

As the Academic Union prepared for its important second congress, at the end of August, many of the organization's leaders wanted to put more distance between the professors and the Union of Unions. In July 1905 Professor Vernadskii flatly declared in a widely publicized newspaper article that "the professors' 'strike' was not an act of political protest. . . . It took place against the will of the professoriate. . . . No possible political gain can outweigh the academic losses already incurred."[81] The professors, Vernadskii pointed out, had been forced to choose between "the police and revolutionary terror." But they would return to teaching in the fall if the government would agree to the short-term compromise of decreeing changes in the administrative structure of the universities, which would at least allow the senior faculty to elect its own rectors.

Although Vernadskii did not know it when he wrote the article, the government was about to give the professoriate exactly the temporary powers it had been asking for. On 7 August, the day after the proclamation of the Bulygin Duma, Tsar Nicholas ordered a ministerial conference to decide whether the universities and other institutions of higher education should reopen on 1 September.[82]

The conference opened with a bitter argument between Glazov and D. F. Trepov, the governor-general of Saint Petersburg. Glazov had asked Trepov to ensure police cooperation in maintaining order in the universities if and when they reopened in the fall. But Trepov, in a surprise move, declared that the police would no longer enter the premises of the institutions of higher education. He told the conference that the basic problem was the bankruptcy of the Ministry of Education: it had no policy. The police could no longer be expected to rescue the Ministry of Education from the results of its mistakes. Past experience, Trepov

80. Galai, *Liberation Movement*, p. 260.
81. "Tri zabastovki."
82. This report of the conference is taken from TsGIA, f. 922, op. 1, d. 219.

argued, had shown that repression only aggravated student unrest. The Ministry of Education had had nine months to develop a creative policy toward higher education. It had failed to do so.

Trepov made two proposals to the conference. First, he urged it to void the threat of 16 April to dismiss the professors en masse if they failed to return to teaching in the fall. Since there were not enough professors anyway, Trepov pointed out, making good on the threat meant destroying higher education in the country. (This was all somewhat disingenuous, since the original threat had been Trepov's idea.) His second suggestion was that the government issue temporary rules for the governance of the institutions of higher education until a new university statute could be presented to the Duma. The government, he argued, had nothing to lose. Things could not get any worse in the universities. Perhaps if the professors were given more responsibilities, they might succeed where the government had failed and keep order in the *VUZy*.

V. N. Kokovtsev, the minister of finance, agreed with Trepov. He reminded the conference that the government would suffer a serious loss of prestige if the universities did not reopen on 1 September. It was important, at the same time, to shift basic responsibility for university discipline to the professoriate. If the universities were forced to close again, the government should ensure that the onus for student unrest fell on the faculty, not the state.

After some debate the conference recommended that the *VUZy*—that is, all institutions of higher education, regardless of ministerial affiliation—reopen under new temporary rules. These regulations received the tsar's approval and were published on 27 August 1905. The 27 August Temporary Rules remained in force, along with the 1884 University Statute, until 1917. This marked a major turning point in the government's higher-education policy.

The Temporary Rules granted the senior faculty many of its most important demands.[83] Henceforth, faculty councils could elect rectors and assistant rectors. Individual departments could elect their own deacons. All electees, however, had to be confirmed by their respective ministries. The new rules gave the faculty councils the responsibility for maintaining order in the *VUZy*. They could, in extreme circumstances, ask the minister to suspend classes. Jurisdiction over student discipline was vested in the faculty disciplinary courts, whose functions continued to be defined by the rules of 24 August 1902.

83. The text of the new rules appeared in *Russkie Vedomosti*, 27 August 1905.

The Temporary Rules would begin a new era in the history of Russian higher education. Yet in the end they would fail either to "normalize" the universities or to put faculty-government relations on a harmonious footing. By issuing the rules, the government seemed to be admitting the failure of its previous policies. In making the internal governance of the universities the responsibility of the faculty councils, the government continued a basic trend of university policy begun in 1887: the piecemeal abrogation of the 1884 Statute. The failure of the state examination commissions, the professors' disciplinary courts, the 1901 and 1902 rules allowing student organizations, and now the 27 August Temporary Rules meant that few of the basic features of the statute remained in force.

Yet a crucial problem lurked just beneath the surface: the legal relationship of the 27 August Rules to the 1884 Statute. The 27 August Rules were not as clear-cut as they at first seemed. Did they actually supersede the 1884 Statute or confer autonomy on the universities? It was unclear whether the faculty councils had gained authority over the curriculum or whether the new rules were merely an administrative device for relieving the government of the embarrassing responsibility for student discipline. Another point left vague was whether *only* the faculty council could send police into the universities. These uncertainties were to poison relations between the government and the professors until 1914.

The Temporary Rules were supposed to remain in effect only until the new Duma could legislate a replacement for the 1884 Statute. But this was never to be. The government, unlike the professors, saw the 27 August Rules not as an organic reform of higher education but, rather, as a political concession to help restore a sense of normalcy to the country. The context in which the rules were issued is significant. They followed the signing of the Portsmouth Peace Treaty ending the Russo-Japanese War and the 6 August rescript proclaiming the granting of a consultative Duma. As the record of the 11 August conference shows, the Temporary Rules were another tactical move in the government's overall strategy of regaining control over events.

Indeed it seemed, by the end of August, that the Revolution of 1905 might be over before it had really begun. The labor movement was showing signs of abating. The Bulygin rescript had split the liberal camp. The revolutionary parties, at least in central Russia, had not yet shown that they enjoyed significant mass support. In this context Kokovtsev was correct when he warned that a continuation of the academic strike could only harm the government's prestige and enhance the impression that a revolution was still going on.

As events would show, the 27 August Temporary Rules proved to be a major miscalculation. Far from ending the revolution, they gave it new impetus.

THE SECOND CONGRESS
OF THE ACADEMIC UNION

On the eve of its second congress, which was scheduled for 25 August, the Academic Union had to decide two very important and interrelated questions: whether to return to classes, and whether to accept the Bulygin Duma. If the professors did both, albeit with reservations, they would be saying in effect that the revolution was over. But if the students—or other groups—did not agree, then there would be trouble in September. Yet another problem was the continued rationale for the union. Now that the Kadet party had given liberal professors the chance to make individual political choices, what need was there for a political Academic Union? But if the Academic Union was to become a purely professional union, how could a balance be struck between its two basic constituencies, senior and junior faculty members? The latter had been organizing ever since the end of 1904 and saw the union as a forum from which to press their own demands for a wider role in university governance and guarantees that "autonomy" would not merely substitute subordination to professors for subordination to government curators.

Just before the congress met, *Osvobozhdenie* published an article written by an anonymous member of of the Academic Union.[84] The author warned his colleagues not to beat too hasty a retreat from their political commitments of the previous spring. The revolution was not yet over, and the professors could guarantee future stability in the universities only by creating a "democratic" atmosphere, which would ensure good relations with students and junior faculty. The article admitted that the professors had been "unwilling politicians" from the start; their main concern had been the defense of the universities from both the government and the revolutionary left. But that job was not yet over: the Academic Union had to continue fighting. The article called for an unwritten pact between the professoriate and the liberation

84. "K predstoiashchemu akademicheskomu s"ezdu," *Osvobozhdenie*, no. 76 (1905).

movement. The latter would respect the special situation of the universities while the academic community would remain committed to the anti-government coalition.

The Academic Union's second congress, which opened on 25 August, attracted 129 delegates from thirty-nine institutions of higher education.[85] The first item on the agenda was what to do in September. Professor Vernadskii made a speech urging his colleagues to return to the classroom. He admitted that some of the basic conditions for a normal academic life had not been met. But by returning to the universities, the professors would gain an important base from which to pressure the government for further political reforms. If the government granted freedom of speech and of the press, then it was likely that the student movement would lose its former importance. Reforms, Vernadskii argued, could create a new climate wherein political tensions could move outside the universities.[86]

The speech touched off a lively debate. Several delegates argued that returning to class would violate the pledge made by the "Declaration of the 342." Since the government had made no concessions—if one did not count the Bulygin Duma—then Vernadskii's proposal was tantamount to capitulation. But the congress voted overwhelmingly to approve Vernadskii's motion. The final resolution declared that by returning to the classroom the professors would be implementing the basic principles of academic freedom as well as "freedom of speech, association, public meetings, and the inalienable rights of the citizen."[87] The resolution went on, however, to warn that if the police engaged in repression of students or faculty, the professors would immediately stop lecturing. The academic community would no longer defer to government threats.

On this issue as well as others, signs of a rift between senior and junior professors in the Academic Union began to emerge. The latter were proving to be more radical than their senior comrades.[88] For example, on the eve of the second congress, a straw vote of Moscow University junior faculty approved the decision to return to class by a margin of only one vote. The meeting, which elected P. N. Sakulin and M. M.

85. TsGAOR, f. DO, ed. kh. 999, 4ch. 1905.

86. GPB im. V. I. Lenina, f. 264 (P. N. Sakulin), folder 41, ed. kh. 21 ("zapis' o vtorom s"ezde akademicheskovo soiuza").

87. Ibid.

88. Professor Brandt, for example, worried that the growing rift between the junior and the senior faculty was becoming a major threat to the Academic Union (*List'ia pozheltelye*, p. 28).

Garnet as representatives to the second congress, called for a change in the rules of the Academic Union, to allow student participation.[89]

Garnet and Sakulin, true to their instructions, raised the issue of student participation at the second congress. Sakulin warned his colleagues that unless the Academic Union reached out to the students—themselves about to decide what to do about resuming normal studies—its decisions would remain a dead letter. The revolutionary parties, Sakulin pointed out, were going to compete with the professors for the loyalty of the *studenchestvo*. The *VUZy* could work again only if the Academic Union took the initiative and made some conciliatory gestures to overcome the suspicions of the past. But Vernadskii and Grevs, representing the central bureau of the Academic Union, rejected the suggestion of student participation in the union's deliberations. What was at stake, of course, was not just the nature of the Academic Union but the underlying principles of future university governance. The senior faculty was beginning to see that a prolonged revolutionary situation could lead to calls for "democratizing" the universities as well as the nation's political institutions.

The issue of the Bulygin Duma caused more controversy at the congress. Brandt and Moscow University's A. A. Manuilov moved for a resolution accepting the Duma, but several delegates argued against a debate on the grounds that the Academic Union was supposed to "enlighten the nation," not pass "political" resolutions.[90] This debate on a debate ended with a declaration that the "interests of science were too closely linked to the political life of the nation" for the Academic Union not to take a stand. The final resolution expressed some dissatisfaction with the Bulygin Duma but urged participation in the forthcoming elections on the grounds that the Duma was a first step toward the "liberation of the people from the yoke of the police regime." Without committing the Academic Union to support any particular political party, the congress called on its members to work for the election of "enlightened" delegates to the Duma.

The collective obligation of the academic profession toward colleagues who were suffering from police repression was the major topic of the 26 August session. Several specific cases were before the congress, which now discussed the general issue of professional solidarity. *Privatdozent* N. N. Parfent'ev of Kazan University had been discharged by

89. There is a summary of this meeting in GPB im. V. I. Lenina, f. 264, folder 45, ed. kh. 5.

90. TsGAOR, f. DO, ed. kh. 999, 4ch. 1905, l. 41.

the curator of his educational district for having attended a student *skhodka*. *Privat-dozenty* R. M. Orzhentski and L. A. Tarasevich had been fired from Odessa University. Professor L. V. Khodskii of Saint Petersburg University, who served as the editor of the progressive daily *Nasha Zhizn'*, had been forced to take early retirement. Trepov had recently forbidden the eminent sociologist M. M. Kovalevskii, just returning from many years of exile, to accept an invitation to teach at the Saint Petersburg Polytechnic Institute.[91]

The congress agreed that the ministers of education and the curators should no longer have the right to discharge faculty and called on all members to refuse to replace any colleagues discharged by the administration. The congress also discussed the very basis of Russian higher education—the state-controlled university. Professor E. Trubetskoi called on the academic community to establish "free universities" which would supplement, and, if need be, replace, the state-controlled institutions of higher education. Trubetskoi explained that no matter what changes the government made in its policy, the professoriate had to admit that

> the state universities did not satisfy the need of the Russian people for higher education. . . . A free university would be a valuable supplement to the state institutions. . . . They would be more flexible since they would not be bound by the government teaching plans and the fixed distribution of faculty chairs. . . . Free universities would advance higher education by introducing new subjects and new methods of teaching.[92]

He also pointed out that "free universities" would eliminate the religious, national, and sexual barriers that plagued Russian higher education. And they would stand ready to replace the state universities if the latter were "temporarily forced out of existence during the present period of struggle for renewal of the national order."

The congress approved Trubetskoi's proposal and called on the Saint Petersburg and Moscow chapters to prepare a detailed project for a free university in time for the next congress of the Academic Union. The local chapters of the Academic Union were encouraged to seek zemstvo and municipal-council support for the project.

The second congress ended just as the news arrived that the government had issued the 27 August Temporary Rules. As the delegates dispersed to return to the classroom, many were doubtless asking themselves whether the long cycle of disruption and repression that had

91. *Russkie Vedomosti*, 29 August 1905.
92. Ibid.

plagued Russian higher education was now about to end. The resignations from the disciplinary courts, the formation of the Academic Union, the "Declaration of the 342," and the faculty councils' refusal to resume teaching after Bloody Sunday all reflected the professoriate's reluctant move toward confrontation with the government. Yet by the end of the summer, the fragile consensus represented by the Academic Union was about to crack. There were many areas of potential conflict—the political versus the professional character of the Academic Union; acceptance of the Bulygin Duma and the 27 August Rules as justifying a return to classes; relations between junior and senior faculty—but they all pointed to some fundamental differences between the situation of the professoriate and that of other professions during the Revolution of 1905. Professors depended on and felt responsible for a vulnerable and complex institution—the university—but had no easy means to convince other involved parties to recognize their claims to authority. Government, outsiders, junior faculty, and students had their own views on how the universities should function during a political crisis. For the professoriate, the short-lived professional assertiveness marked by the "Declaration of the 342" would soon be tested by the bitter realities of the revolution.

CHAPTER 6

1905

By the end of August 1905 the autocracy seemed to have recovered its political balance. The Portsmouth treaty ended the war, and the rescript on the Bulygin Duma divided the liberal opposition. Popular unrest still worried the authorities on the periphery—especially in Poland and the Caucasus. But riots in Lodz or Baku could not threaten the existence of the regime as long as the revolution did not spread to the vital nerve centers of Saint Petersburg and Moscow or to the restive peasantry of the central Russian provinces, and the capitals seemed relatively stable.

By the middle of October, however, the autocracy was facing a serious crisis. A general strike had paralyzed the country and forced the tsar to issue—very grudgingly—a manifesto promising fundamental civil liberties and what seemed to be the beginnings of a constitutional monarchy.

The reopening of the universities and other *VUZy* played a key role in unleashing the chain of events that would culminate in the October general strike. Both Witte and Lenin emphasized the importance of the 27 August Temporary Rules in transforming the political situation. Witte saw the rules as a "first breach through which the revolution, having matured underground, emerged into the broad light of day."[1] In oddly similar language, Lenin concluded that "new revolutionary waves flowed into this breach with unexpected force. This miserable

1. Quoted in John L. H. Keep, *The Rise of Social Democracy in Russia* (Oxford, 1963), p. 217.

concession . . . actually resulted in a tremendous intensification of the struggle."[2] Under the new rules, Russia's *VUZy* reopened at the beginning of September. But they would not even finish out the semester; by the end of October the nation's system of higher education was once again paralyzed.

This chapter will show how the universities were drawn into the maelstrom of the revolution and will analyze how the student movement, the professoriate, and the junior faculty faced the issue of what role universities should play during a period of intense political crisis. All three groups acted in a dual capacity, as members of the general society and as participants in an internal conflict concerning the future nature and course of Russia's system of higher education. The students had to reconcile their own interests with those of the surging labor movement. As the revolution turned the universities into open meeting halls, the senior faculty saw itself as the beleaguered guardian of a fragile national institution, engaged in a desperate struggle for autonomy and even survival against both the forces of order and the revolutionary crowds. Meanwhile, the revolution intensified the internal conflict between the professors, the student movement, and the younger faculty. At issue were two major questions. The first was the extent to which the university *as such* should join the liberation movement. The second issue was whether "democracy" should be extended to the universities themselves, with the professoriate sharing its newly won power with both the students and the younger faculty.

"AUTONOMY": A CAUTIOUS WELCOME

The professoriate gave the new rules a cautious welcome. Leading academic spokesmen were quick to spot some of the legal ambiguities of the new decree and raised questions that were to complicate the professors' relations with the state right up to the beginning of World War I. Were the rules intended merely to turn the professors into effective policemen of unruly students? Or did they signal the government's final abandonment of the 1884 Statute and the beginning of a new era of academic autonomy in Russia? These two questions were to constitute the nub of the so-called university question as it emerged during and after the Revolution of 1905.

2. V. I. Lenin, "Uroki Moskovskikh sobytii," in his *Sochineniia,* 3d ed. (Moscow, 1936), vol. 8, p. 313.

Soon after the rules appeared, Ivan Grevs, the major spokesman for the Academic Union, warned his colleagues that they had won at best only a tactical victory, a victory that could well turn into a trap. The rub was that the professors would find themselves saddled with the onus of keeping the students in line while lacking the powers and prerogatives crucial to achieving real academic autonomy. After all, the minister of education still retained veto power over the elected rectors and deacons. Furthermore, no one could say for sure whether the ministry had given up its authority to approve all teaching appointments.[3] The faculty council of Saint Petersburg University also showed its misgivings by issuing a collective statement warning that without wider political reforms the new government initiative would have little value.[4]

Some leading curators also attacked the new rules for being too liberal. S. F. Speshkov, the influential curator of the Kazan Educational District, blasted the rules for turning the universities over to the "illegal Academic Union." They were untimely, he complained, and ran counter to the government's real interests. A. N. Schwartz, curator of the Warsaw Educational District (who would later earn a reputation as a notoriously reactionary minister of education), complained that the professors tended to interpret the new rules according to the time-tested principle of "squatters' rights" (*zakhvatnoe pravo*). The professoriate confused autonomy with "extraterritoriality" and served the ends of the revolutionary movement by trying to turn the universities into a "state within a state."[5]

The early September elections to university rectorships were the first test of the new rules—and the liberal press hailed the results as marking a clear defeat for the autocracy and the conservative professors. With the exception of the rector of Tomsk University, who was relatively liberal, all the government-appointed incumbents were defeated.[6] Newly elected rectors included I. I. Borgman at Saint Petersburg University, S. N. Trubetskoi at Moscow, N. M. Tsitovich at Kiev, A. V. Reinhart at Kharkov, I. M. Zanchevskii at Odessa, N. M. Liubimov at Kazan, Ia. F. Karskii at Warsaw, and E. V. Passek at Iur'ev.

3. "Vremennye pravila 27ovo avgusta," *Pravo,* no. 36 (1905).

4. Imperatorskii Sankt-Peterburgskii Universitet, *Zhurnaly zasedanii soveta za 1905g.* (Saint Petersburg, 1906), p. 64.

5. On Speshkov, see A. E. Ivanov, "Universitety Rossii v 1905om godu," *Istoricheskie Zapiski,* no. 88 (1971): 130; on Schwartz, TsGIA, f. 733, op. 226, d. 137, l. 13. Schwartz's comments are taken from a memorandum written after he was appointed minister of education in 1908.

6. *Nasha Zhizn',* 4 September 1905.

In his widely reported maiden speech to the Moscow University Faculty Council, rector Trubetskoi euphorically announced that the "university has gained a great moral victory. What have we to fear now? In one stroke we have received all that we could have wished. We have conquered the forces of reaction."[7] Trubetskoi expressed the hope that the students would now obey the professors and stop disrupting the universities. Within one week events would shatter Trubetskoi's optimism.

The results of the new elections raised hopes in the provincial universities as well. The fourth-year juridical students at Kiev University sent a delegation to Professor Tsitovich to tell him that they considered his election as rector to be a victory for progressive ideals. Professor Shchepkin, a prominent member of the Academic Union in Odessa and a close associate of the new rector, Zanchevskii, implied that the professoriate now had a mandate to initiate far-reaching reforms of the curriculum.[8]

The faculty councils now faced the frustrating task of discovering— or guessing—the actual extent of their new powers under the Temporary Rules. Initially there was intense public pressure on the faculty councils to abolish restrictions on the admission of women and Jews. But most of the councils concluded that unilateral action was illegal. As rector Tsitovich explained in his first lecture at Kiev on 22 September, "The public thinks that the professoriate has received very broad new powers. In reality its powers are quite limited. For example, it is erroneous to think that the professors have the right to admit all who wish to enter the universities."[9]

The essence of the problem was whether the new rules implied the abolition of the key provisions of the 1884 Statute and subsequent legislation affecting the universities. The professors' quandary emerged quite clearly in the debate that took place in the Saint Petersburg University Faculty Council on 13 September. Rector Borgman told the council that thirty-seven Jewish applicants, the 3 percent allowed by law, had been accepted for admission to the university. This left eighty-four Jews who

7. *Russkie Vedomosti*, 3 September 1905.
8. Shchepkin complained in a 13 September newspaper interview that "our history faculties lack geography and economics . . . our law students study the history of law without grounding in proper historical method . . . there is no place for sociology. . . . If a student wants to master a particular subject he must still spend two-thirds of his time satisfying compulsory requirements. . . . An economics student must maneuver between Roman and Canon law . . . a historian must spend two years studying classical and Russian philology" (*Odesskie Novosti*, 16 September 1905).
9. *Odesskii Listok*, 25 September 1905.

had not been accepted. The problem was very clear. In rejecting the eighty-four Jewish students, Borgman was complying with the Statutes of the Committee of Ministers of 5 December 1886 and 26 June 1887. But Borgman also declared that the faculty council should no longer be expected to enforce this discriminatory legislation. Therefore he proposed that the faculty council authorize him to *petition* the minister of education to admit the remaining Jewish applicants. Two professors, A. A. Markov and V. M. Shimkevich, vigorously protested. Markov insisted that the faculty council should admit the Jewish students on its own authority. When the council decided to petition the ministry, Markov resigned his seat on the newly established "commission" which was supposed to serve as the executive arm of the council.[10] In an interview with *Syn Otechestva* Markov explained his resignation by remarking that "the 'new course' is very little different from the old one."[11]

Faculty councils at other universities also balked at unilaterally abrogating the *numerus clausus*. Some rectors drew a distinction between overriding circulars of the Ministry of Education and ignoring statutes of the Committee of Ministers. Thus rector Zanchevskii told a meeting of Odessa students on 24 September that the faculty would on its own authority admit Jews as auditors, since restrictions in this area were established by circular, not statute. For the same reason, Zanchevskii explained, the faculty council would abolish the restrictions on the admission to the university of students from other educational districts, as well as readmit students previously expelled by administrative action.[12] The Moscow University Faculty Council also remained within "the law." On 20 September rector Trubetskoi petitioned the minister of education to allow the council to admit sixty-two Jews who were residents of the Moscow Educational District.[13] Caught between their distaste for discrimination in university admissions and their unwillingness to violate established legal procedures, the liberal professoriate experienced a preview in miniature of the problems that would beset the universities in the next month.

The faculty councils also had to face another problem: demands from junior faculty for more power in university governance. After all, why call for democratic suffrage in the country and deny the same prin-

10. Imperatorskii Sankt-Peterburgskii Universitet, *Zhurnaly zasedanii soveta za 1905g.*, p. 87 (meeting of 13 September 1905).
11. *Syn Otechestva*, 17 September 1905.
12. *Odesskie Novosti*, 25 September 1905.
13. *Russkie Vedomosti*, 20 September 1905.

ciple in the university? After the reopening of the universities, junior faculty members intensified their calls for a greater voice in university governance. A major source of junior-faculty strength in September was the Academic Union, where faculty members had equal voting rights irrespective of rank. This in turn led to a growing divergence of interest between the union and otherwise liberal senior faculty who could not accept the principle of equal representation on faculty councils.

On 8 September a meeting of the Saint Petersburg University junior faculty hailed the Temporary Rules as "the first victory of the Academic Union" but warned that this only "increased the union's obligation to strive for further political concessions from the government." What the universities had won was not enough. They should not be willing to become an "oasis . . . in a desert of arbitrariness." The Saint Petersburg junior faculty specified three major goals now facing the Academic Union: the struggle for a democratic Russia with a representative government and an administration accountable to the parliament, equal rights for junior faculty in university governance, and the democratization of university admissions.[14]

On 24 September this same group met to consider a model university statute drawn up by the Saint Petersburg branch of the Academic Union. The draft statute gave junior faculty the right to elect representatives with voting rights to the faculty councils. On 21 September, a general meeting of the junior faculty of Saint Petersburg University asked the faculty council to accept junior faculty delegates with voting rights in meetings both of the faculty council and of individual departments. The junior faculty told the faculty council that this was a "necessary development of the concept of an autonomous university and therefore can neither be rejected nor postponed without a basic contradiction . . . of the idea of autonomy."[15] The junior faculty's demands were relatively modest. A general assembly of junior faculty would elect four delegates with voting rights to participate in the meetings of the individual faculties. These same delegates, along with the president and two vice-presidents of the junior faculty assembly, would participate in the meetings of the faculty council. In its meeting of 31 October the faculty council accepted, by a vote of 36 to 1 with 6 abstentions, "in principle,"

14. *Russkie Vedomosti*, 10 September 1905.
15. Imperatorskii Sankt-Peterburgskii Universitet, *Zhurnaly zasedanii soveta za 1905g.*, pp. 172–178.

junior-faculty representation in individual department meetings, but narrowly rejected such participation in the meetings of the faculty council.[16]

Such tensions were even worse in some of the provincial universities. The Kazan junior faculty demanded legally guaranteed entry into the professors' corporation (*uchenaia korporatsiia*). Professors would no longer be in a position to blight promising careers out of personal pique. The junior faculty also demanded that both department and faculty council meetings be open to the public, or at least to zemstvo and municipal council representatives.[17]

The controversy made clear the lack of consensus within the academic community regarding the meaning of *autonomy*. Senior faculty warned that university governance was not the same as "pure democracy." Professors who supported democratic and universal suffrage in national politics argued that in the universities it was essential to preserve the rule that only merit and proven scholarly achievement should be the major determinants of power and position. According to Professor Evgenii Trubetskoi, the "university has always been and will continue to be the sanctum of a spiritual aristocracy: otherwise it will cease to exist." Far from contradicting the idea of democracy, this conception of the university was a sine qua non for a successful democratic society. "Only a university based on this principle," he warned, "can serve the interests of the people. . . . The nation and the people need a university that will get its job done."[18]

But even more than the junior-faculty issue, the vexing question of professor-student relations brought the revolution into the universities and accelerated the polarization of the academic community. In September, just before the students returned, the faculty councils were cautiously optimistic that they would be able to "control" the students. In most universities the councils elected special commissions to apply the 27 August Rules and deal directly with student organizations in the regulation of student affairs and discussion of student grievances. These commissions, as will be seen, quickly brought the university inspectorate under faculty control and removed many of the most irksome restrictions of the 1884 Statute. Some of the commissions would go to

16. Ibid.
17. M. K. Korbut, *Kazanskii gosudarstvennyi universitet* (Kazan, 1930), vol. 2, p. 218.
18. "K nachalu uchebnovo goda," *Moskovskii Ezhenedel'nik*, no. 34 (1907).

great lengths to consult with the students about the specific role the universities should play during the growing political crisis.[19] But on one important issue, students and faculty would find it hard to reach a compromise: the issue of using the universities as a base for meetings and political agitation.

THE STUDENTS AND THE REVOLUTION

What would the students do? The February *skhodki* that proclaimed the student strike had all stipulated that the *studenchestvo* would consider its future course of action in September. During the summer, an article in the Menshevik *Iskra* appealed to the students to end the strike and return to the universities. Theodore Dan, the author of the article, argued that the strike was a passive weapon that had outlived its usefulness. The students should "seize" the universities and turn them into centers of revolutionary agitation. *Iskra* called on the students to "systematically violate the . . . rules, drive out inspectors and spies of every type, open the doors of the auditoriums to all citizens who wish to enter them, and transform the universities into centers for popular assembly and political meetings."[20]

The Mensheviks, moreover, openly recognized the debt Russian Social Democracy owed to the student movement. A year before, Paul Axelrod had written in *Iskra*:

> History did not wait for the moment when the proletariat, under the direct prod of its natural antagonism to the employers, would enter into the struggle with the autocracy on its own account. . . . Completely unexpectedly, history *pushed* the workers and the Social Democrats themselves into this struggle and for this purpose used not the labor movement but the student movement. The student disorders . . . [of 1899 and 1901] were the direct trigger of an outburst of massive political discontent. . . . Far from being the initiators of the struggle, the Social Democrats were drawn into it.[21]

P. A. Garvi, who was in Moscow at the time, recalls that the *Iskra* article provoked heated debate among the returning students.[22] But

19. This included, at least in the cases of Moscow, Saint Petersburg, and Odessa universities, joint meetings with elected student organizations.
20. *Iskra*, 29 July 1905.
21. Quoted in G. Engel', "1905g. i studencheskoe dvizhenie v Peterburge," *Krasnaia Letopis'*, no. 2 (1925).
22. P. A. Garvi, *Vospominaniia sotsial-demokrata* (New York, 1946), p. 530.

this was more a function of many students' natural impatience with prolonged inactivity than it was a sign of Menshevik influence in the universities.

On the initiative of the Central University Organ of Moscow University and the coalition council of Saint Petersburg University, a fourth all-Russian student congress met in Vyborg, Finland, on 1 September 1905 to discuss the students' options.[23] Representatives of twenty-three student organizations participated in the congress; only six had an affiliation with any of the revolutionary parties. On the first day the congress debated the advisability of organizing a single bureau to direct a unified student movement but rejected the idea of central control and instead issued a vague call to students to collaborate with "the revolutionary parties." The appeal asked students to end the academic strike and turn the universities into centers of anti-government agitation. In addition, it asked students to prepare for an eventual armed uprising against the government.[24]

Although the Vyborg congress did manage to attract student delegates from all over Russia, it was clear that a centrally organized student movement was out of the question. The events of the previous academic year showed just how hard it was to control and channel student unrest during a period of political tension. The heady rhetoric regarding armed uprisings and preparation for revolution masked a complete lack of any specific plan outlining how the universities would help bring this about. But despite the absence of an organized center, the *studenchestvo* quickly evolved a largely uncoordinated but surprisingly uniform response to the new issues facing the universities—the issue of ending the strike, the question of turning the universities into sanctuaries for public political meetings, as well as the questions regarding relations with the professoriate, curricular reform, and increased student participation in university governance. The pattern of events in the major central universities was strikingly similar to the process in the provinces. In all the universities, there was the same complex interplay of academic and political concerns, the same complicated relationship between student organizations and the general student body.

In Saint Petersburg University, the major student organization at the

23. Rafael Vydrin, *Osnovnye momenty studencheskovo dvizheniia v Rossii* (Moscow, 1908), p. 59; cf. TsGAOR, f. 102, op. 5, ed. kh. 00, 3ch. 25/1905, l. 11.
24. The communiqué of this congress can be found in *Krasnyi Arkhiv*, no. 74 (1935): 197.

beginning of the academic year was the coalition council. The council had helped convene the Vyborg congress and, because of its location, was obviously one of the most important of the country's student organizations. Yet the coalition council was a surprisingly casual and loosely organized group at the beginning of September. It obviously had not recovered from the reverses of the previous year.

Vladimir Voitinskii's memoirs provide a valuable glimpse into the evolution and workings of the coalition council during the fall of 1905 and show the important interconnection between outside pressures and student corporate interests. When Voitinskii returned to the university at the end of August, he decided to join the Social Democratic student faction, which dominated the coalition council. He asked Boris Brazol', the secretary of Sviatlovskii's political-economy study group, to enroll him in the Social Democratic student group. Brazol' took Voitinskii to A. Ia. Kaplan (whom Voitinskii called the "gnome"), a former leader of the Partisans of Struggle group who was now a member of the coalition council and a leader of the student Bolshevik faction.

> The gnome did not waste words but bluntly asked me, "You want to join the RSDRP?" These letters meant nothing to me, but he explained that they stood for the Russian Social Democratic Workers' Party. When I said yes, he asked whether I was a Bolshevik or a Menshevik. I confessed my ignorance about the difference between the two factions. "That is simple," he replied. "The Bolsheviks are for the revolution while the Mensheviks seek a compromise with tsarism and are ready to betray the workers." Obviously the gnome was a Bolshevik. Since I had no intention of betraying the workers I told him that according to his definition I was a Bolshevik![25]

Kaplan told Voitinskii to read some of Lenin's pamphlets. Although Voitinskii confessed some doubts about the relevance of Lenin's ideas to the current situation, the student Bolsheviks invited him to join their faction. A few days later they told Voitinskii to represent the Bolshevik student faction at the forthcoming general student *skhodka* which would decide the crucial question of whether to continue or cancel the student strike in force since the previous February.

> The committee brushed aside my objection that I was unfamiliar with the party's views. Obviously I was picked up as a figurehead because of my reputation among students who did not belong to any organization. When I asked whether I was to represent the entire party or only its Bolshevik faction, I was told that "we have a common line—to open the university in the

25. Vladimir Voitinskii, *Gody pobed i porazhenii* (Berlin, 1923), p. 37.

interests of the revolution and to keep it under control. You will represent both factions. The fight is between us and the Social Revolutionaries."[26]

Within two weeks, Voitinskii, who had had little idea of the difference between a Bolshevik and a Menshevik, became a leading representative of the coalition council and its Bolshevik faction. Obviously ideological fanaticism counted for little in student politics. Even if one accepts his explanation of why he received such major responsibilities so quickly, it is hard to escape the conclusion that the student movement at the beginning of September was a highly casual affair. The most important point, as will be shown below, was that the coalition council, dominated by the Social Democratic students, knew that it could maintain its position of leadership in the university only to the extent to which it served the needs and answered the demands of the vast majority of students who saw themselves as part of the *studenchestvo*, not as members of any particular revolutionary party. This pattern was generally true of other *VUZy* as well.

The first important issue the students had to decide was whether to end the strike. The Social Democrats, both Mensheviks and Bolsheviks, wanted the universities to open. The Social Revolutionaries wanted them to stay closed. On 13 September more than two thousand students jammed the main auditorium of Saint Petersburg University to decide the issue. A student named Norskii argued the position of the Social Revolutionaries by calling on the students to continue the academic strike and to go into the villages in order to radicalize the peasantry. The factors that had impelled the *studenchestvo* to strike in Feburary still held: the autocracy was still in power and the revolution had not yet been won.

After Norskii had finished, Voitinskii strode to the rostrum and replied for the Social Democrats. In arguing for a reopening of the university, Voitinskii made two fundamental points. The first was that the social gulf between the *studenchestvo* and the peasantry was so wide that few students would make successful agitators in the countryside. The second argument disputed the Social Revolutionary contention that little had changed since February. Voitinskii reminded the student audience that the announcement of the Bulygin Duma had destroyed the fragile coalition between the liberals and the labor movement. The workers were now alone and needed help. Furthermore, the revolution

26. Ibid.

would be decided in the cities, not in the villages. Although the students, unlike other groups in the political arena, were not a clearly defined socioeconomic class, their concentration in the major urban centers gave them a vital role to play in the revolution. The immediate task, Voitinskii continued, was to consolidate the student movement and give it a sense of direction. This could be achieved only if the universities stayed open.[27]

Just after Voitinskii finished his speech, a young worker named Peter Starostin unexpectedly asked for permission to address the meeting. Starostin appealed to the students to cooperate with the working class and reminded them that if they reopened the universities, they could play an important role in the future course of the political struggle. Notwithstanding years of past rhetoric about student-worker cooperation, this was the first time that most of the students present had been addressed by a real worker, and Starostin's speech made a vivid impression.[28]

The students voted 1,702 to 243 for the Social Democratic resolution favoring the reopening of the university. The resolution stipulated that the strike would be adjourned until such time as it "became useful from the point of view of revolutionary tactics." The university would be opened to prepare for the "forthcoming decisive struggle. . . . May our open university be more dangerous for the autocracy than it was when it was on strike!" The resolution also called for the convening of a constituent assembly after the successful conclusion of an armed uprising against the government.[29]

Other VUZy voted similar resolutions. In Moscow University a general student meeting convened on 7 September. It attracted more than four thousand students. The crowd was so large that the Central University Organ directed the students into four different meeting halls. There were four resolutions on the agenda. The first called for the reopening of the university "solely for revolutionary agitation among the masses," thus ruling out the continuation of normal academic work. The third resolution called for a continuation of the strike, and the fourth advocated the opening of the university "for academic work and political education." But 1,202 of the 1,719 students who stayed until the final vote opted for the so-called second resolution, which advocated reopening the university as a "revolutionary base" (ochag), with the auditoriums to be used for the purposes of political education. The second

27. D. [A. Diakonov], 1905 i 1906gg. v Peterburgskom Universitete (Saint Petersburg, 1907), pp. 23–24.
28. Voitinskii, Gody pobed i porazhenii, pp. 55–57.
29. Diakonov, 1905 i 1906gg., pp. 23–24.

resolution emphasized that "there is room in the university for those who wish to study."[30] In fact there was little difference between the second and the fourth resolutions except for one crucial point—the psychological impact of justifying the decision to end the strike in revolutionary rather than liberal rhetoric.

The victorious resolution came to be known as the Second Moscow Resolution and served as a model for students in such provincial universities as Odessa, where a student *skhodka* approved the platform in its entirety after discussing all the alternative Moscow resolutions.[31] At Kazan University the students passed a similar motion.[32] Political demands featured the rejection of the Bulygin Duma and the convening of a constituent assembly. There were some exceptions: the institute of communications, for instance, rejected a motion allowing nonstudents to attend meetings.

The students' decision to end the strike helped trigger a chain reaction of events that exploded into the great general strike of mid-October. By the end of September the universities would become huge public meeting halls, wherein the working class could discover its revolutionary potential and forge new links to the liberal and radical intelligentsia. But did either the students or the revolutionary parties act with a blueprint detailing how the universities would radicalize the working class?

The reopening of the universities was to give the Social Democrats a badly needed opportunity to improve links with the Russian working class, which had until autumn shown little inclination to lend them consistent support. The November 1904 street demonstrations had mainly attracted radical students, not workers. Bloody Sunday had ignited a massive series of strikes but failed to consolidate the position of the revolutionary parties in the factories. Social Democratic calls for May Day demonstrations had met a disappointing response in the central Russian cities; the *Potemkin* uprising failed to spark larger protest. In the non-Russian areas, the government had a harder time. Jewish and Polish workers built barricades in the streets of Lodz, and a general

---

30. POA, XIIIc(2), folder 6C.
31. *Odesskie Novosti*, 4 October 1905.
32. *Odesskii Listok*, 6 October 1905. The Soviet historian A. E. Ivanov, tabulating the voting results from eleven *VUZy* (including seven universities), shows that 8,660 students (75.4 percent) favored ending the strike. Slightly over 40 percent of the total student body voted, a high figure considering the unsettled conditions in mid-September. (See "Demokraticheskoe studenchestvo v revoliutsii 1905–07gg.," *Istoricheskie Zapiski*, no. 107 [1982]: 184.)

strike broke out in Tiflis. In the central Russian cities, the spring and summer of 1905 saw significant organizational activity on the part of the workers but relatively little political confrontation, especially compared with the non-Russian areas.[33]

The end of the summer saw the Marxist left in general disarray. A September conference called by the Bund and attended by representatives of the major Social Democratic factions agreed on a strategy of boycotting the elections to the Bulygin Duma, a boycott which, it was hoped, would spark a general strike.[34] There seems to have been no specific discussion of using the universities to galvanize the working class, nor does it appear that there were representatives of student organizations at the conference.

Soviet historians assert that the students ended the strike in response to a Bolshevik appeal.[35] Years later Leonid Martov held that the strike ended because of the Mensheviks' *Iskra* article. But Garvi and Voitinskii, both of whom were to join the Mensheviks, admit that Martov exaggerated the impact of the *Iskra* article.[36] And Nikolai Rozhkov, a celebrated Soviet historian who was a *privat-dozent* in Moscow University in 1905 and had close links to the Bolshevik party, insisted in his memoirs that at the beginning of September, most students were unwilling to make an active commitment to the revolutionary parties.[37]

The Second Moscow Resolution, therefore, was not part of a coordinated political plan. The students, always sensitive to the issue of police brutality and conscious of the political traditions of the intelligentsia,

33. On the labor movement, see Victoria E. Bonnell, *Roots of Rebellion: Workers' Politics and Organizations in St. Petersburg and Moscow, 1900–1914* (Berkeley and Los Angeles, 1983), esp. pp. 106–192. Bonnell notes that "the pace of unionization in 1905 was directly correlated with political conditions. In contrast to party circles, which could be conducted clandestinely by a small number of people, trade unions, to be effective, required a mass membership and opportunities for open assembly and freedom of speech and the press. A modicum of civil liberties was the indispensable precondition for an organized labor movement in Russia. Prior to September, however, workers were seldom able to obtain permission for public meetings, and clandestine gatherings were vulnerable to police and the fearsome Cossack troops" (p. 124).

34. Sidney Harcave, *The Russian Revolution of 1905* (London, 1964), p. 168.

35. This view is advanced by P. S. Gusiatnikov (*Revoliutsionnoe studencheskoe dvizhenie*, p. 159), A. E. Ivanov ("Universitety Rossii"), and T. P. Bondarevskaia ("Bolshevistkaia organizatsiia universiteta v revoliutsii 1905–07gg.," in *Peterburgskii Universitet i revoliutsionnoe dvizhenie v Rossii* [Leningrad, 1979], pp. 67–81). These historians of course ignore the *Iskra* article and the fact that the Mensheviks were the first to propagandize the political advantages of open universities.

36. Garvi, *Vospominaniia sotsial-demokrata*, p. 530; Voitinskii, *Gody pobed i porazhenii*, p. 55. The Bolshevik appeal to the students, "Ko vsei uchashcheisia molodëzhi," appeared in mid-September: TsGIA, f. 733, op. 152, d. 173, l. 421.

37. N. A. Rozhkov, *1905 god: Istoricheskii ocherk* (Moscow, 1926), pp. 75–76.

wanted to make some sort of oppositional gesture. The nature of this gesture was determined by the inherent conflict between the self-interest of the students as a group and their principal protest tactic, the strike. The strike was the weapon wielded most easily by the *studenchestvo,* but it was a weapon that caused the government little immediate harm, dispersed the students, and nullified the universities as a political force. Furthermore, continuing the strike would have meant the loss of more study time and, for many, the chance of earning a degree.

How could Russia's students return to the classroom without giving the impression that they were "surrendering"? (Many had doubtless just had long discussions with their parents about accepting the Bulygin Duma.) The Second Moscow Resolution, and similar resolutions passed at other universities, solved this problem by linking the decision to end the strike with an overt commitment to radical, not liberal, politics. This was especially clear in the political resolutions calling for the convening of a constituent assembly along with preparation for an armed uprising. To be sure, the commitment was rhetorical. Rozhkov was right: few students were willing to take the risks of active involvement in the revolutionary movement. The same students who enthusiastically called for turning the universities into "bases of the revolution" were surprised to see thousands of workers actually take over the lecture halls. But the decision to embrace radical resolutions provides valuable insight into the psychology of the *studenchestvo.* And events would soon show how important the gesture was.

In voting for the Second Moscow Resolution the students were rejecting the liberal position of a university "above politics." Liberal resolutions calling for using the universities as centers of political education provided that academic activities continued unhindered were too bland for most students' tastes. One reason for this rejection of the liberal position was that the *studenchestvo* believed liberal politics connoted cowardice and surrender, as epitomized by the professors' willingness to work under the 1884 Statute. Furthermore, the liberals did not seem to recognize the students as being a group with specific economic, social, and even academic needs. The second congress of the Academic Union had shown that the professors were still hoping for a European university where they would govern and the students would study. If Russia attained political freedom, the student movement would presumably melt away. The professors did not realize, at least in their public statements, that student unrest had a social as well as a political dimension. Many students felt that this liberal conception of the university, which posited a paternalistic relationship between faculty and students, was more suited to countries where universities drew an entrenched economic and social elite and were in a less ambiguous position.

The appeals that several leading professors addressed to the *studenchestvo* at the beginning of September to safeguard the universities and end the strike were clearly based on the supposition that the *studenchestvo*, like the professoriate, had a vested interest in seeing an early end to political uncertainty and confrontation politics; they hoped the focus would shift away from the streets and toward the forthcoming Duma.[38] Meanwhile, leading professors argued, the universities would help develop political freedom in two ways. First, they would nurture Russian science and train an educated class, thus laying a secure foundation for freedom and progress. A second liberal argument emerged at the second congress of the Academic Union and in a September *Pravo* article by Ivan Grevs.[39] Grevs contended that merely by resuming their normal functions, the universities would expand the parameters of political freedom in the nation by constantly probing for chinks in the government's armor. For example, the universities would sponsor public lectures and thereby achieve a de facto victory in the struggle to guarantee freedom of speech. Professors would be bolder in their lectures and thereby win more academic freedom. "We should take what we have," Grevs urged, "and fight for more." But these appeals went largely unheeded in September, as the *studenchestvo* made demands and took positions that threatened the professors' position within the university and endorsed the direct involvement of the universities in the revolution.

In voting for the Second Moscow Resolution, the students had rejected not only the views preferred by their professors but also those put forward by the Social Revolutionary party to carry the revolution to the villages. On the face of it, the Social Revolutionaries certainly had a respectable case. In the summer of 1905 there was a marked upsurge of peasant unrest in European Russia.[40] As the academic year started, the countryside was beginning to emerge as a political force. Student opposition to the Social Revolutionary position largely derived from the fact that the Social Revolutionaries were calling on the students to sacrifice their university education in favor of revolutionary action.

38. See the public appeals to the students by Professors Gol'tsev and Kovalevskii, published in *Russkie Vedomosti*, 4 and 8 September 1905. On 7 September, *Russkie Vedomosti* published a stern lead editorial warning the *studenchestvo* to remember their responsibilities to the nation and to refrain from actions that would endanger the universities.

39. "Vremennye pravila 27ovo Avgusta," *Pravo*, no. 36 (1905).

40. Harcave, *Russian Revolution*, p. 171.

Thus the students returned to the universities with no clear sense of what they wanted or what kind of situation they would face. At the same time they had rejected both the liberal position of the professoriate and the total commitment of the Social Revolutionaries.

THE POLITICAL MEETINGS

Sometime in mid-September, a worker appeared at a student meeting at Saint Petersburg University and scolded the students for discussing their own problems when a revolution was going on. At first singly, then in groups, curious workers began to enter the "free university." The coalition council did not know what to do with them and decided to entrust Voitinskii with the job of organizing evening meetings for the workers. At first he tried to arrange lectures on the history of the labor movement. The idea failed because Voitinskii could not find enough student lecturers who could hold the attention of their audiences. But the workers continued to come, and soon the coalition council opened all the larger classrooms as well as the main hall of the university to accommodate the crowds at the evening meetings.[41]

Describing the first large workers' meeting at the university, Voitinskii recalled:

> We had neither agenda nor speakers. I began with a few words of welcome, suggested that we discuss the current political situation, and turned the meeting over to the floor. The ensuing discussion was utterly chaotic. Some of the volunteer speakers were wholly inarticulate. The next day we arranged to have a dozen speakers from various leftist organizations on whom we called intermittently, with volunteers from the floor.[42]

News of the meetings in the universities and other VUZy rapidly spread through the factories; workers would tell their comrades that the police were not interfering. So the crowds grew steadily larger. Why did the workers come? In mid-September, at least, the major reason was curiosity. The workers had little patience for hearing arguments between the various revolutionary parties, but they showed avid interest in using the meetings for education and self-expression. It was not unusual for workers to ask for the floor in order to read their own poetry. Soon whole factories would turn up at the university without notice. Harried representatives of the coalition council would scurry to find a large enough

41. Voitinskii, *Gody pobed i porazhenii*, p. 57.
42. Ibid.

room, and the task became steadily more difficult. On the evening of
11 October, for example, ten thousand railroad workers streamed into
Saint Petersburg University, and the faculty council worried that the
buildings would collapse under the weight of the throng. Even *drozhki*
drivers, the age-old scourge of Saint Petersburg students, asked the
coalition council to give them a place to meet.

In the universities, the various groups of Russian urban society, previously isolated from one another, met on equal terms. Whether lawyer
or worker, the participant at the university meetings was experiencing a
sense of personal political freedom for the first time. In a confidential
memorandum to Witte written in November 1905, a highly placed government official made the telling point that the meetings in the universities wrought profound psychological changes in the Russian working
class. By day rudely treated and deprived of respect, the Russian workers became, as soon as they crossed the threshold of the university,
people who were treated with consideration and even deference.[43] The
contrast with the routine of the factories became more jarring.

One account, quite typical, portrays the atmosphere of these meetings:

> The people . . . come from varied backgrounds . . . university students, high
> school students, thousands of workers, soldiers, sailors, and officers, the very
> poor, and even drifters [*bosiaki*]. The thousands of workers assembled at the
> meeting show a great sense of decorum and restraint! One would think that
> we have had a free political life for a long time! The hall is packed, the people
> stand on window sills. The crowd listens with rapt attention. It does not stir
> for hours at a time. A bad speaker provokes grumbling, noise, and protests.
> But there are good orators, the revolution has spawned them, and the crowd
> hears them with exalted expressions and fervent gazes. After the speech:
> cries of applause, the sound of the president's bell, quiet. A new orator grasps
> the attention of the audience. After the end of the meeting, after having sung
> the "Marseillaise" and the "Varshavianka" . . . the throng is in a holiday
> mood. It leaves in smaller groups, agitatedly discussing what it heard and
> promising to call new comrades to the next meeting.[44]

43. *Materialy k istorii russkoi kontrrevoliutsii* (Saint Petersburg, 1908), p. 60. This
memorandum, written by someone who had extensive access to confidential police files,
from which he quoted at length, gives an interesting account of why the government lost
control in 1905. He sees the issuance of the 27 August Rules as being a major turning
point in the development of the revolution.

44. "Narodnye mitingi v Peterburge," *Proletarii*, no. 25 (1905). Trotsky commented:
"Here the orators of the Revolution reigned unchallenged. Here Social Democracy bound
together with an indissoluble living political bond the countless atoms that comprised the
people and translated the mighty social passions of the masses into the refined language of
revolutionary slogans." According to John Keep, Trotsky wrote with "pardonable exaggeration." (Quoted in Keep, *Rise of Social Democracy*, p. 218.)

One Menshevik recalled that "for the first time in the history of the liberation movement the barriers separating the university from the factory and the educated strata from the masses of the workers began to crumble by themselves."[45] New possibilities opened up before the revolutionary parties. They now had broader opportunities for contact with the workers, and from the middle of September onward, as one observer noted, a dynamic relationship developed between the *VUZy* and the outlying workers' districts: the meetings would radicalize the workers, who in turn would return to the *VUZy* in even greater numbers and radicalize the meetings. The barriers that had separated the revolutionary parties from the mass of the workers did not disappear completely. But, in the words of Evgenii Maevskii, a Menshevik historian of the Revolution of 1905, they began to weaken. Before September, the average worker was only dimly aware of the "secret and strange 'committees.' Now he saw their orators face to face."[46]

Perhaps nowhere was the revolutionary impact of the meetings in the universities felt more than in Moscow. At the beginning of 1905 the Moscow working class was even more conservative than its Saint Petersburg counterpart; in July, workers in one of the largest textile mills in the city had refused even to listen to agitators advocating an eight-hour day. But in the latter part of September it was the Moscow working class that touched off the central Russian strike movement.[47] The strike wave spread to Saint Petersburg and other Russian cities by the beginning of October. When the all-important Union of Railway Workers paralyzed the nation's transport, the tsar wavered, considered the possibility of establishing a military dictatorship, and then split the liberation movement by issuing the manifesto of 17 October.

Although the universities played an important role in the politici-

45. Garvi, *Vospominaniia sotsial-demokrata*, p. 532.

46. For an assessment of the student movement and the meetings from a Menshevik point of view, see E. Maevskii, "Obshchaia kartina dvizheniia," in L. Martov, ed., *Obshchestvennoe dvizhenie v Rossii*, (Saint Petersburg, 1910), vol. 2, part 1, pp. 73–76.

47. A fine work on the Moscow working class is Laura Engelstein's *Moscow 1905* (Stanford, 1982). She notes that although the September strike movement began peacefully, over work-related issues, it soon changed. "There were two specific reasons for this: first the concentration of workers in the downtown areas; and second, the state of political agitation that had seized the Moscow University student body in the wake of the August 27 autonomy decree. As a result of this geographic coincidence, politics moved into the open, under the very nose of the anxious and watchful authorities. It was not long before persons of all social classes found themselves shoulder to shoulder in public places, before the hostile eye of the police, who attempted, unsuccessfully, to send them home. This was the incendiary mix that the government perceived as most threatening to its own political safety" (p. 87).

zation of the major Russian urban centers, the police and the military respected the 27 August Rules and did not stop the meetings inside the *VUZy*. But the principle of holding political meetings in the universities sharply divided the professoriate from the *studenchestvo* and the organized junior faculty. If the professors acquiesced in the use of academic premises as mass meeting halls, they risked government closing of the universities. Nor did they like turning the universities over to the urban crowds. This violated their notion of the proper relationship between university and society. Both students and professors realized, however, that stopping the meetings would cripple the labor movement, which would thus lose its physical base at a crucial time. In the ensuing confrontation over the issue of meetings, the professoriate would find itself isolated from the rest of the academic community, and the universities would close for another year.

STUDENT POLITICS

The student movement in the fall of 1905 presents a striking example of the close interrelationship between academic and general politics. The radical student leaders began to see that the universities were playing an important part in the developing revolutionary situation; they wanted to make sure that they would stay open. But they also knew that their ability to control the situation in the universities depended in large part on their relationship to the mass of the student body. Most students embraced the rhetoric of the revolutionary movement, but they also had their own corporate interests, chief among which were reform of the system of higher education, continuation of their studies, more financial aid, and a greater voice in university governance. The radical activists had to concern themselves with these corporate aspirations in order to ensure that the *studenchestvo* would support them in a confrontation with the government or the professoriate over the question of meetings.

At Saint Petersburg University, Vladimir Voitinskii continued to work as a liaison between the coalition council and the student body. "Probably the students did not need the representatives of the leftist parties to handle their academic affairs," he recalls. "But as long as we did our academic job properly in the morning we were sure of our grip on the masses of students and could keep our hands on the university after dusk [when the workers came for meetings]."[48]

In order to consolidate its authority in the student body, the coalition

48. Voitinskii, *Gody pobed i porazhenii,* p. 56.

council called a mass meeting for 15 September to discuss academic affairs. The agenda included the issues of major concern to the students: more electives, abolition of the uniform, changes in university disciplinary procedures, a possible boycott of certain "reactionary" professors, and, most important, the questions of university admissions and financial aid.[49]

Almost as soon as it began the meeting erupted in turmoil. The Zionist student group demanded a resumption of the strike until the government abolished the *numerus clausus,* and they wanted an explanation as to how the *studenchestvo* could have rallied so impressively in 1899 and then failed to strike after the 1903 Kishinev pogrom. Now, the Zionists insisted, the *studenchestvo* had a pressing moral obligation to help Jewish youth. The president of the meeting, Engel', interrupted the Zionist speakers. There was no such thing as a separate Jewish question, he insisted. The fight against religious and national discrimination had to be part of a general struggle against political repression. The chair rejected the Zionist demand and the meeting broke up in chaos.[50]

It resumed on 19 September. The previous incident did not cool the enthusiasm of the student body; the main hall of the university was packed. This time the Zionists proposed a motion of no confidence in the coalition council, but the students rejected this overwhelmingly. The agenda then turned to the issue of university admissions. A schoolteacher appealed to the meeting to help those who were barred from the universities because they lacked the required gymnasium diploma. The students also heard a representative of a workers' aid society, who asked them to help the workers get a higher education. Other speakers warned the students against allowing themselves to become co-opted by a "system" that needed the universities to serve its own ends. The meeting passed a series of resolutions that called for important changes in the structure of Russian higher education. The most important demand was for the removal of all existing restrictions on the admission of Jews and women. The students also called for courses in European constitutional law, and for history courses dealing with the nineteenth century. In addition, they passed a motion advocating university extension courses, a return to a curriculum based primarily on elective courses, and open admissions to graduates of all secondary schools.[51]

49. Diakonov, *1905 i 1906gg.,* pp. 24–27.
50. Ibid., pp. 20–29.
51. Ibid.

The meeting also called for a boycott of seven professors branded as "reactionaries" by the coalition council.[52] The faculty council, which had been looking the other way during the evening meetings at the university, told the *studenchestvo* that it would not tolerate the boycott, which it saw as a serious threat to its position in the university as well as to the doctrine of academic freedom. The faculty council demanded a showdown with the coalition council on the boycott issue. At a tense meeting, Professor L. I. Petrazhitskii, a legal authority who won the respect even of the radical students, told the representatives of the coalition council that if they did not rescind the boycott, the professors would close the university immediately. Petrazhitskii also appealed to the students' sense of justice; none of the accused professors had received a "fair trial." As for the student demand that the university appoint such "progressive" figures as Struve or Miliukov, Petrazhitskii replied that faculty appointments were the concern of the professors, not the students.[53]

Aside from the issue of the boycott, where the faculty zealously defended the principle of student noninterference in faculty affairs, the faculty council gave the student proposals a positive if cautious response. The council agreed in principle to the demands for the end of admissions restrictions and for fundamental curricular reform, but warned of the legal obstacles that had to be negotiated. The council told the student delegates that henceforth student representatives would participate in financial-aid decisions. Furthermore, the managing board of the university dining hall would include six students, three representatives of the senior faculty, and three from the junior faculty.[54]

On 27 September the coalition council called off the boycott and admitted that it had not accorded the seven professors fair treatment.[55] The incident underscored the fact that the student movement could not be judged solely on the basis of its radical rhetoric. Obviously the students, including the radical organizations, were still open to the influence of the professoriate, especially when the latter appealed to their sense of fairness and seemed to be meeting major student corporate demands. Furthermore, the coalition council had demanded that the proscribed professors be replaced not by noted revolutionaries but, rather, by such pillars of Russian liberalism as Struve, Miliukov, and Kovalev-

52. Ibid.
53. Voitinskii, *Gody pobed i porazhenii*, pp. 79–83.
54. Ibid.
55. Diakonov, *1905 i 1906gg.*, pp. 40–41.

skii. Obviously there were limits to the students' readiness to accept the call by the revolutionary parties to wrest control of the universities from the professoriate.

The coalition council was in a vulnerable position. It had to direct academic politics, to keep the university open for meetings, and to supervise the increasing numbers of citizens who were flocking to the evening rallies. As the political tension grew, there were signs of increasing polarization within the student body. On 27 September a group of dissident left-wing students demanded a halt to all discussion of academic matters and the complete mobilization of the university for political purposes. This was a serious attack on the coalition council and its recognition of the importance of academic politics. The council sent to the meeting a speaker who implored the leftists not to jeopardize the unity of the student body. The speaker emphasized that the political consciousness and unity of the *studenchestvo* drew on dissatisfaction not only with the general regime but also with the students' place in the universities. Concentration on specific political issues to the exclusion of corporate concerns would fracture this unity. The *skhodka* rejected the leftist position.[56]

That same day the council announced upcoming elections for a new student government to direct academic affairs; henceforth the council would devote most of its attention to organizing the meetings and other political issues. Practical reasons motivated the decision: the burden of directing the student meetings, negotiating with the professors, and supervising the allocation of rooms for the evening meetings was becoming too heavy.

The new student government was to be headed by a Council of Student Elders, elected by the whole student body and consisting of one delegate for every 250 students. This Council of Elders would answer to the general *skhodka*.[57]

The resulting election campaign showed that some basic currents of the student movement retained their importance: a deep mistrust of liberal slogans, verbal support of Social Democracy, and a strong sense of corporate identity and interest. Four major political groupings competed for support in the election: the Academists, the Kadets, the Social Democrats, and the Social Revolutionaries.

The Academists, whom the students generally associated with the po-

56. Ibid.
57. Ibid., p. 43.

litical right, campaigned on a platform calling for the complete separation of the universities and politics. They had opposed the strike at the
beginning of the year and now demanded a halt to public meetings in
the university. In addition they wanted the abolition of the traditional
skhodka, arguing that it was dominated by left-wing students and did
not reflect the true sentiments of the student body as a whole. But they
carefully avoided formulating any specific political platform.[58]

On 24 September, representatives of various Academist organizations met in Moscow to draft a statement of principles. The meeting
issued the following appeal to Russia's students:

> In this very difficult period it behooves the Russian *studenchestvo* and each
> individual student, who is also a citizen of his country, to demonstrate a se-
> rious . . . sense of reality. The nation needs cadres of well-educated people
> who are prepared for self-sacrifice. The universities must remain open in
> order to guarantee the future supply of these cadres. Anyone wishing to serve
> the nation or engage in public life must possess a solid educational founda-
> tion. Academic life must not be jeopardized. If it is, the possibility of an open
> university becomes unthinkable; so does any possibility of students coming
> together to discuss their own interests, whatever they may be. There is
> no doubt that the present unstable situation in the universities will lead to
> their closing.[59]

This statement was noteworthy for its seeming moderation and toler-
ation of all political activity that did not directly threaten the existence
of the universities. Furthermore, the Academists recognized and appealed to the students' sense of corporate self-interest and tried to use
this as a way of detaching the students from their rhetorical allegiance
to the revolutionary parties. But when the Academists at Saint Petersburg
University called a campaign meeting on 4 October, only sixty students
came. Nevertheless, the speakers put on a brave front. They told the audience that the majority of the student body was hostile to the "dictatorship" of the coalition council but was too unorganized to do anything about it: hence the need for a real alternative in the university. But
even the small audience turned hostile. The Academists lost control over
their own meeting and left in disarray. The major reason for the cool
reception was widespread feeling that they had acted as informers for
the inspectorate and belonged to the right. The student body did not
accept the protestations of the Academist speakers that their group had

58. For a sympathetic discussion of Academism in the fall of 1905, see A. S. Budilovich,
Nauka i politika (Saint Petersburg, 1905).
59. Ibid., p. 133.

nothing in common with the old Dennitsa, a reactionary, anti-Semitic student organization which had received strong government support in the 1903–1904 academic year.[60]

The newly formed Constitutional Democratic or Kadet student group offered yet another alternative to the revolutionary student parties. On 11 October, Veselovskii, the group's representative, outlined its platform before five hundred students of the juridical faculty. The political section of the platform featured four points: support of basic civil liberties, a parliamentary government with legislative control over the Council of Ministers and the budget, a constituent assembly to be called by the Duma, and free, equal, secret, and direct suffrage. The Kadets' academic platform offered clear alternatives to both the revolutionary factions and the Academists. In a major challenge to the revolutionary student groups, the Kadets denied the future usefulness of the traditional *skhodka*. This issue of the *skhodka* was to become a major dividing line between liberal and leftist student politics. In calling for a student parliament based on proportional representation to replace the *skhodka*, the Kadets rejected the traditional idea that student affairs could be settled on the basis of direct democracy. But the difference between the Kadets and the revolutionary parties over the *skhodka* really spoke to a more fundamental issue, that of the continued survival of the notion of the *studenchestvo* in a time of political and social change. The Kadet rejection of the *skhodka* proceeded from the assumption that the Russian universities would come to resemble their European counterparts as the country continued its course of political liberalization and social development. And like European students, Russian students would come to dissociate the university from their political activities. To be sure, a student government would still be needed to deal with academic issues, but the old ties that bound the Russian students to the traditions of the *studenchestvo* would erode and disappear, victims of the growing political and social differentiation of the student body.

At the same time the Kadet speakers rejected the Academist call for a complete separation of the universities from politics. In a direct reference to the Academist platform, one Kadet speaker warned that "cadres of well-educated people" had no business staying in the classroom while the political battle deciding the nation's fate raged around them. The universities should further the political education of the nation, a goal to be accomplished without disturbing their purely academic activities.[61]

60. Diakonov, *1905 i 1906gg.*, p. 52.
61. Ibid., pp. 58–59.

The Kadets challenged the right of the Social Democrats to speak for the majority of students. Recent massive votes in favor of Social Democratic resolutions, they argued, were only superficial guides to the real mood of the students. Veselovskii warned that "the ideals of Social Democracy have not fully penetrated the consciousness of the majority of the students. If a decisive moment comes, this majority will either abstain from political action and fade away, or it will serve merely as cannon fodder for others."[62] If they stopped to think about it, the Kadets told the students, they would realize that they did not have as much in common with the Social Democrats as they seemed to believe.

Replying for the Social Democrats (and for the coalition council), Voitinskii defended the Marxist cause and reminded the students of the differences between the liberals and the Social Democrats. He appealed to the students' deep-seated suspicions of liberalism. Unlike the Social Democrats, Voitinskii argued, liberals were ready to make a "deal" with the autocracy and abandon the fight for the final victory of the revolution. Moreover, Voitinskii challenged the Kadet assertion that the real interests of the *studenchestvo* were bound up with liberalism and that because of differences in psychological temperament and social position there was no real basis for an alliance between the students and the revolutionary camp. Voitinskii told the meeting that

> Social Democracy aims for a unified movement of the proletariat where there is room for all those who share its views, regardless of whether one is a member of the intelligentsia or a worker. The determining factor is not merely an arbitrary label; it is psychological awareness. This awareness can be attained by the intelligentsia as well as by the workers. . . . Once a person has reached this political consciousness he has no choice but to join the ranks of the proletarian masses. . . . The *studenchestvo*, which is also striving for the liberation of the people, should not be tempted by the blandishments of parties like the Kadets.[63]

The Social Revolutionary speaker made a bristling speech calling on the students to involve themselves more directly in the revolutionary struggle. The speaker also explained that his faction's decision to participate in the student elections did not conflict with its view that the *studenchestvo* should place politics ahead of corporate interests. The Social Revolutionary representative explained that the "Council of Student Elders is a political as well as an academic organization. We will

62. Ibid., p. 59.
63. Ibid., p. 60.

participate in the consideration of academic matters since we look at
them from the political point of view." He promised that they had "no intention of obstructing academic life." The faction's political platform featured a democratic republic, a constituent assembly, self-determination
for non-Russians, and socialization of the land.[64]

The elections ended in clear victories for the Social Democrats. The
students of the juridical faculty gave the Social Democrats 478 votes,
the Social Revolutionaries 85, the Kadets 105, and a nonaligned "wild"
faction 98 votes.[65] The Social Democratic leadership of the coalition
council also served on the Council of Student Elders. Despite the fact
that it had proposed the bifurcation of the student government into a
coalition council and the Council of Student Elders, the Social Democratic students obviously did not want to surrender their key position in
the regulation of academic affairs.

Thus despite the Kadets' sweeping political demands and the Social
Revolutionaries' promise to respect the academic functions of the university, one month after the end of the strike the students still threw
their support to the Social Democrats. The Social Democrats clearly
understood the mood of the students—rhetorical radicalism, suspicion
of liberalism, and a strong desire to keep studying even during the general political crisis. By its skillful handling of September's student meetings, the coalition council demonstrated its recognition of the necessity
not only of protecting the university's role as the center of the city's political life but also of safeguarding and advancing the students' corporate interests.

MOSCOW

Student politics at Moscow and other universities demonstrated
marked similarities to the pattern shown in Saint Petersburg.[66] In sharp
contrast to the behavior of the Saint Petersburg Faculty Council, however, who had decided to accept the meetings in the university and avoid
confrontation with the students and junior faculty, the Moscow pro-

64. Ibid.
65. The Social Democrats received 60 percent of the vote among the natural sciences
faculty.
66. On events at Kazan University, see Korbut, *Kazanskii Gosudarstvennyi Universitet*, vol. 2, pp. 219–226; for Tomsk University, M. I. Matveev, *Studenty Sibiri v revoliutsionnom dvizhenii* (Tomsk, 1966), pp. 157–162. There is a useful survey in A. E. Ivanov,
"Universitety rossii."

fessors tried to stop them and thereby stumbled into a bitter fight with both groups. In the process, the professors' attempt to split liberal from leftist students ended in dismal failure.

When Moscow University's students returned to classes, the Central University Organ, which had been constituted during the 1904–1905 academic year, called a general student meeting on 12 September for the purpose of forming a student government. The basic proposals of the CUO strongly resembled those which the coalition council of Saint Petersburg University would advance two weeks later. The CUO suggested two organizations: a coalition council, and a new Central University Organ.[67] The coalition council would consist of two representatives from each of the three student revolutionary factions: Bolshevik, Menshevik, and Social Revolutionary. They were to "direct the revolutionary movement" in the university, coordinate student political action with the labor and peasant movements, call political meetings in the university, and, if the necessity arose, convene purely student-based meetings. The council's decisions were not to be binding on any of the three constituent groups. Perhaps the most interesting feature of the proposed council was that it was not to be subject to the directives of the *skhodka*. The politically committed students obviously distrusted the revolutionary fervor of the student masses and wanted to enjoy a maximum degree of freedom of action in the event of a crisis.

The Central University Organ would "regulate student life within the university." It was to consist of twenty-six delegates, one from each faculty course (first-year juridical students, second-year medical students, and so on) who were to be elected by secret suffrage. Unlike the coalition council, the Central University Organ was to be directly responsible to the *skhodka*. Basic duties of the CUO included "liaison between students, professors, and junior faculty . . . the organization of a student court, the compiling of data on police repression of students, etc."[68]

In a series of meetings in September, the student body elected twenty-six delegates to the new Central University Organ. The new CUO soon split into two groups: a majority of eighteen and a moderate minority of eight delegates who called themselves the Delegate Council.[69] Like the Kadet student faction at Saint Petersburg University, the Delegate Council made the role of the traditional *skhodka* one of the major issues, calling into question the *skhodka*'s continued legitimacy as a source of

67. TsGAOR, f. 102, 3ch. 32/1905, l. 36.
68. Ibid.
69. *Russkie Vedomosti*, 8 October 1905.

authority in student affairs. Nonetheless, while the Delegate Council disputed the binding authority of *skhodka* resolutions, it refused to accept the Academist call for a university "above politics." In its published platform the Delegate Council explained that the universities had a dual character: they were academic institutions which also occupied an important place in Russian public life.[70] Neither academic nor political functions could be sacrificed without fundamentally compromising the function and mission of the university. The group called for the establishment of a "cohesive academic community," a student government independent of political parties, the speedy implementation of an elective curriculum, reorganization of academic departments, and the removal of sexual, national, and religious restrictions on university admissions.

In short, two interrelated processes marked student politics in the fall of 1905. First, the students began to see that their resolutions of early September actually had made an impact, and therefore they felt a strong obligation to keep the universities open. Second, they began to use the revolutionary process to assert their own demands for changes within the higher-education structure. Both processes had unsettling implications for a senior faculty which had hoped that the 27 August Rules had finally given it the chance to govern the universities.

THE PROFESSORS IN THE MIDDLE

The Delegate Council's hopes for a cohesive academic community quickly foundered on the issue of on-going political meetings in the university. The faculty council alternately pleaded with and warned the students that the meetings were intolerable and that, if they continued, the professors would close the university. The faculty council clearly hoped that the majority of students would listen and join the call for a halt to the meetings. Speaking in a faculty council meeting, rector Trubetskoi told his colleagues: "We can save the university if we stick together . . . the faculty council is now the boss [*khoziain*]."[71]

Trubetskoi's optimism was somewhat premature. With some exceptions, the increasing tempo of public meetings in the university did not interfere with normal academic life. As a matter of principle, however,

70. Ibid.
71. The minutes of the Moscow University Faculty Council are an especially valuable source for following the dilemmas of the professoriate in the fall of 1905. On Trubetskoi's statement, see TsGIAM, f. 418, op. 249, ed. kh. 95 (meeting of 2 September 1905).

the faculty council would not tolerate the university's new role as a popular meeting hall, especially after the outside crowds sharply increased as a result of the 19 September printers' strike. As the university became the focal point of Moscow's political life, the faculty council, unlike its Saint Petersburg counterpart, decided to take a firm stand.

On 22 September the council voted to close the university. Explaining the action to the students, assistant rector Manuilov warned that "the university will function as a university or it will not function at all. . . . [The Second Moscow Resolution] is in fact unworkable." At the same time Manuilov took pains to reassure the students that their professors had not become reactionaries. "We are all," he said, "fighters for political freedom. We may differ . . . about the tactics necessary to achieve it . . . but we all want it. Let us all work together to save the university for our common purpose." Trubetskoi also pleaded with the students to cooperate with the professoriate and accept the faculty's jurisdiction. He announced that the "university is not the place for political meetings. It cannot and should not be a public square, and by the same token a public square cannot be a university. Any attempt to turn the university into a popular meeting place will destroy it."[72] Both Trubetskoi and Manuilov were shaken by the warning they had just received from the Moscow chief of police: if any meeting spilled out into the streets surrounding the university, troops would fire on the crowds.[73]

Trubetskoi and Manuilov sought to rally a solid majority of students to their side by closing the university. They hoped that the moderates would put pressure on the leftists of the coalition council to stop the meetings. Instead, the faculty's action backfired. The professors had misread the students' mood, as they admitted at a gloomy faculty meeting hastily convened on the evening of 22 September.

For years the professoriate had been telling the government that giving it control of the universities would be a major step in solving the problem of student unrest. Now, three short weeks after the announcement of the 27 August Rules, Moscow University was closed, not by order of the minister of education or because of a student strike, but at the insistence of the professors themselves.

The Moscow professors agonized over their future course of action. They knew that, whether they liked it or not, the university had become a major factor in the developing political situation. They recognized

72. *Russkie Vedomosti*, 19 September 1905.
73. TsGIAM, f. 418, op. 249, ed. kh. 95, l. 252.

that their decisions had more than academic significance, and most were uncomfortable at the growing rapport between the students and the onrushing labor movement. At the 22 September meeting of the faculty council, Professor M. A. Menzbir mused aloud that "somehow we have to separate the student movement from the labor movement."[74] B. K. Mlodzievskii and others bemoaned the apparent weakness of the moderate students.

The consensus of the 22 September faculty council debate was that the majority of students would support the faculty position on meetings if only they could be allowed to submit the Second Moscow Resolution to a new vote, this time to be conducted by secret ballot and by student course. In other words, the professors hoped that resolutions approved by the *skhodka* did not represent the true sentiment of the student body.

The new student elections, held on 24 September, convincingly rebutted liberal illusions about the student movement. The level of participation was extremely high: out of 4,700 students in the university, 4,300 voted. The major question on the ballot was the Second Moscow Resolution. Every course in the university reiterated its support of the earlier resolution.[75] Considering that students in eight out of the twenty-six courses in the university had elected moderate representatives in the earlier elections to the Central University Organ, the 24 September results demonstrate an impressive degree of agreement concerning the political obligations of the *studenchestvo* in a time of political crisis.

The faculty council met on the evening of 24 September in an atmosphere of obvious disappointment with the results of the student vote. The rector recommended that the university remain closed "until the workers quiet down."[76] But Professor Vernadskii argued that such a step would put the professors in an impossible position. They had to make some sort of political gesture "toward satisfying the demands of the public." Only then could they announce steps to exclude nonstudents from meetings. Vernadskii recommended that the faculty council solve its problem by publicly petitioning the government to allow freedom of assembly. If that were granted, the universities might be spared further direct involvement in the political struggle.

The 24 September faculty meeting underscored the difficult position faced by the professoriate at a very delicate juncture of the escalating political crisis. The Moscow professors were worried about the very sur-

74. TsGIAM, f. 418, op. 249, ed. kh. 95, l. 255.
75. TsGAOR, f. 102, 3ch. 32/1905, l. 60.
76. TsGIAM, f. 418, op. 249, ed. kh. 95, l. 262.

vival of the university. They did not know how long the local authorities would continue to refrain from direct intervention to stop the meetings. Such intervention would probably have two important and immediate consequences: violent clashes between the students and the police, and a forcible closing of the universities by the government. Such a closing, barely one month after the proclamation of the 27 August Rules, could deal a death blow to any hopes of lasting academic autonomy in Russia. The professors also feared longer-term implications. Reactionaries would cite the September 1905 experience as furnishing conclusive proof that the professoriate was incapable of running the universities.[77] There was also the real fear that the government would decide to abolish the university altogether as an institutional form of higher education. The professors could not hide their own fears of the street. Trubetskoi echoed the sentiments of many of his colleagues when he voiced the hope that the labor movement would "quiet down."

In the third week of September the labor movement was beginning to emerge as a serious factor in central Russia. In closing the university the Moscow professors (as well as their colleagues in Kazan, who did the same thing) seriously jeopardized the workers' position, by depriving them of a sanctuary and making it harder for them to meet without risking police repression. After the faculty council decision, street violence escalated sharply. The fact that the professoriate, not only in Moscow but in other cities as well, petitioned the government to allow freedom of assembly only confirmed the suspicions, shared by many opponents of the regime, that the professors' fear of confrontation politics and their determination not to depart from established legal norms showed political naiveté and even an innate hostility to the liberation movement.

Lenin's 4 October article on the Moscow professoriate, sharply attacking the professors' closing of the university, reflected sentiments held not just by Bolsheviks but by wide segments of the student body and the junior faculty as well. Lenin called the professors the "best elements of liberalism and the Constitutional Democratic party; they are the most idealistic, the most disinterested in material gain." But how did these professors use the powers given to them by the 27 August Rules? They closed the university and tried to cripple the labor movement. The

---

77. At the 22 September faculty meeting, Professor Th. I. Sinitsyn somewhat sarcastically asked his colleagues whether they were happy with the autonomy they had wanted for so long. Trubetskoi replied that the universities may indeed have gotten autonomy too late, but with a revolutionary movement raging in the country, the professors had to think about saving the university rather than indulging in useless recriminations.

professors, Lenin taunted, "are already afraid of the revolution, they fear a sharpening and intensification of the popular movement, they are already putting out the fire and trying to calm things down." But these "philistines of bourgeois science" made a major miscalculation when they decided to close the university.

> They closed the university in Moscow because they feared a bloodbath [*boinia*] there. But by their action they caused a far greater bloodbath in the streets. They wanted to extinguish the revolution in the university, but they ignited the revolution in the streets. These professors have stumbled into a real vise, along with Messrs. Trepov and Romanov, whom they are now trying to convince to grant freedom of assembly. If you close the university you get fighting in the streets. If you open the university you also open a tribune for the popular revolutionary meetings which prepares new and more determined fighters for freedom.[78]

At about the same time that Lenin was writing his article, D. F. Trepov was telling the tsar, in similar terms, that the popular meetings in the nation's *VUZy*, rare at first, had become more and more frequent, with the professors unable to influence the students to stop them. "The moment is not far off," Trepov warned, "when under the pressure of the revolutionaries who now control the universities, the disorders there will spill into the street."[79]

In a last-ditch attempt to restore order in the university, Trubetskoi went to Saint Petersburg on 28 September. Acting on the mandate of the Moscow University Faculty Council, he went to plead with the government to allow freedom of assembly. The next evening he suffered a heart attack, and he died shortly thereafter. Trubetskoi's last mission was the defense of the Russian universities, a goal to which he had dedicated much of his life. Only a month before, he had radiated optimism that a better era had finally dawned for Russian higher education. When he died, his own university was closed; a few days later, his funeral was to become the scene of a major outbreak of street violence.

Trubetskoi's funeral turned into a major demonstration of the liberation movement's growing strength. On 3 October, a crowd of students, professors, and members of the public met the coffin at the Nikolaevskii station and accompanied it to the university chapel. The procession then marched back toward the university. On the way, mounted Cos-

---

78. V. I. Lenin, "Politicheskaia stachka i ulichnaia bor'ba v Moskve," in his *Sochineniia*, vol. 8, p. 294.

79. P. Gorin, *Ocherki po istorii Sovetov rabochikh deputatov v 1905g.* (Moscow, 1925), p. 14.

sacks attacked the crowd and arrested several marchers. The attack infuriated the public and further isolated the government.[80]

September had indeed been a cruel month for the Russian professoriate. Conflicts on the issue of meetings put a growing strain on the Academic Union and on relations between senior and junior faculty. In Moscow the junior faculty members of the Academic Union endorsed the principle of political meetings in the universities, as did the Saint Petersburg branch of the Academic Union, which was increasingly dominated by the junior faculty.[81]

As the professors struggled to keep control of the universities, the Ministry of Education continued to live in its dream world. In late September, Glazov, relying on a 1902 circular, reminded professors that they were to allow student meetings only if they were convened by faculty course. He also warned the faculty councils that they were stretching the 27 August Rules in admitting Jews and women as auditors. On 8 October, as huge crowds were already swamping the universities, Glazov outdid himself, scolding the faculty councils for communicating with him directly. After all, the 1884 Statute stipulated that all messages between the faculty councils and the minister of education had to pass through the curators.[82]

That same day, events overtook the illusions of the minister of education. Moscow's railroad workers struck. The railroad strike was especially dangerous to the government because the Central Bureau of the Union of Railway Workers made political as well as economic demands. The strike spread to other railroads and by 13 October had turned into a general strike that paralyzed the country. The government's back was to the wall. On 12 October, it rather lamely allowed limited freedom of assembly, but there were so many strings attached that this concession was totally ignored.

The general strike pushed even greater crowds into the universities. The crowds now seemed to overshadow all else. One member of the coalition council of Saint Petersburg University wrote on 13 October:

> For the last few days, the "autonomous" university has been transformed into an awesome, turbulent political tribune. Thousands of workers flock either to general meetings or meet separately, according to occupation, to

80. Engelstein, *Moscow 1905*, pp. 95–96.
81. *Russkie Vedomosti*, 9 October 1905. The senior faculty felt differently. A citywide caucus of the Moscow Academic Union voted 129 to 61 (with 13 abstentions) that meetings in the universities were undesirable.
82. TsGIA, f. 733, op. 153, d. 173, l. 35.

discuss the question of professional organization. During this period the *studenchestvo* has disappeared as an independent entity. It has submerged into the huge masses of workers, helping the proletariat in word and deed, by organizing and propagandizing.[83]

POGROMS

The numerous members of Russia's petty bourgeoisie whose livelihoods were directly and adversely affected by the general strike viewed the situation from a radically different perspective. The *studenchestvo*, far from disappearing, was considered to be, along with the Jews, a chief source of their problems. Like the Jews, the student symbolized a strange outside force that threatened the traditional world of large sections of Russia's urban strata. As the revolution reached a crescendo during the week of the general strike, the universities became not only centers for huge revolutionary meetings but also lightning rods attracting the fury of counter-revolutionary mobs. In Odessa, Kazan, Kiev, and Kharkov, rightist crowds attacked the universities, forcing the students and workers inside to erect barricades.[84] The Odessa chief of police, D. B. Neidhart, neatly summed up the situation in a talk with rector Zanchevskii: "The lecture halls might belong to you, but the streets belong to us. There will be no pity there. Blood will flow."[85]

It was now dangerous to walk the streets in student uniform, and professors appealed for donations of "civilian" clothing to enable students to avoid vicious beatings by roaming gangs of the Black Hundred thugs. In Moscow, a horde of butchers and milkmen, thrown out of work by the general strike and historically antagonistic to the students, besieged the university on 15 October after viciously beating everyone they saw whom they suspected of being a student. An eyewitness who mingled with the mob reported that they blamed the students for the general strike and "wanted to teach them a lesson."[86] The mob prepared to attack the university buildings and the students inside prepared to defend themselves. But Professor Manuilov, who had taken Trubetskoi's place as rector of the university, saved the students from the impending

83. Diakonov, *1905 i 1906gg.*, p. 67.

84. *Odesskii Universitet za 75 let (1865–1940)* (Odessa, 1940), pp. 60–61; Korbut, *Kazanskii Gosudarstvennyi Universitet*, vol. 2, pp. 221–222; A. Cherevanin (pseud. of F. A. Lipkin), *Das Proletariat und die russische Revolution* (Stuttgart, 1908), pp. 50–64; Matveev, *Studenty Sibiri*, pp. 162–164; *Khar'kovskii Gosudarstvennyi Universitet imeni A. M. Gor'kovo za 150 let* (Kharkov, 1955), pp. 176–177.

85. *Die Judenpogrome in Russland* (Cologne, 1910), vol. 2, p. 113.

86. *Russkie Vedomosti*, 16 October 1905.

danger by intervening with the military authorities who escorted the students out of the university the following day.[87] In Kharkov, a last-minute intervention by the faculty persuaded the chief of police to call off a planned attack on the students entrenched inside the university. These students were also allowed to leave unharmed and were then escorted to safety.[88] But the growing counter-revolutionary backlash among artisans, shopkeepers, and certain groups of unskilled workers created ominous problems for the universities.

On 13 October, a special meeting of government ministers finally decided to end the hands-off policy toward the universities. The government ordered the faculty councils either to keep nonstudents out of academic buildings or to close the universities altogether.[89] This was a direct challenge to the professoriate just when the authority of the government was tottering under the impact of the growing general strike. The Saint Petersburg branch of the Academic Union voted to ignore the order and resolved that the "meetings are vital to the nation."[90] A group of Saint Petersburg University professors, including E. D. Grimm, M. I. Rostovtsev, I. A. Pokrovskii, V. M. Shimkevich, and A. A. Markov, urged the faculty council to protest the new measure by submitting a collective resignation. Before the Saint Petersburg professors could decide what to do, D. F. Trepov, the governor-general of Saint Petersburg, surrounded all the *VUZy* with troops and halted the meetings going on there. The last meeting at Saint Petersburg University took place on 15 October, the same day that Black Hundred mobs besieged Moscow University. Few suspected then that these universities, as well as most of Russia's other *VUZy*, would not reopen until September 1906.

The government's decision to close the universities came too late to halt either the revolution or the general strike. On 15 October, a beleaguered tsar called his close advisors to Peterhof. In a tense and somber atmosphere the tsar had to make a fundamental choice: political concessions or military dictatorship. Witte urged major political concessions and Trepov warned that brute force alone could not restore the government's authority. Finally on the evening of 17 October, Tsar Nicholas signed the imperial manifesto that promised to

87. *Russkie Vedomosti,* 1 November 1905.
88. V. Buzeskul, "Dni barrikad v Khar'kove v Oktiabre 1905g.," *Golos Minuvshevo,* nos. 7–8 (July–August 1917).
89. TsGAOR, f. 102, 3ch. 32/1905, l. 51.
90. Imperatorskii Sankt-Peterburgskii Universitet, *Zhurnaly zasedanii soveta za 1905g.,* p. 133 (14 October 1905).

grant the people the unshakeable foundations of civic freedom on the basis of genuine personal inviolability, freedom of conscience, speech, assembly and association; to admit immediately to participation in the State Duma, without suspending the scheduled elections and insofar as it is feasible in the brief period remaining before the convening of the Duma, those classes of the population that are now completely deprived of electoral rights, leaving the further development of the principle of universal suffrage to the new legislative order.[91]

The 17 October manifesto held out the promise of a constitutional monarchy. But the news of the manifesto led to an orgy of bloodshed which served as a chilling reminder that Russia was not England. The nation had already been dislocated by the week-long general strike. Local officials were frightened and confused; contact with the capital was halted by the strike. In many areas there had already been bitter confrontations between the urban lower-middle classes and workers, students, and Jews. So the manifesto was proclaimed in an atmosphere of confusion and suspicion. Rumors spread among the loyalist elements of the urban population that Jews and/or students were holding the tsar hostage, forcing him to sign the manifesto. Triumphant demonstrations by liberals and leftists exacerbated the tension in dozens of Russian cities. These street parades of marchers carrying the red flag attracted the "progressive" elements of urban Russian society—professionals, high school and university students, Jews, and zemstvo or municipal council employees.

But what of the small merchants, petty artisans, day laborers, and others whose economic interests had been sorely threatened by the general strike and the revolution? Their world was the other side of urban Russia, a world virtually untouched by the labor movement and the spread of secondary and higher education. It was not difficult to mobilize these strata against the "progressive" demonstrations. Fear of economic ruin, anti-Semitism, anti-intellectualism, and fear of the unknown all combined to set off a bloody conflagration. The week following the October manifesto was supposed to be the Week of Freedom. It turned into a week of pogroms.

Some historians assert that the pogroms were probably prepared and organized by the government. This claim requires serious modification. There is no evidence that the central government structured the pogroms;

91. Harcave, *Russian Revolution*, p. 196.

indeed, in the middle of October it was too disorganized and frightened to be able to do so even if it had wanted to. It is more probable that certain local officials played a role, as did the local police. After all, the police wielded considerable power over urban shopkeepers and artisans through, for example, their authority to issue and revoke licenses.

The pogroms were essentially counter-revolutionary riots by urban crowds who both feared rapid political and social change and were too disorganized to participate in such regular political activity as the formation of parties or strong pressure groups.[92] Overall, Jews suffered more than any other group, but some of the worst pogroms broke out in cities with a relatively small Jewish population. In Tver, for example, a mob burned down a building where zemstvo employees were meeting.

There were several types of pogroms. For example, there were "military" pogroms, instigated and executed by the local garrisons. Such pogroms occurred in Sebastopol, Minsk, Belostok, and Tiflis. In the last three of these cities, the urban population was mainly non-Russian and was less likely to participate willingly in "patriotic" demonstrations. The targets of these pogroms were mainly Jews but included high school students as well. A second type was the "intelligentsia" pogrom. These riots were aimed mainly against students, professionals, and zemstvo employees and occurred in towns with a small non-Russian population. Students walking the streets in uniform risked severe beatings and even death. In Tomsk these two forms combined; the pogrom began against the intelligentsia and ended in an anti-Semitic orgy. A mob surrounded the railroad administration building and killed employees who tried to flee; local troops also participated. There were "mixed" pogroms, intentionally aimed at both Jews and intellectuals. Finally, there were the "Jewish" pogroms, which were especially common in the Ukraine. In Odessa over five hundred Jews were to die in a wave of violence and terror, a horror depicted in Isaac Babel's "The Story of My Dovecoat."[93]

While much of a terrified Jewish population hid in cellars, Odessa University students joined Jewish workers in forming a self-defense or-

92. The best analysis of the pogroms is *Die Judenpogrome in Russland*. This study was published by the Zionist Central Bureau in Germany. For a sociological discussion, see vol. 1, pp. 328–404. See also Heinz-Dietrich Löwe, *Antisemitismus und reaktionäre Utopie: Russischer Konservatismus im Kampf Gegen den Wandel von Staat und Gesellschaft, 1890–1917* (Hamburg, 1978), pp. 87–98.

93. *Die Judenpogrome in Russland*, vol. 1, pp. 187–223. See also Robert Weinberg's excellent article "Workers, Pogroms, and the 1905 Revolution in Odessa" (*Russian Review*, no. 1 [1987]).

ganization to fight the mobs. It had some initial successes, but then was smashed by the military.[94]

The wave of pogroms had important consequences for the Russian universities. Even before the proclamation of the manifesto, many of the major universities had found themselves besieged. The pogroms re-emphasized the ominous fact that wide sections of Russia's urban population viewed the academic community and especially the *studenchestvo* as representative of a hostile social force, interlopers from an alien world. The liberal professoriate had been hoping to remove the universities from direct involvement in the political fray, but the pogroms were a bitter reminder of the tremendous obstacles faced by the professoriate in its struggle to Europeanize Russia's universities.

REOPEN THE UNIVERSITIES?

After the proclamation of the manifesto and the wave of pogroms, the chasm separating the senior faculty from the junior faculty and the students widened even further. Junior faculty and students wanted to reopen the universities; senior faculty wanted to keep them closed. The political situation created by the proclamation of the manifesto was a major factor fanning dissension over this issue. The revolution was far from over, especially in Moscow and Saint Petersburg, where the workers continued to struggle for economic as well as political rights under the leadership of the newly formed Soviets.

The senior faculty had to reckon with the likelihood that if it reopened the universities, workers would renew their meetings there, thus increasing the danger of police or military intervention. Nor could the senior faculty forget that the political situation was likely to generate new challenges to its control of the universities from the students and the junior faculty. Finally, there was the constant threat from rightist mobs.

On 24 October, a meeting of the rectors of the various institutions of higher education in Saint Petersburg agreed that "this was not the right time to petition for the reopening of the institutions of higher education."[95] Both the junior faculty and the coalition council of Saint Peters-

94. Ibid., vol. 2, pp. 109–132.
95. Imperatorskii Sankt-Peterburgskii Universitet, *Zhurnaly zasedanii soveta za 1905g.*, p. 162 (meeting of 24 October 1905).

burg University asked the faculty council to reopen the university on its own authority, but the latter endorsed the rectors' decision. (Responding to an appeal from the coalition council for money to buy arms for student defense against rightist mobs, the faculty council decided to hand out old clothes instead.)

In Moscow University tensions were even sharper, as the Central University Organ engaged in bitter recriminations with the faculty council over its closing of the university on 15 October. On that day, the Central University Organ had seized control of the university and erected barricades in order to provide at least one secure refuge from roving rightist thugs who were attacking students on the streets.[96] Five days later, Cossacks attacked a crowd of workers and students returning from the funeral of Nicholas Bauman, touching off an outbreak of massive violence on the city streets. In order to provide a sanctuary for students and "progressives," the CUO seized the university again and re-erected the barricades. It also organized first aid for the wounded and collected civilian clothing so that students could walk the streets unrecognized by the Black Hundreds.

Replying to the professors' request that the CUO leave the university, the CUO said that it would do so only if the faculty council acceded to four demands. First, the CUO wanted the faculty council to allow a general student *skhodka* on 29 October so that the CUO could "consult with its electorate" about reopening the university and discuss the general political position of the *studenchestvo*. Second, the CUO wanted the faculty council to guarantee it a secure meeting place. Third, the faculty had to promise that it would reopen the university soon. The last demand, which must have been especially irksome to the professors, called on the faculty to meet with the students in order to "work out a detailed constitution for the governance of the university." An informal delegation of professors met with the CUO to discuss the demands but reached no formal agreement. That same day, 28 October, the CUO bowed to the threats of the Moscow military governor and left the university.

On 1 November the Central University Organ bitterly attacked the professors' conduct in an "Open Letter to the Faculty Council." The "Open Letter" reviewed the events of the past months and discussed the problem of faculty-student relations. It reiterated the student lead-

96. *Russkie Vedomosti*, 1 November 1905; TsGIAM, f. 418, op. 249. ed. kh. 95, ll. 305–307.

ers' determination that the revolution should transform not only the nation at large but the universities as well. The CUO declared: "For the past month the university has been seeing a repetition in miniature of what has been going on in the country at large. . . . The old ways which until now have bound [our] life do not satisfy the demands of young Russia, which is surging forward and throwing off the chains of slavery. And it is precisely these narrow customs, which have outlived their usefulness, which have been jolted [*narusheny*] in Moscow University."[97]

The CUO used the "Open Letter" to question the professors' sincerity. "You professors," the letter stated, "who so many times have advertised yourselves as the defenders of an autonomous university, sold out this autonomy in the interests of your own security. . . . You delivered the university and those found within it into the hands of the [local authorities]." The faculty council had been protesting that it had closed the university to protect the students from the Black Hundreds. The CUO rejected this explanation. "The university has served and still could serve as a powerful base, where [progressive] Moscow and the *studenchestvo* in particular could find constant support and protection; in addition the organized *studenchestvo* would have a center." The CUO concluded the "Open Letter" with a defiant query to the faculty council. "Who gave you the right to protect us?" it asked. "It is time for you to abandon forever this outmoded system of chaperonage!"

The CUO received direct support from the junior faculty and the moderate Delegate Council for its demand that the faculty council reopen the university immediately. In addition to voicing this demand, the junior members of the mathematics faculty renewed their call for the professors to open faculty council meetings to delegates from the junior faculty and the student body. They also asked the council to create a new governing body to decide important matters affecting the university. The junior members of the medical faculty sent the faculty council a message declaring that its decision to close the university contradicted "the demands of the present political situation as well as the country's educational needs." The message told the professors that junior faculty, as well as students, should participate in decisions concerning the opening and closing of the university.[98]

On 5 November, the faculty council met to consider reopening the university. The professors were in an apprehensive mood fostered both

97. *Russkie Vedomosti*, 1 November 1905.
98. *Russkie Vedomosti*, 3 November 1905.

by the political situation and by the militant demands of the students and the junior faculty. *Russkie Vedomosti,* Moscow's leading liberal daily, had just run a lead editorial supporting the professors' right to control the university, but the assembled professors feared the worst. P. E. Sokolovskii warned his colleagues that "sooner or later the students, represented by the CUO, will present us with the bill; they will demand participation in the administration of university affairs, since they have taken an active part in the political movement and sacrificed themselves . . . while we professors were drawing our salaries."[99]

Manuilov, the rector, asked the rest of the faculty council to stand firm, to keep the university closed and to resist the pressures coming from the students and the junior faculty. Manuilov rejected the idea of negotiating with the CUO, declaring that "it is impossible to entertain the thought that the university should be run by anybody except by the faculty council. . . . If we reopen the university now it will be seized by the revolutionary crowd. The only way out of the present situation is to firmly uphold the idea that . . . the university should serve only academic purposes."[100] Vernadskii warned his colleagues that if the faculty council decided to keep the university closed, it had better issue a good explanation, since such a step would be widely seen as "being directed against the liberation movement."

On 7 November, the faculty council voted 61 to 5 to keep the university closed until 15 January and issued a public statement explaining its actions. The major reason the university would stay closed, the council explained, was that it had turned into "an arena and weapon of political battle." The council declared:

> The participation of the university as such in the political fray . . . is impermissible. . . . The very nature of political activity is incompatible with the essence, purposes, and spirit of the academy. . . . The university should unite people on the basis of scientific and educational interests and direct them to the service of science and enlightenment. . . . But such a union is possible only on the basis of academic interests . . . it would collapse immediately as soon as politics were introduced into the university. Neither the teaching staff nor the *studenchestvo* is a homogeneous group from the political point of view, so any attempt to unite the academic community on the basis of a common political platform is doomed to failure. . . . The university can and should, while not forgetting its primary purpose, serve the cause of freedom. By struggling for the freedom of science and teaching and for the principle of

99. TsGIAM, f. 418, op. 249, ed. kh. 95, l. 318.
100. Ibid.

academic autonomy . . . and by defending the free development and spread of knowledge, the university itself serves the cause of freedom and progress.[101]

The controversy in Moscow University over whether to reopen classes was repeated, with very minor differences, in the other institutions of higher education in the country.[102] Students and junior faculty wanted the universities to reopen after the proclamation of the manifesto; senior faculty wanted them to remain closed. With a few exceptions, Russia's institutions of higher education closed after the proclamation of the manifesto and remained closed until September 1906.[103]

THE *VUZy* IN 1905: AN OVERVIEW

Several conclusions can be drawn from the turbulent experiences of September and October. More by default than through legal sanctions, the senior faculty enjoyed the academic autonomy for which it had so long clamored; the government was too preoccupied to interfere in academic affairs. But events showed that the students and the junior faculty would not accept the professors' claim that autonomy meant senior-faculty predominance in university governance. At this time when various groups in Russian society were joining to demand political and economic reforms, the universities were not immune—nor could they be—from internal dissension. Various social groups used the revolution to advance specific corporate as well as general political demands. Even the senior faculty acted in this manner in March 1905, when the various faculty councils passed resolutions refusing to renew classes. Once the professors had received major concessions from the government—in particular, the 27 August Rules—they stood determined to defend their own conception of what the universities should be.[104]

101. *Russkie Vedomosti,* 8 November 1905.
102. A useful overview of this issue is the speech given by Professor A. Brandt to the third congress of the Academic Union in January 1906. See "Polozhenie vysshikh uchebnykh zavedenii v sviazi s voprosom o mitingakh," *Tretii delegatskii s"ezd akade-micheskovo soiuza* (Saint Petersburg, 1906), pp. 15–19.
103. On 19 October the Council of Ministers ordered the closing of almost all the nation's *VUZy.* There were brief attempts to reopen some universities and institutes in the spring semester, but they were largely unsuccessful.
104. A clear example is the report of the commission appointed by the Moscow University Faculty Council in the fall of 1905 to study the demands of junior faculty for a larger role in university governance. The commission warned that allowing junior faculty to have permanent representation on the faculty council would lead to a "new type of university" that would soon result in "the total collapse of academic life" (TsGIAM,

Thus a collision between senior faculty and the rest of the academic community was inevitable, although the intensity of the clash varied depending on local circumstances. As has been indicated above, the professors found it difficult to define their specific role in the Russian liberation movement. When they did decide on specific actions, the Academic Union was more restrained and moderate in its political demands than other professional unions. For example, at no time did the Academic Union demand a constituent assembly.

The events of September and October indicate that one explanation for the moderate behavior of the professors, and especially their opposition to political meetings, was a real fear for the future of the university as a form of higher education in Russia. Even the faculties of the technical institutes looked to the universities for scientific leadership, and the professors feared that the existence of the university was endangered on all sides. The government seemed indifferent to threats to its existence and was, the professors suspected, quite capable of replacing it with specialized institutes. The students were always too ready to put their immediate demands ahead of the ultimate welfare of the universities, thus exposing the latter to reprisals from the government as well as from right-wing crowds. Moreover, other professional groups in Russian society, such as the medical and legal professions, were apt to overlook the long-range interests of the universities in their drive for immediate political reform. Junior faculty would not accept the idea that political democracy did not necessarily mean democracy in the academy. Finally, there was a long tradition of town-gown strife in Russian cities. The professors clung to the vision of the universities as apolitical institutions, but they could not ignore the fact that the backward strata of Russian urban society associated the universities with the evil of revolution and the threat of social change. When the government began to lose control in September and October, the universities became lightning rods attracting both left-wing and rightist crowds. The former used the universities as organizational havens and as meeting places that served as an indispensable educational and propaganda resource. For the right, the universities were the symbols for the new, foreign, and little-understood forces threatening to change traditional Russian life irrevocably. The Black Hundreds had hardly more tolerance for the students than they had for the Jews.

f. 418, op. 249, ed. kh. 97 ["Doklad sovetskoi komissii po voprosu o polozhenii v universitete mladshikh prepodavatelei"]).

These factors all contributed to the senior faculties' fear of confrontation politics and their determination to act within the framework of established law. This fear separated the professors from the rest of the academic community, leading to a growing polarization within the Academic Union and preventing the professoriate as a group from engaging in direct political action.

The professors felt that they had little to gain from a continuation of the revolution after the issuance of the Bulygin rescript and the 27 August Rules. It is true that most would have preferred a more democratic electoral law, and the second congress of the Academic Union resolved to press on with the cause of winning freedom of speech and assembly. As a whole the professoriate sincerely wanted these freedoms, just as it sympathized with many of the most important demands of the student movement. The experience at Saint Petersburg and other universities shows that the professors were willing to endorse calls for breaking down religious, national, and sexual barriers to university admissions, changes in the student disciplinary system, student participation in the distribution of financial aid, curricular reform, and a lowering of admissions barriers for the graduates of nonclassical secondary schools. But in September 1905 the professors were determined not to break the law. Rather than force change, the faculty councils preferred to petition the Ministry of Education.

The professors feared the street. Street violence threatened the interests of the professoriate more directly than it did those of other sections of the Russian "bourgeoisie"—with the conspicuous exception of the industrialists. The political situation as it appeared at the time must be recalled. The war was over; the universities seemed launched on the road to autonomy; above all, the government had promised the Bulygin Duma. Before the first week of October, few foresaw the probability of a general strike. The major issue facing the liberal and the leftist opposition was whether to "boycott" the elections to the forthcoming Bulygin Duma. The liberal camp, as we have seen, split over this issue. The Union of Liberation recommended using the Duma as a base from which to demand more reforms, a position endorsed by the Academic Union, whereas the Union of Unions joined the revolutionary parties in demanding a boycott. When the students returned in the fall, most of their resolutions endorsed the boycott and demanded a constituent assembly. The beginning of the academic year, then, found the students and professors in opposite political camps.

These differences are seen as vital when we remember that, until the middle of October, developments in the universities were widely considered to be a crucial test of whether the Bulygin Duma itself held out any promise of real political and social reform. There was a clear parallel in public opinion between the 6 August rescript and the 27 August Rules.

Vladimir Lenin, for example, interpreted the situation in the universities as proving that Russian liberalism, having received a few concessions from the government, would "sell out" the working class. Referring to the behavior of the Moscow professors, he warned that their example is "instructive . . . for an assessment of our State Duma. Doesn't the experience of the institutions of higher education make it clear that the liberals and Kadets will worry as much for the 'fate of the Duma' as these pathetic cavaliers of exalted science fret about the 'fate of the universities'? Isn't it now clear that the liberals and Kadets will only be able to utilize the Duma as an even larger and more putrid platform for the propagation of peaceful, legal freedom?"[105]

The experience of the universities in the fall of 1905 is one important test case of the ability of Russian liberalism to face and solve important political problems. There is little doubt that Russian liberalism, which placed so much faith in such institutions as the zemstvos, universities, and the press, must be judged and studied not only by the performance of the political parties that arose in 1905 but also by its ability to maintain a position in local government and the institutions of higher education.

As the experiences of September and October 1905 show, one major factor frustrating the liberal faculty was the opposition of the student movement. The student political organizations did not return to the universities with a clear plan for using them as political forums, despite the wording of the various September resolutions voted by the *studenchestvo*. The decision to end the strike, like the original decision to strike after Bloody Sunday, reflected the feelings of the majority of the *studenchestvo* and was not dictated from outside the universities by any revolutionary group. By September the majority of students wanted to return to their studies, if they could do so without seeming to renege on the revolutionary resolutions passed in January and February.

On the surface the student movement appeared to be a revolutionary force. Certainly there is seemingly convincing evidence to support this contention. The students voted overwhelmingly for the Social Democrats in all the major Russian *VUZy*. The coalition councils, Central

---

105. Lenin, "Politicheskaia stachka," p. 294.

University Organs, and other student bodies helped organize workers' meetings, erected barricades against the Black Hundreds, and helped defend Jews during the Odessa and Kiev pogroms. Indeed, several writers and historians see the fall of 1905 as the apogee of the Russian student movement.

Nonetheless, in reviewing the turbulent events of September and October, it is easy to overlook other important aspects of the student movement. First, it became clear that the political student groups could not entirely manipulate the *studenchestvo*. They could keep control of the student government only so long as they addressed themselves to and were able to express the corporate demands of the student majority. Like other groups in the Revolution of 1905, the students acted as much from corporate identification as from loyalty to a particular political platform. In other words, they did not suddenly abandon the familiar terrain of corporate identity for the novel and untested notion of behavior determined by political party. Nor should the large voting margins won by the Social Democrats lead us to the conclusion that the *studenchestvo* was on the brink of taking to the streets in a mass effort to topple the government. As we have seen above, the Social Democrats were the only group calling for an end to the university strike that did not break with the oppositional and anti-liberal attitudes of the *studenchestvo*, attitudes that had been steadily growing since the fall of 1901.

An essential aspect of the students' corporate identity was the aura of being an oppositional group. This aura of opposition was an integral part of a student subculture that heightened the students' self-esteem, made it easier for them to adapt to the various economic and social difficulties of student life, and served to register the students' preliminary protests at the prospect of becoming acquiescent civil servants or professionals in a repressive and arbitrary system. As long as the government enforced admissions barriers, tampered with the university curriculum, or harassed the *studenchestvo* in petty ways, the Russian student would reject as dishonorable the liberal ideas that the university was an institution standing above the political maelstrom or that repression should be met by petitions rather than by strikes or defiant resolutions. For the Russian students, the events of 1905 reaffirmed the close relationship between political and corporate issues. If the senior faculty minimized the urgency of finding adequate solutions and recommended patience and restraint, then they would reject that leadership. The same held true for the students' relationship to the revolutionary parties or to their own student organizations. The students would follow them only as long as they believed that they were not being used as pawns and that their own interests were not being disregarded.

This suspicion of outside manipulation surfaced after the proclamation of the manifesto, when various student government organizations had to answer charges of usurpation of authority. In September, and especially after the outbreak of riots and pogroms in October, student organizations in a number of towns showed resourcefulness and even heroism under very difficult circumstances. The Moscow Central University Organ had seized and barricaded the university on 15 October; the Odessa and Kharkov coalition councils had played an important part in defending students and Jews during the pogrom. Because of the widespread violence, these bodies had to make immediate decisions without having the opportunity of convening a *skhodka* to consult with the student body. As a result these student organizations had to answer charges that they had exceeded their authority: the tradition of the *skhodka* was as strong as ever.

At the beginning of November the Moscow Central University Organ and the coalition council of Odessa University, for example, called *skhodki* to answer these charges and submit to a vote of confidence from the students. They received votes of confidence, but accounts of the discussions showed that many students complained of being manipulated to serve the purposes of the revolutionary parties or other groups outside the university. The Odessa coalition council had to reiterate that it considered itself to be a purely student organization whose authority came from the *skhodka,* not from outside political groups.[106] At a jammed *skhodka* on 7 November, which was closed to nonstudents, the coalition council explained its difficult position during the pogrom and why it was unable to convene a *skhodka*. It emphasized that it was not acting as the tool of any political party.

In Moscow the Central University Organ delivered its report and got a vote of confidence on 1 November. It had to face the same charge made against the Odessa coalition council: usurpation of authority. A major issue at this meeting was the feasibility of consultation with the student body during periods of intense political crisis and street violence.[107]

These meetings show that the hold of traditional student politics was still tenacious. Underneath the tumult of the revolution, the Russian student movement maintained very strong links to its past. The change

106. *Odesskii Listok,* 9 November 1905, printed the full text of the report that the coalition council of Odessa University delivered to the student *skhodka.*
107. *Russkie Vedomosti,* 4 November 1905.

was in the emergence of new and more important social groups on the political scene, as well as the beginning of organized political parties and new opportunities for political expression afforded by the institution of the state Duma. Would the student movement lose its political significance and raison d'être now that the country was entering a new phase of political development? This was a major question confronting the students when they finally returned to the classroom in September 1906.

CHAPTER 7

New Possibilities, 1906–1910

Russia's institutions of higher education stayed closed until September 1906. When they reopened, the great transformation brought about as a result of the Revolution of 1905 was clearly visible: the curriculum had become much more flexible, student enrollment in the universities had nearly doubled, and barriers to the admission of Jews and women had all but disappeared. But the legal basis for all these changes rested on the professoriate's liberal interpretation of the 27 August 1905 Temporary Rules. Once the government recovered its balance, it remembered that the 1884 Statute remained in force, ready for use as the legal justification for a counteroffensive against the universities. The main theme of this chapter is how the Revolution of 1905 changed the universities and why the government, unable to accept the new situation, tried to reassert its control.

The aftermath of the revolution revealed important changes in both the professoriate and the student movement. The sobering experiences of 1905 had weakened the cautious but unmistakable corporate political commitment that had led more than half the academic profession to sign the "Declaration of the 342" and form the Academic Union. After a futile struggle against the growing indifference of the senior faculty, the Academic Union petered out. Meanwhile, conservative elements among the professoriate recovered from their 1905 disarray, especially in the provincial universities. Most of the professoriate wanted a new university statute that would guarantee wide professional autonomy and senior faculty preeminence in the universities. In 1906 a landmark conference called by the Ministry of Education seemed to put this goal within reach—all the more reason for the professoriate to revert to its traditional preference for a cooperative rather than a confrontational relationship with the government.

At first the government cooperated with the professors, but after Peter Stolypin became prime minister in 1906, the Ministry of Education charted a tougher course toward both the students and the professors. A major source of friction was the differing interpretations of the 27 August 1905 Rules: the faculty councils read them as supplanting the 1884 Statute, whereas the government, with increasing frequency, argued that except for making the faculty responsible for student discipline and the election of rectors, the rules in no way changed the status quo ante in the universities.

As before, the student movement complicated relations between the professoriate and the government. Stolypin charged that the student movement enabled the revolutionary parties to use the universities for their own ends, while the senior faculty (except in some provincial universities) contended that the students were losing interest in politics, a healthy trend that would continue as long as the government stayed out of the VUZy and left disciplinary matters to the faculty.

In fact the post-1906 period saw major changes occurring within the student movement. The new Duma, for all its imperfections, afforded Russia some semblance of an open political life and thus undermined one of the major bases for student protest. Many students argued that they no longer had any obligation to "wake up" society and incite wider social protest. And after the massive general strike of 1905 students could no longer delude themselves about the significance of the student movement compared to the labor movement. Moreover, student life itself was in flux. Enrollment had doubled, financial aid became even more of a problem, and the relaxed regulations in the universities led to open elections to student governments and political campaigns. A conspicuous student press became a new factor in university life. New agendas emerged, and extensive debate developed about the rationale and future of the student movement, the place of the *skhodka* in student affairs, and the merits of a "political" versus a "professional" student movement. But growing government interference in the universities eventually forced the students back into direct political confrontation with the state.

Complicating the university question was the ambiguous political system that emerged in Russia after 1905. Had the October manifesto, the new laws establishing a Duma, and other changes in the Fundamental Laws made Russia a constitutional or even a semi-constitutional monarchy? Could the clock be turned back, or did the government have to widen its base of support to adapt to the new political situation? These ambiguities created a tense situation that helped the far right gain influence over the tsar and made political leaders such as Peter Stolypin extremely vulnerable to political attacks from that direction. Under the circumstances the university question assumed outsize significance as a gauge of the prime minister's zeal in defending the prerogatives of the autocracy.

A NEW MINISTER OF EDUCATION

After two months of anguish, Russia's professoriate finally heard good news at the end of October 1905. Count Witte appointed a respected moderate, Count I. I. Tolstoi, as the new minister of education. A former secretary of the Russian Archeological Society and a vice-president of the Imperial Academy of the Arts, Tolstoi was a longstanding critic of the Ministry of Education. He was also known as a leading advocate of equal rights for Russia's Jews.[1]

Less than two months after his appointment, Tolstoi charted a major reform program embracing all levels of Russian education. In a memorandum to Witte, Tolstoi outlined some of his major goals: state support for universal primary education, an end to the Russification policies of the Ministry of Education, a greater role for private education, and the abolition of restrictions on Jewish students in secondary and higher education.[2] To show that he was serious, Tolstoi began to clean house, forcing the resignation of the two key officials in charge of higher-education policy, A. A. Tikhomirov and S. M. Lukianov. Their replacements, O. P. Gerasimov and P. P. Izvol'skii, enjoyed the reputation of being more progressive.[3]

In a major departure from past policy, Tolstoi took some important steps to ensure better relations between the professoriate and the government. Agreeing that the immediate priority in higher-education pol-

---

1. A biographical sketch of I. I. Tolstoi can be found in *Odesskii Listok,* 2 November 1905.
2. Gosudarstvennaia Publichnaia Biblioteka imeni M. E. Saltykova-Shchedrina, Otdel Rukopisei (hereafter referred to as GPB im. M. E. Saltykova-Shchedrina), f. 781 (I. I. Tolstoi), ed. kh. 115.
3. GPB im. M. E. Saltykova-Shchedrir.a, f. 781, ed. kh. 568 ("vospominaniia I. I. Tolstovo za vremia evo upravleniia Ministerstvom Narodnovo Prosveshcheniia"), l. 34.

icy was to replace the 1884 Statute, Tolstoi decided to involve the faculty councils in all stages of the process. First he sent the statute draft, just completed by Glazov's commission, to all the councils. Without exception they rejected it.[4] In December, Tolstoi then invited all the universities' faculty councils to elect delegates to a conference to draft a new statute. The first meeting of the conference took place on 5 January 1906. In addition to Tolstoi, the conference included all nine university rectors and thirty-five professors representing various departments. Tolstoi made a brief welcoming address in which he promised the delegates that the Ministry of Education would exert no pressure on them.[5]

Tolstoi's initiative made Witte and other government officials nervous; they feared that the conference would turn into an anti-government demonstration.[6] Indeed, to quote Tolstoi's unpublished memoirs, "only five or six [of the delegates] were conservatives. Most of the elected professors were 'radicals' in the European sense; in Russia they would be called progressives."[7] Yet, far from being an oppositional forum, the Tolstoi Conference, as it came to be called, proved that the professoriate, given half a chance, preferred to work with the government rather than to fight it.

Although its draft statute got no further than the archives—the victim of rapidly changing political circumstances—the Tolstoi Conference was a major landmark in the history of the Russian academic profession and higher education. For the first time ever, the freely elected representatives of the professoriate could meet under the auspices of a sympathetic minister of education. But the conference also showed that it was much easier for the professors to unite against the old statute than to agree on the details of a new one.

The most controversial issues at the conference concerned whether the professor was a civil servant, or a professional who received no decorations from the state; the rights of the junior faculty; procedures for electing professors; professional prerequisites for a teaching career; student rights and discipline; the relationship between the faculty council and the individual departments; and the nature of the state's supervisory power over the universities. Recent events had obviously left their mark. The delegates quickly agreed that the universities should be defined as

4. TsGIA, f. 733, op. 153, d. 173, ll. 64–74.
5. TsGIA, f. 733, op. 226, d. 121 ("zhurnaly soveshchaniia po reforme universitetov obrazovannovo pri MNP v Ianvare 1906ovo goda") (meeting of 5 January 1906).
6. GPB im. M. E. Saltykova-Shchedrina, f. 781, ed. kh. 568, l. 83.
7. Ibid.

institutions dedicated to both research and teaching, but they engaged in a bitter debate on the relationship of the academic profession to the state and whether the word *autonomous* should be used to define the universities.[8] Quoting Pirogov on the scholar's inherent need for independence, Professor V. A. Steklov of Kharkov University argued against Article 14 of the proposed draft, which stipulated that professors would continue to enjoy the rights, privileges, and decorations conferred on them by their civil service status. But he failed to sway the conference. Professor N. M. Bubnov of Kiev University pointed out that getting decorations from the kaiser hardly compromised the German professoriate; in fact, it increased their prestige. Twenty-six delegates voted for Article 14 and only twelve for Steklov's substitute ("A professor is not a civil servant and enjoys neither rank nor decorations").[9]

The issue of required ministerial approval for academic appointments sparked another controversy. Warsaw's G. Th. Voronoi, supporting the minister's prerogatives, told his colleagues that "if we get paid by the government, then we should be subject to ministerial veto." By the very narrow margin of 22 to 20 the delegates voted to have the minister of education confirm professorial appointments voted by the faculty council. But the only grounds for nonconfirmation were to be clear violations of legal procedures by the faculty council; and such nonconfirmation would have to be accompanied by a written explanation. By the same vote, the conference agreed that rectors elected by the faculty councils were to be confirmed by the tsar.

The delegates also had difficulty coming to an agreement on another problem that tended to separate liberal from conservative professors: the relationship between the faculty council and the individual departments. Liberals tended to advocate a strong faculty council. It was, they argued, the fundamental institution of professional autonomy, since it symbolized the principle of the unity of knowledge. If individual departments had the right to bypass the faculty council in recommending appointees, the universities would be replaced by a random collection of departments with no claim to authority, autonomy, or respect. Proponents of departmental powers cited the example of the German universities and argued that the best judges of a candidate's merit were colleagues in the discipline.[10] The greater the role of the faculty council, the

8. TsGIA, f. 733, op. 226, d. 121 (meeting of 16 January 1906).
9. Ibid.
10. For a strong defense of this position, see V. Sergeevich, "Germanskie universitety i nashi," *Vestnik Evropy*, no. 3 (1905).

more likely that political rather than academic considerations would influence the decision.[11] In the end the conference compromised by giving the ultimate decision to the faculty council unless the department unanimously supported one particular candidate. But the issue would surface again, a reminder that the Russian professoriate was deeply divided about the very structure of university governance.

The conference reached many other important decisions. It rejected a proposal from Professor D. A. Goldhammer of Kazan University to guarantee the university's extraterritoriality by expressly forbidding entry to police without the permission of the rector; instead, the conference voted that "police and troops cannot enter the grounds of the university without the knowledge of the rector."[12] Although the delegates called for an elective curriculum to replace the restrictive course system, they rejected Goldhammer's request to include chairs of anthropology and sociology in the draft statute. The Kazan professor had argued that the universities had forfeited their intellectual influence on Russian youth by adhering to an overly restrictive curriculum which slighted the social sciences. Russian students, he warned, got their education from the "thick journals" and ignored professors' lectures. Reflecting the sharp divisions within the professoriate about the merits of these disciplines, the conference compromised by leaving the question of new chairs to be decided by direct negotiations between the Ministry of Education and the faculty councils. And although the faculty councils would be allowed to spend income from student fees and endowments as they saw fit, any expenditures requiring government outlays and any action affecting the universities' physical plant would require ministerial approval.

After another sharp debate the conference smoothed the road to an academic career by abolishing the two-thesis requirement. It restored the official *dozenty,* abolished by the 1884 Statute, and recommended sharply increased salaries for both senior and junior faculty. The delegates also voted to abolish all admission bars to the professoriate and the student body based on religion, nationality, or sex. After a long argument about faculty responsibility for student discipline, the conference voted to include faculty disciplinary courts in the draft statute.

In another liberal move, the delegates voted to end the privileged

11. This was the argument used by Professor Th. Th. Zelinskii of Saint Petersburg University in "Universitetskii vopros v 1906 godu," in *Zhurnal Ministerstva Narodnovo Prosveshcheniia,* no. 8 (1906): 121.

12. TsGIA, f. 733, op. 226, d. 121 (meeting of 20 January 1906).

position of the classical gymnasia; graduates of all secondary schools would be eligible to enter the universities. Faculty councils, however, could still stipulate specific requirements, such as Latin and Greek. As expected, the delegates abolished the requirement that the faculty councils route all communication with the Ministry of Education through the curators. But the conference deadlocked on the thorny issue of abolishing the legal privileges connected with the university degree. Advocates of abolition argued that the government would then have less reason to interfere in university affairs. Besides, the quality of the student body would improve, for "careerists" would presumably have less reason to seek a diploma. But Professor D. D. Grimm of Saint Petersburg University marshalled the counterarguments: it was overly idealistic to expect universities to attract students motivated only by love of learning. The national interest demanded an educated civil service and a guaranteed position for the universities. And even if such special privileges as elevation from the subject estates, better status during military service, and a guaranteed entry rank into the civil service were abolished, Grimm argued, a university degree should at least remain a prerequisite for the state civil-service examination. This was necessary to "secure for the universities a certain position in our national life, as is the case in France and Germany. To abolish these privileges for university graduates and keep them for graduates of the specialized technical institutes would be unfair to the former."[13] Torn between idealism and realism, the conference could reach no decision, another sign that the Russian professoriate was not unanimous in its vision of the relationship between the universities and the wider society.

The issue of junior faculty rights produced one of the most serious disagreements at the conference. A small liberal bloc proposed to allow elected delegates from the junior faculty to enjoy voting rights at faculty council meetings.[14] But this proposal attracted only seven votes. As before, the junior faculty had no right to participate in or vote in faculty council meetings. *Dozenty,* however (who would now be required to hold a doctorate), would be able to attend—but not vote in—department meetings, except when academic appointments were under consideration.

On the whole the delegates had reason to be happy with the results of the Tolstoi Conference. The minister accepted the crucial first article

13. Ibid. (meeting of 23 January 1906).
14. Ibid. (meeting of 25 January 1906).

containing the professors' definition of the university as an autonomous institution dedicated to research and teaching and endorsed their conviction that the universities should stand at the center of the nation's educational system. Indeed, the draft charter proposed raising government expenditures on the universities from 5 to 13.5 million rubles a year.[15] The draft statute produced by the Tolstoi Conference provided for a university that would be more open than ever but where the professors, not the junior faculty or the students, would rule. Although divided on the exact relationship of the university to the state, the delegates mirrored the senior faculty's eagerness to accept the principle of the state university, especially when the government showed signs of finally respecting the professors' professional aspirations. At the same time, the university outlined in the draft statute was a Russian institution, not one fashioned after the German or any other foreign model.[16] Clear examples were the central role of the faculty council in university governance and the call for an end to discrimination based on religion or sex. One foreign professor commented that the draft statute would give Russian universities an independence from outside control that no other universities, even in the United Kingdom or the United States, enjoyed.[17] Nevertheless, the sharp debates at the conference showed some clear divisions within the professoriate.

A DIVIDED ACADEMIC UNION

To drive the point home, the third congress of the Academic Union, which was meeting at the same time, drafted a radically different university statute. The Academic Union's statute gave the delegates from the junior faculty an equal vote in the faculty councils, declared that professors had no civil-service status, and abolished the ministry's veto power over professorial appointments.[18] The delegates to the third congress also refused to define the universities as state institutions. The dif-

---

15. D. E. Bagalei, "Ekonomicheskoe polozhenie russkikh universitetov," *Vestnik Evropy*, no. 1 (1914): 231.

16. The critical comments of foreign professors such as Germany's Friedrich Paulsen emphasize important differences between the draft statute of the Tolstoi Conference and university governance in Prussia. The most signficant was the Russian professors' preference for a strong faculty council. See "Otzyvy nemetskikh i gollandskikh professorov o proekte universitetskovo ustava grafa I. I. Tolstovo," *Zhurnal Ministerstva Narodnovo Prosveshcheniia*, nos. 3–4 (1910).

17. Ibid., p. 10.

18. P. N. Sakulin, "Novyi proekt universitetskovo ustava," *Vestnik Vospitaniia*, no. 4 (1906).

ferences from the Tolstoi Conference draft were painfully obvious and showed the widening polarization within the academic profession. One member of the Academic Union, P. N. Sakulin, complained in Russia's leading journal of education that "the participants of the Tolstoi Conference, raised in the spirit of the 1884 Statute, did not have the courage to carry through the idea of academic autonomy in all its purity and integrity."[19]

By this time, however, the Academic Union was clearly in trouble. One major reason was the junior faculty's strong influence within the organization. Many senior faculty could not forget that, in the chaos of the previous fall, the junior faculty had largely supported the meetings in the universities and the student resolutions. They feared that the Academic Union was becoming a forum for pressing junior faculty demands for more rights in university governance. Besides, by the beginning of 1906 many professors saw ample grounds for optimism about both the general political outlook and the specific prospects for better relations between the professoriate and the government.

The defenders of the Academic Union, however, reminded their colleagues of the original reasons for the "Declaration of the 342" and warned against premature optimism. Despite all the promises of a Duma and the hopes generated by the Tolstoi Conference, the autocracy could not be trusted. This was the main theme of Nikolai Kareev's introductory speech to the union's third congress.[20] Tensions between junior and senior faculty, Kareev admitted, clouded the future of the Academic Union, but academic autonomy had not been won, the nation's political future was still uncertain, and Russia's academics badly needed an organization that would unite them regardless of what rank they held and in which institution of higher education they taught. After some debate, in which Professor A. A. Brandt urged the union "to get to work and seize power in the universities," the congress passed the following resolution:

> Since political conditions in the country have undergone no fundamental change, and since as a result academic freedom and autonomy are not secure, it follows that the Academic Union should adhere to its previous political platform. At the same time it should [refrain from endorsing platforms of specific parties] in order to secure the . . . collaboration and unity of its members belonging to various progressive groups.[21]

19. Ibid.
20. *Tretii delegatskii s"ezd akademicheskovo soiuza* (Saint Petersburg, 1906) (meeting of 14 January 1906).
21. Ibid. (meeting of 17 January 1906).

As in 1905, therefore, the Academic Union reflected a profession unable to unite on any but the most general political platform. The political ambivalence of even the most radical wing of the professoriate was underscored by the debate on another thorny issue: the current relation between the Academic Union and the Union of Unions. The latter was still demanding a constituent assembly and a boycott of the upcoming Duma elections. Professors Brandt and Zernov led the fight for a resolution dissociating the Academic Union from the Union of Unions, reminding the delegates that the Academic Union had gone its own way in 1905 and questioning whether it had ever actually been part of the Union of Unions. Furthermore, they argued, a fundamental principle of the Academic Union, full autonomy for local chapters, ruled out specific political resolutions that presumed to speak for all members. Opponents countered with warnings against excessive professional cowardice. By the narrow margin of 39 to 35 the third congress voted that the Academic Union was not a member of the Union of Unions. The closeness of the vote reflected the growing isolation of the Academic Union. Many of the senior faculty who had played such a key role in the first and second congresses had by now lost interest. Had they been there, the margin would have been much wider.

The third congress was the last gasp of the Academic Union, and nothing came of its resolutions. The Russian professors were abandoning the hesitant steps toward corporate union begun in December 1904. Attempts to hold the Academic Union together after the third congress were unsuccessful. On 11 May 1906, Professor Brandt resigned as president of the Central Bureau and was replaced by Professor D. S. Zernov, who tried to convene a fourth congress in Moscow in August but failed.[22] In 1907 the decline of the Academic Union continued. The Central Bureau, located in Saint Petersburg, continued to raise money to help members of the academic community arrested by the police and reminded reluctant colleagues that "in the past two years political repression of academics has actually increased."[23] But contributions declined. At the end of 1907 the union held an unofficial conference in Saint Petersburg which attracted only twenty-three delegates, mainly from the junior faculty. The conference resolved that the Academic Union was needed more than ever, especially because of the government's crackdown on the academic profession. The problem, of course,

22. GPB im. V. I. Lenina, f. 264, folder 41, ed. kh. 27 ("otchët tsentral'novo biuro akademicheskovo soiuza za 1906–07gg.").
23. Ibid.

was convincing the senior faculty. The conference called on professors to "remember the academic resolution passed by the first congress of the Academic Union and, if the circumstances dictate, to be ready to resign collectively [in order to defend academic freedom]."[24] But by this time the Academic Union was clearly moribund.

The decline of the Academic Union underscored Vernadskii's characterization of the professors as "reluctant politicians" during the Revolution of 1905. There was a strong feeling of ambivalence about the Academic Union from its inception, reflecting a lingering belief that the status of independent scholar was incompatible with participation in an organization aiming for the attainment of collective goals.

Professors also realized that the revolution presented them with problems that other professional groups, such as doctors and lawyers, did not have to face. Unlike other professions, the professors depended on the survival of a highly visible and vulnerable institution, the university. Tactics that might be acceptable for other segments of the educated public were too risky for the academics. Preferring to cooperate with the government, many professors refused to admit to themselves that many of the gains they thought they had won at the beginning of 1906 had come about as a result of the pressure tactics of others. The autocracy had granted the October manifesto under the pressure of the general strike and had issued the 27 August Temporary Rules for tactical reasons—such as concern about student unrest—not out of any newfound respect for the professoriate. The consensus of the senior faculty was that only "revolution from above" could deliver reforms without the urban violence so dangerous to the universities. But reforms born of expediency rather than conviction could hardly provide a stable base for the renewal of the universities.

Trusting in the stability of the new constitutional structure, most professors now hoped that the university question would simply fade away. The Duma would replace university auditoriums as the nation's political forum, and all citizens, including students, would be free to vote and join political parties. Presumably the student movement would then disappear, and the universities might finally achieve what so many professors envied the German universities for—a safe harbor "above politics." As Professor Sergei Trubetskoi had put it, a year and a half before his death:

24. Ibid.

If only the Russian public would realize that the university is the key to a better future . . . then the attacks on its integrity would be unthinkable. In Germany it is impossible to imagine any upheaval, either political or social, that would threaten the independence and inviolability of the universities. There both conservatives and reformers realize that the university is the ancient and holy Palladium of the nation, the guarantee of its success and strength, spiritual growth, health, and freedom. . . . But in Russia the public does not leave the university alone. The university cannot serve two masters. It can serve *only* its own purposes.[25]

Of course Trubetskoi lacked a crystal ball to peer into 1933. But his statement is important for its unspoken assumption, shared by many of his colleagues, that when a society reached a certain level of culture and sociopolitical development, its universities would attain a secure position protected by a solid consensus concerning their indispensability. The corollary was that the university question was a function of political backwardness and social immaturity. Now that Russia had entered on a "new era," its universities could move closer to the stability shared by their European counterparts.

Unfortunately for the professors, they could not make a unilateral decision to take the universities out of politics. The real issue was whether the government would cooperate. Past experience had shown the strong dependence of the government's university policy on its general political line; the liberalism of early 1906 might last no longer than the tsar's temporary loss of self-confidence. The professors might proclaim their status as servants of science, but what defense did they have if the government chose to reverse course and treat them as potential subversives? Was it naive to think that the status of the universities could be divorced from the ultimate issue of power?

Ironically, one of the professors' major gains turned out to be a potential snare. The new electoral law regarding the State Council gave the faculty councils and the Academy of Sciences the right to elect six delegates. This made the professors a handy target for the emerging extreme right, since the election results, according to Moscow's leading liberal daily, showed their loyalty to the Kadet party.[26] After Stolypin became

25. *Russkie Vedomosti*, 12 January 1904.
26. *Russkie Vedomosti*, 11 April 1906. In the first State Council, the academic community was represented by professors I. I. Borgman, A. S. Lappo-Danilevskii, V. O. Kliuchevskii, D. I. Bagalei, V. I. Vernadskii, and A. A. Shakhmatov. Delegates to the second State Council included Vernadskii, E. N. Trubetskoi, A. A. Manuilov, M. M. Kovalevskii, and A. V. Vasil'ev. With the exception of Kovalevskii, who had been abroad at the time, all were signers of the "Declaration of the 342."

prime minister, the conviction that the professoriate was part and parcel of the "disloyal" Kadet party was to serve as a major justification for a crackdown against the gains of 1905.

TOLSTOI DEPARTS

Meanwhile, a month after the January conference, I. I. Tolstoi began to sense that the political winds were about to change direction and that his days were numbered. On 2 February 1906, he wrote to Witte that the tsar trusted neither of them. But he tried to enlist Witte's support for his projected education reforms, reminding him that "the struggle with the revolution not only consists of repression but also demands the formulation of a creative policy, especially in the field of education."[27] But Witte had other worries. While he sympathized with Tolstoi's proposals for university reform, he advised him that they had little chance of getting through the State Council.

Tolstoi also encountered heavy opposition on the Council of Ministers. On 20 January he asked the council to recommend to the tsar the abolition of all restrictions on the admission of Jewish students to the universities.[28] Witte supported the proposal, but P. N. Durnovo, the minister of the interior, was firmly opposed. He told Tolstoi that he was not, of course, an anti-Semite:

> I know and respect most Jews. When they come and ask me for such favors as allowing them to live outside the Pale of Settlement or getting them into a school I usually help them. And you can do the same. But it would be a great mistake to solve the [Jewish question] in principle, especially now. For one thing, we still do not know what the policy of Duma will be. There is much more anti-Semitism in Russia than you think.[29]

Tolstoi ignored Durnovo's advice and pushed ahead. But although most of the ministers, including Witte, supported him, the tsar refused to abrogate the *numerus clausus*. "The Jewish question," he declared, "will be settled in its entirety only when I feel the time is ripe."[30]

Meanwhile Tolstoi moved on his own to liberalize the universities.

27. V. P. Iakovlev, "Politika samoderzhaviia v universitetskom voprose, 1905–11," Kandidat dissertation, Leningrad State University, 1970, p. 61.
28. GPB im. M. E. Saltykova-Shchedrina, f. 781. ed. kh. 568, l. 171. The tsar told Tolstoi that while he favored equal rights for Jews in theory, in practice he had to consider the problems of "protecting Russians."
29. Ibid.
30. Ibid.

On 14 December he issued a circular allowing the graduates of seminaries to attend universities. On 8 February 1906 he rescinded Bogolepov's order forcing high school graduates to attend the university closest
to their educational district, and on 18 March he issued a circular that
allowed graduates of nonclassical high schools (*realuchilishcha*) and
commercial high schools to enter the universities upon passing a Latin
examination.[31] These circulars opened the doors of the universities to
new classes of students. The effects were dramatic. The number of university students rose from 19,563 in 1904 to 35,329 in 1908. Russian
universities had never been as accessible as they were during the years
1906–1908.

But the tenure of one of the most liberal ministers of education ever
to serve in Imperial Russia came to an abrupt end when the tsar forced
Witte's resignation as prime minister in April 1906. After a short interlude, Peter Stolypin became the new prime minister. Stolypin, a complex
figure, was no reactionary. The new prime minister, himself a graduate
of Saint Petersburg University, fought conservative calls for cutbacks in
educational expenditures. A Russian patriot, Stolypin understood how
important education was for the national welfare, but he was also determined to restore order and liquidate what was left of the revolutionary
movement. The universities were state institutions, and Stolypin would
demand that they show their loyalty to the state. He would have little
patience with the student movement or overt opposition from the faculty councils.

PETER VON KAUFMANN

The new minister of education, a holdover from the short-lived
Goremykin cabinet that replaced Witte, was Peter M. von Kaufmann, a
career bureaucrat with little experience in the field of education.[32] Von
Kaufmann was a pragmatic conservative who did not let his personal
biases stand in the way of education policy. As far as higher education
was concerned, his chief priority was seeing the universities reopen in
the fall of 1906 with a minimum of student unrest.

In a 30 July memorandum to the Council of Ministers, von Kaufmann recommended the immediate approval of some of the key recom-

---

31. TsGIA, f. 733, op. 152, d. 195, ll. 97–110.
32. A biographical sketch of von Kaufmann can be found in M. L. Levenson, *Gosudarstvennyi Sovet* (Petrograd, 1915), pp. 97–110.

mendations of the Tolstoi Conference: admission of women, abolition
of the inspectorate, and recognition of the right of the faculty councils
to implement an elective curriculum.

The memorandum was an interesting document. The new minister
left no doubt that he was holding his nose as he endorsed some of the
Tolstoi proposals. For example, he justified the recommendation about
women by arguing that past restrictions had forced many young women
to seek an education abroad, from whence they returned "corrupted
both morally and politically." Although admitting women might be
dangerous, von Kaufmann told his colleagues, "[the situation] could
not get much worse anyway. . . . I could bar women but this would lead
to disorders." He also recommended the abolition of the Jewish quota,
for pragmatic reasons:

> I am convinced that . . . Jewish youth are a bad influence on Christian stu-
> dents. They infect them with a spirit of materialism and cosmopolitanism.
> The Jews spread an attitude that ends justify any means. . . . Nevertheless, I
> do not think it useful to maintain [the restrictions]. . . . The harm that they
> cause is not so much the result of their religion as it is . . . of the characteris-
> tics of their nationality. The readiness with which a Jew will convert for utili-
> tarian ends . . . shows the futility of the quota, which is based on religious
> criteria and merely gives the Jews an excuse for complaining of oppression.[33]

The best solution to the problem was the complete exclusion of "racial"
Jews from all Russian educational institutions. But the government
could do this, von Kaufmann explained, only if the Russian people demanded it, just as southern whites in the United States demanded the
exclusion of blacks. Until that happened, however, political expediency
dictated the abolition of the Jewish quota.

Except for agreeing to abolish the university inspectorate, the Council of Ministers failed to approve von Kaufmann's recommendations.[34]
The council decided to leave the issues of Jews and women to the discretion of the minister of education, pending final action by the Duma on a
new university statute. The council pointedly refrained from recommending that von Kaufmann introduce for Duma consideration the
statute drafted by the Tolstoi Conference.

On 16 August von Kaufmann convened a conference of university
rectors to assess the chances for an orderly resumption of classes in Sep-

33. TsGIA, f. 733, op. 226, d. 122 ("O vremennykh pravilakh po upravleniiu univer-
sitetami i rassmotrenie voprosov, vozbuzhdennykh professorskim soveshchaniem").
34. TsGIA, f. 1276, op. 2, d. 515 ("Osobyi zhurnal soveta ministrov, 17ovo Avgusta,
1906g.").

tember.[35] The new minister was affable and conciliatory. Liberal rectors such as Moscow's Manuilov and Iur'ev's Passek argued that the best way to fight the student movement was for the government to adopt a policy of benign neglect, avoiding overreaction to student disorders. At the same time Passek and Manuilov urged that the government could ensure the decline of the student movement by promptly reconvening the Duma and guaranteeing freedom of assembly for the public. Conservative rectors such as Professor Tsitovich of Kiev University were more pessimistic and warned von Kaufmann that they might have to ask for police help in controlling the students.

The minister's political pragmatism led him to side with the liberal rectors. Student *skhodki,* he told the meeting, did not concern him unless the students gave outright aid and cover to revolutionary organizations. Unless outside elements were involved, the government would not hold the professoriate responsible for stopping student meetings. Furthermore, the government would warn local authorities not to send police or troops into the universities unless they informed the rectors first. Von Kaufmann also announced the lifting of existing restrictions on student dining halls. But he warned the rectors that "the coming year will decide the fate of higher education in Russia."

BACK TO CLASS: CHANGES
IN THE UNIVERSITIES

After a long hiatus Russia's *VUZy* reopened in September 1906. Nobody could predict whether the student movement would again soon force the closing of the universities. The political situation was still tense. The Duma was prorogued while the government imposed emergency rule on most of the country. To counter a wave of terror against government officials, Stolypin responded with military courts and executions.

Conflict between students and professors began immediately after the reopening of classes and forced some of the universities to close for various periods. (The student movement will be considered in more detail below.) But there was no nationwide academic strike, no repetition of the chaos of 1905. Students protested over academic and local rather than political issues.

Legally the universities were in an uncertain situation. The 1884 Statute was still the legal basis of university life, but the 27 August 1905

35. TsGIA, f. 733, op. 152, d. 176.

Rules, Tolstoi's circulars, and von Kaufmann's promises to the professors gave the faculty councils the impression that they could start making important changes. The professoriate took advantage of this situation by transforming curricular and admissions policy. This was especially true in the central universities. One of the most important curricular reforms was the transition to an elective system, the impact of which was greatest on the two faculties most severely affected by the 1884 Statute: law, and history and philology. By abolishing many of the onerous requirements in canon, police, and trade law, the legal faculty of Moscow University was able to give its students much more latitude.[36] They could now major in one of three subgroups: civil law, political science (*gosudarstvennaia nauka*), or economics. Given the choice, most law students preferred civil law, a traditional career path, to more "relevant" cycles. As of 4 November 1906, 67 percent of the law students were specializing in civil law, a field considered to offer better career prospects; 26 percent specialized in economics; and only 7 percent in political science (most of the latter had also switched to civil law by the end of the academic year).[37]

The history and philology faculty also established new subgroups for student majors. George Vernadsky, who was a history student at Moscow University in 1906, recalled the marked improvement in the academic atmosphere and the establishment of closer ties between faculty and students.[38]

As before, most students entered the juridical faculty. Figures for the 1908–1909 academic year show a total of 36,195 students in the Russian universities. Of these, 15,416 were enrolled in a juridical faculty, 8,400 in medicine, 3,100 in history and philology, 5,239 in natural sciences, 3,740 in mathematics, and 120 in theology.[39] More students would have studied medicine, but the universities limited enrollment because of a lack of suitable facilities. Competition for the specialized technical institutes remained as severe as ever. In 1908 the mining institute received 1,480 applications for 200 places; the Saint Petersburg Technological Institute received 1,500 applications for 260 openings.

The Revolution of 1905 had another, even more important effect on

36. M. Kuz'min, "Nasha predmetnaia sistema," *Moskovskii Ezhenedel'nik,* 12 May 1907.

37. Ibid.

38. George Vernadsky, "Iz vospominanii," *Novyi Zhurnal,* no. 100 (1970): 201.

39. Ministerstvo Narodnovo Prosveshcheniia, *Otchët za 1908 god* (Moscow, 1909). No field of study is given for the remaining 180 students.

the university curriculum: a great increase in the number of "scientific circles." These gave the universities an opportunity to explore almost any scientific problem or even controversial social or political question in an atmosphere of close faculty-student contact. Many of these circles functioned under the direction of some of the nation's leading scholars. Maxim Kovalevskii led a circle on constitutional and administrative law; Leonid Petrazhitskii sponsored a group on the philosophy of law. These circles met two to four times a month; a student would prepare an essay to be criticized by the circle as a whole.[40]

These scientific circles brought pressing political and social issues into the academic structure of the universities. The ongoing debate between populists and Marxists attracted a good deal of attention. In Saint Petersburg University, M. Tugan-Baranovskii directed a circle on political economy; students prepared papers on "The Marxist Theory of Value" and held a forum on "Agrarian Disorders in Russia." V. V. Sviatlovskii supervised a circle on labor economics that sponsored debate between populists and Marxists. The work here included tours of local factories.[41] Circles sprang up to discuss every conceivable subject. One group in Saint Petersburg University concentrated on mysticism; weekly discussion topics included the "purpose of life," "God," "woman," and "suicide."

The impact of the circles was not limited to the central universities. In Kiev, rector Tsitovich held a three-hour open debate on scientific socialism. After the debate, the rector took questions from the floor. The debate attracted more than a thousand students.[42] The government refrained from interfering with these groups, at least until Stolypin began to suspect some of them of providing fronts for revolutionary organizations (see below).

Another sign of a new era in the universities was the return of several prominent exiles, including Maxim Kovalevskii, Pavel Vinogradov, and Nikolai Kareev. Kovalevskii's first lecture in Saint Petersburg University filled the main auditorium. When he started to speak, the students' repeated applause forced him to stop.[43] At that time, Kovalevskii stood to

40. *Studenchestvo*, no. 2 (1906).
41. *Studenchestvo*, no. 1 (1906).
42. Ibid. *Studenchestvo*, four issues of which appeared in Saint Petersburg in the fall of 1906, is a superb source on student life during this period. For Moscow's *VUZy*, an excellent counterpart is *Studencheskaia Gazeta*, sixteen issues of which appeared between 1906 and 1908.
43. D. [A. Diakonov], *1905 i 1906gg. v Peterburgskom Universitete* (Saint Petersburg, 1907), p. 105.

the right of the Kadet party and was an obvious example of the bourgeois professors against whom *Iskra* had tried to incite the students in 1905.

Meanwhile the Ministry of Education allowed the faculty councils a good deal of leeway. But there were clouds on the horizon during the 1906–1907 academic year. The 1884 Statute was technically valid; what the ministry granted by circulars, it could likewise take away. More ominously, von Kaufmann relied on the legal force of the statute to appoint politically reliable professors; a case in point was the appointment of Professor Merezhkovskii to the Kazan University medical faculty in October 1906.[44] The Kazan University Faculty Council had opposed Merezhkovskii, whereupon von Kaufmann told the professors that the 27 August Rules did not supersede the right of the minister of education, defined in Article 100 of the 1884 Charter, to appoint professors on his own. For the time being, the ministry did not interfere with the two major universities, but the provincial universities faced a far different situation. These universities were at the mercy of such local governors-general as Kiev's V. A. Sukhomlinov and Odessa's I. N. Tolmachev, who made wide and usually arbitrary use of the powers granted them under the extraordinary decrees. In short, the legal basis for the new policy of liberalization in higher education remained insecure, especially as the ministry made no move to introduce the Tolstoi Conference draft statute into the Duma.

Of course, higher-education policy ultimately depended on the overall policies of the government. Stolypin had already set the stage for a showdown with the professoriate by issuing a 14 September 1906 circular forbidding all "government employees" from joining "political parties, societies, and unions" that showed a "tendency to incite conflict between the government and the population."[45] In Stolypin's eyes, the Kadet party obviously belonged in this category after its celebrated appeal to the population not to pay taxes, as a protest of the dissolution of the first Duma. Two leading professors, L. Petrazhitskii and P. Novgorodtsev, signed the appeal and thus forfeited their professorial chairs.[46] Stolypin's growing distrust of the Kadets held ominous implications for the relations between the professoriate and the government. But the

44. M. K. Korbut, *Kazanskii gosudarstvennyi universitet imeni V. I. Ul'ianova-Lenina za 125 let, 1804/5–1929/30* (Kazan, 1930), vol. 2, p. 242.
45. TsGIA, f. 733, op. 154, d. 160, l. 9.
46. They were, however, permitted to teach as *privat-dozenty*.

most immediate cause of strain was, as usual, sharp conflict between the government and the professors over how to handle the students.

THE STUDENT MOVEMENT

The salient features of the Russian student movement in 1906–1908 were failing confidence in the independent political potential of the *studenchestvo*, confusion about the proper role to be played by students in the newly "autonomous" universities, and a growing realization that the tremendous numerical expansion of the student body posed a fateful challenge to the whole concept of the *studenchestvo* as a distinct estate bound together by common interests, traditions, and principles.

When the universities and other *VUZy* reopened in September 1906 the students seemed, at least on the surface, to have lost little of the political radicalism of the previous fall. Judging by the elections to student government organizations, run on party lines, the *studenchestvo* still preferred Social Democracy—university-style—to the Kadet brand of liberalism. At Saint Petersburg University, for example, the Social Democratic group put twenty delegates on the Council of Elders, compared to four each from the Kadets and the Social Revolutionaries, three from the Polish Socialist party (PPS), and two each from the Trudoviki and nonparty students.[47]

Elections in Moscow University attracted a large turnout—more than 60 percent. The Social Democrats received 2,044 votes, the Kadets 1,462, and the Social Revolutionaries 1,258. The new Central University Organ included twelve Social Democrats, eight Kadets, and seven Social Revolutionaries.[48] Election results indicated greater radicalism among science majors and students from the younger courses. Results from several specialized technical institutes also showed strong leftist sentiment. The institute of civil engineers gave the Socialist bloc 256 votes to the Kadets' 132. In the forestry institute, the student body elected

---

47. *Studenchestvo*, no. 3 (1906).

48. *Studencheskaia Gazeta*, no. 3 (1906). Fragmentary figures permit some insight into the voting patterns of individual departments. From the history and philology faculty, the Social Democrats received 405 votes; the Kadets, 380; and the Social Revolutionaries, 243. Returns from third-, fourth-, and fifth-year medical students gave the Social Democrats 255 votes; the Kadets, 183; and the Social Revolutionaries, 157. First- and second-year medical students, whose returns were combined with students from the natural sciences faculty, gave the Social Democrats 681 votes; the Kadets, 353; and the Social Revolutionaries, 426. From the law faculty, 703 students supported the Social Democrats, 546 voted for the Kadets, and 435 for the Social Revolutionaries.

five Social Democrats, three Trudoviki, two Social Revolutionaries, and only one Kadet to the student government. The students of the Saint Petersburg Mining Institute put four Social Democrats, three Social Revolutionaries, and only two Kadets on the student council. In some places the Kadets made a better showing. In the Saint Petersburg Polytechnic, the student elections gave 508 votes to the Social Democrats, 466 to the Kadets, and 207 to the Social Revolutionaries. In the communications institute, with a 90 percent turnout, the Kadets won four seats on the student council, compared to three each for the Social Democrats, the Social Revolutionaries, and the "academic" party.[49]

But, as in the fall of 1905, the strident rhetoric of the *skhodki* masked the students' fundamental ambivalence about committed activism and their political role. Addressing the inaugural *skhodka* of the 1906–1907 academic year, a leader of the Saint Petersburg University Council of Elders discussed the lessons of the Revolution of 1905 and its political implications for the student movement: "The revolutionary year has transformed the position of the students. The role of [the *studenchestvo*] as a lonely political fighter, which we indeed had until last year, is now part of the past. . . . The revolutionary army has grown and, unlike in the past, it no longer needs constant 'initiatives.'"[50] But the workers and the peasants were now retreating from their violent confrontations with the autocracy, under the impact of fatigue, punitive expeditions, and martial law. As the popular movement ebbed, what should the students do? Should they take up their self-proclaimed role as "lonely fighters" once again, or should they use the revolutionary experience to rethink the place of the student movement?

The students were eager to maintain their verbal alliance with the revolutionary movement as long as this did not preclude their getting back to the classroom and making up for lost time. Boris Frommet, a veteran of the Saint Petersburg student movement, summed up the mood of the *skhodki* in September 1906:

49. These figures come from various issues of *Studenchestvo* and *Studencheskaia Gazeta*. The Soviet historian A. E. Ivanov tabulated voting results from eight *VUZy* with a total enrollment of 25,677 students: the military medical institute, the mining institute, the womens' medical institute, the Tomsk Technological Institute, and Kiev, Tomsk, Moscow, and Saint Petersburg universities. The number of students voting was 12,996, about half the total. Social Democrats received 5,372 votes, Social Revolutionaries 3,278, Kadets 2,680, and Trudoviki 434; other lists received the remaining 1,232 votes ("Demokraticheskoe studenchestvo v revoliutsii 1905–07gg.," *Istoricheskie Zapiski*, no. 107 [1982]: 209). This article must be used with some caution, especially because it tends to confuse "Social Democrat" with "Bolshevik" and fails to make any use of the contemporary student press, a source that would have acted as a corrective.

50. Diakonov, *1905 i 1906gg.*, p. 73.

[The students] elected socialists to the Council of Elders and warmly applauded inflammatory speeches. . . . They liked the idea that the leaders of
the revolutionary parties were using the universities as meeting places. On
the one hand, this made it seem to them that they were in fact helping the
cause of [political] liberation but, on the other hand, they themselves would
be left free to study. *The studenchestvo was happy that nobody kept it from
studying.* This was the clear impression of those who experienced the 1906–
1907 academic year, attentively observed the dominant mood, and participated in both the revolutionary and the student movement.[51]

The ambivalent attitude toward the revolutionary movement affected
even the relatively more committed students who joined the party factions, especially those of the Social Democrats. One speaker at a meeting of the Saint Petersburg University Social Democrats complained of
their complete isolation from the regular Saint Petersburg City Social
Democratic Committee. Some members of that faction called for a more
active political stance; others saw the group's primary mission to be
propagandizing the "Marxist viewpoint in all areas of university life."
The faction, after some debate, adopted a resolution supporting the primacy of "cultural" over "political" work and elected a bureau composed of three Bolsheviks, three Mensheviks, and two Bundists. One
observer of the student Social Democrats noted that their heroes were
Struve and Tugan-Baranovskii, not Lenin and Plekhanov.[52]

It is not surprising, then, that the Russian Social Democratic party,
hard-pressed to maintain its standing and organizations after the decline of the revolution, tried and failed to harness the nominally Social
Democratic students for its own purposes. In the spring of 1907, after
the arrest of the Social Democratic deputies to the second Duma, the
Central Committee of the party called on the students to strike in support of the deputies and demonstrate against Stolypin. Student government organs in the city's *VUZy*, mostly dominated by Social Democrats, decided to ignore the order.[53]

51. B. Frommet, *Ocherki po istorii studenchestva v Rossii* (Saint Petersburg, 1912),
p. 85 (italics in original). The resolution passed at Saint Petersburg University by 1,203 to
141 was typical: "Whereas the strike as a form of passive protest no longer corresponds to
the present needs of the revolution; whereas an open university, as the past year showed,
plays an enormously positive role in the further development of the revolutionary struggle;
whereas the interests of the general revolutionary movement demands the concentration
of the *studenchestvo* in the large cities and its mobilization as one of the legions of
revolutionary democracy: therefore, the general student *skhodka* resolves to open the
university."
52. *Studencheskaia Rech'*, 15 November 1907; Alexei Iarmolovich, *Smert' Prizrakov*
(Saint Petersburg, 1908), p. 9.
53. *Delo soveta studencheskikh predstavitelei Kievskovo Universiteta* (Kiev, 1908),
p. 9.

Within Saint Petersburg University itself the domination of the left in student politics started to erode during 1906–1907 and 1907–1908. In September 1907 the Kadets boosted their representation on the Council of Elders from four to twelve. (This new council consisted of eighteen Social Democrats, twelve Kadets, and eleven Social Revolutionaries.) According to a contemporary pamphlet, "student socialism was not quite Bernsteinism and not quite Kadetism, but to put it quite simply, bourgeois radicalism."[54]

The reappraisal of the potential political role of the *studenchestvo* can be followed in the student press, which became an important factor in Russian student life after the Revolution of 1905.[55] With so many new students, how could anyone still speak of the *studenchestvo?* One student newspaper wrote:

> Students face a dilemma. The old methods of struggle have been rejected . . . but the struggle against the autocracy is not finished. . . . The tactic of the student strike has already been condemned. . . . We had enough unity to protest but not enough to follow through a struggle for the attainment of definite aims. . . . The sociopolitical differentiation of the *studenchestvo* is now obvious to everyone. . . . The loud slogan of the "united *studenchestvo*" as the "vanguard of the revolutionary democracy" figured, with impressive consistency, in all the resolutions of the old *skhodki*. But now it has become an obvious fiction.[56]

There were other signs of this "crisis of the *studenchestvo*." In the fall of 1906 the Council of Elders of Saint Petersburg University rejected an appeal from the student governments of Iur'ev and Kharkov universities for united student action to protest the repressive policies of local authorities against students and professors at those universities. The Saint Petersburg Council of Elders replied that it did not believe in a "united student movement."[57]

The student movement also came in for increasing attack from the liberal camp, especially in A. S. Izgoev's article in the controversial collection of essays entitled *Vekhi*.[58] Izgoev attacked the students for their

54. Iarmolovich, *Smert' Prizrakov*, p. 9.
55. An excellent overview of the student press can be found in S. G. Svatikov, ed., *Put' studenchestva* (Petrograd, 1916), pp. 221–240.
56. M. Podshibiakin, "Staroe i novoe v studenchestve," *Studencheskaia Rech'*, 15 November 1907; on the same theme, see N. Tikhonovich, "Politicheskaia differentsiatsiia studenchestva," *Studenchestvo*, no. 3 (1906).
57. "Ocherednoi vopros," *Studencheskaia Rech'*, 15 November 1907.
58. A. S. Izgoev, "Ob intelligentnoi molodëzhi," *Vekhi: Sbornik statei o russkoi intelligentsii* (Moscow, 1910), pp. 97–124.

intolerance of dissenting viewpoints in their peer group; for their physical weakness in comparison to West European students; for their sexual promiscuity and tendency to masturbate; for their lack of family ties; and for their laziness and unwillingness to take their studies seriously. Izgoev's article approvingly quoted V. V. Rozanov's assertion that Russia's students resembled the old Zaporozhe Cossacks "with their unique customs and unique lifestyle."

In no other country, he complained, did the surrounding society so idealize a separate student subculture. But this subculture, Izgoev asserted, harmed the interests of the Russian nation by crippling the spirit of the professional classes. The average *intelligent*, "upon leaving this subculture, remains in limbo; he doesn't enter any other culture. . . . As long as he is in the university he feels that he has [an identity] but when he leaves he feels that he doesn't have anything." Izgoev thanked the students for their past services in the liberation movement but reminded them that now the Russian public had other priorities. A functioning Duma and political parties had now enabled adults to assume the students' former burden. Times had changed: "The Russian public demands [of the *studenchestvo*] knowledge, willingness to work, and moral restraint."[59]

One of the most important developments of the post-revolutionary period was the Kadet-led attack on the authority of the *skhodka* and, by implication, on the whole notion of *studenchestvo*. The student Kadet factions claimed that the *skhodka* was an anachronistic holdover from days when universities were much smaller and students felt that they had more in common. The *skhodka*, they asserted, gave a distorted picture of student opinon and tended to favor extremists. Open voting and the chaotic atmosphere discouraged dissent and dissuaded moderate students from attending. They proposed replacing the *skhodka* with closed-ballot referenda to decide major matters such as strikes. Student government organs, elected on the basis of proportional representation, would handle routine matters. The Social Democrats and Social Revolutionaries protested the Kadet proposals—and the *skhodka* emerged as a major issue in student politics during the 1906–1907 academic year.

The left argued that the *skhodka* was the most important tradition of

59. In the same vein, see V. Levchenko, "Krizis universitetskoi zhizni," *Russkaia Mysl'*, no. 5 (May 1908); E. N. Trubetskoi, "K nachalu uchebnovo goda," *Moskovskii Ezhenedel'nik*, no. 25 (1906). Levchenko attacked the student subculture for its conformity and intolerance of dissenting viewpoints. Trubetskoi asserted that student disorders had lost their point, except as a demonstration of the "mass suicide of the intelligentsia."

the *studenchestvo*, a reminder that it possessed a "general will" that
found expression in direct democracy and that could unite the *studenchestvo* in immediate and collective action to defend its rights. The Kadets proclaimed that the "university should not be sacrificed for the agitational demands of the moment," but the Social Democrats and Social
Revolutionaries warned that

> the struggle over the *skhodka* will settle the question of whether the time has
> come for the *studenchestvo* to stop participating in the political life of the
> country and whether the battle for academic rights is finished. A rejection of
> the *skhodka* would mean a historic turning point in the history of the student
> movement. It would show that the professional interests of the students are
> fully satisfied by the existing [university autonomy] and that finally the professors' dream of Russia's students accepting a peaceful academic life has
> been realized.[60]

A showdown election on the issue at Moscow University gave the left
2,402 votes to the Kadets' 1,765.[61]

The "crisis of the *studenchestvo*" reflected in part the tension between the political and social changes brought about by the Revolution
of 1905, and traditional concepts of student identity. But on a deeper
level this period of reevaluation was less of a break with the history of
the *studenchestvo* than appeared at first glance. The students' perennial
insecurity about their place, political and social, had not changed. Just
as the students of 1899 had envied the alleged moral superiority of the
generation of the 1870s, so too did the post-1905 students exaggerate
the political dedication and importance of the 1899–1902 student
movement and bemoan their inability to live up to the allegedly higher
standards of an earlier era.

But the post-1905 reevaluation did produce a new ideology of the
student movement: "student professionalism," or the view that the best
way for the student movement to fulfill its democratic obligations was
to concentrate on the economic needs of the *studenchestvo*, even at the
cost of foregoing direct political confrontation with the government on
nonstudent issues. As has been shown, the Revolution of 1905 made
higher education more accessible, but the large influx of new students
aggravated the chronic competition for financial aid and part-time jobs.

60. For a good exposition of the Kadet student viewpoint, see George Vernadsky,
"Pis'mo iz Moskvy," *Studencheskaia Rech'*, 15 November 1907; also *Studencheskaia
Gazeta*, no. 11 (1906). The case for the *skhodka* can be followed in Rafael Vydrin,
Osnovnye momenty studencheskovo dvizheniia v Rossii (Moscow, 1908), p. 63.
61. *Russkie Vedomosti*, 10 March 1907.

Newly formed student cooperatives, along with the older *zemliachestva*, struggled to fill the gap.

Student mutual aid had, of course, long been a mainstay of Russian university life. What was new was the ideological ratification, by some leading student newspapers and commentators, of "student professionalism" as *the* raison d'être of the student movement. One observer noted that "[mutual aid] organizations existed before but the students are like Molière's bourgeois who spoke prose all his life and did not know it."[62]

There were some good reasons for the students to act like Molière's bourgeois, all of which were closely connected with the inner dynamics of the student movement. By its very nature, the *studenchestvo* was constantly in flux, especially during the hectic period following the revolution. The ideas of the student movement that had penetrated the secondary schools gave a somewhat romanticized picture of student life, focusing on the political role of the student movement and the radical nature of the student government organs.

In fact the changes in university affairs brought about by the revolution gave these formally radical bodies a new and important function: working with the professors to determine which students most deserved economic help. These organs of student government, dominated by Social Democrat and Social Revolutionary majorities, clung to the rhetorical slogan of "using the universities for the revolution when the time was ripe," but in fact they became vital intermediaries between the faculty councils and the student body on such issues as scholarships, control over the dining halls, and the status of various student organizations in the universities.[63] These bodies also tried, largely unsuccessfully, to regulate the chaotic student employment market by asking students seeking tutoring and other posts to register at central exchanges which would allocate available jobs according to need.

These changes reinforced a growing view that the student movement had at last found a purpose consistent with its character, constituency, and political strength. By 1908, students from various *VUZy* were

62. Frommet, *Ocherki po istorii studenchestva*, p. 93.
63. There are many references to the fact that the political student organizations actually devoted much of their time to serving students' professional interests. For a professor's account of the cooperation between the leftist-dominated student government and the Saint Petersburg University Faculty Council, see Ivan Grevs, "Stroitel'stvo i razrushenie v nashei vysshei shkole," *Pravo*, nos. 29, 31 (1908). For an account of the activities of the Kiev University student government, see the protocol of the trial of its leading members in 1908 (*Delo soveta studencheskikh*, pp. 20–42, 83–86).

organizing conferences to discuss this new "student professionalism."[64] Clearly, traditional *zemliachestva* and new types of mutual aid societies were showing what many observers considered to be surprising vitality. A major conference of this type met in Saint Petersburg in March 1908 to discuss the problems of the *zemliachestva* and the new student credit associations.[65]

During the 1907–1908 academic year there were 134 *zemliachestva* in Saint Petersburg University alone. Of these, 62 reported a combined membership of 1,581 students. Forty-three of these *zemliachestva* reported giving out more than 20,000 rubles in aid; this compared with 110,000 rubles in aid and scholarships from the university and 14,000 rubles from the Society to Aid Needy Students. In Moscow University in 1909 there were 77 mutual help organizations, mostly *zemliachestva*.

As was the case in the pre-1905 period, the *zemliachestva* received 60 to 90 percent of their income from balls and other charitable affairs organized in the provinces. They thus continued to constitute a major link between the *studenchestvo* and provincial Russian society. But some observers, especially student newspapers such as *Studencheskii Mir* and *Golos Studenchestva,* began to point out the defects of the *zemliachestva*. Too many students, they said, failed to pay back loans; *zemliachestva* depended too much on charity and did too little to develop self-reliance.[66] They called for the institution of new kinds of student organizations.

Indeed, the post-1905 period saw the development of student credit associations and consumer cooperatives. They differed from the *zemliachestva* in that they were not based on the members' common origin in a particular locality but, rather, were open to all students in the particular university town. Some of these organizations became quite large. By 1912, the credit union of the Moscow University juridical faculty operated enterprises grossing over 50,000 rubles a year.[67] All these organizations faced harassment by local authorities.[68]

The advocacy of student professionalism opened a new debate. Some

---

64. The best single account of "student professionalism" is P. Trofimov, "Itogi i perspektivy studencheskovo ekonomicheskovo dvizheniia: 1905–1915," in Svatikov, ed., *Put' studenchestva,* pp. 168–180.

65. *Trudy soveshchaniia predstavitelei studencheskikh ekonomicheskikh organizatsii o nuzhdakh studenchestva* (Saint Petersburg, 1908).

66. In 1909, for example, the Perm *zemliachestvo* of Saint Petersburg University had 267 debtors owing 12,124 rubles in bad debts.

67. Frommet, *Ocherki po istorii studenchestva,* p. 98.

68. If they met off the premises of the *VUZ* all student organizations had to register, to fulfill the requirements of the 4 March 1906 Rules on Organizations and Meetings.

leftists charged that the growing interest in corporate concerns was a betrayal of the student traditions of self-sacrifice and political involvement. The students were aping the general drift of the intelligentsia from altrustic concern for the poor toward bourgeois selfishness; the "crisis of the *studenchestvo*" replicated the "crisis of the intelligentsia" in miniature. Indeed, critics charged, Russian students were finally taking the bourgeois road of their post-1848 German counterparts.

Leading organs of the new student press, especially *Studencheskii Mir* and *Golos Studenchestva,* rose to the defense of the new ideology. Rafael Vydrin, the editor of *Golos Studenchestva,* attacked the view that student professionalism betrayed older traditions. "At the present time," he wrote, "the *studenchestvo* is as far away from the naive academism of the 1860–1890 period as it is from the political messianism of 1900–1905." The autocracy had punctured the "academic illusions" that the student movement could obtain academic and corporate reforms outside the context of more general political reform. But the Revolution of 1905 showed that student demonstrations had little independent political force: "Student professionalism combines two stages of the student movement: the academic and the sociopolitical [*obshchestvennyi*]. Any struggle for a free school [cannot be separated from] the struggle for a free state and [vice versa]."[69] The social composition of the *studenchestvo* guaranteed that the student movement, even while fighting for the attainment of student corporate interests, would not abandon the wider goal of a democratic Russia:

> Three factors make student professionalism a synthesis of the political and academic movements: the lack of firm constitutional guarantees in the country, the democratic composition of the student body, and the rich experience of the student professional movement. . . . The experience of the student movement, which has worked out the methods of struggle for the democratization of higher education, should guarantee that the *haute bourgeoisie* will not come to dominate higher education, as was the case in the West after the student disturbances of 1848.[70]

Vydrin's basic point, that student professionalism continued rather than violated the students' traditional view of themselves as "adversaries of the system," was corroborated by the results of the various elections during this period as well as by the findings of such surveys as the Saint Petersburg Technological Institute census conducted during

69. *Golos Studenchestva,* 9 December 1910.
70. Ibid.

the 1908–1909 academic year.[71] The census showed the continued strength of leftist sympathies but also demonstrated that incoming students were somewhat more moderate than their older colleagues. In response to the question "With which of the following political parties are you most sympathetic?" 25.3 percent answered that they sympathized with the Social Democrats, 20.7 percent favored the Kadets, 20.6 percent professed no party sympathies, 12.4 percent supported the Social Revolutionaries, and 10 percent favored an undefined "left." The anarchists, the Octobrists, the "moderate right," the Union of the Russian People, and other minor parties drew the support of 3 percent, 2.3 percent, 1.9 percent, 1 percent, and 2 percent, respectively. The census also showed some correlation between political preference and both financial status and anti-Semitism. Students who said that they supported the Social Democrats or the Social Revolutionaries indicated that they lived on an average budget of 33 rubles a month, while Kadets spent 40 rubles a month, and Octobrists, 44. Whereas 84.5 percent of the Social Democrats and 74.2 percent of the Social Revolutionaries favored equal rights for the Jews, barely half of the Kadets, one-third of the nonpartisan students, and only 8.7 percent of the Octobrists did so.

Despite the students' political preferences, the overwhelming majority, when asked about their reading habits, preferred fiction to social science and philosophy. Responding to the question "Which of the following do you ordinarily read?" 80.3 percent indicated fiction, 39.1 percent the technical sciences, 38 percent the social sciences, and 30 percent philosophy. Figures for students preferring Social Democracy still showed that 82 percent ordinarily read fiction, only 29 percent read the technical sciences, 38 percent the social sciences, and 30 percent philosophy. However, 40 percent of the Kadet students, 48 percent of the Octobrists, 53 percent of the moderate right students, and 51 percent of the nonpartisan students indicated that they read in the technical sciences. Given the fact that the census was conducted in a technical institute, this may imply some correlation between political moderation and certainty about career plans.

Indeed, only 39.6 percent of the students said that they had definitely

71. M. V. Bernadskii, ed., *K kharakteristike sovremennovo studenchestva* (Saint Petersburg, 1910). The response rate to this census exceeded 50 percent: 1,021 students submitted completed questionnaires. In 1906 the student government at the institute included six Social Democrats, four Kadets, and three Social Revolutionaries. Corresponding figures for 1908 were four Social Democrats, three Kadets, three Social Revolutionaries, one "Socialist," and two nonparty students.

decided on a technical career (33 percent of the Social Democrats, 44.4 percent of the Kadets, and more than half of the rightist students). A comparison of this uncertainty with a 1903 census taken at the same institute is instructive. In 1903, 27 percent of the first-year students indicated that they were unhappy with their course of studies, and this jumped to 45 percent for fourth-year students and 68 percent for fifth-year students. In view of the fact that schools such as the Saint Petersburg Technological Institute offered better and more highly paid employment opportunities than did the universities, at least for first jobs, and were more selective in their admissions policy, the assumption is warranted that this high level of uncertainty about career prospects and dissatisfaction with the curriculum was at least as strong in the universities.

The census also showed that the tradition of the student *skhodka* remained strong at the institute, although less so than in the past, according to the census's editor. Of the students, 70.2 percent indicated that they usually attended *skhodki:* 81.5 percent of the Social Democrats, 87.6 percent of the Social Revolutionaries, 62.2 percent of the Kadets, 52 percent of the Octobrists, and 53 percent of the nonpartisan students.

The census gained wide acceptance in both the student and the general press as a reliable indicator of student moods. The editor's assertion that the students at the technological institute reflected the general mood and social physiognomy of the *studenchestvo* as a whole provoked no argument. The editor concluded that despite important changes in the *VUZy* since 1905, "the general mood of the *studenchestvo* has not changed." The *studenchestvo* still reflected Russia's middle classes, uneasily perched between the masses and the government. "Despite the great diversity of social ideals and the conflict of various political views, one fact basically remains: [Russian society and the *studenchestvo*] have in essence [refused to accept] Stolypin's policy of 'normalization.'"[72]

If few students were willing to jeopardize their lives by engaging in direct revolutionary action, the *studenchestvo* as a whole had little use for any party to the right of the Kadets. In short, student radicalism remained; what changed was its political context.

STOLYPIN AND THE STUDENTS

Although the students were less inclined than ever to protest over political issues, the development of student professionalism portended

72. Bernadskii, *K kharakteristike sovremennovo studenchestva,* p. viii.

sharp conflicts between the students and the government if the latter tried to erase the gains of the Revolution of 1905. A vital determinant of government education policy after 1905 was to be Prime Minister Stolypin's determination to crush the student movement. Seemingly unaware of the preoccupation of the student movement with internal concerns, Stolypin framed his policies on the assumption that the student movement was giving aid and comfort to the revolutionary movement and hindered the restoration of the government's authority.

From the beginning of the 1906–1907 academic year, Stolypin and the Ministry of the Interior took an intense interest in what was going on in the institutions of higher education. They were especially concerned about continued use of university premises for secret meetings by nonstudents and revolutionary organizations, as well as about frequent *skhodki,* which disrupted the normal functioning of classes.

During the first few months of the academic year there were scattered sharp conflicts between the student government organs and the faculty councils. The most important of these conflicts took place in Moscow University, which closed for brief periods in October and December over disputes between the Central University Organ and the faculty council concerning the time and place of *skhodki* and the role of the CUO in university governance.[73] Problems arose in Kazan and Kharkov universities over student boycotts of rightist professors and in Kiev over the decision of the faculty council to reintroduce an equivalent of the old inspectorate. Much of the tension between students and professors grew out of economic issues. Many students, for example, needed certificates of good standing from the faculty councils in order to get police permission to remain in the university towns, especially Moscow and Saint Petersburg. But the faculty councils refused to issue these certificates unless the students had paid all their outstanding bills. Martial law in the university towns complicated an already touchy situation.

To an increasing extent, government policy toward the student movement became intertwined with Stolypin's general course of suppression of the revolutionary movement in the country. Almost immediately Stolypin showed that he took seriously the bombastic *skhodki* resolutions about "using the universities in the interests of the revolution when the time is ripe." The prime minister quickly began bombarding von Kaufmann with letters reiterating his concern and urging firm ac-

73. *Studencheskaia Gazeta* wrote that these conflicts underscored the "alienation of the student movement from the liberal camp."

tion by the Ministry of Education. At the beginning of October, Stolypin complained to von Kaufmann that although most students were willing to get down to serious academic work, "the revolutionary minority is still in charge. . . . Students at Saint Petersburg University are so used to being free to hold meetings and discussions in the university that the latter has become a 'Republic in the Capital of the Autocracy.'" Stolypin hailed the decision by the Kiev governor-general to use troops to break up a *skhodka* that nonstudents were suspected of attending and pointed out to the minister of education that this had had a "sobering effect on students and teachers."[74]

In addition to Stolypin's pressure on von Kaufmann, the local governors kept threatening to send troops into the universities if the rectors did not prevent disorders; these threats in turn made professors especially sensitive to the timing and location of *skhodki* and created additional friction between the faculty councils and the student government organs. Relations between the local authorities and the universities were especially poor in Moscow and Odessa and served to remind the faculty councils of the increasingly parlous position of the 27 August Rules —or at least of their interpretation of them.

On 16 October, Glagolev, the temporary governor-general of Odessa, told professor Zanchevskii, the rector of Odessa University, that the 27 August Rules "did not give the university the right of extraterritoriality." Stolypin supported Glagolev and told von Kaufmann to make sure that the faculty council cooperated with the Odessa administration. A. A. Makarov, the assistant minister of the interior, told von Kaufmann that the university was in the hands of a "group of revolutionary students acting in league with the junior faculty."[75] For good measure he complained that the university was the scene of frequent sexual orgies.

Stolypin also rejected Zanchevskii's petition to permit Professor E. N. Shchepkin, a leading member of the Academic Union, to return to Odessa. Shchepkin had been expelled by the local administration at the beginning of 1906, and his difficulties illustrated the extent to which the situation of the provincial universities was adversely affected by the broad powers granted to local administrations under the provisions of

74. TsGIA, f. 733, op. 153, d. 213, l. 48. On continued use of VUZy premises by outsiders and revolutionary organizations, see Ivan Korel', "Peterburgskii Universitet v 1905 godu," *Leningradskii Universitet,* 21 January 1939; A. E. Ivanov, "Demokraticheskoe studenchestvo," p. 210.
75. TsGIA, f. 733, op. 153, d. 267, l. 111.

martial law. Apparently the safeguards of the 27 August Rules were already a dead letter in some of the provinces. When Odessa and Iur'ev universities were searched by troops in the spring of 1906, neither the Ministry of Education nor the local rector was informed beforehand. Furthermore, continuing efforts to secure the return of Kharkov University's Professor Gredeskul, sentenced to four years of exile in December 1905, were unsuccessful.[76]

Tensions between the local authorities and the university also rose in Moscow, where A. A. Reinbot, the Moscow governor-general, warned rector Manuilov to stop *skhodki* at all costs—including calling in troops to restore order. Worried by this implied threat, the faculty asked for an urgent meeting with Stolypin on 3 October. Stolypin promised the faculty delegation that the local authorities would leave the university alone as long as the professors agreed to keep outsiders away from the university premises. But the guarantees did not improve matters.[77] On 13 December 1906, governor-general Reinbot told rector Manuilov that he had no right to negotiate with the student Central University Organ and demanded that Manuilov give him a list of its members. Manuilov refused, and the Moscow authorities directed their fire at von Kaufmann, asking him in a sharply worded note whether it was the policy of the Ministry of Education to tolerate "clearly revolutionary organizations" (meaning the CUO) in the universities.[78]

On 2 April 1907, von Kaufmann, under growing pressure from the government, summoned the nine university rectors to a high-level meeting to discuss the student movement and student organizations. The minister opened the conference by stating that he was aware that most students had settled down to hard work during the current academic year. But von Kaufmann warned the rectors to expect an imminent change in government university policy, especially because they seemed incapable of expelling "revolutionary organizations" from the universities.

> I do not tremble when I read the resolutions of the . . . *skhodki* in the newspapers; I do not get worried when students boastingly call themselves Social Democrats and Social Revolutionaries. . . . But I am really distressed when I hear that the revolutionary organizations have penetrated the institutions of

---

76. On the exile of Gredeskul, a prominent member of the Academic Union and the Kadet party, see TsGIA, f. 733, op. 153, d. 164. The then minister of the interior, P. N. Durnovo, rejected I. I. Tolstoi's appeal to free Gredeskul. Gredeskul, according to Durnovo, was a "prominent Social Democrat" and a ringleader of the revolutionary movement.

77. For the correspondence between Reinbot and rector Manuilov concerning the situation in Moscow University from 1906 to 1908, see GPB im. V. I. Lenina, f. 158, folder 3.

78. TsGIA, f. 733, op. 153, d. 553, l. 7.

higher education. I am distressed when I learn that these groups, few in number, hold in terror the majority that wants to study.[79]

Von Kaufmann then warned the rectors that they bore a major share of the blame, especially because they tended to misinterpret the 27 August 1905 Rules.

The rectors' replies showed an interpretation of the student movement radically different from that held by Stolypin. Professor I. I. Borgman of Saint Petersburg University declared that the Council of Elders at the university posed no problem, since it pursued academic and professional rather than political goals. Moscow's Manuilov told the conference that the Central University Organ "seemed political on the surface but really had goals of a fundamentally academic and corporate character—more specifically, the attainment of an equal role for students in the running of the university." Manuilov warned against a repressive policy. The student movement was in the process of shifting away from politics toward concern with corporate issues; in time, Manuilov continued, the *zemliachestva* and the credit unions would displace the influence of such central student government organs as the CUO. The right course was to sit and wait, not overreact. With the exception of Kiev's Tsitovich, the provincial rectors backed Borgman and Manuilov.[80]

The conference also discussed such matters as allocation of financial aid, rules governing student *skhodki,* and the question of auditors. Both von Kaufmann and Assistant Minister of the Interior Makarov, Stolypin's deputy attending the 7 April session, told the rectors that the government was unhappy about several issues in the universities. Von Kaufmann warned that the "influx of auditors was an anomaly which should cease." He also announced that the ministry was about to draft new rules governing the professors' disciplinary court. Several rectors rejoined that student discipline was the business of the faculty, not the ministry. The rectors also opposed Makarov's and von Kaufmann's suggestion that student *skhodki* be outlawed.

NEW RULES

A few weeks later the Council of Ministers met and decided to show the professors "where the rights granted by the *ukase* of 27 August

79. TsGIA, f. 1276, op. 3, d. 800, ll. 56–87.
80. Iur'ev's rector Passek described with some exaggeration the growing political moderation of the students: "The typical first-year student is a Social Revolutionary. The second-year student is a Social Democrat. The third-year student is a Kadet, and the

1905 end and where the direct abuse of these rights begins."[81] According to the council, the 27 August Rules did no more than allow the faculty councils to elect rectors and deacons to assume jurisdiction over internal academic affairs. The professors had abused their mandate by using the cover of autonomy to condone anti-government student organizations. Many professors had become "carried away" during the recent revolution (*smuta*) and allowed student organizations to tell them what to do.

In a sweeping attempt to suppress the student movement, the Council of Ministers issued new guidelines on student organizations, the 11 June 1907 Rules. The new rules banned university or institutionwide student government organizations and barred faculty councils from contact with such organizations. They allowed only those student meetings that had a clearly "academic character," and they gave the police the right to attend meetings and stop them when they strayed from their stated agenda. All student meetings required the approval of the rector, who had to record his decision and the subject of the proposed meeting in a book that was open to police inspection. Students could attend meetings only at their own institution. Furthermore, the 11 June Rules affected all *VUZy*, not just those associated with the Ministry of Education. The council warned the professors to expect further "clarifications" of the 27 August Rules "with a view toward inculcating in [the faculty] a consciousness of the responsibilities they bear for the maintenance of the orderly course of academic life."[82]

The Russian public linked the new rules to Stolypin's coup d'état of 3 June, which unilaterally changed the Duma electoral law to strengthen the influence of the landowners. The new university action appeared to be an integral part of a wider policy aimed at crippling potential opposition and forging a firmer base of support for the regime. In any event, it appeared as if Stolypin had succeeded in his gamble. The 3 June bombshell failed to spark significant protest, and nobody expected any major student reaction to the 11 June Rules. Besides, it was summer vacation.

Only one party, the Social Revolutionaries, tried to goad the students into massive protest.[83] But the returning students turned a deaf ear to

---

fourth-year student already stands to the right of the Kadets" (TsGIA, f. 1276, op. 3, d. 800, l. 61).

81. TsGIA, f. 733, op. 226, d. 122, ll. 20–26 ("Osobyi zhurnal Soveta Ministrov po proektu pravil o studencheskikh organizatsiiakh i ob ustroistve sobranii v stenakh VUZov").

82. Ibid.

83. *Znamia Truda*, 30 August 1907. In pleading with the students to take to the streets in September, the Social Revolutionaries emphasized that, unlike the Marxists,

the party's appeal. A powerful deterrent to united student protest, apart from the realization that they would be acting alone and with scant hope of success, was the discovery of a large loophole in the 11 June Rules. The rules barred all student organizations based on universitywide vote but said nothing about forbidding the faculty councils to deal with student organizations elected by faculty or course. Keeping this in mind, the various student *skhodki* in September 1907 voted against a national student protest strike. The leftist factions, of course, responded to this attitude with loud disapproval. Social Revolutionary orators accused the students at Moscow University of "profound political apathy." A *skhodka* called for 12 September fell five hundred students short of the two thousand required to make its resolutions binding on the student body.[84] At Saint Petersburg University a coalition of Mensheviks and Kadets derailed a Social Revolutionary- and Bolshevik-sponsored strike resolution. The situation was no different at other VUZy. The Odessa *Studencheskii Golos* complained of the *studenchestvo*'s spirit of "meek submission."[85]

There was more willingness to support individual students who were arrested, but these short protest strikes remained localized. On 9 October Moscow University students struck for one day to protest the execution of two students from the Moscow Technological Institute on charges of terrorism. There were other short strikes, for similar reasons, in the Kiev Polytechnic Institute, the Tomsk Technological Institute, and Iur'ev University.[86]

Trouble soon came from another direction—the professors' disciplinary court of Kiev University, now firmly in conservative hands. As has been stated above, the provincial universities were in a much worse position than their central counterparts, especially when the local right enjoyed close contacts with the police and military government authorities. At the end of October the Kiev branch of the Union of the Russian People charged that the students were planning a commemoration of Balmashev's 3 November 1902 execution. On 1 November the police arrested the twenty-six members of the Kiev University Council of Student Representatives. Student protesters then marched into the university and began disrupting classes. On 5 November the police surrounded the

---

they had never seen the students only as a "reservoir whose sole value was to furnish potential recruits for the party." Instead they reiterated their respect and appreciation for the student movement as an independent force.

84. GPB im. V. I. Lenina, f. 158, folder 3, ed. kh. 42.
85. *Studencheskii Golos*, no. 1 (1907).
86. *Vestnik Vospitaniia*, no. 4 (1908).

building and took down the names of all suspected demonstrators.[87] The faculty council then voted to close the university until 12 November.

An angry Stolypin now intervened, lambasting the professors for their decision to close the university instead of solving the problem by a blanket expulsion of all suspected troublemakers.[88] Closed universities, he argued, reflected poorly on the government and raised doubts about its ability to maintain control.

The faculty council took Stolypin at his word. When classes resumed and the students called a new *skhodka* on 17 November to discuss the fate of their arrested comrades, police surrounded the meeting and transmitted the names of all the participants to the professors' disciplinary court. The court then voted to suspend 719 students for one year, an unusually severe punishment.

The Kiev affair touched off short strikes and *skhodki* in other *VUZy* and led to a nationwide conference to discuss the political situation of the *studenchestvo*.[89] The conference, which met in Saint Petersburg on 26 and 27 January 1908, attracted more than seventy delegates from various *VUZy*, including thirty-four Social Democrats, twenty-four Social Revolutionaries, and twelve Kadets. The delegates' reports gave a revealing picture of the student movement at various institutions of higher education, but the meeting could not reach consensus on what tactics the *studenchestvo* should pursue on a national scale. The Social Revolutionaries wanted an activist policy, arguing that students should fan local conflicts with professors and police in order to set off a national academic strike. But the Social Democratic delegates repeated the familiar argument that the era of independent student action was gone: the students had to wait for the workers. The Kadets also opposed a strike. They recognized the seriousness of Stolypin's attack on the gains of 1905 but warned that the students were too isolated to make any effective protest. Unable to agree on a plan, the conference dispersed, after calling for another meeting in September.

Meanwhile, in the aftermath of the Kiev affair, the right escalated its attacks on von Kaufmann (and, by implication, Stolypin), accusing the minister of laxity in dealing with the threatening student movement. The leading editorial writer of the influential *Novoe Vremia*, M. O. Men'shikov, emerged as von Kaufmann's most dangerous critic. Men'shi-

---

87. TsGIA, f. 733, op. 154, d. 192.
88. TsGIA, f. 1276, op. 1, d. 731.
89. TsGIA, f. 733, op. 154, d. 159, l. 5.

kov even attacked the mass suspension from Kiev University, on the grounds that the students, free to go elsewhere, would start trouble in other universities and thus "give the Kadets [*sic*] exactly what they wanted."[90] The criticism hit home. A nervous Stolypin told von Kaufmann to make sure that the suspended students were not admitted to other universities.[91] The prime minister also forwarded to von Kaufmann the barrage of protest telegrams from the Union of the Russian People, charging professors and students at various universities with treason, terrorism, and other offenses.[92]

By now the university question had joined anti-Semitism as a staple of right-wing politics. Stolypin worried about this new threat to his flanks. After all, the tsar wore the lapel pin of the Union of the Russian People, an organization that cordially detested the prime minister for his efforts to work with the Duma. Furthermore, Stolypin's attempt to curtail the power of the aristocracy in local government won him few friends in the influential Council of the United Nobility. Another problem for Stolypin was the conservative group in the State Council, headed by P. N. Durnovo and V. F. Trepov.[93] With so many enemies after his political hide, Stolypin could not afford "disorders" in the *VUZy* and grew more impatient with the Ministry of Education.

At year's end, leading professors were worried about the new crusade against the universities and how it would affect Stolypin's policies. V. I. Vernadskii, in a year-end review in *Rech'*, warned his colleagues that although the historic threat from the revolutionary movement had ebbed, the universities faced a dangerous challenge from the right. The big question now, Vernadskii emphasized, was whether the government would resist this pressure or would cave in and follow the lead of the Union of the Russian People.[94]

A. N. SCHWARTZ

Stolypin did not make Vernadskii wait long for his answer. In a New Year's surprise, Stolypin fired von Kaufmann and replaced him with A. N. Schwartz, a former classics professor at Moscow University who

90. Quoted in *Vestnik Vospitaniia*, no. 4 (1908).
91. TsGIA, f. 733, op. 154, d. 84, l. 21.
92. TsGIA, f. 733, op. 153, d. 213; TsGIA, f. 733, op. 154, d. 159.
93. On Stolypin's political position, see Roberta Manning, *The Crisis of the Old Order in Russia* (Princeton, 1982).
94. *Rech'*, 1 January 1908.

had subsequently served as the curator of the Riga and the Warsaw educational districts, where he earned a reputation as a hard-nosed Russifier and conservative.[95]

Stolypin complained to Schwartz that von Kaufmann had been ineffectual in suppressing the student movement and keeping order in the VUZy. The former minister had shifted the burden of keeping discipline to the local authorities, thus "contradicting a basic principle of the 27 August Rules."[96] Clearly Stolypin saw the rules not as a guarantor of university autonomy but, rather, as a procedural order charging the professors rather than the police with the major responsibility for university discipline. Furthermore, von Kaufmann had been too lax with the professors. By letting them suspend classes rather than fight student disorders with mass expulsions, von Kaufmann had compromised the prestige of the government and fostered the impression that it was too weak to keep order. If the professors did not meet their responsibilities, Stolypin wrote to his new minister, they should be fired. Many of them, Stolypin complained, were poor servants of a state "which secures their material existence and gives them career privileges." Stolypin summarized his charge to Schwartz in two words: "Be hard!"[97]

On 7 March 1908, Stolypin asked Schwartz to outline how the Ministry of Education could tailor its policies to a "general plan of defending the state."[98] In response, Schwartz submitted a ten-point proposal that represented a sharp break with Tolstoi's liberalism and von Kaufmann's cautious pragmatism. Schwartz emphasized Russification—the ministry would play a crucial role in "exerting an assimilatory influence on the non-Russian population." Schwartz promised to abandon the "mistaken" policy of granting too many concessions to the non-Russian peoples. He also told Stolypin that the ministry favored a strict quota for Jewish enrollment at all levels of education and, of course, a large increase in its own budget.[99]

95. Von Kaufmann had expected to stay on, and the firing took him by surprise. Assistant Minister Gerasimov, a liberal appointee of Tolstoi's and a specialist in higher-education matters, followed von Kaufmann into retirement (*Russkie Vedomosti*, 1 January 1908). Schwartz himself, in a letter to a friend (which the police intercepted), emphasized that he tried to dissuade Stolypin from appointing him. See "Iz otchëta o perliustratsii del politsiei za 1908 god," *Krasnyi Arkhiv*, no. 28 (1928).

96. TsGIA, f. 733, op. 154, d. 192, l. 79.

97. Ibid.

98. TsGIA, f. 733, op. 196, d. 198.

99. Other aspects of Schwartz's plan included giving special attention to building schools in the Russian areas of the empire ("where most supporters of the state are concentrated") and sharp curbs on the expansion of private education.

Shortly thereafter, the new minister of education submitted to the Council of Ministers a remarkable memorandum on higher-education policy. The crux of Schwartz's argument to the council was that the students and much of the professoriate represented a real danger to the security of the state; the relative laxity of the post-1905 period had to give way to stricter controls.[100]

Schwartz warned his colleagues not to underestimate the students; far from being harmless, they were in fact "the only organized force able to keep up systematic mass disorders in order to maintain pressure on the government." But the students needed and received the help of the professoriate. Until 1905 the professors had been content to make "timid and diffuse statements." But things had changed with the Academic Union. Now the professors saw the universities as playing a major role in politics and proceeded to undermine the government by a willful distortion of the 27 August Rules, which the professors took as license to establish a "state within a state." One flagrant example, Schwartz argued, was the deliberations and draft statute of the 1906 Tolstoi Conference.

Perhaps the most remarkable feature of the memorandum was the charge that the professoriate was consciously collaborating with the revolutionary movement in a plan to topple the government. Schwartz "proved" this charge by questioning the motives of many faculty councils in admitting Jews and women and establishing an elective curriculum:

> We should not assume that the faculty councils did all these things because of inexperience . . . without the presence of an ulterior motive. The jamming of the universities with all kinds of students, including many completely unprepared for higher study, was a conscious step aimed at concentrating large numbers of young *intelligenty* in the large urban centers for the purpose of political indoctrination and the eventual use of this organized mass in bringing about the revolution. Such is the plan of the main revolutionary staff and it is being executed in all its details by the autonomous faculty councils.

Why did the professors institute the elective curriculum, if not to allow students to devote more time to revolutionary activities? Another danger was the professors' tolerance of the *zemliachestva* and other student "economic" organizations which in fact also pursued political ends.

---

100. The text of the memorandum is found in TsGIA, f. 733, op. 226, ed. kh. 137, l. 11 ("Zapiska ot imeni Ministra Narodnovo Prosveshcheniia A. N. Shvartsa o merakh bor'by s volneniiami studentov i politicheskimi partiiami v vysshikh uchebnykh zavedeniiakh posle 1907ovo goda").

This was all part of a plan to prepare the students for socialism. "All of these organizations . . . and the *skhodka* . . . prepare in miniature the [aspects] of the social system in Russia that the revolutionary parties seek."

Thus while political hotheads in the universities were decrying "student professionalism" as a betrayal of the revolutionary traditions of the student movement, and shortly after a student conference had decided that the *studenchestvo* was too isolated and disorganized to take united action, the new minister of education, ignoring all indications to the contrary, depicted the student movement as a dangerous threat to the state. The now moribund Academic Union, whose history showed how difficult it was for the professoriate as a body to collaborate with the Union of Unions, not to mention the revolutionary parties, became living proof that the professors were collaborating with the left. The Tolstoi Conference, which signaled the end of the Academic Union as an important force and the development of a modus vivendi between the senior professoriate and the Ministry of Education, was transformed by Schwartz into a radical gathering dominated by the Academic Union. Schwartz concluded with three specific recommendations: the drawing up of a new university statute, a clear definition of the 27 August Rules "to preclude [their] arbitrary interpretation by the professoriate," and the "complete expulsion of student organizations from the confines of institutions of higher education."

Schwartz's memorandum pleased Stolypin, who forwarded it to Gurliand, editor of the semi-official *Rossiia*, along with instructions to begin a press campaign against the professoriate and mobilize support for the government's crackdown on the universities. To remove all doubts, Stolypin emphasized that "this is the policy not just of the Ministry of Education but of the government as a whole."[101] It was time, the prime minister warned, to show the professors who was boss. Basically, most students were political innocents who had fallen under the harmful influence of the professoriate. Now the professors and the *VUZy* would return to normal: "We must root politics [out of the universities] and replace it with legality [*zakonnost'*]. . . . The government must be firm. It cannot ignore the recent lessons taught us by the Academic Union and the student organizations. No barrage of protests can force the government to allow petty political dabblers [*polikanstvuiushchie*]—left-wing professors—to mold students [as they wish]."[102]

101. TsGIA, f. 1662, op. 1, d. 86.
102. Ibid.

The first step in the crusade against the universities and other *VUZy* was to remind the faculty councils that the government, not the professors, decided what the 27 August Rules really meant. To make his point, Schwartz told the faculty councils to accept his interpretation of the 11 June Rules and stop cooperating with student organizations. Article Four of the 11 June Rules had forbidden organizations representing the student body as a whole, but most faculty councils continued to recognize student government organs elected on the basis of course or faculty. A few days before his dismissal, von Kaufmann had indicated his acceptance of this policy. But shortly after taking office, Schwartz told the Saint Petersburg, Moscow, and Kharkov faculty councils to close down the student organizations.[103]

This order came as a heavy blow to professors, who had felt that they were slowly winning the trust and confidence of the *studenchestvo*. At Saint Petersburg University, for example, the faculty council had managed to establish very close ties with the Council of Elders, and the Saint Petersburg delegates to the January 1908 student conference cited this good relationship as a major reason why they had opposed calls from the provinces for a nationwide student movement or protest.[104] When Schwartz, on 14 February, ordered the organization closed down, five thousand students packed the dining hall to protest. A worried rector F. A. Braun told Schwartz that this was the biggest *skhodka* since 1905, all the more impressive because it drew more than three-quarters of the student body actually in residence.[105]

The faculty councils charged the minister with violating the 27 August Rules which, they felt, gave them the major responsibility for ensuring the orderly continuation of the academic and disciplinary process. The Saint Petersburg Faculty Council protested that Schwartz's policies would turn it "into a passive observer" of events in the university. If the minister insisted on his new course, then the council would have to consider resigning all responsibility for university affairs.[106]

Schwartz also began to attack the post-1905 liberalization of university admissions. On 19 February the Council of Ministers directed him to review the whole question of Jewish enrollment in the institutions of secondary and higher education in the empire; Stolypin wanted a uniform policy that would also guide educational institutions not under

103. TsGIA, f. 733, op. 226, d. 93, ll. 267–269.
104. TsGIA, f. 733, op. 154, d. 159, l. 5.
105. TsGIA, f. 733, op. 154, d. 159, l. 13.
106. *Rech'*, 12 September 1908.

the direct control of the Ministry of Education.[107] The prime minister proposed a flat 4 percent quota on admission of Jews to institutions of secondary and higher education financed by the government, while Schwartz advocated a 3 percent quota in the Moscow and Saint Petersburg districts, 10 percent in educational districts of the Pale of Settlement, and 5 percent in the remaining districts. Furthermore, he told the council that an effective way to combat revolution was to make access to gymnasia and universities available only to the children of rich Jews; the rest would go to lower-level schools. The proposed restrictions drew a protest from the minister of trade and industry, who felt that the *numerus clausus* in the commercial institutes would hurt the efforts of his ministry to develop commercial education in the country. After some debate the Council of Ministers voted, in its meeting of 19 August, to apply Schwartz's plan to Russia's institutions of higher education.[108] The result was the beginning of a sharp drop in Jewish enrollment.

The government also attacked the educational gains of groups such as seminarists, women, and auditors. A 16 May circular revoked Tolstoi's concessions by forcing seminarists to pass additional examinations in order to be admitted to a university.[109] The provisions affecting auditors in effect barred women from attending the universities. Furthermore, Schwartz changed the status of auditors already in the universities. Until the 16 May circular, they had de facto student status and could receive de jure status upon passing examinations in Latin and Greek. (Most auditors had not attended classical gymnasia.) The faculty councils had made these examinations a precondition of graduation but not of admission. Women auditors were in the same position, except that they were designated as *vol'noslushatel'nitsi* (unofficial auditors) rather than *postoronnye slushateli* (official auditors). But the 16 May circular made these examinations a precondition for admission itself. Furthermore, any auditor had to obtain a certificate of political reliability from the police, and the circular decreed that the Jewish quota would apply to auditors as well as students. Any auditor currently enrolled who had not completed all the requirements of the circular would have to withdraw after the end of the 1907–1908 academic year.

107. "Osobyi zhurnal Soveta Ministrov 19ovo Avgusta 1908ovo goda po voprosu ob ustanovlenii protsentnykh norm dlia priëma v uchebnye zavedeniia lits iudeiskovo proiskhozhdeniia," in "Spravka po evreiskomu voprosu" (n.d.). This unpublished compilation of official documents is located at the Hoover Institution, Stanford, California.

108. Ibid.

109. TsGIA, f. 733, op. 152, d. 195, l. 240. These restrictions did not apply to seminarists who wished to enter Warsaw University. The Ministry of Education tried to counter the effect of the Polish boycott by filling that university with Russian seminary graduates.

On 4 September the Council of Ministers met to consider the question of women in the universities. Here Stolypin wanted to go further than Schwartz, who favored allowing women currently enrolled to finish their course (a softening of his May position). But the council, noting that the professors had been admitting women "in violation of the law," insisted that they could remain only if the faculty met the onerous condition of giving them separate lectures duplicating the regular courses. Meanwhile, *Rossiia*, echoing Stolypin, charged the professors with hypocrisy and reiterated that Schwartz acted in the name of the whole government.[110]

After a few weeks the government made a small concession to public opinion by allowing women and auditors currently enrolled to finish their studies. But this did not really alter the dramatic impact of Schwartz's circulars on the student population. The number of auditors and Jewish students began a sharp decline.

In another move that antagonized the professoriate, Schwartz began to curtail faculty jurisdiction over the curriculum. When the natural sciences faculty of Moscow University protested the order to cut down on assigned reading in foreign languages, Schwartz replied that the ministry "had not only the right but the duty" to inspect course offerings and reading lists and issue requisite instructions to the professors.[111] Schwartz also undermined the post-1905 curricular changes by forcing candidates for secondary-school teaching posts to take special examinations keyed to the 1896 examination rules.[112]

Schwartz's moves now began to provoke opposition not only from the left and the liberals but also from the Octobrists. In the 1908 budgetary commission debate on higher-education policy, the leading Octobrist spokesman in this area, V. K. von Anrep, complained that Schwartz's policies were leading to a "Tsushima" of higher education.[113] The Octobrists directed most of their fire at Schwartz's foot-dragging in response to Duma calls for the building of new universities and the expansion of existing ones. The Duma called on the ministry to facilitate the planned opening of a new university at Saratov, add new faculties to

110. The Council memorandum is quoted from TsGIA, f. 1276, op. 2, d. 515. The Council of Ministers declared that "the girls have a right to feel betrayed [by the unlawful decision of the professors to admit them in the first place]. . . . Those professors who do not wish to read separate lectures will only prove that they are more willing to break the law at the government's expense than on their own time." *Rossiia* was cited in *Rech'*, 6 September 1908.

111. *Vestnik Vospitaniia*, no. 7 (1908).

112. TsGIA, f. 733, op. 152, d. 195, l. 251.

113. Gosudarstvennaia Duma, Tretii Sozyv, *Stenograficheskii Otchët* (Saint Petersburg, 1908), pervaia sessiia, 3ch., p. 2384.

Tomsk University, and spend more funds on training additional professors.[114] In passing the ministry's budget, the Duma added a charge to
Schwartz to rescind the restrictions on the admission of seminary graduates and increase expenditures for financial aid, but although he promised to do something about Saratov University and the shortage of
qualified professors, Schwartz rejected the Duma's call for widening access to higher education. Russia needed quality, not quantity. "Higher
education," he told the deputies, "is not for everybody."[115]

In short, significant elements of the moderate right did not want the
policy of quelling student protest, a policy they supported, to serve as an
excuse for pursuing a course detrimental to Russia's economic development and international status. Keep troublemakers in line, they said, but
open new universities and satisfy Russia's need for trained specialists.
The conflict between the search for stability and educational and economic imperatives—epitomized by Octobrist opposition to Schwartz's
policies—reached the Council of Ministers itself. In August Stolypin rejected a request from the Ministry of Trade and Industry that graduates
of commercial high schools be allowed to enter universities.

In the summer of 1908 another controversy embroiled Schwartz with
the professoriate when Tolmachev, the governor-general of Odessa, expelled four liberal professors from the city. Tolmachev's use of the state
of martial law to effect this action was another example of the vulnerability of the provincial universities to arbitrary measures by the local authorities. Schwartz played a duplicitous role. On 28 July he assured the
four—rector Zanchevskii, E. F. Vas'kovskii, V. A. Kossinskii, and B. F.
Verigo—that he had nothing to do with the matter.[116] But at the same
time Schwartz wrote to urge Tolmachev to take advantage of the absence
of the four liberals to install the reactionary professor S. V. Levashev
as rector.[117] Schwartz also pressed charges against Zanchevskii and
Vas'kovskii for alleged dereliction of duty and anti-government activities during the Revolution of 1905. On the basis of testimony by their
more conservative colleagues on the faculty council, the Senate found
Zanchevskii and Vas'kovskii guilty, ousting the former rector from the
civil service and suspending Vas'kovskii for three years.[118] Meanwhile,

114. Ibid., p. 2783.
115. *Rech'*, 11 June 1908.
116. TsGIA, f. 733, op. 154, d. 162, ll. 22–29.
117. Ibid.
118. For a right-wing account of what happened at Odessa University in 1905, see
Revoliutsionnoe gniezdo (Saint Petersburg, n.d.).

the ministry brought the same charges against rector Passek of Iur'ev University, who also lost his post.

As the 1908–1909 academic year began, the policy outlined in Schwartz's memorandum was in full swing. Restrictions on the admission of Jews, women, and seminarists, retaliation against professors affiliated with the Kadet party,[119] reprisals against faculty members who had played a prominent part in the Revolution of 1905, suppression of student organizations, and collaboration with local authorities to ensure conservative domination of provincial faculty councils all showed that Schwartz was executing a systematic policy with the direct support of Stolypin.

The liberal professoriate protested Schwartz's policy but stopped short of direct defiance. When rector Borgman of Saint Petersburg University submitted his protest resignation on 3 September, he was persuaded by his colleagues to rescind it. Moscow's Manuilov also protested but remained at his post and enforced the new circulars. The liberal professoriate, heartened by the recent coolness between Octobrists and Schwartz, now pinned its hopes on the Duma. Many professors feared, with reason, that Schwartz would soon seek to cap his new university policy by introducing for Duma consideration a new draft statute even worse than the discredited 1884 Statute. The liberal professoriate now had one major fear—that an outbreak of massive student unrest would abort this growing Duma support of the professoriate and play into the government's hands. Therefore as the students returned for the start of classes, the liberal press appealed to them to stay calm and leave the defense of the university to the professors.[120]

THE 1908 STRIKE

Never before had the *studenchestvo* been so directly challenged, and never had its dilemma been so great, as in the fall of 1908. The students had now become the objects of direct government repression. Fellow students were being thrown out of the universities because of their sex, reli-

---

119. On 18 August 1908, Schwartz told his curators that professors who signed the 1906 Vyborg manifesto had to swear, as a condition of their remaining in government service, that they were not members of any anti-government party or organization. The teachers directly affected by Schwartz's order—Kadet party members S. A. Muromtsev, G. S. Shershenovitch, Novgorodtsev, and Petrazhitskii—signed the disclaimer. TsGIA, f. 733, op. 154, d. 192, l. 26.

120. *Rech'*, 3 September 1908.

gion, or educational background, and the Ministry of Education had ordered the liquidation of what was left of the student government organs.

The history of the student movement had shown that direct attacks on student interests were the surest way to provoke student unrest. But 1908 was not 1899 or 1905. This time the students knew that their protest would fail to arouse even public sympathy. The liberal press, the Kadet party, and the professoriate clearly opposed student unrest. The workers and peasantry were politically dormant and the revolutionary parties were at a low ebb. In the words of one observer, the *studenchestvo,* in making the decision to fight Schwartz, "had to choose between a Sedan and a Waterloo."[121] Most students realized that a Russian public who meekly accepted Stolypin's revision of the Duma electoral law cared little about student demands.

But a decision not to strike would mean a fateful break with those traditions of the *studenchestvo* that called for student solidarity, mutual help, and a constant readiness to fight for student interests. For the past two years *skhodki* and the student press had been debating the future of the *studenchestvo.* Students had accused their comrades of cowardice and careerism; articles bemoaned the fact that Russian students were following the bourgeois road taken by their German counterparts after 1848. Now in September 1908, the students knew that they were facing a moment of truth.

Between 4 and 7 September an ad hoc group of Saint Petersburg students from various *VUZy* in the capital and representing a number of political factions and *zemliachestva* met to consider the options open to the *studenchestvo.* The group sent delegates to other university towns, decided to call a nationwide student protest strike, and issued an "Appeal to Russian Society."[122]

This "Appeal" became the basic document of the 1908 student strike and served as the model for resolutions adopted in other *VUZy.* Couched in very moderate terms, the "Appeal" was a plea for public support, which the students knew they did not have. It began by analyzing the significance of student protest in Russia before 1905: "Before 1905, the student movement was basically a protest against the restraints that the bureaucracy placed on Russian society. . . . The student movement,

---

121. A. Iarmolovich, *Smert' Prizrakov,* p. 33. It is assumed that Iarmolovich was comparing the students with the French side.
122. "Dokumenty studencheskovo dvizheniia," *Znamia Truda,* no. 14 (December 1908).

although in essence dictated by the academic interests of the students, thus also became a political movement at the same time, achieving social significance and serving as a barometer of . . . the mood of the Russian public."

Since 1906, both students and professors had settled down to the serious job of making Russian higher education work. But then the government began a crusade against the universities, which it regarded as "having no cultural value, . . . [as being] fomenters of constitutional illusions and a threat to public order." The war against the students and the professors received the same priority as the struggle against the revolutionary left. The latest circulars were the last straw. The *studenchestvo* had tried to protect its rights by legal means but now "the illegal measures of the government have deprived it of the opportunity of seeking legal recourse." Schwartz was trying to turn the universities into "diploma factories . . . mills spewing out petty bureaucrats."

The "Appeal" admitted that the only hope for student victory lay in the support of an aroused Russian public. The students concluded by outlining their fundamental demands: the right of the *studenchestvo* to its own organizations, and the right of professors to enjoy full academic autonomy—construed as meaning that the professors would control the academic and economic affairs of the universities. Therefore government controls on university admissions were incompatible with the exercise of real academic freedom. The "Appeal" ended with a call for a nationwide academic strike.

On 13 September a crowded *skhodka* met in the main auditorium of Saint Petersburg University to discuss the "Appeal" and its call for a strike. At first many students were indecisive, weighing their moral obligation to Jews, women, and seminarists against their fear of expulsion from the university for participating in a protest action. What finally convinced the Saint Petersburg students to fight was a direct appeal to the traditions of the Russian *studenchestvo* and the students' sense of honor.

"The strike," one eyewitness reported, "broke out not because the masses really wanted it but because of a direct appeal to the students' sense of their own past [and traditions]."[123] One student told the *skhodka* that unless it voted to protect students' rights, the notion of the *studenchestvo* would be gone forever.[124] The *skhodka* voted 2,398 to 77 to

123. Iarmolovich, *Smert' Prizrakov*, p. 48.
124. Ibid.

strike.[125] The strike began on 20 September and quickly spread to most of the other institutions of higher education in Saint Petersburg.

Meanwhile Moscow's students were following the events in Saint Petersburg closely. Descriptions of the 13 September *skhodka* in Saint Petersburg festooned the walls of Moscow University.[126] The Central University Organ called a *skhodka* on 19 September to consider whether the Moscow University students should join the strike. The student Kadets, however, strongly opposed the CUO action and launched a vigorous pamphlet campaign to convince the students to heed *Rech'*, the Kadet newspaper, to refrain from striking and give the professors a chance to mobilize support in the Duma. The Duma, given a chance, could pressure Schwartz into beating a retreat. The students themselves, the Kadets argued, had long since lost their political importance and should therefore save their one weapon, the academic strike, for a truly decisive occasion.[127]

The Moscow *skhodka* met on 19 September and attracted more than four thousand students. The speakers concentrated almost exclusively on the students' academic demands, making virtually no references to the general political situation. A high point came when a delegate from Saint Petersburg took the floor and appealed for the support of Moscow. The *skhodka* passed, 2,106 to 548, a pro-strike resolution modeled on the Saint Petersburg "Appeal." The students knew they would probably lose, but they could not reject the traditions of student honor, which called for a gesture to be made. The result was a curious mixture of enthusiasm and ambivalence: "One moment everybody was hesitating. And then suddenly they shook their heads, waved their arms and said, 'Hell, I don't want to think anymore! If we have to strike, then let's strike!'"[128]

On 22 September, the Moscow University students established an Executive Committee to direct the strike, and this committee in turn joined an all-Moscow coalition council.[129] That same day a large *skhodka* in Kharkov University endorsed the strike. The strike also spread to Ka-

125. TsGIA, f. 733, op. 154, d. 159, l. 184.

126. TsGAOR, f. 102, op. 117, ed. kh. 42, 5ch. 1/A/1908, ll. 6–8.

127. These Kadet student pamphlets can be found in GPB im. V. I. Lenina, f. 158, folder 6, no. 127.

128. Iarmolovich, *Smert' Prizrakov*, p. 48.

129. TsGAOR, f. 102, op. 117, ed. kh. 42, 5ch. 1/A/1908, l. 16. A noticeable feature of these two organizations, compared with past years, was the prominent role now played by the student "economic organizations"—*zemliachestva* and credit societies.

zan, Kiev, and Odessa, though it achieved only limited success, because of immediate police interference.

The Social Revolutionaries wholeheartedly endorsed the strike, but the Social Democrats were much less enthusiastic. One observer expressed a common sentiment when he noted that the student Social Democrats were "in the piquant position of claiming to represent a proletarian party fighting for the class interests of a bourgeois university."[130] The student strike did not arouse one iota of worker support in Saint Petersburg or any other city. The Saint Petersburg Committee of the Social Democratic party sent a letter to the city's student Social Democratic organizations telling them that they would get no regular party support until they fought for "general as well as only student demands."[131]

The moderate Saint Petersburg "Appeal" was a major source of friction. The Saint Petersburg City Social Democratic Committee complained that it was an "Octobrist-Kadet document . . . permeated through and through with the stupidest [poshlyi] kind of bourgeois liberalism."[132] Proletarii, a Geneva-based Bolshevik journal, acidly noted that the students were going to extreme lengths to avoid any identification with the revolutionary parties: "After years of leftist predominance [in the student movement], we now see the students issue an 'Appeal' directed at Mom and Dad [Momasham i Popasham] promising 'no politics if you'll only get us autonomy.'"[133]

As was the case in 1899, many student Social Democrats found themselves in a dilemma: they did not want to support their classmates' "bourgeois protest" but at the same time they did not want to desert their comrades or stand on the sidelines. Furthermore, in 1908 the labor movement had not recovered from the revolution: the students were the only social group doing any protesting at all. Seeking advice, a group of student Social Democrats wrote to V. I. Lenin.

Lenin quickly published an open letter to his student correspondents, entitled "The Student Movement and the Present Political Situation."[134] Lenin chided his colleagues for taking an overly pedantic view of the current strike and emphasized that the 1908 protest, while academic

130. Iarmolovich, Smert' Prizrakov, p. 29.
131. TsGIA, f. 733, op. 154, d. 159, l. 188.
132. TsGIA, f. 733, op. 154, d. 159, l. 190.
133. Proletarii, no. 36 (1908).
134. Ibid.

rather than political in character, could still play a positive role in politicizing the student masses. Characterizing the broad social significance of the student movement, Lenin emphasized that the students were "connected by thousands and millions of strands with the middle and lower bourgeoisie, the petty bureaucracy, and certain strata of the peasantry and the clergy." Viewed in this light, the strike was the symptom of growing tension between these groups and the Stolypin government. The current student generation had come into the universities after 1905 and had, until 1908, gravitated toward the Kadets and their liberal mistrust of direct action. Therefore, Lenin explained, the 1908 strike, with all its imperfections, nevertheless marked an anti-government protest that the student Social Democrats should not ignore. On the contrary, Lenin explained, the Social Democrats' task was "to explain to the mass of the protesters the objective meaning of this movement and to make it consciously political."

Meanwhile the students were losing whatever hope they had had of rallying public support for the strike. The Kadet party, along with virtually the entire professoriate, called on the students to return to class and leave the defense of the universities to adults. The Octobrists, notwithstanding earlier disagreements with Stolypin over education policy, wholeheartedly supported the government. Even relatively radical faculty members such as Saint Petersburg University's Sviatlovskii and Tugan-Baranovskii ignored student appeals to stay away from the lecture halls. When asked by his students to cancel a lecture, Moscow's Evgenii Trubetskoi replied that the students were giving the government more help than the Black Hundred movement was. The strike, Trubetskoi complained, had compromised the position of the professors. "Up to now," he told his audience, "the professors could at least say that when there was autonomy the students trusted them and listened to their advice. But now we cannot make that claim."[135] Furthermore, he warned, the students were turning the Duma against the universities.

The government appreciated the potential political windfall from the strike and carefully avoided repressive actions that might generate sympathy for the students. In a circular sent to subordinates in all university towns, the director of the Department of Police, N. P. Zuev, outlined his main concern: keeping the student disorders off the street. As long as there were no signs of active collusion between the student movement and the revolutionary movement, the police should keep a low profile,

135. TsGAOR, f. 102, op. 117, ed. kh. 42, 5ch. 1/A/1908, l. 21.

taking care to enter university premises only at the express invitation of academic authorities and arresting only those students who were clearly involved with revolutionary elements.[136] As the strike dragged on, with no visible results, morale sagged and the students began to look for a way out of the impasse. On 1 October a *skhodka* at Saint Petersburg University voted to send a delegation to the Duma and its president, A. I. Guchkov, asking for support. When this overture failed, most student Social Democrats joined the Kadets in calling for an end to the strike.[137] The next day the Saint Petersburg coalition council, which included representatives from ten city *VUZy*, voted 11 to 7 to sponsor resolutions ending the strike. In Moscow a student referendum voted 3,522 to 1,420 to end the strike.

Although the resolutions ending the strike tried to make the best of a bad situation, there was no hiding the overwhelming reaction of the students: they had been defeated, mainly because the public remained indifferent to their cause. Two years later a leading student newspaper offered the following post-mortem of the 1908 strike—and, it believed, of the whole Russian student movement:

> Look at the last great strike of 1908. This presents the historian of the Russian student movement with one of its most interesting chapters. All agree now that the strike was unsuccessful. To be sure, it was, but not in the usually understood sense. If you look at the 1908 strike from the purely quantitative point of view it attracted more student participation than any other action with the exception of 1905. Tens of thousands of students stayed on strike for more than two weeks. And what was the public significance of such an extraordinary event? None. Not small—none. If the student strike had had only a small effect there might be some hope for the future [of the student movement]. But the result was such that in fact there can be no such hope.[138]

Events were soon to show this gloomy appraisal to be unduly pessimistic; the turbulent student disorders of 1910–1911 erupted soon after the appearance of the article. But the analysis confirmed what many students felt: without public support, student protests were little more than a quixotic bow to the past.

In many respects the 1908 strike was a unique chapter in the history

---

136. TsGAOR, f. 102, op. 117, ed. kh. 42, 5ch. 1/A/1908, l. 44. But in Kiev, Kazan, and Odessa universities, the academic authorities called in the police as soon as *skhodki* met to discuss the strike.

137. "Dokumenty studencheskovo dvizheniia."

138. *Golos Studenchestva*, no. 12 (1910).

of the Russian student movement. Its purposes, demands, and basic nature were more closely linked to the students' corporate interests than
was the case in any other coordinated student protest. In a sense the
students had come full circle, back to 1899, leaving the streets to return
to protest within the universities. But the 1899 strike had advanced a
broader issue, one with which wider sections of the Russian public
could sympathize: the principle of personal inviolability. The 1908
strike, however, raised only the corporate demands of the students.
Carefully avoiding identification with the revolutionary left, the students sought the support of what was widely regarded to be a reactionary Duma, dominated by the Octobrist party and elected on the basis of
the newly revised electoral law.

Another important feature of the 1908 student strike was its relatively high level of organization. This time the student action was not an
impulsive act of rage against police brutality. The students had had the
whole summer to ponder the meaning of Schwartz's circulars and the
cruel fact that while most students were left unscathed, certain groups
of students might lose their chance of receiving a higher education. The
issue was group solidarity versus individual self-interest. When the students returned in September, however, there was no mood of fervent
outrage, as had been the case after the 1899 beatings or the Bloody Sunday massacre. Instead, the student masses waited to be challenged by
some organized initiative that would awaken their sense of moral obligation. This was the role of the ad hoc group of Saint Petersburg students who issued the "Appeal" and recommended that the strike begin.
The strike itself was the result of calm and deliberate consideration. The
Saint Petersburg *skhodka* that approved the strike had stipulated that
there be a five-day waiting period in order to enlist the cooperation of
the various student *zemliachestva* and economic organizations. Like
past student movements, the action of one of the two central universities
served as a signal for the rest of the *studenchestvo*. Because of conditions of martial law and immediate use of police power, however, the
strike did not really get off the ground in Odessa, Kiev, or Kazan.

One of the most significant features of the 1908 strike was that it
showed once again the strong hold that the student past and the traditions of the *studenchestvo* still had on the student masses, even those
who could not remember the pre-1905 universities. Perhaps the major
reason for the strike was the widespread determination to meet the stern
test imposed by these traditions, although many students probably
would have preferred not to strike. But once most students realized that

the strike was attracting little public support, enthusiasm quickly waned. Some cynics, reporting on the mood of the *skhodki* that decided to end the strike, remarked that the gesture had been made and now it was time to get back to business. Again, however, it would be most fair to say that, as in the past, the student movement walked a fine line between moral obligation and self-interest, and between the need to protest and the inadequacy of available methods.

The strike also showed that the division of students into formal political factions after 1905 did not mean that the *studenchestvo* had lost its corporate identity, as many feared (or hoped), or that the interests of the national political parties overshadowed academic and corporate concerns. Although Kadet and Octobrist factions opposed the decision to strike in the two central universities, they nonetheless joined it during the first week, out of a feeling of solidarity with a corporate decision of the *studenchestvo*.[139] Despite opposition from the local Social Democratic party, student Social Democrats played a leading role in the Saint Petersburg student movement. Indeed, the tension between student and adult Social Democrats had also been apparent in 1899 and 1901, but now, in 1908, this friction was emphasized by the decline of worker interest in the student movement.

If the students gained little from the strike, neither did the professors. Some prominent leftist journals charged the professoriate with cowering on the sidelines while the students defended the *VUZy* against Schwartz.[140] Ironically, the government agreed with the leftist assessment of professorial spinelessness. In a confidential report to Stolypin on the strike, Assistant Minister of the Interior Makarov concluded that the professors had really welcomed the strike, because they preferred to let the students fight their battles for them.[141]

NEW LEGISLATION

Schwartz soon gave the professoriate a sharp reminder that its antistrike stand earned it little credit from the government. His new draft statute, announced on 4 October 1908, confirmed the worst fears of the professoriate.[142] Unlike the Tolstoi Conference draft, to which the

139. GPB im. V. I. Lenina, f. 158, folder 6, no. 127.
140. V. Miakotin, "Tragediia vysshei shkoly," *Russkoe Bogatstvo*, no. 10 (1908); I. Larskii, "Na granitse akademizma," *Sovremennyi Mir*, no. 10 (1908).
141. TsGIA, f. 733, op. 154, d. 160, l. 89.
142. For a full and critical discussion of the draft statute, see *Vestnik Vospitaniia*, no. 8 (1908).

Schwartz project was diametrically opposed, there was no attempt to involve the professoriate in framing the statute. The new statute defined the universities primarily as teaching institutions preparing future civil servants and professionals. This was fundamentally different from the Tolstoi Conference emphasis on the research functions of the university. In reverting to the 1884 definition of the university, the ministry laid the groundwork for justification of extensive state interference in the *VUZy*. Centrally appointed curators would continue to supervise the universities and, in extraordinary circumstances, could "exceed their specified authority." In a concession to the 27 August Rules, the new draft retained the faculty council's right to elect rectors, but the rectors' main role was to ensure internal discipline. Yet professors would lose their disciplinary functions to a reformed inspectorate. Teaching had to conform to study plans approved by the ministry. New professors could either be appointed by the minister himself or be elected by the department. In the latter case the minister had to approve the department's choice. Thus the draft deprived the faculty council of any role in faculty appointments. The new statute required two degrees for the holder of any faculty position and abolished the rights and privileges associated with the university degree. Entering students had to be males graduating from Ministry of Education gymnasia or presenting certificates proving they had completed an equivalent course of study. The statute banned student meetings in the universities and directed rectors to call police to enforce this rule. Although students were allowed to form organizations, they could meet only off campus and were subject to general legislation. Schwartz called for a major hike in university fees, as well as an annual state allotment of 7 million rubles to the universities. This was well below Tolstoi's recommendation of 13 million.

A few days later Schwartz met the rectors of Saint Petersburg and Moscow universities to discuss the new draft statute. Even the official minutes of the meeting between Schwartz and the rectors convey a tense and bitter atmosphere as Schwartz outlined the main features of the project.[143] Borgman, the rector of Saint Petersburg University, charged that the projected draft entailed the "total destruction of the Russian university." By abolishing the important prerogatives of the faculty council, especially in faculty appointments, Schwartz was destroying the principle that distinguished a university from a mere school or insti-

---

143. The minutes of the meeting are found in TsGIA, f. 733, op. 154, d. 269, l. 2.

tute. As Manuilov put it, the draft statute contradicted "the fundamental basis of the *universitas scholarum-litterarum*. Scientific education cannot be split into separate parts, because science is a unity, the [basis of] . . . the concept of the university. . . . And the unity of the university is epitomized by the participation of all professors, as a faculty council, in the election of their colleagues." Manuilov also reminded Schwartz that it was strange to see the government returning to the spirit of 1884 after the student disturbances of the past ten years had demonstrated the fundamental backruptcy of that statute and had forced its piecemeal revision.

A few weeks later the professoriate suffered another setback as the state Senate upheld Schwartz's interpretation of the 27 August Rules.[144] The 27 November 1908 ruling rejected the contention of the Moscow and Saint Petersburg faculty councils that the 27 August Rules had superseded the 1884 Statute. The rectors of these universities had held that by charging the professoriate with the duty of ensuring the "proper functioning of academic life," the 27 August Rules had in fact abolished the provisions of the 1884 Statute dealing with academic affairs and student discipline and had guaranteed the faculty council freedom from government interference in the regulation of student life and internal university discipline. But the Senate, while emphasizing that the rules gave the professoriate much responsibility, refused to back the faculty council's claim to enhanced power. In matters pertaining to student life, financial aid, admissions, and rules about the status of student organizations, the Ministry of Education would have the final word. Faced with Schwartz's project and stung by the Senate ruling, few liberal professors could dispute Vernadskii's New Year's prediction that 1908 would turn out to be a hard year for the universities.

CONCLUSION

The toughening of the government's policy after 1907 clearly shows the close link between the situation of the universities and Stolypin's general political policies. Without actually repealing the 1884 Statute, the government at first allowed the professors to make major changes in university teaching, admissions, and governance. But after the dissolution of the second Duma and the promulgation of a new restrictive elec-

144. TsGIA, f. 1276, op. 3, d. 800, l. 177.

toral law on 3 June 1907, university policy also shifted in ways directly dictated by the prime minister. Stolypin, as has been shown, took a close interest in the university question. Why?

Labeling Stolypin a reactionary does not answer the question. In fact there is solid evidence to show that on occasion the prime minister understood and defended the nation's interest in higher education. A clear example is the April 1907 Council of Ministers debate on the question of opening a new university. (Various cities had offered sites and partial funding.)[145] Conservatives on the council objected to any new universities because of fear of student unrest. But a majority of the council, including Stolypin, supported funding a new university in Saratov.[146] One reason cited in the council journal was that it was important to stem the outflow of young talent from the provinces into the overcrowded central universities. Furthermore, the council majority agreed that "no matter how unsatisfactory the present state of the universities happens to be . . . we [refuse] to close them . . . because we are convinced that higher education in the empire is necessary and useful."

Stolypin's university policy derived from four basic factors: his conception of the relationship between the university and the state, his determination to crush the revolutionary movement, his firm belief in strong state authority, and his own political vulnerability to rightist attacks. Stolypin saw the universities as state institutions, the professors as civil servants, and the students as young men whose role was to study and graduate. Unable to appreciate the complexity of the institution and unwilling to accept the professoriate's ideological justifications for an autonomous, research-oriented university, he overreacted to the continuing student disturbances and the professors' seeming inability to control them. He failed to appreciate that almost all professors, liberal as well as conservative, feared the revolutionary movement. Like many in the Russian government, Stolypin, for all his constructive vision, failed to see the opportunities presented by pursuing a policy of benign neglect, which might have slowly depoliticized the universities. Unrest, in his view, undermined the prestige of the state and demonstrated the government's inability to maintain order, the professors' duplicity, and the students' unreliability. Whatever his other qualities, Stolypin could not free himself from the "politics of order" in dealing with the university question.

145. "Osobyi zhurnal soveta ministrov ob osnovanii novovo universiteta v Rossii" (10, 13 April 1907). This unpublished source is located at the Hoover Institution.
146. The new university opened in 1909 with only a medical faculty. It also had to overcome strong conservative opposition in the State Council.

CHAPTER 8

Confrontation

Between 1910 and 1914 there was a paradoxical juxtaposition of growing government concern for education with a major crisis in state-university relations.[1] While the government reiterated its preference for technical higher education, the professoriate pressed its claim that the universities should be the centerpiece of the nation's system of higher education. Meanwhile the government showed little regard for the professoriate's prerogatives as it initiated a ruthless campaign to suppress student unrest, which revived after Lev Tolstoi's death in November 1910. The result was a major crisis epitomized by the mass resignations of the Moscow University faculty in 1911 and mass expulsions of students.

New elements were modifying this by-now-familiar pattern of three-sided confrontation. As the state provided a steadily declining percentage of Russia's university budgets, private philanthropy became more

---

1. During this period the Russian government made an unprecedented effort to increase expenditures on education. Between 1906 and 1914 the Ministry of Education's share of the state budget rose from 1.4 percent to 4.4 percent. Between 1896 and 1914 the percentage of Russia's population going to some kind of school more than doubled, from 2.3 percent to 5.5 percent. Yet state outlays on the universities remained constant. Russia was far ahead of England and Germany on the proportion of GNP spent per student (although it lagged far behind in per-capita educational expenditure in absolute terms). The government saw educational expansion as contributing to economic development, but Michael Kaser has argued that precisely the opposite was true: Russia's rapid economic development began without the basic literacy levels widely assumed to be an essential precondition of economic growth. It was the growth of national income that led to the rapid expansion, on all levels, of Russian education ("Education in Tsarist and Soviet Development," in Chimen Abramsky, ed., *Essays in Honor of E. H. Carr* [London, 1974]).

important. And for the first time private institutions of higher education, such as Moscow's Shaniavskii University, emerged as real alternatives to the traditional state university.

There was no crisis in Russian higher education or in Russian science
on the eve of World War I. In both areas Russia had achieved un-
paralleled strength and diversity, largely as a result of the contributions
of private individuals and the efforts of the Ministry of Finance and the
Ministry of Trade and Industry in establishing their own network of
VUZy. The real problem was the crisis in relations between the universities and the state. The policies of the Ministry of Education did much
to undermine the prestige of the autocracy in the eyes of the Russian
professoriate and wide sections of the Russian bourgeoisie, already repelled by the anti-Semitic carnival of the Beilis trial and the growing role
of Rasputin at the court. Nor did the ministry achieve its major aim, the
elimination of student unrest in the country. By 1914 the crisis of the
universities was seen as part of a deeper, more serious issue, that of
the growing friction between the autocracy and the Russian public.

THE COUNCIL OF MINISTERS
AND THE DRAFT STATUTE

During 1909 and 1910 the Council of Ministers met several times to
discuss Schwartz's draft statute before its submission to the Duma. Public pressure and a generally hostile press reception forced some changes
in the original 1908 project, but the council finally approved the entire
draft on 13 January 1910. The record of these discussions illustrates
significant trends in the government's higher-education policy.[2] The
Council of Ministers agreed that the 1884 Statute had outlived its
usefulness, but it also lashed out at the Russian professoriate for its attempts to stretch the meaning of the 27 August Rules and turn the "universities into a state within a state." Pointing to the example of "the
West," the council complained that the professors' definition of autonomy far exceeded the freedoms their counterparts enjoyed in other
countries. The Russian universities were state institutions and the state
had to ensure that they served its interests.

The council also stressed the need to deemphasize the central role of
the universities and encourage students to seek education in other directions. In the past the Russian government had taken steps to encourage

2. The record is found in TsGIA, f. 733, op. 154, d. 471, ll. 182–198.

students to enter the universities, but the time had now come to recognize that the national interest was no longer served by a massive influx of students prompted by considerations of social mobility rather than love of learning or dedication to a useful profession. In endorsing the provision in Schwartz's draft calling for the abolition of the privileges associated with university degrees, the council noted:

> The population now recognizes the value of higher education and [no longer needs state encouragement]. . . . On the contrary, it is much more important to raise the quality of education and improve the intellectual and moral level of the student body. [The government must try to] curb the widespread and excessive striving for higher education as a means of gaining entry into the civil service and the liberal professions: this demand for higher education is very dangerous from the social point of view.[3]

For the same reason, the council supported Schwartz's stipulation that entry into the universities be restricted to graduates of Ministry of Education gymnasia. It thus overruled the argument of the Ministry of Trade and Industry that graduates of commercial and other secondary schools should be allowed to matriculate at universities. The council noted that commercial and other specialized secondary schools were established for a reason; it would not serve the "interests of the state" if their students could easily abandon their chosen careers and enter a university.

An interesting aspect of the deliberations on the Schwartz statute was the Ministry of Finance's opposition to Schwartz's call for sharp increases in faculty salaries and in the state's contribution to the universities' operating budgets.[4] (Poor Schwartz could not win. The rectors attacked him for destroying university autonomy, while the Ministry of Finance accused him of coddling the faculty!) State grants to the universities had lagged far behind student enrollments; between 1880 and 1912, state expenditure per student declined from 311 rubles to 166 rubles. The state share of annual university budgets had declined from 77 percent in 1894 to 60 percent in 1912. And, as was shown earlier, faculty salaries were grossly distorted by the unfair honorarium system.[5] But the minister of finance argued that the universities spent their funds inefficiently, that professors received plenty of vacation time to

---

3. Ibid.
4. TsGIA, f. 733, op. 154, d. 471, l. 114.
5. D. I. Bagalei, "Ekonomicheskoe polozhenie russkikh universitetov," *Vestnik Evropy*, no. 1 (1914): 232; "Rossiia-Prosveshchenie," in E. A. Brokhaus and I. A. Efron, eds., *Entsiklopedicheskii slovar'* (Saint Petersburg, 1913), vol. 27.

make up for their allegedly low salaries, and that rather than throw more money into the universities the state should force them to make better use of the funds they already had.[6] Too many university students, the minister of finance complained, were rejects from the specialized technical institutes and did not really know what they wanted to do with their educations.

Clearly the Council of Ministers had no use for the vision of the universities developed at the Tolstoi Conference, nor was it willing to spend anything like the 13 million rubles a year that the 1906 conference called for. Schwartz, Stolypin, and the majority of the Council of Ministers all believed that the liberal professoriate's claims for the universities were ill-defined, unrealistic, and self-serving.[7] Schwartz published comments by such leading German professors as Friedrich Paulsen that pointed out that the Tolstoi Conference draft would have given the Russian professors powers that far exceeded those of their colleagues at other universities. He and Stolypin were convinced that the professors' slogan of "a research university above politics" was a cover for anti-government activity by professors as well as students. The Council of Ministers did not want to spend state funds preparing students for vague and undefined roles. Instead, while recognizing the defects of the 1884 Statute, it demanded a precise, workable, and utilitarian definition of the universities' role and purpose. This was exactly what Schwartz tried to provide in his draft statute. His major theme was "quality over quantity." As far as he and Stolypin were concerned, it was the government, not the faculty councils, that wanted to raise academic standards, take the universities out of politics, and ensure that they did what they were supposed to do.[8]

In the spring of 1910, Schwartz finally introduced the draft statute into the Duma. Not only the Kadets but also major spokesmen of the Octobrist party attacked the plan and warned that the new statute would cripple the universities.[9] Relations between Schwartz and N. A. Khomiakov, the Octobrist president of the Duma, became severely strained. In addition, Schwartz, like his predecessor, now began to be attacked by the extreme right because of the inability of the Ministry of Education to control student unrest. V. M. Purishkevitch, the leader of the Union of the Russian People, subjected the Ministry of Education to

6. TsGIA, f. 733, op. 154, d. 471, l. 114.
7. TsGIA, f. 733, op. 154, d. 471, ll. 182–198.
8. Ibid.
9. *Vestnik Vospitaniia*, no. 5 (1910).

a number of interpellations regarding alleged violations of the law by both students and professors. Nor did the Nationalist faction in the Duma, more important than ever to a politically beleaguered Stolypin, particularly like Schwartz. One of its leaders, A. A. Bobrinskii, noted in a September 1910 diary entry that Schwartz was a "fine person, a rightist of firm principles, but, like any other professor, seems unsuited to the tasks of the Ministry of Education. The [routine] of the job seems to have paralyzed him." [10] Meanwhile, a major conservative daily, the *Novoe Vremia,* attacked both Schwartz's draft statute and his allegedly dangerous policy of opening up too many new high schools. [11]

Unable to afford additional political liabilities, Stolypin decided once again to change ministers of education. The new appointee was also a professor, L. A. Kasso, who had taught on the juridical faculty of Moscow University. A member of the Bessarabian nobility, Kasso brought with him a reputation as an arch-conservative. [12] One immediate result of Kasso's appointment was that the government withdrew Schwartz's draft statute from the Duma, despite the objections of a group of rightist professors, led by Odessa's A. P. Kazanskii, who met in January 1911 to reaffirm their support for the project. [13]

In an interview with *Novoe Vremia* Kasso announced a new turn in the government's university policy. The Ministry of Education now proclaimed that it could live with the 1884 Statute. "It is abnormal," Kasso explained, "for the statute to change every twenty years. We can get along perfectly well with the present statute and the 27 August Rules." [14]

On that note, Kasso began a four-year tenure marked by controversy and confrontation. Within a month of his taking office, the renewal of student unrest gave him and Stolypin a chance to try new policies to

10. "Dnevnik A. A. Bobrinskovo," *Krasnyi Arkhiv,* no. 26 (1928).
11. As reported in *Golos Studenchestva,* no. 1 (1910).
12. Professor P. I. Novgorodtsev, a longtime colleague at Moscow University, characterized Kasso as a "man who, though himself a professor, was by his spirit and breeding absolutely alien to the spirit and traditions of the Russian universities. . . . He came from a Rumanian family in Bessarabia and was educated abroad. If his predecessors did not always look with sufficient reverence on Russian learning, then he was . . . completely indifferent to national achievements and to the peculiarities of the Russian universities. He did not hesitate to dismiss . . . the best Russian scholars, to interfere with the work of the most eminent scientific institutions. . . . He viewed university teaching from the viewpoint of scholastic professionalism, which he wanted to implant in the Russian universities, thus killing their independence and originality" (P. N. Ignatiev, P. I. Novgorodtsev, and D. M. Odinets, *Russian Schools and Universities in the World War* [New Haven, 1929], p. 149).
13. *Rech',* 7 January 1911.
14. As reported in *Rech',* 3 February 1911.

cow the faculty councils and the students. But this time the government would find itself more isolated than at any time since 1905.

THE STUDENT MOVEMENT AND
THE TOLSTOI DEMONSTRATIONS

The collapse of the nationwide student strike in the fall of 1908 did not signal the end of student unrest in the country, but only the re-emergence of a series of local, uncoordinated confrontations. A number of student strikes occurred in 1909 and 1910 because of disputes with academic authorities over such matters as scholarships and examination schedules. Two of the most serious disputes erupted at the elite forestry institute and the Saint Petersburg Mining Institute. In both cases Stolypin directly intervened and reaffirmed Plehve's policy that the technical institutes would get the same treatment as the universities.[15]

But these were isolated incidents, and in March 1910 Assistant Minister of the Interior P. G. Kurlov expressed some guarded optimism that the students were beginning to lose their taste for confrontation.[16] He was especially encouraged by what he saw as their growing interest in sports and religion. Kurlov's assessment was echoed in the student press, which continued to decry the students' "cowardice" and *embourgeoisement*. A typical complaint, printed in 1910 in *Golos Studenchestva*, emphasized that "the problem does not lie in the so-called political differentiation of the *studenchestvo*. No, the real issue is that now a 'new *studenchestvo*' has appeared, a new kind of 'complacent student' [*studenta-obyvatelia*]. . . . For students of this kind, Sanine, Vaininger, and the libretto of the theater . . . have replaced Marx and Mikhailovskii."[17] The trend toward student professionalism, first noted after 1906, continued, but the *zemliachestva*, credit societies, and other student economic organizations still had to contend with chronic lack of funds and frequent demoralization and apathy.[18] In some cases scandals erupted over allegations of financial misdealings.

15. *Vestnik Vospitaniia*, no. 1 (1909): TsGIA, f. 1276, op. 20, d. 42. In the case of the forestry institute, the dispute concerned the elective curriculum; in the mining institute, the issue was the implementation by the Ministry of Trade and Industry of Stolypin's order banning student participation in the determination of financial aid. After a reduction in the financial-aid budget, the students declared a strike in January 1910 and the cuts were cancelled. As a result, Stolypin ordered that Professor E. S. Fedorov, Russia's leading crystallographer, be dismissed from the directorship of the mining institute.

16. TsGIA, f. 733, op. 201, d. 158.

17. *Golos Studenchestva*, no. 7 (1910).

18. An informative description of this problem can be found in "Vzaimopomoshch' i solidarnost' studenchestva," *Studencheskii Mir*, no. 1 (1910).

Despite all these hardships, however, the basic sense of a *studenchestvo* tradition continued. When the rightist deputy Purishkevitch attacked students' sexual mores in a Duma speech, there were protest *skhodki* in several *VUZy;* some students at Saint Petersburg University even wanted to challenge him to a duel.[19] The threat of Schwartz's draft statute was a powerful unifying factor. It also made students pay more attention to their professors' warnings that large-scale student disorders would play into Schwartz's hands by convincing the Octobrists to support the project.

The student press, which encountered difficulties after the abortive 1908 strike, revived in 1910. The most important student newspapers to emerge during this year were *Studencheskaia Zhizn'*, *Studencheskii Mir,* and *Golos Studenchestva.* A basic theme of the student press was the continued survival of the *studenchestvo* as a unique group with its own traditions and goals: "The Russian *studenchestvo* now constitutes an army of 100,000. . . . Though it is scattered all the way from Saint Petersburg to Tomsk, the *studenchestvo* remains a single entity and possesses common properties."[20] Economic need, wider educational access, and the democratization of the country ensured that student professionalism, advocated by most of the student press, became a complement of, rather than a substitute for, political commitment. This argument was made especially strongly in *Golos Studenchestva.* Its editorial staff included Rafael Vydrin, V. M. Friche, and S. G. Svatikov, who had all written extensively about the history of the Russian universities and the *studenchestvo.*

The student press and its propagation of student professionalism met with a cool reception from the revolutionary movement. A report on the students published in *Znamia Truda,* the organ of the Social Revolutionary party, complained that professional interests and economic concerns had replaced politics as the students' chief preoccupations.[21] *Znamia Truda* placed much of the blame on the student press. It concluded that the 1910–1911 academic year promised to be disappointingly quiet.

This prediction turned out to be totally wrong. The catalyst for the renewal of large-scale student unrest was the death of the writer Lev Tolstoi on 7 November 1910. The next day, students in *VUZy* all over the country spontaneously held memorial services and passed resolutions

---

19. TsGIA, f. 733, op. 201, d. 158.
20. *Studencheskii Mir,* no. 1 (1910).
21. *Znamia Truda,* no. 32 (1910).

calling on the students to honor Tolstoi's memory by leading the fight
against capital punishment.[22] During that week enthusiasm ran high, especially in Saint Petersburg, where police repeatedly dispersed thousands of students trying to demonstrate on the Nevskii Prospekt. When
the prorector of Saint Petersburg University, Professor I. D. Andreev,
went to the university embankment to convince the students to disperse,
the crowd lifted him off his feet and continued to march and sing.

The government was worried by the demonstrations. The head of
the Saint Petersburg Okhrana told Stolypin that the mood of the students reminded him of 1905.[23] Unlike 1908, students were marching in
the streets. Stolypin feared a possible fusion of the student and labor
movements.[24]

Had he known the students better he might have rested easier. The
student organizations that emerged in November to direct the marches
against capital punishment were ad hoc affairs, composed of self-
appointed representatives of political factions and a few delegates from
the *zemliachestva*.[25] Students sympathetic to the revolutionary movement were skeptical of the demonstrations and stayed on the sidelines.[26]
Most of the enthusiasm for the November demonstrations came from
freshmen and sophomores.[27] The few attempts made to attract worker
support for the student demonstrations ended in complete failure.[28]
Various district committees of the RSDRP advised the workers to stay
away, warning them not to trust the transient enthusiasms of the students.[29] But considering the disarray of the Social Democratic party, it is

22. A useful collection of documents describing the students' reaction to Tolstoi's
death can be found in "Politicheskaia bor'ba vokrug smerti Tolstovo," *Literaturnoe
Nasledstvo*, no. 69 (1961): 321–402.
23. Ibid., pp. 338–339.
24. TsGAOR, f. 102, d. 12, ed. kh. 59 LB, l. 30.
25. *Znamia Truda*, no. 33 (1911). A letter received by the *Znamia Truda* editorial
staff from someone at Moscow University stated that "in 1905 and 1906 the student
movement signaled the beginning of a broad popular political movement. But now . . .
alas! The student movement has caught the revolutionaries napping. The 'factions' of the
various political parties in the university did not lead the movement and in most cases
could barely keep up with it. They usually wavered and in some cases even hid."
26. *Rabochaia Gazeta*, 18 December 1910.
27. Ibid. "One of the most notable features of the demonstrations was the absence of
the older 'active' students. They were either completely absent or they used the *skhodki* to
speak against the demonstrations. The weight of the demonstrations . . . was borne by . . .
the younger students. . . . Now there are no leaders among the students. The factions of
the Social Democrats and Social Revolutionaries are weak and barely do anything. But it
is enough to say that a student is speaking in the name of a revolutionary group and the
other students listen to him."
28. "Politicheskaia bor'ba vokrug smerti Tolstovo," p. 372.
29. See, for example, an RSDRP pamphlet urging the workers to ignore the student
movement ("Politicheskaia bor'ba vokrug smerti Tolstovo," pp. 332–333). The pamphlet

probable that worker disinterest, not party pamphlets, lay behind the complete absence of proletarian involvement. Furthermore, the demonstrations themselves assumed a mass character only in Moscow and Saint Petersburg. Students in the provincial cities, all too aware of the whims of the local authorities, preferred memorial *skhodki* within the grounds of the *VUZy*.

By 15 November the Tolstoi demonstrations were over. The student organizations which arose that week in the capitals tried to maintain the momentum of the student movement by using two new issues to fan further protest: the release of students arrested during the demonstrations, and the suicide of a certain Sazonov, a political prisoner in the Novyi Zerentui prison. But calls for protest strikes in Saint Petersburg and Moscow failed.

As students dispersed for their vacations, there seemed little reason to expect an abnormal second semester. The liberal press saw the failure of the strike calls as further proof that the era of political student protest was finally over. Responsibility for this welcome development was attributed to the moral influence of the professoriate and its efforts to convince well-meaning but immature students that unrest in the universities only helped the right and jeopardized the existence of a vital national institution. Further peace in the universities depended on the government's willingness to respect the leadership of the professoriate and widen the parameters of academic autonomy.[30]

The right, however, drew radically different conclusions from the November demonstrations. And at the end of 1910, Stolypin was in no position to alienate the Nationalist party, his firmest ally in the Duma, as was evident from his decision to dismiss Schwartz. The Nationalists were frightened that the student demonstrations presaged a repeat of 1905. Prince A. A. Bobrinskii, one of their leaders, noted in his diary entry of 10 December that the "revolution is going forward . . . and the aristocracy must again prepare to defend its property. . . . All this is going on with the negligent connivance of the government."[31] On 11 December M. O. Men'shikov, in *Novoe Vremia*, urged Stolypin to crush the student movement by mass expulsions. He warned that the "second round of the revolution had already begun." The influential journalist

---

reminded the workers that in the past the students had cared little for their fate. Even if now the students were marching to protest capital punishment, it did not mean that the workers should be deluded by the "unstable, transitory moods of the intelligentsia."

30. *Vestnik Vospitaniia*, no. 1 (1911): 97–113.

31. Cited in A. Ia. Avrekh, *Stolypin i tret'ia Duma* (Moscow, 1968), p. 314.

reminded his conservative readers that the Revolution of 1905 had also begun with student demonstrations.[32]

Stolypin's response came quickly. On 11 January the government issued a circular that banned student meetings on the premises of *VUZy* and directed the police not to wait for an invitation from the faculty councils before breaking up *skhodki* and arresting participants. The circular also ordered the professors to call in the police at the first sign of trouble.[33] In a secret explanation of the circular, Stolypin told the governors-general and chiefs of police that the student movement was no longer corporate but political.[34]

It is possible that the prime minister was influenced by a special Okhrana report on the student movement that glumly warned that "the center of gravity in the revolutionary movement has passed to the students." The report emphasized the crucial importance of suppressing any student demonstrations before they spread to the working class.[35] But Stolypin clearly overreacted to the Tolstoi demonstrations and the scattered student activity at the end of November. Although masses of students had taken to the streets in Saint Petersburg, their slogans focused mainly on the issue of capital punishment and contained no revolutionary demands.

The professors, shocked at this further attenuation of their rights, protested the circular. *Russkie Vedomosti,* in a common reaction, complained that the circular abolished "university self-rule. There is no longer a trace of university autonomy."[36] Under the 27 August Rules, the option of calling police into the *VUZy* rested with the faculty councils, who exercised it when the need arose. Now professors had no choice. But despite grave misgivings, the professors prepared to comply with Stolypin's latest orders. Although they did not like the circular, such rectors as Moscow's Manuilov ignored calls to resign in protest. Such a step, he explained, might be construed as encouraging student disorders.[37] As in 1905, the professors wanted to avoid any hint of collaboration with the student movement.

32. Ibid.
33. TsGIA, f. 1276, op. 3, d. 800, l. 187.
34. TsGAOR, f. 102, d. 12, ed. kh. 59 LB, l. 30.
35. TsGAOR, f. DP, ed. kh. 59, 1911, l. 4.
36. *Russkie Vedomosti,* 14 January 1911.
37. Manuilov's report on these events is in GPB im. V. I. Lenina, f. 158, folder 5, ed. kh. 16. On 17 January the rectors of the Saint Petersburg *VUZy* met with curator Musin-Pushkin to complain about the circular. But they promised to "remain at their posts" (TsGIA, f. 733, op. 201, d. 205, l. 128).

THE 1911 STRIKE

Meanwhile the students' corporate interests were under direct attack. The ban on meetings on the premises of *VUZy* threatened to destroy the *zemliachestva* and credit societies. Rentals of outside buildings were costly, and police interference was a constant threat. Furthermore, the government dealt very harshly with some of the students arrested in the fall demonstrations. Twenty-four Saint Petersburg university students were expelled by government order, a procedure that completely bypassed the faculty disciplinary court. Five were exiled to remote regions of the country for terms ranging from two to five years.[38] The last time the government had treated student demonstrators so severely was in February 1902.

The Christmas vacation ended amid the general expectation of a strike for the second semester. Many students agreed with *Golos Studenchestva* that not only the students but also the professoriate faced a moment of truth. Self-interest alone, the newspaper editorialized, would force the professors to make common cause with the students. Just before Christmas vacation, a tense confrontation at Odessa University resulted in bloodshed when a rightist student shot a classmate. On the first day of the new semester the police arrested 373 students in Tomsk Technological Institute for attending a *skhodka*.[39]

As in 1908, Saint Petersburg took the lead in organizing student action. Pamphlets posted in various *VUZy* asked students to await a signal from Saint Petersburg.[40] Plans for a semester strike crystallized at a 23 January meeting of the newly organized Saint Petersburg City Coalition Council, which included representatives of the capital's *VUZy* as well as a Moscow delegate.[41] Once again there was a proclamation that would serve as a model for similar appeals in other cities. The Saint

38. *Russkie Vedomosti,* 1 January 1911.
39. On the Odessa incident, see *Vestnik Vospitaniia,* no. 1 (1911); on the Tomsk Technological Institute, see *Rech',* 22 January 1911. To make matters worse, the curator of the Tomsk Educational District, L. A. Lavrentiev, insulted various faculty members in front of students because the teachers were allegedly lax in trying to break up the *skhodka.*
40. A report on the mood of the *studenchestvo* at the beginning of the semester can be found in *Golos Studenchestva,* no. 3 (1911).
41. Of the thirty-one students on the City Coalition Council, eighteen considered themselves to be Social Democrats, nine were Social Revolutionaries, and four were Kadets (TsGAOR, f. DO, 1910–11, 53a, ll. 10–16). Cf. Z. S. Kruglova, "Studencheskaia zabastovka 1911ovo goda i eë politicheskoe znachenie," *Uchënye Zapiski Moskovskovo Oblastnovo Pedagogicheskovo Instituta* 135 (1964): 8.

Petersburg proclamation admitted that "our chances for victory in the upcoming struggle are slight." Nonetheless, the students could seriously embarrass the government by fighting for the principles of freedom of speech and of assembly, and liberty from police repression.[42] Another proclamation, issued on 22 January by the Kharkov coalition council, admitted that the students' situation was desperate but emphasized that there was little choice but to fight:

> The ban on *skhodki* and other meetings means the liquidation of the *zemliachestva* and mutual aid societies. . . . The *studenchestvo*, which is mostly poor, has been put into a terrible position. . . . With cold-hearted and premeditated cruelty the government is provoking the *studenchestvo;* it is pushing us onto the path of stubborn and difficult battle and we knowingly choose that path, because we have no choice. We have no illusions about the support we can expect from the Duma. In the defense of its rights the *studenchestvo* has to rely on itself alone.[43]

But along with a feeling of resignation, many of the proclamations demonstrated an undercurrent of hope that this time the student movement might generate more support than in 1908. In 1911 there was a clearer sense of the government's growing isolation in the Duma, where even the Octobrists were taking an increasingly critical stance toward many of Stolypin's policies. The 1911 student movement was based on corporate issues: the January circular, and the police repression against other students. But unlike the 1908 strike, which erupted in protest against a crackdown on the admission of Jews and women to universities, these issues could be fairly easily related to the general liberal demand for legal order and guarantees of personal inviolability. The students' corporate demands now had a decidedly political tinge.

Furthermore, leftist students tried to instruct their comrades on the political significance of the strike. In a 26 January proclamation, the Saint Petersburg Social Revolutionary Student Committee urged the *studenchestvo* to go beyond corporatism. "The student movement," the committee proclaimed, "should now drop its present goal, the struggle for academic autonomy, and fight for the overthrow of the whole system."[44] Of course, the chances for immediate success were remote. But

42. TsGAOR, f. DO, 1910–11, 53a, ll. 10–16.
43. TsGIA, f. 733, op. 201, d. 205, l. 150. For the text of a similar proclamation by the Moscow City Coalition Council, see GPB im. V. I. Lenina, f. 158, folder 6, no. 58.
44. TsGIA, f. 1282, op. 1, d. 731, l. 3. Student Social Revolutionary proclamations in Moscow and Saint Petersburg played heavily on the theme of the *studenchestvo*'s glorious tradition of protest.

by their sacrifice, the students could set an example and "reawaken Russian society." A Social Democratic group in Moscow University told the students that precisely because the peasants and the workers were so passive, the student movement was poised to play a decisive role in reawakening the masses.[45] Besides, a semester strike would harm the "system" by depriving it of educated cadres.

By the first week of February, the strike had become nationwide, involving both universities and the specialized technical institutes. Students themselves, as their purloined letters show, were surprised by the sudden resurgence of the *studenchestvo*'s spirit and determination. An informal nationwide student conference, which met during the Christmas vacation, ensured a high degree of coordination at the beginning of the semester.[46]

Once again the professoriate found itself in a quandary. Opposing both the 11 January circular and the strike, the professors continued to lecture. Students responded by obstructing classes; even popular teachers with liberal reputations (E. D. Grimm, M. Ia. Pergament, I. A. Pokrovskii) were hooted down. Bitter over the professors' opposition to the student strike, on 5 February the coalition council of Saint Petersburg University issued an "Open Letter to the Faculty" which set the tone for similar statements at other universities:

> A few days ago you asked the students to resume classes peacefully but you can see that you were unsuccessful. . . . You were not with us when we marched in the streets after Tolstoi's death. You even accept [the 11 January circular]. . . . You have closed the student employment bureau and the student financial aid commission. . . . Where, then, is your defense of the interests [of the universities]? . . . In your condemnation of the strike? In your toadyism? No, kind sirs! People of true convictions do not act in such a way. You do not even take yourselves seriously. Remember your brave pronouncements during the 1908 strike that you would defend academic autonomy? . . . What right do you have after this to hinder us in our fight for the dignity of the university? What alternative do you have to offer?[47]

As incidents multiplied, faculty councils in several major *VUZy* asked for temporary cessation of classes in order to prevent further violence.

45. TsGIA, f. 1282, op. 1, d. 731, l. 2.

46. A file of student letters purloined by the police can be found in TsGAOR, f. DP, DO 59, 46ch., LB. 1911. On the student conference, see the unsigned agent's report in TsGAOR, f. DP, ed. kh. 59, 1911, l. 66. On 28 January 1911, rector Manuilov told the Moscow University Faculty Council that on 18 January an announcement had been posted in the corridors of the university telling the students that contact had been established with the coalition councils of other *VUZy* throughout the country.

47. TsGIA, f. 733, op. 201, d. 168, l. 27.

The government, determined to smash the strike by mass arrests, refused, sending in police to guard the lecture halls. Many students asked
their teachers whether they had already forgotten the "Declaration of
the 342," in which they had proudly asserted that lecturing under such
circumstances was beneath their dignity.

On 1 February *Russkie Vedomosti* described a typical scene at Saint
Petersburg University, where, by the evening of 31 January, more than
410 students had been arrested: "There are many police with rifles and
fixed bayonets ranged along the long corridors of the university; professors, along with small numbers of students, are escorted by armed
police to lectures. Armed police stand in the lecture halls. Students
storm in, trying to interrupt lectures with whistles, noxious gases, and
the singing of revolutionary songs."[48] One professor, accosted by a
striking student, was said to have suffered a hysterical fit and had to be
carried away.[49]

In Moscow University, the situation escalated rapidly. Rector Manuilov was prepared to cooperate with the authorities. But as police stormed
into the university uninvited, to apprehend students taking part in
banned meetings, they arrested innocent bystanders as well as activists.
These actions, as Manuilov complained to the faculty council, not only
deterred moderate students from coming to classes but also had a radicalizing effect on the whole student body.[50] When their efforts to curb
police interference failed, Manuilov, assistant rector M. A. Menzbir,
and prorector P. A. Minakov decided to resign. On 28 January, the rector explained to the faculty council that although the police tried to behave correctly the 11 January circular had created an "intolerable state
of dual power in the university."[51] The three resigned their administrative, not their academic, posts and offered to continue serving in the former until replacements could be found.

Now came the surprise. Minister of Education Kasso, after consulting Stolypin and the tsar, dismissed the three professors from their university duties. Stolypin had the semi-official *Rossiia* warn that the government considered the resignations "political demonstrations," which
were intolerable on the part of state employees.[52] The Moscow University Faculty Council, in a 2 February emergency meeting, told the gov-

48. *Russkie Vedomosti*, 1 February 1911.
49. Ibid.
50. GPB im. V. I. Lenina, f. 158, folder 5, ed. kh. 16.
51. TsGIA, f. 733, op. 201, d. 168, l. 37, contains a valuable record of the faculty
council's 28 January meeting.
52. As reported in "Krizis vysshei shkoly," *Russkaia Mysl'*, no. 3 (1911): 134–164.

ernment that unless the three professors were reinstated, many of their colleagues would be forced to resign.[53] But Stolypin refused to compromise, and Moscow University tottered on the brink of ruin. By 20 February twenty-five full professors and seventy-four junior faculty members had resigned from the university—more than one-third of the teaching staff. The natural sciences faculty was especially hard-hit.[54] Most of those who resigned did not return to Moscow University or, indeed, to service in any *VUZy* controlled by the Ministry of Education. Many did, however, find positions in the independent Shaniavskii University, the Moscow Commercial Institute, or the *VUZy* not attached to the Ministry of Education. The government did not interfere with these appointments.[55]

The year 1911 came to be known as the year of the "destruction [*razgrom*] of Moscow University." Professor Evgenii Trubetskoi, in a widely quoted "plague on both your houses" article, explained that his and his colleagues' resignations in no way connoted any support for the student movement. During any period of political confrontation, "the university should enjoy the same status as a Red Cross hospital on the battlefield and should not be shot at from either side. . . . We resigned . . . because neither side respected the neutrality of the university."[56] In another comment on the resignations, Peter Struve, writing in *Russkaia Mysl'*, lamented that the current crisis, "the worst faced by Moscow University in its 150-year existence," had fundamental political as well as academic implications. Struve emphasized that, unlike past crises in the universities, this one seemed to offer no shreds of hope, no grounds for ultimate optimism.[57]

Many students and large sections of the Russian public hailed the mass resignations as an act of moral courage, but the Moscow City Coalition Council, coordinating strike activities there, reminded the

53. TsGIA, f. 733, op. 201, d. 161, l. 135.

54. The 6 February issue of *Russkie Vedomosti* reported that of the 21 full professors who had resigned by that date, 1 was from the history and philology faculty, 10 were from the physics and mathematics faculty, 3 were from the law faculty, and 7 were from the medical faculty. Of the 69 *privat-dozenty* on the natural sciences faculty, 36 resigned. Corresponding figures for the medical, juridical, and history faculties are 18 out of 124, 16 out of 38, and 9 out of 39. A full list of those resigning can be found in V. I. Vernadskii, "1911 god v istorii russkoi umstvennoi kul'tury," *Ezhegodnik Gazety Rech' za 1911 god* (Saint Petersburg, 1912).

55. On alternatives available to professors in other *VUZy* not under the Ministry of Education's control, see M. M. Novikov, *Ot Moskvy do N'iu-Iorka* (New York, 1952), pp. 94–100; N. V. Speranskii, *Krizis russkoi shkoly* (Moscow, 1914), pp. 182–183.

56. *Rech'*, 23 February 1911.

57. "Krizis vysshei shkoly," p. 163.

studenchestvo that the professors did not leave the university out of sympathy with the students. They had looked on impassively while the government moved to curtail student rights and disband their organizations. In resigning, the Moscow professors demanded the reinstatement of their three comrades but kept silent about the return of expelled students or the rights of students to organize and meet. The coalition council concluded its commentary with a warning to students that they could not count on faculty support and would have to maintain their struggle alone to the end.[58]

Nor could students expect much help from what was left of the regular Social Democratic organizations in the capitals. At the beginning of February the Saint Petersburg City Social Democratic Committee adopted a set of "theses" on the student movement that opposed trying to involve workers in the students' struggle—although it welcomed the student movement as a sign of strained intelligentsia-government relations, which would weaken Russia's prestige in Europe. The committee also reminded student Social Democrats that their first task was to help the regular party; work on behalf of the student movement was of secondary importance.[59] Other Social Democratic groups were no more encouraging, with the possible exception of Trotsky's *Pravda*. The latter admitted that the student movement historically owed little to outside influence or direction but claimed that its spontaneity and vitality were potential political assets to the Social Democratic movement if the latter could only find a way to channel the students' energies into regular party work.[60]

A lead editorial in the Bolshevik *Zvezda* on 29 January was an important barometer of the relationship between the revolutionary and the student movements. *Zvezda* stressed the basic social differences between the student movement and the labor movement and echoed the statements made elsewhere in the left-wing press that students with clear revolutionary views or party affiliations had largely ignored the student movement.[61] *Zvezda*'s analysis of the student movement stressed its unique sociological characteristics and offered some still-useful insights into the place of the universities in prerevolutionary Russian society. Most of the students involved in the strike, the editorial asserted,

58. TsGAOR, f. 102, op. 12, ed. kh. 59, 46A/1911, l. 88.
59. TsGAOR, f. 102, op. 12, ed. kh. 65, 3/1911.
60. See the copy of a circular discussion letter on the student movement sent by the editorial board of *Pravda,* in TsGAOR, f. DP, ed. kh. 59, 1911, l. 106.
61. *Zvezda,* 29 January 1911.

were young arrivals from the provinces, where there was even less political freedom than in the capitals. These students reflected the seething
but impotent discontent of their fathers, the "formless mass of middling
and petty citizenry." Student disorders were inchoate and undefined,
but they would continue until "those classes from which the students
come stop being discontented."

While the *Zvezda* analysis minimized some of the genuine corporate
concerns of the *studenchestvo,* its description of the student movement
as a function of the wider discontent of the middle classes underscored a
crucial clue to the political significance of the 1911 strike: the relationship between the student movement and Russian liberalism in a tense
period when widespread disillusionment with the political situation in
the country had replaced the high hopes raised by the 17 October manifesto. And it was precisely these middle classes from which the *studenchestvo* came: the petty bureaucrats, clerks, schoolteachers, and merchants who also represented the chief potential social base of the Kadet
party.

A major reason why the student movement was important was that
in many respects it represented a spontaneous but nonetheless conspicuous attack on some of the central assumptions of Russian liberalism.
This was the thrust of a provocative analysis published by Nikolai
Iordanskii, a prominent journalist and moderate Social Democrat who,
as we have seen, had himself been a leader of the 1899 student strike.[62]
He reminded his readers that the current student movement posed a direct challenge to the consciences and beliefs of those very groups in Russian society, including the liberal professoriate and the Kadet party, who
felt that "after 17 October 1905, Russia had crossed the Rubicon and
begun a course of social development on the European model." The student movement threw them into "perplexity and confusion. . . . Liberalism sympathizes with many of the demands of the student movement,
such as academic freedom and autonomy for the universities. But the
students' tactics of [direct confrontation] are very different from the liberal tactic of compromise, and the student movement inspires fear in the
liberal camp, especially because liberalism cannot help seeing in the student movement a strong element of democratic social radicalism." The
professoriate opposed the student movement, in part from the sincere
conviction that student protest would jeopardize the future of Russian
higher education, play into the hands of the right, and lead the govern-

62. Nikolai Iordanskii, "Ottsy i deti," *Sovremennyi Mir,* no. 2 (1911).

ment to rescind some of the gains won by the professors after 1905. While the student movement defended academic autonomy by direct confrontation, the professors preferred the liberal tactic of compromise. But was this realistic in the Russia of 1911?

> The liberal tragedy reaches its highest stage precisely in the area where fathers clash directly with the children: in the sphere of the professors' relations with the students. The professors cannot dodge having to give direct answers to the accursed questions raised by the students, but in a confrontation they must make a choice and at the same time be ready to take firm action. But this itself is foreign to the political character of Russian liberalism.[63]

It was only natural, Iordanskii continued, for the professoriate to compensate for its lack of real power by striving for the removal of the university from the arena of power and politics, defending the integrity and importance of "pure science," and asking all sides to respect the "neutrality" of the university. And even after more than one-third of the faculty of Moscow University resigned, the professors were still careful to emphasize that they were protesting the violation by the students as well as the government of the idea that the university should be "above politics."

In a suggestive counterpoint to Iordanskii's article, A. S. Izgoev's analysis of the university crisis, published in Struve's *Russkaia Mysl'*, also saw the wider stakes involved, but from a different perspective. Whereas Iordanskii clinically analyzed the implications of the university crisis for Russian liberalism, Izgoev, in a passionate defense of the professoriate, attacked not only the students and the government but also the Russian educated public. For Izgoev, the real question was whether Russia's thin reserves of culture and civic values could survive constant blows from right and left, as well as the indifference of an educated public that failed to understand the significance of the universities for the nation's future. Only the professoriate, Izgoev argued, understood what was at stake and was fighting to protect the *VUZy*.[64]

The students were forcing both the professoriate and the Kadet party to face the harsh realities of the role of power in political and academic life—and to take a second look at the notion that the university could somehow lead a life uniquely above the political fray. The Kadets had to consider the issues raised by the student movement at their May 1911

63. Ibid.
64. A. S. Izgoev, "Nebyvalyi razgrom," *Russkaia Mysl'*, no. 3 (1911): 146–147.

party conference. One item on the agenda was the relationship between the party and its student groups. Kadet student representatives told the conference that they were fighting the left for influence among the students and needed clear guidelines from the central party. Was the university only a cultural center, the students asked, or did it have a political role?

Many members of the party, including Paul Miliukov, himself a former academic, found themselves torn between their opposition to student strikes in principle and their awareness of the usefulness of student unrest as a convenient way of causing the government political embarrassment. The underlying issue, as Miliukov recognized, was whether Russian liberalism should respond to the government's overall policies by abandoning the polite tactics of a "loyal opposition" and returning to the direct confrontation of 1905.

It was a strained discussion. Some members, such as N. V. Nekrasov, suggested that the party follow the example set by the students: why follow constitutional tactics when the government did not even respect the promises of the 17 October manifesto? Besides, did not the Duma itself, and even the Kadet party, come out of the 1905 general strike? Yes, other delegates responded, but that was an exceptional case. Now the party had to condemn the student strike explicitly. How could they try to build respect for law, culture, and learning, and simultaneously endorse student strikes?

Professor Nikolai Gredeskul saw the student movement as forcing the Kadet party to face the vital question of the incompatibility between the liberal goal of a constitutional Russia and the use of "unconstitutional tactics."[65] He urged the party to condemn student strikes. Until 1905 the student movement had "carried the torch" against the autocracy, but now it only undermined the effort to give culture and learning a secure place in Russian society.

In the end Miliukov advised the conference to avoid taking a stand and to refuse to issue guidelines to the Kadet students. By straddling the issue, Miliukov conceded that the party was putting itself in a two-faced situation, unwilling to support the students but loath to condemn them. Nonetheless, the party followed Miliukov's advice. In the words of Soviet historian A. Ia. Avrekh, the "Kadets, as a constitutional party op-

---

65. TsGAOR, f. 523, op. 1, ed. kh. 11/1911, ll. 34–36 (minutes of 9 May 1911 meeting of Kadet Central Committee). Another important meeting of the Kadet Duma faction on the subject of the student movement took place on 16 January 1911 (TsGAOR, f. 523, op. 1, ed. kh. 3). See also Avrekh, *Stolypin i tret'ia Duma*, pp. 441–442.

posed in principle to revolutionary tactics, could not approve student demonstrations, but they were not averse to using them for their own purposes."[66]

This time, the students did not lose heart after a few days and peacefully return to the classroom, as they did in the 1908 strike. To break the strike the government resorted to mass expulsions and suspensions on an unprecedented scale, expelling 1,871 students and suspending 4,406.[67] Those students previously exiled as a result of the Tolstoi demonstrations suffered harsh treatment. *Rech'* reported that few of the exiles to the Arkhangel'sk region had sufficient money or warm clothing. Many students had to march twenty versts a day to their ultimate destinations.[68] The authorities also conducted mass arrests of student coalition councils, and these arrests thwarted a planned student conference in April to discuss the overall situation of the *studenchestvo*.[69] As a final blow, Kasso warned students on financial aid that if they did not start attending classes, they would lose their scholarships. Nevertheless, the strike continued to be highly effective until the beginning of April.

One way the government hoped to combat the student movement was to encourage the formation of rightist student groups. Representatives of these groups were granted private audiences with Stolypin and the tsar in February and March. There was more concrete inducement as well, such as preference in financial aid or the promise of state posts after graduation.[70] In Odessa the prorector asked for and received a consignment of pistols to distribute to rightist students—which resulted in the shooting of a student. But in the central universities the membership of these organizations remained extremely small. It was only in Odessa and Kiev, where the rightist professors used the protection of the local authorities to gain control of the faculty councils, that the right-wing student groups were a significant factor.[71]

Although the government, as the students themselves foresaw, suppressed the strike, that victory came at a price. The wholesale arrests and the mass resignations from Moscow University occurred at a time

66. Avrekh, *Stolypin i tret'ia Duma*, p. 441.

67. A tabulation of those expelled and suspended in the spring of 1911 can be found in TsGIA, f. 733, op. 201, d. 206, l. 167.

68. *Rech'*, 18 February 1911.

69. TsGAOR, f. DP, ed. kh. 59/1911, l. 116.

70. On 30 December 1913, Minister of the Interior Makarov sent a long report to Prime Minister Kokovtsev outlining the history of the rightist student groups in the *VUZy* and government attempts to help them. See TsGIA, f. 1276, op. 3, d. 800, l. 187.

71. Ibid.

when Stolypin was already becoming more estranged from some of his former supporters, such as the industrialists and the Octobrists. Along with the nettlesome western zemstvo crisis,[72] the university problem both underscored and increased his political isolation and demonstrated just how dependent Stolypin had become on the Council of the United Nobility, which bore him no great love, and the Nationalists.

A conspicuous sign of the political effects of the university crisis and the growing dissatisfaction with Stolypin's policies was the public protest signed by the sixty-six leading industrialists in the middle of February; they were very upset over the apparent destruction of Moscow University. The industrialists condemned some of the worst excesses of the strike but put most of the blame for the university crisis on the government:

> During the past few years the revolutionary wave was ebbing [in the universities] . . . and the students became more serious about their studies; one can say with certainty that only a few months ago the overwhelming mass of Russian students were far from any idea of active protest. If, as a result of the measures of the government, this protest arose and assumed, in many cases, rude forms, does this mean that [the government] can, with a clear conscience, take revenge on the university itself? In important matters of national interest, wrath is a poor guide for policy.[73]

Many Octobrists also attacked the government's handling of the university problem. The party met on 12 February to discuss the issue. N. P. Shubinskii read a report on the student movement covering the period from November until February; he concluded that the present strike did not have a revolutionary character and that the whole mass movement was the result of Stolypin's overreaction to the Tolstoi demonstrations. Most students, he told the meeting, wanted to defend university autonomy, not overthrow the regime. Another delegate, V. K. von Anrep, supported Shubinskii and saw the university crisis in the context of a

---

72. In March 1911 an amended version of a Stolypin proposal introducing zemstvos into five western provinces was rejected by the conservative State Council. In order to increase Russian influence at the expense of the Poles in these projected zemstvos, the bill proposed a voting law that severely limited the power of the Polish nobility. The State Council, in a bitter rebuke to Stolypin, rejected the proposal because, to quote Richard Charques, "the nobility there might be entirely Polish, but nobility they remained and as such had a prescriptive right . . . to the privileges of their class." Stung by the rebuke, Stolypin forced the grudging assent of the tsar to the removal from the State Council of two of his right-wing foes and the implementation of the bill under Article 87. This high-handed action further weakened his political position. See Richard Charques, *The Twilight of Imperial Russia* (London, 1965), pp. 184–185.

73. For the text of the protest, see *Vestnik Vospitaniia*, no. 2 (1911).

growing gulf between even the loyalist elements in the country and the Stolypin regime. But the party itself, already on the verge of disintegration, was deeply split on the issue, as its votes on the Duma interpellations (discussed below) would show.[74]

Between 22 January and 8 February the Duma discussed the university question. The Kadets were in a very delicate position, torn as they were between their opposition to the government and their scruples about a "university above politics"; at first they hoped that the matter could be kept out of the Duma altogether. But the Social Democrats and the Trudoviki pressed the issue by introducing formal interpellations of the government's policy. This forced the Kadets to take a stand.[75] I. P. Pokrovskii, representing the Social Democrats, challenged the liberal view of the student movement by linking some of the underlying causes of student unrest to the genuine economic problems of much of the *studenchestvo*.[76] He also questioned the moral integrity of a professoriate that had enforced, albeit reluctantly, government circulars abridging university autonomy.

The Kadets finally introduced an interpellation of their own, based on the alleged legal incompatibility between the 11 January circular and the 1905 Temporary Rules. V. A. Maklakov, the major Kadet speaker, emphasized that student unrest had been on the wane in Russia until the government, whose motives he questioned, needlessly provoked the students with the January circular. Until then, the students had rebuffed all pleas from "outside agitators" for revolutionary demonstrations; the students were "sick of politics"; the "professoriate, irrespective of political affiliation, stood up to the revolutionaries and despite all abuse . . . protected the university for learning." And, he continued, "just when it appeared that the agitation from the left had failed, troublemakers appeared from the right and our government stabbed . . . the professors in the back."[77]

The Duma defeated the Kadet interpellation by a margin of 160 to 109. The vote was narrower than expected, and it foreshadowed the ministerial crisis of March 1911, the disintegration of the Octobrist party, and the growing polarization in the Duma between a center-left bloc of Kadets and Progressives and a right-wing bloc of conservative Octobrists, Nationalists, and the extreme right.

74. Iordanskii, "Ottsy i deti."
75. Ibid.
76. *Rech'*, 6 February 1911.
77. *Russkie Vedomosti*, 9 February 1911.

Another result of the 1911 university crisis was a further deterioration in relations between the government and the professoriate. Many
professors in other institutions agonized over whether they should join
their Moscow colleagues in resigning their posts but were dissuaded
from doing so after it became clear that the Ministry of Education welcomed resignations from professors with a liberal reputation.[78] The
1911–1914 period was a low point in the relations between the Ministry of Education and the professoriate. Between 1907 and 1909 the ministry followed the recommendations of the faculty councils in appointment decisions on all but five occasions. But in 1911 the ministry made
twenty-one appointments that conflicted with the wishes of the faculty
councils and in 1913 it made thirteen more appointments of which the
faculty councils disapproved.[79]

Kasso dealt ruthlessly with professors who publicly questioned the
policies of the Ministry of Education. A favorite tactic was to transfer
professors from the central universities to schools in the provinces,
where they would be at the mercy of local authorities less hesitant to
employ the police powers granted them by the 1881 special decrees.
Kasso disingenuously argued that his main aim was to raise the quality
of the provincial universities. In this way he proceeded to break up the
prestigious juridical faculty of Saint Petersburg University. In the summer of 1911 he ordered Professor M. Ia. Pergament to transfer to Iur'ev
University. Pergament refused and resigned. In August 1912 he transferred I. A. Pokrovskii to Kharkov University.[80] In 1913 D. D. Grimm
resigned his professorship rather than accept a transfer to Kharkov
University.[81]

In turn conservative professors were transferred from the provinces
to the central universities. A notable example was Professor P. P. Migulin,
who was transferred from Kharkov to Saint Petersburg to lecture in financial law. His first lecture, which took place on 23 January 1912, set
off a sizable student demonstration. Migulin was hooted down and not
permitted to finish his lecture. The next month Professor V. A. Udintsov,
whom Kasso took from Kiev University to fill Pergament's civil law
chair at Saint Petersburg, received similar treatment and lectured under

78. V. R. Leikina-Svirskaia, "Iz istorii bor'by Peterburgskovo Universiteta s ministerstvom Kasso," *Vestnik Leningradskovo Universiteta*, no. 4 (1947).
79. V. P. Iakovlev, "Politika samoderzhaviia v universitetskom voprose, 1905–11,"
Kandidat dissertation, Leningrad State University, 1970, p. 197.
80. Leikina-Svirskaia, "Iz istorii bor'by."
81. V. I. Vernadskii, "Vysshaia shkola v Rossii," *Ezhegodnik Gazety Rech' za 1914
god* (Petrograd, 1915), p. 312.

constant police guard.[82] In another blow aimed at the Saint Petersburg juridical faculty, Kasso forbade *privat-dozenty* from giving courses already being offered by full professors. This sudden move prevented an extremely popular and able group—A. Kaufman, M. P. Chubinskii, V. A. Lazarevskii, and I. V. Gessen—from offering their courses.[83]

ON THE EVE OF THE WAR

After Stolypin's assassination in September 1911, the state's university policy remained in Kasso's hands until his own death in 1914. The rift between the state and the professoriate continued to grow. In a move ostensibly made to train more professors and alleviate the serious problem of "vacant chairs," Kasso proposed, in November 1911, the opening of special seminars for selected graduate students in Berlin, Tübingen, and Paris. Modeled on a similar scheme in the 1880s, Kasso's plan undermined the right of Russian professors to train their successors. To add insult to injury, the candidates would be chosen by the Ministry of Education rather than by the professors themselves. The Academy of Sciences labeled the scheme a "needless abasement of the dignity of Russian science."[84] But even in the face of intensely hostile public opinion, the Council of Ministers approved Kasso's scheme, albeit with a marked lack of enthusiasm.[85]

The shortage of qualified professors was one reason the minister of education cited for opposing requests from numerous zemstvos and cities for more universities. On 20 January 1911, the Council of Ministers ordered Kasso to report on the future direction of the nation's higher-education policy. The directive recognized a special need to expand facilities in higher technical education.[86]

On 9 February 1912, the Council of Ministers met to consider Kasso's conclusions. Kasso stated that there was a particular need for medical, veterinary, and agricultural education but argued against a general policy commitment to the expansion of higher education. The study group chaired by Kasso considered requests for new universities in Rostov and Tiflis; polytechnics in Samara, Perm, Ekaterinburg, and Nizhni-Novgorod; the expansion of Tomsk University, new veterinary institutes

82. *Vestnik Vospitaniia*, no. 4 (1912).
83. *Vestnik Vospitaniia*, no. 3 (1914).
84. *Rech'*, 16 October 1911.
85. TsGIA, f. 733, op. 155, d. 201, ll. 4–9.
86. TsGIA, f. 1276, op. 20, d. 49.

in Tomsk and Omsk; and new agricultural institutes in Kursk, Novo-Nikolaevsk, and Krasnoiarsk. Kasso rejected most of these requests, recommending only an agricultural institute in Voronezh, a mining institute in Ekaterinburg, and a medical faculty in Rostov. The council rejected strong pressure for a university in Tiflis because it feared the consequences of establishing an institution of higher education in the Caucasus. At its February 1912 meeting the Council of Ministers approved Kasso's recommendations.[87]

When Nicholas II reviewed the record of the 9 February meeting of the Council of Ministers, his written comments both described the past trend of the state's policy toward higher education and strongly indicated what future policy would be. The tsar endorsed the specific recommendations of the Council of Ministers, including the proviso that henceforth the government would only pay the yearly expenses while the locality would have to pay the construction costs of any new institution of higher education. In endorsing the recommendations the tsar wrote: "I agree. I think that Russia needs higher technical institutions and *even more so* intermediate technical and agricultural schools, but the already existing universities are sufficient. Take this resolution to be my guiding order."[88] In short, the tsar decreed that there would be no more universities in Russia, only additional specialized institutes.

Although the government and the Ministry of Education discouraged the establishment of new universities, it would be wrong to infer that the 1905–1914 period saw the erosion of Russia's system of higher education. On the contrary, in this period the numbers of *VUZy* and students reached an all-time high. A major reason for this was the growing initiative of other ministries and private individuals in starting new *VUZy* and supporting existing ones.

Two of the most important of these new *VUZy* were the Saint Petersburg Psychoneurological Institute and Moscow's Shaniavskii University. Both these institutions were started and funded by private sources, an indication that the rise of a new Russian bourgeoisie was beginning to generate enough capital to challenge the traditional hegemony of the

87. Ibid. For a critical appraisal of the government's refusal to establish a new university in Tiflis, see Speranskii, *Krizis russkoi shkoly*, p. 184. Although most ministers opposed establishing a *VUZ* in Tiflis, Viceroy Vorontsov-Dashkov's arguments in favor of such a move received Prime Minister Kokovtsev's support. Finally, the tsar approved the establishment of a polytechnic there, but nothing was accomplished before the outbreak of World War I.

88. Sovet Ministrov, "Ob otkrytii novykh vysshikh uchebnykh zavedenii i o rasshirenii sushchestvuiushchikh," *Osobyi Zhurnal*, 9 February 1912.

state.[89] Neither had an easy time gaining government approval to begin operations, and outside interference remained a constant problem.[90] But these new *VUZy* indicated the beginning of significant new trends in Russian higher education.

Shaniavskii University, for example, broke new ground in university governance and curriculum.[91] The faculty, recruited from the staffs of nearby *VUZy* and from those professors who had resigned from Moscow University, enjoyed excellent relations with the students. The Shaniavskii curriculum was geared to the needs of zemstvo workers, municipal employees, schoolteachers, and other groups who needed a new kind of higher education. Prospective students did not face the admissions barriers that complicated the quest of seminary graduates, Jews, and women for a university education. Courses included public administration, the cooperative movement, public health, pedagogic theory, and other areas not strongly represented in the traditional university curriculum. There was a fundamental tension within Shaniavskii University between the traditional concept of the Humboldtian elite university and the notion of practical higher education aimed at a mass constituency.[92] But the tension was creative and hinted at a new willingness to reconsider the traditional role of university education. Although Shaniavskii's degrees did not confer the same privileges as those granted by state institutions, its graduates found that employers respected their academic credentials.[93]

There were several other indications of the growing diversity of Russian higher education on the eve of World War I. The Ministry of Trade and Industry fostered the rapid expansion of higher commercial education: in 1913 the Moscow Commercial Institute, the biggest such school, had more than four thousand students. The network of polytechnic institutes continued to attract more students. By 1910 there were more than twenty *VUZy* for women, with a total enrollment of over twenty thousand. According to *Ezhegodnik Rossii* 74,783 students were enrolled in state *VUZy* in 1914. University students made up

89. On the Psychoneurological Institute, see Alexander Vucinich, *Science in Russian Culture* (Stanford, 1970), vol. 2, p. 322. A useful survey of the growing role of private contributors can be found in *Vestnik Vospitaniia*, no. 4 (1914).

90. Speranskii, *Krizis russkoi shkoly*, pp. 147–184.

91. Ibid.; A. A. Kizevetter, *Na rubezhe dvukh stoletii* (Prague, 1929), pp. 470–494; Silke Spieler, *Autonomie oder Reglementierung* (Cologne, 1981), pp. 188–212.

92. For example, see Professor A. I. Chuprov's comments on the relationship between the projected Shaniavskii University and the more traditional universities, quoted in Speranskii, *Krizis russkoi shkoly*, p. 160.

93. Kizevetter, *Na rubezhe dvukh stoletii*, pp. 492–493.

about half this total. Adding enrollment in non-state institutions, Russia's student population in 1914 exceeded one hundred thousand.[94] Leading universities such as Saint Petersburg and Moscow universities were among the largest in the world.

But this expansion of Russian higher education did not soothe the growing resentment of the professoriate. Leading professors pointed out that most of this expansion was a result of private initiative or the efforts of other ministries. The Ministry of Education, they complained, was doing practically nothing. Most important, the state had apparently turned its back once and for all on the professors' claim for the elite Humboldtian university as the cornerstone of Russia's system of higher education.

In 1914, Professor V. I. Vernadskii published a severe criticism of the state's higher-education policy. The concentration on specialized technical institutes, Vernadskii warned, was a mistake that would seriously affect the future of Russian higher education:

> The creation in the nation of a system of higher education in which specialized institutes predominate over universities has no precedent in any country . . . and will have important and widespread consequences. One should not deny some useful benefits from the creation of multi-department higher technical schools. They introduce much that is valuable and new into Russian life. But at the same time the influence of general education, imparted by the universities, is lost. The respect of the Russian public for pure learning diminishes. I think that the structure of the [university] provides more of a basis for the proper organization of academic life than does a structure based on technical, commercial, and agricultural schools. In any case the university has stood the test of experience and represents a known quantity. It is no accident that the educational system of other countries has been based on the universities, and that includes such practically oriented peoples as the English and the Americans. But Russia is embarking on another path, is making a new experiment, but it is doing so accidentally, only because of the unfortunate character of its central ministry in charge of education.[95]

Despite the great increase in private giving and local support of higher education, the university professoriate knew that ultimately the universities needed the financial and moral commitment of the state. On the eve of World War I, this goal seemed more elusive than at any time since 1884.

---

94. In "Vysshaia shkola v Rossii," Vernadskii cited a total figure of 137,000 students in 1912. This included students in people's universities and other institutions that did not confer the state-recognized privileges associated with the degree.

95. As cited in ibid.

THE *STUDENCHESTVO*, 1911–1914

Right up until the beginning of the war, the Russian government maintained its pressure on the *studenchestvo*, but it failed to pacify the *VUZy*. The *studenchestvo* did not forget the 1911 crackdown nor did it forgive the government for the unprecedented expulsions and suspensions. Between 1911 and 1914 several outbreaks of student unrest occurred, most confined to specific *VUZy*, a few escalating to nationwide protests. There were strikes and sympathy demonstrations over a mass repression of the students of the military-medical academy; *skhodki* to protest the Beilis trial and the Lena massacre; and, most frequent of all, constant demonstrations against unwelcome professors foisted on the universities by the Ministry of Education.

As in the past, the *studenchestvo* was quicker to protest attacks on comrades than to react to events outside the *VUZy*. For example, the reaction to the events in the military-medical academy involved many more students than did the protests against the Beilis trial and the Lena Goldfields massacre—although the latter made the Okhrana very nervous.[96]

The assault on the military-medical academy was another example of the gratuitously repressive policies that alienated the Russian government from the educated public on the eve of World War I. The students at the academy had long been divided into two groups, those with a future military obligation and those whose status differed little from students in other *VUZy*. (The first group had state scholarships.) On 14 December 1912, V. A. Sukhomlinov, the minister of war, issued an order requiring all students at the academy to salute officers—even in the street. The students were outraged by the militarization of their status, and most refused to give the required salute. One officer responded by striking a student with a saber, and his victim then attempted suicide. Four hundred students promptly resigned from the academy. Unfazed, on 12 March 1913, Sukhomlinov announced a new statute that turned the school into a full-fledged military institution. In response, more than a hundred thousand students participated in short protest strikes.[97]

But Russian student life during this period was marked by more than

96. "Kak otozvalis' studenchestvo i obshchestvo na sobytiia v voenno-meditsinskoi akademii," *Studencheskie Gody,* no. 3–4 (1913); *Studencheskoe Delo,* no. 5–6 (1912); TsGIAM, f. 11, op. 5, ed. kh. 454, l. 112.

97. "Kak otozvalis' studenchestvo"; A. Ia. Avrekh, *Tsarizm i chetvërtaia Duma* (Moscow, 1981), pp. 64–67.

just protests and demonstrations. The processes that had begun after the Revolution of 1905 continued, and so did the problems. More students than ever—more than one hundred thousand—attended *VUZy* in 1914, with an especially large influx from the peasant estate. The vast majority crowded into Saint Petersburg and Moscow, where they continued the fierce competition for jobs, housing, and scholarships. As we have seen (see Chapter 7), this large increase in numbers, along with new political realities, made it increasingly difficult to talk about the *studenchestvo* as a close-knit family held together by common moral and economic interests. Besides sheer numbers, unmistakable signs of growing intellectual heterogeneity strained old traditions and definitions. One notable example was the growth of a students' Christian Movement, with numerous chapters and international ties.[98] This religious movement, condemned by the Synod, had nothing to do with state-sponsored rightist student organizations, but its growth, as several respected observers of university life pointed out, showed that new processes were at work within the *studenchestvo*.[99]

Most discussions of "where the *studenchestvo* is going," however, stopped with questions, not answers. Typical was Vernadskii's cautious appraisal that the "*studenchestvo* stood at a crossroads."[100] Few observers repeated the prediction, so common in 1907–1908, that the Russian students would follow the bourgeois road of their post-1848 German counterparts.

One reason for this caution was that amid the growing signs of intellectual heterogeneity, there were also clear indications of centripetal forces at work within the *studenchestvo*. In many important respects student organizations and traditions were showing unmistakable resilience and vitality. After all, the old problems—loneliness, economic need, intellectual confusion—remained, and the students needed their organizations more than ever. In the period just before the war, student organizations such as *zemliachestva* and cooperative societies enjoyed impressive growth, although their instability was a source of constant concern.[101] The *zemliachestva*, for all their drawbacks, maintained their central place in student life and relied heavily on the mystique of the stu-

98. V. I. Vernadskii, "Vysshaia shkola i nauchnye organizatsii," *Ezhegodnik Gazety Rech' za 1913 god* (Saint Petersburg, 1914), pp. 366–367.

99. L. Kleinbort, "Sovremennaia molodëzh': Prezhde i teper'," *Sovremennyi Mir*, 10 (1914): 138.

100. Vernadskii, "Vysshaia shkola i nauchnye organizatsii," pp. 366–367.

101. *Russkie Vedomosti*, 5 January 1914; P. Trofimov, "Itogi i perspektivy studencheskovo ekonomicheskovo dvizheniia," in S. G. Svatikov, ed., *Put' studenchestva* (Petrograd, 1916), pp. 167–193.

dent traditions to integrate entering freshmen into the student culture.[102]

The student organizations still faced formidable problems. The 1911 circulars banning all but student "scientific circles" from university premises forced the *zemliachestva* and student economic organizations off campus. They faced manifold challenges in finding suitable meeting places and obtaining legal recognition on the basis of the 4 March 1906 Rules on Voluntary Associations.[103] All the while the old problems continued to bedevil the *zemliachestva* and other student economic organizations: lack of funds, over-reliance on a diligent few, and so forth.[104]

Continuing a trend of which everyone but the government and the extreme right seemed to be aware, the center of student concerns continued to shift away from purely political organizations and toward the problems of student professionalism. (Although, as we have seen, the students' alleged obsession with politics had always been misunderstood.) The student political groups survived, but their place in student life depended, as before, on their relationship to and involvement in issues specific to the *studenchestvo*. And within the political groups themselves, especially the student Social Democrats, there was little patience with the doctrinal disputes dividing the adult parties.[105] Of course, this did not mean that the *studenchestvo* as a whole was indifferent to politics. What the students were looking for were answers to the problems of relating larger political and moral issues to their own experiences and situation, something the revolutionary parties per se could not offer.

Perhaps the major issue of student life just before the war was the ongoing debate concerning student professionalism and moral commitment. Would the student economic organizations renounce any kind of political, moral, or educational mission and confine themselves to organizing inexpensive dining halls and discount bookstores? Or would they use the framework created by the students' economic and fraternal needs to inculcate in their members the *studenchestvo*'s traditional concern with justice and democracy? This question was fought out on the pages of the student press and within the *zemliachestva* and student cooperatives. Two new weeklies, Moscow's *Studencheskie Gody* (founded

102. An example is the May 1912 appeal of the Serpukhov *zemliachestvo* of Moscow University to entering freshmen (TsGAOR, f. 102, op. 13, ed. kh. 59, 46ch. B/1912, l. 25).

103. Trofimov, "Itogi i perspektivi"; "Neskol'ko slov k voprosu o studencheskom dome," *Studencheskie Gody,* no. 2 (1913).

104. "Zemliachestva ili kooperatsiia?" *Studencheskoe Delo,* no. 1 (1912).

105. For example, see the 3 April 1913 Okhrana report on the student movement in TsGIAM, f. 111, op. 5, ed. kh. 455, l. 179.

in 1912) and Saint Petersburg's *Studencheskoe Delo* (founded in 1913), emerged as the most energetic proponents of a morally committed student professionalism.[106] Another student newspaper, *Golos Polytekhnika*, argued that students' main responsibility was to work hard, acquire useful skills, and serve the nation by doing their jobs well. Student organizations should limit themselves to immediate economic matters and leave wider questions to the discretion of their individual members. The old *studenchestvo*, *Golos Polytekhnika* asserted, was gone.[107]

This debate coincided with a growing tendency toward larger student organizations operating on a citywide rather than an institutional basis.[108] This trend affected both cooperative societies and *zemliachestva*. An important example was the campaign launched in Moscow in 1912 for a Student House. The Student House would be built with funds raised by the students themselves and would serve as a physical base for citywide student organizations and enterprises. Proponents pointed out that such an enterprise would teach the students how to manage a large-scale project themselves and wean them away from their over-reliance on handouts and charity balls.[109] As the Student House campaign spread to Saint Petersburg, a committee emerged to define its ultimate purposes. Some members of the Student House committee saw it as a totally apolitical center open to all students, but a group centered in the staff of Moscow's *Studencheskoe Delo* saw the Student House as a base for the "democratic *studenchestvo*." While avoiding identification with any particular party, it would nonetheless support a nonpartisan but left-wing "democratic professionalism." The paper emphasized that its aim was "that every students' organization should always regard itself as part of a general student movement, that it should teach its members to aspire to great and important ends, instead of confining itself to paltry calculations."[110]

106. "Ot redaktsii," *Studencheskie Gody* (February 1913); "Studenchestvo i ekonomicheskie organizatsii," *Studencheskie Gody* (April 1914); "Ot redaktsii," *Studencheskoe Delo* (February 1912); V. Vetrov, "Moskovskii Studencheskii Dom," in Svatikov, ed., *Put' studenchestva*, pp. 241–243. *Studencheskoe Delo*, while not denying the legitimacy of student party organizations, remained—as S. G. Svatikov, one of its editors, recalled—firmly committed to the notion of nonpartisan "democratic professionalism" worked out by *Golos Studenchestva* in 1910–1911. *Studencheskie Gody* grew increasingly impatient with nonpartisan professionalism and by 1914 openly called for a more politically committed student movement.
107. As cited in *Studencheskie Gody* (February 1913).
108. Trofimov, "Itogi i perspektivi," pp. 181–182.
109. V. Vetrov, "Moskovskii Studencheskii Dom," in Svatikov, *Put' studenchestva*, pp. 194–212.
110. Quoted by Ignatiev et al., in *Russian Schools and Universities*, p. 139.

On the eve of the war, therefore, it was clear that the students still maintained their ongoing dialogue with themselves and the past over their identity and their place in Russian society. For many the concept of *studenchestvo* still served not only as a vital psychological and intellectual construct but as a sign of their heritage and their links to previous student generations.

THE FIRST YEARS OF WORLD WAR I

Shortly after the outbreak of World War I and the death of L. A. Kasso in November 1914, the direction of the government's higher-education policy took yet another turn. After a short interlude, Kasso was replaced by Count Pavel Nikolaevich Ignatiev, a scion of a prominent family and a former governor of Kiev who had been serving as assistant minister of agriculture. Ignatiev, who would remain minister of education until December 1916, pursued policies that earned him the respect, if not always the agreement, of the liberal press and the majority of the professoriate. Influenced by the Slavophile tradition, Ignatiev believed in breaking down the "bureaucratic walls" that allegedly separated the tsar from the people. In a government alienated from the Duma and the educated public, the Ministry of Education became something it had rarely been before—a bastion of relative enlightenment. Though by no means a liberal, Ignatiev was still quite explicit about his determination to remove the odium from the ministry by working with the Duma and by paying closer attention to public opinion. This did little to endear him to the empress or to Rasputin. Asked later by a Provisional Government commission how he had survived so long at his post and how he managed to turn his ministry into an "oasis," Ignatiev replied that he probably owed his tenure to an old personal association with the tsar: they had served together in the Preobrazhenskii Regiment, and there had been close family ties as well. On assuming his appointment, Ignatiev recalled, he resolved to change the "terrible state of affairs where precisely that ministry which should be the beloved child of the entire nation is instead despised." [111]

In higher-education matters Ignatiev undertook two major initiatives: a master plan for the expansion of higher education, and a new draft statute. Shortly after his appointment, Ignatiev told the budget

111. Chrezvychainaia sledstvennaia komissiia vremennovo pravitel'stva, *Padenie tsarskovo rezhima* (Moscow, 1926), vol. 6, pp. 4–5; see also, Silke Spieler, *Autonomie oder Reglementierung* (Cologne, 1981), pp. 40–44.

committee of the Duma that, unlike Kasso, he agreed on the urgency of replacing the 1884 Statute, and he promised close collaboration with the Duma.[112] A year later, speaking to the same committee, Ignatiev emphasized that "the ministry must meet halfway the wishes of the nation; it must draw into its work the whole community, all the living forces of the country. It must create conditions for lasting and fruitful work in this field."[113]

Ignatiev worked quickly. A project was ready by the middle of 1915. Although many of its provisions did not satisfy the professoriate, even Ignatiev's critics appreciated his willingness to listen to and often to accept new opinions. More than any of his predecessors, Ignatiev was willing to meet a key demand of the professoriate by emphasizing the mission of the universities as research institutions and by stressing the primacy of method over content in university teaching. In his introductory remarks to the draft statute, he criticized the past tendency to stress the role of the universities as training grounds for civil servants. Only by dedicating themselves to the imperatives of research and eschewing the temptation to impart "practical" education and training could the universities prepare the kind of civil service that the state needed.[114]

The new draft largely eliminated the powers of the curator and greatly strengthened those of the rector, who would be elected by the faculty council. The minister could appoint professors if the individual department had failed twice to elect a suitable candidate or if he twice found the department's choice unacceptable. After some indecision on the role of the faculty council in electing professors, the ministry finally favored bypassing the faculty council in favor of the individual department, a move that caused some consternation on the part of many academic critics.[115] Students could organize academic and cultural societies within the *VUZy,* but all other student organizations would be subject to general statutes. The new statute would have greatly expanded the faculty,

112. Ignatiev et al., *Russian Schools and Universities,* p. 195.

113. Ibid., p. 196.

114. TsGIA, f. 1037, op. 1, ed. kh. 6 ("Obiasnitel'naia zapiska po proektu ustava imperatorskikh rossiiskikh universitetov").

115. See, for example, the critical article by Professor M. M. Novikov of Moscow University that appeared in *Russkie Vedomosti* on 12 January 1917 (after Ignatiev had already resigned). Novikov, who had worked closely with Ignatiev while serving on the Duma's Education Committee, respected the minister but believed that the draft statute constituted "a serious threat to university autonomy." Ignatiev's draft statute invested the departments with the power of electing professors, but on 3 July 1916 a decree went into effect that, besides raising academic salaries, clarified procedures for electing professors and associate professors. According to this decree, the electing body was the faculty council, not the department. The final word in the debate was to have rested with the

abolished the honorarium, and raised faculty salaries. The course of study on all but the medical faculty would be cut from four to three years. But students interested in pursuing teaching careers, in either secondary schools or universities, would stay a fourth year, write a specialized thesis, and receive a Kandidat degree.[116]

Shortly after assuming his post, Ignatiev instructed N. O. Palachek, now the ministry's chief specialist in higher-education affairs, to prepare a study of the nation's future needs in this area.[117] In his report, submitted in the spring of 1916, Palachek noted that despite decades of commissions and studies, the Ministry of Education had lacked a coherent strategy governing the development of higher education in the empire. Although spending for lower and secondary education had sharply increased, and many new specialized technical institutes had been opened, the universities were languishing. There were serious shortages of physicians and high school teachers, and too many of the existing institutions of higher education were concentrated in Moscow and Saint Petersburg, an anomaly that caused a drain of talent from the provinces to the capitals. Palachek linked the case for more universities with the imperative of regional development, as well as with the need to utilize Russian culture as a unifying force on the periphery of the empire. Building a new university at Vitebsk or Minsk, for example, would help counterbalance the cultural influence of the Polish nobility. Moscow University was overcrowded and could not meet the needs of the teeming central Russian provinces. Palachek called for at least ten new universities in cities such as Voronezh, Irkutsk, Tashkent, Rostov, Perm, and Samara. He also recommended careful consideration of a new type of university—a "mixed" institution along the lines of American state universities, which would combine "pure" subjects with de-

Duma. For discussion of the 3 July decree, as well as additional arguments in favor of faculty council as opposed to department powers, see *Russkie Vedomosti*, 26 August 1916.

116. The draft statute also abolished the two-degree requirement for university teachers (now only the doctorate was required) and substituted the *dozent* rank, abolished by the 1884 statute, for the category of extraordinary professor. This move would have greatly reduced the size of the faculty council, since *dozenty* would have voting power only in departments, not on matters affecting appointments. For a sympathetic discussion of the draft, see two articles by E. D. Grimm: "Organizatsiia universitetskovo prepodavaniia po proektu novovo ustava," *Russkaia Mysl'*, no. 4 (1916); "Organizatsiia universitetskovo upravleniia po proektu novovo ustava," *Russkaia Mysl'*, no. 5 (1916).

117. Palachek's report, entitled "Blizhaishie zadachi Ministerstva Narodnovo Prosveshcheniia v oblasti vysshevo obrazovaniia," can be found in TsGIA, f. 733, op. 226, d. 206. For a positive evaluation of this official, see Novikov, *Ot Moskvy do N'iu-Iorka*, p. 207.

partments teaching technology and other applied skills.[118] (This had the support of such key members of the Duma Education Committee as Professor M. M. Novikov.) In all, Palachek estimated that 40 million rubles would be needed to renovate existing universities and 160 million would be needed to implement an optimal program of building new universities and new specialized institutes.

On 16 June 1916, Ignatiev presented a memorandum to the tsar that argued for an expansion of the system of higher education. He made a careful case for favoring universities over specialized institutes as the linchpin of the nation's system of higher education. As an interim measure Ignatiev asked the tsar to approve the transformation of Tomsk and Saratov into full-fledged universities and the building of new universities in Rostov and Perm. In the latter two cities, the municipalities and the zemstvo had agreed to pay the start-up costs. On 30 June 1916, four years after he had opposed the building of new universities, Tsar Nicholas reversed his stand. Approving Ignatiev's memorandum, he wrote that it would be beneficial to found new universities and other institutions of higher education, "especially in smaller cities."[119] This imperial decision served as another reminder that the autocracy's higher-education policy was not so much reactionary as it was inconsistent. The tsar could indeed be swayed by arguments appealing to the national interest, especially in wartime, and temporarily put aside his fear of creating new bastions of troublesome student unrest. Nevertheless, student unrest remained the major criterion for the autocracy's evaluation of higher-education policy.

In the end, however, Ignatiev was no more successful than I. I. Tolstoi had been in holding on to his post. Rasputin and the empress resented his policies and wanted to replace him with someone who would follow the policies of Kasso. In turn, Ignatiev minced no words in telling the tsar of the need for major changes in personnel and policy.[120] For some time, Tsar Nicholas refused to fire Ignatiev. One reason, according to the testimony that Minister of the Interior A. D. Protopopov gave before the Provisional Government investigating commission, was that Ignatiev

118. For an interesting discussion of this concept, see Novikov, *Ot Moskvy do N'iu-Iorka*, pp. 198–199.

119. TsGIA, f. 1037, op. 1, ed. kh. 6 ("Vsepodaneishii doklad Ministra Narodnovo Prosveshcheniia, 30ovo Iunia, 1916").

120. P. N. Ignatiev, "Sovet Ministrov v 1915–16 godakh," *Novyi Zhurnal*, nos. 8, 9 (1944).

had succeeded in keeping the students quiet.[121] But by the end of 1916 Ignatiev's time had run out and a favorite of Rasputin's, Professor N. K. Kulchitskii, became the empire's last minister of education (just when Rasputin himself met his untimely end). Kulchitskii began his short tenure by sharply criticizing Ignatiev's policies and his "failure to take heed of the law." [122] Nevertheless, Kulchitskii promised to let the Duma consider Ignatiev's projects.

World War I also had a major impact on the student movement. From the outbreak of the war through the Revolution of 1917, one basic point united the professoriate with the vast majority of the *studenchestvo:* the need for national defense. The imperative of helping the war effort overshadowed most other problems, especially dissatisfaction with the government's higher-education policy. This is not to say that student demonstrations and *skhodki* ceased. As before the war, there were frequent incidents sparked by dissatisfaction with internal issues— unpopular professors, the scheduling of examinations, and so forth. But the context of student unrest changed as events outside the universities impinged on the students' lives more than ever before.

Russia's students returned from their 1914 summer vacation under the shadow of the crushing defeat suffered by the Russian army at Tannenberg. As a February 1915 Okhrana report noted, the general mood of the *studenchestvo* at the very beginning of the academic year was clearly patriotic.[123] L. Kleinbort, who had written several articles on student affairs for the leftist journal *Sovremennyi Mir,* published a widely quoted article in November 1914 on the students' patriotism.[124] This, Kleinbort emphasized, was a "different war," in part because students keenly felt the Germans' contempt for Russian culture.

To be sure, there were dissenting voices. A lead article in the 15 March 1915 issue of *Studencheskie Gody* complained about the Kleinbort piece as well as about excessive chauvinism in the universities. Singling out the participation of some students in anti-German street violence, *Studencheskie Gody* insisted that such actions were atypical of the *studenchestvo* as a whole. Indeed, right-wing student groups tried but failed to exploit the war in order to gain massive student support. A January 1916 Okhrana report noted that the Moscow Academic Club

121. Chrezvychainaia sledstvennaia komissiia, *Padenie tsarskovo rezhima,* vol. 4, pp. 321–322.

122. Quoted in Ignatiev et al., *Russian Schools and Universities,* p. 218.

123. TsGAOR, f. DP 00, op. 1915, ed. kh. 59, 57ch.

124. L. Kleinbort, "Molodëzh' i voina," *Sovremennyi Mir,* no. 11 (1914).

might have to liquidate its activities because of insufficient funds. In response the Moscow chief of police urged that the Ministry of the Interior increase its subsidy of the organization.[125] In March of 1916, forty-eight Petrograd University *zemliachestva* and other student organizations signed a petition calling on students to boycott the Academists, who had just helped the police arrest five students accused of participating in a *skhodka*.[126]

Outright opposition to the war was limited to a tiny minority of Bolshevik and radical Social Revolutionary supporters, but the influence of these party groups continued to decline. Bolshevik students in Saint Petersburg organized the United Committee of Social Democratic Organizations, but it wielded scant influence.[127] According to Okhrana reports, most Bolshevik sympathizers in the *VUZy* abandoned their work in the universities to participate in outside political activity. Protest *skhodki* called to support the arrested Bolshevik Duma deputies in the fall of 1914 failed to attract much student interest.[128] Most Menshevik and Social Revolutionary sympathizers followed their adult parties in supporting the war as a matter of national defense.[129] They also played a leading role in the student war-relief and economic self-help organizations.

As the war dragged on, however, and the confrontation between society and the government deepened, student unrest began to reemerge. After the Progressive Bloc announced its program on 21 August 1915, the government responded by proroguing the Duma. Public outrage was quickly reflected in various resolutions emanating from such groups as the Union of Zemstvos and Towns and the war-industry committees. In September 1915 a massive one-week strike broke out in Moscow's larger institutions of higher education—the university, the commercial institute, and the technological institute—to protest the proroguing of the Duma, the anti-Semitic policies of the high command, and repression of workers' organizations. The *skhodki* demanded the reconvening of the Duma, the replacement of the Council of Ministers by a govern-

125. TsGAOR, f. DP 00, op. 1915, ed. kh. 59, 46ch. l. 5.

126. TsGAOR, f. DP 00, op. 1915, ed. kh. 59, 57ch. l. 45.

127. For a somewhat biased but still useful account of Bolshevik activity in Petrograd *VUZy* during the 1914–1917 period, see I. P. Leiberov, "Revoliutsionnoe studenchestvo Petrogradskovo Universiteta nakanune i v period pervoi mirovoi voiny," in *Ocherki po istorii Leningradskovo Universiteta*, (Leningrad, 1968), vol. 2, pp. 3–40.

128. TsGAOR, f. DP 00, op. 1915, ed. kh. 59, 57ch. l. 42.

129. See, for example, the 9 November 1915 Okhrana report on the student movement, in TsGAOR, f. DP 00, ed. kh. 59, 46ch. LB, l. 88.

ment answerable to the Duma, and a general amnesty. (A major factor contributing to the strike was the shooting of a Moscow University student by the police.)[130] But at the same time that the students voted these resolutions, they were rejecting more extreme calls for a constituent assembly and urging Moscow workers not to strike. To be sure, the student resolutions were to the left of the program announced by the Progressive Bloc. But clearly the consensus on national defense and the growing rift between the government and the public were altering the relative position of the student movement. An October 1915 Okhrana report identified a similar trend in Petrograd. The *studenchestvo*, the report noted, was showing greater readiness to support mainstream liberal rather than extreme revolutionary demands.[131]

More than ever, the center of gravity of student life continued to shift to the *zemliachestva* and economic organizations. In large part, this reflected the staggering practical problems the students encountered as a result of the war. In addition to inflation, the students faced an unprecedented housing crisis, following an influx of refugees into Petrograd and Moscow. Spiraling inflation weakened the ability of the student self-help organizations to cope with the situation and made the role of outside philanthropy all the more important. But this development undercut one of the most important goals of student professionalism, that of developing student self-reliance and initiative. Tension developed between outside philanthropic organizations, which tried to raise money to help needy students, and student groups who insisted on the imperative of student self-reliance but lacked the means to do much about it.[132]

By 1916, the deteriorating economic situation began to affect student enrollment. In June 1916 the Ministry of Education was forced to limit entering classes in Petrograd, Moscow, Iur'ev, Kiev, and Kharkov. Meanwhile, growing numbers of students either left for the army or were forced to leave the universities because of shortages of housing and the worsening inflationary situation. For example, on 1 January 1916, 11,184 students were enrolled in Moscow University; on 1 January 1917, only 6,680 were enrolled.[133]

One point of continuity with the prewar period was the persisting student problem of self-definition. An issue that had preoccupied the

130. TsGAOR, f. DP OO, op. 1915, ed. kh. 59, 46ch. (Okhrana report of 18 September 1915).

131. TsGAOR, f. DP OO, op. 1915, ed. kh. 59, 57ch. l. 30 (10 October 1915 report on the Petrograd student movement).

132. See A. A. Kizevetter, "Studenchestvo i obshchestvennyi dolg," *Russkie Vedomosti,* 12 September 1916.

133. Ignatiev et al., *Russian Schools and Universities*, p. 209.

student movement on the eve of the war—whether student cooperatives and economic organizations should limit themselves to economic tasks or see their role as providing "moral leadership" and "unity" for the *studenchestvo*—continued to foment controversy. For example, after some disagreement, the new Petrograd Kassa Vzaimopomoshchi, which arose at the end of 1915 to unite student self-help groups, proclaimed that a basic purpose of the organization was not only to disburse funds but also to give the *studenchestvo* a sense of purpose and cohesion. The students were in danger of becoming a random group of "individual visitors" to the university, the *kassa* warned. It was time for a real effort to restore unity.[134]

Those who argued for the necessity of linking student economic organizations to larger moral purposes, such as maintaining the democratic traditions of the *studenchestvo,* had other organizational bases. One was *Studencheskie Gody,* which the government finally closed down at the end of 1915. Another was the Moscow Committee for a Student House. In 1916 this group, which included such historians of the *studenchestvo* as S. G. Svatikov and Rafael Vydrin, issued the important collection of essays *Put' Studenchestva,* which discussed the history and prospects of the *studenchestvo.* In the introduction Svatikov admitted that the outbreak of the war had diverted the students' attention from their own concerns. But whereas in other countries the war strengthened the links between government and society, in Russia the test of war had exposed the system and brought about the demand for far-reaching political changes. The war would bring about the liberation of Russian society, and when that moment came, the *studenchestvo* had to be ready.[135] The essays emphasized fundamental divergences of interest between the *studenchestvo* and the professoriate. History had repeatedly shown that professors were all too prone to forget about student concerns once they felt that they were about to win their own goals—faculty power and higher salaries.[136] The student agenda—more scholarships, rights of assembly and organization, economic self-help,

134. "Khronika," *Vestnik Vospitaniia* 4 (1916): 91–92. On 11 March 1916, the minister of the interior sent a letter to Ignatiev complaining about the harmful influence of the new Kassa Vzaimopomoshchi. By that time, 1,032 students had already signed up for membership. See TsGIA, f. 733, op. 155, d. 1191, l. 137.

135. Svatikov, ed., *Put' studenchestva,* p. iv. Although Minister of Education Ignatiev supported the Student House idea, the Okhrana heatedly opposed legalizing the enterprise. A 15 May 1915 memorandum argued that the Student House committee dreamed of "uniting the *studenchestvo* of all of Russia" to fight against the government. See TsGAOR, f. DP 00, ed. kh. 59, 46ch. LB.

136. See the essays by Rafael Vydrin, "Studenchestvo i obshchestvo," and A. Kovrin, "O reforme vysshei shkoly," in Svatikov, ed., *Put' studenchestva.*

liberalized admissions—demanded that the *studenchestvo* develop the organization and determination to fight for its interests.

Protected from conscription until they had completed their studies, many students nonetheless felt a moral obligation to aid the war effort.[137] In 1914, Moscow students had already started the Moscow Students' Hospital Organization to help the wounded and organize their transport from trains to local hospitals. Similar efforts developed in other cities. In Petrograd the students organized the General Student Committee to Help Victims of the War, which eventually included more than one hundred different student groups, including *zemliachestva* and self-help organizations.[138]

Professor Pavel Novgorodtsev estimates that by the end of 1915 about 10 percent of Russia's students had volunteered for officers' training schools.[139] As early as September 1914, the minister of war had been empowered to draft students, but he deferred action for the first year of the war. On 15 September 1915 an interministerial conference discussed the issue of drafting the students. The minister of war favored immediate conscription, but Ignatiev submitted a memorandum urging that only in "exceptional cases" should students be drafted before they had graduated.[140] After all, the minister of education argued, the nation would desperately need trained professionals once the war was over. But in the spring of 1916, conscription was initiated, beginning with the youngest students and exempting medical students and students in their last year at the university or last two years at technical schools. Call-ups proceeded by lots, which were drawn in the presence of all prospective conscripts. According to Professor Novgorodtsev, the initial mood of these meetings was one of "patriotic harmony." But as the war dragged on, he recalled, the mood grew more sullen, although outright opposition to conscription was still confined to a minority.[141]

1917

The sudden fall of the Romanov dynasty met an enthusiastic response from faculty councils and students alike. Classes spontaneously

137. For example, see a purloined letter written by a Moscow student on 27 September 1914: "All student organizations are working as before, but now all want to salve their conscience and do something for the wounded" (TsGAOR, f. DP 00, 1914, 59, 46ch. LB, l. 148).

138. *Studencheskie Gody,* 15 March 1915.

139. Ignatiev et al., *Russian Schools and Universities,* p. 190.

140. Ibid., p. 191.

141. Ibid., p. 217.

halted as both faculty and students gave in to the prevailing excitement of the revolution. In several *VUZy* student *skhodki* passed resolutions calling for a suspension of classes so that students could engage in unspecified political or educational work. For many this political work consisted of participating in election campaigns for municipal elections, responding to zemstvo calls for lectures in the countryside, and preparing to work in the planned inventory of land holdings and food reserves.[142] Even when classes resumed for the remainder of the semester, attendance was small.

Shortly after the fall of the dynasty, several professors called for the revival of the Academic Union. In a 12 May article published in *Rech'*, Nikolai Kareev stressed the importance of the Academic Union in 1905–1906 and argued that it had a role to play even in a democratic republic. Governments, be they autocratic or democratic, had a tendency, Kareev warned, to take a "utilitarian" approach to higher education. Even public opinion could not be trusted to safeguard the interests of the universities. It was up to the professoriate to defend the interests of "pure science." Moreover, professors—whose profession was defined by a disinterested seeking after truth—had a responsibility to the nation to provide proper political leadership. In Kareev's words, *"noblesse oblige."* No matter what political party they belonged to, they had to ensure that politics did not serve "narrow class interests."[143]

The fourth congress of the Academic Union (so numbered to stress the basic continuity with the Academic Union of 1905 and 1906) convened in Petrograd in June 1917. The seventy delegates heard reports on faculty-student relations, the relationship between the government and the universities, and the nagging issue of junior-faculty rights. They adopted a collective statement calling on all citizens to show "discipline," support the war effort, and fight against the growing anarchy in the nation.[144]

The revolution also saw the election of new student government organs. Although the parties of the moderate left maintained their majority, the elections showed some gain in popularity by the Kadets.[145]

---

142. See *Vestnik Vospitaniia*, no. 4–5 (1917): 27–28.
143. *Rech'*, 12 May 1917.
144. "Iz zhizni vysshei shkoly," *Vestnik Vospitaniia*, no. 6–7 (1917): 77–82; *Russkie Vedomosti*, 11 June 1917.
145. One possible explanation, noted by Professor Novgorodtsev in Ignatiev et al., *Russian Schools and Universities*, p. 222, was that committed leftists left the universities to engage in political work and were thus unlikely to participate in student politics. The elections to the Temporary Council of Student Elders of Petrograd University gave the Kadets six seats, the Trudoviki four, the Social Democrats (Mensheviks) four, and a "unifica-

The student resolutions supported fighting the war and preparing for a transfer of power to the constituent assembly. Pro-Bolshevik slogans made little headway.[146]

Although the attention of students and professors alike was focused on the tumultuous events occurring outside the *VUZy*, in several universities conflicts did erupt between the two groups.[147] In Kiev, the students called for a boycott of several professors accused of rightist views. The students in Odessa University called for an investigation into the 1911 shooting incident where a student lost his life, and they demanded curricular reforms and a student role in running the university. In Kharkov University as well, the students pressed their claims for a greater role in internal governance. In Kiev and Kharkov, students had active help from the newly organized junior faculty, who advanced their own claims.[148] At Kazan University, the faculty council gave in to student demands for delegates at department meetings but turned down the call for student representation at faculty council meetings.[149] In the central universities, relations appeared to be better, as negotiations proceeded on the principle that joint faculty-student committees would consider all matters directly affecting the *studenchestvo*.

The Provisional Government appointed a new minister of education, former Moscow University rector A. A. Manuilov. Manuilov (later succeeded by Sergei Oldenburg), who had been fired by Kasso and Stolypin in 1911, immediately ordered the reappointment of all those professors who had lost their jobs that year as well as the removal of all those professors who had been appointed to their posts by the Ministry of Education without the consent of the faculty councils (the latter could, if they

---

tion" group one. At the Petrograd Polytechnic the Kadets won five seats, the Social Revolutionaries four, the Trudoviki two, and the Social Democrats one (*Rech'*, 9 May 1917). In Odessa the student governing board was composed of twenty-two "Socialists," sixteen representatives of a nationalities bloc, and twelve Kadets (*Rech'*, 19 May 1917).

146. On student hostility to anti-war propaganda, see reports in *Russkie Vedomosti*, 9 and 24 March 1917, and *Rech'*, 13 April 1917. Shortly after the revolution the Student House group called for ending the war but was explicitly repudiated by the newly formed Moscow Committee of Student Deputies.

147. Still, one cannot agree with Marc Ferro's assertion that "the professor had within a few weeks become as discredited as the priest, the bureaucrat and the judge." See Marc Ferro, *The Bolshevik Revolution* (London, 1980), p. 66. According to Novgorodtsev, the net effect of the revolution was to increase the authority of the professoriate over the students, especially as both groups began to perceive a common enemy—the Bolsheviks (in Ignatiev et al., *Russian Schools and Universities*, p. 222).

148. "Iz zhizni vysshei shkoly," p. 77.

149. M. K. Korbut, *Kazanskii Gosudarstvennyi Universitet imeni V. I. Ul'ianova-Lenina za 125 let, 1804/5–1929/30* (Kazan, 1930), vol. 2, pp. 294–295.

wished, ask these colleagues to stay). Manuilov also announced the convening of a conference on the needs of higher education that would include representatives not only from the senior faculty but from the junior faculty and the students as well. The conference convened in June 1917 and discussed several issues, including a future university statute, relations between students and faculty, and the role of younger faculty in university governance. Basic principles of agreement included joint faculty-student committees to consider matters affecting student life, abolition of the minister's ultimate veto power over faculty appointments, and somewhat increased representation of younger faculty in internal governance. *Privat-dozenty* and assistants could participate in department meetings and send representatives to meetings of the faculty council. Students received the right to maintain their organizations within the *VUZy*. Professor Novikov recalled that the student delegates had arrived in a somewhat belligerent mood, prepared to fight for student interests. But the conference proceeded smoothly, and a good working relationship developed among all the groups.[150]

In the summer of 1917, the professoriate began to speak out more clearly on political as well as academic issues. The Moscow University Faculty Council issued a hard-hitting statement implicitly attacking the Provisional Government for not doing more to maintain order. The Kiev University Faculty Council criticized the Provisional Government's willingness to negotiate with Ukrainian separatism.

In August 1917 the universities were invited to send delegates to the State Conference called by Kerensky to shore up the tottering government. Speaking for the professoriate, Professor D. D. Grimm attacked the Provisional Government for its lack of determination to fight anarchy and safeguard the national interest. Soon, Grimm warned, Russia would turn into a "jungle society" (*budet podlinno chelovek cheloveku volk*). There was too much concern with rights and freedom, not enough regard for duty, obligation, and work.[151]

By the fall of 1917, conditions had deteriorated so much that the Provisional Government, in order to relieve the demand on the limited food supplies in Moscow and Petrograd, called for the cancellation of the academic year. Loud protests helped countermand this decision, but relatively few students returned for classes in September.

What was left of the *studenchestvo* joined the faculty in attacking

---

150. Novikov, *Ot Moskvy do N'iu-Iorka*, pp. 275–276.
151. *Rech'*, 14 August 1917.

the Bolshevik seizure of power in November 1917. On 8 November a huge *skhodka* convened in Moscow which included representatives of all student political groups and all the city's *VUZy*. The *skhodka* condemned the Bolsheviks for betraying socialism and "betraying the popular masses." The *skhodka* proclaimed that the "*studenchestvo* will dedicate all its strength to defending the rights of the people and to struggling for the ideals of democracy and socialism." [152]

The Soviet regime did not achieve immediate control of the universities; that took at least three years. [153] The young Soviet state bitterly complained of the counter-revolutionary tendencies of the *studenchestvo* and set about altering the social composition of the student body. For their part, the students joined forces with the faculty to fight for academic autonomy. In an ironic turn, the professoriate actually began asking for a greater student role in university governance, and the students fought back against efforts to curb the powers of their elective bodies. Student *skhodki* demanded that the regime respect student rights, and the *studenchestvo* even organized street demonstrations, complete with the singing of traditional student songs. The Council of Elders in Petrograd University organized evenings where new students, especially working-class recruits to the new Rabfak, could become acquainted with the traditions of the *studenchestvo*. A new organization appeared in Petrograd University to fight the Bolsheviks: the Staroe Organizovannoe Studenchestvo (the old organized *studenchestvo*). But now both students and professors were confronting a much more efficient opponent.

152. *Russkie Vedomosti*, 8 November 1917.

153. A good source on student-Bolshevik relations is Sergei Zhaba, *Petrogradskoe studenchestvo v bor'be za svobodnuiu vysshuiu shkolu* (Paris, 1922). Zhaba was a student leader in Petrograd University in the 1918–1922 period. Cf. V. Stratonov, "Poteria Moskovskim Universitetom svobody," and M. M. Novikov, "Moskovskii Universitet v pervyi period bol'shevitskovo rezhima," in V. B. El'iashevich, A. A. Kizevetter, and M. M. Novikov, eds., *Moskovskii Universitet 1755–1930: iubileinyi sbornik* (Paris, 1930), pp. 156–242. Also see J. C. McClelland, "Bolsheviks, Professors, and the Reform of Higher Education in Soviet Russia: 1917–1921," Ph.D. diss., Princeton University, 1970.

Conclusion

The history of the Russian universities in the last decades of the autoc racy reflects the strained relations between the educated classes and the government and reveals the difficulties the universities faced in reconciling their complex and often contradictory functions. The universities also epitomized the paradoxical nature of the Russian autocracy as it struggled, unsuccessfully, to reconcile two contradictory roles. One role was to be the revolutionary creator of a new Russia; the second was to be the preserver of a traditional society based on the tsar's personal authority, official orthodoxy, the primacy of the landed aristocracy, and the principle that a person's status depended on estate rather than talent, wealth, or educational achievement.

In its first role, the autocracy created institutions of higher education, encouraged industrial development, fostered the ascendancy of a service bureaucracy over the landed nobility, emancipated the serfs, and instituted zemstvos and trial by jury. Some of its more imaginative statesmen, such as Stolypin, even planned to reform local government and create the basis of a modern relationship between subject and state that was not mediated by estate barriers. In its second role, it undercut statesmen such as Stolypin and Witte, tried to shore up the privileges of the landed nobility, clung to the estate principle, and belatedly attempted to enforce contol over the very institutions—such as the universities—it had itself created.

Despite its many successes, which even now have not won sufficient recognition from historians, the autocracy failed in one basic way: it could not conceptualize a stable ideology that could both recognize the impact of the social and economic changes it had set in motion and create the basis for a modern concept of citizenship and partnership between civil society and the state. This failure made the state less stable, less able to handle the shocks of international competition, and it certainly undercut the chances of accomplishing what would have been in any case a very difficult task, that of integrating the peasant masses into a civil society. The relationship between the universities and the state is a case study of this failure to formulate a new relationship between state and society.

A creature of the state, the Russian university was founded to train civil servants, teachers, and doctors. But during the nineteenth century, the new ideal of service to society began an uneasy coexistence with the principle of service to the state. The relationship between these ideals might have been fairly harmonious, but in fact it was mostly competitive. In Germany the imperatives of service to state and service to society were reconciled—after a fashion—in a tacit bargain between the state and the professoriate.[1] The former would support learning, while the latter, building on the traditions of German idealism, made the university into a "theoretical sponsor and defender" of the Prussian state.[2] In Russia such a bargain was also possible, but to the very end the autocracy regarded the professoriate with suspicion. Furthermore, an important ideological underpinning of the German bargain—the *Rechtsstaat*—was compromised by the post-1881 turn toward an inefficient police state based on emergency decrees.[3]

Especially after 1881, there was an unmistakable congruence between the autocracy's university policy and its general political course. The 1884 Statute had its counterpart in the zemstvo and municipal government counter-reforms, and Vannovskii's "benevolent supervision" (*serdechnoe popechenie*) and Temporary Rules paralleled the police-sponsored unions in labor policy. The turn to tighter state control of all *VUZy* in 1903–1904, despite a slackening of the student movement, was an integral part of Plehve's general policy. The 27 August 1905 Rules were a natural counterpart to the Bulygin Duma edict issued a few weeks earlier. The liberal course pursued by Tolstoi in the winter of 1905–1906 was of a piece with the conciliatory policies advocated by

---

1. See Fritz Ringer, *The Decline of the German Mandarins: The German Academic Community, 1890–1933* (Cambridge, Mass., 1969), esp. chapters 1 and 2.
2. Ibid., p. 116.
3. See Richard Pipes, *Russia Under the Old Regime* (New York, 1974), p. 315.

Witte during the same period. Finally, the 11 June 1907 Rules on Student Organizations followed by one week Stolypin's unilateral alteration of the Duma electoral law. True, Ignatiev's tenure as minister of education was out of tune with the general alienation of the last governments from the Duma and educated public opinion, but he too finally resigned.

Although the policy toward the universities paralleled general government policy, the university as such failed to find a stable source of support within the state bureaucracy. Meanwhile, other forms of higher education did find powerful advocates. Between 1865 and 1914 the government founded fourteen new technical institutes and only two new, incomplete universities. The impetus for the establishment of these institutes came from specific ministries and special-interest groups. For example, the Ministry of Finance fostered the development of the polytechnics, while the Ministry of Trade and Industry fought for the interests of the commercial institutes. In this they got solid backing from merchants and industrialists. Aside from professors, the major advocates of new university construction were particular towns. The immediate economic value of the universities was not as readily apparent, and the professoriate found it difficult to convince the government to give university education as high a priority as the expansion of primary or technical education.

It would be stretching the point, however, to insist that the government was "against the universities," for within the ruling strata there were wide differences of opinion on university policy. When Katkov advocated strict curricular control through a state examination system, he faced the opposition not only of the State Council majority but also of arch-reactionary Pobedonostsev. Furthermore, the 1884 Statute became law only because the tsar overrode the majority opinion of the State Council. It was true, nonetheless, that some arch-conservatives dreamed of eliminating the universities altogether and replacing them with specialized institutes scattered in various towns. There was also less radical opposition from conservatives. Many clung to the vision of universities attended only by the very rich, and, as we have seen, in 1912 Tsar Nicholas endorsed the conservative opposition to the establishment of new universities.

However, the government always stopped short of enacting the most extreme anti-university proposals. Indeed it could not do so. There was constant opposition within the government to these calls for the breakup of the universities or for a total halt to their expansion. General Glazov, for example, opposed arguments for the breakup of the universities and emphasized the need to build additional universities in non-Russian areas. His conservative assistant, Professor A. Tikhomirov, became a strong advocate of increased scholarship assistance to needy students. In 1907 Stolypin threw his vote against those conservatives in the Council of Ministers who tried to stop the establishment of Saratov University. For all his shortcomings, Schwartz did try to secure higher government outlays on the universities. In 1911, Kokovtsev, as minister of finance, opposed Kasso's proposal to establish seminars for the training of politically reliable professors in Western Europe.

The tsar himself, of course, was hardly consistent. For the most part he took a hard line, but in 1899–1901 he often urged a moderate stance toward the students and looked for ways, as his appointment of Vannovskii shows, to reform the university structure. The tsar did not hide his dislike of the professoriate, but three short years after his rejection of new universities in 1912, he supported Ignatiev's 1915 project of a more liberal university statute and vastly increased university construction. And Kasso and Schwartz were, after all, former university professors who believed they were only protecting the universities' standards from the attempts of their liberal ex-colleagues to turn them into political clubs. In other words, what critics of the government regarded as reactionary, they themselves saw as steps to protect the universities.

The only common denominator of the government's university policy was paternalistic authoritarianism aimed at ensuring order. Apart from this there was no coherent policy, only an inconsistent succession of half-measures in alternating periods of reaction and comparative liberalism. Generals, conservative professors, and liberal reformers alternated as minister of education. The archives bulge with draft statutes and recommendations that would never become law: Vannovskii's 1901 questionnaire; the 1902 Commission; the draft statutes of Glazov, von Kaufmann, and Schwartz; the minutes of the 1906 Tolstoi Conference.

A fundamental determinant of the government's university policy was the tension between the autocracy's efforts to ensure control and the fact that in many ways the development of the universities was influenced and shaped by factors that resisted such manipulation and control. The development of new academic disciplines, the achievements of Russian scientists, the growing conviction of Russian parents and young people that some kind of higher education was essential to social and economic success—all of these resulted in pressures and changes that kept the universities in flux. The state could regulate an institution where professors wanted to do nothing but teach and where students wanted only to study hard and become doctors, lawyers, teachers, and civil servants. It could not as easily control an institution where students were much more sure about what they did not want to be—provincials with a useless high-school diploma—than they were about future career choices. Nor could it regiment a professoriate that was coming to believe that questions of university governance were an essential part of its professional prerogative.

The autocracy's utilitarian view of the universities need not have precluded compromise with the professoriate. The conciliatory policies of Tolstoi and Ignatiev showed that dialogue was possible; but the government, though willing to give up control temporarily, could not institutionalize such a surrender. Issues such as demands for powerful faculty councils, faculty disciplinary courts, and the elimination of curators raised the specter of "extraterritoriality." The state was always willing to recognize the professor as a teacher and scholar. What it could never do was to concede to him a professional identity that linked professors across the disciplines in a relationship of shared responsibility for university governance and structural safeguards of academic freedom. The basic problem was not the state's inability to agree temporarily to periods of university autonomy but its lack of willingness to accede to some form of permanent and manifest institutionalization of such autonomy. The autocracy's "ideology of order" crippled its political vision and its ability to govern a rapidly changing society. The universities were critical nodal points where many of the tensions generated by the clash of official paternal authoritarianism and autonomous social developments converged in a pattern of misunderstanding and confrontation.

The fate of the 1884 Statute shows how difficult it was for the government to exert close control of university teaching and student discipline. The new examination rules failed to ensure state regulation of the curriculum. Higher tuition fees did little to change the social composition of the student body. The attempted appropriation of the supposed advantages of German *Lehrfreiheit* and *Lernfreiheit* through the introduction of the honorarium and *privat-dozenty* yielded disappointing results.

After the outbreak of large-scale student unrest in 1899, the autocracy admitted the need to replace the statute. In a total departure from one of the statute's basic principles, the government turned to the professors and asked them to help deal with the problem of student unrest. Here, too, fear of losing control quickly got the upper hand. The fiasco of the Vinogradov Commission and the effective nullification of the newly established professors' disciplinary courts underscored the difficulties the government met in pursuing a fundamentally new approach to problems of university governance. By August 1905, the 1884 Statute appeared finally to have lapsed. The government issued the 27 August 1905 Temporary Rules and promised a new statute—but in the end let the 1884 law stand until the Revolution of 1917.

Founded by the state and financially dependent on it, the universities needed clear definitions of their prerogatives, administrative structure, and legal relationship to the government. Many issues that in Oxford or Cambridge could be settled by tradition here required the explicit definition of a statute. Until the very end of the Romanov dynasty, the legal position of the universities rested on the highly unstable foundation of the 1884 Statute, which the government itself admitted had failed but which it was unable to replace.

The statute had to regulate such diverse areas of university life as the number of chairs on each faculty, pay scales, tuition fees, and student discipline. In practice the entire statute came to be judged by one criterion: whether the students were quiet. The failure to replace the 1884 Statute stymied the enactment of important and overdue reforms in such diverse areas as faculty compensation, new chairs, and the position of the younger faculty.

Another fundamental problem was defining the exact relationship between the 27 August Temporary Rules and the 1884 Statute. The confusing legal situation of the universities reinforced their dependence on the government's general political line and tended to politicize the question of replacing the 1884 Statute. This dependence was accentuated by two other factors: the powers granted local governors-general by the 1881 emergency decrees, and the political uncertainties generated by the Revolution of 1905 and its quasi-constitutional aftermath. The emergency decrees certainly affected the status of such provincial universities as Odessa, where local satraps could engineer wholesale purges of suspect professors. And while the central universities suffered much less from the impact of the emergency decrees, they certainly had to contend with the new political context of the university question in the aftermath of the events of 1905. The tsar had long mistrusted the professoriate. Now Stolypin accepted the accusations of malicious anti-government activity contained in the 1908 Schwartz memorandum and set about reasserting the state control over the universities that he felt had been lost in the aftermath of 1905. The extreme right stood ready to attack him if he did not.

Politically the university question was another liability for the autocracy. More students attended *VUZy* in 1914 than ever before; spending on all levels of education had reached unprecedented levels; various ministries were promoting new trends in higher education. But blunders such as those that led to the 1911 Moscow University fiasco isolated the government and undercut its position with hitherto supportive groups. By 1911, even such relatively moderate journals as Struve's *Russkaia Mysl'* were bitterly comparing the situation to the dark days of M. L. Magnitskii and S. S. Uvarov in the first half of the nineteenth century. During the tenure of those ministers of education, however, the Russian professoriate had felt little sense of its professional worth. This had changed fundamentally by the eve of World War I, when the Russian professoriate keenly resented the way it was being treated by the government and the Ministry of Education.

Just before the war began, Professor Vernadskii wrote a revealing article on this growing tension between professional self-confidence and anger at government tutelage. Attendance at international scientific conferences taught Russian professors, Vernadskii argued, that they were winning growing stature in the eyes of their non-Russian colleagues. Yet they had to put up with inexcusable treatment from the Ministry of Education.

> We can say openly that as long as the Russian professor strives for scientific achievement, all the attempts of the Ministry of Education to turn him into a lackey will be in vain. This is because we know that it is *we*, and not the Ministry of Education, who are performing tasks of national and human significance. We know that Russian scientists have done their work despite the state system, in the face of the absence of the most elementary safeguards of public legality.[4]

Vernadskii's complaint epitomized the tension between the professoriate's scientific and academic freedom. Enjoying, with rare exceptions, the former, Russian professors registered solid achievements in scholarship and scientific research. But if professional identity within the discipline was relatively secure, the status of the professoriate as a group suffered to the very end from a frustrating relationship with the

---

4. V. I. Vernadskii, "1911 god v istorii russkoi umstvennoi kul'tury," *Ezhegodnik Gazety Rech' za 1911 god* (Saint Petersburg, 1912), p. 327.

state and a sense of responsibility for a fragile institution that answered demands and was buffeted by forces beyond the control of the professors. The situation of the Russian professor was far from desperate. Even if he lost his post at a university, he could continue his research in a *VUZ* under the control of some other ministry. As time went on, private support for research grew as well. But, given the conditions of Russian life, there was no real substitute for the state university—thus the need for reaching some kind of agreement between the professoriate and the state on the nature of their relationship.

Growing professional self-confidence only heightened resentment at state tutelage. With the benefit of hindsight, it is possible to be critical of many of the professors' complaints. Russian professors, to judge from many of their writings, tended to idealize the degree of academic freedom in other countries and the amount of respect with which other societies viewed academics. And while the government failed to implement the recommendations of the Tolstoi Conference, it might be remembered, as Germany's Professor Paulsen pointed out, that the 1906 draft statute would have given Russian professors privileges and governance powers that many of their foreign colleagues would have envied. The resentment expressed by many professors that state encouragement of technical institutes came at the expense of the universities has to be balanced against a counterargument that an elite Humboldtian university was not necessarily the highest priority of Russian educational policy. The universities, it can be argued, had reached a level at which they could take care of themselves while the state attended to the more pressing needs of elementary and technical education. Certainly, there was strong resistance in government circles to the recommendation of the Tolstoi Conference that the state's yearly grant to the universities rise from 5.5 to 13 million rubles just when the government was about to embark on a costly program to develop primary and secondary education. And although most Russian professors agreed that the 1884 Statute had to go, there was less agreement on exactly what should replace it. Finally, at least some of the anger of the Russian academic profession stemmed from inevitable structural ambiguities inherent in the nature of the university, and especially in a university dependent on state support.

Yet there were many quite legitimate reasons for professorial discontent. An underlying problem was the ambiguous legal position of the Russian universities, resulting in the absence of clear legal foundations for academic freedom. The professor's relationship to the state was marked by a debilitating uncertainty about his powers within the university and about whether he was a civil servant or an independent professional scholar. If the kind of high-handedness that characterized the 1911 Moscow crisis was the exception rather than the rule, the fact remained that the government always had the option of treating the professor as a lowly subordinate.

The tension between the professors' status as state employees and their claims to the roles not only of independent professional scholars but also of respected leaders of public opinion and Russian society came to a climax during the turbulent years of 1905 and 1906. After having long told the students to "take the long view" and "study hard," after having clung to the notion that creative universities were compatible with the autocratic system, the professoriate now faced a hard choice. Staying aloof from the liberation movement meant forfeiting claims to social leadership and professional self-respect. Involving the universities as such in the escalating struggle against the government and making an explicit professional commitment to the liberation movement risked jeopardizing a vital claim to the universities' status "above politics."

Complicating the choice was the unwillingness of other members of the universities—students and junior faculty—to accept the professors' assertion that more democracy in the nation at large was perfectly compatible with continued authoritarian rule in the academy—with the faculty council replacing the state-appointed curator and rector as tyrant. As political tensions escalated, the universities were drawn into direct political involvement, whether the professors liked it or not.

Little wonder, then, that the Academic Union became one of the most moderate of the 1905 unions, a study in professional ambivalence. Desire for political reform clashed with a keen sense that the Russian universities were in a fragile position and that if the professors did not worry about their welfare and protect them—not only from the encroachments of the streets but also from the alleged immaturity of the students and the junior faculty—then no one would. Vernadskii was right: the year 1905 proved that the professors were "unwilling politicians." In 1906 the professoriate jumped at the first opportunity to resume collaboration with the government and lost interest in the fading Academic Union. But it quickly relearned the lesson that the status of the Russian universities very much depended on power and politics. The concessions won in 1905 resulted from a political crisis faced by the government rather than from a sudden decision by the autocracy to accept the professors' professional claims. As the government recovered its balance, it took away many of those gains and the professors found themselves forced to confront a basic issue raised by the student movement: how, except by direct confrontation, could the members of the universities defend their prerogatives?

A major reason for the strained relations between the autocracy and the professoriate was the student movement. One of the most significant conclusions to emerge from a survey of student unrest in tsarist Russia is that the Russian student movement must be viewed as a separate form of collective mass protest. Even when students voted revolutionary slogans, they maintained their separate collective identity, apart from the revolutionary parties. The common view that the student movement served as a reservoir for the revolutionary movement must therefore be modified somewhat. The students were certainly overrepresented in the revolutionary movement compared to their percentage of the population. But their relative weight in the revolutionary movement steadily declined between 1860 and 1914.[5]

A comparison of the Russian student movement with the mass student protest that engulfed the United States and Western Europe in the late 1960s reveals significant differences as well as similarities. The student movements of the late 1960s, especially in Western Europe, developed a utopian critique of the political system, a critique that emphasized the gulf between the claims of political parties and social institutions and the alienation they supposedly produced or defended. The 1968 French student movement, for example, aimed much of its fire at the "bureaucratization" inherent in the structures of mature industrial society and put forward the vision of a counterculture based on the ideal of close communal interaction. In the view of student leaders, the traditional left and, certainly, the Communist party were no less guilty than the Gaullists. The "impersonal system" that quashed spontaneity and individual expression included socialist as well as capitalist societies.

The Russian student movement, however, had neither a Tom Hayden nor a Daniel Cohn-Bendit. It failed to develop an original critique of Russian society. When students began to hold open elections after 1906, most voted party lists, a sign that adult politics had not become

---

5. According to data collected by V. R. Leikina-Svirskaia, students comprised more than 60 percent of the political arrestees in the 1860s and more than 35 percent in the 1870s. For the 1884–1890 period, students comprised 25.4 percent of the total. The proportion dropped to 9.6 percent for the years 1901–1903. (*Intelligentsiia v Rossii vo vtoroi polovine 19ovo veka* [Moscow, 1971], pp. 289, 317.) A survey of the *Vedomost' Doznanii* for the years 1894 through 1897 shows that, of the 4,083 individuals arrested for political crimes, 418, or 10.2 percent, were students (POA, file 16, nos. 22–23).

delegitimized. And Russian students were quite ambivalent about their potential political role. While there was always a strong current in the student movement that tended to glorify the *studenchestvo* as a vanguard, there was also a strong tendency to readily accept the argument that the students were an inherently weak force, especially when compared to such social groups as the workers or the peasantry. Lewis Feuer thus errs in calling the Russian student movement the "classical exemplar of all modern student movements."[6] But Gianni Statera is also mistaken when he minimizes the distinctiveness and the independent identity of the Russian student movement.[7] Student unrest in tsarist Russia was not merely an example of the "wider . . . political mobilization of intellectuals and the bourgeoisie," to use Statera's phrase, but reflected the doubly ambiguous position in which Russian students found themselves as students, and as future members of a professional class or civil servants.

The Russian student movement found itself in an ongoing identity crisis, torn between the pressure to live up to the ideals of the *studenchestvo* and the fear of succumbing to acquiescent philistinism (*meshchanstvo, obyvatel'shchina*) after graduation. The underlying backdrop to this dilemma was the dissonance between the world of the universities and the claims of a government system that until 1905 allowed little overt opposition and even afterward pursued contradictory and often repressive policies. The conflict between these two ideals was intensified and mediated by the nature of student life—and constant confrontation with authority—within the universities. Furthermore, the roles for which the universities and specialized technical institutes prepared their students—government posts, teaching positions, traditional professions such as medicine and law, emerging professions such as engineering—all promised at least some material security. But in varying degrees, they also reflected the unresolved issue of state power versus social autonomy. The free professions were still struggling against government tutelage.[8] High school teachers had many reasons

6. Lewis Feuer, *The Conflict of Generations* (New York, 1969).

7. Statera writes that "the Russian, the Bosnian and the Italian student movements of the nineteenth and the beginning of the twentieth century were nothing but particular aspects of wider phenomena of political mobilization of intellectuals and the bourgeoisie. The German, the French, the English and Italian student movement of the last years are phenomena which directly involve students as students" (*Death of a Utopia: The Development and Decline of Student Movements in Europe* [New York, 1975], p. 46).

8. The consensus that the relationship between the various professions and the state was deteriorating between 1900 and 1917 emerged at a conference on Professions in Tsarist Russia that took place at the University of Illinois at Urbana in June 1982.

to resent the policies of the Ministry of Education. Civil service demanded at least a modicum of political acquiescence. In short, the universities and institutes prepared their students for roles that, to borrow a point from Joseph Ben-David, still lacked stable models in the wider society.[9]

The relationship between the student movement and wider political agendas was extremely complex and in constant flux. As we have seen, the events of 1899–1905 assume critical importance. Student defiance and anger alternated with hopes that the government would grant meaningful reforms. The 1899 strike crossed a fine line from a corporate to a public protest, but most students had some hope for the Vannovskii investigation. The early 1901 strikes and demonstrations broke out in response to the July 1899 Temporary Rules, but most students believed that Vannovskii's appointment as minister of education marked the beginning of a better era. The students were not an oppositional force a priori. It was the policies of the authorities that fueled the process of making them so. Each year a new cohort arrived and confronted, in the myriad details of the university experience, the interplay of hope and frustration, freedom and regimentation. From the lowly inspector, to the mounted policeman with a whip, to the minister of education, the student's confrontation with authority was part of a cumulative, collective, and formative experience. It was an authority tyrannical enough to cause deep anger and resentment, but one that lacked the brutality to crush the students. For the most part, the tsarist authorities preferred to suspend, not expel; to beat, rather than kill.

The confrontation with authority was mediated by the interplay of changing political contexts with recurring student corporate concerns. One result was a blurring of the line between corporate and public issues. (Protesting the beating of comrades was a case in point.) In 1899–1902 the students acted largely alone, which led many to consider the feasibility of conceptualizing the student movement as a catalyst for wider social protest. In 1904 and 1905, student unrest coincided with war and revolution as students ignored calls for disciplined subordination to the revolutionary parties, shut down the VUZy in response to Bloody Sunday, returned to class in September, and defined their place within the universities by embracing the rhetoric of radical rather than liberal politics. All the while, they could see how their decision to keep the universities open for political meetings transformed the general political situation, and they resented their teachers' opposition to this extramural use of the classrooms. A conflict between students and professors over meetings symbolized the gulf between differing perceptions and agendas: the professors feared for the life of the universities, the students (and junior faculty) feared for the fate of the liberation movement if the meetings were forced into the streets. After 1906, the students once again acted alone in fighting back against government policies, and they responded to the post-1905 political situation by creating an ideology of student professionalism. The new circumstances spawned conflicts not only with the government but with the professoriate as well. In 1917 there was no longer a repressive government. Instead, there was a growing tendency for both students and professors to agree that now there was a common—political—enemy. But the revolution did not stop the students from disputing faculty authority or demanding what they considered their due on university issues.

A constant feature of the Russian student movement was the unending argument about its nature and purpose. Students asked themselves whether they were politically important, whether they were justified in defending their corporate interests, whether the student movement could and should serve as a catalyst for the mobilization of larger social groups. Aware of their alleged weakness and isolation, the students kept surprising everybody, including themselves, by continuing to fight, even when they knew in advance that they would lose. All the while they kept searching for an ideology of the student movement—which they never quite found.

None of the established oppositional groups in Russia could give students the answers they were seeking. Liberals and professors castigated the students for jeopardizing, by their protests and strikes, the fragile position of the universities. But there were also occasions when they used the student movement to try to wrest concessions from the government; and when relations between liberals and the government became even more strained than usual, liberal hostility to the student movement often gave way to tolerance or even interest. In 1911, many important leaders of the Kadets, while unwilling to support the students publicly, in private welcomed student protest because it embarrassed the autocracy.

Most Marxists had been saying ever since the 1890s that the student movement was a waste of time. If students wanted to achieve results, they should join the revolutionary movement. The unexpected student strike of 1899, the street demonstrations of February and March 1901, and the big student protests of 1902 forced a temporary change in attitude. Lenin urged Social Democrats to support the students in 1901, attacked his rivals in the movement for not doing so, and came to see the student movement as a convenient process for radicalizing potential recruits. Basically, however, the Social Democratic attitude was hostile or, at best, skeptical. Students interested in Social Democracy still felt uncomfortable with the implication that because they were not workers, they had only second-class status in the ranks of this Marxist movement.

Only the Social Revolutionaries showed a consistently sympathetic attitude toward the student movement. They kept reminding the students that they respected their role more than did the Marxists; their party, after all, did not look at people through the rigid prism of objectively determined class identity. But more than the liberals or the Marxists, the Social Revolutionaries stressed the moral duty to make a real commitment to revolutionary activity. The party's doctrine left less room for fellow-travelers.

At the beginning of the 1906 academic year, student elections confirmed the strong position of Social Democracy. The Social Revolutionaries made a disappointing showing, and in several *VUZy* they even trailed the Kadets. One major reason for the popularity of the student Social Democrats in the *VUZy* was that by voting for them, students could make a rhetorical commitment to radicalism and proclaim their frustration with liberalism, but still continue to study. Although the Social Revolutionaries supported the student movement, they emphasized that in moments of political crisis students would have to shut down the universities and devote themselves to the revolution. Student Social Democrats did not ask their fellow students to make this commitment, and in September 1905, the student Social Democrats, unlike the Social Revolutionaries, wanted the universities to remain open.

In other words, the student Social Democratic groups were only theoretically revolutionary. Voitinskii and Iarmolovich—reliable observers—agreed that this was "pamphlet social democracy," where Struve and Tugan-Baranovskii were more popular than Lenin. In 1911 Trotsky's *Pravda* admitted that the student movement had always eluded outside control—a point already made by Struve in 1904.

A significant question is why students, in 1905 and 1906, seemed to prefer Social Democracy to the Kadets. After all, many of the most important demands of the Russian student movement, such as calls for academic autonomy, personal inviolability, and more accessible universities, were of a liberal rather than a revolutionary nature. As we have seen, some student Social Democratic pamphlets were quite explicit about using Social Democracy as a means to achieve an end—not the dictatorship of the proletariat, but a society characterized by liberty, freedom, and legality. Here, too, we must look at the underlying context of student unrest—in this case how the autocratic system affected the *perception* of liberalism, a perception honed by the students' collective experience in the universities. And we might note that after the fall of the dynasty in 1917, the fortunes of the Kadets in student politics began to improve. To be sure, the moderate left still attracted more votes for student governments, but the dead hand of the autocracy was no longer compromising the basic tenets of Russian liberalism.

A major key to understanding the dynamics of student unrest in tsarist Russia is provided by a recurrent theme in the student sub-culture: the fear of becoming an ineffectual "Chekhovian hero." A very high proportion of students—about two-thirds—came from middle-class provincial families. Many realized that graduation meant a return to the provinces and to jobs that did not permit the relative independence of the university experience. Many students feared that graduation from the university marked the beginning of a life of impotence, compromise, and boredom.[10]

The *studenchestvo* was a group in transition. In terms of social background, the students were as far from the *narod* as they were from their roots in the provincial middle class or from the political elite. Their experience in the *VUZy* had helped to cut the ties to home, but if they looked ahead, they faced problems of how to define their future identity. The student movement rejected the notion that the students were the future members of a Russian bourgeoisie, or even of a professional middle class, in part because the prevailing options gave these terms a pejorative meaning. Nonetheless, only a few students could live up to the ideal of the self-sacrificing intellectual. The students were, therefore, suspended between an identity based on a traditional category—the

10. G. B. Sliozberg, reflecting on his university experience, wrote: "For the student, life was full of disappointments and unpleasantness. If he came from a civil service family he tended to see his father as a bureaucratic cog in a large machine, a cog deprived of any individual substance . . . if he were the son of a merchant then everything he saw at home repelled him; he looked for moral purity and this search took place where there was none, against the backdrop of a dusty provincial town. Even worse was the situation of the student who was the son of a small tradesman or artisan" (Sliozberg, ed., *Pamiati russkovo studenchestva* [Paris, 1934], p. 89).

ideal of the self-sacrificing intellectual—and an identity-to-be that was tainted with all the political and social weakness of Russian liberalism and the Russian professional classes.

It is now possible to explain why the Russian student movement marched under a radical rather than a liberal banner. For many students, the universities afforded a last chance to rebel against the prospect of political impotence. As long as they were in the universities, the collective solidarity of the student experience gave individual students a chance to protest in a semi-protected and socially sanctioned fashion. The university experience was also a microcosm of the restrictions and choices the students would face later, a constant struggle against petty restrictions imposed by a government unable to follow a consistent policy. And it would not be too far-fetched to say that for many students, the concrete embodiment of liberalism was the seemingly timid professor who resented state interference but refused to engage in direct confrontation with the authorities.

The universities offered a preview of the choices faced by educated, politically concerned citizens in the last years of the autocracy. Students anticipated three options, apart from total political passivity. Upon graduation, they could support the established order, which itself was torn between reform from above and a last-ditch defense of the interests of the landed nobility. They could join the revolutionary movement. Or they could settle down, do "small deeds," and hope for the best. The government might have had student support at one time—1899 to 1901 is an example—but pursued policies that discredited those who urged students to trust the intentions of the regime. Only a tiny minority would join the revolutionary movement. Most students knew they would follow the third road, but for many it was an uninspiring and emotionally unsatisfying option.

Student protest, therefore, not only was directed against the Russian autocracy, but also represented an often spontaneous but emphatic challenge—as Nikolai Iordanskii pointed out in his 1911 article—to many of the assumptions of Russian liberalism. It was in the universities that many of these assumptions came under close scrutiny, as both students and professors confronted a basic question: how does one defend one's "rights"? Paul Miliukov had pointed out that the Kadets preferred to be the loyal opposition of His Majesty rather than be in opposition to His Majesty. But how was it possible to be a loyal opposition when the government imposed martial law or reneged on implied promises of academic autonomy? If a Peter Stolypin failed to prevail against the entrenched power of the landed nobility and had to concede the failure of his ambitious plans for reform of local government and the creation of a political system less tied to the narrow interests of the landowning aristocracy, then what could liberal parties such as the Kadets hope to achieve? The Kadet party told the *studenchestvo* that the Kadets were their future social base. By means of the student movement, the *studenchestvo* told the professors and the Kadets that they found the prospect unappealing.

In its wider policies as well as in the universities, the government pursued a course that confronted liberals with the problem of having to consider radical tactics to defend liberal goals. Student protest pointed up this dilemma. While the students and professors could agree on many ultimate ends, the student movement, with its constant determination to resort to the tactics of direct protest—strike or demonstration—exposed the Achilles' heel of Russian liberalism. To borrow a point made by Michael Miles about the American student movement in the 1960s, the Russian student movement had not only an actual but also a symbolic dimension.[11] It symbolized, through its constant confrontation with the professoriate within the universities, both the lack of consensus that hampered the coalescence of a strong civil society and the difficulty of developing effective political strategies that could exert effective pressure on the autocracy.

If Russian students registered doubts about their future identities, they had a strong sense of their past. The *studenchestvo* was constantly comparing itself to its predecessors, usually to the advantage of the latter. In their pamphlets and leaflets students repeatedly exaggerated the courage, heroism, and determination of earlier student generations. This tendency became especially marked after 1899, when students began to fear that the *studenchestvo* would fade away and be replaced by an apathetic bourgeois studentry, as had happened, they felt, in Germany after 1848. During the 1908 and 1911 strikes, numerically the most impressive protests in the history of the Russian student movement, the students referred back to 1899–1901 as a time when students were more courageous. As has been shown, a major reason for the 1908 strike was a feeling that the students had to live up to the example of earlier student generations or forfeit their claim to be a part of the *studenchestvo*. And in 1899 and 1901, students compared themselves unfavorably to their predecessors from the 1860s and 1870s.

11. Michael Miles, *The Radical Probe: The Logic of Student Rebellion* (New York, 1971).

Clearly, a central feature of the Russian student movement was a collective memory of the protests of successive student generations. There was no nationwide organization to lend continuity to the student movement. The notion of a continuous student movement came from the mystique of the *studenchestvo*. It was a mystique that was hard to live up to, and students were constantly afraid that it had no future. This tension between mystique and reality gave student protest much of its continuous character.

One important reason for this widespread anxiety about the future of the *studenchestvo* was the continual expansion in the size of Russia's student population. By 1910, Moscow and Saint Petersburg were among the largest universities in the world. This increase in numbers, as well as the introduction of an elective system of instruction after 1906, made the student body seem much less closely knit. Such basic student institutions as the *skhodka* came under increasing attack as liberals called for the replacement of "direct democracy" by a "parliamentary system" in student government. This was another way of saying that there was no such thing as a unified *studenchestvo* with a "general will," expressed in the *skhodka*, that was binding and could react instantaneously to challenges from without. Marxist students renewed their assertions that the *studenchestvo* was nothing more than a loose amalgam of individuals from various social classes who happened to be at the university at the same time. Thus in a real sense the "crisis of the *studenchestvo*"—the main theme of the student press—was part of a wider crisis in Russia, a conflict between traditional forms of social perception and tensions generated by rapid social change.

A second reason for anxiety about the future of the *studenchestvo* was the emergence of new groups on the political scene, especially during the Revolution of 1905. Compared to the proletariat or the peasantry, students felt weak and unimportant. A third reason was the emergence of the Duma. For all its drawbacks, the Duma provided a forum for the articulation of political views; many students believed, with reason, that as a result, the public no longer followed student unrest with interest or tacit sympathy.

One response to the "crisis of the *studenchestvo*" was the suggestion that student professionalism should become the main focus of the student movement. This view held that students should concentrate on economic self-help, defend their corporate rights, and forget the alleged political messianism of the 1899–1901 period. According to this view, students still had a political role, but this could best be fulfilled if the students fought for their own interests—the right to organize, open admissions, more financial aid—and thus demonstrated the objective conflict between the autocracy and the democratic classes in Russian society. But here, too, student professionalism was less a new ideology of the student movement than it was a symptom of the basic ambivalence of the students' position. The political messianism of the 1899–1901 period was less extreme than it appeared to be ten years later, and the doctrine of student professionalism had been articulated before, at least implicitly, in the *zemliachestva* of the 1880s and 1890s.

It is significant that on the eve of, and during, World War I, the students were still debating many of the same issues they had been struggling over ever since the 1860s. It was noted earlier that many historians have tended to impose an artificial structure on the student movement that tends to ignore underlying processes of self-definition which were hardly unilinear, logical, or predictable.

To discuss the psychological context of the student movement or its lack of real commitment to the revolutionary parties is not to imply that the student movement was unimportant—quite the opposite. On the whole, the student movement had far more impact than its participants realized. Perhaps the most important political effect of the student movement was its slow, corrosive effect on the legitimacy of the autocracy. The very fact of student protest in Russia's large urban centers challenged and embarrassed an autocracy which saw the maintenance of public order as one of its major goals. Concentrated in the nerve centers of the empire and based in institutions that gave it a common, if temporary, identity, the *studenchestvo* proved to be a hard nut to crack. No one, and least of all the students themselves, could predict when the universities would erupt. Obviously the student movement lost much of its political significance when other groups were actively battling or confronting the autocracy or when general political mobilization was in progress. Thus from a purely political point of view, the student movement was less important in 1917 or even 1906 than it had been in 1899 or 1901. But the fact that most major student unrest occurred when other social groups were comparatively quiet was, from the point of view of the government, a mixed blessing. Students were rarely a *direct* political threat but the 1899, 1901, 1902, 1908, and 1911 strikes destroyed any illusion that the system had complete control.

The student movement forced the autocracy to abandon piecemeal the 1884 Statute, and it kept the government's higher-education policy in a constant state of flux. Insofar as the government saw the student movement as a threat to its prestige, student protest was an important factor in contributing to a growing estrangement between the state and the educated classes. This was especially true in 1899–1902 and 1910–1911.

The student movement was politically significant in still another way. It is true that, for the most part, student protest did not spread to other social groups—although there were major exceptions, such as the Kazan Square demonstration of 1901, which, contrary to the views of some historians, was organized exclusively by students to protest student concerns. However, the constant recurrence of student protest served as a steady corrective to narrow ideological views of the dynamics of Russian society. In that sense, the student movement certainly influenced the evolution of Russian Social Democracy between 1899 and 1902, as well as the self-definition of the Kadets in 1911. And some observers make the link between the unsettling effect of the 1899–1902 student movement and the development of the Social Revolutionary party.

Largely spontaneous, basically impervious to outside manipulation and control, often unpredictable, the Russian student movement reminded not only the government but also the political opposition of the constant tension between a priori political slogans and the realities of Russia's political and social development. Last but not least, the student movement underscored some important psychological obstacles faced by Russian liberalism as its potential constituency struggled to reconcile a symbol of traditional self-definition—the notion of *studenchestvo*—with the vague and threatening prospect of membership in an as-yet-undefined professional middle class.

Appendix A: Russian University Students

TABLE A-1   REGIONAL ORIGINS OF MOSCOW
UNIVERSITY STUDENTS, 1891, 1904, 1913

Educational District	1891	1904	1913
Moscow	49.1%	61.9%	60.0%
Saint Petersburg	1.8	2.0	2.0
Kazan and Orenburg	6.8	5.2	7.0
Ukraine (Kiev, Kharkov, Odessa)	20.4	16.1	12.0
Siberia and Turkestan	2.2	0.9	2.0
Caucasus	5.6	5.5	7.0
Vilna, Dorpat, Riga	10.1	6.3	5.0
Warsaw	2.9	1.7	3.0
Foreign	1.1	0.4	1.0

SOURCE: Imperatorskii Moskovskii Universitet, *Otchët za 1891 god* (Moscow, 1892); Imperatorskii Moskovskii Universitet, *Otchët za 1904 god* (Moscow, 1905); Imperatorskii Moskovskii Universitet, *Alfavitnyi spisok studentov* (Moscow, 1913).

NOTE: Because only main categories are shown here, the figures do not total exactly 100 percent.

TABLE A-2   SOCIAL ORIGINS OF STUDENTS, 1880

	University								
Social Origin	Saint Petersburg	Moscow	Kharkov	Kazan	Iur'ev	Warsaw	Odessa	Kiev
Hereditary nobles	26.4%	19.8%	21.1%	10.6%	23.6%	45.2%	12.1%	20.6%
Personal nobles	28.2	27.3	18.1	21.1	21.9	17.1	10.1	24.4
Clerics	23.0	22.0	38.6	42.3	8.5	8.9	51.7	25.1
Honorary citizens and merchants	9.6	9.9	8.5	8.4	12.9	3.2	5.5	9.5
Meshchane, artisans, raznochintsy	9.6	11.2	7.5	7.2	12.4	2.2	12.1	15.9
Peasants and cossacks	1.8	3.3	1.2	3.7	6.5	2.1	2.0	1.8
Foreigners	0.9	6.0	4.9	6.7	14.1	1.2	6.3	2.7
Total number of students (N = 8,120)	1,647	1,876	656	706	949	804	346	1,136

SOURCE: V. R. Leikina-Svirskaia, *Intelligentsiia v Rossii vo vtoroi polovine 19ovo veka* (Moscow, 1971), p. 62.

NOTE: Because only main categories are shown here, the figures do not total exactly 100 percent.

TABLE A-3   SOCIAL ORIGINS OF STUDENTS, 1900
(EXCLUDING KIEV)

Social Origin	University								
	Saint Petersburg	Moscow	Kharkov	Kazan	Iur'ev	Warsaw	Odessa	Tomsk	Total
Nobles and civil servants	68.3%	56.1%	45.6%	50.0%	19.6%	39.0%	48.2%	15.3%	50.4%
Clerics	4.2	5.5	3.8	8.2	41.9	4.8	4.9	60.5	11.4
Honorary citizens and merchants	11.7	13.7	17.7	8.2	11.3	2.4		4.0	
Meshchane, artisans, raznochintsy	10.9	17.3	23.4	28.4	16.7	49.2	43.0	12.7	36.5
Peasants and cossacks	3.5	5.5	7.4	4.5	9.7	2.8		6.0	
Foreigners	1.3	1.8	1.9	.04	0.8	1.7	3.7	0.5	1.9
Total number of students	3,584	4,025	1,234	823	1,543	1,127	663	549	13,548

SOURCE: V. R. Leikina-Svirskaia, *Intelligentsiia v Rossii vo vtoroi polovine 19ovo veka* (Moscow, 1971), p. 64.
NOTE: Because only main categories are shown here, the figures do not total exactly 100 percent.

TABLE A-4   SOCIAL ORIGINS OF STUDENTS, 1912

Social Origin	University										
	Saint Petersburg	Moscow	Kharkov	Kiev	Kazan	Iur'ev	Warsaw	Odessa	Tomsk	Saratov	Total
Nobles and civil servants	46.1%	37.7%	28.4%	37.4%	37.7%	27.5%	14.7%	33.4%	25.0%	27.7%	35.6%
Clerics	5.9	8.1	8.2	8.2	9.2	15.0	48.0	5.7	30.3	6.0	11.4
Honorary citizens and merchants	7.5	15.5	12.1	12.3	10.8	11.2	2.2	10.7	7.2	8.3	11.0
Meshchane, artisans, raznochintsy	24.8	22.2	27.2	31.7	24.2	23.0	21.4	29.0	22.1	29.4	25.1
Peasants and cossacks	14.3	9.9	15.6	9.2	15.0	22.1	13.1	10.1	12.3	25.0	12.8
Foreigners and others	1.3	6.6	8.4	1.1	3.0	1.2	0.6	11.1	3.1	3.6	4.1
Total number of students	7,282	9,390	3,002	4,857	2,012	2,251	2,415	2,025	892	412	34,538

SOURCE: These figures were compiled by the author on the basis of the 1912 *Otchët* of the Ministry of Education.
NOTE: Because only main categories are shown here, the figures do not total exactly 100 percent.

TABLE A-5 SOCIAL ORIGINS OF STUDENTS BY FIELD OF STUDY, 1894, MOSCOW UNIVERSITY

Social Origin	Natural Science	Mathe-matics	History and Philology	Medicine	Law
Nobles and civil service	46.4%	46.3%	51.2%	38.2%	54.2%
Clerics	3.2	6.1	12.0	6.9	6.2
Honorary citizens and first guild merchants	9.1	7.4	6.6	5.2	6.2
Meshchane, second guild merchants, artisans	29.0	28.0	22.0	37.8	22.6
Peasants	6.9	7.4	3.8	5.8	4.7
Total number of students (N = 3,693)	373	311	258	1,182	1,569

SOURCE: Imperatorskii Moskovskii Universitet, *Otchët za 1894 god* (Moscow, 1895).
NOTE: Because only main categories are shown here, the figures do not total exactly 100 percent.

TABLE A-6 SOCIAL ORIGINS OF STUDENTS BY FIELD OF STUDY, 1904, MOSCOW UNIVERSITY

Social Origin	Natural Science	Mathe-matics	History and Philology	Medicine	Law
Nobles and civil service	47.6%	49.3%	49.6%	43.3%	53.3%
Clerics	5.4	4.5	6.7	5.5	4.0
Honorary citizens and first guild merchants	16.1	12.3	9.7	13.8	15.4
Meshchane, second guild merchants, artisans	5.4	5.5	6.3	5.6	20.2
Peasants	22.9	26.2	25.6	28.0	4.0
Total number of students (N = 5,070)	731	590	491	1,306	1,952

SOURCE: Imperatorskii Moskovskii Universitet, *Otchët za 1904 god* (Moscow, 1905).
NOTE: Because only main categories are shown here, the figures do not total exactly 100 percent.

Appendix B:
Russian University
Professoriate

TABLE B-1 LISTED PROPERTY OF PROFESSORIATE

	1902	1913
No listed property	74.7%	83.5%
One house	12.2	7.7
Two houses	0.9	0.3
1–50 desiatines of land	0.3	1.4
51–200 desiatines of land	2.2	2.3
201–500 desiatines of land	3.6	1.2
501–1,000 desiatines of land	2.4	0.6
1,001–2,500 desiatines of land	2.6	1.4
2,501–5,000 desiatines of land	0.9	0.3
Over 5,000 desiatines of land	0.0	0.3
Unspecified "landed estate"	0.0	1.1

SOURCE: Ministerstvo Narodnovo Prosveshcheniia, *Spisok lits sluzhashchikh po vedomstvu Ministerstva Narodnovo Prosveshcheniia* (Saint Petersburg, 1913).

NOTE: Because only main categories are shown here, the figures do not total exactly 100 percent.

TABLE B-2 THE RUSSIAN PROFESSORIATE BY SOCIAL BACKGROUND AND SPECIALTY, 1913

Social Origin	Natural Science	Mathematics	History and Philology	Medicine	Law	Theology[a]	Total
Hereditary nobility	37.0%	48.1%	39.8%	29.3%	44.1%	16.7%	36.1%
Civil service	10.2	7.4	9.8	9.6	8.1	8.3	9.3
Clergy	9.4	3.7	19.5	20.9	16.2	66.7	17.3
Honorary citizens	3.1	7.4	0.0	3.6	2.8	0.0	2.8
Merchants	5.5	0.0	4.5	8.0	6.3	0.0	6.1
Meshchanstvo	9.4	7.4	6.7	11.6	7.2	0.0	9.2
Peasants	3.1	3.7	2.3	1.2	1.8	0.0	2.0
Military	14.9	3.7	7.5	9.6	9.0	0.0	9.8
Foreign	3.1	0.0	3.8	0.8	0.9	16.7	2.0
Total number of professors	127	27	133	249	111	6	653

SOURCE: Ministerstvo Narodnovo Prosveshcheniia, *Spisok lits sluzhashchikh po vedomstvu Ministerstva Narodnovo Prosveshcheniia* (Saint Petersburg, 1913).

NOTE: Because only main categories are shown here, the figures do not total exactly 100 percent. The service list includes full and associate professors as well as some retired professors and junior faculty teaching required courses. It does not include most of the junior faculty. The list includes only university faculty.

[a] Iur'ev University.

TABLE B-3   RUSSIAN PROFESSORS WHO
PREPARED AT EITHER MOSCOW UNIVERSITY
OR SAINT PETERSBURG UNIVERSITY

	1902	1913
Natural sciences	50.4%	58.3%
Mathematics	65.2	51.8
History and philology	48.0	48.8
Medicine	31.2	28.5
Law	46.6	43.2

SOURCE: Ministerstvo Narodnovo Prosveshcheniia, *Spisok lits slu-zhashchikh po vedomstvu Ministerstvo Narodnovo Prosveshcheniia* (Saint Petersburg, 1913).

Bibliography

I. ARCHIVAL SOURCES

Leningrad

Gosudarstvennaia Publichnaia Biblioteka imeni M. E. Saltykova-Shchedrina.
  Otdel Rukopisei (GPB im. M. E. Saltykova-Shchedrina)
    fond 781, I. I. Tolstoi
Tsentral'nyi Gosudarstvennyi Istoricheskii Arkhiv (TsGIA)
    fond 733, Ministry of Education
    fond 740, Legal Department of the Ministry of Education
    fond 922, V. G. Glazov
    fond 1276, Council of Ministers
    fond 1282, Ministry of the Interior
    fond 1662, P. A. Stolypin

Moscow

Arkhiv Biblioteki Moskovskovo Gosudarstvennovo Universiteta imeni M. V.
  Lomonosova (BMGU)
    fond V. I. Orlova
Arkhiv Instituta Istorii Akademii Nauk SSSR (AIISSSR)
    fond 5, M. N. Pokrovskii
Gosudarstvennaia Publichnaia Biblioteka imeni V. I. Lenina. Otdel Rukopisei
  (GPB im. V. I. Lenina)
    fond 119, N. I. Kareev
    fond 158, A. A. Manuilov
    fond 264, P. N. Sakulin
Tsentral'nyi Gosudarstvennyi Arkhiv Oktiabrskoi Revoliutsii (TsGAOR)
    fond 102
    fond 124

fond 646, Grand Duke Sergei Alexandrovich
fond DO
fond DP
Tsentral'nyi Gosudarstvennyi Istoricheskii Arkhiv Moskvy (TsGIAM)
fond 418
fond 459

Stanford, California
Hoover Institution, Boris Nikolaevskii Collection
Hoover Institution, Paris Okhrana Archive (POA)

II. PRINTED OFFICIAL AND
    UNIVERSITY MATERIALS

Gosudarstvennaia Duma. Tretii Sozyv. *Doklady Biudzhetnoi Komissii.* Saint Petersburg, 1908–1912.
———. *Stenograficheskie Otchëty.* Saint Petersburg, 1908–1912.
Gosudarstvennyi Sovet. *Otchëty.* Saint Petersburg, 1884–1905.
Imperatorskii Khar'kovskii Universitet. *Suzhdeniia Soveta Imperatorskovo Khar'kovskovo Universiteta po voprosam kasaiushchimsia ustroistva universitetov.* Kharkov, 1901.
Imperatorskii Moskovskii Universitet. *Doklad Komissii izbrannoi sovetom Imperatorskovo Moskovskovo Universiteta 28ovo fevralia, 1901ovo goda dlia vyiasneniia prichin studencheskikh volnenii i mer k uporiadocheniiu universitetskoi zhizni.* Moscow, n.d.
———. *O peresmotre ustava i shtatov Imperatorskikh Rossiiskikh Universitetov.* Moscow, 1901.
———. *Alfavitnyi spisok studentov.* Moscow, 1902, 1903, 1909, 1913.
———. *Otchëty.* Moscow, 1902–1914.
Imperatorskii Sankt-Peterburgskii Universitet. *Otchëty.* Saint Petersburg, 1900–1914.
———. *Zhurnaly zasedanii soveta.* Saint Petersburg, 1900–1912.
Komissiia po preobrazovaniiu vysshikh uchebnykh zavedenii. *Trudy.* 5 vols. Saint Petersburg, 1903.
Ministerstvo Narodnovo Prosveshcheniia. *Otchëty.* Saint Petersburg, 1900–1914.
———. *Spisok lits sluzhashchikh po vedomstvu Ministerstva Narodnovo Prosveshcheniia.* Saint Petersburg, 1902, 1912.
Polnyi Svod Zakonov Rossiiskoi Imperii. Saint Petersburg, 1911.
Schwartz, A. N. *Ob"iasnitel'naia zapiska k proektu obshchevo ustava Imperatorskikh Rossiiskikh Universitetov.* Saint Petersburg, 1908.
Sovet Ministrov. *Osobye Zhurnaly.* Saint Petersburg, 1908–1914.
———. *Spravka po evreiskomu voprosu.* Saint Petersburg, n.d.

III. PERIODICALS AND NEWSPAPERS

Byloe   *Golos Minuvshevo*
Dela i Dni   *Golos Studenchestva*

Iskra
Istoricheskie Zapiski
Istoricheskii Vestnik
Istoriia SSSR
Krasnaia Letopis'
Krasnyi Arkhiv
Minuvshie Gody
Mir Bozhii
Nakanune
Nasha Zhizn'
Nashi Dni
Obrazovanie
Odesskie Novosti
Odesskii Listok
Osvobozhdenie
Pravo
Proletarii
Proletarskaia Revoliutsiia
Rabochaia Gazeta
Rech'
Revoliutsionnaia Rossiia
Russkaia Mysl'
Russkie Vedomosti

Russkii Arkhiv
Russkoe Bogatstvo
Sovremennyi Mir
Studencheskaia Gazeta
Studencheskaia Rech'
Studencheskie Gody
Studencheskii Mir
Studencheskoe Delo
Studenchestvo
Student
Syn Otechestva
Vestnik Evropy
Vestnik Russkoi Revoliutsii
Vestnik Vospitaniia
Voprosy Istorii
Voprosy Zhizni
Vperëd
Vsemirnyi Vestnik
Zhurnal Ministerstva Narodnovo
    Prosveshcheniia
Znamia Truda
Zvezda

IV. MEMOIRS AND PERSONAL ACCOUNTS

Anisimov, A. "Kniaz' S. N. Trubetskoi i Moskovskoe studenchestvo." *Voprosy Filosofii i Psikhologii*, no. 1 (1906).

Astrov, N. I. *Vospominaniia*. Paris, 1941.

B—a. B. "Vospominaniia peterburzhtsa o vtoroi polovine 80-kh godov." *Minuvshie Gody*, nos. 10, 11 (1908).

Boborykin, P. A. *Za polveka: Moi vospominaniia*. Moscow, 1929.

Bobrinskii, A. A. "Dnevnik A. A. Bobrinskovo." *Krasnyi Arkhiv*, no. 26 (1928).

Brandt, A. A. *List'ia pozheltelye: Peredumannoe i perezhitoe*. Belgrade, 1930.

Bukhbinder, N. "Studencheskie volneniia v Kieve v 1884om godu." *Katorga i Ssylka*, no. 66 (1930).

Buzeskul, V. "Dni barrikad v Khar'kove v Oktiabre 1905g." *Golos Minuvshevo*, nos. 7—8 (July—August 1917).

Chernov, V. M. *Zapiski sotsialista-revoliutsionera*. Berlin, 1922.

Chicherin, B. N. *Vospominaniia: Moskovskii Universitet*. Moscow, 1929.

Chulkov, G. I. *Gody stranstvii: Iz knigi vospominanii*. Moscow, 1930.

D. [A. Diakonov.] *1905 i 1906gg. v Peterburgskom Universitete*. Saint Petersburg, 1907.

Doroshenko, N. V. "Vozniknovenie bol'shevistskoi organizatsii v Peterburgskom Universitete i pervye gody eë sushchestvovaniia." *Krasnaia Letopis'*, no. 2 (1931).

Garvi, P. A. *Vospominaniia sotsial-demokrata*. New York, 1946.

Ianzhul, I. I. *Vospominaniia.* Saint Petersburg, 1910.
Iordanskii, N. "Missiia P. S. Vannovskovo." *Byloe,* no. 9 (1907).
Ivanov-Razumnik, R. V. *Tiur'my i ssylki.* New York, 1953.
Kamenskii, S. *Vek minuvshii.* Paris, 1967.
Kizevetter, A. A. *Na rubezhe dvukh stoletii.* Prague, 1929.
Levitskii, V. *Za chetvert' veka.* Moscow, 1926.
Maklakov, V. A. *Vlast' i obshchestvennost' na zakate staroi Rossii.* Paris, 1936.
Martov, Iu. *Zapiski sotsial-demokrata.* Berlin, 1922.
Mavrodin, V. V., and V. A. Ezhov, eds. *Leningradskii Universitet v vospomina-niiakh sovremennikov,* volume 2. Leningrad, 1982.
Medem, V. *Fun mayn lebn.* 2 vols. New York, 1923.
Mel'gunov, S. P. *Vospominaniia i dnevniki.* Paris, 1964.
Miliukov, P. N. *Vospominaniia, 1859–1917.* New York, 1955.
Mitskevich, S. I. *Revoliutsionnaia Moskva, 1888–1905.* Moscow, 1940.
Mogilianskii, M. N. "V devianostye gody." *Byloe,* nos. 23, 24 (1924).
Na puti k pobede. Leningrad, 1925.
Naumov, A. N. *Iz utselevshikh vospominanii, 1868–1917.* 2 vols. New York, 1954.
Nestroev, G. *Iz dnevnika maksimalista.* Paris, 1910.
————. "K istorii studencheskovo dvizheniia v Rossii." *Katorga i ssylka,* nos. 28–29 (1926).
Novikov, M. M. *Ot Moskvy do N'iu-Iorka.* New York, 1952.
Pantaleev, L. F. *Vospominaniia.* Moscow, 1958.
Polovtsev, A. A. "Dnevnik A. A. Polovtseva." *Krasnyi Arkhiv,* no. 3 (1923).
Posse, V. A. *Moi zhiznennyi put'.* Moscow, 1929.
Rozanov, V. "Iz studencheskikh vospominanii." *Katorga i ssylka,* no. 51 (1929).
Strumilin, S. G. *Iz perezhitovo, 1897–1917.* Moscow, 1957.
Titov, A. *Vospominaniia o studencheskom dvizhenii 1901ovo goda.* Moscow, 1907.
Trubetskaia, O. *Kniaz' S. N. Trubetskoi: Vospominaniia sestry.* New York, 1953.
Tyrkova-Williams, A. *Na putiakh k svobode.* New York, 1953.
Vernadskii, G. "Iz vospominanii." *Novyi Zhurnal,* no. 100 (1970).
Vishniak, M. *Dan' proshlomu.* New York, 1954.
Voitinskii, V. *Gody pobed i porazhenii.* Berlin, 1923.
Witte, S. Iu. *Vospominaniia.* Moscow, 1960.
Zaionchkovskii, P. A., ed. *Moskovskii Universitet v vospominaniiakh sovremen-nikov.* Moscow, 1956.

V. ARTICLES

A. L. "Naselenie universitetov." *Vestnik Evropy,* no. 9 (1896).
Ashevskii, S. "Russkoe studenchestvo v epokhu 60-kh godov." *Sovremennyi Mir,* nos. 6–11 (1907).
B. G. "V. I. Sergeevich i studencheskie bezporiadki v 1899 godu." *Istoricheskii Vestnik,* no. 113 (1911).
Bagalei, D. I. "Ekonomicheskoe polozhenie russkikh universitetov." *Vestnik Evropy,* no. 1 (1914).

Ben-David, J., and R. Collins. "A Comparative Study of Academic Freedom and Student Politics." In S. M. Lipset, ed., *Student Politics.* New York, 1970.

Braun, J. "Położenie i ruch organizacyjny młodzieży akademickiej na uniwersytecie warszawskim w latach 1890–1904." *Roczniki Uniwersytetu Warszawskiego,* vol. 5 (1963).

"Brozhenie v vysshikh uchebnykh zavedeniiakh." *Osvobozhdenie,* nos. 15–16 (1904).

Bulgakov, S. "Bez plana." *Voprosy Zhizni,* no. 1 (1905).

Chicherin, B. N. "Zapiska po studencheskomu voprosu." *Byloe,* no. 8 (1907).

D. K. O. "Studencheskoe dvizhenie i zadachi oppozitsii." *Osvobozhdenie,* no. 56 (1904).

Dubovnikova, A. N. "Pis'ma k Chekhovu o studencheskom dvizhenii 1899–1902." *Literaturnoe Nasledstvo,* vol. 68. Moscow, 1960.

Dudgeon, R. "The Forgotten Minority: Women Students in Imperial Russia, 1872–1917." *Russian History,* no. 9 (1982).

"Dva razgovora: iz dnevnikov V. G. Glazova." *Dela i Dni,* no. 1 (1920).

Eimontova, R. G. "Universitetskaia reforma 1863evo goda." *Istoricheskie Zapiski,* no. 70 (1965).

Engel', G. "1905g. i studencheskoe dvizhenie v Peterburge." *Krasnaia Letopis',* no. 2 (1925).

Famintsyn, A. "Nakanune universitetskoi reformy." *Mir Bozhii,* no. 1 (1903).

Filippov, A. "Moskovskoe studenchestvo." *Russkoe Obozrenie,* nos. 2–6, 12 (1897).

Fortunatov, A. Th. "Zachem liudi idut v vysshuiu shkolu." In A. Th. Fortunatov, *Po voprosam nauchnoi shkoly.* Moscow, 1916.

Frommet, B. "Ekonomicheskoe polozhenie studenchestva." *Zhizn' Dlia Vsekh,* no. 10 (1910).

Glinskii, B. B. "Universitetskie ustavy." *Istoricheskii Vestnik,* nos. 1–2 (1900).

Gordon, G. "K voprosu o material'nom polozhenii nashevo studenchestva." *Vestnik Vospitaniia,* no. 7 (1914).

Gredeskul, N. A. "Rol' universiteta v sovremennom dvizhenii." *Pravo,* no. 40 (1905).

Grevs, I. "Stroitel'stvo i razrushenie v nashei vysshei shkole." *Pravo,* nos. 29, 31 (1908).

———. "Vozroditsia u nas podorvannoe nauchnoe prosveshchenie?" *Pravo,* no. 9 (1905).

———. "Vremennye pravila 27ovo Avgusta." *Pravo,* no. 36 (1905).

Grimm, E. "Organizatsiia universitetskovo prepodavaniia po proektu novovo ustava." *Russkaia Mysl',* no. 4 (1916).

Guerrier, V. I. "Nauka i gosudarstvo." *Vestnik Evropy,* no. 10 (1876).

Iordanskii, N. "Ottsy i deti." *Sovremennyi Mir,* no. 2 (1911).

Iukhneva, N. V. "Studencheskoe dvizhenie v Peterburgskom universitete i pervye demonstratsii 1901ovo goda." *Ocherki po istorii Leningradskovo universiteta.* Leningrad, 1962.

Ivanov, A. E. "Demokraticheskoe studenchestvo v revoliutsii 1905–07gg." *Istoricheskie Zapiski,* no. 107 (1982).

———. "Rossiiskie universitety i russko-iaponskaia voina." In Akademiia Nauk S.S.S.R., Institut Istorii, *Problemy otechestvennoi istorii.* Mosow, 1973.

————. "Universitety Rossii v 1905om godu." *Istoricheskie Zapiski,* no. 88 (1971).
Izgoev, A. S. "Nebyvalyi razgrom." *Russkaia Mysl',* no. 3 (1911).
————. "Ob intelligentnoi molodëzhi." *Vekhi: Sbornik statei o russkoi intelligentsii.* Moscow, 1910.
"Iz otchëta o perliustratsii del politsiei za 1908 god." *Krasnyi Arkhiv,* no. 28 (1928).
K. P. "K universitetskomu voprosu." *Russkaia Mysl',* no. 5 (1901).
Kaminka, A. "Tretii akademicheskii s"ezd." *Pravo,* no. 4 (1906).
Kapnist, P. "Universitetskie voprosy." *Vestnik Evropy,* nos. 11, 12 (1903).
Kaufman, A. "Anketa o molodëzhi." *Russkaia Mysl',* no. 2 (1911).
————. "Russkaia kursistka v tsifrakh." *Russkaia Mysl',* no. 6 (1912).
"Kazënnyi patriotizm i russkaia molodëzh'." *Osvobozhdenie,* no. 18 (1904).
Khvostov, V. "Vopros ob avtonomii universitetov na s"ezde professorov." *Russkaia Mysl',* no. 3 (1906).
Kleinbort, L. "Molodëzh' i voina." *Sovremennyi Mir,* no. 11 (1914).
————. "Russkaia kursistka." *Sovremennyi Mir,* no. 9 (1914).
————. "Sovremennaia molodëzh': Prezhde i teper'." *Sovremennyi Mir,* no. 10 (1914).
Korel', I. "Peterburgskii Universitet v 1905 godu." *Leningradskii Universitet,* 21 January 1939.
"Krizis vysshei shkoly." *Russkaia Mysl',* no. 3 (1911).
Kruglova, Z. S. "Studencheskaia zabastovka 1911ovo goda i eë politicheskoe znachenie." *Uchënye Zapiski Moskovskovo Oblastnovo Pedagogicheskovo Instituta,* no. 135 (1964).
Kuz'min, M. "Nasha predmetnaia sistema." *Moskovskii Ezhenedel'nik,* 12 May 1907.
Larskii, I. "Na granitse akademizma." *Sovremennyi Mir,* no. 10 (1908).
Lazarson, M. "Studenchestvo i minuvshii akademicheskii krizis." *Obrazovanie,* no. 4 (1909).
Leikina-Svirskaia, V. R. "Iz istorii bor'by Peterburgskovo Universiteta s ministerstvom Kasso." *Vestnik Leningradskovo Universiteta,* no. 4 (1947).
Levchenko, V. "Krizis universitetskoi zhizni." *Russkaia Mysl',* no. 5 (1908).
Mel'gunov, S. P. "Studencheskie organizatsii 80–90kh godov v Moskovskom Universitete." *Vestnik Vospitaniia,* no. 4 (1907).
Metzger, W. P. "Academic Freedom and Scientific Freedom." *Daedalus* 107, no. 2 (1978).
Miakotin, V. "Dliashchaiasia tragediia." *Russkoe Bogatstvo,* no. 3 (1911).
————. "Khoziacva universiteta." *Narodno-Sotsialisticheskoe Obozrenie,* no. 2 (1906).
————. "Tragediia vysshei shkoly." *Russkoe Bogatstvo,* no. 10 (1908).
Mironov, A. M. "Pravovoe i material'noe polozhenie privat-dozentov v russkikh universitetakh." *Vestnik Vospitaniia,* no. 1 (1906).
"Moskovskoe studenchestvo i professora nakanune Fevral'skoi revoliutsii." *Krasnyi Arkhiv,* no. 58 (1933).
Nikolaevskii, B. "I. G. Tseretelli." *Sotsialisticheskii Vestnik,* no. 7 (1959).
Orlov, V. I. "Studencheskoe dvizhenie 1901ovo goda." *Krasnyi Arkhiv,* no. 75 (1936).

"Otzyvy nemetskikh i gollandskikh professorov o proekte universitetskovo ustava grafa I. I. Tolstovo." *Zhurnal Ministerstva Narodnovo Prosveshcheniia*, nos. 3–4 (1910).

Pavlitskaia, N. I. "Peterburgskii Universitet v revoliutsii 1905–07gg." *Vestnik Leningradskovo Universiteta*, no. 11 (1948).

Podshibiakin, M. "Staroe i novoe v studenchestve." *Studencheskaia Rech'*, 15 November 1907.

Pokrovskii, M. M. "K universitetskomu voprosu." *Russkaia Mysl'*, no. 11 (1906).

"Politicheskaia bor'ba vokrug smerti Tolstovo." *Literaturnoe nasledstvo*, vol. 69. Moscow, 1960.

Pollard, A. "The Russian Intelligentsia." *California Slavic Studies*, no. 3 (1964).

Rashin, A. G. "Gramotnost' i narodnoe obrazovanie v Rossii v 19om i nachale 20ovo vekakh." *Istoricheskie Zapiski*, no. 37 (1951).

"Razgrom Khar'kovskovo Tekhnologicheskovo Instituta." *Osvobozhdenie*, no. 56 (1904).

Rokov, G. "Iz noveishei istorii studencheskikh volnenii." *Vestnik Vospitaniia*, no. 3 (1906).

Sakulin, P. N. "Novyi proekt universitetskovo ustava." *Vestnik Vospitaniia*, no. 4 (1906).

Savich, S. E. "Zabastovka v vysshikh uchebnykh zavedeniiakh." *Pravo*, no. 11 (1905).

Sergeevich, V. "Germanskie universitety i nashi." *Vestnik Evropy*, no. 3 (1905).

Shchetinina, G. I. "Universitety i obshchestvennoe dvizhenie v poreformennyi period." *Istoricheskie Zapiski*, no. 84 (1969).

Statkovskii, P. "Sankt-Peterburgskoe Okhrannoe Otdelenie v 1895–1901 godakh." *Byloe*, no. 16 (1921).

"Stranitsa iz zhizni Moskovskovo Universiteta." *Russkyi Arkhiv*, no. 1 (1913).

Struve, P. B. "Chto zhe teper'?" *Osvobozhdenie*, no. 56 (1904).

Svatikov, S. G. "Opal'naia professura 80-kh godov." *Golos Minuvshevo*, no. 2 (1917).

Syromiatnikov, A. "Moskovskii Universitet v Oktiabrskie dni 1905ovo goda." *Krasnyi Arkhiv*, no. 74 (1936).

Tikhonovich, N. "Politicheskaia differentsiatsiia studenchestva." *Studenchestvo*, no. 3 (1906).

Trubetskoi, E. N. "K nachalu uchebnovo goda." *Moskovskii Ezhenedel'nik*, no. 25 (1906).

———. "K nachalu uchebnovo goda." *Moskovskii Ezhenedel'nik*, no. 34 (1907).

———. "Universitetskii Vopros." *Pravo*, no. 50 (1904).

Trubetskoi, S. "Universitet i studenchestvo." *Russkaia Mysl'*, no. 4 (1897).

Ukraintsev, V. "Nekotorye voprosy iz istorii dorevoliutsionnoi vysshei shkoly." *Trudy Kalininskovo Torfianovo Instituta*, no. 9 (1958).

Vagner, V. "Universitet kak shkola prepodavatelei." *Russkaia Mysl'*, no. 11 (1898).

Vernadskii, V. I. "Blizhaishie zadachi akademicheskoi zhizni." *Pravo*, no. 24 (1905).

———. "1911 god v istorii russkoi umstvennoi kul'tury." *Ezhegodnik Gazety Rech' za 1911 god.* Saint Petersburg, 1912.

———. "O nachale akademicheskikh zaniatii." *Pravo,* no. 24 (1905).

———. "O professorskom s"ezde." *Nashi Dni,* 20 December 1904.

———. "Tri zabastovki." *Russkie Vedomosti,* 5 July 1905.

———. "Vysshaia shkola i nauchnye organizatsii." *Ezhegodnik Gazety Rech' za 1913 god.* Saint Petersburg, 1914.

———. "Vysshaia shkola v Rossii." *Ezhegodnik Gazety Rech' za 1914 god.* Petrograd, 1915.

Vernadsky, G. "Iz vospominanii." *Novyi Zhurnal,* no. 100 (1970).

———. "Pis'mo iz Moskvy." *Studencheskaia Rech',* 15 November 1907.

Vinogradov, P. G. "Politicheskie pis'ma." *Russkie Vedomosti,* 5 August 1905.

———. "Uchebnoe delo v nashikh universitetakh." *Vestnik Evropy,* no. 10 (1901).

Vydrin, R. "Nakanune novovo universitetskovo ustava." *Sovremennyi Mir,* no. 2 (1910).

Wildman, A. K. "The Russian Intelligentsia in the 1890's." *American Slavic and East European Review,* no. 9 (1960).

Zelinskii, Th. Th. "Universitetskii vopros v 1906 godu." *Zhurnal Ministerstva Narodnovo Prosveshcheniia,* no. 8 (1906).

Zhivovo, S. "Chevo nedostaët v universitete nashim budushchim iuristam?" *Russkaia Mysl',* no. 10 (1902).

VI. BOOKS

Abramsky, C., ed. *Essays in Honor of E. H. Carr.* London, 1974.

Alston, P. *Education and the State in Tsarist Russia.* Stanford, 1969.

Avrekh, A. Ia. *Stolypin i tret'ia Duma.* Moscow, 1968.

———. *Tsarizm i chetvërtaia Duma.* Moscow, 1981.

Bazylow, L. *Polityka wewnętrzna caratu i ruchy społeczne w Rosji na początku XX wieku.* Warsaw, 1966.

Bernadskii, M. V., ed. *K kharakteristike sovremennovo studenchestva.* Saint Petersburg, 1910.

Besançon, A. *Education et société en Russie dans le second tiers du 19ᵐᵉ siècle.* Paris, 1974.

Bonnell, V. E. *Roots of Rebellion: Workers' Politics and Organizations in St. Petersburg and Moscow, 1900–1914.* Berkeley and Los Angeles, 1983.

Brockhaus, E. A., and I. A. Efron, eds. *Entsiklopedicheskii slovar'.* Saint Petersburg, 1897–1903.

Brower, D. *Training the Nihilists: Education and Radicalism in Tsarist Russia.* Ithaca, 1975.

Budilovich, A. S. *Nauka i politika.* Saint Petersburg, 1905.

Buzeskul, V. *Istoriia Khar'kovskovo Universiteta pri deistvii ustava 1884ovo goda.* Kharkov, 1905.

Chanbarisov, Sh. Kh. *Formirovanie sovetskoi universitetskoi sistemy.* Ufa, 1973.

Cherevanin, A. (pseud. of F. A. Lipkin). *Das Proletariat und die russische Revolution.* Stuttgart, 1908.

Chertkov, V. *Russkie studenty v osvoboditel'nom dvizhenii*. Moscow, 1908.

Chlenov, M. A. *Polovaia perepis' Moskovskovo studenchestva i eë obshchestvennoe znachenie*. Moscow, 1909.

Chrezvychainaia Sledstvennaia Komissiia Vremennovo Pravitel'stva. *Padenie tsarskovo rezhima*. 7 vols. Moscow, 1924–1927.

Delo soveta studencheskikh predstavitelei Kievskovo Universiteta. Kiev, 1908.

Dzhanshiev, G. A. *Epokha velikikh reform*. Moscow, 1900.

El'iashevich, V. B., A. A. Kizevetter, and M. M. Novikov, eds. *Moskovskii Universitet 1755–1930: iubileinyi sbornik*. Paris, 1930.

Emmons, T. *The Formation of Political Parties and the First National Elections in Russia*. London, 1983.

Engel', G., and V. Gorokhov. *Iz istorii studencheskovo dvizheniia 1899–1906*. Moscow, 1908.

Engelstein, L. *Moscow 1905*. Stanford, 1982.

Erikson, E. *Childhood and Society*. New York, 1950.

Erman, L. K. *Intelligentsiia v pervoi russkoi revoliutsii*. Moscow, 1966.

Feuer, L. *The Conflict of Generations*. New York, 1969.

Frieden, N. M. *Russian Physicians in an Era of Reform and Revolution, 1856–1905*. Princeton, 1981.

Frommet, B. *Ocherki po istorii studenchestva v Rossii*. Saint Petersburg, 1912.

Galai, S. *The Liberation Movement in Russia, 1900–1905*. Cambridge, England, 1973.

Gorin, P. *Ocherki po istorii Sovetov rabochikh deputatov v 1905g*. Moscow, 1925.

Gusiatnikov, P. S. *Revoliutsionnoe studencheskoe dvizhenie v Rossii*. Moscow, 1971.

Hans, N. *A History of Russian Educational Policy, 1701–1917*. London, 1931.

Harcave, S. *The Russian Revolution of 1905*. London, 1964.

Iarmolovich, A. *Smert' Prizrakov*. Saint Petersburg, 1908.

Ignatiev, P. N., P. I. Novgorodtsev, and D. M. Odinets. *Russian Schools and Universities in the World War*. New Haven, 1929.

Istoriia Leningradskovo Universiteta. Leningrad, 1969.

Istoriia Moskovskovo Universiteta. 2 vols. Ed. M. N. Tikhomirov. Moscow, 1955.

Istoriia Tartusskovo Universiteta. Tallinn, 1982.

Ivanov, P. *Studenty v Moskve: Byt, nravy, tipy*. Moscow, 1918.

Jarausch, K., ed. *The Transformation of Higher Learning, 1860–1930*. Chicago, 1983.

Die Judenpogrome in Russland. 2 vols. Cologne, 1910.

Kablukov, N. A. *Studencheskii kvartirnyi vopros v Moskve*. Moscow, 1908.

Keep, J. L. H. *The Rise of Social Democracy in Russia*. Oxford, 1963.

Khar'kovskii Gosudarstvennyi Universitet imeni A. M. Gor'kovo za 150 let. Kharkov, 1955.

Kirpichnikov, S. D. *Soiuz soiuzov*. Saint Petersburg, 1906.

Kiss, G. *Die gesellschaftspolitische Rolle der Studentenbewegung im vorrevolutionaeren Russland*. Munich, 1963.

Kol'tsov, N. *K universitetskomu voprosu*. Moscow, 1909.

Konovalovskii konflikt. Saint Petersburg, 1905.

Korbut, M. K. *Kazanskii gosudarstvennyi universitet imeni V. I. Ul'ianova-Lenina za 125 let, 1804/5 – 1929/30.* 2 vols. Kazan, 1930.

Leikina-Svirskaia, V. R. *Intelligentsiia v Rossii vo vtoroi polovine 19ovo veka.* Moscow, 1971.

———. *Russkaia intelligentsiia v 1900 – 1917 godakh.* Moscow, 1981.

Lenin, V. I. *Sochineniia.* 3d ed. Moscow, 1936.

Libanov, G. M. *Studencheskoe dvizhenie 1899 goda.* London, 1901.

Lifton, R. J. *Explorations in Psychohistory.* New York, 1974.

Lipset, S. M., ed. *Student Politics.* New York, 1970.

———. *Students in Revolt.* New York, 1970.

McClelland, J. C. *Autocrats and Academics: Education, Culture, and Society in Tsarist Russia.* Chicago, 1979.

Manning, R. *The Crisis of the Old Order in Russia: Gentry and Government.* Princeton, 1982.

Margolin, D. *Spravochnik po vysshemu obrazovaniiu.* Petrograd, 1915.

Martov, L., ed. *Obshchestvennoe dvizhenie v Rossii.* 4 vols. Saint Petersburg, 1910.

Materialy k istorii russkoi kontrrevoliutsii. Saint Petersburg, 1908.

Matveev, M. I. *Studenty Sibiri v revoliutsionnom dvizhenii.* Tomsk, 1966.

Menshikov, L. *Okhrana i revoliutsiia.* Moscow, 1925.

Miles, M. *The Radical Probe: The Logic of Student Rebellion.* New York, 1971.

Ocherki po istorii Leningradskovo Universiteta, volume 2. Leningrad, 1968.

Odesskii Universitet za 75 let (1865 – 1940). Odessa, 1940.

Orlov, V. I. *Studencheskoe dvizhenie Moskovskovo Universiteta v 19om stoletii.* Moscow, 1934.

Ozerov, I. Kh. *Na temy dnia.* Moscow, 1912.

Pinchuk, B.-C. *The Octobrists in the Third Duma.* Seattle, 1974.

Pintner, W., and D. K. Rowney, eds. *Russian Officialdom: The Bureaucratization of Russian Society from the Seventeenth to the Twentieth Century.* Chapel Hill, 1980.

Pozner, S. *Evrei i obshchaia shkola.* Saint Petersburg, 1914.

Rieber, A. J. *Merchants and Entrepreneurs in Imperial Russia.* Chapel Hill, 1982.

Ringer, F. *The Decline of the German Mandarins: The German Academic Community: 1890 – 1933.* Cambridge, Mass., 1969.

Rothblatt, S. *The Revolution of the Dons: Cambridge and Society in Victorian England.* London, 1969.

Rozhdestvenskii, S. V. *Istoricheskii obzor deiatel'nosti ministerstva narodnovo prosveshcheniia.* Saint Petersburg, 1902.

Rozhkov, N. A. *1905 god: Istoricheskii ocherk.* Moscow, 1926.

Schneiderman, J. *Sergei Zubatov and Revolutionary Marxism.* Ithaca, 1976.

Shchetinina, G. I. *Universitety v Rossii i ustav 1884ovo goda.* Moscow, 1976.

Sinel, A. *The Classroom and the Chancellery: State Educational Reform in Russia under Count Dmitry Tolstoi.* Cambridge, Mass., 1973.

Sliozberg, G. B., ed. *Pamiati russkovo studenchestva.* Paris, 1934.

Solov'ëv, I. *Russkie universitety v ikh ustavakh i vospominaniiakh sovremennikov.* Saint Petersburg, 1914.

Solov'ëv, Iu. B. *Samoderzhavie i dvorianstvo v kontse 19 veka.* Leningrad, 1973.
Speranskii, N. V. *Krizis russkoi shkoly.* Moscow, 1914.
Spieler, S. *Autonomie oder Reglementierung.* Cologne, 1981.
Statera, G. *Death of a Utopia: The Development and Decline of Student Movements in Europe.* New York, 1975.
Stavrou, T. G., ed. *Russia Under the Last Czar.* Minneapolis, 1969.
Svatikov, S. G., ed. *Put' studenchestva.* Petrograd, 1916.
Sviatlovskii, V. V. *Studenchestvo v tsifrakh.* Saint Petersburg, 1909.
Tkachenko, P. S. *Moskovskoe studenchestvo v obshchestvenno-politicheskoi zhizni Rossii vtoroi poloviny 19ovo veka.* Moscow, 1958.
Venturi, F. *Roots of Revolution.* New York, 1966.
Vezhbitskii, V. G., ed. *Materialy po istorii Rossii v period kapitalizma.* Moscow, 1976.
Vucinich, A. *Science in Russian Culture.* 2 vols. Stanford, 1970.
Vydrin, R. *Osnovnye momenty studencheskovo dvizheniia v Rossii.* Moscow, 1908.
Wildman, A. *The Making of a Workers' Revolution.* Chicago, 1967.
Zaionchkovskii, P. A. *Rossiiskoe samoderzhavie v kontse 19ovo stoletiia.* Moscow, 1970.
Zhaba, S. *Petrogradskoe studenchestvo v bor'be za svobodnuiu vysshuiu shkolu.* Paris, 1922.

VII. DISSERTATIONS

Iakovlev, V. P. "Politika samoderzhaviia v universitetskom voprose, 1905–11." Kandidat dissertation, Leningrad State University, 1970.
Ivanov, A. E. "Universitetskaia politika samoderzhaviia nakanune pervoi russkoi revoliutsii." Kandidat dissertation, Moscow State University, 1975.
Latysheva, S. I. "Moskovskii Universitet v revoliutsionnoi bor'be v period pervoi russkoi revoliutsii." Kandidat dissertation, Moscow State University, 1954.
Schmidt, C. "Pushed into Politics: The Radicalization of Women Students in Saint Petersburg from 1889 to 1901." B.A. thesis, Harvard University, 1986.
Veselaia, G. A. "Massovye obshchestvennye vystupleniia Moskovskovo studenchestva v kontse 19ovo–nachale 20ovo veka." Kandidat dissertation, Moscow State University, 1974.

Index

Academic freedom, 38–40, 211, 394–395; and political reform, 198–199, 209, 217–221, 333
Academic Union, 6–7, 222–236, 272, 286, 326, 395; first congress of, 222–225; formation of, 216–222, 236; fourth congress of, 383; and junior faculty, 242, 270; and other unions, 226–228, 281, 295, 326; and politics, 226, 280–281; Schwartz on, 325–326; second congress of, 232–236, 251–252; and students, 234; third congress of, 293–296
Academists, 259–261, 265, 378–379
Academy of Sciences, 99, 220, 297
Adamov, Vasilii, 127
Admissions, university: control over, 46, 327–328, 341; restrictions on, 57–58, 198, 240–241, 257–258, 265, 281, 283. See also Jews; Seminary graduates; Women
Adzhemov, M. E., 150
Alexander II, 23, 28, 54, 80, 133
Alexander III, 29
Alexandrovich, Grand Duke Sergei, 99, 104, 137, 165–166
Alexandrovskii Lycee, 19, 27, 195, 212
American student movement, 396, 403
Andreev, I. D., 350
Anichkov, E. V., 74
Anisimov, A., 143 n.1, 146–147, 173 n.96
Annensky, N. F., 128

Anti-intellectualism, 273–274
Anti Semitism, 271–274, 314, 323, 344, 379. See also Jews
Arrests. See Students: arrested
Astrov, N. I., 59
Autocracy. See Government
Avrekh, A. Ia., 361–362

Bailes, Kendall, 39, 41 n.67
Batiushkov, Th. D., 101
Beketov, N. N., 98–99
Ben-David, Joseph, 41, 44 n.76, 398
Bestuzhev-Riumin courses, 23, 24 nn.28,29
Bloody Sunday protest, 206–207, 236
Boborykin, P. A., 53
Bobrinskii, A. A., 347, 351
Bogolepov, N. P., 7, 30 n.39, 37, 39, 72, 99, 115, 126, 299
Bolsheviks, 188, 384, 386; and professors, 268; and students, 335, 358; students as, 246–247, 264, 379. See also Lenin, Vladimir; Social Democrats
Bonnell, Victoria E., 250 n.33
Borgman, I. I., 239–241, 297 n.26, 319, 331, 340
Bourgeoisie: and state, 171; and students, 52, 83–84, 102–105
Brandt, A. A., 219–220, 223 n.57, 228, 233 n.88, 234, 294–295
Braun, F. A., 327
Brower, Daniel, 55–56

Bulgakov, S. N., 139, 214
Bulygin Duma, 209, 228–237, 247, 252,
    281, 388; boycott of, 249–251, 281,
    295. See also Duma
Bunge, N., 66–67
Buzeskul, V., 29

Caucasus: higher education in, 367; pro-
    test in, 237; students from, 80–81
Central University Organ. See Moscow
    University Central University Organ;
    Saint Petersburg University Central
    University Organ
Charques, Richard, 363 n.72
Chekhov, Anton, 50–51
Chernov, Victor, 82 n.108, 83–86
Chicherin, Boris Nikolaevich, 27, 215
Chlenov, M. A., 63–64
Christian Movement, 371
Chubinskii, M. P., 201, 366
Chulkov, G. I., 148, 150, 152, 162,
    168–170
Chuprov, A. I., 43 n.73, 76
Civil service, 17 n.8, 18 n.10, 292, 398
Classics, study of, 30, 31, 71
Closed schools, 19, 27, 194–195, 212
Clowes, Edith, 51
Coalition councils, student, 180, 183–
    194, 262–264, 282–283. See also
    Student government
Collins, R., 44 n.76
Commercial education, higher, 17 n.5,
    21–23, 368–369, 389
Commercial high school graduates, 299,
    330, 345
Conservatives: and student groups, 323,
    362; and tsar, 288
Constituent assembly, demand for, 164,
    195–196, 263, 280, 384
Constitutional Democratic party, 229.
    See also Kadet party
Cooperative societies, 373
Council of Elders. See Saint Petersburg
    University Council of Elders
Council of the United Nobility, 323, 363
Courts, student, 146, 152
Credit associations, 154, 312–313
Curators, 36, 270, 375, 391
Curriculum, 31–32; control of, 283,
    300, 329; elective, 209, 265, 291,
    325; reform of, 258, 281

"Declaration of the 342," 6, 219–222,
    226, 233, 236, 286, 294, 297 n.26,
    356
Delianov, I. D., 28, 30, 31

Demonstrations. See Street demon-
    strations
Dennitsa, 182–183, 186, 261
Dining halls, 71–72, 107, 258, 311, 327;
    restrictions on, 154–155, 187, 301
Disciplinary courts. See Faculty disciplin-
    ary courts
Discipline, student. See Faculty disciplin-
    ary courts; Student discipline
Dorpat University, 53
Dozenty, 291–292
Dudgeon, Ruth, 24 n.29
Duma, 287–288, 296, 300–301, 304,
    323; arrest of deputies to, 307; elec-
    toral law for, 320, 338, 341–342,
    389; participation in, 273; professori-
    ate and, 331; proroguing of, 379; and
    Schwartz, 329–330, 334; and univer-
    sities, 336–337, 364, 404. See also
    Bulygin Duma
Durnovo, P. N., 298, 318 n.76, 323

Elections, student. See Student gov-
    ernment
Elective system, 209, 257, 302, 404
Electrotechnical Institute (Moscow), 20
Engel', G. A., 156–157, 179, 181–182,
    185, 237
Engelstein, Laura, 255 n.47
Enrollment, university, 16, 22; growth of,
    53, 198, 286, 287, 299, 404; and
    World War I, 380
European universities, 26–27, 158, 251,
    261. See also German universities
Examination system, 31, 44, 45, 76–77,
    110, 209, 231, 329, 348, 389, 391
Exile, students sentenced to, 159–160,
    167–172, 176, 362
Expulsion. See Professors: expulsion of;
    Students: expulsion of

Faculty. See Junior faculty; Professors
Faculty councils, 7, 26–28, 207–210,
    391; and boycott of professors, 258;
    conservatives on, 331; and depart-
    ments, 290–291, 375; and Ministry
    of Education, 45; powers of, 28, 39,
    224, 297, 395; and student meetings,
    265; and student strikes, 194; and
    Temporary Rules, 27 August, 230–
    231, 240–241, 317; and Tolstoi,
    289–293
Faculty disciplinary courts, 46, 173, 181,
    193, 200–207, 230–231, 291; at-
    tacks on, 196, 353, 391–392; resig-
    nations from, 201–202, 236

Ferro, Marc, 384n.147
Feuer, Lewis, 397
Financial aid, 67–70, 287, 319, 330; control over, 72, 98, 258, 281, 362; discrimination in, 362. *See also* Scholarships
Forestry Institute (Saint Petersburg), 20n.16, 305–306, 348
Frieden, Nancy, 60
Frommet, Boris, 306–307

Garvi, P. A., 244–245, 250
German students, 10, 45, 52, 53, 403
German universities, 17n.7, 25–26, 296–297, 388, 391
Glazov, V. G., 17n.7, 194, 202n.4, 229, 389–390; and faculty, 204–206, 210–213, 270, 289
Goremykin, I. L., 72, 99
Gorokhov, V. A., 156–157
Government: higher education policy of, 15–37, 203–204, 210–214, 374, 377; and public, 344; and student movement, 3 4, 47, 137, 164–174, 205, 331–332, 405–406; and universities, 14–15, 27, 272, 287, 326–327, 339–341, 344–349, 387, 391. *See also* Ministry of Education; Nicholas II; Temporary Rules of 29 July 1899; Temporary Rules of 27 August 1905; Temporary Rules on Student Organizations; *names of individual ministers of education; and names of individual statutes*
Graduates, university: legal and civil privileges for, 16–18, 23–24, 45, 292, 340, 345; and state, 61–62
Gredeskul, N. A., 98, 199, 201, 244, 361; exile of, 318
Grevs, Ivan, 30n.39, 43n.74, 214, 217–218, 221, 234, 239, 252, 311n.63
Grimm, D. D., 292, 365, 385
Grimm, E. D., 41n.65, 272, 355
Gusiatnikov, P. S., 170n.85, 190n.138
Gymnasia graduates, 257, 292, 340, 345

Higher education, 15–24. *See also* Technical institutes; Universities; *VUZy*
Historical-Philosophical Society of Moscow University, 43n.75, 173
History and philology faculty, 24–25, 30, 32, 61; enrollment in, 58–59, 302; and strikes, 111–112, 134, 168
Honorarium system, 32–34, 36, 45, 114, 345–346, 376, 391

Ianzhul, I. I., 42–43, 82n.107
Ignatiev, Pavel Nikolaevich, 374–378, 382, 390–391
Inspectorate, 73–74, 98, 146, 340, 398; protest to, 81, 98, 300
Institute of Civil Engineers (Saint Petersburg), 20n.16, 305
Institute of Communications (Saint Petersburg), 20n.16, 95
Institute of Law, 19
Intelligentsia, 144, 177, 215, 250
Iordanskii, Nikolai, 78, 79, 92–96, 101–102, 106–109, 116, 359–360, 402
Iskra, 94, 125–128, 132–135, 159–160, 170–171, 175
Iur'ev University, 24–25, 58, 206, 208, 218, 239, 321, 331, 365
Ivanov, A. E., 249n.32, 306n.49
Ivanov, P., 70n.67, 77n.86
Ivanov-Razumnik, R. V., 128–131
Izgoev, A. S., 308–309, 360

Jews: admission to higher education restricted for, 57, 143, 146, 240–241, 257, 270, 286, 288, 298, 300, 324–332, 354; barred from professoriate, 33; and higher education degree, 18; and pogroms, 271–274; support for equal rights for, 314. *See also* Anti-Semitism
Junior faculty, 35–36, 206, 289, 292, 384; in Academic Union, 242, 293–294; and "Declaration of the 342," 220; and senior faculty, 6, 199, 238, 241–243, 256, 270, 279n.104
Juridical faculty. *See* Law, study of

Kadet party, 6, 346, 402–403; professors in, 6–7, 232, 297–298, 331; and strike in 1908, 334, 336–339; in student elections, 8–9, 259, 261–263, 305–310, 314, 383–384, 400; and student movement, 322, 332, 359–364, 399, 406
Kaplan, A. Ia., 246
Kareev, Nikolai, 30n.39, 223n.60, 294, 303, 383
Kaser, Michael, 15nn.2,3, 343n.1
Kassa Radikalov, 150, 152, 156–160, 174–176; exile of, 168–171
Kassa Vzaimopomoshchi, 85–87, 158, 381; and 1899 strike, 92–94; and student movement, 102–104, 107, 122–123, 161
Kasso, L. A., 7, 39, 347, 362, 367, 384; and professors, 356, 365–366

Katkov, Mikhail, 28, 29, 389
Kazan Square demonstration, 127–136
Kazan University, 24, 239, 271; professors at, 206, 234–235, 304, 316, 384; student movement at, 53–54, 194, 243, 249, 268
Kharkov Technological Institute, 153, 183, 202–204
Kharkov University, 24, 239, 271–272, 327; demonstrations at, 153, 170 n.82, 201, 203; professors at, 26, 30, 45–46, 63, 316, 365; strike in 1899 at, 97–98; students at, 121, 132–133, 143, 153, 284, 308, 334, 354, 384
Kharkov Veterinary Institute, 153, 160
Khovrin, A. A., 148, 169–170
Kiev Institute (commercial), 21
Kiev Polytechnic Institute, 21, 175, 321
Kiev University, 24, 77, 239–240, 271, 303, 362; professors at, 30, 33 n.48, 45, 206, 316, 384–385; and strike in 1899, 96, 106–107, 110, 117–118; and strike in 1908, 335, 338; students at, 53, 55, 119–120, 143, 158, 175, 178, 194, 283, 306, 317, 321
Kistiakovskii, Bogdan, 7
Kizevetter, A. A., 13–14, 69, 76, 79
Kliuchevskii, V. O., 13, 43 n.73, 69, 76, 82 n.107, 191, 297 n.26
Kokovtsev, V. N., 230–232, 367 n.87, 390
Konovalov, D. P., 203–204
Kostomarov, N. I., 27, 54
Kovalevskii, M. M., 7, 30, 76, 225, 235, 252 n.38, 258–259, 297 n.26, 303
Kulchitskii, N. K., 378
Kuropatkin, A. N., 99, 114

Labor movement, 231, 247, 250 n.33, 273, 335; and student movement, 102, 238, 267–268, 287, 358–359. See also Workers
Law, study of, 21 n.23, 24–25, 30–32, 58–60, 302
Law students: arrested, 134, 168; and 1899 strike, 111–112
Lazarev Institute of Eastern Languages, 20 n.16
Lenin, Vladimir, 7, 186, 246; on professors, 268–269, 282; on student movement, 125, 335–336, 400; on Temporary Rules of 1905, 237–238
Levchenko, V., 309 n.59
Levin-Stankevich, Brian, 60 n.38
Levitskii, Vladimir, 124–126
Liberalism, Russian, 188, 214–215, 225,

282, 401; and student movement, 5–6, 11, 54, 184–185, 359–361, 399, 402–406; students' suspicion of, 43, 176, 251, 262
Lukianov, S. M., 201, 202 n.5, 205, 213, 288

McClelland, James C., 15 n.3, 19 n.15, 386 n.153
Makarov, A. A., 317, 319, 339
Maklakov, V. A., 79, 188 n.133, 364
Manning, Roberta, 60 n.36
Manuilov, A. A., 234, 266, 271–272, 278, 297 n.26, 356, 384–385; and Schwartz, 331, 341; and student movement, 301, 318–319, 352
Markov, A. A., 241, 272
Marxism, 108, 250; on student movement, 9, 82–83, 93, 103, 117, 127–128, 171, 175–178, 399–400; students' interest in, 86, 161, 164, 186, 262, 303
Mathematics faculty, 111–112, 134, 168, 302
Medem, Vladimir, 77, 82, 96
Medical faculty, 24–25, 32, 77; enrollment in, 58, 302; students in, 44, 60–61, 111–112, 134, 168
Meetings. See Skhodki; Universities: political meetings at
Mel'gunov, S. P., 31 n.45, 173–174 n.96
Mendeleev, D. I., 30, 43 n.73
Mensheviks, 188, 379; and student movement, 244–245, 250, 255, 264. See also Social Democrats
Men'shikov, M. O., 322–323, 351–352
Menzbir, M. A., 76, 267, 356
Merchants, 20, 34, 42 n.71, 51–52, 62
Meshcherskii, Prince, 144–146
Metzger, Walter, 4, 38
Miles, Michael, 11, 403
Military-Medical Academy, 20, 306 n.49, 370
Military service: deferment from, 18, 382; forced conscription for, 48, 114, 115, 120–121, 136, 138, 161, 196; and scholarships, 370; status in, 292
Miliukov, Paul, 183–184, 188, 227–228, 258, 361, 402
Mining Institute. See Saint Petersburg Mining Institute
Ministers of education, 28, 390. See also names of individual ministers
Ministry of Education, 18–20, 204–206, 230, 270, 374; and faculty councils, 304. See also Government
Ministry of Finance, 344, 389

Ministry of Trade and Industry, 21–23, 344, 389
Minsk, 17 n.6, 274
Mogilianskii, M. N., 85–86, 92–94, 102–104, 108, 117
Moscow: local authorities in, 317–318; student movement in, 132–133, 191–193, 357–358, 382. See also Moscow University
Moscow Commercial Institute, 21, 357, 368
Moscow Executive Committee, 160–164; exile of, 168–170
Moscow Juridical Society, 38 n.60, 42 n.71
Moscow Technological Institute, 321
Moscow University, 24, 30, 74; "destruction" of, 357, 363, 393; junior faculty at, 233; professors' closing of, 266–269; professors from, 34, 415; rector of, 239–240; size of, 69, 369, 371, 404; strike of 1899 at, 95–96, 102, 111–113; strike of 1905 at, 193–195; strike of 1911 at, 356–357; student government at, 263–265, 305–306, 310 (see also Moscow University Central University Organ); student movement at, 54–55, 84, 130, 145–146, 180–181, 192; students of, 63–66; Tat'ianin Den' at, 13–14, 69, 82; zemliachestva in, 78–85, 312
Moscow University Central University Organ, 245, 264–265, 284, 318–319; and faculty, 276–278, 316–317; makeup of, 267, 305; and strike of 1908, 334
Moscow University Executive Committee, 143, 147–155
Moscow University Faculty Council, 45–46, 155–156, 202 n.4, 241, 356–357; and politics, 193, 208–210, 263–270, 385; on student movement, 73–74, 136–137, 194–195, 206, 327
Moscow University United Council, 84, 180–181, 192
Muromtsev, S. A., 30, 38 n.60, 43 n.73, 331 n.119

Nationalists, 347, 351, 363
Natural sciences and mathematics faculty, 24–25, 32, 58–59, 61, 77, 302; students of, 111–112, 134, 168
Naumov, A. N., 31 n.43, 74
Nekrasov, P. A., 137, 145, 210–213, 224
Nestroev, Grigorii, 170 nn.82,85, 178–179

Nicholas I, 52–53
Nicholas II: and Glazov, 204–206; and strike of 1899, 99, 116; and strike of 1905, 227–229, 255, 272–273; and student unrest, 82, 137–138, 166–167; on universities, 16 n.4, 367, 377, 389–392
Nobility, 387; professors from, 34–35
Non-Russian areas, 228, 263, 324; education in, 15 n.3; protest in, 249–250; students from, 77; universities in, 17, 390
Nosar, Gregorii, 93
Novgorodtsev, P. I., 214, 226–227, 304, 331 n.119, 347 n.12, 382, 383 n.145, 384 n.147
Novikov, M. M., 18 n.9, 375 n.115, 385
Novocherkassk, 21 n.22
Numerus clausus. See Jews: admission to higher education restricted for

October 1905 manifesto, 272–273, 287–288, 296
Octobrists: and government, 329–331, 336, 338, 346, 354, 363–364; and students, 314, 339
Odessa: local authorities in, 317–318, 330, 392; Organization Committee at, 121; pogroms in, 271–275, 283
Odessa conference, 179–190, 196
Odessa University, 24, 239–241; disciplinary court at, 201, 206; firing of faculty at, 30, 235, 330; and strike in 1905, 208 n.21, 249; and strike in 1908, 335, 338; student movement in, 190, 194, 284, 321; unrest at, 353, 362
Okhrana, Moscow, 147, 162–163; and professors, 223 n.57, 228; on student movement, 166, 352. See also Police
Orlov, V. I., 75 n.81, 147–150, 152, 162, 176 n.105
Ozerov, I. Kh., 42 n.71, 43 n.73

Panteleev, L. F., 53 n.12, 101
Partizany Bor'by, 174, 181–182, 186
Passek, E. V., 239, 301, 331
Paulsen, Friedrich, 293 n.16, 346, 394
Peasantry, 247, 332, 355, 388, 404; professors from, 34; students from, 20–21, 72, 371; unrest of, 247, 252
Pergament, M. Ia., 355, 365
Perkin, Harold, 41
Petrazhitskii, L. I., 25, 186, 258, 303, 304, 331 n.119
Petrograd University, 382–383, 386
Petrovskii Agricultural Academy, 20 n.16

Pirogov, N. I., 2, 26–27, 55, 290
Plehve, V. K., 47, 60 n.36, 183, 202–205, 216, 348, 388
Pobedonostsev, K. P., 29, 114, 137 n.144, 153, 389
Pogroms, 271–275, 284
Pokrovskii, I. A., 355, 365
Pokrovskii, M. K., 186
Poland, 228, 237, 376; students from, 53, 112–113, 305
Police, 74–75, 123, 316, 321; and pogroms, 271–274; Political, 115; and strike of 1908, 335–337; and student meetings, 127, 320, 340, 352–353; in universities, 110, 229, 231, 291, 301
Police brutality, 92, 95, 99, 114, 129–132, 193–194
Police repression, 98, 106–107, 153, 157, 233–235, 264. See also Okhrana, Moscow
Polytechnic institutes. See Technical institutes
Populism, 54, 82, 84, 303
Press: liberal, 332; student, 308, 313, 349, 372–373
Primary education, 15–16, 288, 376
Privat-dozenty, 32, 35 n.54, 36, 366, 391. See also Junior faculty
Private funding of VUZy, 343–344, 367–368, 394
Professoriate, admission to, 33, 291
Professors: appointment of, 4, 28–30, 45, 290, 293, 340–341, 384–385; autonomy of, 198–199, 238–243, 278; boycott of, 257–258, 316, 384; as civil servants, 6, 39, 199–200, 217, 289, 342, 394–395; conservative, 39, 365–366; disciplinary power of, 213; education of, 33–35, 415; election of, 33–35, 415; expulsion of, 330; and government, 4–5, 30, 37–47, 210–215, 226, 344, 365–366, 393–394; and intelligentsia, 7, 225–226; isolation of, 256, 275; and junior faculty, 36, 243, 270; and Kadet party, 6–7, 232, 297–298, 331; liberal, 6–7, 39, 54, 253; and politics, 7, 200, 206–209, 214–223, 236, 280–283, 295, 385; property of, 413; protests by, 193, 201–203, 241; resignations by, 201, 203–204, 343, 356–359, 365; and Revolution of 1905, 265–270, 275–279; salaries of, 34, 35, 45, 291, 345–346, 376, 381; and Schwartz, 325–327; shortage of, 33; social

background of, 34–35, 414; and strike of 1908, 336; and strike of 1911, 355–356; and student movement, 5–6, 136–137, 221–222, 238, 332, 339, 381, 399; and students, 37, 43–44, 54, 77, 145, 243, 256, 283, 301; transfers of, 365; and University Statute (1884), 4, 37–40. See also Academic Union; "Declaration of the 342"; Faculty councils; Faculty disciplinary courts; Junior faculty
Progressive Bloc, 379–380
Proskuriatov, E. K., 48, 123
Provinces, 61, 113; students from, 113
Provincial universities, 286, 365; local authorities at, 304, 321, 330; strike of 1899 in, 95–98, 106–107

Radicals. See Revolutionary movement; Student Radicalism
Rashin, A. G., 15 n.3
Rasputin, 344, 374, 377–378
Rectors: and discipline, 73, 206; election of, 45, 209, 224, 229, 230, 239, 320, 340, 375; and student movement, 319; tsar and, 290
Revolutionary movement, 332; and government, 281–282, 316; and student movement, 180, 184, 350, 358–359, 405; and students, 2, 79, 250–251, 264, 283–284, 307, 372, 402
Revolution of 1905, 1–2, 182–194, 237–238; effects of, 286–287, 302–303, 331, 392; and student movement, 10, 244–265, 269–270, 280–285, 305–315, 404. See also Strike of 1905
Revolution of 1917, 382–386, 399
Rieber, Albert, 42 n.71
Riga Polytechnic Institute, 180–181
Right-wing politics. See Conservatives
Rostov, 367, 377
Rozhkov, Nikolai, 250–251
Rules of 11 June 1907, 321, 327, 389
Russo-Japanese War: professors and, 203, 214–216, 226–227, 231; students and, 182–183, 187, 201

Saint Petersburg: demonstrations in, 119; Social Democrats in, 133, 188, 190, 358; strike of 1901 in, 132; strike of 1905 in, 255; strike of 1911 in, 350–351; students' "Appeal" from, 332–333, 338
Saint Petersburg City Coalition Council, 353–354
Saint Petersburg Mining Institute, 20,

183, 202–203, 302, 306; strikes at, 348
Saint Petersburg Polytechnic, 21, 306
Saint Petersburg Psychoneurological Institute, 367
Saint Petersburg School of Engineering, 20 n.16
Saint Petersburg Technological Institute, 20 n.16, 302, 313–315
Saint Petersburg University, 24, 34; faculty at, 30, 33 n.48, 235; junior faculty at, 242, 270; juridical faculty of, 365–366; political meetings at, 253–255; professors from, 34, 415; size of, 53, 69, 369, 371, 404; Social Democrats at, 305; strike of 1899 at, 90–105; strike of 1905 at, 245–247; strike of 1911 at, 356; student government at, 143, 151–152, 306 n.49; student movement at, 55–57, 107, 116, 127, 144–145, 321, 353–355; women's courses at, 181; *zemliachestva* at, 78–79, 85–87, 312. *See also* Kassa Radikalov; Kassa Vzaimopomoshchi; Saint Petersburg University Faculty Council
Saint Petersburg University Central University Organ, 186–187
Saint Petersburg University Coalition Council, 245–246, 256–259, 270–271, 275–276
Saint Petersburg University Council of Elders, 259, 262–263, 305, 306, 307, 308, 319, 327
Saint Petersburg University Faculty Council, 45, 98, 155–156, 239–241, 263, 327
Saint Petersburg University Mutual Aid Society. *See* Kassa Vzaimopomoshchi
Saltykov, Sergei, 93, 95–96, 101
Sanger, G. E., 47, 201
Saratov, 17 n.6, 24, 329–330, 342, 377, 390
Savich, S. E., 221–222
Schmidt, Catherine, 140 n.150
Scholarships, 36, 67–70, 312, 381, 390; control over, 28, 72; state, 205, 370; strikes over, 348. *See also* Financial aid
Schwartz, A. N., 7, 23 n.26, 39, 323–331, 351; draft statute of, 339–341, 344–349; and professors, 201, 239, 346; and students, 332–333
"Scientific circles," 303
Secondary education, 15–16, 137 n.144, 327–328, 376
Second Moscow Resolution, 249–252, 267

Seminary graduates: admission of, 299; discrimination against, 57–58, 143, 328–331
Senior faculty. *See* Professors
Shaniavskii University, 344, 357, 367–368
Shchepkin, E. N., 240, 317
Siberia. *See* Exile, students sentenced to
Sipiagin, D. S., 47, 115, 120–121, 137 n.144, 153, 154, 162, 165
Skhodki, 20, 54–56, 261, 264–265, 284, 287, 315; debate on, 309–310, 404; political, 143; restrictions on, 57, 110, 153–155, 173, 196, 301, 317, 319, 340, 353–354
Sliozberg, G. B., 76, 401 n.10
Social Democrats: and Duma, 250, 364; in Moscow, 162, 355; and Radicals, 157; and revolutionary parties, 186; in Saint Petersburg, 125, 185–189, 339; and strike of 1908, 335–337; in student government, 8, 246–248, 259–263, 282–283, 305–311; and student movement, 102, 125, 132–133, 139, 142, 170, 174–185, 189, 192, 314, 350; students as, 307, 322, 358, 372, 400–401; and workers, 249. *See also* Bolsheviks; Mensheviks
Social Revolutionaries, 94, 142, 188; and strike of 1905, 247, 252–253; and strike of 1908, 335; in student government, 259, 262–263, 305–311; and student movement, 174–177, 314, 320–321, 349, 400, 406; students as, 192, 264, 322, 379
Society for the Aid of Needy Students, 69, 71–72
Soiuz Bor'by, 125–128
Soviet regime, 386
Specialized technical institutes. *See* Technical institutes
State Council, 297–298
Statera, Gianni, 397
Stolypin, Peter, 7, 287–288, 299, 301, 315–331, 366, 384, 387, 389; and conservatives, 351, 362–363, 392–393, 402–403; on professors, 304, 318, 322, 329, 346; and student movement, 303, 315–317, 323–324, 348, 351–352; university policy of, 342
treet demonstrations, 9, 121–140, 161, 249, 386; effect of, 90, 399–400; Social Democrats and, 185, 188–189; workers and, 125, 135–136, 156–157, 162–163, 191–192, 350
Strike of 1899, 50, 88–119, 398–400;

Strike of 1899 (*continued*)
    effect of, 74, 104–109, 116–118,
    136; as protest against autocracy,
    104–105; resumption of, 107–112;
    and revolutionary movement, 116;
    students arrested during, 99–102,
    106–107, 110, 112, 115–116
Strike of 1905: effect of, 361; general, 2,
    237, 249–250, 255 n.47, 270–273,
    287; students', 194–196, 221, 244–
    253, 282–283
Strike of 1908, 331–339, 348
Strike of 1911, 353–365
Strikes: academic, 2, 9, 136, 157–159,
    166, 251; local, 132, 321, 348; work-
    ers', 86, 249–250, 255 n.47, 270–
    273. See also *individual strikes*
Struve, Peter, 128, 130, 139, 171, 183–
    186, 188, 191, 214, 216, 258, 307,
    357, 360, 393, 400
Studenchestvo, 2, 8–11, 14, 82–87, 157,
    370–374, 397; and Bolsheviks, 386;
    and politics, 174–180, 193–194,
    267, 305–307; social origins of,
    62–66, 359, 391; solidarity of,
    48–58, 331–332, 338–339; tradi-
    tion of, 149, 261, 349, 374, 403–406
Student congress, all-Russian, 245–246
Student discipline, 73, 194, 257, 281,
    289; faculty control of, 27, 45, 57,
    224, 230–231, 287; government con-
    trol of, 52–53, 203–204, 319. See
    also Faculty disciplinary courts
Student government, 265, 284; elections
    for, 8, 263, 287, 305–308, 400; and
    1917 revolution, 383–384. See also
    Moscow University: student govern-
    ment at; Saint Petersburg University:
    student government at
Student House, Moscow, 373, 381
Student meetings. See *Skhodki*
Student movement: as academic, 115;
    control of, 205, 245; government per-
    ception of, 113–114, 217–218,
    319–320, 348–352; government pol-
    icy on, 47, 171–172; ideology of,
    117, 259, 310–316, 354, 400; inde-
    pendence of, 177, 180, 193; and lib-
    eralism, 5–6, 11, 54, 251, 359,
    400–401; political importance of,
    88–90, 103, 184; and political par-
    ties, 174–182, 193; and politics,
    142–162, 256–263; and professors,
    8, 54, 98, 238, 287, 296; radicalism
    of, 142–151, 400–403; and revolu-
    tionary movement, 8–9, 109, 142,
    184, 191, 245, 283, 396, 405; and

Revolution of 1905, 10, 244–265;
    and strike of 1899, 29; and workers,
    3, 102, 118, 139, 149, 165, 238, 271
Student organizations, 71–73, 348, 385;
    control over, 151, 154–155, 203,
    231, 341, 375; faculty and, 327; sup-
    pression of, 72–73, 114, 331–332,
    372. See also Student government
Student professionalism, 310–316, 372,
    380, 399, 404–405; and revolution-
    ary movement, 326, 349
Student protest, 9, 36–37, 57, 142,
    160–162, 185, 364, 403, 406;
    against professors, 82 n.107, 257–
    258, 316, 384; local, 174, 185. See
    also Street demonstrations; Strikes;
    Student movement
Student Radicalism, 156–160, 174–192
Students: arrested, 99–118, 127, 130–
    134, 159–172, 187, 196, 321, 351–
    353, 356; as corporate group, 54–56,
    73, 114, 141–143, 154, 172, 263, 283;
    executed, 321; exiled, 159–160, 167–
    172, 176, 362; expulsions of, 83,
    110, 112, 120, 143, 146, 148, 152–
    153, 160, 206, 343, 351, 358, 362;
    finances of, 21 n.19, 66–67, 310–
    312; housing for, 71, 114; number of,
    305, 367–369; and politics, 174, 372;
    and professors, 37; regional origins
    of, 407; and revolutionary parties,
    250–251, 258–259, 283; rights of,
    27, 116, 289; social origins of, 24 n.28,
    57–58, 62–66, 112–113, 401, 408–
    411; solidarity of, 10, 96; suspension
    of, 181–182, 206, 322–323; and
    workers, 89, 94, 149, 176, 397; and
    World War I, 378–379, 382. See also
    Financial aid; Military service; *Stu-
    denchestvo;* Student movement
Svatikov, S. G., 349, 373 n.106, 381
Sviatlovskii, V. V., 186, 246, 303, 336
Sviatopolk-Mirskii, Prince, 172, 183,
    194

Tat'ianin Den', 13–14, 69, 82
Teachers: high school, 61, 397–398; re-
    quirements for, 289, 329, 376; short-
    age of, 32–33; women as, 24 n.27
Technical institutes, 4, 16, 17 n.5, 19–21,
    25, 95, 202, 302; state's concentra-
    tion on, 343, 366–369, 376–377,
    389, 394
Temporary Rules of 29 July 1899,
    114–115, 120–124, 137–138, 166;
    protest against, 128–134, 140, 398
Temporary Rules of 27 August 1905,

228–232, 235–239, 256, 270, 279–282, 388, 392; Lenin on, 237–238; and police, 352; professors' interpretation of, 240–242, 265, 281, 286–287, 301–302, 317; state interpretation of, 287, 296, 304, 317–321, 324–327, 340–341, 344
Temporary Rules on Student Organizations (1901), 151–155, 160, 203
Theaters, 75
Theology, 25, 302
Tiflis, 17 n.7, 250, 274, 367
Tikhomirov, A. A., 102, 110, 205, 213, 288
Timberlake, Charles, 17 n.8
Timiriazev, K. A., 76, 222
Tolmachev, I. N., 304, 330
Tolstoi, I. I., 18, 288–289, 298, 318 n.76, 324, 377, 388, 391
Tolstoi, Lev, 343, 349–350
Tolstoi Conference, 289–293, 300, 346, 390, 394; draft statute of, 304, 325–326, 339–340
Tomsk, 132, 274, 377
Tomsk Technological Institute, 67, 306 n.49, 321, 353
Tomsk University, 24, 58, 67, 239, 330, 366
Trepov, D. F., 166, 223 n.57, 229–230, 235, 269, 272
Trubetskoi, Evgenii, 7, 17 n.8, 216–217, 225, 228, 235, 243, 297 n.26, 309 n.59, 336, 357
Trubetskoi, Sergei, 43 n.75, 45 n.80, 147, 173, 195, 215, 227, 239–240, 265–269, 296–297
Trudoviki, 305, 306, 364
Tsar. See Alexander II; Alexander III; Nicholas I; Nicholas II
Tseretelli, Iracli, 148–150, 152, 161–162
Tsitovich, N. M., 239–240, 301, 303, 319
Tugan-Baranovskii, M. I., 128–129, 139, 303, 307, 336, 400
Tuition fees, 35, 56–57, 68–70, 340, 391–392
Tver, 274
Tyrkova-Williams, Ariadna, 129–130

Ukraine, 274, 385
Uniforms, student, 53, 72, 74–75, 257, 271, 274
Union of Liberation, 142, 183, 188, 209, 214, 218–229, 281
Union of the Russian People, 314, 321, 323, 346

Union of Unions, 6, 219; and Academic Union, 226–228, 281, 295, 326
Universities: as apolitical, 205–206, 213, 222, 360, 395; autonomy of, 4–5, 26–27, 40–41, 45, 141, 209–210, 391; "free," 235, 253; funding of, 16–17, 205, 343, 389; and government, 3–4, 15, 25–26, 56, 158–159, 289, 387–388; liberal concept of, 251–252; new, 376–377, 389; political meetings at, 238, 244–245, 249, 253–270, 316, 399; purpose of, 2–3, 40–41, 208–209; as research institutions, 4, 289–290, 293, 375; as state institutions, 194, 293, 342, 344, 388; as teaching institutions, 4–5, 289–290, 293, 340. See also Admissions, university; Government; and names of individual University Statutes and Temporary Rules
University Statute of 1863, 23, 27–28
University Statute of 23 August 1884, 28–29, 138, 286, 301–302, 304, 346–347, 375, 389–392; abrogation of, 173, 195, 198, 231; opposition to, 4, 36–40, 46, 81, 85–86, 116, 206–208; and professors, 4, 37–47, 200–201, 210–211, 251; and student corporate identity, 116, 143, 145, 154, 172; and Temporary Rules of 27 August 1905, 230–231, 240, 243, 341, 392; and tuition fees, 57

Vannovskii, P. S., 37, 47, 106, 110, 142–149, 153–154, 164, 388, 390, 398; rules by, on student organizations, 154–155, 160, 203; on student movement, 115–116
Vannovskii Commission, 99–102, 104–108, 113–115, 196
Vannovskii questionnaire, 45–46, 200, 208, 390
Vernadskii, V. I., 26, 43 n.73, 214–218, 224–229, 233–234, 267, 278, 296, 297 n.26, 323, 341, 369, 371, 393, 395
Vernadsky, George, 302
Vinogradov, P. G., 7, 33 n.48, 41 n.66, 76, 145–147, 202, 214–215, 225, 303, 392
Vishniak, Mark, 77 n.86, 150, 191–192
Voitinskii, Vladimir, 185–186, 246–250, 253, 256–257, 262, 400
Von Kaufmann, Peter M., 299–304, 327, 390; and rectors, 318–319; and Stolypin, 316–317, 322–323
Voronezh, 17 n.6, 367

VUZy, 1, 18–24. *See also* Technical institutes; Universities
Vyborg congress, 245–246, 331 n.119
Vydrin, Rafael, 313, 349, 381

Warsaw, 106–107, 110
Warsaw University, 24, 58, 201, 239
West, James, 42 n.71
Wildman, Allan, 139
Witte, S. Iu., 32; resignation of, 299; and strike of 1905, 272; on student movement, 165; on student protest, 99, 114, 137 n.144, 153–154; and Temporary Rules of 27 August 1905, 237; and Tolstoi, 288–289, 298, 388–389
Women: admission of, to universities, 57, 143, 240, 257, 270, 286, 300, 327–331, 354; and demonstrations, 121, 140; enrolled in higher education, 22–24, 368–369; and professoriate, 33
Women's Medical Institute, 23, 306 n.49

Workers: and Social Democracy, 162, 176; and strike of 1905, 248–257; and student demonstrations, 125, 135–136, 156–157, 162–163, 191–192, 350; and student movement, 94, 118, 125, 144, 179–181, 282, 332, 339, 355, 358. *See also* Labor movement
World War I, 374–382; and student movement, 378–379, 382

Young, George, 42

Zanchevskii, I. M., 239–241, 271, 317, 330
Zemliachestva, 54, 77–87, 114, 118, 186, 312, 353, 371–373, 380; ban on, 153, 180; in prison, 167; Schwartz on, 325–326; and strike of 1908, 338; United Council of, 81–86
Zemstvos, 214, 219, 282

Compositor: G & S Typesetters, Inc.
Printer: Braun-Brumfield, Inc.
Binder: Braun-Brumfield, Inc.
Text: 10/13 Sabon
Display: Sabon